CRITICAL ACCLAIM FOR

ON THE EDGE OF DEAF CULTURE

"I am impressed with the scope and diversity of the materials compiled here. This book is an excellent resource for professional service students, teachers, and researchers involved in fields related to Deaf Studies, Interpreting, Multicultural Education/Ethnic Studies, Disability Studies, and Human Relations/Family Studies. Hearing children of Deaf parents as well as Deaf parents who have hearing children will certainly want to add this book to their libraries. In fact, anyone with an interest in the culture of Deaf people will benefit from this book. It's a valuable contribution to our knowledge about this unique and integral part of our community and culture."

Glenn Anderson, Ph.D., Director of Training, Rehabilitation Research and Training Center for Persons who are Deaf or Hard of Hearing, University of Arkansas and Chair, Gallaudet University Board of Trustees

"This is a much anticipated resource book for codas, Deaf parents of kodas (hearing kids of deaf adults), and professionals working with Deaf people. We hope this comprehensive bibliography will contribute to codas' understanding of the bilingual and bicultural aspects of their lives, families, and communities; enlighten the community at large of the rich literature relating to the language and cultural aspects of Deaf parenting; explode the myths surrounding the assumption of deficit parenting; and unite codas, Deaf parents, and kodas in the political arena."

James E. Tucker, Superintendent, Maryland School for the Deaf and Karen Sheffer-Tucker Deaf parents of Bradford (hearing coda) and Claire (Deaf)

"Finally, the resource everyone has been waiting for: a comprehensive bibliography on the subject of deaf parents/hearing children. Looking through the pages of this book, one cannot help but be amazed at the resources that we, as deaf parents of hearing children, can seek out. This is a labor of love and a must for anyone who is involved in this field, especially deaf parents who have hearing children."

Stephen F. Weiner, Ed.D., Dean, School of Undergraduate Studies, Gallaudet University Mary (Tammy) Weiner, Ph.D., Assistant Professor, Psychology, Gallaudet University

"The need for this project has existed for decades. Many of us have had tremendous difficulty and frustration locating information about Deaf-parented families, whether for personal or professional use. I commend you for your dedication to this worthwhile undertaking. My heartfelt gratitude for the countless hours you've devoted to creating this gift for the international professional and lay community. I am extremely impressed!"

Elaine Jones, Ph.D., R.N., Associate Professor, Maternal-Child Nursing Director of Clinical Scholarship, University of Arizona College of Nursing

"The National Association of the Deaf (NAD) is delighted that such a compendium is now available. This new publication will prove to be an invaluable resource for parents and professionals alike. One of the 'quality of life' issues of concern to the NAD is the deaf/hearing family relationships that are an integral part of our lives. With this gold mine of information, our knowledge base has expanded significantly. This is, without a doubt, an outstanding achievement!"

Nancy J. Bloch, Executive Director, National Association of the Deaf

"The amount and variety of the material is amazing. In fact, it is overwhelming."

William C. Stokoe, Jr., Ph.D., Professor Emeritus, Gallaudet University

"In searching for materials related to hearing children of deaf parents we are likely to be led astray due to the complicated nature of how variously this unique group of people are categorized. Now we have a reference book which is extremely useful for such varied fields of interest as Deaf Studies, disability studies, studies of children of immigrants, etc. This annotated bibliography is a researcher's dream."

Ben Bahan, Ph.D., Chair, Deaf Studies Department, Gallaudet University

"This book is a must for all who are deaf and who are involved with deaf individuals. We need to learn that hearing children of deaf parents are different from the majority of hearing children of hearing parents. I strongly believe that learning about them will make us, deaf parents, better parents for them and will let them enjoy their childhood in both worlds. This publication is the only one of its kind available."

Rachel E. Stone, Ph.D., Assistant Professor, Deaf Education
Assistant Coordinator, ASL Specialist Program, Western Maryland College

"Rarely do I have the pleasure of giving my unqualified and enthusiastic endorsement to a work, but this one deserves no less from me. *On the Edge of Deaf Culture* is the most comprehensive bibliography that I have ever seen on the topic of growing up as a hearing person in a deaf family. I cannot imagine any institution or program that is committed to serious investigation of this topic being without this book."

Lou Fant, Lead Instructor, Interpreter Training Program, Seattle Central Community College

"An impressive book and its scope is unparalleled. It will be helpful to researchers and others who are interested in learning more about the experience of growing up hearing in a Deaf household. This book will appeal to students of all ages."

Gertrude R. Schafer, President, Children of Deaf Adults (CODA) International

"This is a unique contribution to the literature for anyone interested in deafness. A resource that is impressive in its breadth and depth, this book belongs in every library, and on the shelf of any serious student or scholar in the field."

Kathryn P. Meadow-Orlans, Ph.D., Professor Emerita, Gallaudet University
Former Senior Research Scientist, Gallaudet Research Institute

"This bibliography focuses on a primary adult role - parenting - and catapults the reader into an awareness that deaf children do grow up. An important document for many potential audiences: professionals who are involved in preparing teachers, audiologists, counselors to work with deaf people, those working with parents of deaf children and deaf parents, students in a variety of classes, and parents."

Loraine DiPietro, Director, National Information Center on Deafness, Gallaudet University

"This book provides us with informative and valuable resources and insights into the experiences of hearing children who have deaf parents. Our youngest son is the only hearing member of our family and a coda. He has had the benefit of a well-rounded education both at home and at school having been raised in our bilingual family. This book gives him and us tremendous insight into the Deaf World that we live in!"

Laurene Gallimore, Coordinator/Assistant Professor, Western Oregon University

"This book is a welcome resource for deaf parents of hearing children and hearing parents of deaf children, researchers, university professors, undergraduate and graduate students. The content is broad and covers such disciplines as psychology, genetics, sociology, linguistics, audiology, cultural anthropology, and history. An excellent guide to research in Disability Studies and Deaf Studies. A masterpiece!"

Yerker Andersson, Ph.D., Professor Emeritus, Gallaudet University
Past President, World Federation of the Deaf, Member, National Council on Disability

"This is an impressive bibliography which is much needed in the Deaf Community. Its amazing and gratifying to see the amount of information available related to coda issues. As we try to increase awareness about all aspects of deafness, this book documents the progress we've made to develop literature that validates Deaf Culture. This is a valuable and convenient resource for a variety of purposes."

Howie Seago, actor, co-star *Beyond Silence*, Coordinator, Shared Reading Project
Deaf Connection/Puget Sound Educational Services District, Seattle

"Your work is to be highly commended and is an excellent choice for inclusion in the reference section of most libraries. A wonderful tool for program planners observing Mother, Father Deaf Day in April and all other Deaf Community annual events throughout the year."

Alice L. Hagemeyer, Founder, Friends of Libraries for Deaf Action (FOLDA)

"This bibliography gives evidence that hearing children of deaf parents have a place in the consciousness of deaf people. A lot has been written on this subject over time which reflects a preoccupation with children who hear in a culture of people who don't. The sheer weight of the bibliography also indicates how much hearing children of deaf parents have been concerned with their relationship to the deafness of their parents in addition to their relationship to their parents. The many publications here that try to express these relationships are testimony to the strong hold these relationships have over hearing adults in particular. Deaf parents and their children have a special bond that can only be understood through deep introspection and study. This bibliography provides a good resource for anyone wanting to do such study. An excellent work!"

Tom Humphries, Ph.D., Department of Communication and Teacher Education Program
University of California, San Diego
Carol Padden, Ph.D., Associate Professor, Department of Communication, and
Associate Director, Human Development Program, University of California, San Diego

On the Edge of Deaf Culture

Nathie
Thanks heaps
for keeping me
"on the edge."

Hugs & Smacks

Tom

Hearing Children/Deaf Parents

Annotated Bibliography by

Thomas Bull

On the Edge of Deaf Culture
Hearing Children/Deaf Parents
Annotated Bibliography

PRESS

Deaf Family Research Press
DFR Press, P.O. Box 8417
Alexandria, Virginia 22306-8417
E-mail: tomthe@aol.com
E-mail: Tom.Bull@Gallaudet.edu
http://www.gallaudet.edu/~gisweb/Tom.html

©Thomas H. Bull

Library of Congress Catalog Card Number: 98-72707

ISBN 0-9665152-1-8 (paper)

This book is printed on acid-free paper.

The paper used in this publication meets the minimum
requirements of the American National Standard for Information Sciences—
Permanence of Paper for Printed Library Materials
ANSI Z39.48-1984

On the Edge of Deaf Culture—Photographs on the covers

Front, (*shown top to bottom*):
Goodstein family–(*left to right*), Matt (21), Harvey, Astrid, Ryan (16), and Jon Brett (22); **Margolin family**–(*left to right*), Justin (22 months), Murray, and Anjali; **Walker family**–(*left to right*), Joshua (14), Kris (12), Kristina (Leitch), Stephanie (12), and Steven; **Duhon family**–(*left to right*), Dean (15), Sherry, Andrew, and Chad (17).

Back, (*shown top to bottom*):
Feggins family–(*clockwise from top right*), Audrey, Robert L. (12), Rachel (7), Marvin (9), Tracy (10), and Robert J.; **Talbert family**–(*left to right*), Lisa (Jacobs), Darby Cortlynn (24 months), and Allen; **Madan family**–(*left to right*), Graziella (3) and Cecilia; **Lowe family**–(*left to right*), Andrew, Catherine (Kitty) (9 months), Shelby.

Cover Design by Wendelin A. Daniels

TABLE OF CONTENTS

The following types of materials are listed here: monographs, reports, brochures, booklets, manuscripts, handbooks, internet articles, unpublished, difficult-to-obtain or unavailable papers. Materials from the Gallaudet University Archives such as vertical, manuscript, subject, biographical and other files are also included here.

PREFACE

Deaf people are no longer the invisible minority they once were. Deaf characters appear on soap operas and *Star Trek*. One deaf woman wins an Oscar as Best Actress. Another becomes Miss America. Closed captioning and TTYs provide an increasing number of interactions between deaf and hearing people. Although deaf people may have become more visible, media and technology frequently mask significant cultural differences between Deaf people and Hearing people. How much do hearing people really understand the day-to-day lives of ordinary deaf people?

One of the aspects of Deaf life that has received increasing attention is family life -- but not just families of hearing parents and their deaf children. Many deaf children grow up to raise families of their own. Deaf-parented families are especially noteworthy among the infinite variations and configurations of parent-and-child. Almost 90% of deaf parents have hearing children -- and this sets into motion an unprecedented interplay between two cultures within one family.

Hearing children of deaf parents represent a unique paradigm because we straddle two worlds, incorporate two visions, and often speak two significantly different languages. Our cross-cultural experience has generated interest not only among outsiders, but among ourselves as well. As we struggle to understand ourselves in the midst of the innumerable versions created by linguists, psychologists, educators, and curious onlookers, we have added our own voices, too. We have shared stories of our lives and our families in articles, essays, interviews, plays and novels. We don't always agree about the story of our lives -- because each of our stories is a little different. But it is from these many perspectives that our ongoing story unfolds.

Trying to find materials on hearing children of deaf parents is challenging for a number of reasons. Professional publications on hearing children of deaf parents (increasingly referred to as "codas") are scattered across many disciplines -- each with its own network of publication vehicles, indices, references and archives. You might think library databases or internet search engines would address this multidisciplinary problem. But, a simple search for "hearing children of deaf parents" invariably produces hundreds or even thousands of listings -- on "hearing parents of deaf children." In this case, word order makes two generations' of difference.

There is also a more insidious problem inherent in locating these materials. Much of the "known" literature is decidedly biased, but this bias doesn't just refer to those writers and researchers who look for pathology in our lives. There is also the more subtle and seductive bias of professionalism. Libraries and bibliographies typically emphasize literature that has been filtered through academic channels and established publications. This self-selecting process eliminates many additional sources of information including newspaper articles, class papers, self-published books and conference proceedings. Non-written materials -- such as videotaped interviews or even live presentations -- are also frequently forgotten resources. These latter exclusions are especially notable when considering the importance and immediacy of visual communication among the Deaf.

Given these challenges, it takes great effort to come up with a truly broad cross section of materials which encompasses many disciplines and many perspectives. Tom Bull's endeavors to create the definitive bibliography on hearing children of deaf parents have paid off. This annotated bibliography is simply the most comprehensive resource on hearing children of deaf parents that exists. This book encompasses a wide variety of academic and popular citations on hearing children of deaf parents as well as valuable up-to-date resources for parents and professionals. On the surface, this publication represents many years of dedication and just plain old hard work. Tom has methodically and persistently tracked down even the faintest reference to hearing children of deaf parents.

When I was beginning fieldwork for my own book on hearing children of deaf parents, it took months to find even a fraction of the materials accumulated here. In his search for source materials, Tom has spent years networking among Deaf communities and hearing children of deaf parents. But he has ventured beyond being merely a gatherer and cataloger. True to his heritage, Tom has also taken on the role of cultural guide. He has read and summarized these works and, as guide, he is both thorough and fair.

At Through the Looking Glass' National Resource Center for Parents with Disabilities, we share Tom's zeal for recognition and understanding of our families. Deaf and disabled parents represent more than 8 million American parents, and millions and millions more throughout the world. My own involvement in this first National Center came about through the intersections of our families. Deaf parents. Disabled parents. Our parents. There are, to be sure, significant differences between our families -- but there is also much that we share. I think my colleague Megan Kirshbaum expressed it best: "Our families," she wrote, "are profoundly ordinary." At our Center, one major goal is to promote understanding about deaf and disabled parents through information -- information about the viability, the variety and the ordinariness of our families. We seek to share our histories, challenge misconceptions, and document our lives in ways both representative and fair. Tom Bull's work here is an important contribution to this effort.

As a researcher on deaf families, this is the first book I'll reach for. Tom's book is a must for anyone interested in deafness -- as well as biculturalism, bilingualism, disability studies, infant development and family studies. As a fellow coda, I want to thank Tom for his gift to our community. The extensive breadth of materials accumulated here provides a rich resource for many people, but especially deaf parents and their hearing children. This book should be in libraries and schools across the country.

Paul Preston, Ph.D.
Author, *Mother Father Deaf: Living between Sound and Silence*
Co-Director, National Resource Center for Parents with Disabilities
Through the Looking Glass
Berkeley, California

INTRODUCTION

Hearing children with deaf parents (codas) live half their life in the Deaf World and half in the Hearing World. They often wonder whether they are hearing or deaf. This identity conflict is not unusual for those raised in a bilingual and bicultural family, for those who grow up "hearing" in the Deaf World. In fact, it is typical of people who are raised with two or more cultures. This experience is expressed in a variety of ways: "I felt like I visited two homes but had no place for myself"; "I'm caught in between"; "I'm neither one nor the other." Identity development is impossible without a sense of community. Deaf and hard-of-hearing people know this. As adults, some of us hearing children of deaf parents are finding an identity that helps us know our place in the world. This identity comes from a community of those like us. This community is CODA, Children of Deaf Adults. I am deaf-hearing-coda, always on the edge of Deaf Culture.

There are no statistics on the number of codas. In 1989 the National Institute on Deafness and Other Communication Disorders (NIDCD) estimated there were approximately 2 million profoundly deaf Americans. Approximately 90% of the children born to deaf parents are hearing.[1] Dr. Robert Hoffmeister, a fellow coda and Chair of Programs in Deaf Studies at Boston University, and I have calculated that there are at least 1.5 million codas in the United States. Of course, this figure depends on how wide a net one casts (from profoundly to moderately deaf and late-deafened parents) and assumptions about birth rate.

Some years ago, those of us who are hearing and who were born into a family with deaf parents were labeled "HCDPs" (hearing children of deaf parents). Since 1983, there has been a significant spread in the use of the term coda which, by definition, implies the *hearing* offspring of at least one deaf parent. That term was coined by Millie Brother, founder of the now international organization CODA (Children of Deaf Adults). The acronym has its origins in the musical term *coda*, which is the concluding section of a piece of music that reflects, yet differs from, the main structure. Millie chose this word because of her strong musical background.

I recall practicing classical music pieces for symphony orchestra concerts and having conductors explain the term *coda*. In a musical composition, it was the concluding segment dependent upon the preceding musical development; yet, it was an altered version of the original. In my eyes, I was the human analogy to this musical form.[2]

In my case, I am the second child of deaf parents. My father was born deaf, from unknown causes, in Nebraska in 1903. He attended the Kansas School for the Deaf in Olathe because it was closer to his home than the Nebraska school. When he was 10 years old, my grandparents moved to the San Joaquin Valley in California and he attended the California School for the Deaf in Berkeley. He excelled in sports, learned the shoe repair trade, and in 1922 became the second deaf person in the United States to become an Eagle Boy Scout. The school only provided up to an 8th grade education at the time, so he "mainstreamed" back to his rural hometown public high school where he played football and completed 2 more years of education. He went on to manage his own shoe repair shop in his hometown for 18 years. My family moved to the San Francisco Bay Area during the Second World War where factory jobs were plentiful, and my dad became a member of the United Auto Workers Union.

My mother was born hearing in Missouri in 1904 and became deaf from a series of illnesses contracted between the age of 2 and 3 years. Her speech was neither very intelligible nor grammatical, but because she had some apparent speech capability, her family took the "oral" route educationally. Her family also moved to California where she eventually entered the California School for the Deaf at the age of 15, an apparent "oral failure." I assume that her educational potential was wasted over these "oral" years because she was functionally illiterate. It was difficult for her to understand the meaning of newspaper articles, and she held a pen awkwardly. She never drove a car. As far as I know, deafness is not hereditary in my family.

If you are familiar with the book *In This Sign* by Joanne Greenberg,[3] the deaf couple there, Janice and Able Ryder, were born in 1900 and raised their hearing children during the Depression and the Second World War. If you saw the 1986 Hallmark Hall of Fame movie, *Love Is Never Silent*,[4] which was based on Greenberg's novel, then you have a good sense of the life and times of my parents and deaf people in that period. It's uncanny how many aspects of Janice and Able Ryder's family life are similar to my story. They lived in New York City and had two children, Margaret and Bradley, who were 6 years apart, and they communicated at home in American Sign Language. My parents communicated most readily in American Sign Language. My sister was 6 years old when I was born, and during her early years my family lived with our hearing grandmother in California farm country. Bradley Ryder was 4 years old when he climbed out onto a fire escape in their tenement building and fell to his death. Margaret was 10 years old and interpreted for her parents in selecting a "coffin" and dealing with the funeral director. As my paternal grandmother crossed a rural highway at dusk, she was hit by a driver in a pickup truck and died. I was 12 years old, and helped my parents select the casket and communicate with mortuary personnel. Able Ryder was a blue-collar worker and at his 25-year retirement party received a yellow-gold watch. When my father retired from his union after 25 years, he also received a yellow-gold watch. Like Janice, who worked for many years as a seamstress in a sheltered workshop, my mother, too, labored as a piecework seamstress at Goodwill Industries.

Margaret Ryder married and had a son who, as a young adult, became involved in the Civil Rights Movement and went South. He had seen enough of oppression and discrimination in the case study of his deaf grandparents over the years. I was a student at the Pacific School of Religion in Berkeley, California, preparing for ministry in the United Methodist Church, when Dr. Martin Luther King, Jr., called for volunteers. In response, I boarded a bus with 41 other seminary students from the Bay Area. We eventually marched from Selma to Montgomery out of our concern for those who were being discriminated against and out of our commitment to social justice. Having deaf parents was, for me, definitely a factor as well. (Remember, when I was growing up there was no legislation like the Americans with Disabilities Act, there were no certified Sign Language interpreters, no telephone access using TTYs or relay operators, and no closed captioning of television programs.) There are other parallels between my family and Margaret's in the book. I marvel that Joanne Greenberg could write such a candid depiction of deaf family life with such insight.

It may seem strange to introduce myself to the reader in this manner. There are many characteristics of Deaf culture. One in particular - long introduction rituals - is worth explaining here. Storytelling is an integral part of Deaf culture but is also characteristic of introductions in the deaf community. The authors of *A Journey into the DEAF-WORLD* describe the reasons in their chapter, "Welcome to the DEAF-WORLD:"

> When members of the DEAF-WORLD meet, they introduce themselves and their companions [by giving a] capsule life-histor[y] so that each can see how the others are connected to the DEAF-WORLD network. For unlike other cultures, Deaf culture is not associated with a single place, a "native land"; rather, it is a culture based on relationships among people for whom a number of places and associations may provide common ground.[5]

My involvement in the CODA organization began in 1984, and I attended the first CODA conference in 1986. I have attended every annual conference since and have edited 5 years of conference proceedings as well as helped establish the Washington, D. C., CODA chapter. A bibliography I compiled has been distributed since 1993 by the National Information Center on Deafness at Gallaudet University.[6] It is 20 pages long and is a precursor to this book. I am now steeped in my "coda heritage." Even my personalized license plates declare I am a "coda." However, for all of my childhood and most of my adult years, I never knew this was my identity.

Until my first CODA conference, I thought I was alone. That meeting helped me realize more clearly my identity as a coda. That conference was and remains a significant milestone. As I said on a panel at the Denver, Colorado, CODA Conference in July 1997:

> Coming to CODA has helped bring a lot of the parts of my life together in a way that I wish had happened much earlier.... There are many people who don't fully realize who they are until later in life. It makes me think of a story I heard of a person whose parents never told him he had Usher's syndrome. He's deaf and has a vision problem. He doesn't find out he's going to become blind until he's 25 years old, but his parents knew he had Ushers when he was 12 years old. What an identity crisis.[7]

No one ever told me I was unique because I was a koda (kid of deaf adults). I have wandered for many years "in the wilderness" alone. I have always had a sense of being different from others because my parents were deaf. I recall a Cub Scout banquet where I interpreted for my parents. I was 8 years old. Before that, I remember thinking they were just fooling me and wishing that they could hear. I even tested them. I would yell or clap my hands and sometimes they would turn around just enough so that, as a young child, I believed the evidence before my own eyes. When our telephone was installed (I was 9 years old) my sister and I spent the entire day calling our friends. I had embarrassing moments as a kid, signing in American Sign Language to my parents in front of peers. But at some point in my lonely journey I made the conscious decision not to feel embarrassed signing in public. I saw my father's helplessness in arousing neighbors at 2 a.m. when my sister fainted at home after having dental surgery and it is not a pleasant memory. I wondered "What's wrong with me?" in high school when others didn't hold eye-contact with me. I needed eye-contact in return and didn't understand that about myself until I was 47 years old. On my weekly bus trips home from college, it didn't feel right to simply shake hands with my dad. I made a conscious decision to embrace him. Within the Deaf community, the affectionate hug is a culturally appropriate greeting. I now realize that I was, at that time, caught in a cultural wasteland of confusion between the Deaf and Hearing worlds. It has just been within the past few years that I have come to understand myself as a bilingual and bicultural person.

Are these the thoughts and painful memories I feared would come loose and cascade down upon me when I attended my first CODA conference in 1986? Perhaps. It's fairly commonplace to hear stories of deaf or hard-of-hearing students who never realize their full identity (as deaf or hard-of-hearing) until they find others "like them." So many of us in CODA have had a similar experience. My experience was personally dramatic. For me the sense of isolation and aloneness yielded to the camaraderie and joy I found. Over the last few years, I have shared what I thought were the experiences of a jaded personality with my coda brothers and sisters. I now realize that my experiences are, in fact, the common denominator of what it means to be hearing on the edge of Deaf Culture amidst the richness we now call American Sign Language. My search has brought me ultimately to the printed page here.

As a graduate student, then teacher, and now staff member at Gallaudet University, for 30 years it's been a privilege to vicariously witness the metamorphoses of self-esteem and accomplishments within the Deaf community. First came pride in learning that American Sign Language (which is my language, too) is not a "bastardized" form of English, where the appropriate emotion should be shame. ASL is now offered for foreign language credit in many high schools, colleges and universities. Then came the Deaf President Now movement which broke down many personal and attitudinal barriers, as well as barriers associated with accessibility and human rights. When Jack Gannon published, in 1981, his seminal volume *Deaf Heritage*,[8] he said, "There is a Deaf Culture." Today, Deaf Studies is a field of study and there are international Deaf history conferences. That sense of connection with the past and with deaf people from around the world has had a profound impact on deaf individuals and the Deaf World. Indeed, it's had a powerful impact on me.

For example, my mother was born in 1904 and was orally educated. She died at the age of 69 unable to read or write English at a minimal level. Those facts came to mind when I attended a showing of the documentary film *In the Land of the Deaf* in 1994.[9] It's about the French Deaf community and was filmed between 1989 and 1992. What I saw on the screen was the emphasis on speech training and lipreading without visual support (Sign Language). The most poignant moments I identified with were the wedding and the newlyweds' search for an apartment using a "hard-of-hearing" friend as their "interpreter." I thought to myself, "In 90 years [1904-1994], not much has changed." Knowledge of history and a film like that can be powerful mobilizers and catalysts for change.

Deafness is a low-incidence disability. But that disability has created a whole world of unique experiences for deaf and hard-of-hearing individuals. Could it be that the hearing children born into these families also share a unique universe to be proud of? My parents were born in 1903 and 1904. As deaf children and later deaf adults, what was their world like? My story is inextricably bound up with their history. Their world was one in which their language (American Sign Language) was suppressed. They had to fight for the right to drive and obtain automobile insurance. Although they may not have been cognizant of it, they had to fight against Aristotle's dictum of 355 B.C. and the attitudes that it perpetuated: "Those who are born deaf all become senseless and incapable of reason."[10] The Deaf community in the United States has had to fight for the right to marry and parent, adopt and rear hearing children. That struggle continues even today.[11] Society's stigma, placed on deaf and hard-of-hearing parents, has rubbed off onto us, their hearing children. Often, people wonder and ask, "Can 'normal' hearing children learn English in an environment that's different?" "How?" Many of these issues become part of the repartee, folklore and heritage that is shared within the community of CODA.

The wealth of knowledge brought together in this bibliography should be helpful to codas and those inside and outside the Deaf community. In so many doctoral dissertations and master's theses the author begins by saying, "There is a dearth of information and research on deaf families with hearing children." While we may have qualms about the quality of that research, the sheer number of references listed in this bibliography (over 2,200) refute that statement today. American Sign Language and the Deaf community are topics of widespread interest now in American society. Along with that, there is more interest in the "hearing of deaf" community than ever before. For example, in the period 1971-1976 there were only four Ph.D. or M.A. theses on this subject. In the period 1992-1997, there were at least 21.

An outstanding collection of historical materials on deafness is housed within the Gallaudet University Archives. On a wall in the Archives office hangs a photograph. There are several Indians kneeling on the ground warming themselves around a fire. A Sioux saying is quoted at the bottom of the picture: "A people without history is like the wind on the buffalo grass." Indeed, people are lost without a sense of history and pride in that history. I am a person with a stake in the Deaf community. Although I am hearing, many consider that I am, to some extent, also a member of the Deaf community. Where is my history? I am not deaf, so to some extent the impact of Deaf history on me will be different. Where is the history of those born hearing into the Deaf World?

Our story as a people necessarily begins with the personal stories of individuals and families. Lou Ann Walker wrote the first autobiographical account of growing up hearing in a deaf family that I know of. Her book was published in 1986. There have been six other such autobiographies since (Abrams[12], Barash,[13] Crowe,[14] Davis,[15] Miller-Hall,[16] Sidransky[17]), several novels (Glickfeld,[18] Greenberg,[19] Jeffers[20]), and a number of important studies (Preston,[21] Thurman,[22] and any of the 81 citations listed in the "Ph.D. dissertations and M.A. theses" section of this book). My isolation and loneliness began to ebb as I read these stories. These authors and the many others who have shared their stories, have had a normalizing effect on me. The importance of storytelling is echoed in the following quotes.

Tell someone a fact and you reach their minds; give them a story and you touch their souls.
Hasidic Proverb

In his classic *Reaching Out*, Dutch theologian Henri Nouwen writes of the importance of becoming "sensitive and obedient to our own stories." ...Rooted in the Latin *surdus*, absurdity refers to a kind of deafness, incongruity, not being capable of perceiving sound and meaning. In this sense, it seems that obedience has an open quality, of questions and process, listening and receiving, while absurdity has a closed quality, of "answers" and indifference, distraction and denial. Nouwen concluded that though our own story "can be hard to tell, full of disappointments and frustrations, deviations and stagnations...it is the only story we have and there will be no hope for the future when the past remains unconfessed, unreceived, and misunderstood."

Cynthia Hirni[23]

Stories are our protectors, like our immune system, defending against attacks of debilitating alienation. They are the connective tissue between culture and nature, self and other, life and death, that sew the worlds together, and in telling, the soul quickens and comes alive.

Joan Halifax[24]

Telling our stories may be the most human thing we do. By telling stories, we remember our past, invent our present, and envision our future. Then, by sharing those stories with others, we overcome loneliness, discover compassion, and create community with kindred souls.

Sam Keen, philosopher, theologian and poet[25]

As my search for identity and self began with others like me at my first CODA conference, so my search for community and a sense of history is carried on in my interest in stories from the past. How far back does the coda historical record go? Were those other codas like me? What have researchers "found out" about codas? What is the depth of our uniqueness in American and Deaf society? Are there common ties we have with codas from other cultures and other times? Is there a "coda heritage" that goes beyond the boundaries of race, religion, culture, and national origin? Do we have our own language, literature, values, beliefs, and shared characteristics that are unique enough to draw us together? I began this bibliography to find answers to questions like these.

Codas and the Deaf community are inextricably woven together. I didn't realize this until I began to travel. The summer after my first year in college, I was 19 years old and went 3,000 miles across the country to work at the Delaware State Hospital, a hospital for the mentally ill. They were doing a lot of experimentation with new pharmacological drugs like phenobarbital and others. I met a deaf patient there, and no one was able to communicate with him. Before long, we were in our own world of American Sign Language. On another summer venture during my seminary days, I worked as an assistant pastor of a small church in Hawaii. One of my duties was door-to-door canvassing in the community. I came to a house where there was a note above the door bell that said, "Press and hold for 30 seconds." I knew it was a deaf family. I knew the light signals inside would flash off and on for 30 seconds getting the deaf householder's attention. I made friends there and had a wonderful time over the summer as a result. It's uncanny how a person can go so far away from home and still feel the warmth and closeness of (Deaf) community. Similar things have happened to countless other coda friends.

Codas from other generations have also discovered their strong emotional tie to the Deaf community in remote places. During the Second World War the National Association of the Deaf raised money to purchase a Clubmobile (a canteen on wheels) as one of their contributions to the war effort.[26] This letter, written by a coda, touchingly illustrates how that contribution made him proud of his connection to the Deaf community:

Mother, your National Association of the Deaf has contributed to the Red Cross and it bought Clubmobiles with the money. The other day, one came here and on the door was printed "FROM THE DEAF OF THE UNITED STATES THROUGH THE N.A.D.!!" I got a thrill out of seeing that and after rubbing off the mud, took a picture of the car.

I thought you and your [deaf] friends might like to know YOUR car is here in Italy where it will do a lot of good spreading cheer and hot coffee to many tired soldiers and greeting thousands of pilots back from missions.

I know I speak for a couple of thousand soldiers - both enlisted men and officers - when I say to you and your GRAND NATIONAL ASSOCIATION OF THE DEAF: "THANKS SO MUCH."
Wally [Oldfather from Iowa, 1943][27]

One of the most inventive individuals of the 20th century was Alexander Graham Bell. His mother was deaf, which makes him a coda. Incidentally, his wife was also deaf. However, his legacy in the Deaf community makes me uncomfortable. He was a prominent opponent of the ideas of Edward Miner Gallaudet, president of Gallaudet College at that time. They were both codas but on opposite sides of the oral/manual debate. Bell was also against intermarriage of the deaf. As unpleasant as it is, these ideas are a part of deaf heritage and my coda history. This quote from Bell makes me realize that ignorance can lead even a coda to promulgate mistaken ideas.

If the laws of heredity that are known to hold in the case of animals also apply to man, the intermarriage of congenital deaf mutes through a number of successive generations should result in the formation of a deaf variety of the human race.[28]

When I tell people my parents are deaf, they invariably ask a lot of questions. Sometimes they are thoughtful questions, and people seem genuinely interested. One of the most common questions is, "How did you learn to talk?" However, the novelty of answering these same questions over and over again wears off. It's a source of irritation to realize that American society's general knowledge of the Deaf world remains so minimal. People do ask dumb questions like, "Do your parents know braille?" I have once heard a story about a flight attendant who brought a wheelchair for the deaf passenger!

The Deaf community as well, has had to deal with any number of mistaken ideas or myths about being deaf. One I have already mentioned is about the inheritability of deafness. Based on this "theory" people in turn advocated that a deaf person should not marry another deaf individual. The related myth - about their children - has had an impact on my life and the lives of codas. In his "Public Opinion" column in the April 1918, *Silent Worker*, Dr. J. H. Cloud quotes from page 5 of Amy Eliza Tanner's book, *The Child*, on the subject of the causes of degeneracy:

As the causes of degeneracy are studied, more and more do we realize how the sin or defect of the parent is "visited upon the children even unto the third and fourth generation." Like begets not like but similar. The parent with any form of nervous defect passes on, but in the child it may assume almost any other form. For example, statistics on the children of parents, one or both of whom were congenitally deaf, show that their children, a much higher percent than normal were not deaf, but imbecile, epileptic, and criminal.[29]

Cloud goes on to say, "It would be interesting to know how the author manipulated statistics in reaching such an unfair conclusion as regards the deaf...the sins of authors, of which the above is a glaring illustration, are limited only by the circulation of their books."[30] In my research, it was a surprise to learn that these questions about the hearing children of deaf parents are not unique to my generation. Here's evidence, from a 1905 issue of The Silent Worker to illustrate how the common denominator of the "coda experience" persists:

My Dear Mr. Editor:

The pictures of "typical children of deaf parents," appearing frequently in your excellent paper have been a source of great interest to me, for where is the person who can fail to delight in the charming sweetness of childhood in its pictured loveliness. The cute pictures of pretty Lucille Berg, in the December number, had an added interest for me in that her parents were both school-mates of mine in the long ago of merry Hoosier days. It is quite a treat to see the young faces of all those "typical children of deaf parents," and, especially, when they happen to belong to old school mates of youthful days. So go on with the good work! And to help it on, I send you photographs of two little representatives of the great Middle West and hope others will send more too. The large picture is of Edith Una Long, the eldest daughter of Mr. J. Schuyler Long, of Council Bluffs, Iowa.... Her parents are semi-mutes and Mr. Long is head teacher of the Academic Dep't [sic] of the [Iowa] State School [for the Deaf]. The small picture is of little Beth Thompson.... [She] is just seven, and in the second grade at school where she easily holds her own with the best. Her parents are both deaf-mutes.... Both children show the usual bright cleverness of children of deaf parents and lead their classes at school in reading and spelling and also show great taste for music and drawing.

Now, if more deaf parents would send pictures of their little ones that are of school age to your paper, there would be enough to collect together in book form which they could buy and distribute to such hearing acquaintances as ask the fool question, "Can your baby hear?" "How can it ever hear or speak when you cannot?" etc. Such a little book might be a good thing in public libraries where hearing people could read it and disabuse their minds of the popular fallacy that intermarriage of the deaf resulted in either deaf or idiotic offspring. It would certainly be choice reading for Dr. Bell and make him reflect before he furnished any more conclusions concerning deaf [people] to a confiding public. With all good wishes for the continued success of your highly interesting paper and the compliment of the season. I am Sincerely, E. F. L.[31]

One characteristic of Deaf culture and the deaf community is a high interest in young deaf children, the future generation. For example, a deaf couple living down the street from a family where the parents are hearing and have a deaf child, the deaf couple might take a special interest in that family and in that deaf child. They feel a special bond with the future generation. In the same way, many of us in CODA feel a bond with the "little ones" as someone put it. This poem by a deaf father describes their experiences and is simply titled, "My Hearing Children's Dilemma":

> Daddy, why are the kids at school
>   always making fun of me
>   because of you and Mommy?
> Daddy, what is it
>   that they're laughing about?
> They think you have *funny* speech
>   because of the button in your ear.
>   They think I'm not as smart as they are
>   because you're not like their parents.
> Daddy, why are they doing this to me?
>   Dad, it's not fair.
> Daddy, is it because you're deaf?[32]

In our pluralistic society, there is still room for improvement, especially in the patronizing, condescending and paternalistic attitudes people have toward the disabled and people who are deaf and hard-of-hearing. In her piece, "Don't Forget the Children - The hearing children born to deaf parents" JoAnn McCann writes: "they are the ones who bore for you the taunts and jeers of other kids on the playground who don't understand the magic of your signs...."[33] Bonnie Kraft, in her storytelling videotape, said she felt the oppression of her deaf parents and friends. "Family is family." She went on to say that even though her ears can hear, her heart is Deaf.[34] Through such efforts as the Millie Brother Scholarship Fund and the Mother Father Deaf Day activity, CODA and codas are laboring to dispel society's myths about deaf parenting.[35] Some codas are actively involved in encouraging deaf/Deaf parents to form KODA chapters. It would be wonderful, I think, if the Deaf community and CODA community could find ways to work together so that the difficulties kodas experience could be further alleviated. It was fascinating to find the same sentiment voiced back in 1977 by Israel Sela. He presented a paper at the Vth World Conference on

World Conference on Deafness in Copenhagen, Denmark, and described the Israeli system of exclusively oral education for the deaf and other developments in his country. In the last paragraph from that paper, he gives a challenge to the audience:

> Yesterday, a nice lady from Canada, a daughter of deaf parents, talked about the problems of hearing children with deaf parents (I am [one], too). I want to ask the leaders, managers, the President, Dr. Magarotto [who is also a coda and the founder of the World Federation of the Deaf], Dr. Vogoti, and other people here, to decide to create, here and now, a committee of hearing children of deaf parents who work with the deaf - we are very few but we exist. I think that today, with all the professionals who come to work with the deaf - why not use us, we the professionals, to help contribute to the World of the Deaf. And I hope that at the next Congress [of the World Federation of the Deaf], in Bulgaria, this committee will function.[36]

I am not aware of any tangible result from Sela's appeal, but I hope something like this will happen some day. The history of the Deaf community cannot be considered something separate from coda heritage. I was very glad to see a section in Jack Gannon's *Deaf Heritage* devoted to the hearing children born to deaf parents.[37] My history as a coda is bound up with the history of the Deaf World. The Deaf World cannot cut itself off from its hearing sons and daughters. Somehow, we must find a way to work together. There are many members of CODA who are very eager to work with the Deaf community. This lyrics from this song, *At the Same Time,* describe a wonderful world vision. When I hear it, I think of all the koda children, koda hearts, koda eyes and hands out in the world. I also think of their deaf/Deaf parents and members of the deaf community who are unaware that their hearing children are kodas.

> Think of all the hearts, beating in the world, at the same time.
> Think of all the faces, and the stories they could tell, at the same time.
> Think of all the eyes, looking out into this world, trying to make some sense of what we see.
> Think of all the ways we have of seeing, think of all the ways there are of being.
>
> Think of all the children, being born into this world, at the same time.
> Feel your love surround them, through the years they'll need to grow at the same time.
> Just think of all the hands that will be reaching for a dream, think of all the dreams that could come true.
> If the hands we're reaching with could come together joining me and you.
>
> When it comes to thinking of tomorrow, we must protect our fragile destiny.
> In this precious life there's no time to borrow, the time has come to be a family.
> Just think of all the love pouring from our hearts at the same time.
> Yes, think of all the light our love can shine around this world at the same time.
>
> Just think what we've been given and then think what we can lose, all of life is in our trembling hands.
> It's time to overcome our fears, and join to build a world that loves and understands.
> It helps to think of all the hearts beating in the world, and hope for all the hearts beating in the world,
> There's a healing music in our hearts, beating in this world at the same time, at the same time.[38]

In the meantime, this book is dedicated to the millions of those young kodas and adult codas in the world who don't know their rich heritage. Be proud of it as I have become. You are the future generations who will fill the pages of coda and Deaf history with your contributions to the Deaf World, writings, stories, wisdom, and insight. I hope someday we can forever leave behind the medical and pathological model of Deaf parenting and begin to ask a whole new set of questions. Enhancing our knowledge base should help. That is what I am about here.

NOTES

1. J. D. Schein, & M. T. Delk, Jr. (1974). Civil status, family composition, and fertility. In The Deaf Population of the United States (pp. 35-46). Silver Spring, MD: National Association of the Deaf.

2. M. Brother (Ed.). (1983, November). <u>CODA Newsletter [Introductory issue]</u> (p. 1). Santa Barbara, CA: Children of Deaf Adults.

3. J. Greenberg. (1970). <u>In This Sign.</u> New York: Holt, Rinehart and Winston.

4. *Love Is Never Silent.* Hallmark Hall of Fame: NBC-TV. (1985, December 1). New York: Hallmark Hall of Fame.

5. H. Lane, R. Hoffmeister, & B. Bahan. <u>A Journey into the DEAF-WORLD</u> (p. 5). San Diego, CA: DawnSignPress.

6. T. H. Bull (Ed.). (1993). <u>Hearing Children with Deaf Parents</u> [Bibliography]. Washington, DC: National Information Center on Deafness.

7. J. Powell (Ed.). (1977). Opening panel: What keeps you coming back to CODA? In R. Shipman (Ed.). <u>"Once upon a time....:" Proceedings of the twelfth annual International CODA Conference, Denver, Colorado, July 10-13, 1997</u> (p. 66). Santa Barbara, CA: Children of Deaf Adults.

8. J. R. Gannon. (1981). <u>Deaf Heritage: A Narrative History of Deaf America.</u> Silver Spring, MD: National Association of the Deaf.

9. *In the Land of the Deaf.* (1992/1994). Distributed by International Film Circuit Inc., New York.

10. R. E. Bender. (1981). <u>The Conquest of Deafness: A History of the Long Struggle to Make Possible Normal Living to the Handicapped by Lack of Normal Hearing</u> (p.21). Danville, IL: Interstate Printers and Publishers. (Bender goes on to explain that while this quote was distorted and taken out of context, nevertheless "this pronouncement was especially disastrous to the deaf, since the writings of Aristotle were accepted without question for hundreds of years, down through the Middle Ages.")

11. See the *Dateline: Hear No Evil* program entry in the "Video and Audio Tapes" section of this bibliography for a description of the custody battle of Keri Knickerbocker and Gerald Webb who lost custody of their hearing daughter, Angie, in 1992.

12. C. Abrams. (1996). <u>The Silents.</u> Washington, DC: Gallaudet University Press.

13. H. L. Barash, & E. Barash-Dicker. (1991). <u>Our Father Abe: The Story of a Deaf Shoe Repairman.</u> Madison, WI: Abar Press.

14. D. I. Crowe. (1993). <u>Dummy's Little Girl.</u> New York: Carlton Press.

15. L. J. Davis. (in press). <u>The Sense of Silence: A Memoir of a Childhood with Deafness.</u> Chicago: University of Illinois Press. Manuscript in preparation.

16. M. Miller-Hall. (1994). <u>Deaf, Dumb and BLACK: An Account of an Actual Life of a Family.</u> New York: Carlton Press.

17. R. Sidransky. (1990). <u>In Silence: Growing Up Hearing in a Deaf World.</u> New York: St. Martin's Press.

18. C. L. Glickfeld. (1989). <u>Useful Gifts: Stories by Carole L. Glickfeld.</u> Athens, GA: The University of Georgia Press.

19. J. Greenberg. (1970). <u>In This Sign.</u> New York: Holt, Rinehart and Winston.

20. A. Jeffers. (1995). <u>Safe as Houses.</u> New York: Faber and Faber.

21. P. M. Preston. (1994). <u>Mother Father Deaf: Living Between Sound and Silence.</u> Cambridge, MA: Harvard University Press.

22. S. K. Thurman, (Ed.). (1985). <u>Children of Handicapped Parents: Research and Clinical Perspectives.</u> Orlando, FL: Academic Press.

23. C. Herni. (1994, January). <u>The Ridgeleaf</u> (p. 1). Newsletter published occasionally by the Kirkridge Center, Bangor, Pennsylvania.

24. J. Halifax. (1994). <u>The Fruitful Darkness: Reconnecting with the Body of the Earth.</u> San Francisco: Harper.

25. Taken from the narrative of an interview with Sam Keen, part of *The World of Ideas* series produced and conducted by Bill Moyers, in 1991.

26. Victory Fund Goes to Red Cross: One of Three Clubmobiles in Army Show. (1943, November 24). <u>The Buff and Blue,</u> <u>52</u> (3), p. 1.

27. I want to thank Dr. Barbara Kannapell for this quotation which is on film footage in the following presentation. Source unknown. B. M. Kannapell. The forgotten people: Deaf people's contributions during World War II. In Gallaudet University, College of Continuing Education (Ed.), <u>Deaf Studies IV: "Visions of the Past - Visions of the Future,"</u> <u>Conference Proceedings, Woburn, Massachusetts, April 27-30, 1995</u> (pp. 111-123). Washington, DC: Gallaudet University, College for Continuing Education and Outreach.

28. A. G. Bell. (1884/1969). <u>Memoir Upon the Formation of a Deaf Variety of the Human Race</u> (p. 4). Washington, DC: Alexander Graham Bell Association for the Deaf.

29. J. H. Cloud. (1918, April). Public Opinion [Column]. <u>The Silent Worker, 30</u> (7), 23-24.

30. Ibid., p. 24.

31. E. F. Long. (1905, February). Typical Children of Deaf Parents [Letter to the Editor]. <u>The Silent Worker, 17</u> (5), 76. (The letter is from E. Florence Long and is dated December 27, 1904)

32. C. Robbins. (1993). (Personal communication. I'm grateful to Curt for permission to reprint this poem.)

33. McCann, J. A. (1992, Aug/Sept). Don't forget the children - the hearing children born to deaf parents. <u>CODA</u> <u>Connection, 9</u> (3), 4.

34. *Tomorrow Dad will Still be Deaf and Other Stories.* (1997). San Diego, CA: DawnSignPress.

35. See especially <u>Dispelling Myths about Deaf Parenting.</u> (1996). This is only one of the pieces of literature disseminated through the Mother Father Deaf Day program spearheaded by Trudy Schafer. See references in the "Miscellaneous" section of this bibliography.

36. I. Sela. (1978). Response. In L. von der Lieth (Ed.), <u>Life in Families with Deaf Members: Proceedings of the Vth World</u> <u>Conference on Deafness, Copenhagen, Denmark, 1977</u> (pp. 134-135). Copenhagen, Denmark: National Federation of the Deaf in Denmark.

37. J. R. Gannon. (1981). The 1970s. <u>Deaf Heritage: A Narrative History of Deaf America</u> (pp. 413-414). Silver Spring, MD: National Association of the Deaf.

38. From the 1997 album *Higher Ground* by Barbra Streisand. <u>AT THE SAME TIME,</u> by Ann Hampton Callaway. © 1997 WB Music Corp. (ASCAP), Halaron Music (ASCAP), Emmanuel Music Corp. (ASCAP) and Works of Heart Publishing (ASCAP) All Rights o/b/o Halaron Music, Emmanuel Music Corp. & Works of Heart Publishing administered by WB Music Corp. All Rights Reserved. Used by Permission. WARNER BROS. PUBLICATIONS U.S. INC., Miami, FL 33014

GUIDE TO REFERENCES

The present bibliography is considerably more inclusive than the list I compiled in 1993.[1] Some conventions utilized in references here may not be readily apparent. In general usage, capital "CODA" will refer to the organization Children of Deaf Adults, and the lower case "coda" will refer to individuals whether or not they are affiliated with the organization. No organizational affiliation is implied in using "coda." It is simply a convenient and meaningful acronym to identify individuals as hearing offspring/adults with at least one deaf parent. Deaf parents are meeting for mutual support and learning opportunities and to provide activities for their hearing children. KODA is an acronym referring to these deaf parent groups forming across the United States and means "Kids of Deaf Adult(s)." A hearing child below the age of 18 may be referred to as a "koda," or "kid of deaf adult(s)."

Citations are formatted here generally according to the style manual of the American Psychological Association.[2] There are instances where I have added more information for the sake of completeness. For those who want an updated search for materials relevant to this topic, check the Gallaudet University Library's online "Pathfinder" series. A copy of their pathfinder on "Deaf Parents with Hearing Children" is available at the end of this book and online at <http://www.gallaudet. edu/~library/new/deafguid.html>.

Brackets [ ] following a citation contain information about the location of the item at the Gallaudet University Merrill Learning Center (the library). Here are some examples of designations inside brackets: books may be found in Gallaudet's outstanding deaf collection [DEAF 612.78 L4v, 1965]; articles may be available in the periodicals section [UNIV DEAF Periodicals]; and dissertations available on microfilm will be designated in this way [DEAF Microfilm 260 1976]. Some materials may also be found at the Gallaudet library reference desk [UNIV Index].

Citations are embedded occasionally with notes within parentheses ( ) and an annotation within braces { }. A note or annotation may include a further reference that will be cited within the ( ) or { }. The initial citation's Gallaudet location in [ ] will follow information in ( ) and { }. Some of the materials listed may be available from your public library or educational institution through its interlibrary loan system. The Gallaudet University Library electronic catalog (known as ALADIN - Access to Library and Database Information Network) can be accessed through the World Wide Web at <http://www.gallaudet.edu/~library>.

Here is a summary of the symbols used:

[ ]	Brackets at the end of a citation contain the Gallaudet Library catalogue number.
[*]	Identifies an item not yet available at the Gallaudet Library.
[C]	This item is available from Gallaudet through the WRLC Consortium interlibrary loan system.
(#)	Editor needs additional information about this reference.
(##)	Editor needs a copy of this item.
(*)	Item is referenced in more than one section because the topic overlaps.
( )	Parentheses contain additional notes on the citation.
{ }	Braces contain a brief annotation, comments, or quote.

Because there is a continuum of functional deafness - and hearing (the amount of hearing loss or acuity as displayed on an audiogram) and cultural deafness (the degree to which one either identifies oneself as deaf or feels identified with the Deaf community), it's difficult to make these distinctions in the many citations listed here. Where the intention seemed reasonably clear, the attempt is made to add the distinction (small "d" deaf or capital "D" Deaf) in a reference.[3]

Over a long period of time, I have become aware of a variety of articles related to the subject of hearing children of deaf parents. Some of these materials on the following topics are included here: deaf/hearing relationships (including marriage); studies of dyadic interaction (mother/caretaker-child pairs) in American Sign Language (ASL); the dynamics of ASL acquisition in the early years; social and cultural marginality and identity issues; language processing of ASL in bilinguals; parenting and child-rearing issues for disability groups other than deaf/Deaf; heredity and genetics; cultural literacy for speakers of English as a second language; immigrant experiences and literature; relevant cross-cultural and deaf studies topics; hearing parents teaching signs to hearing infants, etc. Let me know at the address given below of other things that should be included.

Some materials are cited here for their historical significance. For example, Joanne Greenberg wrote *In This Sign* in 1970. It was a ground-breaking piece of fiction about a deaf family with hearing children. She is also the author of several other pieces it's important to be aware of. They are included here. I have listed books, articles, and films about or starring famous persons who had at least one deaf parent: Alexander Graham Bell, Albert Camus, Lon Chaney, Loren Eiseley, Edward Miner Gallaudet, and Prince Philip have been the subject of many authors. I have only selected a few items about them for inclusion here. A few references about grandchildren of deaf adults (godas) are also included. For example, Lon Chaney, Jr., was nearly as famous in his own right as an actor, as his coda father. It's a wonderful film about his life and also refers to his relationship to his father.[4] That is included here. I have not cited books, articles, films, etc., simply because they were written or produced by a coda. That's a whole other book, to be sure. While I have tried to obtain accurate citation information from the actual documents and materials or from reliable sources, the errors here are solely my responsibility.

My present research efforts are in several directions: (1) to get hard copies of Ph. D. dissertations and M.A. theses into the Gallaudet library to encourage research and their use; (2) to obtain translations of the foreign-language articles listed here; (3) to make sure that the Gallaudet Library has as complete a collection of these materials as possible; (4) to publish the following: (a) dissertation and theses abstracts, (b) abstracts of journal and research articles, and (c) an assemblage of "coda stories," literature from the "hearing side" of Deaf culture. Someday, I hope to extend the present bibliography to include more of the historical literature that exists in Deaf community publications. Let me know if you would like to help in any of these activities. If you have other relevant materials to add, and especially if you have a copy of items marked (##) that I don't have and need, please send them with complete citation information to: Thomas H. Bull, Gallaudet University, P.O. Box 2352, 800 Florida Avenue, N.E., Washington, DC 20002-3695.

NOTES

1. T. H. Bull (Ed.). 1993. Hearing Children with Deaf Parents Bibliography. Washington, DC: Gallaudet University, National Information Center on Deafness.

2. American Psychological Association (Ed.). (1994). Publication Manual of the American Psychological Association, 4th ed. Washington, DC: American Psychological Association.

3. See the following for a clear description of the origins of and intention in making these "d" and "D" distinctions: J. C. Woodward. (1972). Implications for Sociolinguistics Research Among the Deaf. Sign Language Studies, 2, 1-7. C. Padden & T. Humphries. (1988). Deaf in America: Voices from a Culture (pp. 2-4). Cambridge, MA: Harvard University Press. P. Preston. (1995, June). Mother Father Deaf: The Heritage of Difference. Social Science and Medicine, 40 (11), 1461-1467 (especially page 1466).

4. *Biography: Lon Chaney, Jr., Son of a Thousand Faces*. (1995). Produced by the Art and Entertainment Television Network.

I

BOOKS

Check on the availability of these books at Amazon Books: <http://www.amazon.com>

Abbott, D., & Kisor, H. (1994). <u>One TV blasting and a pig outdoor.</u> Illustrated by Leslie Morrill. Morton Grove, IL: Albert Whitman & Company. {Conan's dad is deaf and he recounts what it's like to have a deaf dad. "Life with a deaf father is just like life with a hearing father - except, for Dad, there's no sound at all. And that can make life with him very interesting"} [DEAF 812.54 A19o, 1994]

Abrams, C. (1996). <u>The silents.</u> Washington, DC: Gallaudet University Press. (Autobiography: The author is hearing and has deaf parents) [DEAF 920 A27Zs, 1996]

Ackerman, F. J. (1983). <u>Lon of 1000 faces!</u> Beverly Hills, CA: Morrison, Raven-Hill Company. (Lon Chaney was hearing and had deaf parents) [*]

Acredolo, L., & Goodwyn, S. (1996). <u>Baby signs: How to talk with your baby before your baby can talk.</u> Chicago: Contemporary Books. {Advocates teaching up to 60 gestures/signs to hearing babies} [DEAF 649.122 A37b, 1996]

Anderson, R. G. (1971). <u>Faces, forms, films: The artistry of Lon Chaney.</u> New York: A. S. Barnes and Company. (Lon Chaney was hearing and had deaf parents) [*]

Baldwin, S. C. (1993). <u>Pictures in the air: The story of the National Theatre of the Deaf.</u> Washington, DC: Gallaudet University Press. {Lou Fant is hearing and had deaf parents. He's prominent throughout the book as one of the original founders and performers in the National Theatre of the Deaf} [DEAF 792.0872 B34p, 1993]

Barash, H. L., & Dicker, E. B. (1991). <u>Our father Abe: The story of a deaf shoe repairman.</u> Madison, WI: Abar Press. (Autobiography: The authors are hearing siblings with deaf parents) [DEAF 920 B372b, 1991]

Becker, G. (1980). <u>Growing old in silence.</u> Berkeley, CA: University of California Press. [DEAF 362.6 B4g, 1980]

Benderly, B. L. (1980/1990). <u>Dancing without music: Deafness in America.</u> Washington, DC: Gallaudet University Press. [DEAF 302.22 B4d, 1990]

(*) Blackman, J. A. (1986). <u>Warning signals: Basic criteria for tracking at-risk infants and toddlers.</u> Washington, DC: National Center for Clinical Infant Programs. (13 pages) [DEAF 618.9209 B52w, 1986]

Blake, M. F. (1993). <u>Lon Chaney: The man behind the thousand faces.</u> Vestal, NY: Vestal Press, Ltd. [DEAF /791.43028 C42Zb, 1993]

Blake, M. F. (1995). <u>A thousand faces: Lon Chaney's unique artistry in motion pictures.</u> Vestal, NY: Vestal Press, Ltd. [DEAF 791.43028 C42Zb, 1995]

(*) Brabham, B. T. (1994). <u>My mom is handicapped: A "grownup" children's book.</u> Illustrated by Caleb Tims Brabham. Virginia Beach, VA: Cornerstone Publishing. (16 pages - Proceeds go to support the Muscular Dystrophy Association: <www.mdausa.org> or <http://www.educ.kent.edu/deafed/viiib8.html> P.O. Box 7972, Louisville, KY 40257 (812) 544-2577) {A beautiful book for children written by a mother with muscular dystrophy and illustrated by her 9-year-old daughter} [*]

Bragg, B., & Bergman, E. (1980). <u>Tales from a clubroom.</u> Washington, DC: Gallaudet College Press. [DEAF 813.54 B69t, 1980]

Brislin, R. W. (1981). <u>Cross-cultural encounters: Face-to-face interaction.</u> New York: Pergamon Press. [DEAF

302 B74c, 1981]

Bruce, R. V. (1973/1990). <u>Bell: Alexander Graham Bell and the conquest of solitude.</u> Ithaca, NY: Cornell University Press. (Considered by some to be the definitive Bell biography) [The Gallaudet University Library has the 1973 edition: DEAF 920 B45b, 1973. The 1990 edition is available. [C]

Bull, T. H. (Ed.). (1998). <u>On the edge of Deaf Culture: Hearing children/Deaf parents annotated bibliography.</u> Alexandria, VA: Deaf Family Research Press. (356 pages - Order from D. F. R. Press, P.O. Box 8417, Alexandria, VA 22306-8417) [On order]

(*) Bunde, L. T. (1979). <u>Deaf parents - hearing children: Toward a greater understanding of the unique aspects, needs and problems relative to the communication factors caused by deafness.</u> Washington, DC: Registry of Interpreters for the Deaf, Signograph Series No. 1. (Also available from Ephphatha Services, American Lutheran Church, 422 S. 5th Street, Minneapolis, MN 55415 - 83 pages [*]) [DEAF 306.87 B87d, 1979]

(*) Burns, K. (1989). <u>Our Mom.</u> New York: Franklin Watts. (A book for children with black and white photographs - 48 pages) {The author, paraplegic since an automobile accident in 1968, is pictured throughout with her four children doing a variety of daily activities to care for her family. A wheelchair helps her get about} [*]

Camus, A. (1995). <u>The first man.</u> New York: Alfred A. Knopf. {Thought to be somewhat autobiographical: "...tells the story of Jacques Cormery, a boy who lived a life much like [Camus'] own. [He] summons up the sights, sounds, and textures of a childhood circumscribed by poverty and a father's death yet redeemed by the austere beauty of Algeria and the boy's attachment to his nearly deaf-mute mother. The result is a moving journey through the lost landscape of youth that also discloses the wellsprings of Camus's aesthetic powers and moral vision." From the jacket} [C]

Chester, K. (1996). <u>Hear no evil: A time of fear.</u> New York: Scholastic, Inc. (One in a series of mysteries for children with deaf and coda characters. Other titles in the "Hear no evil" series are: <u>Missing, A time of fear</u>, and a number of others) {Sara Howell is deaf and communicates in American Sign Language. Her boyfriend is a hearing coda} [On order]

Chism, S. C. (1997). <u>Little girl lost and found again, the road never taken: A search for identity.</u> (A letter from the author in the May, 1997, issue of the <u>CODA Connection, 14</u> (2), 6 [UNIV DEAF Periodicals] mentions that the book is in progress) Manuscript in preparation.

Corfmat, P. (1990). <u>"Please sign here": The world of the deaf.</u> Worthing, West Sussex, England: Churchman Publishing Limited. (162 pages - The author is hearing and has deaf parents. Available from the family of Rev. Percy Corfmat, 7 Granville Road, St. Albans, Aerts AL1 5BE) [DEAF 305.741 C67p, 1990]

Crowe, D. I. (1993). <u>Dummy's little girl.</u> New York: Carlton Press. (Autobiography: The author is hearing and has deaf parents) [DEAF 920 C78d, 1993]

Davis, L. J. (1995). <u>Enforcing normalcy: Disability, deafness, and the body.</u> New York: Verso Press. (The author is hearing and has deaf parents) [DEAF 303.38 D38e, 1995]

Davis, L. J. (Ed.). (1997). <u>Disability studies reader.</u> New York: Routledge. (The editor is hearing and has deaf parents) {The introduction contains biographical information} [*]

Davis, L. J. (in press). <u>The sense of silence: A memoir of a childhood with deafness.</u> Chicago: University of

Illinois Press. (Autobiographical: The author is hearing and has deaf parents) Manuscript in preparation.

Davis, L. J. (Ed.). (in press). Love and misunderstanding: The love letters of Eva Weintrobe and Morris Davis, 1936-1938. Washington, DC: Gallaudet University Press. (The editor is hearing and has deaf parents) Letters were written when his father was in the United States and his mother was in England. Introduction by Leonard Davis and preface by his brother, Gerald Davis} Manuscript in preparation.

Eiseley, L. (1975). All the strange hours: The excavation of a life. New York: Charles Scribner's Sons. (Autobiography: The author, a renowned anthropologist, poet and writer, was born in 1907 and died in 1977. A note in the Gallaudet catalogue says "the author had a hearing loss in one ear") {At one point he describes his mother as "stone deaf" and "untutored, [a] talented artist [who] left me, if anything, a capacity for tremendous visual impressions just as my father, a one-time itinerant actor, had in that silenced household of the stone age - a house of gestures, of daylong facial contortion - produced for me the miracle of words when he came home." When he was ten years old and with friends her "rasping voice of deafness ordered me home....She could not hear, she was violently gesticulating without dignity, and her dress was somehow appropriate to the occasion."} [DEAF Copy 1: 500.824 E5a, 1975]

English, J. (1985). My Mommy's special. Chicago: Childrens Press. (A book for children with black and white photographs of the author and her mother - 32 pages) {The author, Jennifer English, is 7 years old and her mother has multiple sclerosis. Jennifer describes with pride when her mother was crowned Miss Wheelchair Virginia. They are pictured in their daily life activities together where Jennifer helps her mommy and her mommy helps her in things she can't do as well} [*]

Follain-Grisell, V., Leitch-Walker, K., & Morton, D. (Eds.). (1998). Building bridges: Strengthening home and school relationships for Deaf parents and their hearing children, conference proceedings, Gallaudet University, Washington, D. C., May 1-3, 1997. Washington, DC: Gallaudet University, College for Continuing Education. {This book and videotape package includes the following: keynote addresses by Dr. Paul M. Preston, Through the Looking Glass, and Dr. Mary T. Weiner, Psychology Department, Gallaudet University; and papers from various sessions} Manuscript in preparation.

Gallaudet, E. M. (1907/1983). History of the college for the deaf, 1857-1888, 1888-1907. Washington, DC: (publisher unspecified). (356 pages - Published again in 1983: L. J. Fischer & D. L. de Lorenzo (Eds.), History of the college for the deaf, 1857-1907. Washington, DC: Gallaudet College Press, 1983. (Edward Miner Gallaudet was president of Gallaudet College for 47 years. He was hearing and his mother, Sophie Fowler, was deaf. [DEAF 378.753 G32h, 1983]) [DEAF Copy 1: 378.753 G29h, 1907]

Gannon, J. R. (forthcoming). Daddy! Get your elbow off the horn. (The author is deaf and has hearing children. The book will have a chapter of "deaf/hearing family" anecdotes) Manuscript in preparation.

Glickfeld, C. L. (1989). Useful gifts. Athens, GA: University of Georgia Press. (Fiction: The author is hearing and has deaf parents. Winner of the Flannery O'Connor Fiction Award) [DEAF 813.54 G5u, 1989]

Greenberg, J. (1964). I never promised you a rose garden. New York: Penguin Books. (Originally published under a pseudonym, Hannah Green - Greenberg went on to write *In this sign* about a deaf family with hearing children and *Of such small differences* about deaf-blindness) [UNIV Gen 813.54 G7i, 1964]

Greenberg, J. (1970). In this sign. New York: Holt, Rinehart and Winston. {Fiction: Janice and Abel Ryder are deaf and have two hearing children. This is their oldest hearing daughter, Margaret's, story. Hallmark Hall of Fame produced the film version, *Love is Never Silent*, in 1985} [DEAF 813.54 G7i, 1970]

17

Greenberg, J. (1988). <u>Of such small differences.</u> New York: Holt, Rinehart and Winston. {About deaf-blindness} [DEAF 813.54 G7o, 1988]

Grosjean, F. (1982). <u>Life with two languages: An introduction to bilingualism.</u> Cambridge, MA: Harvard University Press. {There are at least 18 pages of anecdotes from native American Sign Language/English bilinguals} [DEAF 420 G761, 1982]

Grosvenor, E. S., & Wesson, M. (1997). <u>Alexander Graham Bell: The life and times of the man who invented the telephone.</u> Foreword by R. V. Bruce, Professor Emeritus of History, Boston University. New York: Harry N. Abrams, Inc. (304 pages) [C]

Guccione, L. D. (1996). <u>Hear no evil: Death in the afternoon.</u> New York: Scholastic, Inc. (One in a series of mysteries for children with deaf and coda characters. Other titles in the "Hear no evil" series are: *Missing, A time of fear*, and a number of others) {Sara Howell is deaf and communicates in American Sign Language. Her boyfriend is a hearing coda} [On order]

(*) Haseltine, F. P., Cole, S. S., & Gray, D. B. (Eds.). (1995). <u>Reproductive issues for persons with physical disabilities.</u> Baltimore: Paul H. Brookes. (368 pages) [C]

(*) Higgins, P. C. (1980). <u>Outsiders in a hearing world: A sociology of deafness.</u> Beverly Hills, CA: Sage Publications. (Also see listing under "Ph.D. dissertations and M.A. theses" section - The author is hearing and has deaf parents) [DEAF 305 H5o, 1980]

Hirsch, E. D., Jr. (1987). <u>Cultural literacy: What every American needs to know.</u> New York: Houghton Mifflin Company. {Useful resource for bilingual families} [UNIV GEN 370.19 H57c, 1987]

Hirsch, E. D., Jr. (Ed.). (1989). <u>A first dictionary of cultural literacy: What our children need to know.</u> Boston: Houghton Mifflin Company. {Useful resource for bilingual families. This book is designed for younger children} [C]

Hirsch, E. D., Jr., Kett, J. F., & Trefil, J. (1988). <u>The dictionary of cultural literacy: What every American needs to know.</u> Boston: Houghton Mifflin Company. {Useful resource for bilingual families} [UNIV REFERENCE 973.03 H5d, 1988]

Homer, S. (1939/1978). <u>My wife and I: The story of Louise and Sidney Homer.</u> New York: Da Capo Press. (269 pages - The author was hearing and had deaf parents) [*]

Jeffers, A. (1995/1998). <u>Safe as houses.</u> New York: Faber and Faber. (Fiction: The 1998 edition is a paperback published by Gay Men's Press, London. See <http://www.people.hbs.edu/ajeffers/safe.html> for more information about Alex Jeffers and an excerpt from this book and other writings. Jeffers was inspired to write this after reading Harlan Lane's book *When the Mind Hears*) {A gay novel about family values. The central character, Allen, had deaf parents who attended the Pennsylvania School for the Deaf} [DEAF 813.54 J43s, 1995]

Johnson, H. P. (1977). <u>Hands can say hello.</u> Illustrations by Amy Beckwith. Atlanta: Home Mission Board. {A book for children in grades 4-6. Mr. and Mrs. Henderson, who are deaf, and their hearing children, Jamie and Becky, move to a new town and are befriended by the Norman family. They attend the Norman's church which has a deaf ministry. After becoming active members they attend a convention of the Southern Baptist Conference for the Deaf in New Mexico} [DEAF 266.09 J6h, 1977]

(*) **Kannapell, B. M. (1993).** Language choice reflects identity choice: A sociolinguistic study of deaf college students. Burtonsville, MD: Linstok Press. (Also see listing under "Ph.D. dissertations and M. A. theses" section) [DEAF 306.44 K3la, 1993]

Levi, D. H. (1992). A very special sister. Illustrations by Ethel Gold. Washington, DC: Kendall Green Publications, Gallaudet University Press. (34 pages) {A book for children} [DEAF 813.54 L48ve, 1992]

Lindenov, H. (1945). The etiology of deaf-mutism: With special reference to heredity. Translated from Danish by Axel Andersen. Copenhagen, Denmark: Einar Munksgaard. (268 pages) [DEAF 573.21 L5e, 1945]

Litchfield, A. B. (1980). Words in our hands. Illustrations by Helen Cogancherry. Chicago: Albert Whitman and Company. (32 pages - see the article "CODA in the classroom" in the February, 1986, issue of the CODA Newsletter, 3 (1), 3, for a letter from A. B. Litchfield) {A children's book that describes life in a family with deaf parents} [DEAF 813.54 L57w, 1980]

Lottman, H. R. (1979). Albert Camus: A biography. Garden City, NY: Doubleday. {There are two chapters that in particular discuss his last book and his deaf mother: "The First Man" (pp. 1-13) and "Family Dramas" (pp. 14-25)} [C]

Mackenzie, C. (1928). Alexander Graham Bell, the man who contracted space. Boston: Houghton Mifflin Company, the Riverside Press, Cambridge. (Bell's mother and wife were deaf) [DEAF 920 M321a, 1928]

Marrero, R. (1993). Vintage monster movies. Key West, FL: Fantasma Books. {About Lon Chaney} [*]

(*) **Mathews, J. (1992).** A mother's touch: The Tiffany Callo story. New York: Henry Holt & Company. (265 pages) {Tiffany Callo, a cerebral-palsied mother, fought the State of California for custody of her two sons} [C]

Miller-Hall, M. (1994). Deaf, dumb and BLACK: An account of an actual life of a family. New York: Carlton Press - A Hearthstone book. (Autobiography - out of print) {Mary Miller-Hall was born in Columbus, Ohio. The daughter of two deaf parents, she had ten siblings. "This is a book about dysfunction within a family of two deaf parents. They are also black, with very little education. Eleven children were born to the couple. This family or their ancestors had moved up from the deep South, seeking freedom and a better life. This is a tale of deprivation, hate, prejudice, restitution, incest, assault, fraud, theft of life, love, and death. It covers many decades. It speaks to the setbacks and daily trials of this family." - Author's foreword} [DEAF 920 M545d, 1994]

Moore, M. S., & Levitan, L. (1993). For hearing people only: Answers to some of the most commonly asked questions about the Deaf community, its culture, and the "Deaf reality" (2nd ed.). Rochester, NY: Deaf Life Press. [DEAF 305.773 M66f, 1993]

(*) **Parks, S. (Ed.). (1984).** HELP: When the parent is handicapped. Palo Alto, CA: VORT Corp. (278 pages) {Adapted version of the Hawaii Early Learning Profile - HELP - activity guide, introduction and bibliography} [DEAF 649.1 P371h, 1984]

Perez, J. E. (1985). A sign of love. Glenn, CA: Author. Privately published by the author. Write Janet Enos Perez, Rt. 1, P.O. Box 678, Glenn, California 95943 (Autobiography: The author is hearing and has deaf parents) [*]

Peterson, J. W. (1977). I have a sister my sister is deaf. Illustrations by Deborah Kogan Ray. New York: Harper and Row. {A book for children} [DEAF 362.71 P4i, 1977]

(*) Preston, P. M. (1994). <u>Mother father deaf: Living between sound and silence.</u> Cambridge, MA: Harvard University Press. (The author is hearing and has deaf parents - Also see listing under "Ph.D. dissertations and M. A. theses" section) {"Based on 150 interviews with adult hearing children of deaf parents throughout the United States...[this book] is rich in anecdote and analysis, remarkable for its insights into a family life normally closed to outsiders." - *Booklist* "I have no doubt that Preston's work is now the major study on this topic and will be so regarded by researchers in deafness and anyone interested in the study of culture and its transmission through the family...Preston's interviews will lay to rest many of the stereotypes and myths that exist in both the media and the literature of deafness." John S. Schuchman, Gallaudet University - book jacket. Highly recommended} [DEAF 306.874 P73m, 1994]

Richards, L. A. (1896). <u>Isla Heron.</u> Illustrated by Frank Timerrill. Boston: Colonial Press, Charles Simonds and Company. (109 pages) {Fiction: The oldest book-length work we know of that deals with deaf/hearing family relationships} [UNIV Archives Deaf Rare, non-circulating]

Riley, P. J. (1985). <u>London after midnight.</u> New York: Cornwall Books. {About Lon Chaney} [*]

Riley, P. J. (1988). <u>A blind bargain: Ackerman Archives Series Vol. 2, Atlantic City, New Jersey.</u> Brigantine Island, NJ: MagicImage Films. {About Lon Chaney} [*]

Robbins, C. (forthcoming). <u>Numinous sounds [Poems].</u> (The author is deaf and has hearing children) Manuscript in preparation.

(*) Rogers, J., & Matsumura, M. (1995?). <u>Mother-to-be: A guide to pregnancy and birth for women with disabilities.</u> Demos Vermande. [*]

Ross, N. L. (1981, 1988). <u>Lon Chaney - master craftsman of make believe.</u> Los Angeles: Quality RJ Publishers. [*]

(*) Rutherford, S. D. (1993). <u>A study of American deaf folklore.</u> Burtonsville, MD: Linstok Press. (156 pages - Also see listing under "Ph.D. dissertations and M. A. theses" section) [DEAF 398.2 R87s, 1993]

Sante, L. (1998). <u>The factory of faces.</u> New York: Pantheon Books. {The articles listed elsewhere, "Living in tongues" and "Heart without a country" were excerpted from this book: A bilingual family's experiences in America}

Schreiber, K. (1981). <u>Dear Beth: Poems to an absent daughter.</u> Washington, DC: K. Schreiber. (The author is deaf and her daughter is hearing) [DEAF 813.54 S37d, 1981]

Schuchman, J. S. (1988). <u>Hollywood speaks: Deafness and the film entertainment industry.</u> Urbana, IL: University of Illinois Press. (The author is hearing and has deaf parents) [DEAF 791.43 S3h, 1988]

Sidransky, R. (1990). <u>In silence: Growing up hearing in a deaf world.</u> New York: St. Martin's Press. (Autobiography: The author is hearing and has deaf parents) [DEAF 306.874 S52i, 1990]

Sidransky, R. (1992). <u>Wenn ihr mich doch hören könntet: Kindsein in einer stummen Welt</u> [In silence: Growing up hearing in a deaf world]. Bern, Switzerland: Scherz Verlag. (In German. The German translation of the title is considered bad: "If you just could hear me - childhood in a mute world") [*]

(#) Sidransky, R. (1992?). <u>Een wereld van stilte</u> [In silence: Growing up hearing in a deaf world]. Baarn,

Netherlands: De Kern. (Dutch translation) [*]

Slocombe, A. (1996). My parents' voice. Surrey, England: A. Slocombe. (75 pages - Autobiography: The author is hearing and had deaf parents) [DEAF 306.874 S56m 1996]

Stenross, B. (forthcoming). Connecting: Hard of hearing in a hearing world. {Will have a chapter on family life} Manuscript in preparation.

Thurman, S. K. (Ed.). (1985). Children of handicapped parents: Research and clinical perspectives. Orlando, FL: Academic Press. [DEAF 306.874 C4, 1985]

Toward, L. M. (1984). Mabel Bell, Alexander's silent partner. New York: Methuen. [DEAF 920 B42t, 1984]

Walker, L. A. (1986). A loss for words: The story of deafness in a family. New York: Harper and Row. (Autobiography: The author is hearing with deaf parents) [DEAF 306.874 W3l, 1986]

Walker, L. A. (1989). Lou Ann - Leben in einer Stummen Welt [A loss for words: The story of deafness in a family]. Munchen, Germany: Doremersche Verlagsanstalt. (In German) [*]

Wallisfurth, M. (1979/1982). Sie hat es mir erzählt [She told me about it]. Freiburg im Breisgau: Herder Verlag. {Maria, the author, was born in 1927 and is the only child born to "deaf and dumb" parents. She passes on stories from interviewing her mother about her experience growing up deaf in Germany in the first third of this century. "Her mother grew up on a farm...had a lot of brothers and sisters, some of them being deaf as well. She visited an oral school in the city, found a job and met a lot of deaf people by going to a deaf club. She married one of them even though a lot of people told her not to because his voice was hard to understand, whereas hers was very clear. During World War I and the depression she and her husband had to go through a very hard time, but they managed fairly well. They got pregnant with Maria and were very happy when they found out that she was hearing. Then Hitler came to power and with him laws that forced people with disabilities to get sterilized. Maria's mother, after protesting and proving that in spite of her and her husband's deafness her children don't necessarily have to be deaf as well, in the end she gave in and was sterilized." From Melanie Cromwell in Germany} [DEAF 920 G53w, 1982]

Wiggins, J. (1980). No sound. New York: The Silent Press. [DEAF 920 W53ln, 1980]

Williams Wilson, M. J. (1989). HELP for children from infancy to adulthood: A national directory of hotlines, helplines, organizations, agencies, and other resources (5th ed.). Shepherdstown, WV: Rocky River Publishers. [*]

(*) Winefield, R. (1987). Never the twain shall meet: Bell, Gallaudet, and the communications debate. Washington, DC: Gallaudet University Press. (Also see listing under "Ph.D. dissertations and M. A. theses" section) [DEAF 371.301 W5n, 1987]

21

II

JOURNAL ARTICLES

AND BOOK CHAPTERS

Check out the Pathfinder series of reference guides on a variety of topics available at the Gallaudet University Library. One guide to searches is titled "Deaf parents with hearing children" and can be accessed on the World Wide Web at <http://www.gallaudet.edu/~library/new/deafguid.html>. Also at the end of this book.

You may conduct searches utilizing the OCLC Data Bases (Online Computer Library Center) in Ohio: <http://www.ref.oclc.org:2000/> You must be a subscriber or login under a subscriber's license (University or other provider).

The ERIC system is another valuable source for relevant information: <http://www.edrs.com>

Abrahamsen, A., Cavallo, M. M., & McCluer, J. A. (1985, April). Is the sign advantage a robust phenomenon? From gesture to language in two modalities. Merrill Palmer Quarterly, 31 (2), 177-209. [UNIV Periodicals]

Accardo, P. J., & Whitman, B. Y. (1990). Children of parents with mental retardation: Problems and diagnoses. In B. Y. Whitman & P. J. Accardo (Eds.), When a parent is mentally retarded (pp. 123-131). Baltimore: Paul. H. Brookes Publishing Co. [C]

Ackerman, J., Kyle, J., Woll, B., & Ezra, M. (1990). Lexical acquisition in sign and speech: Evidence from a longitudinal study of infants in deaf families. In C. Lucas (Ed.), Sign Language research: Theoretical issues (pp. 337-345). Washington, DC: Gallaudet University Press. [DEAF 420 S533, 1990]

Adamson, L., Als, H., Tronick, E., & Brazelton, T. B. (1977). The development of social reciprocity between a sighted infant and her blind parents. Journal of the American Academy of Child Psychiatry, 16, 194-205. [*]

Aguilar, C., & Rodriguez-Sullivan, M. E. (1998). Tri-lingual/Tri-cultural Latino deaf families in the USA. In V. Follain-Grisell, K. Leitch-Walker & D. Morton (Eds.), Building bridges: Strengthening home and school relationships for Deaf parents and their hearing children, conference proceedings, Gallaudet University, Washington, D. C., May 1-3, 1997. Washington, DC: Gallaudet University, College for Continuing Education. Manuscript in preparation.

Ainoda, N., & Suzuki, S. (1977). Environmental influence upon the language development of a normal hearing child brought up by deaf parents. In International Congress on Education of the Deaf (Ed.), Proceedings of the International Congress on Education of the Deaf, Tokyo, 1975 (pp. 695-697). Tokyo: The Organizing Committee, International Congress on Education of the Deaf. [DEAF 370 I57p, 1975]

Allen, G. D., Wilbur, R. B., & Schick, B. B. (1991, Fall). Aspects of rhythm in ASL. Sign Language Studies, 72, 297-320. [UNIV RESERVE]

Anderson, C. V. (1996, April). Life in sound and silence [Book review of *Mother father deaf: Living between sound and silence* by Paul Preston]. Contemporary Psychology: A Journal of Reviews, 41 (4), 381. [UNIV Periodicals]

Anonymous. (1975). Panelist: Adult hearing children of deaf parents. In Gallaudet College, Department of Sociology, Social Work Program (Ed.), An orientation to deafness for social workers: Papers from the workshop, Washington, DC, March 18-20, 1975 (pp. 45-46). Washington, DC: Gallaudet College Press. [DEAF 361 G3o, 1975]

Anthony, D. A. (1995). A S L write right rite wright. In M. D. Garretson (Ed.), Deafness, life and culture II: A Deaf American monograph, 45 (pp. 1-3). Silver Spring, MD: National Association of the Deaf. [UNIV RESERVE]

Arlow, J. A. (1976). Communication and character: A clinical study of a man raised by deaf-mute parents. Psychoanalytic Study of the Child, 31, 139-163. [DEAF 155.924 A7c, 1976]

Arneson, S. M. (1987). Responses to Bienvenu and Sherwood. In M. McIntire (Ed.), Journal of Interpretation, 4, 25-27. Rockville, MD: Registry of Interpreters for the Deaf, Inc. [UNIV RESERVE]

Artman, D. (1978). Family counseling and treatment of families with deaf members. In L. von der Lieth (Ed.), Life in families with deaf members: Proceedings of the Vth World Conference on Deafness, Copenhagen, Denmark, 1977 (pp. 195-198). Copenhagen, Denmark: National Federation of the Deaf in Denmark. [DEAF 306.87 W651,

1978]

Artmann, D. S. (1988). Hearing children with deaf parents. In R. Ojala (Ed.), <u>Program, X World Congress of the</u> <u>World Federation of the Deaf: One world one responsibility, proceedings, Espoo, Finland, July 20-28, 1987, Vol.</u> <u>2</u> (pp. 741-746). Helsinki, Finland: Finnish Association of the Deaf. (The editor is hearing and has deaf parents) [DEAF 366 W6, 1987]

Ayoub, N. C. (Ed.). (1994, June 8). New scholarly books, psychology: *Mother father deaf, living between sound and silence* by Paul Preston. <u>The Chronicle of Higher Education, 40</u> (40), A12. [UNIV Periodicals]

Backenroth, G., & Hanson, G. (1978). Crisis intervention with parents of deaf and hard of hearing children. In L. von der Lieth (Ed.), <u>Life in families with deaf members: Proceedings of the Vth World Conference on Deafness,</u> <u>Copenhagen, Denmark, 1977</u> (pp. 213-219). Copenhagen, Denmark: National Federation of the Deaf in Denmark. [DEAF 306.87 W651, 1978]

Bahan, B. (1994, Fall). Comment on Turner. <u>Sign Language Studies, 85,</u> 241-249. [UNIV RESERVE]

(*) Bail, S., & Littlefield, D. (1993). Setting up a parent education program. In S. Polowe-Aldersley (Ed.), <u>Pride</u> <u>is with us: Proceedings of the 56th biennial meeting, Convention of American Instructors of the Deaf and the 64th</u> <u>annual meeting of the Conference of Educational Administrators Serving the Deaf, Baltimore, Maryland, June, 1993</u> (pp. 116-118). Bedford, TX: Convention of American Instructors of the Deaf. [Gallaudet University Archives]

(##) Baker, A., Bogaerde, B. v. d., Coerts, J., & Rooijmans, C. H. (1997). Methodological issues in sign language research on child language acquisition: A Manual. In <u>Amsterdam Series in Child Language Studies.</u> Amsterdam: Institute for General Linguistics and the Human Capital and Mobility Programme "Inter-Sign," EU. [*]

(##) Baker, A. E., & Bogaerde, B. v. d. (1996). Language input and attentional behavior. In C. E. Johnson & J. H. V. Gilbert (Eds.), <u>Children's language, Vol. 9</u> (pp. 209-217). Mahwah, NJ: Lawrence Erlbaum Associates. [*]

Baker, E. D. (1998). Making it work: Classroom strategies that spell successful outcomes for deaf parents, their hearing children, and professionals. In V. Follain-Grisell, K. Leitch-Walker & D. Morton (Eds.), <u>Building bridges:</u> <u>Strengthening home and school relationships for Deaf parents and their hearing children, conference proceedings,</u> <u>Gallaudet University, Washington, D. C., May 1-3, 1997.</u> Washington, DC: Gallaudet University, College for Continuing Education. Manuscript in preparation.

Baker-Shenk, C. (1992). The interpreter: Machine, advocate, or ally? In J. Plant-Moeller (Ed.), <u>Expanding</u> <u>horizons: Proceedings of the twelfth National Convention of the Registry of Interpreters for the Deaf, Bethesda, MD,</u> <u>August 6-11, 1991</u> (pp. 120-140). Silver Spring, MD: RID Publications. [DEAF 420.802 R43e, 1991]

Bakker, P. (1987, October). Hearing children of deaf parents. In <u>Autonomous languages: Signed and spoken</u> <u>languages created by children in the light of Bickerton's Language Bioprogram Hypothesis, University of Amsterdam,</u> <u>Institute for General Linguistics, No. 53</u> (pp. 26-30). Amsterdam: University of Amsterdam. (97 pages - Slightly different version of this thesis was written in 1985-1986 at the University of Amsterdam) [DEAF 401.93 B34a, 1987]

(*) Baranowski, E. (1983, March-April). Childbirth education classes for expectant deaf parents: Because of communication barriers and cultural differences, expectant deaf parents need childbirth education classes adapted to their situation. <u>American Journal of Maternal Child Nursing, 8</u> (2), 143-146. [DEAF 618.24 B3c, 1983]

Bard, B., & Sachs, J. S. (1977). Language acquisition patterns in two normal children of deaf parents. Paper presented at the second annual Boston University Conference on Language Development, Boston, Massachusetts, September 30-October 1, 1977. (ERIC Document Reproduction Service No. ED 150 868 - 16 pages - Summarized in de Villiers and de Villiers book, Early language (pp. 103-105). [UNIV Gen 401.9 D4e, 1979]) [REFERENCE DESK]

Basova. A. G. (1970). Deaf parents and their children. In World Federation of the Deaf (Ed.), Fifth congress of the World Federation of the Deaf/Polish Association of the Deaf, Warsaw, Poland, August 10-17, 1967 (pp. 378-379). Warsaw, Poland: Polish Scientific Publishers. [DEAF 366 W6, 1967]

Bean, B. T. (1967, July). Hearing children of deaf parents. Deaf Welfare, 4 (8), 137-142. [UNIV DEAF Periodicals]

Beardslee, W. R., Bemporad, J., Keller, M. B., & Klerman, G. L. (1983, July). Children of parents with major affective disorder: A review. The American Journal of Psychiatry, 140 (7), 825-832. [UNIV Periodicals]

Beattie, R. G. (1994). [Book reviews] In silence: Growing up hearing in a deaf world by Ruth Sidransky. The ACEHI Journal, 20 (3), 125-126. (The official journal of the Association of Canadian Educators of the Hearing Impaired) [UNIV DEAF Periodicals]

Beazley, S., & Moore, M. (1996). Family lives of hearing children with deaf parents. In M. Moore, J. Sixsmith, K. Knowles, C. Kagan, S. Lewis, S. Beazley & U. Rout (Eds.), Children's reflections on family life (pp. 81-99). Washington, DC: Falmer Press. [C]

Bechinger, E. (1974). Mixed marriages (between deaf and hearing partners). In D. H. Pokorny (Ed.), My eyes are my ears: A collection of papers delivered at the first International Ecumenical Seminar on the Pastoral Care of the Deaf, Geneva, Switzerland, 1971 (pp. 139-144). New York: MSS Information Corporation. [DEAF 261 I5m, 1974]

Becker, G. (1980). Family life. In Growing old in silence (pp. 51-63). Berkeley, CA: University of California Press. [DEAF 362.6 B4g, 1980]

Bell, A. G. (1884/1969). Memoir upon the formation of a deaf variety of the human race. Washington, DC: Alexander Graham Bell Association for the Deaf. (49 pages - A paper presented to the National Academy of Sciences at New Haven, Connecticut, November 12, 1883. First published in 1884: "Upon the formation of a deaf variety of the human race," National Academy of Sciences Memoirs, 2 (4), 179-262. [Gallaudet University Archives, DEAF Rare]) [DEAF 301.42 B4m, 1969]

Bell, A. G. (1891, March 12). "Upon marriage." Dr. Bell defines his position. Silent World, 5 (6), 1-4. (Also published in 1887/1969 as Marriage: An address to the deaf. - "An address delivered to the Members of the Literary Society of Kendall Green, Washington, D. C., March 6, 1891" - 14 pages - see the second edition [Gallaudet University Archives] which has three additional pages: "Appendix. Consanguineous Marriages." Dated May 22, 1891. [DEAF 306.81 B44m, 1891]) [Gallaudet University Archives - DEAF Rare]

Bellugi, U., & Fischer, S. (1972). A comparison of Sign Language and spoken language. Cognition, 1 (2-3), 173-200. (French résumé) [DEAF 428 B3c, 1972]

Bellugi, U., van Hoek, K., Lillo-Martin, D., & O'Grady, L. (1993). The acquisition of syntax and space in young deaf signers. In D. Bishop & K. Mogford (Eds.), Language development in exceptional circumstances (2nd ed., pp. 132-149). Hillsdale, NJ: Lawrence Erlbaum Associates. (The Gallaudet University Library also has the 1988 edition

[DEAF 401.93 L36, 1988]) [DEAF 401.93 L36, 1993]

Benderly, B. L. (1980a/1990). Community and identity. In Dancing without music: Deafness in America (pp. 218-239). Washington, DC: Gallaudet University Press. [DEAF 302.22 B4d, 1990]

Benderly, B. L. (1980b/1990). Growing up deaf. In Dancing without music: Deafness in America (pp. 39-66). Washington, DC: Gallaudet University Press. [DEAF 302.22 B4d, 1990]

Benderly, B. L. (1980c/1990). Who are the deaf? In Dancing without music: Deafness in America (pp. 9-23). Washington, DC: Gallaudet University Press. [DEAF 302.22 B4d, 1990]

Bene, A. (1977). The influence of deaf and dumb parents on a child's development. Psychoanalytic Study of the Child, 32, 175-194. [DEAF 306.874 B4i, 1977]

Bernstein, J. E., & Fireside, B. J. (1991). Angela, Vanessa, and Ryan Stewart. In Special parents, special children (pp. 48-63). Morton Grove, IL: Albert Whitman and Company. [*]

Bettger, J. G., Emmorey, K., McCullough, S. H., & Bellugi, U. (1997, Fall). Enhanced facial discrimination: Effects of experience with American Sign Language. Journal of Deaf Studies and Deaf Education, 2 (4), 223-233. [UNIV DEAF Periodicals]

Bialystok, E. (1991). Introduction. In E. Bialystok (Ed.), Language processing in bilingual children (pp. 1-9). New York: Cambridge University Press. [*]

Bienvenu, MJ. (1987). The third culture: Working together. In M. L. McIntire (Ed.), Journal of Interpretation, 4, 1-12. Rockville, MD: Registry of Interpreters for the Deaf, Inc. [UNIV RESERVE]

Bloch, P. (1995, Spring). *Mother father deaf: Living between sound and silence* by Paul Preston [Abstract]. Exceptional Child Education Resources, 27 (1), 78. (Council for Exceptional Children - Abstract No. 901663) [UNIV Index]

(##) Bogaerde, B. v. d. (1992). Aandacht voor Gebarentaal: Interactie tussen dove moeders en hun kinderen [Attention for Sign Language: Interaction between deaf mothers and their children]. Gramma/TTT, jrg. 1 (3), 179-191. [*]

Bogaerde, B. v. d. (1994). Attentional strategies used by deaf mothers. In I. Ahlgren, B. Bergman & M. Brennan (Eds.), Perspectives on sign language usage: Papers from The Fifth International Symposium on Sign Language Research, Vol. 2, Salamanca, Spain, May 25-30, 1992 (pp. 305-317). Durham, England: Deaf Studies Research Unit, University of Durham. (Paper originally presented at the "Symposium sobre el Sords," Barcelona, Spain, September, 1992) [DEAF 420 I65p, 1994]

Bogaerde, B. v. d., & Baker, A. E. (1996). Verbs in the language production of deaf and hearing children of deaf parents. Poster presented at the Fifth International Conference on Theoretical Issues on Sign Language Research, Montreal, Canada, September, 1996. (Authors are at the University of Amsterdam) [*]

Bogaerde, B. v. d., & Baker, A. E. (1996). Verbs in the input of a deaf mother to one deaf and one hearing child. Paper presented at the Child Language Seminar, University of Reading, United Kingdom, April, 1996. (10 pages - Authors are at the University of Amsterdam) [DEAF Copy 1: 401.93 B63v, 1997]

(##) Bogaerde, B. v. d., & Blankenstijn, C. (1990). Tweetalige aspecten in het taalaanbod van drie dove moeders aan hun horende kinderen [Bilingual aspects in the language input of three deaf mothers to their hearing children]. Netwerk Bundel, 19-28. (The authors are at the University of Amsterdam) [*]

(##) Bogaerde, B. v. d., Knoors, H., & Verrips, M. (Eds.). (1994). Language acquisition with non-native input: The acquisition of SLN (Sign Language of the Netherlands), No. 62. Publication of the Department of General Linguistics, University of Amsterdam, Amsterdam. [*]

Bogaerde, B. v. d., & Mills, A. E. (1994). Word order in language input to children: SLN (Sign Language of the Netherlands) or Dutch. In M. Brennan & G. H. Turner (Eds.), Word-order issues in sign language/working papers (pp. 133-157). Durham, England: The International Sign Linguistics Association. [DEAF 415 W67, 1994]

Bogaerde, B. v. d., & Mills, A. (in press). Propositional content in different modes: An analysis of the language production of deaf and hearing children of deaf parents. In Proceedings of the Child Language Seminar, Bristol, England, April, 1995. (9 pages) [*]

Bonvillian, J. D., Cate, S. N., Weber, W. R., & Folven, R. J. (1988, Fall). Early letter recognition, letter naming, and reading skills in a signing and speaking child. Sign Language Studies, 60, 271-294. [UNIV RESERVE]

Bonvillian, J. D., Orlansky, M. D., & Folven, R. J. (1994). Early Sign Language acquisition: Implications for theories of language acquisition. In V. Volterra & C. J. Erting (Eds.), From gesture to language in hearing and deaf children (pp. 219-232). Washington, DC: Gallaudet University Press. [DEAF 401.93 F76, 1994]

Bonvillian, J. D., Orlansky, M. D., & Novack, L. L. (1983a, December). Developmental milestones: Sign Language acquisition and motor development. Child Development, 54 (6), 1435-1445. [UNIV Periodicals microfilm]

Bonvillian, J. D., Orlansky, M. D., & Novack, L. L. (1983b). Early Sign Language acquisition and its relationship to cognitive and motor development. In J. G. Kyle & B. Woll (Eds.), Language in sign: An international perspective on Sign Language (pp. 116-125). London: Croom Helm. [DEAF 419 L36, 1983]

Bonvillian, J. D., & Richards, H. C. (1993, Spring). The development of hand preference in children's early signing. Sign Language Studies, 78, 1-14. [UNIV RESERVE]

Bonvillian, J. D., Richards, H. C., Dooley, T. T., Kinzler, S., Mayer, L. E., Maynard, A. E., Saah, M. I., & Slavoff, G. R. (1993, March). Hand preference in young children's early signing. Paper presented at the biennial meeting of the Society for Research in Child Development, New Orleans, Louisiana, March, 1993. (ERIC Document Reproduction Service No. 360 765 - 13 pages) [REFERENCE DESK]

Boothroyd, B. (1971). Alice of Battenberg. In Prince Philip: An informal biography (pp. 100-109). New York: The McCall Publishing Company. [C]

Bornstein, M. H. (1989). Between caretakers and their young: Two modes of interaction and their consequences for cognitive growth. In M. H. Bornstein & J. S. Bruner (Eds.), Interaction in human development (pp. 197-214). Hillsdale, NJ: Lawrence Erlbaum Associates. [C]

Bouvet, D. (1983). Bilingual education for deaf children. In W. Stokoe & V. Volterra (Eds.), SLR '83: Proceedings of the III International Symposium on Sign Language Research, Rome, June 22-26, 1983 (pp. 64-71). Silver Spring, MD: Linstok Press. [DEAF 410 I5s, 1983]

JOURNAL

Bowe, F. G. (1996, October). *A journey into the Deaf-World*: Media review [Book review]. American Annals of the Deaf, 141 (4), 277. [UNIV DEAF Periodicals]

Braddock, G. C. (1975). Notable deaf persons No. 61 - Mr. and Mrs. George Homer. In F. B. Crammatte (Ed.), Notable deaf persons (pp. 106-108). Washington, DC: Gallaudet College Alumni Association. (Reprinted from the January, 1942, edition of The FRAT: Official Publication of the National Fraternal Society of the Deaf, 39th year, No. 6, 3. [UNIV DEAF Periodicals]) [DEAF 920 B685, 1975]

Brill, R. G. (1963, September). Deafness and the genetic factor. American Annals of the Deaf, 108 (4), 359-373. {An analysis of apparent causes of deafness in 819 children attending the California School for the Deaf, Berkeley, between 1948 and 1962} [UNIV DEAF Periodicals]

Brooks, D. K. (1996). In search of self: Experiences of a postlingually deaf African-American. In I. Parasnis (Ed.), Cultural and language diversity and the Deaf experience (pp. 246-257). New York: Cambridge University Press. [DEAF 305.773 C84, 1996]

Brother, M. (1987). [Review of *A loss for words* by Lou Ann Walker]. In M. L. McIntire (Ed.), Journal of Interpretation, 4, 109-111. Rockville, MD: Registry of Interpreters for the Deaf, Inc. [UNIV RESERVE]

Brother, M. (1991, March). Book World Review [of the book *In silence* by Ruth Sidransky]: In silence, in sound, as a hearing daughter of deaf parents, Ruth Sidransky knew early on that there was a purpose for her life, and that she *had* to succeed. The World and I: A Chronicle of Our Changing Era, 6 (3), 399-405. (Washington, DC: The Washington Times Publications) [*]

(*) Brown, D. (1981). All in the family: Disabled persons are parents, too. Disabled U.S.A., 4 (3), 32-35. (Quarterly publication of the President's Committee on Employment of the Handicapped, Washington, DC 20120 The author is on the Communications staff of the President's Committee) {"The five mobility impaired parents interviewed for this article demonstrate skill in adapting to the demands of parenting. Further, in varying degrees, the lives of their children seem to have been enriched."} [*]

Bruce, R. V. (1973, March). Excerpts from BELL: Alexander Graham Bell and the conquest of solitude. Volta Review, 75 (3), 146-154. [UNIV DEAF Periodicals]

Brundidge, H. T. (1930/1977). Lon Chaney (1883-1930). In Twinkle, twinkle, movie star! (pp. 220-230). New York: Garland Publishing, Inc. [*]

Buchino, M. A. (1990, February). Hearing children of deaf parents: A counseling challenge. Elementary School Guidance and Counseling, 24 (3), 207-212. [UNIV Periodicals]

Buchino, M. A. (1993, January). Perceptions of the oldest hearing child of deaf parents: On interpreting, communication, feelings, and role reversal. American Annals of the Deaf, 138 (1), 40-45. [UNIV DEAF Periodicals]

Buck, F. M. (1995). Parenting by fathers with physical disabilities. In F. P. Haseltine, S. S. Cole & D. B. Gray (Eds.), Reproductive issues for persons with physical disabilities (pp. 163-185). Baltimore: Paul H. Brookes. [C]

Buck, F. M., & Hohmann, G. W. (1981, September). Personality, behavior, values, and children of fathers with spinal cord injury. Archives of Physical Medicine and Rehabilitation, 62, 432-438. [*]

Buck, F. M., & Hohmann, G. W. (1982, June). Child adjustment as related to severity of paternal disability. Archives of Physical Medicine and Rehabilitation, 63, 249-253. [*]

Buck, F. M., & Hohmann, G. W. (1983). Parental disability and children's adjustment. Annual Review of Rehabilitation, 3, 203-241. [*]

Bull, T. H. (1998). Deaf family issues: Codas and identity. In V. Follain-Grisell, K. Leitch-Walker & D. Morton (Eds.), Building bridges: Strengthening home and school relationships for Deaf parents and their hearing children, conference proceedings, Gallaudet University, Washington, D. C., May 1-3, 1997. Washington, DC: Gallaudet University, College for Continuing Education. Manuscript in preparation.

Bunde, L. T. (1980a). Unique interpersonal dynamics of deaf parents/hearing children [Abstract]. In International Congress on Education of the Deaf (Ed.), Abstracts of papers to be presented at the International Congress on Education of the Deaf, Hamburg, August 4-8, 1980 (p. 44). Hamburg, Germany: International Congress on Education of the Deaf, German Congress Secretariat. (The author is listed as affiliated with Ephphatha Services for the Deaf and the Blind, The American Lutheran Church, Minneapolis, Minnesota) [DEAF 370 I57a, 1980]

Bunde, L. T. (1980b). Unique interpersonal dynamics of deaf parents/hearing children. In Proceedings of the International Congress on Education of the Deaf, Hamburg, 1980, Vol. 1 (pp. 721-726). Heidelberg: Julius Groos Verlag. (Moderator of panel #124, Interaction between deaf parents and their children, was G. Rammel of Germany) [DEAF 370 I57pro, 1980, v. 1]

Bunde, L. T. (1984). Parents and their hearing-impaired [sic] children [Abstract]. In R. G. Brill (Ed.), International congresses on education of the deaf: An analytical history, 1878-1980 (pp. 356-357). Washington, DC: Gallaudet College Press. {The title of this article is incorrect since the abstract is about Lawrence Bunde's "study of the interpersonal dynamics of deaf parents with their hearing children."} [DEAF 370 B74i, 1984]

Burke, T. G. (1994, September). Understanding and assisting hearing children of deaf parents: A review of the literature. (ERIC Document Reproduction Service No. ED 375 550 - 15 pages - Ms. Burke was at Loyola College) [REFERENCE DESK]

(*) Burns, K. (1989). Our Mom. New York: Franklin Watts. (A book for children with black and white photographs - 48 pages) {The author, paraplegic since an automobile accident in 1968, is pictured throughout with her four children doing a variety of daily activities to care for her family. A wheelchair helps her get about} [*]

Burton, D. K. (1978). Family counseling and therapy with families containing deaf members. In L. von der Lieth (Ed.), Life in families with deaf members: Proceedings of the Vth World Conference on Deafness, Copenhagen, Denmark, 1977 (pp. 177-193). Copenhagen, Denmark: National Federation of the Deaf in Denmark. [DEAF 306.87 W651, 1978]

Calhoun, J. (1986). Lon Chaney, Jr., 1906-1973, American actor, son of Hollywood's first great horror performer, and the star of a great many terror films himself. In J. Sullivan (Ed.), The Penguin encyclopedia of horror and the supernatural (pp. 76-78). New York: Viking. [C]

Caligiuri, F. A. (1975, April). The telephone and the deaf. Journal of Rehabilitation of the Deaf, 88 (4), 1-3. [UNIV RESERVE]

Carroll, C., & Mather, S. M. (1997). Glimpse of a deaf princess: Alice of Battenberg, 1885-1969. In Movers and shakers: Deaf people who changed the world, twenty-six tales of genius, struggle, perseverance and heroism, (pp.

1-6). San Diego, CA: DawnSignPress. (See the related teacher's guide and student bilingual workbook under Mather and Carroll) {In chapter 1, it's mentioned that Alice was born deaf, had a son, Prince Philip, who married Elizabeth who became Queen of England, and that Prince Philip is considered a "coda."} [DEAF 920 M68, 1997]

Cartwright, D. (1991). How to prepare a presentation on deaf awareness. In World Federation of the Deaf (Ed.), Equality and self-reliance: Proceedings of the XI World Congress of the World Federation of the Deaf, Tokyo, July 2-11, 1991 (pp. 639-660). Tokyo: Japanese Federation of the Deaf. [DEAF 366 W6, 1991]

Carty, B. (1994). The development of deaf identity. In C. J. Erting, R. C. Johnson, D. L. Smith & B. D. Snider (Eds.), The deaf way: Perspectives from the International Conference on Deaf Culture, Washington, D. C., 1989 (pp. 40-43). Washington, DC: Gallaudet University Press. [DEAF 305.773 D42, 1994]

Caselli, M. C., & Volterra, V. (1994). From communication to language in hearing and deaf children. In V. Volterra & C. J. Erting (Eds.), From gesture to language in hearing and deaf children (pp. 263-277). Washington, DC: Gallaudet University Press. [DEAF 401.93 F76, 1994]

Champlin, C., & Klinger, L. (1994). Lon Chaney. In Legends of the silent screen: A collection of U.S. postage stamps (pp. 24-27). Washington, DC: U.S. Postal Service. [*]

Chan, L. M., & Lui, B. (1990, October). Self-concept among hearing Chinese children of deaf parents. American Annals of the Deaf, 135 (4), 299-305. [UNIV DEAF Periodicals]

Chaney, L. (1924). What is characterization. In L. A. Hughes (Ed.), The truth about the movies by the stars (pp. 198-199). Los Angeles: Hollywood Publishers. [*]

Chaney, L. (1929a). Make-up. In The Encyclopaedia Britannica, 14th edition: A New Survey of Universal Knowledge, Vol. 15 (Mary, Duchess of Burgundy to Mushet Steel) (pp. 864-865). New York: Encyclopaedia Britannica, Inc. [*]

Chaney, L. (1929b). Methods of make-up. In The Encyclopaedia Britannica, 14th edition: A New Survey of Universal Knowledge, Vol. 15 (Mary, Duchess of Burgundy to Mushet Steel) (p. 865). New York: Encyclopaedia Britannica, Inc. [*]

Chaney, L. (1983a). My darkest hour (as told to Maude Cheatham). In F. J. Ackerman (Ed.), Lon of 1000 faces (p. 209). Beverly Hills, CA: Morrison, Raven-Hill Company. [*]

Chaney, L. (1983b). Why I prefer grotesque characters. In F. J. Ackerman (Ed.), Lon of 1000 faces (pp. 47-48). Beverly Hills, CA: Morrison, Raven-Hill Company. [*]

Chaney, L., Jr. (1983c). My father Lon Chaney. In F. J. Ackerman (Ed.), Lon of 1000 faces (p. 237). Beverly Hills, CA: Morrison, Raven-Hill Company. [*]

Charlson, E. S. (1990, November). Hearing children of the deaf. Paper presented at the 52nd annual congress of the National Council on Family Relations, Seattle, Washington, November 13, 1990. (ERIC Document Reproduction Service No. ED 334 804 - 14 pages) [REFERENCE DESK]

Charlson, E. S. (1991). Social cognition and self-concept of hearing adolescents with deaf parents: Implications for service providers. In D. Watson & M. Taff-Watson (Eds.), At the crossroads: A celebration of diversity, proceedings of the 12th biennial conference of the American Deafness and Rehabilitation Association, New York,

May 26-29, 1989, Monograph No. 15 (pp. 255-272). Little Rock, AR: American Deafness and Rehabilitation Association (ADARA). [DEAF 362.0425 A8, 1989]

Childress Johnson, S. (1993). The power of sign. In B. Johnson Reagon (Ed.), We who believe in freedom: Sweet Honey In the Rock - still on the journey (pp. 275-283). New York: Doubleday. (Shirley Childress Johnson is hearing and has deaf parents) [DEAF 782.25 R42w, 1993]

Christensen, K. M. (1997). Deaf American culture: Notes from the periphery. In L. L. Naylor (Ed.), Cultural diversity in the United States (pp. 273-277). Westport, CT: Bergin and Garvey. [C]

Christiansen, J. B., & Meisegeier, R. W. (Eds.). (1986). Ronnie Wilbur and Macalyn Fristoe, "I had a wonderful, if somewhat unusual childhood: Growing up hearing in a deaf world, questions." In Papers for the second Research Conference on the Social Aspects of Deafness, Gallaudet College, Washington, D. C., June 8-10, 1986 (pp. 21-25). Washington, DC: Gallaudet College. {A list of 66 questions compiled from conference participants in response to their presentation} [DEAF 303.32 R4p, 1986]

Churn, C. A. (1989, Summer). Books: *Psychotherapy with Deaf and Hard of Hearing Persons: A Systemic Model* [review of the book] by Michael A. Harvey, Adjunct Professor, Boston University, Gallaudet University. Deafness: The Journal of the Sociology of Deafness, 5 (2), 14-15. (Deafness is published by the National Council of Social Workers with Deaf People and the British Deaf Association) [UNIV DEAF Periodicals]

Cicourel, A. V., & Boese, R. J. (1972a). The acquisition of manual Sign Language and generative semantics. Semiotica, 3, 225-256. (A 41-page pre-publication draft is available at the Gallaudet Library [DEAF 428 C5a, 1970]. A condensed version of this paper was presented at the annual meeting of the American Sociological Association, San Francisco, September, 1969, and another version at the International Congress on Education of the Deaf, Stockholm, Sweden, August, 1970) [*]

Cicourel, A. V., & Boese, R. J. (1972b). Sign Language acquisition and the teaching of deaf children. In C. B. Cazden, V. P. John & D. Hymes (Eds.), Functions of language in the classroom (pp. 32-62). New York: Teachers College Press. [DEAF 401 F8, 1972]

Cicourel, A. V., & Boese, R. J. (1972c, February). Sign Language acquisition and the teaching of deaf children, Pt. I. American Annals of the Deaf, 117 (1), 27-33. [UNIV DEAF Periodicals]

Cicourel, A. V., & Boese, R. J. (1972d, June). Sign Language acquisition and the teaching of deaf children, Pt. II. American Annals of the Deaf, 117 (3), 403-411. [UNIV DEAF Periodicals]

(*) Clark, J. G. (1982, August). Counseling in a pediatric audiologic practice. ASHA, 24 (8), 521-526. [UNIV DEAF Periodicals]

(##) Clifford, L. (1976, November). Language problems of children whose parents are deaf. The Bulletin of AASH, 2, 10-13. (Australian Association of Speech and Hearing - now known as Speech Pathology Australia)

(##) Clifford, L. V. (1977). The problem of the normal-hearing child of deaf parents. Special Education Bulletin, 19 (2), 14-17. (Brisbane, Australia)

Coates, D. L., Vietze, P. M., & Gray, D. B. (1985). Methodological issues in studying children of disabled parents. In S. K. Thurman (Ed.), Children of handicapped parents: Research and clinical perspectives (pp. 155-180). Orlando, FL: Academic Press. [DEAF 306.874 C4, 1985]

(##) Coerts, J. A., Mills, A. E., & Bogaerde, B. v. d. (1991). <u>Language input, interaction and the acquisition of Sign Language of the Netherlands.</u> Paper presented to the Fourth European Conference of Developmental Psychology, Budapest, Hungary.

Cohen, H., & Jones, E. G. (1990, October). Interpreting for cross-cultural research: Changing written English to American Sign Language. <u>Journal of the American Deafness and Rehabilitation Association, 24</u> (2), 41-48. [UNIV RESERVE]

Cokely, D. (1981, Fall). Sign Language interpreters: A demographic survey. <u>Sign Language Studies, 32,</u> 261-286. [UNIV RESERVE]

Cokely, D., & Baker, C. (1980). "Language" and the Sign Language teacher. In <u>American Sign Language: A teacher's resource text on curriculum, methods, and evaluation</u> (pp. 1-21). Silver Spring, MD: T. J. Publishers. {Membership in the Deaf community is discussed on pages 15-20} [DEAF 420.07 C6a, 1980]

Coppola, F. (1986/1990). Exploration of cross-cultural barriers: Hearing children and deaf parents. In M. L. McIntire (Ed.), <u>Interpreting: The art of cross-cultural mediation, proceedings of the ninth National Convention of the Registry of Interpreters for the Deaf, San Diego, July 4-8, 1985</u> (pp. 54-55). Silver Spring, MD: RID Publications. (The second edition was published in 1990) [DEAF 420.802 R4i, 1985]

Corbett, E. E., Jr., & Jensema, C. J. (1981). Hearing impairment among teachers. In E. E. Corbett, Jr. & C. J. Jensema, <u>Teachers of the deaf: Descriptive profiles</u> (pp. 15-22). Washington, DC: Gallaudet College Press. [DEAF 371.11 C6t, 1981]

Corfmat, P. T. (1959, November). Childless marriages of the deaf. <u>Deaf Welfare: The Journal of the National Council of Missioners and Welfare Officers to the Deaf: Incorporating the Council of Church Missioners to the Deaf and Dumb, 2</u> (3), 239-243. (The author is hearing and has deaf parents) [UNIV DEAF Periodicals]

Corina, D., & Sandler, W. (1993). On the nature of phonological structure in sign language. <u>Phonology, 10</u> (2), 165-207. [C]

Corina, D. P. (1994). The induction of prosodic constraints: Implications for phonological theory and mental representation. In R. Corrigan, G. Iverson & S. Lima (Eds.), <u>The reality of linguistic rules</u> (pp. 115-145). Philadelphia: John Benjamins. [*]

(*) (##) Corina, D. P., Bellugi, U., Kritchevsky, M., O'Grady-Batch, N. (1990). Spatial relations in signed verses spoken language: Clues to right parietal functions. <u>Academy of Aphasia,</u> Baltimore, Maryland.

(*) (##) Corina, D. P., Kritchevsky, M., Bellugi, U. (in press). Visual language processing and unilateral neglect: Evidence from American Sign Language. <u>Journal of Cognitive Neuropsychology.</u>

Corina, D. P., Vaid, J., & Bellugi, U. (1992, March 6). The linguistic basis of left hemisphere specialization. <u>Science, 255</u> (5049), 1258-1260. [UNIV Periodicals]

Corker, M. (1996a). The bubble and the coal hole. In <u>Deaf transitions: Images and origins of deaf families, deaf communities, and deaf identities</u> (pp. 65-82). London: J. Kingsley Publishers. [DEAF 305.773 C67d, 1996]

Corker, M. (1996b). Coming home. In <u>Deaf transitions: Images and origins of deaf families, deaf communities, and deaf identities</u> (pp. 158-180). London: J. Kingsley Publishers. [DEAF 305.773 C67d, 1996]

Corker, M. (1996c). Swamps and rivers. In <u>Deaf transitions: Images and origins of deaf families, deaf communities, and deaf identities</u> (pp. 123-139). London: J. Kingsley Publishers. [DEAF 305.773 C67d, 1996]

Corker, M. (1996d). Underground rivers. In <u>Deaf transitions: Images and origins of deaf families, deaf communities, and deaf identities</u> (pp. 140-157). London: J. Kingsley Publishers. [DEAF 305.773 C67d, 1996]

Corker, M. (1996e). Windows and toast on beans. In <u>Deaf transitions: Images and origins of deaf families, deaf communities, and deaf identities</u> (pp. 83-122). London: J. Kingsley Publishers. [DEAF 305.773 C67d, 1996]

(*) Cornwell, M. (1975a). Blind and partially sighted parents. In <u>Early years</u> (pp. 138-143). London: Disabled Living Foundation. [UNIV Deaf 649.1 C6e, 1975]

(*) Cornwell, M. (1975b). Deaf and partially hearing parents. In <u>Early years</u> (pp. 144-149). London: Disabled Living Foundation. {Most of the material in this chapter was contributed by Diane Kenyon, a partially hearing mother of hearing children} [UNIV Deaf 649.1 C6e, 1975]

(*) Cornwell, M. (1975c). General considerations [for disabled parents]. In <u>Early years</u> (pp. 6-18). London: Disabled Living Foundation. [UNIV Deaf 649.1 C6e, 1975]

Coutts, K. (1994). "The social worker's role" by Karen Coutts, a hearing child of deaf parents and a Social Worker with deaf people. <u>Deafness: The Journal of the Sociology of Deafness, 10</u> (1), 6-9. (Reprinted in National Council for Social Workers with Deaf People Training Committee (Ed.), <u>Special needs or special breed? Hearing children of deaf adults</u> (pp. 12-20). London: National Council for Social Workers with Deaf People, NCSWDP - Write NCSWDP, 1st floor, Bedford House, 125-133 Camden High Street, London, England NW1 7JR. Transcript of a paper presented at a one day seminar organised [sic] by the London Boroughs Disability Resource Team of the NCSWDP, April 9, 1991 - 24 pages [DEAF 306.874 S632, 1992]) [UNIV DEAF Periodicals]

Covington, V. C. (1980, Fall). Problems of acculturation into the deaf community. <u>Sign Language Studies, 28,</u> 267-285. [UNIV RESERVE]

Critchley, E. (1967a, January). Hearing children of deaf parents. <u>Journal of Laryngology and Otology, 81</u> (1), 51-61. [UNIV DEAF Periodicals]

Critchley, E. (1967b). Language development of hearing children in a deaf environment. <u>Developmental Medicine and Child Neurology, 9,</u> 274-280. [UNIV Periodicals]

Critchley, E. M. R. (1967a). Gesture and the deaf. In <u>Speech origins and development</u> (pp. 95-106). Springfield, IL: Charles C. Thomas Publishers. [DEAF 371.301 C7s, 1967]

Critchley, E. M. R. (1967b). The lessons of childhood speech. In <u>Speech origins and development</u> (pp. 74-94). Springfield, IL: Charles C. Thomas Publishers. [DEAF 371.301 C7s, 1967]

Crittenden, P. M., & Bonvillian, J. D. (1984, April). The relationship between maternal risk status and maternal sensitivity. <u>American Journal of Orthopsychiatry, 54</u> (2), 250-262. [UNIV Periodicals]

Cross, T. G., Nienhuys, T. G., & Morris, J. E. (1980). Maternal speech styles to deaf and hearing children [Abstract]. In International Congress on Education of the Deaf (Ed.), <u>Abstracts of papers to be presented at the International Congress on Education of the Deaf, Hamburg, August 4-8, 1980</u> (p. 62). Hamburg, Germany: International Congress on Education of the Deaf, German Congress Secretariat. [DEAF 370 I57a, 1980]

Daniels, M. (1993, Spring). ASL as a factor in acquiring English. Sign Language Studies, 78, 23-29. [UNIV RESERVE]

Daniels, M. (1994, Summer). Words more powerful than sound. Sign Language Studies, 83, 155-166. [UNIV RESERVE]

Daniels, M. (1996, Spring). Bilingual, bimodal education for hearing kindergarten students. Sign Language Studies, 90, 25-37. [UNIV RESERVE]

Dempsey, M. (1995, May/June). Lon Chaney: A thousand and one faces. Film Comment, 31, 62-67. [C]

Denmark, J. (1994, April). Children of deaf parents. In Deafness and mental health (pp. 24-25). London: Jessica Kingsley Publishers. [DEAF 362.2 D46d, 1994]

Dent, K. A. (1982). Two daughters of a deaf mute mother: Implications for ego and cognitive development. Journal of the American Academy of Psychoanalysis, 10 (3), 427-441. [DEAF 306.874 D4t, 1982]

(*) Deshen, S., & Deshen, H. (1989, Fall). Brief communications: Managing at home, relationships between blind parents and sighted children. Human Organization, 48 (3), 262-267. [C]

de Villiers, J., Bibeau, L., Ramos, E., & Gatty, J. (1993). Gestural communication in oral deaf mother-child pairs: Language with a helping hand? Applied Psycholinguistics, 14 (3), 319-347. [UNIV Periodicals]

de Villiers, P. A., & de Villiers, J. G. (1979). Crucial experiences. In Early language (pp. 96-114). Cambridge, MA: Harvard University Press. [UNIV Gen 401.9 D4e, 1979]

Devlin, L., Goffen, R. L., Allen, A., & Brunner, B. J. (1998). Hearing-speech-language development of preschool children in deaf families. In V. Follain-Grisell, K. Leitch-Walker & D. Morton (Eds.), Building bridges: Strengthening home and school relationships for Deaf parents and their hearing children, conference proceedings, Gallaudet University, Washington, D. C., May 1-3, 1997. Washington, DC: Gallaudet University, College for Continuing Education. Manuscript in preparation.

Dicaprio, N. S. (1971, June). Factors affecting the child's evaluation of the visually handicapped parent. The New Outlook for the Blind, 65, 181-186. (Publication of the American Foundation for the Blind, New York) [C]

DiPietro, R. J. (1977). Code-switching as a verbal strategy among bilinguals. In F. R. Eckman (Ed.), Current themes in linguistics: Bilingualism, experimental linguistics, and language typologies (pp. 3-13). Washington, DC: Hemisphere Publishing Corp., distributed by Halsted Press. (Papers presented at a UWM linguistics symposium, University of Wisconsin - Milwaukee, March 26-28, 1976) [UNIV Gen 410 C8, 1977]

Doe, T. (1994). Multiple minorities: Communities within the Deaf community. In C. J. Erting, R. C. Johnson, D. L. Smith & B. D. Snider (Eds.), The deaf way: Perspectives from the International Conference on Deaf Culture, Washington, D. C., 1989 (pp. 464-469). Washington, DC: Gallaudet University Press. [DEAF 305.773 D42, 1994]

Doig, I. (1990). Motating the high line. In I. Doig, Ride with me, Mariah Montana (pp. 96-210). New York: Atheneum, MacMillan Publishing Company. {Novel of one family's search for the new West and for each other. The third and final of the McCaskill trilogy. There's a fascinating paragraph: "They are Asian delta people, newly come to American mountain headwaters. Their immense journey pivots on the children, especially on the lithe daughter made solemnly older by the presence of two cultures within her. Driver's license, income tax, television,

J
O
U
R
N
A
L

food budget, rock music, all the reckless spill of America must come to her family through the careful funnel of this ten-year-old woman who is now the mother of words to her own parents." (p. 131)} [C]

Duc, D. (1974). Deaf parents and their educational problems. In D. H. Pokorny (Ed.), <u>My eyes are my ears: A collection of papers delivered at the first International Ecumenical Seminar on the Pastoral Care of the Deaf, Geneva, Switzerland, 1971</u> (pp. 122-126). New York: MSS Information Corporation. [DEAF 261 I5m, 1974]

Duhon, S. B, & Leitch-Walker, K. (1998). Everything you wanted to know about deaf parents, but were afraid to ask: Tips for teachers and school principals. In V. Follain-Grisell, K. Leitch-Walker & D. Morton (Eds.), <u>Building bridges: Strengthening home and school relationships for Deaf parents and their hearing children, conference proceedings, Gallaudet University, Washington, D. C., May 1-3, 1997.</u> Washington, DC: Gallaudet University, College for Continuing Education. Manuscript in preparation.

Durnbaugh, C., & Seago, L. (1993). Visual communication strategies for parent-infant interactions. In S. Polowe-Aldersley (Ed.), <u>Pride is with us: Proceedings of the 56th biennial meeting, Convention of American Instructors of the Deaf and the 64th annual meeting of the Conference of Educational Administrators Serving the Deaf, Baltimore, Maryland, June, 1993</u> (pp. 119-120). Bedford, TX: Convention of American Instructors of the Deaf. [Gallaudet University Archives]

Eikeland, T. (1978). Deaf parents and hearing children: The problem of verbal language acquisition. In L. von der Lieth (Ed.), <u>Life in families with deaf members: Proceedings of the Vth World Conference on Deafness, Copenhagen, Denmark, 1977</u> (pp. 57-61). Copenhagen, Denmark: Akademisk Forlag, National Federation of the Deaf in Denmark. [DEAF 306.87 W65l, 1978]

Eiseley, L. (1992). The running man. In J. Schlib, E. A. Flynn & J. Clifford (Eds.), <u>Constellations: A contextual reader for writers</u> (pp. 121-129). New York: Harper Collins. {This is a chapter from his autobiography, *All the strange hours: The excavation of a life* where he struggles with his relationship to his "stone deaf" mother. The editors suggest the student write an essay based on the questions and themes revealed in this chapter} [*]

Elliott, H. (1974, October). Marriage counseling with deaf clients. <u>Journal of Rehabilitation of the Deaf, 8</u> (2), 29-36. [UNIV DEAF Periodicals - on reserve]

Emerton, R. G. (1995, February 22). Deafness, *Mother father deaf: Living between sound and silence* by Paul Preston [Book review]. <u>Journal of the American Medical Association, 273</u> (8), 677. [UNIV Periodicals]

Emerton, R. G. (1996). Marginality, biculturalism, and social identity of Deaf people. In I. Parasnis (Ed.), <u>Cultural and language diversity and the Deaf experience</u> (pp. 136-145). New York: Cambridge University Press. [DEAF 305.773 C84, 1996]

Emmorey, K., & Corina, D. (1993, July). Hemispheric specialization for ASL signs and English words: Differences between imageable and abstract forms. <u>Neuropsychologia, 31</u> (7), 645-653. [*]

Emmorey, K., Corina, D. P., & Bellugi, U. (1995). Differential processing of topographic and referential functions of space. In K. Emmorey & J. S. Reilly (Eds.), <u>Language, gesture, and space</u> (pp. 43-62). Hillsdale, NJ: Lawrence Erlbaum Associates Publishers. [DEAF 428 L35, 1995]

Emmorey, K., Kosslyn, S. M., & Bellugi, U. (1993, February). Visual imagery and visual-spatial language: Enhanced imagery abilities in deaf and hearing ASL signers. <u>Cognition, 46</u> (2), 139-181. [UNIV Periodicals]

Erting, C. J., & Hynes, M. O. (1990/1994). The interactional context of deaf mother-infant communication. In V. Volterra & C. J. Erting (Eds.), <u>From gesture to language in hearing and deaf children</u> (pp. 97-106). Washington, DC: Gallaudet University Press. (Reprint of the 1990 book published by Springer-Verlag, New York [DEAF 401.93 F76, 1990]) [DEAF 401.93 F76, 1994]

Erting, C. J., & Volterra, V. (1990/1994). Conclusion. In V. Volterra & C. J. Erting (Eds.), <u>From gesture to language in hearing and deaf children</u> (pp. 299-303). Washington, DC: Gallaudet University Press. (Reprint of the 1990 book published by Springer-Verlag, New York [DEAF 401.93 F76, 1990]) [DEAF 401.93 F76, 1994]

Evans, C., & Zimmer, K. (1993a). <u>"Kids R Bi-Bi:" Sign Talk Development Project (STDP)</u>. Paper presented at the 27th annual meeting of the Teachers of English to Speakers of Other Languages (TESOL), Atlanta, Georgia, April 13-17, 1993. (ERIC Document Reproduction Service No. ED 362 047 - 10 pages - The Sign Talk Children's Centre is in Winnipeg, Manitoba, Canada) [REFERENCE DESK]

Evans, C., & Zimmer, K. (1993b). Sign Talk Development Project, Winnipeg, Manitoba. <u>ACEHI - Journal 19</u>, 62-70. (The official journal of the Association of Canadian Educators of the Hearing Impaired - the Sign Talk Children's Centre is in Winnipeg, Manitoba, Canada) [UNIV DEAF Periodicals]

Evans, C., Zimmer, K., & Murray, D. (1994). <u>Discovering with words and Signs, Sign Talk Development Project: A resource guide for developing a bilingual and bicultural preschool program for deaf and hearing children</u>. Winnipeg, Manitoba, Canada: Sign Talk Children's Centre. (56 pages - See two other reports: *"Kids R Bi-Bi:" Sign Talk Development Project - STDP* and an ERIC document by Evans and Zimmer. [*]) [*]

Everitt, D. (1986). Lon Chaney, 1883-1930, American silent film actor, particularly in horror roles requiring complex makeup. In J. Sullivan (Ed.), <u>The Penguin encyclopedia of horror and the supernatural</u> (pp. 76-77). New York: Viking. [C]

Fant, L., Jr. (1980). Drama and poetry in Sign Language: A personal reminiscence. In C. Baker & R. Battison (Eds.), <u>Sign Language and the Deaf community: Essays in honor of William C. Stokoe</u> (pp. 193-200). Silver Spring, MD: National Association of the Deaf. [DEAF 420 S52, 1980]

Fant, L. J. (1990). Knots. In <u>Silver threads: A personal look at the first twenty-five years of the Registry of Interpreters for the Deaf</u> (pp. 89-91). Silver Spring, MD: RID Publications, Registry of Interpreters for the Deaf, Inc. [DEAF 420.802 F36s, 1990]

Fant, L. J., Jr., & Schuchman, J. S. (1974). Experiences of two hearing children of deaf parents. In P. J. Fine (Ed.), <u>Deafness in infancy and early childhood</u> (pp. 225-229). New York: Medcom Press. [DEAF 362.7 F5d, 1974]

Finger, A. (1995). Mothers with disabilities. In F. P. Haseltine, S. S. Cole & D. B. Gray (Eds.), <u>Reproductive issues for persons with physical disabilities</u> (pp. 119-124). Baltimore: Paul H. Brookes. [C]

Finton, L. (1996). Living in a bilingual-bicultural family. In I. Parasnis (Ed.), <u>Cultural and language diversity and the Deaf experience</u> (pp. 258-271). New York: Cambridge University Press. [DEAF 305.773 C84, 1996]

Flaxbeard, R., & Toomey, W. (1987, September). No longer deaf to their needs. <u>British Journal of Special Education, 14</u> (3), 103-105. {Compensatory education for hearing children of deaf parents is discussed} [UNIV Periodicals]

Fleischer, L. (1990, August 17). Talk of the trade [Review of *In silence*]. Publishers Weekly, 237 (33), 43. [C]

Folven, R. J., & Bonvillian, J. D. (1991, September). The transition from nonreferential to referential language in children acquiring American Sign Language. Developmental Psychology, 27 (5), 806-816. [UNIV Periodicals]

(*) Ford, N. M. (1984, April). Parent-education services for deaf adults. Journal of Rehabilitation of the Deaf, 17 (4), 1-3. [UNIV DEAF Periodicals]

Frank, H. (1978-79). Psychodynamic conflicts in hearing children of deaf parents. International Journal of Psychoanalytic Psychotherapy, 7, 305-315. [DEAF 155.418 F7p, 1979]

Frankenburg, F. R., Sloman, L., & Perry, A. (1985, March). General papers: Issues in the therapy of hearing children with deaf parents. Canadian Journal of Psychiatry, 30 (2), 98-102. (Paper was originally delivered at the 63rd annual meeting of the Ontario Psychiatric Association, Toronto, Canada, 1982) [DEAF 306.874 F7i, 1985]

Frelich, P. (1991). The many wonderful advances that have so improved the quality of life for the deaf in America. In World Federation of the Deaf (Ed.), Equality and self-reliance: Proceedings of the XI World Congress of the World Federation of the Deaf, Tokyo, July 2-11, 1991 (pp. 89-102). Tokyo: Japanese Federation of the Deaf. [DEAF 366 W6, 1991]

Frishberg, N. (1990). Role, ethics, and etiquette of interpreting. In Interpreting: An introduction (Rev. ed., pp. 59-72). Silver Spring, MD: RID Publications. [DEAF 420.802 F7i, 1990]

Fritsch Rudser, S., & Strong, M. (1986, Winter). An examination of some personal characteristics and abilities of Sign Language interpreters. Sign Language Studies, 53, 315-331. (Reprinted in D. Cokely (Ed.), Sign Language interpreters and interpreting (pp. 15-28). Burtonsville, MD: Linstok Press, 1992 [DEAF 418.02 S53, 1992]) [UNIV RESERVE]

Fuchs, M. G. (1990, October 15). Book review: *In silence: Growing up hearing in a deaf world*. Library Journal, 115 (17), 93. [UNIV Periodicals]

Furth, H. G. (1973). From school to adulthood. In Deafness and learning: A psychosocial approach (pp. 43-51). Belmont, CA: Wadsworth. {Hearing children of deaf parents are listed as one of the categories of people belonging to the Deaf community} [DEAF 370.15 F8d, 1973]

Gaines, R. (1987). The language and communication development of monozygotic preschool deaf and hearing twins. In R. Ojala (Ed.), Program, X World Congress of the World Federation of the Deaf: One world one responsibility, proceedings, Espoo, Finland, July 20-28, 1987, Vol. 2 (pp. 697-701). Helsinki: Finnish Association of the Deaf. (The editor is hearing and has deaf parents) [DEAF 366 W6, 1987]

Gallaudet, E. M. (1890, November 28). The intermarriage of the deaf, and their education. Science: Weekly Newspaper of all the Arts and Sciences, 16 (408), 295-299. (Reprinted in 1891 in the American Annals of the Deaf, 36, 81-83. [UNIV DEAF Periodicals]) [DEAF 306.84 G3i, 1890]

Gannon, J. (1991). The importance of cultural identity. In M. D. Garretson (Ed.), Perspectives on Deafness: A Deaf American monograph, 41 (Nos. 1-2) (pp. 55-58). Silver Spring, MD: National Association of the Deaf. [DEAF RESERVE]

Gannon, J. R. (1981). The 1970s. In Deaf heritage: A narrative history of Deaf America (pp. 377-417). Silver

Spring, MD: NAD Press, National Association of the Deaf. [DEAF 305.773 G3d, 1981]

Gannon, J. R. (1989). Day Five. In <u>The week the world heard Gallaudet</u> (pp. 92-107). Washington, DC: Gallaudet University Press. [DEAF 378.753 G3w, 1989]

(*) Gatewood, J., Thomas, W., Musteen, Z., & Castleberry, E. (1992, Summer). Parenting skills for lower functioning deaf adults. <u>Journal of the American Deafness and Rehabilitation Association, 26</u> (1), 26-29. [UNIV RESERVE]

Gaustad, M. G. (1988). Development of vocal and signed communication in deaf and hearing twins of deaf parents. In M. Strong (Ed.), <u>Language learning and deafness</u> (pp. 220-260). New York: Cambridge University Press. (The author also has published under the name M. A. Gonter) [DEAF 419 L363, 1988]

George, E. (1992, June/July/August). Ruth Sidransky: Wenn ihr mich doch hören könntet - Kindsein in einer stummen Welt [Review of Ruth Sidransky's book, *In silence: Growing up hearing in a deaf world*]. <u>Das Zeichen, 6</u> (20), 216-217. (In German. Need a translation. *Das Zeichen* means "The sign" in German) [UNIV DEAF Periodicals]

Gerner de Garcia, B. (1990). The emerging deaf community in the Dominican Republic: An ethnographic study. In C. Lucas (Ed.), <u>Sign Language research: Theoretical issues</u> (pp. 259-274). Washington, DC: Gallaudet University Press. [DEAF 420 S533, 1990]

Gianino, A., & Meadow-Orlans, K. P. (1987, April). <u>Stress and self-regulation in six-month-old deaf and hearing infants with deaf mothers.</u> Poster session presented at the biennial meeting of the Society for Research in Child Development, Baltimore, Maryland. (10 pages) [DEAF 155.422 G52s, 1987]

Gibson, C. (1988). The impact of early developmental history on cerebral asymmetries: Implications for reading ability in deaf children. In D. L. Molfese & S. J. Segalowitz (Eds.), <u>Brain lateralization in children: Developmental implications</u> (pp. 591-604). New York: The Guilford Press. [DEAF 305.231 B7, 1988]

Gibson, G., & Ludwig, E. G. (1968, February). Family structure in a disabled population. <u>Journal of Marriage and the Family, 30</u> (1), 54-63. [UNIV Periodicals Microfilm]

(*) Gilhool, T. K., & Gran, J. A. (1985). Legal rights of disabled parents. In S. K. Thurman (Ed.), <u>Children of handicapped parents: Research and clinical perspectives</u> (pp. 11-34). Orlando, FL: Academic Press. [UNIV Deaf 306.874 C4, 1985]

(*) Gill-Williamson, L. M. (1991, June). The impact of a visually impaired parent on a family's decision making. <u>Journal of Visual Impairment and Blindness, 85</u> (6), 246-248. [UNIV Periodicals]

Glickfeld, C. L. (1988, Spring/Summer). American Sign Language: Help or handicap to a writer? <u>The Croton Review, 11,</u> 31-34. (Essay prize winner) [*]

Glickfeld, C. L. (1991). What my mother knows. In S. L. Barber (Ed.), <u>Connections: Using multi-cultural, racial and ethnic short stories to promote better writing</u> (pp. 98-107). Dubuque, IA: Kendall/Hunt. [*]

Glickfeld, C. L. (1992). What my mother knows. In C. East (Ed.), <u>The Flannery O'Connor Award: Selected stories</u> (pp. 99-106). Athens, GA: University of Georgia Press. (Winner of the Flannery O'Connor Fiction Award.

Reprinted from Useful gifts. The University of Georgia Press. [DEAF 813.54 G5u, 1989] The author is hearing and has deaf parents) [DEAF 813.0108 F52, 1992]

Glickman, N. (1983, January). A cross cultural view of counseling with deaf clients. Journal of Rehabilitation of the Deaf: Journal of Professional Rehabilitation Workers with the Adult Deaf, 16 (3), 4-12. [UNIV RESERVE]

Glickman, N. S. (1996). The development of culturally Deaf identities. In N. S. Glickman & M. A. Harvey (Eds.), Culturally affirmative psychotherapy with deaf persons (pp. 115-153). Mahwah, NJ: Lawrence Erlbaum Associates, Publishers. [DEAF 616.8914 C84, 1996]

Goldenberg, M., Rabinowitz, A., & Kravetz, S. (1979, August). The relation between communication level and self-concept of deaf parents and their normal children. American Annals of the Deaf, 124 (4), 472-478. [UNIV DEAF Periodicals]

Goldin-Meadow, S., & Morford, M. (1985, April). Gesture in early child language: Studies of deaf and hearing children. Merrill-Palmer Quarterly, 31 (2), 145-176. [UNIV Periodicals - Microfilm]

Goldin-Meadow, S., & Mylander, C. (1991). Levels of structure in a common system developed without a language model. In K. R. Gibson & A. C. Petersen (Eds.), Brain maturation and cognitive development: Comparative and cross-cultural perspectives (pp. 315-344). Hawthorne, NY: Aldine De Gruyter. [C]

Goldin-Meadow, S., & Mylander, C. (1998, January). Spontaneous sign systems created by deaf children in two cultures [Letters to Nature]. Nature, 391 (6664), 279-281. [C]

Gonter, M. A. (1984, April). Early development of vocal and signed language in hearing and deaf fraternal twins. Paper presented at the 68th annual conference of the American Educational Research Association, New Orleans. (ERIC Document Reproduction Service No. ED 249 714 - 38 pages) [REFERENCE DESK]

Goodman, J. F., Cecil, H. S., & Barker, W. F. (1984, February). Early intervention with retarded children: Some encouraging results. Developmental Medicine and Child Neurology, 26 (1), 47-55. {On pages 51-52 there is reference to intervention with hearing children of deaf parents} [UNIV Periodicals]

Goodman, M. (1994, November/December). Pregnant and disabled? Don't assume the professionals will understand. Professional Care of Mother and Child, 4, 227-228. {"The Maternity Alliance [of London] has uncovered a high degree of ignorance about how to treat parents with disabilities. Here are some ideas for remedying uncertainty and prejudice among professionals." For further information: The Maternity Alliance, 15 Britannia Street, London WC1X 9JN} [C]

Gray, D. B., & Schimmel, A. B. (1995). Future directions for research on reproductive issues for people with physical disabilities. In F. P. Haseltine, S. S. Cole & D. B. Gray (Eds.), Reproductive issues for persons with physical disabilities (pp. 339-354). Baltimore: Paul H. Brookes. [C]

Greer, B. G. (1985). Children of physically disabled parents: Some thoughts, facts, and hypotheses. In S. K. Thurman (Ed.), Children of handicapped parents: Research and clinical perspectives (pp. 131-143). Orlando, FL: Academic Press. [DEAF 306.874 C4, 1985]

Gregory, S. (1994). The first signs and words: Language development in a bilingual environment. In J. G. Kyle (Ed.), Growing up in sign and word: Papers from a conference at Centre for Deaf Studies (pp. 29-41). Bristol, England: University of Bristol. [DEAF 371.9721 G76, 1994]

Gregory, S. (1996, November). Book reviews: *A Journey into the DEAF-WORLD.* Deaf Worlds: Deaf People, Community and Society, 12 (3), 31-32. (Former title of this journal was Deafness) [UNIV DEAF Periodicals]

Gregory, S., & Barlow, S. (1989). Interactions between deaf babies and their deaf and hearing mothers. In B. Woll (Ed.), Language development and Sign Language: Papers from the Seminar on Language Development and Sign Language, Monograph No. 1, International Sign Linguistics Association, Centre for Deaf Studies, University of Bristol, Bristol, U. K., 1986 (pp. 23-35). Bristol, U.K.: University of Bristol, Centre for Deaf Studies. [DEAF 480.07 S41, 1986]

(*) Griffith, A., & Scott, D. (Eds.). (1985). Marriage and children. In Looking back - looking forward: Living with deafness (pp. 200-201). Toronto, Canada: Canadian Hearing Society. [DEAF Copy 1: 362 L66, 1985]

Griffith, P. L. (1985, Fall). Mode-switching and mode-finding in a hearing child of deaf parents. Sign Language Studies, 48, 195-222. [UNIV RESERVE]

Griffith, P. L. (1990/1994). Emergence of mode-finding and mode-switching in a hearing child of deaf parents. In V. Volterra & C. J. Erting (Eds.), From gesture to language in hearing and deaf children (pp. 233-245). Washington, DC: Gallaudet University Press. (Originally published in 1990 by Springer-Verlag, New York [DEAF 401.93 F76, 1990]) [DEAF 401.93 F76, 1994]

Groce, N. E. (1996, March). *Mother father deaf. Living between sound and silence.* Paul Preston [Book review]. Medical Anthropology: Cross-cultural studies in health and illness, 10 (1), 102-103. (Publication of the Society for Medical Anthropology) [C]

Grosjean, F. (1982a). Bilingualism in society. In Life with two languages: An introduction to bilingualism (pp. 113-166). Cambridge, MA: Harvard University Press. [DEAF 420 G761, 1982]

Grosjean, F. (1982b). Bilingualism in the United States. In Life with two languages: An introduction to bilingualism (pp. 42-112). Cambridge, MA: Harvard University Press. [DEAF 420 G761, 1982]

Grosjean, F. (1982c). The bilingual person. In Life with two languages: An introduction to bilingualism (pp. 228-288). Cambridge, MA: Harvard University Press. [DEAF 420 G761, 1982]

Grosjean, F. (1985). The bilingual as a competent but specific speaker-hearer. Journal of Multilingual and Multicultural Development, 6 (6), 467-477. [C]

Grosjean, F. (1992, Winter). The bilingual and the bicultural person in the hearing and in the deaf world. Sign Language Studies, 77, 307-320. [UNIV RESERVE]

Grosjean, F. (1996). Living with two languages and two cultures. In I. Parasnis (Ed.), Cultural and language diversity and the Deaf experience (pp. 20-37). New York: Cambridge University Press. [DEAF 305.773 C84, 1996]

Grosvenor, M. B. (1994, Jan/Feb). Life with Alexander Graham Bell. Volta Voices, 1 (1), 5-7. Washington, DC: The Alexander Graham Bell Association for the Deaf. (Edited by P. Feibelman) [UNIV DEAF Periodicals]

Guttentag, R. E., & Schaefer, E. G. (1987, April). Phonological encoding by hearing children of deaf parents. Cognitive Development, 2 (2), 169-178. [DEAF 153.123 G87p, 1987]

Haglund, M., Ojemann, G. A., Lettich, E., Bellugi, U., & Corina, D. P. (1993, January). Dissociation of cortical and single unit activity in spoken and signed languages. Brain and Language, 44 (1), 19-27. [UNIV Periodicals]

Halbreich, U. (1979, February). Influence of deaf-mute parents on the character of their offspring. Acta Psychiatrica Scandinavica, 59, 129-138. [DEAF 616.858 H3i, 1979]

Harris, J., & Hartley, K. (1979, May 1). Children of deaf parents. Social Work Today, 10 (34), 12-13. (British Association of Social Workers journal) {Casework with a family consisting of deaf parents with three hearing daughters} [UNIV Periodicals]

Harris, M., Clibbens, J., Chasin, J., Tibbits, R. (1988). "The third chicken is a duck": Linguistic experience and early Sign Language development. In G. Collins, A. Lewis & V. Lewis (Eds.), Proceedings of the Child Language Seminar, University of Warwick, England, 1988 (pp. 205-216). {Signing strategies Deaf mothers use in free play with deaf children from 7 to 20 months} [*]

(##) Harris, M., Clibbens, J., Tibbits, R., & Chasin, J. (1987). Communication between deaf mothers and their deaf infants. In P. Griffith, A. E. Mills & J. Local (Eds.), Proceedings of the Child Language Seminar, University of York, York, England, 1987. [*]

Harris, M., & Mohay, H. (1997, Spring). Learning to look in the right place: A comparison of attentional behavior in deaf children with deaf and hearing mothers. Journal of Deaf Studies and Deaf Education, 2 (2), 95-103. [UNIV DEAF Periodicals]

Harris, R. I. (1981). Mental health needs and priorities in deaf children and adults: A deaf professional's perspective for the 1980s. In L. K. Stein, E. D. Mendel & T. Jabaley (Eds.), Deafness and mental health (pp. 219-250). New York: Grune and Stratton. [DEAF 362.2 D43, 1981]

Harvey, M. A. (1982, December). The influence and utilization of an interpreter for deaf persons in family therapy. American Annals of the Deaf, 127 (7), 821-828. [UNIV DEAF Periodicals]

Harvey, M. A. (1985, October). Toward a dialogue between the paradigms of family therapy and deafness. American Annals of the Deaf, 130 (4), 305-314. [UNIV DEAF Periodicals]

Harvey, M. A. (1989). Hearing children with deaf parents. In Psychotherapy with deaf and hard of hearing persons: A systemic model (pp. 182-208). Hillsdale, NJ: Lawrence Erlbaum Associates. [DEAF 616.8914 H3p, 1989]

Harvey, M. A. (1997, July). The evolving relationship between interpreter and family therapist. Journal of Interpretation, 63-76. Silver Spring, MD: Registry of Interpreters for the Deaf, Inc. [*]

Harvey, M. A., & Dym, B. (1988, January). An ecological perspective on deafness. Journal of Rehabilitation of the Deaf, 21 (3), 12-20. [UNIV RESERVE]

Haseltine, F. P., Cole, S. S., & Gray, D. B. (Eds.). (1995). Introduction. In Reproductive issues for persons with physical disabilities (pp. xxvii-xxxi). Baltimore: Paul H. Brookes. [C]

(*) Held, M. (1975, May). Oral deaf parents communicate with their deaf infants. The Volta Review, 77 (5), 309-310. [UNIV DEAF Periodicals and DEAF Copy 1: 306.874 H44o, 1975]

Heller, B. (1985). Family composition. In Hearing impairment demographics: Implications for mental health services provision (p. 14). San Francisco: University of California, Center on Deafness. [DEAF 362.2 H4h, 1985]

Hessmann, J. (1991, March). Taubenschlag. Das Zeichen, 5 (15), 103-105. (In German. Need a translation - *Das Zeichen* means "the sign" in German) {This is a segment in a regular column by J. Hessmann, "Schon gehört - unerhört." Discusses examples of the bad English-to-German translation of Lou Ann Walker's book, *A Loss for Words*} [UNIV DEAF Periodicals]

Higgins, P. C. (1979, April). Outsiders in a hearing world: The deaf community. Urban Life: A Journal of Ethnographic Research, 8 (1), 3-23. [C]

Hoffmeister, R., & Harvey, M. A. (1996). Is there a psychology of the hearing? In N. S. Glickman & M. A. Harvey (Eds.), Culturally affirmative psychotherapy with deaf persons (pp. 73-97). Mahwah, NJ: Lawrence Erlbaum Associates. [DEAF 616.8914 C84, 1996]

Hoffmeister, R. J. (1985). Families with deaf parents: A functional perspective. In S. K. Thurman (Ed.), Children of handicapped parents: Research and clinical perspectives (pp. 111-130). Orlando, FL: Academic Press. (The author is hearing and has deaf parents) [DEAF 306.874 C4, 1985]

Holcomb, R. K., Holcomb, S. K., & Holcomb, T. K. (1994). Signing cop. In Deaf culture *our way*: Anecdotes from the Deaf community, (3rd ed., p. 3). San Diego, CA: DawnSignPress. [DEAF 817 H6h, 1994]

Holcomb, T. K. (1993). The construction of Deaf identity. In M. D. Garretson (Ed.), Deafness, 1993-2013: A Deaf American monograph, 43 (pp. 41-45). Silver Spring, MD: National Association of the Deaf. [DEAF RESERVE]

Holmes, K. M., & Holmes, D. W. (1980, Fall). Signed and spoken language development in a hearing child of hearing parents. Sign Language Studies, 28, 239-254. [UNIV RESERVE]

(*) Hoshimi, S. (1975). Programs for parents in early education and cases. In International Congress on Education of the Deaf (Ed.), Proceedings of the International Congress on Education of the Deaf, Tokyo, 1975 (pp. 247-249). Tokyo: The Organizing Committee, International Congress on Education of the Deaf. (The author is at the Sapporo School for the Deaf, Sapporo, Japan) [DEAF 370 I57p, 1975]

Hughes, P. (1995). [Book reviews] *Discovering with words and signs: Sign Talk Development Project, a resource guide for developing a bilingual and bicultural preschool program for deaf and hearing children* by Charlotte Evans, Kyra Zimmer, and Denise Murray. The ACEHI Journal, 21 (1), 69-71. (The official journal of the Association of Canadian Educators of the Hearing Impaired) [UNIV DEAF Periodicals]

Ingram, D. (Ed.). (1974, November). Child Language Newsletter, 1 (2). Linguistic Reporter, 16 (9), 17, 19-21. {Reports the purposes of Naomi Schiff's doctoral study of five hearing children from deaf homes} [UNIV Periodicals]

Ingram, R. M. (1985). Simultaneous interpretation of sign languages: Semiotic and psycholinguistic perspectives. Multilingua, 4 (2), 91-102. [*]

Ingram, R. M. (1988, Spring). Interpreters' recognition of structure and meaning. Sign Language Studies, 58, 21-36. (Reprinted in D. Cokely (Ed.), Sign Language interpreters and interpreting (pp. 99-119). Burtonsville, MD: Linstok Press, 1992 [DEAF 418.02 S53, 1992]) [UNIV RESERVE]

(*) Inoue, K. (1975). What should the school do for the children who have left school to start in life? In

International Congress on Education of the Deaf (Ed.), <u>Proceedings of the International Congress on Education of the Deaf, Tokyo, 1975</u> (pp. 660-661). Tokyo: The Organizing Committee, International Congress on Education of the Deaf. [DEAF 370 I57p, 1975]

Interplay with mother may control deaf child's speech. (1978, August). <u>Clinical Psychiatry News, 6</u> (8), 28-29. {Report from a press conference held by Drs. Eleanor Galenson and Moisy Shopper before the American Psychoanalytic Association meeting. Namely, that "deaf mothers generally do not make good mothers. Deaf mothers often tend to be harsh, unpredictable, aggressive, and intermittent in their relationship with their infants. Whatever signals the deaf mother uses to communicate with her child are usually used for discipline, not pleasure, Dr. Galenson said. Most deaf mothers have attended schools for the deaf that are notably unempathic, and this unempathic, harsh attitude is carried over to the parenting of their own children, Dr. Shopper noted" } [Gallaudet University Archives, "Parent-child relationship - deaf adults" subject vertical file]

Interpreter of the month: Carol J. Bailie. (1993, April/May). <u>The Professional INTERPRETER,</u> 3. (Carol is hearing and has deaf parents) [UNIV DEAF Periodicals]

Israel, J., Cunningham, M., Thumann, H., & Shaver Arnos, K. (1992, June). Genetic counseling for Deaf adults: Communication/language and cultural considerations. <u>Journal of Genetic Counseling, 1</u> (2), 135-153. {Members of the deaf community could utilize genetic counseling services if the issues of communication access and attitude could be overcome} [UNIV Periodicals]

(*) Jackson, A. B. (1996). Pregnancy and delivery. <u>Sexuality and Disability, 14</u> (3), 211-219. [UNIV Periodicals]

Jackson, C. A. (1984, September). Which is MINE/mine? Acquisition of possessives in ASL and English. <u>Papers and Reports on Child Language Development, 23,</u> 66-73. (Department of Linguistics, Stanford University - ERIC Document Reproduction Service No. ED 249 784 - 9 pages) [REFERENCE DESK]

Jackson, C. A. (1989, Spring). Language acquisition in two modalities: The role of nonlinguistic cues in linguistic mastery. <u>Sign Language Studies, 62,</u> 1-22. [UNIV RESERVE]

Jacobs, L. M. (1989). A look back and a look ahead. In L. M. Jacobs, <u>A deaf adult speaks out</u> (3rd ed., pp. 116-129). Washington, DC: Gallaudet University Press. (The author talks about his experience of CODA through his daughter) [DEAF 305.773 J32d, 1989]

Jacobs, S. (1986/1992). Panel discussion summaries on cross-cultural issues: Hearing people who had deaf parents and hearing people who had hearing parents. In M. L. McIntire (Ed.), <u>Interpreting: The art of cross-cultural mediation, proceedings of the ninth National Convention of the Registry of Interpreters for the Deaf, Inc., San Diego, California, July 4-8, 1985</u> (3rd printing, pp. 30-32). Washington, DC: RID Publications. (The Gallaudet University Library has the 1985 edition [DEAF 420.802 R4i, 1985]) [*]

(*) Jacobson, D. S. (1995). Rethinking expectations. In F. P. Haseltine, S. S. Cole & D. B. Gray (Eds.), <u>Reproductive issues for persons with physical disabilities</u> (pp. 49-52). Baltimore: Paul H. Brookes. [C]

(*) Jacobson, N. (1995). Learning about disability from children. In F. P. Haseltine, S. S. Cole & D. B. Gray (Eds.), <u>Reproductive issues for persons with physical disabilities</u> (pp. 63-65). Baltimore: Paul H. Brookes. [C]

Jamieson, J. R. (1994a). Instructional discourse strategies: Differences between hearing and deaf mothers of deaf children. First Language, 14 (Pt. 2, No. 40), 153-171. [UNIV Periodicals]

Jamieson, J. R. (1994b, March/April). Teaching as transaction: Vygotskian perspectives on deafness and mother-child interaction. Exceptional Children, 60 (5), 434-449. [UNIV Periodicals]

Jamieson, J. R., & Pedersen, E. D. (1993). Deafness and mother-child interaction: Scaffolded instruction and the learning of problem-solving skills. Early Development and Parenting, 2 (4), 229-242. [*]

Jeffers, A. (1990). My face in a mirror. In G. Stambolian (Ed.), Men on men 3: Best new Gay fiction (pp. 275-281). New York: Penguin Books. {Short story excerpt from the book Safe as houses} [C]

Johnson, J. M., Watkins, R. V., & Rice, M. L. (1992, March). Bimodal bilingual language development in a hearing child of deaf parents. Applied Psycholinguistics, 13 (1), 31-52. [UNIV Periodicals]

Johnson, M. L. (1971). An investigation of the effect of language input on the child's performance. Unpublished paper, University of Connecticut. {Data collected here were reported in March, 1972, in J. Sachs, Development of oral language abilities from infancy to college: Final report. (ERIC Document Reproduction Service No. ED 065 896 - 60 pages) [REFERENCE DESK] On pages 25-38 Johnson's data is reported and summarized thus: "Effects of reduced language input were observed in a hearing child of deaf parents. The language was quantitatively and qualitatively different from normal children's. Absence of signing suggested that language must be directed to the child to permit acquisition."} [*]

Jones, E. (1987, September/October). Translation of quantitative measures for use in cross-cultural research: Methodology corner. Nursing Research, 36 (5), 324-327. [C]

(*) Jones, E., Strom, R., & Daniels, S. (1989, December). Evaluating the success of deaf parents. American Annals of the Deaf, 134 (5), 312-316. [UNIV DEAF Periodicals]

Jones. E. G. (1995, March/April). Deaf and hearing parents' perceptions of family functioning. Nursing Research, 44 (2), 102-105. [C]

Jones, E. G. (1996, February). Deaf and hearing mothers' interactions with normally hearing infants and toddlers. Journal of Pediatric Nursing, 11 (1), 45-51. [DEAF 306.874 J66d, 1996]

Jones, E. G., & Dumas, R. E. (1996, October). Deaf and hearing parents' interactions with eldest hearing children. American Annals of the Deaf, 141 (4), 278-283. [UNIV DEAF Periodicals]

Jones, E. G., & Kay, M. (1992, May/June). Instrumentation in cross-cultural research: Methodology corner. Nursing Research, 41 (3), 186-188. [C]

Jones, K. D. (1994, March). Deafness [Editorial]. Deafness: The Journal of the Sociology of Deafness, 10 (1), 2. (Deafness is published by the British Deaf Association) [UNIV DEAF Periodicals]

Jones, M. L., & Quigley, S. P. (1979, May). The acquisition of question formation in spoken English and American Sign Language by two hearing children of deaf parents. Journal of Speech and Hearing Disorders, 44 (2), 196-208. [UNIV DEAF Periodicals]

Jones, T. W. (1996). America's first multi-generation deaf families (A genealogical perspective). In M. D. Garretson (Ed.), Deafness, historical perspectives: a Deaf American monograph, 46 (pp. 49-54). Silver Spring, MD:

National Association of the Deaf. [UNIV RESERVE]

Jordan, I. K. (1996). A conversation with Edward Miner Gallaudet. In M. D. Garretson (Ed.), Deafness: Historical perspectives, a Deaf American monograph, 46 (pp. 55-56). Silver Spring, MD: National Association of the Deaf. [UNIV RESERVE]

Kamerling, S. C. (1988). Hearing children of deaf parents and their place within deaf communities. In R. Ojala (Ed.), Program, X World Congress of the World Federation of the Deaf: One world one responsibility, proceedings, Espoo, Finland, July 20-28, 1987: Vol. 2 (pp. 747-752). Helsinki, Finland: Finnish Association of the Deaf. (The editor is hearing and has deaf parents) [DEAF 366 W6, 1987]

Kannapell, B. M. (1995). The forgotten people: Deaf people's contributions during World War II. In Gallaudet University, College of Continuing Education (Ed.), Deaf Studies IV: "Visions of the past - visions of the future," conference proceedings, Woburn, Massachusetts, April 27-30, 1995 (pp. 111-123). Washington, DC: Gallaudet University, College for Continuing Education and Outreach. {A number of references are cited about "the role of hearing children of deaf adults (CODAs) during WWII."} [DEAF 305.77307 D424, 1995]

Kantor, R. (1982, Fall). Communicative interaction: Mother modification and child acquisition of American Sign Language. Sign Language Studies, 36, 233-282. [UNIV RESERVE]

Kantor, R. M. (1978). Identifying native and second-language signers. Communication and Cognition, 11 (1), 39-56. [UNIV Periodicals]

Kawai, I. (1983). Educational consideration based on "an incident" which occurred at a public primary school in Osaka. In C. Magarotto (Ed.), Deafness today and tomorrow: Reality and utopia, proceedings of the IX congress of the World Federation of the Deaf, Palermo, Italy, 1983 (pp. 273-278). Rome, Italy: The Federation. (Isamu Kawai is with the Japanese Federation of the Deaf) [DEAF 366 W6, 1983]

Kelly, K. (1997). Four. In The Royals (pp. 30-56). New York: Warner Books, Inc. {Chapter discusses briefly Prince Philip's (Queen Elizabeth II's husband) family background: "The platinum blond toddler had been born on a kitchen table on the Greek island of Corfu in a house, Mon Repos, with no electricity, no hot water, and no indoor plumbing. He learned sign language to communicate with his mother, who had turned deaf after catching German measles at the age of four. He also learned English, French, and German but did not speak a word of Greek." (page 45). His mother, Alice, Princess of Greece, died while he was young so he went on to live with relatives after the age of 10} [*]

(*) Kelsall, J. (1992, December 1). She can lip-read, she'll be all right: Improving maternity care for the deaf and hearing-impaired. Midwifery, 8, 178-183. [*]

Kersting, S. A. (1997, Fall). Balancing between deaf and hearing worlds: Reflections of mainstreamed college students on relationships and social interaction. Journal of Deaf Studies and Deaf Education, 2 (4), 252-263. [UNIV DEAF Periodicals]

(*) Kirshbaum, M. (1988, June). Parents with physical disabilities and their babies. Zero to Three: A bulletin of the National Center for Clinical Infant Programs, 7 (5), 8-15. Washington, DC: National Center for Clinical Infant Programs. [C]

(*) Kirshbaum, M. (1994, Fall). Family context and disability culture reframing: Through the Looking Glass. The Family Psychologist, 10 (4), 8-12. [*]

(*) Kirshbaum, M. (1995). Serving families with disability issues: Through the Looking Glass. <u>Marriage and Family Review, 21</u> (1/2), 9-28. (Co-published simultaneously in 1995 in D. Guttmann & M. B. Sussman (Eds.), <u>Exemplary social intervention programs for members and their families</u> (pp. 9-28). New York: The Haworth Press) [C]

Koch, H. R. (1975). Panelist: Adult hearing children of deaf parents. In Gallaudet College, Department of Sociology, Social Work Program (Ed.), <u>An orientation to deafness for social workers: Papers from the workshop, Washington, D. C., March 18-20, 1975</u> (pp. 39-41). Washington, DC: Gallaudet College Press. [DEAF 361 G3o, 1975]

(*) Koester, L. S. (1992, October). Intuitive parenting as a model for understanding parent-infant interactions when one partner is deaf. <u>American Annals of the Deaf, 137</u> (4), 362-369. [UNIV DEAF Periodicals]

Korzon, A. (1991). The attitude of deaf youths towards the hearing world, sex education of deaf youth. In World Federation of the Deaf (Ed.), <u>Equality and self-reliance, proceedings of the XI World Congress of the World Federation of the Deaf, Tokyo, 1991</u> (pp. 372-378). Tokyo: Japanese Federation of the Deaf. [DEAF 366 W6, 1991]

Kovacs, S. F. (1992, November/December). Meet Jacqueline Hunter: Kids to look up to. <u>Learning, 21</u> (4), 68. {Jackie Hunter of Holly Hill, Florida, was nominated by Dr. Susan Forbes Kovacs of Holly Hill Middle School as a "shining star" at school and home. She is the oldest hearing child of deaf parents and is in the 6th grade. She is a winner of <u>Learning's</u> Kids to Look Up To program} [UNIV Periodicals]

Kowalewski, F. (1983a). Our boys [Poem]. In <u>You and I: Fifty years of poems, translations and art work by Felix Kowalewski</u> (p. 85). Riverside, CA: California School for the Deaf. [DEAF 811.52 K6y, 1983]

Kowalewski, F. (1983b). Our three [Poem]. In <u>You and I: Fifty years of poems, translations and art work by Felix Kowalewski</u> (p. 59). Riverside, CA: California School for the Deaf. [DEAF 811.52 K6y, 1983]

Kowalewski, F. (1983c). To my small daughter, Nadja [Poem]. In <u>You and I: Fifty years of poems, translations and art work by Felix Kowalewski</u> (p. 93). Riverside, CA: California School for the Deaf. [DEAF 811.52 K6y, 1983]

Kraft, B. S. (1985). Ethics and role in a cultural context. In Registry of Interpreters for the Deaf, Inc. (Ed.), <u>Golden opportunities in interpreting: Proceedings of the 8th National Convention of the Registry of Interpreters for the Deaf, Denver, Colorado, August 9-13, 1983</u> (pp. 140-146). Silver Spring, MD: Registry of Interpreters for the Deaf. [DEAF 420.02 R43, 1983]

Kyle, J., & Ackerman, J. (1989). Early mother-infant interaction in deaf families. In B. Woll (Ed.), <u>Language development and Sign Language: Papers from the Seminar on Language Development and Sign Language, Monograph No. 1, International Sign Linguistics Association, Centre for Deaf Studies, University of Bristol, Bristol, U. K., 1986</u> (pp. 14-22). Bristol, U.K.: University of Bristol, Centre for Deaf Studies. [DEAF 480.07 S41, 1986]

(##) Kyle, J., & Ackerman, J. (1990). Signing for infants: Deaf mothers using BSL in the early stages of development. In W. H. Edmondson & F. Karlsson (Ed.), <u>Sign Language Research '87: The Fourth International Symposium on Sign Language Research</u> (pp. 200-211). Hamburg: Signum Press. [*]

Kyle, J., Ackerman, J., & Woll, B. (1987). Early mother-infant interaction: Language and pre-language in Deaf families. In P. Griffith, A. E. Mills & J. Local (Eds.), <u>Proceedings of the Child Language Seminar, University of</u>

York, York, England, 1987 (pp. 217-226). [*]

Ladd, P. (1988). The modern deaf community. In D. Miles (Ed.), British Sign Language: A beginner's guide (pp. 27-43). London: BBC Books. (Foreword by HRH The Princess of Wales) [DEAF 480.07 M5br, 1988]

Ladd, P. (1989, Autumn). Books: *Never the Twain Shall Meet: The Communications debate* by Richard Winefield, Gallaudet University Press [Review]. Deafness: The Journal of the Sociology of Deafness, 5 (3), 10. (Deafness is published by the National Council of Social Workers with Deaf People and the British Deaf Association) [UNIV DEAF Periodicals]

Lambert, W. E., Havelka, J., & Crosby, C. (1958). The influence of language-acquisition contexts on bilingualism. The Journal of Abnormal and Social Psychology, 56, 239-244. [C]

Lane, H. L., Hoffmeister, R., & Bahan, B. J. (1996a). Deaf culture. In A journey into the DEAF-WORLD (pp. 124-173). San Diego, CA: DawnSignPress. [DEAF 305.773 L3j, 1996]

Lane, H. L., Hoffmeister, R., & Bahan, B. J. (1996b). The future of the DEAF-WORLD. In A journey into the DEAF-WORLD (pp. 369-378). San Diego, CA: DawnSignPress. [DEAF 305.773 L3j, 1996]

Lane, H. L., Hoffmeister, R., & Bahan, B. J. (1996c). Welcome to the DEAF-WORLD. In A journey into the DEAF-WORLD (pp. 3-23). San Diego, CA: DawnSignPress. [DEAF 305.773 L3j, 1996]

Lange, A. J. (1994). Growing up in a deaf family: From an office newsletter. In M. D. Garretson (Ed.), Deafness, life and Culture: A Deaf American monograph, 44 (pp. 65-67). Silver Spring, MD: National Association of the Deaf. [UNIV RESERVE]

Larson, C. A. (1974). Deafness and family planning. In R. E. Hardy & J. G. Cull (Eds.), Educational and psychosocial aspects of deafness (pp. 81-94). Springfield, IL: Charles C. Thomas. [DEAF 362 H3e, 1974]

Lartz, M. N., & Lestina, L. J. (1995, October). Strategies deaf mothers use when reading to their young deaf or hard of hearing children. American Annals of the Deaf, 140 (4), 358-362. [UNIV DEAF Periodicals]

Lauritsen, R. R. (1973). Reflections...hearing children of deaf parents. In G. T. Lloyd (Ed.), The deaf child and his family: Proceedings of National Forum VI, Council of Organizations Serving the Deaf, Williamsburg, Virginia, March 14-16, 1973 (pp. 22-26). Washington, DC: United States Department of Health, Education and Welfare, Office of Human Development, Social and Rehabilitation Service. [DEAF 362 D36, 1973]

(*) Lawrence, I. E. (1972). Is justice deaf: What are the legal and constitutional rights of the deaf. Tallahassee, FL: Florida Registry of Interpreters for the Deaf. (33 pages - Ivan Lawrence is an attorney and associate professor of law) [DEAF 342.085 L3i, 1972]

Lederberg, A. R., & Mobley, C. E. (1990, October). The effect of hearing impairment on the quality of attachment and mother-toddler interaction. Child Development, 61 (5), 1596-1604. [UNIV Periodicals]

(*) Leigh, I. W. (1979, Spring). The support a parent needs from the audiologist and speech pathologist. Hearing Rehabilitation Quarterly, 4 (1), 9. [UNIV DEAF Periodicals]

Leigh, I. W., Marcus, A., & Dobosh, P. (forthcoming). Deaf/hearing identity paradigms. Paper presented at the European Society on Deafness and Mental Health, Fourth Triennial Congress, Manchester, England, October 2-4,

1997. (The second author is hearing and has deaf parents) Manuscript in preparation.

Lenneberg, E. H. (1964a/1966). A biological perspective of language. In New directions in the study of language (pp. 65-88). Cambridge, MA: M.I.T. Press. [UNIV GEN 158 L56n]

Lenneberg, E. H. (1964b). The capacity for language acquisition. In J. A. Foder & J. J. Katz (Eds.), The structure of language: Readings in the philosophy of language (pp. 579-603). Englewood Cliffs, NJ: Prentice-Hall, Inc. [UNIV GEN 410 F65s]

Lenneberg, E. H. (1967). Language in the context of growth and maturation. In Biological foundations of language (pp. 125-187). New York: Wiley. [DEAF 401.9 L4b, 1967]

Lenneberg, E. H., Rebelsky, F. G., & Nichols, I. A. (1965). The vocalizations of infants born to deaf and to hearing parents. Human Development, 8, 23-37. [DEAF 612.78 L4v, 1965]

Leonard, D. L., & Littlefield, D. (1995). Parent education and family support in the Deaf Community. In Gallaudet University, College of Continuing Education (Ed.), Deaf Studies IV: "Visions of the past - visions of the future," conference proceedings, Woburn, Massachusetts, April 27-30, 1995 (pp. 265-271). Washington, DC: Gallaudet University, College for Continuing Education and Outreach. [DEAF 305.77307 D424, 1995]

(*) Levesque, R. J. R. (1996, Spring). Maintaining children's relations with mentally disabled parents: Recognizing difference and the difference that it makes [Update]. Children's Legal Rights Journal, 16, 14-22. (Publication of the Children's Legal Rights Information and Training Program, Washington, DC) [C]

Lewis, V. (1975). Panelist: Adult hearing children of deaf parents. In Gallaudet College, Department of Sociology, Social Work Program (Ed.), An orientation to deafness for social workers: Papers from the workshop, Washington, D. C., March 18-20, 1975 (pp. 42-44). Washington, DC: Gallaudet College. [DEAF 361 G3o, 1975]

Liben, L. S., Nowell, R. C., & Posnansky, C. J. (1978, November). Semantic and formational clustering in deaf and hearing subjects' free recall of signs. Memory and Cognition, 6 (6), 599-606. [DEAF 401.9 L5s, 1978]

Lights out for Lon Chaney. (1930, September). The Literary Digest, 106, 37, 40, 42, 44. {Quotes heavily from the chapter on Chaney in Twinkle, twinkle, movie star! by Harry T. Brundidge} [*]

List of issues and topics from the small group discussions. (1986). In J. B. Christiansen & R. W. Meisegeier (Eds.), [Proceedings of the second] Research Conference on the Social Aspects of Deafness, Gallaudet College, Washington, D. C., June 8-10, 1986 (pp. 21-25). Washington, DC: Gallaudet College. {A list of 66 questions compiled from conference participants in response to their presentation} [DEAF 303.32 R4pr]

Literacy initiatives for families of deaf parents with hearing children: Research report. (1992). Pittsburgh, PA: Western Pennsylvania School for the Deaf. (ERIC Document Reproduction Service No. ED 353 391 - 101 pages - See a related ERIC document: TIPS (Toward Improved Parenting Skills) for deaf parents with hearing children [REFERENCE DESK]) [REFERENCE DESK]

(#) Lit Hits: *Useful gifts* by Carole L. Glickfeld [Review]. (1989, April). Voice Literary Supplement. (Literary Criticism, The Village Voice, New York city, page unidentified) [C]

Lloyd, B. S. (1995, June). *Mother father deaf: Living between sound and silence* by Paul Preston [Book review]. American Anthropologist, 97 (2), 417. [UNIV Periodicals]

Lloyd, G. T. (Ed.). (1972). Seven faces of deafness - a seminar. <u>Deafness Annual, II, 1972</u> (pp. 3-20). Silver Spring, MD: Professional Rehabilitation Workers with the Adult Deaf, Inc. {This is a transcript of a panel moderated by Glenn T. Lloyd and composed of Donnell Ashmore, Victor Galloway, Marvin [sic - Mervin] Garretson, Ausma Herbold, Jack Levesque, James Magness and Judith Williams} [DEAF 362 D42]

Lloyd, G. T. (1973). Group discussion summary. In G. T. Lloyd (Ed.), <u>The deaf child and his family: Proceedings of the National Forum VI, Council of Organizations Serving the Deaf, Williamsburg, Virginia, March 14-16, 1973</u> (pp. 88-90). Washington, DC: United States Department of Health, Education and Welfare, Office of Human Development, Social and Rehabilitation Service. [DEAF 362 D36, 1973]

Lon Chaney: April 1, 1883-August 26, 1930. (1968). <u>Who was who in America with world notables, Vol. 4: 1961-1968,</u> 166. Chicago: Marquis-Who's Who, Inc. {Chaney was a hearing son of deaf parents, born in Colorado Spring, Colorado and starred in many motion pictures. His first name was Alonzo) [UNIV Reference 920.073 W621, v. 4]

Lucas, C. (1989). Introduction. In C. Lucas (Ed.), <u>The sociolinguistics of the Deaf community</u> (pp. 1-8). New York: Academic Press. [DEAF 401.9 S6, 1989]

Lucas, C., & Valli, C. (1989). Language contact in the American Deaf community. In C. Lucas (Ed.), <u>The sociolinguistics of the Deaf community</u> (pp. 11-40). New York: Academic Press. [DEAF 401.9 S6, 1989]

Lucas, C., & Valli, C. (1990). ASL, English, and contact signing. In C. Lucas (Ed.), <u>Sign Language research: Theoretical issues</u> (pp. 288-307). Washington, DC: Gallaudet University Press. [DEAF 420 S533, 1990]

Lucas, C., & Valli, C. (1992a). Contact signing in the context of language contact studies. In <u>Language contact in the American Deaf community</u> (pp. 107-115). San Diego: Academic Press. [DEAF 420 L9l, 1992]

Lucas, C., & Valli, C. (1992b). What happens when languages come in contact. In <u>Language contact in the American Deaf community</u> (pp. 1-48). San Diego: Academic Press. [DEAF 420 L9l, 1992]

Luetke-Stahlman, B. (1984, Spring). Second system code shifting in a hearing two-year old. <u>Sign Language Studies, 42,</u> 13-22. [UNIV RESERVE]

Lumio, J. S., Piirainen, H., & Paljakka, P. (1966, September). Marriages between the deaf and hereditary deafness in Finland. <u>Acta-Oto-Laryngologica, 62</u> (3), 265-276. [UNIV DEAF Periodicals]

(*) Lundh, P. (1986, May). A new baby-alarm based on tenseness of the cry signal. <u>Scandinavian Audiology, 15</u> (4), 191-196. [UNIV DEAF Periodicals]

MacDougall, J. C. (1978). Conditions for growing up for hearing children of deaf parents. In L. von der Lieth (Ed.), <u>Life in families with deaf members: Proceedings of the Vth World Conference on Deafness, Copenhagen, Denmark, 1977</u> (pp. 63-65). Copenhagen, Denmark: Akademisk Forlag, National Federation of the Deaf in Denmark. [DEAF 306.87 W65l, 1978]

Machida, S., & Nozawa, K. (1979, March). Education a donner par les parents sourds a leurs enfants: Problèmes soulevés et mesures à prendre [Information to be given by deaf parents to their children: Issues brought up and steps to be taken]. <u>Bulletin of the Tokyo Metropolitan Rehabilitation Center for the Physically and Mentally Handicapped, No. 53</u> (pp. 47-55). (In French, need translation) {English abstract: "In educating hearing children, deaf parents face special problems which are not fully discussed in literatures. In this article, their major problems, such as a difficulty of communication and a difficulty of teaching speech to their hearing children are discussed."} [Gallaudet University Archives, "Parent-child relationship - deaf adults" subject vertical file]

Maestas y Moores, J. (1980, Spring). Early linguistic environment: Interactions of deaf parents with their infants. Sign Language Studies, 26, 1-13. [UNIV RESERVE]

Maestas y Moores, J., & Moores, D. F. (1980). Interaction of deaf parents with children in the first months of life [Abstract]. In International Congress on Education of the Deaf (Ed.), Abstracts of papers to be presented at the International Congress on Education of the Deaf, Hamburg, August 4-8, 1980 (p. 222). Hamburg: German Congress Secretariat. [DEAF 370 I57a, 1980]

Maestas y Moores, J., & Moores, D. F. (1984). Interaction between deaf parents and their children [Abstract]. In R. G. Brill (Ed.), International congresses on education of the deaf: An analytical history, 1878-1980 (pp. 354-355). Washington, DC: Gallaudet College Press. [DEAF 370 B74i, 1984]

(*) Mallory, B. L., Schein, J. D., & Zingle, H. W. (1991-1992, Winter). Parenting resources of deaf parents with hearing children. Journal of the American Deafness and Rehabilitation Association, 25 (3), 16-30. [UNIV RESERVE]

(*) Mallory, B. L., Schein, J. D., & Zingle, H. W. (1992a, January). Improving the validity of the PSNI [Parental Strengths and Needs Inventory] in assessing the performance of deaf parents of hearing children. American Annals of the Deaf, 137 (1), 14-21. [UNIV DEAF Periodicals]

Mallory, B. L., Schein, J. D., & Zingle, H. W. (1992b, Fall). Hearing offspring as visual language mediators in deaf-parented families. Sign Language Studies, 76, 193-213. [UNIV RESERVE]

Mallory, B. L., Zingle, H. W., & Schein, J. D. (1993, Spring). Intergenerational communication modes in deaf-parented families. Sign Language Studies, 78, 73-92. [UNIV RESERVE]

Mallory, B. L., Zingle, H., Schein, J. D., & Corley, D. J. (1993, April). Home-school communication with deaf parents: Correction. The Canadian School Executive, 12 (10), 19-25. (Originally printed in The Canadian School Executive, 12 (9) but 2 figures had erroneous keys or legends. The editors republished a corrected version here) [*]

(*) Mann, H.G., & Sevigny-Skyer, S. (1989, July). Deaf patients [sic: parents] and children: An innovative organization by and for deaf parents. Journal of the American Deafness and Rehabilitation Association, 23 (1), 14-16. [UNIV RESERVE]

Marcus, A. (1998). Building self-esteem in our children. In V. Follain-Grisell, K. Leitch-Walker & D. Morton (Eds.), Building bridges: Strengthening home and school relationships for Deaf parents and their hearing children, conference proceedings, Gallaudet University, Washington, D. C., May 1-3, 1997. Washington, DC: Gallaudet University, College for Continuing Education. Manuscript in preparation.

Marcus, A., & Myers, R. R. (1995, September). Specialized clinical demands: Mental health considerations for hearing children of deaf or hard of hearing parents. In R. R. Myers (Ed.), Standards of care for the delivery of mental health services to deaf and hard of hearing persons (pp. 14-17). Silver Spring, MD: R. R. Myers Consulting. (Distributed by the National Association of the Deaf, 814 Thayer Ave., Silver Spring, MD 20910-4500 - 185 pages with 211 pages of appendices) {The editor is a coda and describes his "personal perspectives" as a hearing member of a Deaf family} [DEAF 362.2 S72, 1995]

(*) **Marafino, K. (1990).** Parental rights of persons with mental retardation. In B. Y. Whitman & P. J. Accardo (Eds.), When a parent is mentally retarded (pp. 163-189). Baltimore: Paul. H. Brookes Publishing Co. [C]

Markowicz, H., & Woodward, J. (1978). Language and the maintenance of ethnic boundaries in the deaf community. Communication and Cognition, 11 (1), 29-38. (Special issue on Sign Language research edited by Ronnie B. Wilbur) [UNIV Periodicals]

Marschark, M., Everhart, V.S., & Dempsey, P. R. (1991, April). Nonliteral content in language productions of deaf, hearing, and native-signing hearing mothers. Merrill-Palmer Quarterly, 37 (2), 305-323. [UNIV Periodicals]

Masataka, N. (1996, September). Perception of Motherese in a signed language by 6-month-old Deaf infants. Developmental Psychology, 32 (5), 874-879. [UNIV Periodicals]

Mather, S. M., & Bull, T. H. (forthcoming). Pragmatics of eye gaze in deaf classrooms: Attention getting strategies using American Sign Language. Manuscript in preparation.

Mathis, S. L., III. (1976). Hearing children of deaf parents. In F. B. Crammatte & A. B. Crammatte (Eds.), "Full citizenship for all deaf people": VII World Congress of the World Federation of the Deaf, Washington, D. C., July 31-August 7, 1975 (pp. 286-288). Silver Spring, MD: National Association of the Deaf. [DEAF 366 W6, 1975]

Mathis, S. L., III. (1977). Hearing children of deaf parents. In C. E. Williams (Ed.), Educational development research problems: Proceedings of the third Gallaudet symposium on research in deafness, Washington, D. C., January 21-22, 1976 (pp. 135-138). Washington, DC: Office for Research, Gallaudet College. (This study was made while the author held the Powrie Vaux Doctor Chair of Deaf Studies at Gallaudet College, 1973-1974) [DEAF 370.78 G3e, 1976]

Mattock, L., & Crist, P. (1989, December). Hearing impairment: Implications for mother-daughter interaction. Volta Review, 91 (7), 333-340. [UNIV DEAF Periodicals]

Maxwell, M. (1985, June). Some functions and uses of literacy in the deaf community. Language in Society, 14 (2), 205-221. [UNIV Periodicals]

Maxwell, M., Bernstein, M. E., & Mear, K. M. (1991). Bimodal language production. In S. D. Fischer & P. Siple (Eds.), Theoretical issues in Sign Language research: Vol. 2. Psychology (pp. 171-190). Chicago: University of Chicago Press. [DEAF 420 T43]

Mayberry, R. (1976, October). An assessment of some oral and manual language skills of hearing children of deaf parents. American Annals of the Deaf, 121 (5), 507-512. [UNIV DEAF Periodicals]

Mayberry, R., Fischer, S., & Hatfield, N. (1983). Sentence repetition in American Sign Language. In J. Kyle & B. Woll (Eds.), Language in sign: An international perspective on Sign Language (pp. 206-214). London: Croom Helm. [DEAF 419 L36, 1983]

Mayberry, R., & Tuchman, S. (1985). Memory for sentences in American Sign Language: The influence of age on first sign learning. In Wm. C. Stokoe & V. Volterra (Eds.), SLR '83: Proceedings of the III International Symposium on Sign Language Research, Rome, June 22-26, 1983 (pp. 120-125). Silver Spring, MD: Linstok Press. [DEAF 410 I5s, 1983]

Mayberry, R. I., & Eichen, E. B. (1991, August). The long-lasting advantage of learning Sign Language in childhood: Another look at the critical period for language acquisition. <u>Journal of Memory and Language, 30</u> (4), 486-512. [UNIV Periodicals]

McCray, N. (1994, March 15). Voice-over: Listening to the nonhearing world. <u>Audiovisual Media, 28,</u> 1380. (Official journal of the International Council for Educational Media, London) {Reviews a four-part video series that focuses on the deaf community in Australia, *The Nonhearing World.* The films are *Understanding Hearing Loss*, *Signs of Life*, *Signs of Language*, and *Passport Without a Country* which is about the Australian coda community} [C]

McRae, M. J. (1979, Jan./Feb.). Bonding in a sea of silence. <u>American Journal of Maternal and Child Nursing,</u> <u>4</u> (1), 29-34. [DEAF 306.874 M37b, 1979]

Meadow, K. P. (1969, June). Self-image, family climate, and deafness. <u>Social Forces, 47</u> (4), 428-438. [UNIV Periodicals]

Meadow, K. P., Greenberg, M., Erting, C., & Carmichael, H. (1981, June). Interactions of deaf mothers and deaf preschool children: Comparisons with three other groups of deaf and hearing dyads. <u>American Annals of the</u> <u>Deaf, 126</u> (4), 454-468. [UNIV DEAF Periodicals]

Meadow, K. P., Greenberg, M. T., & Erting, C. (1985). Attachment behavior of deaf children with deaf parents. In S. Chess & A. Thomas (Eds.), <u>Annual progress in child psychiatry and child development, 1984</u> (pp. 176-187). New York: Brunner/Mazel. (Originally published in 1983 in the <u>Journal of the American Academy of Child</u> <u>Psychiatry, 22</u> (1), 23-28. [*]) [UNIV GEN 136.7 A61]

Meadow-Orlans, K. P. (1995a, March). <u>Deafness and interaction: Four groups of mothers and infants.</u> Poster presentation at the Biennial Meeting of the Society for Research in Child Development, Indianapolis, Indiana, March 31, 1995. (8 pages) [DEAF 306.874 M4de, 1995]

Meadow-Orlans, K. P. (1995b). Parenting with a sensory or physical disability. In M. H. Bornstein (Vol. Ed.), <u>Handbook of parenting: Vol. 4, Applied and practical parenting</u> (pp. 57-84). Mahwah, NJ: Lawrence Erlbaum Associates. [DEAF 649.1 H36, 1995]

Meadow-Orlans, K. P. (1997, Winter). Effects of mother and infant hearing status on interactions at twelve and eighteen months. <u>Journal of Deaf Studies and Deaf Education, 2</u> (1), 26-36. [UNIV DEAF Periodicals]

Meadow-Orlans, K. P., Erting, C., Day, P. S., MacTurk, R., Prezioso, C., & Gianino, A. (1987). Deaf and hearing mothers of deaf and hearing infants: Interaction in the first year of life. In R. Ojala (Ed.), <u>Program, X World</u> <u>Congress of the World Federation of the Deaf: One world one responsibility, proceedings, Espoo, Finland, July 20-</u> <u>28, 1987, Vol. 2</u> (pp. 692-696). Helsinki, Finland: Finnish Association of the Deaf. (The editor is hearing and has deaf parents) [DEAF 366 W6, 1987]

Meadow-Orlans, K. P., MacTurk, R. H., Prezioso, C., Erting, C., & Day, P. S. (1987, April). <u>Interactions of</u> <u>deaf and hearing mothers with three- and six-month-old infants.</u> Paper presented at the biennial meeting, Society for Research in Child Development symposium on relations between communication and social emotional development, implications from research with deaf children, Baltimore, Maryland. (13 pages) [*]

Meadow-Orlans, K. P., & Spencer, P. E. (1996a, April). <u>Maternal sensitivity to the visual needs of deaf children.</u> Paper presented at the 10th biennial International Conference on Infant Studies, Providence, Rhode Island. [*]

Meadow-Orlans, K. P., & Spencer, P. E. (1996b). Maternal sensitivity and the visual attentiveness of children who are deaf. Early Development and Parenting, 5 (4), 213-223. [*]

Miles, D. (1988). The development of the deaf community. In D. Miles (Ed.), British Sign Language: A beginner's guide (pp. 8-26). London: BBC Books. (Foreword by HRH The Princess of Wales) [DEAF 480.07 M5br, 1988]

(##) Mills, A., Bogaerde, B. v. d., & Coerts, J. A. (1994). Language input, interaction and the acquisition of Sign Language of the Netherlands. In B. v. d. Bogaerde, H. Knoors & M. Verrips (Eds.), Language acquisition with non-native input: The acquisition of Sign Language of the Netherlands, Publication No. 62 (pp. 31-50). Amsterdam: University of Amsterdam, Institute for General Linguistics. [*]

Mills, A. E., & Bogaerde, B. v. d. (1991, October). Input and interaction in Deaf families. Paper presented at the 16th annual Boston University Conference on Language Development, Boston, Massachusetts. [*]

Mills, A. E., & Coerts, J. (1989). Functions and forms of bilingual input: Children learning a Sign Language as one of their first languages. In S. Prillwitz & T. Vollhaber (Eds.), Current trends in European Sign Language research: Proceedings of the 3rd European Congress on Sign Language Research, Hamburg, July 26-29, 1989 (pp. 151-162). Hamburg: Signum Press. [DEAF 419 E4c, 1989]

(##) Mills, A. E., & Coerts, J. A. (Eds.). (1989). Uit de eerste hand: Taalaanbod en interactie in dove gezinnen [Characteristics of input and interaction of deaf mothers]. Research report of the course "Deafness and Sign Languages," 1988-1989, Department of General Linguistics, University of Amsterdam, Amsterdam. [*]

(##) Mills, A. E., & Coerts, J. A. (1990). Language input, interaction and the acquisition of SLN (Sign Language of the Netherlands). Paper presented at the Fourth European Conference on Developmental Psychology, University of Stirling, Scotland, August, 1990. [*]

Minnett, A., Clark, K., & Wilson, G. (1994, October). Play behavior and communication between deaf and hard of hearing children and their hearing peers in an integrated preschool. American Annals of the Deaf, 139 (4), 420-429. [UNIV DEAF Periodicals]

Mogford, K., & Bishop, D. (1993). Five questions about language acquisition considered in the light of exceptional circumstances. In D. Bishop & K. Mogford (Eds.), Language development in exceptional circumstances (2nd ed., pp. 239-260). Hillsdale, NJ: Lawrence Erlbaum Associates. (The Gallaudet University Library also has the 1988 edition [DEAF 401.93 L36, 1988]) [DEAF 401.93 L36, 1993]

Mohsen, R. A. (1993). Communication issues in Deaf/hearing intimate relationships: Toward a better future. In M. D. Garretson (Ed.), Deafness, 1993-2013: A Deaf American monograph, 43 (pp. 99-102). Silver Spring, MD: National Association of the Deaf. [UNIV RESERVE]

Moore, M., Sixsmith, J., & Knowles, K. (1996). Introduction. In M. Moore, J. Sixsmith, K. Knowles, C. Kagan, S. Lewis, S. Beazley & U. Rout (Eds.), Children's reflections on family life (pp. 1-11). Washington, DC: Falmer Press. [C]

Moore, M. S., & Levitan, L. (1993a). Do Deaf parents breed Deaf children? In For hearing people only: Answers to some of the most commonly asked questions about the Deaf community, its culture, and the "Deaf reality" (2nd ed., pp. 182-185). Rochester, NY: Deaf Life Press. (Reprinted from the August, 1988, issue of Deaf Life, 1 (2), 8. [UNIV DEAF Periodicals]) [DEAF 305.773 M66f, 1993]

Moore, M. S., & Levitan, L. (1993b). *"How* did Alexander Graham Bell almost succeed in wiping out Deaf culture?" In For hearing people only: Answers to some of the most commonly asked questions about the Deaf community, its culture, and the "Deaf reality" (2nd ed., pp. 230-233). Rochester, NY: Deaf Life Press. (Reprinted from the June, 1990, issue of Deaf Life, 2 (12), 7. [UNIV DEAF Periodicals]) {Bell proposed banning deaf marriages in order to prevent deaf people from breeding deaf children} [DEAF 305.773 M66f, 1993]

Moore, M. S., & Levitan, L. (1993c). I know that the Deaf community includes both "deaf" and "hard-of-hearing." What other categories are there? In For hearing people only: Answers to some of the most commonly asked questions about the Deaf community, its culture, and the "Deaf reality" (2nd ed., pp. 196-198). Rochester, NY: Deaf Life Press. (Reprinted from the July, 1989, issue of Deaf Life, 2 (1), 7. [UNIV DEAF Periodicals]) [DEAF 305.773 M66f, 1993]

Moore, M. S., & Levitan, L. (1993d). "Is hearing loss common in my family because of heredity, or because my grandmother fell down during her pregnancies?" In For hearing people only: Answers to some of the most commonly asked questions about the Deaf community, its culture, and the "Deaf reality" (2nd ed., pp. 208-211). Rochester, NY: Deaf Life Press. [DEAF 305.773 M66f, 1993]

Moore, M. S., & Levitan, L. (1993e). Should a hearing person write about Deaf Culture? In For hearing people only: Answers to some of the most commonly asked questions about the Deaf community, its culture, and the "Deaf reality" (2nd ed., pp. 224-229). Rochester, NY: Deaf Life Press. (Reprinted from the January, 1990, issue of Deaf Life, 2 (7), 7. [UNIV DEAF Periodicals]) [DEAF 305.773 M66f, 1993]

Moore, M. S., & Levitan, L. (1993f). Why do most deaf parents raise a hearing child better than hearing parents a deaf child? In For hearing people only: Answers to some of the most commonly asked questions about the Deaf community, its culture, and the "Deaf reality" (2nd ed., pp. 192-195). Rochester, NY: Deaf Life Press. (Reprinted from the May, 1992, issue of Deaf Life, 4 (11), 6-7. [UNIV DEAF Periodicals]) [DEAF 305.773 M66f, 1993]

Moore, M. S., & Levitan, L. (1993g). Why don't some deaf people trust hearing people? In For hearing people only: Answers to some of the most commonly asked questions about the Deaf community, its culture, and the "Deaf reality" (2nd ed., pp. 282-285). Rochester, NY: Deaf Life Press. (Reprinted from the June, 1989, issue of Deaf Life, 1 (12), 7. [UNIV DEAF Periodicals] In the original article, "deaf" and "hearing" were capitalized) [DEAF 305.773 M66f, 1993]

Moores, D. F. (1973). Families and deafness. In A. G. Norris (Ed.), Deafness Annual, III, 1973 (pp. 115-129). Silver Spring, MD: Professional Rehabilitation Workers with the Adult Deaf, Inc. [DEAF 362 D42]

Moores, J. M., & Moores, D. F. (1980). Interaction of deaf parents with children in the first months of life. In Proceedings of the International Congress on Education of the Deaf, Hamburg, 1980, Vol. 1 (pp. 718-721). Heidelberg: Julius Groos Verlag. (Moderator of panel #124, Interaction between deaf parents and their children, was G. Rammel of Germany) [DEAF 370 I57pro, 1980, v. 1]

Mottez, B. (1990, Fall). Deaf identity. Sign Language Studies, 68, 195-216. [UNIV RESERVE]

Mowl, G. E. (1996). Raising deaf children in hearing society: Struggles and challenges for deaf native ASL signers. In I. Parasnis (Ed.)., Cultural and language diversity and the deaf experience (pp. 232-245). New York: Cambridge University Press. [DEAF 305.773 C84, 1996]

Mozzer-Mather, S. M., & Carroll, C. (1997a). Glimpse of a deaf princess: Alice of Battenberg, 1885-1969. In Movers and shakers: Deaf people who changed the world, twenty-six tales of genius, struggle, perseverance and heroism, student bilingual workbook (pp. 1-6). San Diego, CA: DawnSignPress. (See the related textbook under Carroll and Mather and the teacher's guide under Mather and Carroll) {This is exercise one where it is mentioned that Alice was born deaf, had a son, Prince Philip, who married Elizabeth who became Queen of England, and that Prince Philip is considered a "coda."} [DEAF 920 M68, 1997 Workbook]

Mozzer-Mather, S. M., & Carroll, C. (1997b). Glimpse of a deaf princess: Alice of Battenberg, 1885-1969. In Movers and shakers: Deaf people who changed the world, twenty-six tales of genius, struggle, perseverance and heroism, teacher's guide (pp. 1-6). San Diego, CA: DawnSignPress. (See the related textbook under Carroll and Mather and student bilingual workbook under Mather and Carroll) {This is exercise one where it is mentioned that Alice was born deaf, had a son, Prince Philip, who married Elizabeth who became Queen of England, and that Prince Philip is considered a "coda."} [DEAF 920 M68, 1997 Guide]

Mudgett-DeCaro, P. (1996). On being both hearing and deaf: My bicultural-bilingual experience. In I. Parasnis (Ed.), Cultural and language diversity and the Deaf experience (pp. 272-288). New York: Cambridge University Press. [DEAF 305.773 C84, 1996]

(*) Mulhern, E. (1988, January). How will you hear the baby cry? The Hearing Journal, 41 (1), 19-20. {A hearing ear dog is the perfect solution for this family} [UNIV DEAF Periodicals]

Murdaugh, J., Spitz, J., & Blatt, H. (1980). Psychological factors in choosing to teach deaf children [Abstract]. In International Congress on Education of the Deaf (Ed.), Abstracts of papers to be presented at the International Congress on Education of the Deaf, Hamburg, August 4-8, 1980 (p. 227). Hamburg, Germany: International Congress on Education of the Deaf, German Congress Secretariat. [DEAF 370 I57a, 1980]

(*) Murkin, R. W., & Womersley, R. (1978). Health and safety. In For young deaf people: A guide to everyday living (pp. 130-183). Melbourne, Australia: Victorian School for Deaf Children. (281 pages) {In a segment titled "Pregnancy and child care" there are four pages in a "special note for deaf parents with a hearing child."} [UNIV DEAF Copy 1: 301.157 M8f, 1978]

Murphy, J., & Slorach, N. (1983, September). The language development of pre-preschool hearing children of deaf parents. British Journal of Disorders of Communication, 18 (2), 118-127. [UNIV DEAF Periodicals]

Murphy, J. E. (1988, June). Language acquisition in normally hearing children of hearing-impaired mothers. Australian Journal of Human Communication Disorders, 16 (1), 97-106. (Journal of the Australian College of Speech Therapists, Glebe, New South Wales) [UNIV DEAF Periodicals]

Murphy, K. (1964). Development of normal vocalisation [sic] and speech. In. C. Renfrew & K. Murphy (Eds.), The child who does not talk, Clinics in Developmental Medicine, No. 13: Report of an international study group on the Development and the Disorders of Hearing, Language and Speech in Children, St. Mary's College, Durham, England, 1963 (pp. 11-15). London: Spastics International Medical Publications in Association with William Heinemann Medical Books Ltd. [*]

Murphy, R. F., Scheer, J., Murphy, Y., & Mack, R. (1988). Physical disability and social liminality: A study in the rituals of adversity. Social Science and Medicine, 26 (2), 235-242. [C]

Muse, A. (Ed.). (forthcoming). Children of deaf adults [Panel presentation]. In National Black Deaf Advocates (Ed.), Black Deaf leadership in the 21st century: Preparing the way, proceedings of the 15th National Black Deaf Advocates conference, Washington, D. C., August 12-17, 1997. (Moderator: Agnes Muse, Washington, D. C. Panelists: Marcellus Hartsfield, Washington, D. C.; Glendia Boon, South Carolina; and Lettie Reid, Ohio)

Manuscript in preparation.

Myers, L. R. (1998). Children of shame? In V. Follain-Grisell, K. Leitch-Walker & D. Morton (Eds.), <u>Building bridges: Strengthening home and school relationships for Deaf parents and their hearing children, conference proceedings, Gallaudet University, Washington, D. C., May 1-3, 1997.</u> Washington, DC: Gallaudet University, College for Continuing Education. Manuscript in preparation.

Myers, R. R. (1995, September). Introduction. In R. R. Myers (Ed.), <u>Standards of care for the delivery of mental health services to deaf and hard of hearing persons</u> (pp. 11-17). Silver Spring, MD: R. R. Myers Consulting. (Distributed by the National Association of the Deaf, 814 Thayer Ave., Silver Spring, MD 20910-4500 - 185 pages with 211 pages of appendices) {The editor is a coda and describes his "personal perspectives" as a hearing member of a Deaf family} [DEAF 362.2 S72, 1995]

Myers, R. R., & Marcus, A. (1993). Hearing. Mother, father deaf: Issues of identity and mediation in culture and communication. In J. Cebe (Ed.), <u>Deaf studies III: Bridging cultures in the 21st century, conference proceedings, Chicago, April 22-25, 1993</u> (pp. 171-184). Washington, DC: Gallaudet University, College of Continuing Education and Outreach. [DEAF 305.77307 D42, 1993]

Myers, R. R., & Shultz-Myers, S. (1992). Family relations: Structural and communication issues in families. In S. J. Larew, K. M. Saura & D. Watson (Eds.), <u>Facing deafness: Proceedings of ALDACON III, the Association for Late-Deafened Adults, Chicago, Illinois, November 6-10, 1991</u> (pp. 102-115). DeKalb, IL: Northern Illinois University, Research and Training Center on Traditionally Underserved Persons who are Deaf, Department of Communicative Disorders. {Both authors are codas and discuss a wide range of family issues regarding hearing children in deaf and hard-of-hearing families} [DEAF 362.0425 A42, 1992]

(##) Neville, H., Corina, D., Bavelier, D., Clark, V. P., Jezzard, A., Prinster, A., Karni, A., Lalwani, J., Rauschecker, J., & Turner, R. (1995). Biological constraints and effects of experience for language: An fMRI study of sentence processing in English and American Sign Language (ASL) by deaf and hearing subjects. <u>Neurosciences.</u> Miami, Florida.

Neville, H. J. (1990, December 31). Intermodal competition and compensation in development: Evidence from studies of the visual system in congenitally deaf adults. <u>The Annals of the New York Academy of Sciences, Vol. 608: The development and neural bases of higher cognitive functions</u> (pp. 71-91). [UNIV Gen 153.4 D48, 1990]

Neville, H. J. (1991). Neurobiology of cognitive and language processing: Effects of early experience. In K. R. Gibson & A. C. Petersen (Eds.), <u>Brain maturation and cognitive development: Comparative and cross-cultural perspective</u> (pp. 355-380). Hawthorne, NY: Aldine de Gruyter. [DEAF 401.93 B72, 1991]

Neville, H. J., Bavelier, D., Corina, D., Rauschecker, J., Karni, A., Lalwani, A., Braun, A., Clark, V., Jezzard, P., & Turner, R. (1998, February 3). Cerebral organization for language in deaf and hearing subjects: Biological constraints and effects of experience. <u>Proceedings of the National Academy of Sciences of the United States of America, 95</u> (3), 922-929. (Includes papers from a National Academy of Sciences Colloquium on Neuroimaging of Human Brain Function) [C]

Neville, H. J., & Lawson, D. (1987, March). Attention to central and peripheral visual space in a movement detection task. III. Separate effects of auditory deprivation and acquisition of a visual language. <u>Brain Research, 405</u> (2), 284-294. [DEAF 152.1425 N4a, 1987]

(*) Newbrough, J. R. (1985). The handicapped parent in the community: A synthesis and commentary. In S. K.

Thurman (Ed.), <u>Children of handicapped parents: Research and clinical perspectives</u> (pp. 181-193). Orlando, FL: Academic Press. [DEAF 306.874 C4, 1985]

Newport, E. L., & Meier, R. P. (1985). The acquisition of American Sign Language. In D. I. Slobin (Ed.), <u>The crosslinguistic study of language acquisition: Vol. 1, The data</u> (pp. 881-938). Hillsdale, NJ: Lawrence Erlbaum Associates. (1992 edition in process at Gallaudet; they also have a monograph reprint [DEAF 420.07 N4a, 1986]) [UNIV Gen 401.9 C7]

Nienhuys, T. G., Horsborough, K. M., & Cross, T. G. (1985, June). A dialogic analysis of interaction between mothers and their deaf or hearing preschoolers. <u>Applied Psycholinguistics, 6</u> (2), 121-140. [C]

Nordén, K. (1978). Conditions of growing up for deaf children of deaf or hearing parents and hearing children of deaf parents. In L. von der Lieth (Ed.), <u>Life in families with deaf members: Proceedings of the Vth World Conference on Deafness, Copenhagen, Denmark, 1977</u> (pp. 31-46). Copenhagen, Denmark: National Federation of the Deaf in Denmark. [DEAF 306.87 W65l, 1978]

Novack, L. L., Folven, R. J., Orlansky, M. D., Bonvillian, J. D., & Holley-Wilcox, P. (1983). Language, cognitive, and cherological development in young children of deaf parents. In C. Magarotto, (Ed.), <u>Deafness today and tomorrow: Reality and utopia, proceedings of the IX congress of the World Federation of the Deaf, Palermo, Italy, 1983</u> (pp. 559-571). Rome, Italy: The Federation. [DEAF 366 W62s, 1983]

(*) Odegard, J. (1993). The Americans with Disabilities Act: Creating "Family values" for physically disabled parents. <u>Law and Inequality, 11</u>, 533-563. (Publication of law students of the University of Minnesota Law School) [C]

Olgas, M. (1974, July-August). The relationship between parents' health status and body image of their children. <u>Nursing Research, 23</u> (4), 319-324. [C]

Orlansky, M. D., & Bonvillian, J. D. (1984, August). The role of iconicity in early Sign Language acquisition. <u>Journal of Speech and Hearing Disorders, 49</u> (3), 287-292. [UNIV DEAF Periodicals]

Orlansky, M. D., & Bonvillian, J. D. (1985, April). Sign Language acquisition: Language development in children of deaf parents and implications for other populations. <u>Merrill-Palmer Quarterly, 31</u> (2), 127-143. [UNIV Periodicals]

Padden, C. (1980). The deaf community and the culture of deaf people. In C. Baker & R. Battison (Eds.), <u>Sign Language and the Deaf community: Essays in honor of Wm. C. Stokoe</u> (pp. 89-103). Silver Spring, MD: National Association of the Deaf. {Hearing children of deaf parents are mentioned on pp. 100-101} (Reprinted in S. Wilcox (Ed.), <u>American Deaf culture: An anthology</u> (pp. 1-16). Silver Spring, MD: Linstok Press, 1989. [DEAF 305.773 A5, 1989]) [DEAF 420 S52, 1980]

Padden, C., & Markowicz, H. (1976). Cultural conflicts between hearing and deaf communities. In F. B. Crammatte & A. B. Crammatte (Eds.), <u>"Full citizenship for all deaf people": VII World Congress of the World Federation of the Deaf, Washington, D. C., July 31-August 7, 1975</u> (pp. 407-411). Silver Spring, MD: National Association of the Deaf. [DEAF 366 W6, 1975]

Panara, R., & Panara, J. (1983). Mabel Hubbard Bell. In <u>Great deaf Americans</u> (pp. 17-19). Springfield, MD: T. J. Publishers. [DEAF 920 P32g, 1983]

Parasnis, I. (1996). On interpreting the Deaf experience within the context of cultural and language diversity. In I. Parasnis (Ed.), Cultural and language diversity and the Deaf experience (pp. 3-19). New York: Cambridge University Press. [DEAF 305.773 C84, 1996]

Pecora, P. J., Despain, C. L., & Loveland, E. J. (1986, January). Adult children of deaf parents: A psychosocial perspective. Social Casework: The Journal of Contemporary Social Work, 67 (1), 12-19. [UNIV Periodicals]

(*) Pelarski, J., Poorbaugh, J., & Hines, J. (1973). Tell it like it is. In National Conference on Program Development for and with Deaf People (Ed.), Proceedings of National Conference on Program Development for and with Deaf People, Washington, D. C., October 9-12, 1973 (pp. 19-21). Washington, DC: Gallaudet College, Public Service Programs. (ERIC Document Reproduction Service No. ED 108 427 - 131 pages) [DEAF 361.8 N3p, 1973 or REFERENCE DESK]

Penman, R., Cross, T., Milgrom-Friedman, J., & Meares, R. (1983, February). Mothers' speech to prelingual infants: A pragmatic analysis. Journal of Child Language, 10 (1), 17-34. [C]

Petitto, L. A. (1989). Knowledge of language in signed and spoken language acquisition. In B. Woll (Ed.), Language development and sign language: Papers from the Seminar on language Development and Sign Language, Bristol, 1986, Monograph No. 1 (pp. 1-13). Bristol, England: International Sign Linguistics Association, Centre for Deaf Studies, University of Bristol. [DEAF 480.07 S41, 1986]

Petitto, L. A. (1992). Modularity and constraints in early lexical acquisition: Evidence from children's early language and gesture. In M. R. Gunnar & M. Maratsos (Eds.), The Minnesota Symposia on Child Psychology, Vol. 25. Modularity and constraints in language cognition (pp. 25-58). Hillsdale, NJ: Lawrence Erlbaum Associates. [UNIV Gen 155.4 M66]

Petitto, L. A. (1993). On the equipotentiality of signed and spoken language in early language ontogeny. In Gallaudet University, College for Continuing Education (Ed.), Post Milan ASL and English literacy: Issues, trends, and research, conference proceedings, Washington, DC, October 20-22, 1993 (pp. 195-223). Washington, DC: Gallaudet University Press. [DEAF 420 P67c, 1993]

Petitto, L. A., & Marentette, P. F. (1991, March 22). Babbling in the manual mode: Evidence for the ontogeny of language. Science, 251, 1493-1496. [UNIV Periodicals]

Pietrulewicz, B. (1975, March-April). Wplyw Srodowiska Rodzin Gluchych na osobowosc dzieci slyszacych [Environmental influence of deaf parents on personality of hearing children]. Psychologia Wychowawcza, 18 (2), 242-249. (In Polish - need translation) [DEAF 155.413 P54w, 1975]

Pietrulewicz, B. (1979, May-June). Inteligencja dzieci Slyszacych Wychowywanych przez Rodzicow Gluchych [Intelligence of hearing children reared by deaf parents]. Psychologia Wychowawcza, 22 (3), 393-400. (In Polish - need translation) {Abstract: "Administered the WISC to 30 normal hearing children reared by deaf parents and a matched group of 30 reared by hearing parents. Those reared by deaf parents scored significantly lower on the full verbal and nonverbal scales as well as on the five subtests. The differences may be due in part to differences in child-parent contact or perhaps to genetic effects."} [DEAF 155.413 P54i, 1979]

(*) Pischke, M. E. (1995). Parenting with a disability. In F. P. Haseltine, S. S. Cole & D. B. Gray (Eds.), Reproductive issues for persons with physical disabilities (pp. 57-60). Baltimore: Paul H. Brookes. [C]

Pitts, M. R. (1991a). Lon Chaney, Jr. In Horror film stars (2nd ed., pp. 42-57). Jefferson, NC: McFarland and Company, Inc. [C]

Pitts, M. R. (1991b). Lon Chaney, Sr., 1883-1930. In Horror film stars (2nd ed., pp. 31-41). Jefferson, NC: McFarland and Company, Inc. [C]

Poizner, H., & Battison, R. (1980). Cerebral asymmetry for Sign Language: Clinical and experimental evidence. In H. Lane & F. Grosjean (Eds.), Recent perspectives on American Sign Language (pp. 79-101). Hillsdale, NJ: Lawrence Erlbaum Associates. [DEAF 420 R43, 1980]

Poizner, H., Newkirk, D., Bellugi, U., & Klima, E. S. (1981, March). Representation of inflected signs from American Sign Language in short-term memory. Memory and Cognition, 9 (2), 121-131. [UNIV Periodicals]

Pollard, R. Q. (1996, April). Professional psychology and deaf people: The emergence of a discipline. American Psychologist, 51 (4), 389-396. [UNIV Periodicals]

Pollock, G. H. (1988, July). View point: The cold nose and the nudge. The Hearing Journal, 41 (7), 34, 36. {Describes the grieving process when deaf parents and hearing children experience the loss of a hearing-ear dog they've had for many, many years} [UNIV DEAF Periodicals]

Potts, P. (1982). Professional "help": The Taylor family. In T. Booth & J. Statham (Eds.), The nature of special education: People, places and change (pp. 71-77). London & New York: Routledge and the Open University Press. [UNIV Gen 371.9 N37, 1982]

Power, D. J., Wood, D. J., & MacDougall, J. (1990). Maternal control over conversations with hearing and deaf infants and young children. First Language, 10 [Pt. 1] (28), 19-35. [UNIV Periodicals]

Preston, P. M. (1994). Is Deaf culture contagious? [Keynote address]. In D. Watson, S. E. Boone & R. White (Eds.), Deaf senior citizens: Our heritage, our future, selected proceedings from the first National Conference for Deaf Senior Citizens, Austin, Texas, May 28-31, 1992 (pp. 9-14). Little Rock, AR: University of Arkansas Rehabilitation Research and Training Center for Persons who are Deaf or Hard of Hearing. (The author is hearing and has deaf parents) [DEAF 362.6 D42, 1994]

Preston, P. M. (1995, June). Mother father deaf: The heritage of difference. Social Science and Medicine, 40 (11), 1461-1467. (The author is hearing and has deaf parents) [*]

Preston, P. M. (1996, April/May). Chameleon voices: Interpreting for deaf parents. Social Science and Medicine, 42 (12), 1681-1690. (The author is hearing and has deaf parents) [*]

Preston, P. M. (1998). Two cultures, one family: Deaf parents and their hearing children [Keynote address]. In V. Follain-Grisell, K. Leitch-Walker & D. Morton (Eds.), Building bridges: Strengthening home and school relationships for Deaf parents and their hearing children, conference proceedings, Gallaudet University, Washington, D. C., May 1-3, 1997. Washington, DC: Gallaudet University, College for Continuing Education. Manuscript in preparation.

Prickett, H. T. (1987, December). [Review of *A loss for words* by Lou Ann Walker]. American Annals of the Deaf, 132 (5), 360. [UNIV DEAF Periodicals]

Prinz, P. M., & Prinz, E. A. (1979a, August). Acquisition of ASL and spoken English in a hearing child of a deaf

JOURNAL

mother and hearing father: Phase I, early lexical development. In Papers and Reports on Child Language Development, 17, 139-146. (Stanford University Department of Linguistics - ERIC Document Reproduction Service No. ED 197 583 - 9 pages) [REFERENCE DESK]

Prinz, P. M., & Prinz, E. A. (1979b, September). Acquisition of ASL and spoken English by a hearing child of a deaf mother and a hearing father: Phase II, early combinatorial patterns of communication. Paper presented at the fourth annual conference on language development, Boston, September, 1979. (ERIC Document Reproduction Service No. ED 193 936 - 12 pages) [REFERENCE DESK]

Prinz, P. M., & Prinz, E. A. (1979c, Winter). Simultaneous acquisition of ASL and spoken English (In a hearing child of a deaf mother and hearing father), Phase I: Early lexical development. Sign Language Studies, 25, 283-296. [UNIV RESERVE]

Prinz, P. M., & Prinz, E. A. (1981, Spring). Acquisition of ASL and spoken English by a hearing child of a deaf mother and a hearing father: Phase II, early combinatorial patterns. Sign Language Studies, 30, 78-88. [UNIV RESERVE]

Pye, C., Wilcox, K. A., & Siren, K. A. (1988, February). Refining transcriptions: The significance of transcriber "errors." Journal of Child Language, 15 (1), 17-37. [UNIV Periodicals]

Rainer, J. D., & Firschein, I. L. (1959, June). Mating and fertility patterns in families with early total deafness. Eugenics Quarterly, 6 (2), 117-127. ("This report is the 13th in a series of publications on the Mental Health Project for the Literate Deaf, which is being conducted by the Department of Medical Genetics of the New York State Psychiatric Institute, Columbia University...[and] was presented as part of an international conference on *Differentiation in Current Mating and Fertility Trends* which was held by the American Eugenics Society at the New York Academy of Medicine on February 14, 1959.") [DEAF 306.872 R34m, 1959]

Rayson, B. (1987a). Deaf parents of hearing children. In E. D. Mindel & M. Vernon (Eds.), They grow in silence: Understanding deaf children and adults (2nd ed., pp. 103-110). Austin, TX: Published for the National Association of the Deaf by Pro-ed Publisher. [DEAF 306.874 M5t, 1987]

Rayson, B. (1987b). Emotional illness and the deaf. In E. D. Mindel & M. Vernon (Eds.), They grow in silence: Understanding deaf children and adults (2nd ed., pp. 65-101). Austin, TX: Published for the National Association of the Deaf by Pro-ed Publisher. [DEAF 306.874 M5t, 1987]

Rea, C. A., Bonvillian, J. D., & Richards, H. C. (1988, December). Mother-infant interactive behaviors: Impact of maternal deafness. American Annals of the Deaf, 133 (5), 317-324. [UNIV DEAF Periodicals]

Reilly, J. S., & Bellugi, U. (1996, February). Competition on the face: Affect and language in ASL motherese. Journal of Child Language, 23 (1), 219-239. [C]

[Review of *In silence: Growing up hearing in a deaf world* by Ruth Sidransky]. (1990, September 1). Kirkus Reviews, 1237. [C]

[Review of *Useful gifts* by Carole L. Glickfeld]. (1989, January 13). Publishers Weekly, 235 (2), 76. (Author is listed as FC) [C]

Rhine, S. A. (1995). Genetic counseling and evaluation of recurrence for people with physical disabilities. In F. P. Haseltine, S. S. Cole & D. B. Gray (Eds.), Reproductive issues for persons with physical disabilities (pp. 153-161).

Baltimore: Paul H. Brookes. [C]

Riekehof, L. L. (1980). Interpreter training: The Gallaudet College Model. In <u>Proceedings of the International Congress on Education of the Deaf, Hamburg, 1980, Vol. 2</u> (pp. 510-519). Heidelberg: Julius Groos Verlag. {In the section on "Sources for recruiting interpreter trainees" Riekehof says the first source "is the family of the deaf person."} [DEAF 370 I57pro, 1980, v. 2]

Rienzi, B. M. (1990, December). Influence and adaptability in families with deaf parents and hearing children. <u>American Annals of the Deaf, 135</u> (5), 402-408. [UNIV DEAF Periodicals]

Rienzi, B. M., Levinson, K. S., & Scrams, D. J. (1992). University students' perceptions of deaf parents. <u>Psychological Reports, 71</u> (3 - Pt. 1), 764-766. {Evaluation of a technique for assessing attitudes toward non-traditional parents. "Applicants' hearing status and gender influenced perceived suitability to adopt a son but not a daughter."} [UNIV Periodicals]

Riley, P. (1994). You are what you know. The culture and social identity of bilingual children. In J. G. Kyle (Ed.), <u>Growing up in sign and word: Papers from a conference at Centre for Deaf Studies</u> (pp. 11-17). Bristol, England: University of Bristol. [DEAF 371.9721 G76, 1994]

(*) Roberson, C. A. (1995). I can do anything. In F. P. Haseltine, S. S. Cole & D. B. Gray (Eds.), <u>Reproductive issues for persons with physical disabilities</u> (pp. 43-46). Baltimore: Paul H. Brookes. [C]

Robinson, L. D., & Weathers, O. D. (1974, June). Family therapy of deaf parents and hearing children: A new dimension in psychotherapeutic intervention. <u>American Annals of the Deaf, 119</u> (3), 325-330. [UNIV DEAF Periodicals]

Rogers, J., & Matsumura, M. (1991). The first step - Deciding whether to have a child. In <u>Mother-to-be: A guide to pregnancy and birth for women with disabilities</u> (pp. 51-91). New York: Demos Publications. [*]

Rogers, J. G. (1995). A guide to pregnancy, labor, and delivery for women with disabilities. In F. P. Haseltine, S. S. Cole & D. B. Gray (Eds.), <u>Reproductive issues for persons with physical disabilities</u> (pp. 83-95). Baltimore: Paul H. Brookes. [C]

Rolfe, U. T. (1990). Children of parents with mental retardation. In B. Y. Whitman & P. J. Accardo (Eds.), <u>When a parent is mentally retarded</u> (pp. 133-146). Baltimore: Paul. H. Brookes Publishing Co. [C]

Rutherford, S. D. (1988). The culture of American Deaf people. <u>Sign Language Studies, 59,</u> 129-147. [UNIV RESERVE]

Sachs, J. (1972, March). <u>Development of oral language abilities from infancy to college: Final report.</u> (ERIC Document Reproduction Service No. ED 065 896 - 60 pages) {Five studies are reported. One of them is titled "Language development in a hearing child of deaf parents" (pages 25-38). The boy, John, was seen in seven sessions between the ages 3.9 and 3.11 years. Data was collected by Marie L. Johnson (Unpublished paper, University of Connecticut, 1971) and was summarized here: "Effects of reduced language input were observed in a hearing child of deaf parents. The language was quantitatively and qualitatively different from normal children's. Absence of signing suggested that language must be directed to the child to permit acquisition."} [REFERENCE DESK]

Sachs, J., Bard, B., & Johnson, M. L. (1981, February). Language learning with restricted input: Case studies of two hearing children of deaf parents. Applied Psycholinguistics, 2 (1), 33-54. Cambridge, MA: Cambridge University Press. [DEAF 155.413 S32l, 1981]

Sachs, J., & Johnson, M. (1976). Language development in a hearing child of deaf parents. In W. von Raffler-Engel & Y. Lebrun (Eds.), Baby talk and infant speech: Proceedings of the International Symposium on First Language Acquisition, Florence, Italy, 1972 (pp. 246-252). Amsterdam, Netherlands: Swets and Zeitlinger. [DEAF 401.9 I5b, 1976]

(*) Sackett, R. S. (1991, Fall). Terminating parental rights of the handicapped. Family Law Quarterly, 25 (3), 253-298. (Publication of the American Bar Association, section of Family Law, proceedings, Chicago, Illinois) [*]

Sainsbury, S., & Lloyd-Evans, P. (1986a). Communication. In Deaf worlds: A study of integration, segregation, and disability (pp. 59-107). London: Hutchinson. [DEAF 302 S3d, 1986]

Sainsbury, S., & Lloyd-Evans, P. (1986b). Conclusion. In Deaf worlds: A study of integration, segregation, and disability (pp. 292-298). London: Hutchinson. [DEAF 302 S3d, 1986]

Sainsbury, S., & Lloyd-Evans, P. (1986c). Family, friends and neighbourhood. In Deaf worlds: A study of integration, segregation, and disability (pp. 178-221). London: Hutchinson. [DEAF 302 S3d, 1986]

(*) Saito, I. (1975). Marriage of the graduates of our school and problems involved. In International Congress on Education of the Deaf (Ed.), Proceedings of the International Congress on Education of the Deaf, Tokyo, 1975 (pp. 675-678). Tokyo: The Organizing Committee, International Congress on Education of the Deaf. [DEAF 370 I57p, 1975]

Schein, J. D. (1968). Civil status, family composition, and fertility. In The deaf community: Studies in the social psychology of deafness (pp. 53-57). Washington, DC: Gallaudet College Press. [DEAF 301.32 S3de, 1968]

Schein, J. D. (1982a). The demography of deafness. In P. C. Higgins & J. E. Nash (Eds.), The deaf community and the deaf population: Social Aspects of Deafness, Vol. 3, proceedings of the Sociology of Deafness Conference, Gallaudet College, Washington, D. C., June, 1982 (pp. 27-62). Washington, DC: Gallaudet College Press. [DEAF 305 D4, 1982a]

Schein, J. D. (1982b). The demography of deafness. In P. C. Higgins & J. E. Nash (Eds.), The deaf community and the deaf population: Pre-conference working papers of Sociology of Deafness Conference, Washington, D. C., No. 3. Washington, DC: Gallaudet College Press. (32 pages) [DEAF 305 D4, 1982a]

Schein, J. D. (1989a). Family life. In At home among strangers: Exploring the deaf community in the United States (pp. 106-134). Washington, DC: Gallaudet University Press. [DEAF 305.773 S3a, 1989]

Schein, J. D. (1989b). Medical, legal, and interpreting services. In At home among strangers: Exploring the deaf community in the United States (pp. 181-196). Washington, DC: Gallaudet University Press. [DEAF 305.773 S3a, 1989]

Schein, J. D., & Delk, M. T., Jr. (1974). Civil status, family composition, and fertility. In The Deaf population of the United States (pp. 35-46). Silver Spring, MD: National Association of the Deaf. (Conducted by the National Association of the Deaf in cooperation with the Deafness Research and Training Center, New York University) {Some census statistics are interesting: "Of the children born [in this study], 88 percent are normal-hearing. The comparable figure for the Metropolitan Washington study was 89.4 percent, and 90.4 percent for New York State.

When data are analyzed by hearing of parents, the rates become progressively greater for combinations of congenitally deaf parents as opposed to those with acquired deafness...Where one parent had normal hearing and the other acquired deafness, 92.5 percent of the offspring were normal-hearing. Where both parents were congenitally deaf, 81.4 percent of the offspring were normal-hearing. Despite the dramatic differences in percentages of deaf children for the various categories, it should be noted that the expectation from all pairings is for normal-hearing children. Genetic counseling can specify more closely the expectations for deaf offspring in particular instances of prospective matings." pp. 44-45} [DEAF 312 S3d, 1974]

Schiff, N. B. (1979, September). The influence of deviant maternal input on the development of language during the preschool years. Journal of Speech and Hearing Research, 22 (3), 581-603. [UNIV DEAF Periodicals]

Schiff, N. B., & Ventry, I. M. (1976, August). Communication problems in hearing children of deaf parents. Journal of Speech and Hearing Disorders, 41 (3), 348-358. [UNIV DEAF Periodicals]

Schiff-Myers, N. B. (1982, June). Sign and oral language development of preschool hearing children of deaf parents in comparison with their mothers' communication system. American Annals of the Deaf, 127 (3), 322-330. [UNIV DEAF Periodicals]

Schiff-Myers, N. B. (1993). Hearing children of deaf parents. In D. Bishop & K. Mogford (Eds.), Language development in exceptional circumstances (2nd ed., pp. 47-61). Hillsdale, NJ: Lawrence Erlbaum Associates. (The Gallaudet University Library also has the 1988 edition [DEAF 401.93 L36, 1988]) [DEAF 401.93 L36, 1993]

Schiff-Myers, N. B., & Klein, H. B. (1985, December). Some phonological characteristics of the speech of normal-hearing children of deaf parents. Journal of Speech and Hearing Research, 28 (4), 466-474. [UNIV DEAF Periodicals]

Schiller, R. (1974). What's the matter, you deaf or something? Deafness Annual, IV, 1974 (pp. 1-7). Silver Spring, MD: Professional Rehabilitation Workers with the Adult Deaf. (Reprinted from the May, 1974, issue of The Christian Herald) [DEAF 362 D42]

Schleper, D. R. (1997). Principles for reading to Deaf children. In Reading to Deaf children: Learning from Deaf adults, a manual for parents and teachers, version 1. Washington, DC: Gallaudet University, Pre-College National Mission Programs. {There is a list of 15 principles Deaf parents incorporate into reading to their children} [*]

Schlesinger, H. S. (1972). A developmental model applied to problems of deafness. In H. S. Schlesinger & K. P. Meadow (Eds.), Sound and sign: Childhood deafness and mental health (pp. 7-30). Berkeley, CA: University of California Press. [DEAF 614.5833 S3s, 1972]

Schlesinger, H. S. (1978). The acquisition of bimodal language. In I. M. Schlesinger & L. Namir (Eds.), Sign Language of the deaf: Psychological, linguistic, and sociological perspectives (pp. 57-93). New York: Academic Press. [DEAF 420 S5, 1978]

School told to provide aide for deaf parents. (1989, November 30). New York Law Journal, 202 (204), 1, 4. {Deaf parents Kenneth and Karen Rothschild filed in White Plains for the Rockland County (New York) school district to provide interpreters for school events. U.S. District Court Judge Gerard Goettel said this access should be limited to "school initiated" conferences for their fourth-grader and high school senior who "can hear normally."} [C]

Schuchman, J. S. (1986). Comment on Ronnie B. Wilbur and Macalyne Fristoe ['s session entitled] "I had a wonderful, if somewhat unusual childhood: Growing up hearing in a deaf world." In J. B. Christiansen & R. W. Meisegeier (Eds.), [Proceedings of the second] Research Conference on the Social Aspects of Deafness, Gallaudet College, Washington, DC, June 8-10, 1986. Washington, DC: Gallaudet College. (5 pages) [DEAF 303.32 R4pr]

Schuchman, J. S. (1993). Oral history and deaf heritage: Theory and case studies. In R. Fischer & H. Lane (Eds.), Looking back: A reader on the history of deaf communities and their Sign Languages (pp. 515-532). Hamburg: Signum Press. [DEAF 305.7 L66, 1993]

Schwam, E. (1980, April). "MORE" is "LESS": Sign Language comprehension in deaf and hearing children. Journal of Experimental Child Psychology, 29 (2), 249-263. [UNIV Periodicals]

Seal, B. C., & Hammett, L. A. (1995, November). Language intervention with a child with hearing whose parents are deaf. Journal of Speech-Language Pathology, 4 (4), 15-21. [DEAF 401.93 S421, 1995]

Searls, J. M. (1993, Summer). Self-concept among deaf and hearing children of deaf parents. Journal of the American Deafness and Rehabilitation Association, 27 (1), 25-37. [UNIV RESERVE]

Searls, S. C., & Johnston, D. R. (1996). Growing up Deaf in Deaf families: Two different experiences. In I. Parasnis (Ed.), Cultural and language diversity and the Deaf experience (pp. 201-224). New York: Cambridge University Press. [DEAF 305.773 C84, 1996]

Seidel, J. V. (1982). The points at which deaf and hearing worlds intersect: A dialectical analysis. In P. C. Higgins & J. E. Nash (Eds.), The deaf community and the deaf population: Working papers No. 3 (pp. 1-33). Washington, DC: Gallaudet College. (Revised version of a paper presented at the Western Social Sciences Association meeting, April, 1980) [DEAF 305 D4, 1982]

Seki, Y., & Machida, S. (1981, March). Communication between a deaf mother and her hearing children - A case study. Bulletin of the Tokyo Metropolitan Rehabilitation Center for the Physically and Mentally Handicapped (pp. 11-22). [*]

Sela, I. (1978). Response. In L. von der Lieth (Ed.), Life in families with deaf members: Proceedings of the Vth World Conference on Deafness, Copenhagen, Denmark, 1977 (pp. 129-135). Copenhagen, Denmark: National Federation of the Deaf in Denmark. {The bulk of the article describes the Israeli system of education for the deaf which is oral and other developments. The last paragraph is of interest here: "I want to conclude with a challenge to the audience: Yesterday, a nice lady from Canada, a daughter of deaf parents, talked about the problems of hearing children with deaf parents (I am, too.) I want to ask the leaders, managers, the President, Dr. Magarotto, Dr. Vogoti, and other people here, to decide to create, here and now, a committee of hearing children of deaf parents who work with the deaf - we are very few but we exist. I think that today, with all the professionals who come to work with the deaf - why not use us, we the professionals, to help contribute to the World of the Deaf. And I hope that at the next Congress [of the World Federation of the Deaf], in Bulgaria, this committee will function."} [DEAF 306.87 W651, 1978]

Shahidi, R. G. (1978). Conditions of growing up for deaf children of deaf or hearing parents and hearing children of deaf parents. In L. von der Lieth (Ed.), Life in families with deaf members: Proceedings of the Vth World Conference on Deafness, Copenhagen, Denmark, 1977 (pp. 47-48). Copenhagen, Denmark: Akademisk Forlag, National Federation of the Deaf in Denmark. [DEAF 306.87 W65l, 1978]

Shaver Arnos, K., Israel, J., & Cunningham, M. (1991). Genetic counseling of the deaf: Medical and cultural considerations. Annals of the New York Academy of Sciences, 630, 212-222. [C]

Sheridan, M. A. (1995). A mother's gift. In M. D. Garretson (Ed.), Deafness, life and culture II: A Deaf American monograph, 45 (pp. 107-109). Silver Spring, MD: National Association of the Deaf. [UNIV RESERVE]

Sherwood, B. (1987a). Sherwood rebuttal. In M. L. McIntire (Ed.), Journal of Interpretation, 4, 59-60. Rockville, MD: Registry of Interpreters for the Deaf. [UNIV RESERVE]

Sherwood, B. (1987b). Third culture: Making it work. In M. L. McIntire (Ed.), Journal of Interpretation, 4, 13-24. Rockville, MD: Registry of Interpreters for the Deaf. [UNIV RESERVE]

Shultz-Myers, S. (1998). Where in the world(s) am I?: Developmental issues of the school-age coda. In V. Follain-Grisell, K. Leitch-Walker & D. Morton (Eds.), Building bridges: Strengthening home and school relationships for Deaf parents and their hearing children, conference proceedings, Gallaudet University, Washington, D. C., May 1-3, 1997. Washington, DC: Gallaudet University, College for Continuing Education. Manuscript in preparation.

Shultz-Myers, S., Myers, R. R., & Marcus, A. (in press). Hearing children of deaf parents: Issues and interventions within a bicultural context. In I. W. Leigh (Ed.), Psychotherapeutic interventions within the deaf community. Washington, DC: Gallaudet University Press. Manuscript in preparation.

Siedlecki, T., Jr., & Bonvillian, J. D. (1993a, Spring). Location, handshape and movement: Young children's acquisition of the formational aspects of American Sign Language. Sign Language Studies, 78, 31-52. [UNIV RESERVE]

Siedlecki, T., Jr., & Bonvillian, J. D. (1993b, Fall). Phonological deletion revisited: Errors in young children's two-handed signs. Sign Language Studies, 80, 223-242. [UNIV RESERVE]

Siple, P. (1985, April). Plasticity, robustness, and language development: An introduction to research issues relating Sign Language and spoken language. Merrill-Palmer Quarterly, 31 (2), 117-126. [UNIV Periodicals - Microfilm]

Siple, P., & Akamatsu, C. T. (1991). Emergence of American Sign Language in a set of fraternal twins. In P. Siple & S. D. Fischer (Eds.), Theoretical issues in Sign Language research: Vol. 2. Psychology (pp. 25-40). Chicago: University of Chicago Press. [DEAF 420 T43, v.2]

Siple, P., Akamatsu, C. T., & Loew, R. C. (1990). Acquisition of American Sign Language by fraternal twins: A case study. International Journal of Sign Linguistics, 1 (1), 3-13. [UNIV DEAF Periodicals]

Slesser, S. F. (1994, November). Deaf adults with hearing siblings - communication and attitudes. Deafness: The Journal of the Sociology of Deafness, 10 (3), 6-10. (Deafness is published by the British Deaf Association) [UNIV DEAF Periodicals]

Sloman, L., Perry, A., & Frankenburg, F. (1987, Fall). Family therapy with deaf member families. The American Journal of Family Therapy, 15 (3), 242-252. [DEAF 616.89156 S56f, 1987]

Söderfeldt, B., Rönnberg, J., & Risberg, J. (1994, Fall). Regional cerebral blood flow during Sign Language perception: Deaf and hearing subjects with deaf parents compared. Sign Language Studies, 84, 199-208. [UNIV RESERVE]

Spencer, P., Koester, L. S., & Meadow-Orlans, K. (1994, December). Communicative interactions of deaf and hearing children in a day care center: An exploratory study. <u>American Annals of the Deaf, 139</u> (5), 512-518. [UNIV DEAF Periodicals]

Spencer, P. E., Bodner-Johnson, B., & Gutfreund, M. K. (1992, Winter). Interacting with infants with a hearing loss: What can we learn from mothers who are deaf? <u>Journal of Early Intervention, 16</u> (1), 64-78. [UNIV Periodicals]

Staehle, S. C., & Witteborg, J. G. (1998). Telling it like it is: Data from interviewing deaf parents and hearing children. In V. Follain-Grisell, K. Leitch-Walker & D. Morton (Eds.), <u>Building bridges: Strengthening home and school relationships for Deaf parents and their hearing children, conference proceedings, Gallaudet University, Washington, D. C., May 1-3, 1997.</u> Washington, DC: Gallaudet University, College for Continuing Education. Manuscript in preparation.

Stein, L. (1942). Mutism. In <u>Speech and voice: Their evolution, pathology and therapy</u> (pp. 93-104). London: Methuen and Company, Ltd. [*]

Steiner, B. (1994, November). A personal journey. <u>Deafness: The Journal of the Sociology of Deafness, 10</u> (3), 11-14. (An excerpt from an essay written for his postgraduate studies at The Deaf Studies Research Unit of Durham University - <u>Deafness</u> is published by the British Deaf Association) [UNIV DEAF Periodicals]

Stevenson, A. C., & Cheeseman, E. A. (1956). Hereditary deaf mutism with particular reference to Northern Ireland. <u>Annals of Human Genetics, 20,</u> 177-207. [C]

Stewart, L. G. (1972). A truly silent minority. <u>Deafness Annual, II, 1972</u> (pp. 1-2). Silver Spring, MD: Professional Rehabilitation Workers with the Adult Deaf. [DEAF 362 D42]

Strom, R., & Cooledge, N. (1984). Parental success as perceived by parents, teachers and children. <u>Child Study Journal, 14</u> (4), 339-347. [UNIV Periodicals]

Strom, R., Daniels, S., & Jones, E. (1988). Child and parent development in deaf families. <u>Australasian Journal of Special Education, 12</u> (1), 34-39. [*]

(*) Stone-Harris, R. (1983). Deaf parents' perceptions of family life with deaf and/or hearing children. In G. D. Tyler (Ed.), <u>Rehabilitation and human services: Critical issues for the eighties, proceedings of the 1980 conference of the American Deafness and Rehabilitation Association, Cincinnati, 1980, Readings in deafness: Monograph No. 6</u> (pp. 5-9). Silver Spring, MD: American Deafness and Rehabilitation Association. [DEAF 361.06 A43m, 1980]

(*) Strom, R., Daniels, S., & Jones, E. (1988, Spring). Parent education for the deaf. <u>Educational and Psychological Research, 8</u> (2), 117-128. [DEAF 649.1 S77p, 1988]

(*) Strom, R., Daniels, S., Wurster, S., & Jones, E. (1985, September). Deaf parents of normal hearing children. <u>Journal of Instructional Psychology, 12</u> (3), 121-126. [*]

(*) Strom, R. D. (1985, April). Developing a curriculum for parent education. <u>Family Relations, 34</u> (2), 161-167. [UNIV Periodicals]

Strong, M., & Fritsch Rudser, S. (1986, Winter). The subjective assessment of Sign Language interpreters. <u>Sign Language Studies, 53,</u> 299-314. (Reprinted in D. Cokely (Ed.), <u>Sign Language interpreters and interpreting</u> (pp. 1-

14). Burtonsville, MD: Linstok Press, 1992 [DEAF 418.02 S53, 1992]) [UNIV RESERVE]

Stuttaford, G. (1990, August 31). [Book Review: *In silence, growing up hearing in a deaf world*]. Publishers Weekly, 237 (35), 57-58. [C]

Sullivan, F. (1981). Frank Sullivan, Mount Prospect, Illinois. In M. D. Orlansky & W. L. Heward (Eds.), Voices: Interviews with handicapped people (pp. 186-191). Columbus, OH: Charles E. Merrill. [DEAF 920 O74v, 1981]

Sutherland, J., & Beattie, R. G. (1994). [Book reviews] *Dancing without music: Deafness in America* by B. L. Benderly. The ACEHI Journal, 20 (3), 122-124. (The official journal of the Association of Canadian Educators of the Hearing Impaired) [UNIV DEAF Periodicals]

Sweeney, A. (1978, July). Genetic counseling in families with hearing impairment. Journal of Rehabilitation of the Deaf, 12 (1), 1-12. [UNIV RESERVE]

Szymoniak, E. (1977, Nov.-Dec., 1978, Jan.-Feb.). Hearing children of deaf parents. Hearing and Speech Action, 45 (6) & 46 (1), 16-19. [UNIV DEAF Periodicals]

Takala, M., & Seppälä, U. (1994, Fall). My life as a deaf person in Finnish society - Stories about being deaf. Journal of the American Deafness and Rehabilitation Association, 28 (2), 31-49. {"Forty-one stories about being Deaf in Finnish society were analyzed and thematicized." The theme of "children" or "family relationships" were never mentioned} [UNIV RESERVE]

Tanaka, S. (1977). Children's attitude towards parents with impaired hearing. In International Congress on Education of the Deaf (Ed.), Proceedings of the International Congress on Education of the Deaf, Tokyo, 1975 (pp. 690-691). Tokyo: The Organizing Committee, International Congress on Education of the Deaf. [DEAF 370 I57p, 1975]

Taska, R., & Rhoads, J. (1981-82, Fall/Winter). Psychodynamic issues in a hearing woman raised by deaf parents. Psychiatric Forum, 10 (2), 11-16. [DEAF 155.924 T3p, 1981]

Taylor, I. (1997). Setting out. In Buddhas in disguise: Deaf people of Nepal (pp. 5-9). San Diego: DawnSignPress. (The author is hearing and has deaf parents) {Irene Taylor is a photographer who spent three years in the Nepalese deaf community. She dedicates the book to "my Mother and Father, for showing me how to live within two worlds."} [DEAF 305.75496 T39b, 1997]

Terrell-Grassman, A. (1994). Hearing people: Who are they? Or it takes two to tango. In M. D. Garretson (Ed.), Deafness, life and culture: A Deaf American monograph, 44 (pp. 113-115). Silver Spring, MD: National Association of the Deaf. [UNIV RESERVE]

(*) Thurman, S. K. (1985). Ecological congruence in the study of families with handicapped parents. In S. K. Thurman (Ed.), Children of handicapped parents: Research and clinical perspectives (pp. 35-46). Orlando, FL: Academic Press. [DEAF 306.874 C4, 1985]

Thurman, S. K., Whaley, A., & Weinraub, M. A. (1985). Studying families with handicapped parents: A rationale. In S. K. Thurman (Ed.), Children of handicapped parents: Research and clinical perspectives (pp. 1-9). Orlando, FL: Academic Press. [DEAF 306.874 C4, 1985]

TIPS (Toward Improved Parenting Skills) for deaf parents with hearing children. (1992). Pittsburgh, PA: Project report by Western Pennsylvania School for the Deaf. (ERIC Document Reproduction Service No. ED 353 392 - 62 pages - See a related ERIC document: Literacy initiatives for families of deaf parents with hearing children, 1992 and the Evans, Zimmer and Murray resource guide in the "Miscellaneous publications" section) [REFERENCE DESK]

Todd, P., & Aitchison, J. (1980, June). Learning language the hard way. First Language, 2 (2), 122-140. [DEAF 401.93 T66l, 1980]

Todd, P. H. (1971). A case of structural interference across sensory modalities in second-language learning. Word, 27 (1-3), 102-118. (Child Language - 1975). [DEAF 155.413 T6c, 1971]

Turner, G. H. (1994a, Summer). *HOW* is Deaf Culture? Another perspective on a fundamental concept. Sign Language Studies, 83, 103-126. [UNIV RESERVE]

Turner, G. H. (1994b, Winter). Response to comments by Bahan, Ladd, Montgomery, and further thoughts. Sign Language Studies, 85, 337-366. [UNIV RESERVE]

Turner, W. W. (1847). Causes of deafness. American Annals of the Deaf, 1 (1), 25-32. (Reprinted in the October, 1997, issue of the American Annals of the Deaf, 142 (4), 316-319) [UNIV DEAF Periodicals]

Vaid, J., & Corina, D. (1989, January). Visual field asymmetries in numerical size comparisons of digits, words, and signs. Brain and Language, 36 (1), 117-126. [UNIV Periodicals]

Vernon, M. (1971). Current status of counseling with deaf people. In A. E. Sussman & L. G. Stewart (Eds.), Counseling with deaf people (pp. 30-42). New York: Deafness Research and Training Center, New York University School of Education. (A complete bibliography for the booklet is listed on pages 150-158) [DEAF 361.06 C6, 1971]

Vernon, M. (1974). Effects of parents' deafness on hearing children, compensating for language deficiency: Can it be done? In P. J. Fine (Ed.), Deafness in infancy and early childhood (pp. 219-224). New York: Medcom Press. [DEAF 362.7 F5d, 1974]

Vernon, M., & Mindel, E. (1978). Psychological and psychiatric aspects of profound hearing loss. In D. E. Rose (Ed.), Audiological assessment (2nd ed., pp. 99-145). Englewood Cliffs, NJ: Prentice-Hall. [DEAF 617.89 A92, 1978]

Vesterager, V. (1978). Hearing children of deaf parents. In L. von der Lieth (Ed.), Life in families with deaf members: Proceedings of the Vth World Conference on Deafness, Copenhagen, Denmark, 1977 (pp. 49-56). Copenhagen, Denmark: Akademisk Forlag, National Federation of the Deaf in Denmark. [DEAF 396.87 W651, 1978]

Vollmar, G. L. (1981). Guy L. Vollmar, DeKalb, Illinois. In M. D. Orlansky & W. L. Heward (Eds.), Voices: Interviews with handicapped people (pp. 20-24). Columbus, OH: Charles E. Merrill. [DEAF 920 O74v, 1981]

Volterra, V. (1981, Winter). Gestures, signs, and words at two years: When does communication become language? Sign Language Studies, 33, 351-362. [UNIV RESERVE]

Volterra, V. (1983). Gestures, signs, and words at two years, or when does communication become language? In

J. Kyle & B. Woll (Eds.), <u>Language in sign: An international perspective on Sign Language</u> (pp. 109-115). London: Croom Helm. [DEAF 419 L36, 1983]

Volterra, V., & Erting, C. J. (1990a/1994). Hearing children and deaf children compared. In V. Volterra & C. J. Erting (Eds.), <u>From gesture to language in hearing and deaf children</u> (pp. 247-248). Washington, DC: Gallaudet University Press. (Originally published in 1990 by Springer-Verlag, New York [DEAF 401.93 F76, 1990]) [DEAF 401.93 F76, 1994]

Volterra, V., & Erting, C. J. (1990b/1994). Hearing children with spoken and Sign Language input. In V. Volterra & C. J. Erting (Eds.), <u>From gesture to language in hearing and deaf children</u> (p. 217). Washington, DC: Gallaudet University Press. (Originally published in 1990 by Springer-Verlag, New York [DEAF 401.93 F76, 1990]) [DEAF 401.93 F76, 1994]

Volterra, V., & Erting, C. J. (1990c/1994). Introduction. In V. Volterra & C. J. Erting (Eds.), <u>From gesture to language in hearing and deaf children</u> (pp. 1-4). Washington, DC: Gallaudet University Press. (Originally published in 1990 by Springer-Verlag, New York [DEAF 401.93 F76, 1990]) [DEAF 401.93 F76, 1994]

Volterra, V., & Erting, C. (1990d/1994). Preface to 1994 Gallaudet University Press edition. In V. Volterra & C. J. Erting (Eds.), <u>From gesture to language in hearing and deaf children</u> (pp. viii-xiv). Washington, DC: Gallaudet University Press. (Originally published in 1990 by Springer-Verlag, New York [DEAF 401.93 F76, 1990]) [DEAF 401.93 F76, 1994]

von der Lieth, L. (1978). Social-psychological aspects of the use of Sign Language. In I. M. Schlesinger & L. Namir (Eds.), <u>Sign Language and the deaf: Psychological, linguistic and sociological perspectives</u> (pp. 315-332). New York: Academic Press. {The "Family constellations of the deaf" section has some discussion of hearing children in deaf families. The exceptional position of the first hearing child in the family is described briefly} [DEAF 420 S5, 1978]

von Tetzchner, S., Siegel, L. S., & Smith, L. (Eds.). (1989). Introduction. In <u>The Social and cognitive aspects of normal and atypical language development</u> (pp. vii-xii). New York: Springer-Verlag. [*]

Wagenheim, H. S. (1985). Aspects of the analysis of an adult son of deaf-mute parents. <u>Journal of the American Psychoanalytic Association, 33</u> (2), 413-435. [DEAF 306.874 W33a, 1985]

Walker, L. A. (1988a). Introduction. In H. Keller, <u>The story of my life</u> (pp. ix-xviii). New York: New American Library. [*]

Walker, L. A. (1988b). The world without sound. In E. Bernstein (Ed.), <u>Encyclopaedia Britannica 1989 Medical and Health Annual</u> (pp. 84-103). Chicago: Encyclopaedia Britannica. [*]

Walker, L. A. (1992). A hearing daughter shares her view about growing up with parents who are deaf. In D. D. Smith & R. Luckasson (Eds.), <u>Introduction to special education: Teaching in an age of challenge</u> (pp. 413-414). Boston: Allyn and Bacon. (Excerpt from *A Loss for Words* by Lou Ann Walker) [C]

Walker, L. A. (1994, Fall). Mr. Walker goes to court: Deaf culture on trial. <u>Hopewell Review: Indiana Literary Review, 6,</u> 63-67. {About Lou Ann Walker's deaf father and uncle and deaf culture in Indiana} [*]

Walsh, C. B., & Beattie, R. G. (1994). [Book reviews] *A loss for words: The story of deafness in a family* by L. A. Walker. <u>The ACEHI Journal, 20</u> (1/2), 64-66. (The official journal of the Association of Canadian Educators

J
O
U
R
N
A
L

of the Hearing Impaired) [UNIV DEAF Periodicals]

Walters, P. (1996a). Mother [Poem]. In <u>Border countries</u> (p. 44). Fredericksburg, VA: The Kirkland Press. [*]

Walters, P. (1996b). Visit [Poem]. In <u>Border countries</u> (p. 35). Fredericksburg, VA: The Kirkland Press. [*]

Watkins, R. V., & Rice, M. L. (1987, November). <u>Grammatical form-class errors in a hearing child of deaf parents.</u> Paper presented at the American Speech-Language-Hearing Convention, New Orleans. (15 pages) [*]

(*) Watts, A. J. (1995, March/April). Sticking it out! Managing a parent support group. <u>Perspectives in Education and Deafness, 13</u> (5), 5-7, 11. [UNIV DEAF Periodicals]

Waxman, R. P., & Spencer, P. E. (1997, Spring). What mothers do to support infant visual attention: Sensitivities to age and hearing status. <u>Journal of Deaf Studies and Deaf Education, 2</u> (2), 104-114. [UNIV DEAF Periodicals]

Weiner, M. T. (1998). How can we as a community help deaf families with hearing children? [Keynote address]. In V. Follain-Grisell, K. Leitch-Walker & D. Morton (Eds.), <u>Building bridges: Strengthening home and school relationships for Deaf parents and their hearing children, conference proceedings, Gallaudet University, Washington, D. C., May 1-3, 1997.</u> Washington, DC: Gallaudet University, College for Continuing Education. Manuscript in preparation.

Weiner, T. (1998). Raising bicultural and bilingual children: Deaf parents' perceptions. In C. Carroll (Ed.), <u>Deaf Studies V: Toward 2000 - Unity and diversity, conference proceedings, Gallaudet University, April 17-20, 1997</u> (pp. 193-228). Washington, DC: Gallaudet University, College for Continuing Education. [On order]

Wells, D. (1994, March). I followed the path that many of us did, became "welfare for the deaf." <u>Deafness: The Journal of the Sociology of Deafness, 10</u> (1), 3. (Paper presented at a one day seminar organized by the Training Committee of the National Council for Social Workers with Deaf People, London, England, April 9, 1991) [UNIV DEAF Periodicals]

Welsh, W. A. (1991, Jan/April). The economic impact of deafness. <u>Journal of the American Deafness and Rehabilitation Association, 24</u> (3-4), 72-80. [UNIV DEAF Periodicals]

(#) Weltman, S. (1994, December). Overview: *Mother father deaf, living between sound and silence* by Paul Preston [Book review]. <u>Readings: A Journal of Reviews and Commentaries in Mental Health</u> (p. 22). [*]

White, C. (1994). "Growing up" by Catherine White, Head of Sign Language Services at the London Boroughs Disability Resource Team. <u>Deafness: The Journal of the Sociology of Deafness, 10</u> (1), 4-5, 13. (Reprinted in National Council for Social Workers with Deaf People Training Committee (Ed.), <u>Special needs or special breed? Hearing children of deaf adults</u> (pp. 4-9). Write NCSWDP, 1st floor, Bedford House, 125-133 Camden High Street, London, England NW1 7JR. (24 pages) {Transcript of a paper presented at a one day seminar organized by the Training Committee of the National Council for Social Workers with Deaf People, NCSWDP, April 9, 1991. [DEAF 306.874 S632, 1992]} [UNIV DEAF Periodicals]

(*) White, G. W., & White, N. L. (1995). The adoptive process: Challenges and opportunities for people with disabilities. In F. P. Haseltine, S. S. Cole & D. B. Gray (Eds.), <u>Reproductive issues for persons with physical disabilities</u> (pp. 107-115). Baltimore: Paul H. Brookes. [C]

White, S. (1993). Book review: *The legal rights of people with disabilities.* <u>Deafness: The Journal of the Sociology</u>

of Deafness, 9 (3), 16-17. (The book is published by Castlemilk Law Centre, Castlemilk, Glasgow. Deafness is published by the National Council of Social Workers with Deaf People and the British Deaf Association) [UNIV DEAF Periodicals]

(*) Whitman, B. Y., Graves, B., & Accardo, P. J. (1990). Parents learning together I: Parenting skills training for adults with mental retardation. In B. Y. Whitman & P. J. Accardo (Eds.), When a parent is mentally retarded (pp. 51-65). Baltimore: Paul. H. Brookes Publishing Co. [*]

Widell, J. (1978). A life of paradoxes. In L. von der Lieth (Ed.), Life in families with deaf members: Proceedings of the Vth World Conference on Deafness, Copenhagen, Denmark, 1977 (pp. 93-97). Copenhagen, Denmark: National Federation of the Deaf in Denmark. [DEAF 306.87 W651, 1978]

Widell, J. (1993). The Danish Deaf culture in European and Western society. In R. Fischer & H. Lane (Eds.), Looking back: A reader on the history of deaf communities and their Sign Languages (pp. 457-478). Hamburg: Signum Press. [DEAF 305.7 L66, 1993]

Wilbur, R. B. (1987). Sociolinguistic aspects of Sign Language and deaf culture. In American Sign Language: Linguistic and applied dimensions (Rev. ed., pp. 227-246). Boston: Little, Brown and Company. {Discusses "Between two worlds: Hearing children of deaf parents" on pages 239-242} [DEAF 420 W5am, 1987]

Wilbur, R. B., & Fristoe, M. (1986). I had a wonderful, if somewhat unusual childhood: Growing up hearing in a deaf world. In J. B. Christiansen & R. W. Meisegeier (Eds.), Papers for the second Research Conference on the Social Aspects of Deafness, Gallaudet College, Washington, D. C., June 8-10, 1986 (pp. 1-48). Washington, DC: Gallaudet College. [DEAF 303.32 R4p, 1986]

Wilbur, R. B., & Jones, M. L. (1974). Some aspects of the acquisition of American Sign Language and English by three hearing children of deaf parents. In M. W. LaGaly, R. A. Fox & A. Bruck (Eds.), Papers from the Tenth Regional Meeting Chicago Linguistic Society, April 19-21, 1974, 10 (pp. 742-749). Chicago: Chicago Linguistic Society. [*]

Wilcox, S., & Wilcox, P. (1991a). American deaf culture. In Learning to see: American Sign Language as a second language (pp. 54-75). Englewood Cliffs, NJ: Regents/Prentice Hall. [DEAF 420 W54l, 1991]

Wilcox, S., & Wilcox, P. (1991b). Special considerations. In Learning to see: American Sign Language as a second language (pp. 109-117). Englewood Cliffs, NJ: Regents/Prentice Hall. [DEAF 420 W54l, 1991]

Williams, D., Nover, R. A., Ward, D. B., Castellan, J. M., Greenspan, S. I., & Lieberman, A. F. (1988). Two infants, a family, and the service system: The Lake family. In S. I. Greenspan, S. Wieder, R. A. Nover, A. F. Lieberman, R. S. Lourie & M. F. Robinson (Eds.), Infants in multirisk families: Case studies in preventive intervention (pp. 81-124). Madison, CT: International Universities Press. (Originally published by the National Center for Clinical Infant Programs in their Clinical Infant Reports No. 3, 1987, pp. 81-124. [*]) [DEAF 362.1968 I53, 1988]

(*) Williams, J. S. (1976, Spring). Bilingual experiences of a deaf child. Sign Language Studies, 10, 37-41. [UNIV RESERVE]

Wilmot, J. (1995, January). Mother father deaf: Living between sound and silence by Paul Preston [Book review]. Disability, Pregnancy and Parenthood International, No. 9, 15. [*]

Wilson, A. (1992, Nov. 1). Video reviews: *My daddy's ears are broken.* Library Journal, 117 (18), 128-129. (See film reference under "Video and audio tapes, films and compact discs" section) [UNIV Periodicals]

Wilson, M., & Emmorey, K. (1997, Summer). Working memory for Sign Language: A window into the architecture of the working memory system [Theoretical and review articles]. Journal of Deaf Studies and Deaf Education, 2 (3), 121-130. [UNIV DEAF Periodicals]

Wolkomir, R. (1992, July). American Sign Language, "It's not mouth stuff - it's brain stuff": Research on how deaf people communicate gives them a stronger hand in our culture, and casts new light on the origin of language. Smithsonian, 23 (4), 30-41. [C]

Woll, B., Kyle, J., & Ackerman, J. (1988). Providing Sign Language models: Strategies used by deaf mothers. In G. Collins, A. Lewis & V. Lewis (Eds.), Proceedings of the Child Language Seminar, University of Warwick, 1988 (pp. 217-228). [*]

Woll, B., & Kyle, J. G. (1989). Communication and language development in children of deaf parents. In S. von Tetzchner, L. S. Siegel & L. Smith (Eds.), The social and cognitive aspects of normal and atypical language development (pp. 129-144). New York: Springer-Verlag. [*]

Woodford, D. (1993). Towards a perception of a "hearing culture" and its relationships with a "deaf culture." Deafness: The Journal of the Sociology of Deafness, 9 (3), 13-15. (Deafness is published by the National Council of Social Workers with Deaf People and the British Deaf Association) [UNIV DEAF Periodicals]

Woodford, D. E. (1994). Towards a perception of a hearing culture and its relationships with a deaf culture. In J. G. Kyle (Ed.), Growing up in sign and word: Papers from a conference at Centre for Deaf Studies (pp. 54-62). Bristol, England: University of Bristol. [DEAF 371.9721 G76, 1994]

Woodward, J. C. (1972). Implications for sociolinguistic research among the deaf. Sign Language Studies, 1, 1-7. [UNIV RESERVE]

Woodward, J. C., Jr. (1973, Fall). Some observations on sociolinguistic variation and American Sign Language. The Kansas Journal of Sociology, 9 (2), 191-200. [DEAF 428 W6so, 1973]

Wright, D. (1969/1994). Eight. In Deafness (pp. 103-117). New York: Stein and Day. (See the 1994 edition, Deafness: An autobiography [DEAF 920 W7d, 1994]) {On page 108 there is an anecdote concerning a hearing child of deaf parents} [DEAF 920 W7d, 1969]

(*) Zola, I. K. (1995a). A father's gift. In F. P. Haseltine, S. S. Cole & D. B. Gray (Eds.), Reproductive issues for persons with physical disabilities (pp. 117-118). Baltimore: Paul H. Brookes. [C]

(*) Zola, I. K. (1995b). And the children shall lead us. In F. P. Haseltine, S. S. Cole & D. B. Gray (Eds.), Reproductive issues for persons with physical disabilities (pp. 67-69). Baltimore: Paul H. Brookes. [C]

(*) Zola, I. K. (1995c). Is it all right to be sad? In F. P. Haseltine, S. S. Cole & D. B. Gray (Eds.), Reproductive issues for persons with physical disabilities (pp. 61-62). Baltimore: Paul H. Brookes Publishing. [C]

(*) Zola, I. K. (1995d). Tell me...tell me. In F. P. Haseltine, S. S. Cole & D. B. Gray (Eds.), Reproductive issues for persons with physical disabilities (pp. 97-102). Baltimore: Paul H. Brookes. [C]

(*) **Zola, I. K. (1995e).** Why Marcia is my favorite name. In F. P. Haseltine, S. S. Cole & D. B. Gray (Eds.), <u>Reproductive issues for persons with physical disabilities</u> (pp. 53-56). Baltimore: Paul H. Brookes. [C]

JOURNAL

III

NEWSPAPER,

MAGAZINE,

PROCEEDINGS AND

NEWSLETTER ARTICLES

At the Gallaudet University Learning Center check their <u>Subject Index to Deaf Periodicals</u> (kept at the front desk). This is an on-going project indexing Deaf Community magazines such as the <u>Deaf American</u>, <u>Deaf American monographs</u>, <u>Deaf Life</u>, <u>DeafNation</u> and the <u>Silent Worker</u>. One of the index subject headings is "Hearing children with Deaf parents."

Abarbanell, A. (1997a, February). Ababab speaks out (how unusual...). <u>CODA Connection, 14</u> (1), 9. [UNIV DEAF Periodicals]

Abarbanell, A. (1997b, May). Dear Codas [Letter to the editor]. <u>CODA Connection, 14</u> (2), 4. {Quotes an Associated Press article: "Teenager one of seven killed in Jordanian massacre." Adi Malka, the hearing daughter of deaf parents, was one of the seven Israeli teenagers slain by a Jordanian soldier while the children were on a field trip to Jordan's 'Island of Peace.'" Abarbanell asks for suggestions of what we (codas and CODA) can do} [UNIV DEAF Periodicals]

Abarbanell, A. R. (1991, November). The wonderful wizard of CODA. <u>CODA Connection, 8</u> (4), 7. [UNIV DEAF Periodicals]

Ability stressed at annual meeting for handicapped. (1963). <u>Electrical Workers' Journal,</u> 1-3. (Official publication of the International Brotherhood of Electrical Workers - AFL-CIO) {Reports on the Annual Meeting of the President's Committee on Employment of the Handicapped held in May in Washington, D. C. President of the union Gordon M. Freeman served as vice chairman of the President's Committee. President John F. Kennedy was the opening day principal speaker. There is a photo of Miss Elizabeth Benson interpreting for the Senior Class from Gallaudet that attended the meeting} [Gallaudet University Archives, "Elizabeth English Benson, interpreter in the Language of Signs" biographical subject vertical file]

Accident claims life of local woman. (1993, January 15). <u>McGehee Arkansas News.</u> [*]

(##) Ackerman, G. (1997, March 14). Anxious wait for news of children. <u>The (Manchester) Guardian Daily,</u> p. 13. (England - Reported from Beit Shemesh, Israel - Associated Press) [C]

Acting in sign language is like acting in French. (1985, December 6). <u>Kennepec Journal.</u> (Augusta, Maine) {Article about *Love is Never Silent* and Mare Winningham's struggle in learning sign language for the part of the hearing daughter in the made-for-TV film} [Gallaudet University Archives, "Love is Never Silent" subject vertical file]

Actor to join in seminar for deaf. (1974, September 18). <u>The Indianapolis News.</u> (Indiana) [Gallaudet University Archives, "Louie Fant" biographical vertical file]

Actresses' deaf parents say plight forced daughter to be expressive. (1976, March 30). <u>Gazette.</u> (Reno, Nevada) [Gallaudet University Archives, "Louise Fletcher" biographical vertical file]

Adams, M. (1966, June 13). Johnson visits Gallaudet graduates. <u>The Evening Star.</u> (Washington, D. C.) {Louis Fant is pictured interpreting the President's Commencement address} [Gallaudet University Archives, "Louie Fant" biographical vertical file]

(#) Adoption rights finally won by deaf. (1961, December 22). (Florida newspaper unidentified) [Gallaudet University Archives, "Court litigation - deaf" subject vertical file]

Adult CODAs tell experiences. (1991, July 22). <u>On the Green: A Weekly Published for Gallaudet University Staff and Faculty, 21</u> (36), 1-2. Washington, DC: Gallaudet University Department of Publications and Production. [UNIV DEAF Periodicals]

Advertising Club honors Dean Benson. (1967, May-June). <u>The Gallaudet Record, 12</u> (7), 2. {Dr. Elizabeth Benson, Dean of Women at Gallaudet College, has been named 1967 Woman of the Year in Education by the

ARTICLES

Women's Advertising Club of Washington} [Gallaudet University Archives and "Elizabeth English Benson, interpreter in the Language of Signs" biographical subject vertical file]

Advocate for deaf speaks for those who are unable. (1985, December 15). Asbury Park Press. (Asbury Park New Jersey) {Story about Adele Belitz, the oldest hearing child in a family where the parents are deaf} [Gallaudet University Archives, "Hearing children of deaf parents" subject vertical file]

After lightning hits dad, 5-year-old son calls 911. (1995, November). CODA Connection, 12 (4), 1, 9. [UNIV DEAF Periodicals]

Aheroni, E. (1997a, May). To Evie [A poem]. CODA Connection, 14 (2), 17. [UNIV DEAF Periodicals]

Aheroni, E. (1997b, May). The President's forum. CODA Connection, 14 (2), 3-4. [UNIV DEAF Periodicals]

Aheroni, E. (1997c, September). President Aheroni's final forum. CODA Connection, 14 (3), 3-4. [UNIV DEAF Periodicals]

Aig, M. (1990, February). Interpreter ordered for deaf parents. The Silent News, 22 (2), 5. (Associated Press article) [UNIV DEAF Periodicals]

Alfred L. Harden [Photo and caption]. (1918, March). The Silent Worker, 30 (6), 107. {Machinists mate U.S. Aviation Corps, Pensacola, Florida, and son of Mr. and Mrs. E. Harden of St. Louis is reported drowned} [UNIV DEAF Periodicals]

Alvarez, L. (1995, October 1). Interpreting new worlds for parents: English puts children in awkward roles. The New York Times (Metro Report), 145 (No. 50,201), pp. 29, 36. (Reprinted in the February, 1996, CODA Connection, 13 (1), 7-8. [UNIV DEAF Periodicals]) [UNIV Newspapers Microfilm]

Anderson, G. (1976, March 31). Jack Nicholson's ship finally comes in. Post-Gazette. (Pittsburgh, Pennsylvania) [Gallaudet University Archives, "Louise Fletcher" biographical vertical file]

Anderson, L. (1980, May 30). Signs of love: Son hears, father doesn't; special bond bridges the silence. The Roanoke Times. (Roanoke, Virginia) [Gallaudet University Archives, "Parent-child relationship - deaf adults" subject vertical file]

Andes, C. (1990, June). A good question [Letter to the editor]. Deaf Life, 2 (12), 5. [UNIV DEAF Periodicals]

Andrews, R. M. (1961, May). Son of deaf parents shows pluck despite his painful burns in accident. The Silent Worker, 13 (9), 15. (Reprinted from the Richmond Times-Dispatch, 1960) [UNIV DEAF Periodicals]

Andrews, R. M. (1982a, May 19). Actress Fletcher knows the estrangement of deafness. Argus Leader, p. 6D. (Sioux Falls, South Dakota) [Gallaudet University Archives, "Louise Fletcher" biographical vertical file]

Andrews, R. M. (1982b, September 30). Actress knows what deafness is like. Marshall Independent, p. 10. (Marshall, Minnesota) [Gallaudet University Archives, "Louise Fletcher" biographical vertical file]

Angelos, C. (1989, October 19). New teacher seen as good sign: College excited to hire expert. The Seattle Times. (Seattle, Washington) [Gallaudet University Archives, "Louie Fant" biographical vertical file]

(#) Angier, N. (n.d.). Study: Deaf tots babble with hands. <u>Sarasota Herald Tribune,</u> pp. 1A, 15A. (Sarasota, Florida) [*]

Anna Witter: Making communication comfortable. (1978, November). <u>The Deaf American, 31</u> (3), 24-25. {Anna Witter is hearing and her parents are deaf. She explains their influence on her work coordinating interpreter services at the National Technical Institute for the Deaf, Rochester, New York} [UNIV DEAF Periodicals]

Annie A. Ugarte [Photo and caption]. (1922, July). <u>The Silent Worker, 34</u> (10), 389. {She is seven months old and the daughter of Mr. and Mrs. E. Ugarte of Toredo, Texas} [UNIV DEAF Periodicals]

Annis, R. (1997, September). How I got to Codarado. <u>CODA Connection, 14</u> (3), 8. [UNIV DEAF Periodicals]

Anonymous. (1990, February). Central issues in our lives as codas and in the life of the CODA organization [Letter to the editor]. <u>CODA Connection, 7</u> (1), 3. [UNIV DEAF Periodicals]

Anonymous. (1993, February). [Letter to the editor]. <u>CODA Connection, 10</u> (1), 5-6. [UNIV DEAF Periodicals]

Another hero. (1944, May). <u>The FRAT: Official Publication of the National Fraternal Society of the Deaf, 42nd year, No. 10,</u> 4-5. {Clipped from the <u>Press-Scimitar</u> (Memphis, Tennessee), about the war-time bravery of Lt. Sidney L. Wallace, Jr., son of Mr. and Mrs. Sidney L. Wallace Sr., Memphis} [UNIV DEAF Periodicals]

Appleby, J. (1996, May). Sign on to a new baby language. <u>Parenting Magazine,</u> 25. [*]

An appreciative audience [Photo and caption]. (1956, January 4). <u>Sun.</u> (Greeneville, Tennessee) {Actress June Havoc signs and dances for students of "Gallaudet College for the Deaf and Dumb in Washington." Elizabeth Benson interprets the song} [Gallaudet University Archives, "Elizabeth English Benson, interpreter in the Language of Signs" biographical subject vertical file]

Armstrong, T., Jr. (1993, May). Sherry Hicks: The queen of Coda cool [Interview]. <u>Hot Wire: The Journal of Women's Music and Culture, 9</u> (2), 2-5. [*]

Army names center for Doctor Benson. (1973, March 10). <u>The News,</u> p. B10. (Frederick, Maryland) [Gallaudet University Archives, "Elizabeth English Benson: Memorials" biographical subject vertical file]

Arnold, G. (1994, October 7). Movies: *Deaf* uses fluent style for message. <u>The Washington Times,</u> p. C16. {Review of the French documentary on the French Deaf community, *In the Land of the Deaf*} [UNIV Newspapers]

(#) **Arthur, E. (1991?).** The Deafpride Mailbox [Letter to the editor]. <u>The Deafpride Advocate, 8</u> (1), 8. [UNIV DEAF Periodicals]

Arthur, N. (1994, October 7). [Review of: *In the Land of the Deaf*, October 7-13]. <u>Washington City Paper.</u> (Washington, D. C.) [*]

Asa, R. (1989, November 1). Hearing is interpreting: Children of deaf parents often become the window to the hearing world. <u>The Oak Park Leaves,</u> pp. 28, 35. (Oak Park, Illinois) [*]

Aschenbrenner, B. (1992, Spring). Book review: *Our Father Abe.* <u>The Endeavor,</u> 17, 20. (The newsletter of the American Society for Deaf Children, Silver Spring, Maryland) [UNIV DEAF Periodicals]

Ashley, D. (1985, December 19). Movie speaks to deaf people. State, pp. 1B, 6B. (Columbia, South Carolina) {An article about *Love is Never Silent* as a "powerful, touching television movie." Concerns that the film's depiction was distorted and might present an overly stereotyped view of the deaf family were expressed by South Carolinians Pat Goff, Alton Brant, Leah Jacques and Caroline Grant who all are hearing and have deaf parents. Dr. Paul C. Higgins, a professor in the sociology department at the University of South Carolina and a coda, was also interviewed} [Gallaudet University Archives, "Love is Never Silent" subject vertical file]

Ask Dr. Deaf. (1991, Aug/Sept). CODA Connection, 8 (3), 5. (Address questions for this column to Dr. Deaf, c/o ALDA News, 2445 W. Cuyler St., Chicago, IL 60618) [UNIV DEAF Periodicals]

Ask them yourself: For the "Ask them yourself" editor. (1976, July 17). The Progress. (Clearfield, Pennsylvania - Reprinted in the Wilmington, North Carolina, Star, July 18, 1976) {Responds to a reader's question: Tell me about Louise Fletcher's family} [Gallaudet University Archives, "Louise Fletcher" biographical vertical file]

Assistant speaker [Photo and caption]. (1964, June 7). The Sunday Star. (Washington, D. C.) {President Johnson addresses the centennial banquet of Gallaudet College with help of sign language from Dr. Elizabeth Benson, dean of women} [Gallaudet University Archives, "Elizabeth English Benson, interpreter in the Language of Signs" biographical subject vertical file]

At last, housing for the deaf [Editorial]. (1981, December 17). Evening Sun. (Baltimore, Maryland) [Gallaudet University Archives, "Rev. Louis W. Foxwell, Jr." biographical vertical file]

Avery, E. (1988, December 4). Valdosta Tech helps educate area people in Sign Language. Valdosta Daily Times. (Valdosta, Georgia) [Gallaudet University Archives, "American Sign Language - teaching" subject vertical file]

Bainbridge, J. S., Jr. (1974, April 4). Police lack "strong leads" in slaying. The Morning Sun, A1, A14. (Baltimore, Maryland) [Gallaudet University Archives, "Louis W. Foxwell" biographical vertical file]

Bakker, D. (1994, October/November). The misfortune that has befallen a deaf Michigan couple makes the point that American justice may well be blind...and deaf. Hearing Health, 10 (6), 18. [UNIV DEAF Periodicals]

Baldridge named Coach of the Year. (1992, March 16). On the Green: A Weekly Published for Gallaudet University Staff and Faculty, 22 (20), 2. Washington, DC: Gallaudet University Department of Publications and Production. [UNIV DEAF Periodicals]

(*) Baldwin, D. R. (1992, Aug/Sept). Winning essay: The 1992 CODA Millie Brother Scholarship. CODA Connection, 9 (3), 5. (Reprinted in D. Prickett & R. Prickett (Eds.), Richness in our diversity: Proceedings of the tenth International CODA Conference, Research Triangle Park, North Carolina, July 27-30, 1995 (p. 121). Santa Barbara, CA: Children of Deaf Adults. [On order]) [UNIV DEAF Periodicals]

Balk, M. J. (1996, November). Reality on the subway: The 1996 Millie Brother Scholarship essay winner. CODA Connection, 13 (4), 4-5. [UNIV DEAF Periodicals]

Balloch, J. (1977, July 1). Mock trial helps explain proceedings if deaf person faces court charges. News-Sentinel. (Knoxville, Tennessee) {Susan Childress is pictured serving as an interpreter} [Gallaudet University Archives, "Court litigation - interpreting for the deaf" subject vertical file]

Barber, M. (1994, January). Mick Barber (hearing person living in a Deaf family). British Deaf News, 25 (1), 11. [UNIV DEAF Periodicals]

Bark, E. (1985, December 9). *Never Silent* will light up the airways [Television review]. Morning News. (Dallas, Texas) {A very positive review of *Love is sever silent*. "Tears were flowing - silently - from the eyes of one who has seen very few television movies of this caliber." This is a "lump-in-the-throat movie." Mare Winningham, who played the title role in the 1984 film *Helen Keller - The Miracle Continues* stars in the role of Margaret, the hearing daughter of deaf parents} [Gallaudet University Archives, "Love is Never Silent" subject vertical file]

Barnhart, M. (1979, September 8). Judge's educated fingers help try a deaf defendant. Daily Mail. (Hagerstown, Maryland) {District Court Judge Daniel Moylan's grandparents were deaf} [Gallaudet University Archives, "Court litigation - interpreting for the deaf" subject vertical file]

Barnwell, E. (1991, March/April). Sweet Honey in the Rock: Music with a message. Washington View, 2 (3), 8-10. (Washington, D. C.) [*]

Bass, J. (1990, Aug/Sept). Young codas: The CODA organization needs to work towards a "young coda program." CODA Connection, 7 (3), 7. [UNIV DEAF Periodicals]

Beck, M. (1976a, March 31). Brenda [Vaccaro] lost award but still "gained" an Oscar [Hollywood Hotline column]. Star-Ledger. (Newark, New Jersey) {About Louise Fletcher and the Academy Awards} [Gallaudet University Archives, "Louise Fletcher" biographical vertical file]

Beck, M. (1976b, March 31). Oscar-loser Vaccaro thrilled by Award results. Chronicle. (Houston, Texas) [Gallaudet University Archives, "Louise Fletcher" biographical vertical file]

Beeson, R. (1992, September). *Please sign here* by Percy Corfmat [Book review]. H-MFD Newsletter, No. 12. (Reprinted in Digest of past mailshots and newsletters of H-MFD 1-4, listed under "Miscellaneous Publications." Reproduced from NEWSLI (12), September, 1992) [*]

Beeson, R. (1998, February). Movie review: *Beyond silence.* CODA Connection, 15 (1), 5. [UNIV DEAF Periodicals]

Belated greetings to these moms. (1969, May 12). Democrat and Chronicle. (Rochester, New York) [Gallaudet University Archives, "Parent-child relationship - deaf adults" subject vertical file]

Bellugi, U. (1971, April). [Book review] *In this sign,* a novel by the author of I never promised you a rose garden: Joanne Greenberg. Psychology Today, 4 (11), 10, 12. [UNIV Periodicals]

Ben Steiner paintings. (1993, September). British Deaf News Supplement, 24 (9), 1. [UNIV DEAF Periodicals]

Bentley-Adler, C. (1989, January 12). American Sign Language: When fingers do the talking. Times Star. (Middletown, California) [Gallaudet University Archives, "Children of deaf adults" subject vertical file]

(*) Bergmann, R. (1994, April). Parent guidance of Deaf parents with deaf children: We need deaf parent counselors. WFD News, No. 1, 28-29. (A publication of the World Federation of the Deaf, founded by Cesare Magarotto who is hearing and whose parents are deaf. This article was also obtained off the internet on January 23, 1997 at <http://dww.deafworldweb.org:80/dww/pub/english/f/counselors.html> from the Deaf World Web) [UNIV DEAF Periodicals]

Berry, H. (1993, May). Opening night: *PHOENIX the.* Hot Wire: The Journal of Women's Music and Culture,

9 (2), 16-17. [*]

Better baby "talk." (1996, September 15). Bottom Line Personal, 10, 10. [C]

Bhatia, S. (1997, March 14). Massacre of the schoolgirls. The (Manchester) Guardian Daily, p. 1. (England) {It was reported that one of the teenagers was Adi Malka, the hearing daughter of deaf parents} [C]

Bienvenu, MJ. (1994, July/August). In celebration of a life: Ronald L. Coffey, August 9, 1960-June 27, 1994 [Photo]. TBC News, No. 69, 7. [UNIV DEAF Periodicals]

The big event: Deaf awareness. (1985, April 2). Democrat and Chronicle. (Rochester, New York) {About Louise Fletcher appearing at the National Technical Institute for the Deaf} [Gallaudet University Archives, "Louise Fletcher" biographical vertical file]

Bildilli, H. (1969, March 21). Handicapped woman lives normally, rears family, receives education. Commercial-News. (Danville, Illinois) [Gallaudet University Archives, "Parent-child relationship - deaf adults" subject vertical file]

Blake, J. (1974, July 4). Deaf parents conquer silent challenge. Herald. (Everett, Washington) [Gallaudet University Archives, "Parent-child relationship - deaf adults" subject vertical file]

Boe, S. (1996a, Aug/Sept). More reflections from Sandy Boe: "Aah, those C-words!" CODA Connection, 13 (3), 10. [UNIV DEAF Periodicals]

Boe, S. (1996b, Aug/Sept). Reflections of CODA-LA '96. CODA Connection, 13 (3), 1. [UNIV DEAF Periodicals]

Boesen, S. L. (1988, June). Lessons learned [Letters to the editor]. The NAD Broadcaster, 10, (6), 3. {An open letter to Linda Hatrak-Cundy in response to her Mother Knows Best column on CODA} [UNIV DEAF Periodicals]

Boesen, S. L. (1993, February). An open love letter to Sheila and Paul [Letter to the editor]. CODA Connection, 10 (1), 5. [UNIV DEAF Periodicals]

Bolinaga, S. (1987, June-July). Deaf mother earns special honor. The V. A. D. Bulletin, 29, 1-2. (Virginia Association of the Deaf newsletter) [UNIV DEAF Periodicals]

Book reviews...*In this sign* by Joanne Greenberg. (1971, February). The Deaf American, 23 (6), 28-29. (Three reviews are included by CAA, JSP and EWP. The second review is by a hearing daughter of deaf parents) [UNIV DEAF Periodicals]

Boothroyd, J. (1993, Summer). Minding the signs: She discovered that deaf infants "babble on the hands." McGill News: Alumni Quarterly, 12-16. (Canada) {About Dr. Laura Ann Petitto's research findings} [*]

Borger, G. (1978, August 5). Deaf expectant mother wins a "voice" in the delivery room: "She wanted...to understand everything going on." Washington Star, p. D1. (Washington, D. C.) [Gallaudet University Archives, "Court litigation - deaf" subject vertical file]

(*) Bourne, F. S. (1994, November). "Your parents are Deaf? I'm sorry. How did you get lucky?" [The 1994 CODA Millie Brother Scholarship winning essay]. CODA Connection, 11 (4), 8. (Reprinted in D. Prickett & R.

Prickett (Eds.), <u>Richness in our diversity: Proceedings of the tenth International CODA Conference, Research Triangle Park, North Carolina, July 27-30, 1995</u> (pp. 125-126). Santa Barbara, CA: Children of Deaf Adults. [On order]) [UNIV DEAF Periodicals]

Boustany, N. (1990, October 28). Lebanese Christians despair of civilian deaths, defeat by Syria. <u>The Washington Post,</u> pp. A1, A25. (Washington, D. C.) [UNIV Newspapers Microfilm]

(*) Bowe, D. W. (1994, November). What my father taught me [The 1994 Millie Brother] Scholarship essay winner. <u>CODA Connection, 11</u> (4), 9. (Reprinted in D. Prickett & R. Prickett (Eds.), <u>Richness in our diversity: Proceedings of the tenth International CODA Conference, Research Triangle Park, North Carolina, July 27-30, 1995</u> (p. 127). Santa Barbara, CA: Children of Deaf Adults. [On order]) [UNIV DEAF Periodicals]

Bowe, F. (1974, September). The DA [Deaf American] interview: James Hanson. <u>The Deaf American, 27</u> (1), 9-10. [UNIV DEAF Periodicals]

Boy actor's agent sues welfare agency for fee. (1954, October 3). <u>Herald.</u> (Bridgeport, Connecticut) [Gallaudet University Archives, "Parent-child relationship - deaf adults" subject vertical file]

Braddock, G. C. (1942, January). Notable deaf persons No. 61 - Mr. and Mrs. George Homer. <u>The FRAT: Official Publication of the National Fraternal Society of the Deaf, 39th year, No. 6,</u> 3. (Reprinted in <u>Notable deaf persons</u> (pp. 106-108) by Guilbert C. Braddock, edited by Florence B. Crammatte. Washington, DC: Gallaudet College Alumni Association, 1975. [DEAF 920 B685, 1975]) [UNIV DEAF Periodicals]

Braddock, G. C. (1943, May). Notable deaf persons No. 77 - Mabel Hubbard Bell. <u>The FRAT: Official Publication of the National Fraternal Society of the Deaf, 40th year, No. 10,</u> 3. [UNIV DEAF Periodicals]

Bradley, A. (1967, May 26). Julia Lee is Ad Woman of the Year. <u>The Evening Star.</u> (Washington, D. C.) {The Women's Advertising Club of Washington presented it's awards yesterday. Among other award recipients was Dr. Elizabeth Benson, dean of women at Gallaudet College, who also received an achievement award} [Gallaudet University Archives, "Elizabeth English Benson, citations and awards" biographical subject vertical file]

Bragg, B. (Ed.). (1953, October). The answer box, question of this month: What are the advantages and disadvantages of your having deaf parents? <u>The Silent Worker, 6</u> (2), 31. (Letters are from Almer Jacobs Allman, Julia Palmer Trenham, Donna and Mary Jane Goode, Edith Long Stevenson, Ralph F. Neesam, Mary Stone and Walter Lester, Jr.) [UNIV DEAF Periodicals]

Breaking the language barrier. (1991, March). <u>News In General,</u> 1-2. (Published bimonthly by the public relations office for employees, volunteers and medical staff of Lutheran General Hospital, Chicago) [*]

Brenda Vaccaro happy Oscar loser. (1976, April 1). <u>State Journal.</u> (Lansing, Michigan) [Gallaudet University Archives, "Louise Fletcher" biographical vertical file]

Brennan, P. (1985, December 8-14). *Love Is Never Silent* breaking barriers, breaking bonds. <u>The Washington Post</u> (TV Week), pp. 10-11. (Washington, D. C.) [Gallaudet University Archives, "Parent-child relationship - deaf adults" subject vertical file]

Brennan, P. (1985, December 6). *Love is Never Silent* speaks louder than words. <u>Bulletin.</u> (Providence, Rhode Island) {A positive review of *Love is Never Silent*. Mentions that Phyllis Frelich, who played the part of Janice Ryder here, recently appeared in *Children of a Lesser God*, for which she won a Tony Award} [Gallaudet University

Archives, "Love is Never Silent" subject vertical file]

Brennan, P. (1985, December 9). *Silent* features deaf actors in prominent roles tonight. Post-Standard. (Syracuse, New York) {A positive review of *Love is Never Silent*. Mentions that 10-year-old Susan Ann Curtis of Seattle who plays the young margaret is the daughter of deaf parents and Cloris Leachman, winner of one Oscar and five Emmy's, plays Margaret's mother-in-law} [Gallaudet University Archives, "Love is Never Silent" subject vertical file]

Bridge, M. (1993a, May). I belong: A poem. CODA Connection, 10 (2), 8. [UNIV DEAF Periodicals]

Bridge, M. (1993b, May). Journey: A poem. CODA Connection, 10 (2), 7. [UNIV DEAF Periodicals]

Bright, S. (1980, August 17). Coping in hearing world: Deaf parents Don and Eleanor Belcher share a closeness with their hearing children. Kentucky-Advocate, pp. 3-4. (Danville, Kentucky) [Gallaudet University Archives, "Parent-child relationship - deaf adults" subject vertical file]

Broadway star son of deaf parents. (1973, March). The Deaf American, 25 (7), 16. [UNIV DEAF Periodicals]

(#) Brodeur, N. (1995, December, 22). A life story spelled out with hands. The News and Observer (Metro section). (City unspecified, North Carolina) [*]

Brody, R. (1987, May). My mother's silent world: As the child of a profoundly deaf woman, the author learned early that family hardships can bring their own special blessings. 50 PLUS, 27, 25-27, 59. [C]

Brody, R. (1990a, Mar/April). Granny nannies: An ageless answer to the child-care crisis. Utne Reader, No. 38, 83. (Excerpted with permission from Special Report on Family, November 1989-January, 1990 [C]) [UNIV Periodicals]

Brody, R. (1990b, October). The reluctant go-between: By depending on me to communicate for her, my deaf mother assumed a power close to tyranny. Glamour Magazine, 88 (10), 288, 301. (Comment on this article in the vertical file at Gallaudet: "Another parent bashing article.") [UNIV Periodicals]

Broecker, B. (1997, June). Betty's potpourri: Now that I have your attention. Silent News, 29 (6), 2. [UNIV DEAF Periodical]

Broecker, C. (1990, November). Hi! [Letter to the editor]. CODA Connection, 7 (4), 3. (Letter is dated June 26, 1990) {Candace writes that she is a coda and works as an interpreter and actress. She appeared in *Bridge to Silence* as Marlee Matlin's best friend "Mary" and that Allison Silva, the little girl that played in the film, was also a coda. She met Whitney Bowe, the hearing daughter of Frank Bowe, shooting a commercial and describes their delight at meeting} [UNIV DEAF Periodicals]

Brother, B. (1961, November). From our readers [Letter to the Rev. Robert L. Johnson, editor of "The Church Page" column]. The Silent Worker, 14 (3), 23. [UNIV DEAF Periodicals]

Brother, M. (Ed.). (1983, November). [Introductory issue]. CODA Newsletter, 1-6. (Vol. 1, number 1, begins with the February, 1984, issue) [UNIV DEAF Periodicals]

Brother, M. (1984, August). CODA cudos [sic]. CODA Newsletter, 1 (3), 3-4. [UNIV DEAF Periodicals]

Brother, M. (1986, August). Open letter to our parents. <u>CODA Newsletter, 3</u> (3), 1-2. [UNIV DEAF Periodicals]

Brother, M. (1987a, May). Love is never silent...or is it? <u>CODA Newsletter, 4</u> (2), 4. [UNIV DEAF Periodicals]

Brother, M. (1987b, Aug/Sept). What CODA is and is not. <u>CODA Newsletter, 4</u> (3), 1-2. (Reprinted in T. H. Bull (Ed.), <u>A CODA Retreat: Coming home, proceedings of the fifth National CODA Conference, Austin, Texas, July 14-17, 1990</u> (p. 8). Santa Barbara, CA: Children of Deaf Adults. [DEAF 306.874 N3, 1990] and in D. Prickett & R. Prickett (Eds.), <u>Richness in our diversity: Proceedings of the tenth International CODA Conference, Research Triangle Park, North Carolina, July 27-30, 1995</u> (p. 8). Santa Barbara, CA: Children of Deaf Adults. [On order]) [UNIV DEAF Periodicals]

Brother, M. (1988, July). CODA welcomes all [Letter to the editor]. <u>The NAD Broadcaster, 10</u> (7), 3. (Reprinted in the November, 1988, issue of the <u>CODA Newsletter, 5</u> (4), 8. [UNIV DEAF Periodicals]) [UNIV DEAF Periodicals]

Brother, M. (1989, Aug/Sept). Deaf Way meets CODA Way. <u>CODA Connection, 6</u> (3), 1. [UNIV DEAF Periodicals]

Brother, M. (1993, May). In memoriam: Eli Savanick. <u>CODA Connection, 10</u> (2), 1. [UNIV DEAF Periodicals]

Brother, M. (1994, November). A CODA Christmas down under! <u>CODA Connection, 11</u> (4), 1-2. [UNIV DEAF Periodicals]

Brother, M. (1996, February). Typhoon CODA hits Tokyo: Millie Brother, soggy but safe. <u>CODA Connection, 13</u> (1), 1. [UNIV DEAF Periodicals]

Brown, M. (1985, December 5). Hollywood slow to hear case of deaf actress. <u>Herald Statesman,</u> pp. C1, C19. (Yonkers, New York) {A positive review of *Love is Never Silent*. Also includes an interview with deaf co-producer Julianna Fjeld who describes her 10-year struggle to get this story to film. "This is a film about a family with universal problems, not just a film about being deaf" she said} [Gallaudet University Archives, "Love is Never Silent" subject vertical file]

Bruno, K. (1992, February). To my dad, Sal. <u>CODA Connection, 9</u> (1), 7. [UNIV DEAF Periodicals]

(#) (##) Buck, F. M. (1982). The influence of parental disability on children [Abstract]. <u>Rehab Brief, 5,</u> 1-4.

Buck, J. (1985a, December 5). NBC drama focuses on deafness in '30s. <u>News Herald.</u> (Morganton, North Carolina) {A positive review of *Love is Never Silent*, a Hallmark Hall of Fame production. Interview with Mare Winningham who plays the part of Margaret Ryder, the hearing daughter of deaf parents in the film} [Gallaudet University Archives, "Love is Never Silent" subject vertical file]

Buck, J. (1985b, December 7). "Hallmark Hall of Fame" airs Monday. <u>Daily Star.</u> (Shelby, North Carolina) {The focus is on Mare Winningham who plays "a young woman in conflict between her world of the hearing and the silent world of her deaf parents."} [Gallaudet University Archives, "Love is Never Silent" subject vertical file]

Buck, J. (1985c, December 8). Daughter the only ears for deaf mother, father. <u>Tennessean.</u> (Nashville, Tennessee) {A positive review of *Love is Never Silent*, a Hallmark Hall of Fame production to air on NBC Monday night. Mentions that Mare Winningham, who plays the part of Margaret Ryder, the hearing daughter of deaf parents in the film, also appeared in *Amber Waves*, her first movie, in 1980, which won her an Emmy for Best Supporting Actress}

[Gallaudet University Archives, "Love is Never Silent" subject vertical file]

Buck, J. (1985d, December 9). Actress "signed up" for film airing on Channel 2 tonight. <u>Post.</u> (Houston, Texas) {An article about *Love is Never Silent* and Mare Winningham's experience as Margaret, the hearing daughter of deaf parents} [Gallaudet University Archives, "Love is Never Silent" subject vertical file]

Building bridges. (1997, Spring). <u>Gallaudet Today, 27</u> (3), 4. [UNIV DEAF Periodicals]

Buildings named.... (1973, March). <u>Gallaudet Alumni Newsletter, 7</u> (5), 1. {Mentions the dedication of a new building at the U.S. Army Medical Training Center at Ft. Sam Houston. It will be named "The Elizabeth E. Benson Dormitory" in recognition for her service to the deaf community and as the first woman to earn a commission in the U.S. Army} [Gallaudet University Archives]

Bull, T. H. (1993, November). An open letter to CODA. <u>CODA Connection, 10</u> (4), 4. [UNIV DEAF Periodicals]

Bulletin. (1974, April 3). <u>On the Green: A Weekly Published for Gallaudet University Staff and Faculty, 3</u> (3), 4. {News about the death of and funeral arrangements for the Rev. Louis Foxwell, pastor of Christ Methodist Church in Baltimore} [Gallaudet University Archives, "Louis W. Foxwell" biographical vertical file]

(#) (##) Bunde, L. T. (1980?). Unique interpersonal dynamics of deaf parents/hearing children. <u>Extension Magazine,</u> 10-12. (Publication of the Catholic Church Extension Society of the United States of America, official organ of the Home Missions - date unspecified) [*]

Burch, D. (1998, May). RID remembers Judie Husted [Eulogy]. <u>Views, 15</u> (5), 6. (Registry of Interpreters for the Deaf newsletter) {RID President Dan Burch's eulogy for coda Judie Husted of Washington state} [UNIV DEAF Periodicals]

Burleigh, B. (1952, May). DORchester 3-4832. <u>World Outlook,</u> 217-220. {About The Rev. Mrs. Constance Elmes, "the nation's only ordained woman preacher to the deaf."} [Gallaudet University Archives, "Constance Elmes" biographical vertical file]

Burr, T. (1997) Lon Chaney. In A. Gwinn (Ed.), <u>Entertainment Weekly: The 100 Greatest Stars of All Time</u> (pp. 156-157). New York: Entertainment Weekly Books, Time, Inc. Specials. [*]

Butler, K. (1987, September 27). Man lends ear to needs of deaf. <u>Port Haywood Daily Press,</u> pp. C1-C3. (Port Haywood, Virginia) [*]

Caley, S. (1994, January). Sheila Caley (hearing person living in Deaf family). <u>British Deaf News, 25</u> (1), 10. [UNIV DEAF Periodicals]

California: Deaf justice. (1966, October 17). <u>Newsweek, 68</u> (16), 37-38. {Wayne and Madeline Christensen of Torrance, California, and their efforts to adopt a 13-month-old boy, Scotty. Judge A. A. Scott decided they would fail as parents because their home "is not a normal home...."} [Gallaudet University Archives, "Wayne Christensen" biographical vertical file]

Callander, J. (1994, August 18). Reviews, *No jeans: Scenes from life and the imagination,* watercolors by Jacquelyn Cavish and oil pastels by Ron Hillas, at the Alley Gallery. <u>The Independent,</u> p. 39. (Santa Barbara, California) {The show will be in Carpinteria, California, through August 31} [*]

Calvert, S. (1994, August). Trusting for a sign: The fruits of her hands, Oh! The lives we have led. <u>Royal Service: A Missions Tapestry for Southern Baptist Women, 88</u> (2), 20-25. (The Magazine for Baptist Women, Woman's Missionary Union, Southern Baptist Convention, Birmingham, Alabama) {About Peggy Keough and her quilting, life, honors, hobbies and retirement. She took nine T-shirts from different International CODA Conferences and created the "CODA Quilt" and two pillows. They were auctioned off in 1994 and the proceeds were designated for the Millie Brother CODA Scholarship fund. Her hearing daughter, Margaret Collier, was very touched when she read her mother's signature piece on the back corner of the quilt: "Chaotic Beginnings......Made by Peggy Keough Mother of a CODA 1994." See Margaret's poem referenced in the "Miscellaneous" section} [*]

Canote, A. (1994, Spring). Late deaf parents are weird. <u>ALDA News: The Official Newsletter of the Association of Late-Deafened Adults, 8</u> (1), 1. (Adam is 12 years old) [UNIV DEAF Periodicals]

Capital cameraman: Clipping the Veep. (1964). <u>Scripps-Howard News, 19</u> (2), 5. {Full-page photo of Vice President Lyndon Johnson as he speaks at Gallaudet College and Elizabeth Benson, interpreter, standing next to him} [Gallaudet University Archives, "Elizabeth English Benson, interpreter in the Language of Signs" biographical subject vertical file]

Carr, S. L. (1992, September 14). Dean's Ocala law firm is a family affair. <u>Ocala Star-Banner.</u> (Ocala, Florida) [Gallaudet University Archives, "Children of deaf adults" subject vertical file]

Carroll, C. (1979, March). Another misconception...: Article belittling deaf mothers causes furor. <u>The Deaf American, 31</u> (7), 13. [UNIV DEAF Periodicals]

Carroll, C. (1986a, April 21). Living through the night: Young, deaf, and Jewish, Rose faced the Nazis with her baby, her husband, and lots of courage. <u>The World Around You: A publication of Pre-College Programs, Gallaudet University, 7</u> (14), 5-6. Washington, DC: Gallaudet University, Pre-College Programs. {The story of Max Feld and Rose Rosman and how they managed during World War II with their hearing daughter Esther. Rose now lives in Los Angeles, California, and is a member of Temple Beth solomon of the Deaf} [Gallaudet University Archives]

Carroll, C. (1986b, December). An island where everyone signs. <u>The World Around You: A publication of Pre-College Programs, Gallaudet University,</u> 8-9. Washington, DC: Gallaudet University, Pre-College Programs. {Why were so many deaf people born on Martha's Vineyard? "Jonathan Lambert was a carpenter and farmer who moved to Martha's Vineyard in 1692. Lambert was deaf himself. He had seven children - two of whom were also deaf. Lambert's deaf children never married. But his hearing children - with Lambert's recessive genes for deafness - did marry. When they had children, they continued to pass on the recessive genes for deafness."} [Gallaudet University Archives]

Carroll, C. (1989, January). Born hearing and trying not to hate it: Sheila Palmer didn't know it for the first seven years of her life, but she was born hearing. <u>World Around You: A publication of Pre-College Programs, Gallaudet University,</u> 8-9, 15. Washington, DC: Gallaudet University, Pre-College Programs. [Gallaudet University Archives]

Carroll, C. (1992, Fall). New directions: NTD's Julianna Fjeld makes her presence felt. <u>Gallaudet Today, 23</u> (1), 5. [Gallaudet University Archives or RESERVE]

Carroll, C. (1993, Fall). A father, a son, and a university: Thomas Hopkins Gallaudet. <u>Preview: Pre-College Programs, Gallaudet University,</u> 12-13. Washington, DC: Gallaudet University, Pre-College Programs. (Also available from the National Information Center on Deafness, Gallaudet University [DEAF 920 G3ca, 1993]) [UNIV DEAF Periodicals]

Carter, B. (1985, December 8). Deafness doesn't stop stars of *Love is Never Silent* [Cover story and television review]. The Baltimore Sun (TV Week), p. 2, cover. (Baltimore, Maryland) {Brief review of the film} [Gallaudet University Archives, "Parent-child relationship - deaf adults" subject vertical file]

Carter, B. (1985, December 9). Winningham and *Love* are special [Television review]. The Baltimore Sun, pp. 1B, 6B. (Baltimore, Maryland) {Review of *Love is Never Silent*. A "warm, moving drama, filled with graceful performances, excellent writing and convincing period atmosphere. It also conveys the details of life inside a community unlikely to be known by many viewers. That element raises this film to a level approaching greatness." Mare Winningham is "one of the most gifted young actresses working today."} [Gallaudet University Archives, "Parent-child relationship - deaf adults" subject vertical file]

Carter, S. M., Jr. (1981). Overview. The Deaf American, 34 (3), 3. [UNIV DEAF Periodicals]

(#) Cason, C. (1994, July 15). About the artist [Photo]. Time Out, p. 10. (City and newspaper unidentified) {There was a cover story in the "Gallery" section, a weekly look at Ventura County (California) visual arts expression} [*]

Cerf, D. (1996, Aug/Sept). My first CODA meeting. CODA Connection, 13 (3), 12. [UNIV DEAF Periodicals]

Cerney, B. (1996, February). Interpreters as cultural allies. Views, 13 (2), 16-17. (Registry of Interpreters for the Deaf newsletter) [UNIV DEAF Periodicals]

Chandler, K. (1995, September 20). Breaking through S I L E N C E [Photos and story]. Star Tribune, pp. E1-E2. (Minneapolis, Minnesota) {Feature story about Elvira and Kelvin Hodson of Coon Rapids, Minnesota. They have two hearing children and belong to a support group for deaf parents sponsored by the Minneapolis chapter of MELD. Diane Leonard, a deaf parent herself, is coordinator of the group} [Gallaudet University Archives, "Parent-child relationship - deaf adults" subject vertical file]

Chaney borne to tomb: Small group of friends hears noted film actor eulogized as "true" and "kind." (1930, August 29). The Los Angeles Times, 49 (part 2), pp. 1, 3. (Los Angeles, California) [*]

Chaney buried: "Laugh, clown, laugh" is dirge - Grind of cameras in movie capital cease as tribute to famed film star. (1930, August 29). The Cleveland Press, No. 16320, p. 17. (Cleveland, Ohio) [*]

Chapman-Smith, A. (1997, February). More comments about CODA-LA 1996! [Letter]. CODA Connection, 14 (1), 10. [UNIV DEAF Periodicals]

Children of Deaf Adults hold first conference. (1986, Nov/Dec). The Endeavor, 2. (The newsletter of the American Society for Deaf Children, Silver Spring, Maryland) [UNIV DEAF Periodicals]

Children of deaf parents find beauty in their silent world. (1986, December 21). The Ocala Star Banner. (Ocala, Florida - The Raleigh, North Carolina, newspaper also reprinted this article) [*]

Children of Mr. Lars M. Larson, Faribault, Minn. [Photos and captions]. (1922, May). The Silent Worker, 34 (8), 288. {These photos of Rosa, Vera and Louis M. Larson were taken about twenty years ago. Rosa now lives in Duluth, Minnesota, with her deaf husband and Vera is in Northfield, Minnesota on a farm demolished by a great tornado two years ago. Louis is now a chemist working in Cincinnati, Ohio} [UNIV DEAF Periodicals]

Children of the deaf. (1950, March). The Silent Worker, 2 (7), 21, cover. {Featured are Connie and Ronnie, the children of Mr. & Mrs. Harry L. Baynes of Talladega, Alabama} [UNIV DEAF Periodicals]

Children of the deaf...A coming educator. (1952, April). The Silent Worker, 4 (8), 5. [UNIV DEAF Periodicals]

Children of the deaf...They shine on the gridiron. (1950, December). The Silent Worker, 3 (4), 9. [UNIV DEAF Periodicals]

Children of the deaf...They stand at the scholastic heights. (1950, September). The Silent Worker, 3 (1), 10. [UNIV DEAF Periodicals]

Children of the deaf...This one aspired to a singing career. (1950, July). The Silent Worker, 2 (11), 11. [UNIV DEAF Periodicals]

Children of the deaf: West Point has them. (1950, June). The Silent Worker, 2 (10), 4. [UNIV DEAF Periodicals]

Childress, M. (1989, May 21). Book review: Beware of s-t-r-a-n-g-e-r-s, review of *Useful gifts* by Carole L. Glickfeld. The New York Times Book Review. [UNIV Newspapers Microfilm]

Childress, R. (1998, February). Gathering sense [Poem]. CODA Connection, 15 (1), 1. [UNIV DEAF Periodicals]

Childress Brown, M. (1987, June 21). The day daddy was arrested changed our lives. Sunday Democrat and Chronicle, p. 19A. (Rochester, New York) {A first-person account of the effect on a family of being Black and deaf. Maxine, the oldest of three girls, was 8 years old when a policeman came to their door with an arrest warrant for her father. "I do recall that [the days that followed] were very difficult for my family and that the resulting stress and confusion changed every member of my family forever." One tangible result is that as an adult she ran for public office and won} [*]

Chism, S. (1997, May). Dear Codas [Letter]. CODA Connection, 14 (2), 6. {Mentions her forthcoming book and asks for information} [UNIV DEAF Periodicals]

Christensen, S. G. (1987, January 26). Of two worlds: Children of deaf parents feel bond. The Clarion-Ledger, pp. 1C-2C. (Jackson, Mississippi) [*]

Christy, M. (1982a, May 20). Conversations: Louise Fletcher's growth through parents' courage. The Boston Globe, pp. 65-66. [Gallaudet University Archives, "Louise Fletcher" biographical vertical file]

Christy, M. (1982b, June 16). Actress draws strength from the sounds of silence. Buck County Courier Times. (Levittown, Pennsylvania - Marian Christy is "of the Boston Globe") [Gallaudet University Archives, "Hearing children of deaf parents" subject vertical file]

Christy, M. (1982c, June 26). Actress unheard: Louise Fletcher's deaf parents taught her courage. Lancaster New Era. (Lancaster, Pennsylvania) [Gallaudet University Archives, "Hearing children of deaf parents" subject vertical file]

Christy, M. (1982d, August 3). Conversations: Dreams and courage from her parents. Washington Times. (Washington, D. C.) [Gallaudet University Archives, "Louise Fletcher" biographical vertical file]

Clark, S. M. (1995, January). KODA group assists families with two cultures. Deaf Community News: Massachusetts State Association of the Deaf, 18 (1), 9. (Boston, Massachusetts) [UNIV DEAF Periodicals]

Cleveland, J. (1974, November 10). They needn't hear their babies cry to know the joys of parenthood. <u>Sun-Telegram,</u> pp. C1, C9. (San Bernardino, California) [Gallaudet University Archives, "Parent-child relationship - deaf adults" subject vertical file]

Cloud, J. H. (1918, April). Public opinion [Column]. <u>The Silent Worker, 30</u> (7), 23-24. {Includes an amazing quote from Amy Elisa Tanner's book, <u>The Child,</u> where she speaks of the causes of degeneracy (p. 5). Also has photos and captions of "Sons of the deaf in the war" including George H. Cloud, Herbert Beurmann, Jack and Howard Pach, Elliott Duprey, and Anthony Capelli, Jr.} [Gallaudet University Archives]

Coco, K. (1994, Spring). My dad, old deaf and dumb. <u>ALDA News: The Official Newsletter of the Association of Late-Deafened Adults, 8</u> (1), 2, 9. (Kevin is 12 years old) [UNIV DEAF Periodicals]

CODA. (1993, June). <u>British Deaf News Supplement, 24</u> (6), 3. [UNIV DEAF Periodicals]

CODA - Children of Deaf Adults. (1990, April). <u>WFD News,</u> No. 1, 21. (World Federation of the Deaf newsletter) [UNIV DEAF Periodicals]

CODA for the UK. (1990, May). <u>Soundbarrier,</u> No. 36, 5. (Publication of the Royal National Institute for the Deaf, London, England) [UNIV DEAF Periodicals]

CODA in the classroom. (1986, February). <u>CODA Newsletter, 3</u> (1), 3. {Ada Litchfield, author of <u>Words in Our Hands,</u> wrote a letter to the editor about her background and reasons for writing this book} [UNIV DEAF Periodicals]

Coda Olympian: Email news from Deaf Digest. (1998, May). <u>CODA Connection, 15</u> (2), 6. {Reports that Alexei Kobelev, a Russian coda, was interviewed at the Nagano Winter Olympics, February 21, 1998. He signed in Russian Sign Language to his deaf parents on television after the slalom event} [UNIV DEAF Periodicals]

CODA on the screen. (1986, February). <u>CODA Newsletter, 3</u> (1), 3. {Various comments of those who viewed *Love is Never Silent* on December 9, 1985, on NBC-TV} [UNIV DEAF Periodicals]

CODA scholarships for hearing children of deaf parents. (1996, April). <u>The NAD Broadcaster, 18</u> (4), 34. [UNIV DEAF Periodicals]

CODA sets a day to honor parents. (1996, April). <u>The Silent News, 28</u> (4), 18. [UNIV DEAF Periodicals]

Cohn, V. (1987, October 20). Typecast as a Medic. <u>The Washington Post (Health section).</u> (Washington, D. C.) {Louise Fletcher talks about her medical roles in films to a symposium on medicine and the arts} [Gallaudet University Archives, "Louise Fletcher" biographical vertical file]

Coleman, L. D. (1985, December 8). A sensitive drama about a family living with deafness and hearing [Commentary]. <u>Des Moines Register.</u> (Des Moines, Iowa) {The author was born in Mississippi, moved to Iowa in 1956 and has worked in the composing room at the Des Moines register for the past 22 years. He and his wife both have been deaf since birth and are the parents of five hearing children. They are active in the Iowa Association of the Deaf and the Des Moines Silent Club. "The film, *Love is Never Silent*, is an invitation for the deaf and the hearing to come together and see each other as important and able people."} [Gallaudet University Archives, "Love is Never Silent" subject vertical file]

College honored by President Johnson. (1964, June). <u>The Gallaudet Record, 9</u> (8), 1-2. {President Lyndon B.

Johnson spoke at the Centennial Banquet of Gallaudet College, June 6. A photo shows Elizabeth Benson interpreting his remarks} [Gallaudet University Archives and "Elizabeth English Benson, interpreter in the Language of Signs" biographical subject vertical file]

Colley, J. (1988, November). Codas speak out. CODA Newsletter, 5 (4), 2-3. [UNIV DEAF Periodicals]

Collier, M. (1997a, May). [Letter to the editor]. CODA Connection, 14 (2), 7. {Response to the proposal for an official "Christian Coda" group session} [UNIV DEAF Periodicals]

Collier, M. (1997b, May). One Coda's journey. CODA Connection, 14 (2), 14, 18. [UNIV DEAF Periodicals]

Collier, M. (1997c, September). More Codarado '97! [Letter to the editor]. CODA Connection, 14 (3), 8. [UNIV DEAF Periodicals]

Collins, G. (1986a, December 15). Children of deaf share their lives. The New York Times (Style), pp. C1, C16. (Also reprinted in The Des Moines Register as "Hearing children of deaf parents share experiences at conference," December, 1986, Des Moines, Iowa [*]) [UNIV Newspapers Microfilm]

Collins, G. (1986b, December 21). Hearing children of deaf parents share experiences at conference. Des Moines Register. (Des Moines, Iowa) {Story about a meeting at Marymount Manhattan College in New York. Annjoy and Alan Marcus, Mike Jacobs, Mary Ann Klein and Lou Ann Walker, all hearing offspring with deaf parents are quoted. Howard Busby and Samuel Landau, deaf parents with hearing children, are also quoted} [Gallaudet University Archives, "Hearing children of deaf parents" subject vertical file]

Collins, G. (1987a, March 31). Children of deaf share experiences. Herald-Journal. (Spartanburg, South Carolina) [Gallaudet University Archives, "Hearing children of deaf parents" subject vertical file]

Collins, G. (1987b, April 3). Children of deaf parents. Post. (Salisbury, North Carolina) {Pictured and interviewed are Alan and Annjoy Marcus, hearing children of deaf parents} [Gallaudet University Archives, "Hearing children of deaf parents" subject vertical file]

Colonomos, B. (1989, May). An open letter to deaf parents, hearing children of deaf parents, and others concerned with deaf people parenting hearing children. TBC News, No. 14, 1-2. (Reprinted in the Aug/Sept, 1989, issue of the CODA Connection, 6 (3), 3, 6. [UNIV DEAF Periodicals]) [UNIV DEAF Periodicals]

Colonomos, B. (1994, July/August). In celebration of a life: Ronald L. Coffey. TBC News, No. 69, 7. [UNIV DEAF Periodicals]

(*) Colonomos, M. (1997a, February). CODA love [Poem]. CODA Connection, 14 (1), 18. (Reprinted in the November, 1997, issue of the CODA Connection, 14 (4), 14. [UNIV DEAF Periodicals] and In R. Shipman (Ed.), "Once upon a time...:" Proceedings of the twelfth annual International CODA Conference, Denver, Colorado, July 10-13, 1997 (p. 107). Santa Barbara, CA: Children of Deaf Adults. [DEAF 306.874 I57o, 1997]) [UNIV DEAF Periodicals]

(*) Colonomos, M. (1997b, February). CODA Oscars [Poem]. CODA Connection, 14 (1), 18. [UNIV DEAF Periodicals]

(*) Colonomos, M. (1997c, May). CODA wall [Poem]. CODA Connection, 14 (2), 17. [UNIV DEAF Periodicals]

(*) **Colonomos, M. (1997d, September).** Coda child [Poem]. <u>CODA Connection, 14</u> (3), 15. [UNIV DEAF Periodicals]

(*) **Colonomos, M. (1997e, September).** Coda voice [Poem]. <u>CODA Connection, 14</u> (3), 15. [UNIV DEAF Periodicals]

Cominel, C. (1956, January 6). Parents deaf, but girl masters ventriloquism. <u>World-Telegram and Sun.</u> (New York) [Gallaudet University Archives, "Parent-child relationship - deaf adults" subject vertical file]

(#) **Commencement address [Photo and caption]. (year unspecified, June 4).** <u>The Washington Post.</u> (Washington, D. C.) {Mary E. Switzer of the Department of Health, Education and Welfare spoke at Gallaudet College's commencement. Elizabeth E. Benson, dean of women, interprets} [Gallaudet University Archives, "Elizabeth English Benson, interpreter in the Language of Signs" biographical subject vertical file]

Communication skills taught at UAB. (1988, January 13). <u>Cherokee County Herald.</u> (Centre, Alabama) {Reports Sue Noblin will teach a manual communication course} [Gallaudet University Archives, "American Sign Language - teaching" subject vertical file]

Community for deaf opposed. (1979, November 20). <u>Cumberland News.</u> (Cumberland, Maryland) [Gallaudet University Archives, "Rev. Louis W. Foxwell, Jr." biographical vertical file]

Compton, S. (1990, November 9). Learning to speak a "tongue of hands" [Book review of *In silence: Growing up hearing in a deaf world* by Ruth Sidransky]. <u>San Francisco Chronicle,</u> p. E12. (California) [*]

Conner, P. (1979, October 12). Daughter acts as voice, ears of deaf parents [Photos and story]. <u>Enterprise,</u> p. 1D. (Beaumont, Texas) {Feature story about Polly Walton, oldest daughter of deaf parents} [Gallaudet University Archives, "Parent-child relationship - deaf adults" subject vertical file]

Conrad, P. (1997, April-June). Stories in the news: Parents' lack of hearing failed to daunt loving family. <u>ACRID Newsletter,</u> 21. (ACRID is the Alberta Chapter of the Registry of Interpreters for the Deaf, Alberta, Canada - Reprinted from the <u>Calgary Herald,</u> April 10, 1996) [*]

Conwell, M. L. (1989, December 1). Fletcher not as wretched as Ratched. <u>The Mobile Press.</u> (Mobile, Alabama) [Gallaudet University Archives, "Louise Fletcher" biographical vertical file]

Coogan, M. (1996, February 5). Pia Walters wins noted poetry award. <u>On the Green: A Publication for Gallaudet University Staff and Faculty, 26</u> (8), 3. [Gallaudet University Archives or RESERVE]

Cooley, J. (1984, July 14). Iverson talks like a ballerina dances. <u>Outlook.</u> (Gresham, Oregon) {Features an interview with Trisha Iverson, daughter of deaf parents} [Gallaudet University Archives, "Hearing children of deaf parents" subject vertical file]

Cooper, C. (1980, April 16). Teacher's knowledge creates awareness of deaf world. <u>The Daily Sundial,</u> pp. 9-10. (Campus newspaper of the California State University, Northridge) {Joyce (Linden) Groode is interviewed about her career as assistant professor of special education at CSUN and about the personal resourcefulness of her deaf parents coping with parenting their hearing daughter} [*]

Cooper, K. (1988, November). Dear CODA members. <u>CODA Newsletter, 5</u> (4), 3. [UNIV DEAF Periodicals]

Corfmat, P. T. (1965, Autumn). Some thoughts of a hearing child of deaf parents. British Deaf News, 5 (1), 4-5. [UNIV DEAF Periodicals]

Cornell, C. (1985, December 9). TV tonight, evening highlights: *Love is Never Silent*. Inquirer. (Philadelphia, Pennsylvania) {A brief review of the Hallmark Hall of Fame special} [Gallaudet University Archives, "Parent-child relationship - deaf adults" subject vertical file]

Corry, J. (1985, December 9). *Love is Never Silent*, on deafness in a family [TV Reviews]. The New York Times. (New York) {This Hallmark Hall of Fame production is "family entertainment," with sentiment that "isn't saccharine," and uplift that "isn't cloying." It's a "tough-minded" and "handsome production...but doesn't quite touch us the way it should."} [Gallaudet University Archives, "Parent-child relationship - deaf adults" subject vertical file]

Cossel, A. (1994, Spring). Mom never gives up. ALDA News: The Official Newsletter of the Association of Late-Deafened Adults, 8 (1), 1-2. (Alissa is 11 years old) [UNIV DEAF Periodicals]

Cossel, L. (1994, Spring). Dear little old mom. ALDA News: The Official Newsletter of the Association of Late-Deafened Adults, 8 (1), 2. (Lori is 13 years old) [UNIV DEAF Periodicals]

Couple can't talk, but TV aids normal baby: Deaf parents "hear" with their hearts. (1955, March 28). Examiner. (Los Angeles, California) [Gallaudet University Archives, "Parent-child relationship - deaf adults" subject vertical file]

(#) Couple devote lives to teaching: See education of the deaf as great cause. (year unspecified, September 13). Utica Daily Press. (Utica, New York) [Gallaudet University Archives, "Warren Fauth" biographical vertical file]

Court decisions not always popular. (1965, January). The Gallaudet Record, 10 (4), 2. {Summary of Mr. Justice Douglas' speech. Accompanying photo shows Dr. Elizabeth Benson interpreting for Mr. Justice Douglas speaking at Gallaudet} [Gallaudet University Archives]

Coutts, K. (1994, September). Deaf parents/hearing children. British Deaf News, 25 (9), 8. {Reports on the "deaf parents hearing children" workshop and discussion at the British Deaf Association Meeting, Reading, England, July, 1994} [UNIV DEAF Periodicals]

Coutts, K., & Townsend-Handscomb, D. (1990, December). New group formed - "Hearing-Mother Father Deaf." British Deaf News, 21 (12), 7. [UNIV DEAF Periodicals]

Cowan, R. (1984, September 7). "Nurse Ratchett" [sic] is back...: Actress Louise Fletcher returns to scene of 1974 Academy Award-winning role. Statesman-Journal, pp. 1D, 5D. (Salem, Oregon) [Gallaudet University Archives, "Louise Fletcher" biographical vertical file]

Cowan, R. (1985, March 15). Made-in-area movie makes TV debut. Statesman-Journal. (Salem, Oregon) {Louise Fletcher appears in *A Summer to Remember*, the CBS-TV movie about the friendship of a deaf boy and an escaped orangutan. Louise Fletcher is a scientist who has taught Sign Language to Casey, the female orangutan} [Gallaudet University Archives, "Louise Fletcher" biographical vertical file]

Cowan, R. (1985, December 6). Movie an exception to rule: *Love is Never Silent* offers sensitive look at the deaf. Statesman-Journal. (Salem, Oregon) {A positive review of the film. "This is no sugar-coated pill, nor is it another tract about how badly we have treated the handicapped. Instead it is a thoughtful look at both sides and an unusual chronicle of how their attitudes have changed over the years."} [Gallaudet University Archives, "Parent-child relationship - deaf adults" subject vertical file]

Cowdrey, K. (1975, July 3). Children learn deaf language. West L.A. Independent. (Los Angeles, California) [Gallaudet University Archives, "Parent-child relationship - deaf adults" subject vertical file]

Cox, J. A. (Ed.). (1994). The health shelf: Paul Preston's *Mother father deaf* [Book review]. The Midwest Book Review. (Oregon, Wisconsin) [*]

Crammatte, F. (1973, Spring). A tribute to "Benny." The Phi Kappa Zetan, 11 (2), 1-2. (Official organ of the Phi Kappa Zeta Sorority) [Gallaudet University Archives, "Elizabeth English Benson: Obituary, memorial service" biographical subject vertical file]

Crash kills interpreter for Clinton: Served as translator for hearing impaired. (1993, January 15). Democrat-Gazette (Press Services). (Little Rock, Arkansas) [*]

Crocker, C. (1997, June). Hospitals in Maryland, New York sued over deaf access: New York attorney files eight lawsuits on behalf of hearing-impaired clients. Newswaves for Deaf and Hard-of-Hearing People, 1 (6), 4, 7. [UNIV DEAF Newspapers]

Croll, L. (1996, November). Can anyone explain to me what CODA is? CODA Connection, 13 (4), 1, 9. [UNIV DEAF Periodicals]

Crosby, J. (1982a, October 28). Fletcher aiding the deaf. Daily Item. (Sumter, South Carolina) {About Louise Fletcher} [Gallaudet University Archives, "Louise Fletcher" biographical vertical file]

Crosby, J. (1982b, November 20). Helper for hearing impaired. The Index Journal. (Greenwood, South Carolina) {About Louise Fletcher} [Gallaudet University Archives, "Louise Fletcher" biographical vertical file]

Cuckoo's Nest **sweeps top Oscars. (1976, March 30).** Review Journal. (Las Vegas, Nevada - From The Washington Post) [Gallaudet University Archives, "Louise Fletcher" biographical vertical file]

Cummins, D. (1986, December). The not-so-quiet sound of silence. St. Benedict's Parish Newsletter. (San Francisco, California) [*]

Dalton, A. (1987, April 12). Visual learning for deaf on brink of extinction? Richmond Times-Dispatch, p. F2. (Richmond, Virginia) [*]

Dalton, A. (1988a, November). Codas speak out. CODA Newsletter, 5 (4), 2. [UNIV DEAF Periodicals]

Dalton, A. (1988b, November). From the mailbox: An advocate speaks out. TBC News, No. 8, 3-4. [UNIV DEAF Periodicals]

Dalton, A. (1991, June). From the mailbox: Anyone else? TBC News, No. 37, 4. [UNIV DEAF Periodicals]

Daniels, R. S. (1994, Aug/Sept). [Letter to the editor and] A poem: Hearing child of deaf adults. CODA Connection, 11 (3), 7. [UNIV DEAF Periodicals]

Daughter of deaf couple plans book. (1983, July 5). Courier-Journal. (Louisville, Kentucky) [Gallaudet

University Archives, "Parent-child relationship - deaf adults" subject vertical file]

Daughter of deaf parents...Louise Fletcher shows promise as dramatic actress, attributes much of her talent to lifetime of familiarity with the Sign Language...has appeared in recent Television shows. (1959, March). The Silent Worker, 11 (7), 3-5, cover. {Includes a reprint of an article by Erskine Johnson ("Deaf parents 'made' star") from the Los Angeles Daily Mirror, January 6, 1959} [UNIV DEAF Periodicals or Archives]

Daughter of deaf parents now instructing in Paris. (1962, December). The Silent Worker, 15 (4), 9. [UNIV DEAF Periodicals]

Daughter of deaf parents receives Bachelor of Laws degree. (1937, June 18). The American Deaf Citizen. (Versailles, Ohio) {On June 10 Elizabeth E. Benson, daughter of Mr. and Mrs. Harry G. Benson, Frederick, Maryland, received her Bachelor of Laws degree from the Washington College of Law. Lists a variety of activities she was involved in during her Law School education} [Gallaudet University Archives and the "Elizabeth English Benson, biographical information and news clippings" biographical subject vertical file]

Daughter of deaf parents writes prize-winning essay on hiring handicapped. (1959, April). The Silent Worker, 11 (8), 12-13. [UNIV DEAF Periodicals]

Daughter returned to deaf couple. (1978, March 3). Philadelphia Bulletin. (Pennsylvania) [Gallaudet University Archives, "Court litigation - deaf" subject vertical file]

Davidson, M. (1990, September 20). "Circula Chase WEE-OOO," one of Ron Hillas's oil paintings on exhibit at Danica House [Photo]. The Independent. (Santa Barbara, California) [*]

Davis, L. J. (1990, August-September). Books [Review of *Useful gifts* by Carole L. Glickfeld]. CODA Connection, 7 (3), 5. [UNIV DEAF Periodicals]

Davis, L. J. (1991, March). About fathers: "I never sang for my father," raised by deaf parents, one dad savors his children's bitter sweet sounds. Parents Magazine, 66 (3), 222, 224. [UNIV Periodicals]

Davis, L. J. (1993, October 4). Hear ye? The prisoners of silence. The Nation, 256 (10), 354-356. {Jose Flores is deaf and was raised in a remote rural area of Puerto Rico. Teodoro Lopez was born in the Dominican Republic and was raised without the benefit of sign language. Charges were dropped against Charles Williams and Charles Graham because of the communication barriers involved. "Warehoused deaf people" have been found languishing in hospital or prison systems unable to communicate. Some of these deaf people are declared mentally incompetent. No consideration has been given to the concept of "linguistic incompetence" within our court systems as of yet. "A broader question is, How can society allow people to reach adulthood without a language?" A brilliant example of investigative reporting by a hearing journalist/academician whose parents were deaf} [*]

Day, C. A. (1975, January). Growing up with deaf parents. The Deaf American, 123 (1), 39-42. [UNIV DEAF Periodicals]

Day, J. P. (1975, October 27). Update: Foxwell's film-making takes new thrust under Griswold's direction. The Evening Sun. (Baltimore, Maryland) [Gallaudet University Archives, "Louis W. Foxwell" biographical vertical file]

"Deaf city" opposed. (1979, November 21). Evening Times. (Cumberland, Maryland) [Gallaudet University Archives, "Rev. Louis W. Foxwell, Jr." biographical vertical file]

Deaf couple face problem in baby. (1955, March 28). Valley Times. (North Hollywood, California) [Gallaudet University Archives, "Parent-child relationship - deaf adults" subject vertical file]

Deaf couple's life bittersweet. (1978, June 9). The News Tribune. (Woodbridge, New Jersey) [Gallaudet University Archives, "Parent-child relationship - deaf adults" subject vertical file]

Deaf couple wanted "baby that hears." (1979, December 2). Journal. (Rapid City, South Dakota) [Gallaudet University Archives, "Parent-child relationship - deaf adults" subject vertical file]

Deaf enter a new life with "Signs." (1955, July 3). Des Moines, Iowa, Register. [Gallaudet University Archives, "Children of deaf adults" subject vertical file]

Deaf, hearing educators at Vista Community College create nation's first standard ASL curriculum: 175 U. S. colleges set to replicate model.... (1988, Spring). The Deaf American, 38 (2), 9-10. [UNIV DEAF Periodicals]

Deaf leader opposes "Deaf City." (1979, November 20). Home like prison, deaf woman testifies. Washington Star. (Washington, D. C.) [Gallaudet University Archives, "Rev. Louis W. Foxwell, Jr." biographical vertical file]

Deaf mother of the year. (1990, Oct.-Nov.). The V.A.D. Bulletin, 31 (2), 1. (Newsletter of the Virginia Association of the Deaf) [UNIV DEAF Periodicals]

Deaf mute couple wins adoption fight [People in the news column]. (1967, September 20). The Evening Star, p. A2. (Washington, D. C.) [Gallaudet University Archives, "Parent-child relationship - deaf adults" subject vertical file]

Deaf pair lose child custody: Husband held to Grand Jury. (1956, March 26). Herald. (Clinton, Iowa) [Gallaudet University Archives, "Parent-child relationship - deaf adults" subject vertical file]

Deaf pair win custody of daughter. (1978, March 4). New Bedford Standard Times. (New Bedford, Massachusetts) [Gallaudet University Archives, "Court litigation - deaf" subject vertical file]

Deaf parent response. (1987, February). CODA Newsletter, 4 (1), 3. [UNIV DEAF Periodicals]

Deaf parents aided actress. (1976, March 31). Cincinnati Enquirer. (Cincinnati, Ohio) [Gallaudet University Archives, "Louise Fletcher" biographical vertical file]

Deaf parents are happy when baby is born deaf. (1995, January). The Silent News, 27 (1), 16. (Reprinted from the Toledo, Ohio, Blade, October 11, 1994) [UNIV DEAF Periodicals]

Deaf parents, attention! (1949, October). The Silent Worker, 2 (2), 17. {The Silent Worker announces the revival of a universally enjoyed feature from the old Silent Worker, photographs and biographical sketches of children of deaf parents. "Nothing so quickly and easily dispelled doubts as to a deaf person's fitness for parenthood as did this pictorial proof of well-kept homes and happy family life."} [UNIV DEAF Periodicals]

Deaf parents: Honor yours. (1996, May). Deaf Life Plus: Supplement to Deaf Life, 8 (11), 6-9. {Includes an announcement about "Mother Father Deaf Day" and related papers: "Some notable children of deaf adults" and "Dispelling myths about deaf parenting."} [UNIV DEAF Periodicals]

Deaf parents influence Stangarone (1972, June-July). NTID Focus, 12, 15. (Publication of the National Technical

Institute for the Deaf, Rochester, New York) [UNIV DEAF Periodicals]

Deaf parents of hearing child in Fla. get NCLD support in custody case. (1986, January 13). On the Green: A Weekly Publication for Gallaudet Staff and Faculty, 16 (12), 1, 3. {Joe and Shirlene Timmons of Okeechobee, Florida, receive help from the National Center for Law and the Deaf to regain custody of their 3-year-old son, Joey. The Florida Department of Health and Rehabilitative Services "contends that because the Timmonses are deaf, their children will not receive enough oral and auditory stimulation."} [Gallaudet University Archives]

Deaf parents played by Ed Waterstreet and Phyllis Frelich [Photo and caption]. (1985, December 9). Press. (Savannah, Georgia) [Gallaudet University Archives, "Love is Never Silent" subject vertical file]

Deaf parents regain child. (1978, March 2). San Francisco Examiner. (California) [Gallaudet University Archives, "Court litigation - deaf" subject vertical file]

Deaf parents watch Louise accept Oscar. (1976, March 31). Journal. (Atlanta, Georgia) [Gallaudet University Archives, "Louise Fletcher" biographical vertical file]

The deaf "speak" at Long Wharf. (1968, September 15). Connecticut Herald. (Fairfield, Connecticut) [Gallaudet University Archives, "Louie Fant" biographical vertical file]

Deaf struggle in 1925 America: December TV drama. (1985, December 12). Living through the night: Young, deaf, and Jewish, Rose faced the Nazis with her baby, her husband, and lots of courage. The World Around You: A publication of Pre-College Programs, Gallaudet University, 7 (6), back cover. Washington, DC: Gallaudet University, Pre-College Programs. {Announcement that *Love is Never Silent* will be on television and stars among others, Susan Ann Curtis, the daughter of deaf parents} [Gallaudet University Archives]

Deaf worshipers aided by "traveling parson." (1958, April 4). The Evening Star. (Washington, D. C.) [Gallaudet University Archives, "Louis W. Foxwell" biographical vertical file]

Dean at Gallaudet: Devotes life to helping the deaf. (1960, July 5). The Globe and Mail, 11. (Toronto, Ontario, Canada) {A general article about Gallaudet College which features Elizabeth Benson, dean of women, who was in Toronto for the Diamond Jubilee Convention of the Ontario Association for the Deaf} [Gallaudet University Archives, "Elizabeth English Benson, biographical information and news clippings" biographical subject vertical file]

Dean Benson retiring after 44 years on Gallaudet staff. (1970, May 21). The News, p. A7. (Frederick, Maryland) [Gallaudet University Archives, "Elizabeth English Benson: Obituary, memorial service" biographical subject vertical file]

Dean Elizabeth Benson honored by BPW. (1965, Feb-March). The Gallaudet Record, 10 (5), 1. {Dr. Elizabeth E. Benson, Dean of Women at Gallaudet, has been named "Woman of the Year" by the Frederick, Maryland, Business and Professional Women's Club and by the Western District of the Maryland Federation of BPW Clubs} [Gallaudet University Archives, "Elizabeth English Benson, citations and awards" biographical subject vertical file]

Dean of Women at Gallaudet appointed to *Annals* staff. (1964, April). AHS Bulletin Board, 2. (Published by the American Hearing Society) {Dr. Elizabeth E. Benson, dean of women at Gallaudet College, has been named associate editor of *The American Annals of the Deaf*} [Gallaudet University Archives, "Elizabeth English Benson, Associate Editor of the American Annals of the Deaf" biographical subject vertical file]

Dean, R. (1961, October 29). Her flying fingers talk. The Sunday Star, p. H6. (Washington, D. C.) {Although the focus of this article is on Elizabeth Benson who "has made working with the deaf her life's work," it's published the day she will interpret Cardinal Spellman's sermon at the Crusade of Prayer for Peace at the Washington Monument grounds} [Gallaudet University Archives and the "Elizabeth English Benson, biographical information and news clippings" biographical subject vertical file]

Dean to speak. (1963, March 16). Star, p. A15. (Washington, D. C.) {Miss Elizabeth Benson, dean of women at Gallaudet College, will be principal speaker at the annual athletic banquet of the Governor Baxter State School for the Deaf in Portland, Maine} [Gallaudet University Archives, "Elizabeth English Benson, Addresses to various organizations" biographical subject vertical file]

Dear Stella [Letter to Stella]. (1996, December). Silent News, 28 (12), 11. (Letter is signed "C.O.D.A. Problem." Reprinted in the February, 1997, issue of the CODA Connection, 14 (1), 18. [UNIV DEAF Periodicals]) [UNIV DEAF Periodicals]

(#) Death takes Lon Chaney, movie star: Master of makeup succumbs to pneumonia in Los Angeles. (1930, August 26). Buffalo Times, p. 1. (Buffalo, New York) [*]

de Courtivron, I. (1997, December 14). Rebel without a cause: Albert Camus would not let himself be forced into taking fashionable positions [Book review of Albert Camus: A life by Olivier Todd]. The New York Times Book Review, 102 (50), pp. 14-15, cover. {There are oblique references to Camus' mother's deafness. She is, for example, described as "the mother whose world consisted of silence, hard work and poverty." (p. 15) If Camus was a coda, it's interesting to know that he received the Nobel Prize for Literature in 1957} [*]

DeLorenzo, K. (1998, March 18). Interpreters discuss their experiences during DPN [Deaf President Now movement in 1988]. On the Green: A Publication for Gallaudet Faculty, Teachers, and Staff, 28 (20), 1-2. {This panel of interpreters discusses their involvement in this historic event ten years ago. Among those on the panel are Brenda Marshall, Sheila Deane and Tom Bull who are codas} [UNIV DEAF Periodicals]

Demmon, C. (1987, September 4). Having deaf parents had its advantages. Monterey Peninsula Herald. (Monterey, California) {Sharon Neumann Solow is featured} [Gallaudet University Archives, "Parent-child relationship - deaf adults" subject vertical file]

Dencker-Hill, D. (1985, December 18). "Bilingual" Bray carries message with her hands. Hacienda Heights Highlander. (Hacienda Heights, California) {About Betty Bray, the hearing daughter of deaf parents} [Gallaudet University Archives, "Hearing children of deaf parents" subject vertical file]

Dicker, E. (1994, November). It's my turn. CODA Connection, 11 (4), 11. [UNIV DEAF Periodicals]

Dickerson, L. B. (1950, August). Children of the deaf: BABY ROYALTY. The Silent Worker, 2 (12), 12. [UNIV DEAF Periodicals]

Dimmock, A. F. (Ed.). (1988, November). A girdle around the earth column: USA. British Deaf News, 19 (11), 9. {In the paragraph on "ETHIOPIA" it's reported that deaf parent members of the Ethiopian National Association of the Deaf who have hearing children are fighting claims that "the verbal abilities of children of deaf parents are not so well developed as those of hearing parents." In the "USA" paragraph it's reported that a Michigan deaf mother is awarded custody of her two young hearing children on appeal. The hearing grandparents were fighting for custody contending the children "needed to be exposed to persons with oral language skills in order to develop their ability to communicate on a regular basis."} [UNIV DEAF Periodicals]

Dimmock, A. F. (Ed.). (1994, December). Girdle: USA. British Deaf News, 25 (12), 17. [UNIV DEAF Periodicals]

Dishneau, D. (1980, January 18). Deaf couple sells 40s home for $1,500, sues. Herald-Leader. (Menominee, Michigan) [*]

Dispelling myths about deaf parenting. (1997, February). CODA Connection, 14 (1), 5. (Excerpts - Reprinted in the May, 1998, issue of The Silent News, 30 (5), B12) [UNIV DEAF Periodicals]

Dixon, Y. (1976, April 29). Stars shine for handicapped. The Washington Star. (Washington, D. C.) {Reports on the Bicentennial festival presented by the President's Committee for the Handicapped at the Kennedy Center. Louise Fletcher was among the participants mentioned} [Gallaudet University Archives, "Louise Fletcher" biographical vertical file]

Does ASL improve spoken English? (1993, August). DCARA News, 12. (Newsletter of the Deafness Counseling, Advocacy and Referral Agency serving the San Francisco Bay Area. Main office in San Leandro, California) [UNIV DEAF Periodicals]

Dole, K. (1961, October 30). Huge crowd prays here for peace: Catholic crusade attracts 125,000 to outdoor Mass. The Washington Post, 84th year, No. 329, p. A1. (Washington, D. C.) {Francis Cardinal Spellman, Archbishop of New York, celebrated the concluding Washington Monument Mass of the Crusade of Prayer for World Peace, an observance by Catholics of the Archdiocese of Washington, D. C. "A Gallaudet dean, Elizabeth Benson, 'signed' his words as fast as he spoke to 50 deaf students near the altar."} [Gallaudet University Archives, "Elizabeth English Benson, interpreter in the Language of Signs" biographical subject vertical file]

(*) Dollard, V. (1988, Winter/Spring). Shared memories. NTID Focus, 24-25. (Publication of the National Technical Institute for the Deaf, Rochester, New York. Reprinted in T. H. Bull (Ed.), Reflections: Codas and cultures, proceedings of the second National CODA Conference, Rochester, New York, August 21-23, 1987 (3rd rev. ed., pp. 74-75). Santa Barbara, CA: Children of Deaf Adults. The Gallaudet University Library also has the first edition [DEAF 306.874 N3, 1987] and the second edition [DEAF 306.874 N3, 1987b]. The third edition is [DEAF 306.874 N3, 1987a]) [UNIV DEAF Periodicals]

Donovan, D. (1988, May 8). Children are sounds of happy household for deaf mother of 12. The Pittsburgh Press. (Pittsburgh, Pennsylvania) [Gallaudet University Archives, "Hearing children of deaf parents" subject vertical file]

Dorin, J. S. (1976, May 2). "I hope we can meet the needs of the deaf." Irving, Texas, News. [Gallaudet University Archives, "Parent-child relationship - deaf adults" subject vertical file]

Dorman, E. (1997, May). [Letter to the editor]. CODA Connection, 14 (2), 9. {Response to the proposal for an official "Christian Coda" group session} [UNIV DEAF Periodicals]

Dorsey, S. H. (1952, October). Children of the deaf...Ruth Oordt, Queen's Attendant, Tulip Festival. The Silent Worker, 5 (2), 10. [UNIV DEAF Periodicals]

Double take: Sitting pretty. (1994, March 9). The Washington Post, 117th year, No. 94, p. F2. (Washington, D. C.) [UNIV Newspapers Microfilm]

Dougan, M. (1985a, December 6). Milestone for deaf [Television review]. Examiner. (San Francisco, California) {An interview with Ed Waterstreet, one of the professional deaf actors in a Hallmark Hall of Fame presentation *Love is Never Silent*} [Gallaudet University Archives, "Parent-child relationship - deaf adults" subject vertical file]

Dougan, M. (1985b, December 9). *Love* breakthrough for deaf actors. <u>Tribune.</u> (Tulsa, Oklahoma) {Interview with Ed Waterstreet, one of the professional deaf actors in the Hallmark Hall of Fame film *Love is Never Silent*} [Gallaudet University Archives, "Parent-child relationship - deaf adults" subject vertical file]

Dougan, M. (1985c, December 9). *Never Silent* is milestone, co-star says. <u>Post-Herald.</u> (Birmingham, Alabama) {Positive review and interview with Ed Waterstreet, one of the professional deaf actors in this Hallmark Hall of Fame presentation} [Gallaudet University Archives, "Parent-child relationship - deaf adults" subject vertical file]

Draft-free mutes prove superior in war jobs. (1944, November). <u>North Dakota Banner.</u> (Publication of the North Dakota School for the Deaf, Devil's Lake, North Dakota. Reprinted from <u>The News and Courier</u> of Charleston, South Carolina) {Explains that one contribution "the silents" have made to the war effort is through their children who "are not similarly afflicted."} [Gallaudet University Archives, "World War II" subject vertical file]

Dr. Benson, educator of the deaf. (1972, December 15). <u>Morning Sun.</u> (Baltimore, Maryland) [Gallaudet University Archives, "Elizabeth English Benson: Obituary, memorial service" biographical subject vertical file]

Dr. Elizabeth Benson, educator of deaf, dies. (1972, December 14). <u>The News.</u> (Frederick, Maryland) [Gallaudet University Archives, "Elizabeth English Benson: Obituary, memorial service" biographical subject vertical file]

Dr. Elizabeth Benson honored. (1967, November). <u>The Nebraska Journal, 97</u> (2), 2. (Publication of the Nebraska School for the Deaf, Omaha. The article by-line is <u>Dee Cee Eyes,</u> deaf community publication from Washington, D. C.) {Dr. Elizabeth E. Benson has been named 1967 Woman of the Year in Education by the women's Advertising Club of Washington, [D. C.]} [Gallaudet University Archives, "Elizabeth English Benson, citations and awards" biographical subject vertical file]

Dr. Elizabeth Benson honored at Fort Sam Houston. (1973, April 15). <u>The Lone Star, 94</u> (14), 1-2. (Publication of the Texas School for the Deaf) {On March 30, a new dormitory complex at the Army Medical Training Center, Fort Sam Houston, was dedicated. "The building which will house members of the Women's Army Corps was named and dedicated *Benson Dormitory* in honor of Dr. Elizabeth English Benson, late dean of women at Gallaudet College."} [Gallaudet University Archives, "Elizabeth English Benson, citations and awards" biographical subject vertical file]

Dr. Benson receives citation. (1971, March 26). <u>The News.</u> (Frederick, Maryland) {Miss Elizabeth E. Benson of Frederick...will be among 20 distinguished members of the National Association of Women Deans and Counselors cited by the association at the[ir] National convention in St. Louis on March 26." The article included the full text of the citation} [Gallaudet University Archives, "Elizabeth English Benson, citations and awards" biographical subject vertical file]

Dr. Elizabeth Benson speaks at our school. (1964, May). <u>The Oregon Outlook, 72</u> (8), 1. (Published by the Oregon State School for the Deaf, Salem Oregon) {Summary of the many opportunities Dr. Benson had to speak with students and professionals, many of whom are her friends and acquaintances} [Gallaudet University Archives, "Elizabeth English Benson, Addresses to various organizations" biographical subject vertical file]

Dr. Elizabeth E. Benson, former Dean at Gallaudet. (1972, December 15). <u>Washington Star.</u> (Washington, D. C.) [Gallaudet University Archives, "Elizabeth English Benson: Memorials" biographical subject vertical file]

Dr. Elizabeth E. Benson, former Dean at Gallaudet. (1972, December 15). The Star and News. (Washington, D. C.) [Gallaudet University Archives, "Elizabeth English Benson: Obituary, memorial service" biographical subject vertical file]

Drozdiak, Wm. (1994, April 26). Camus, a stranger no more: Novelist's last draft reveals personal life. The Washington Post, pp. E1, E4. [UNIV Newspapers Microfilm]

Dumas, A. (1997, August 29). Laughs from the sounds of silence. Rocky Mountain News. (Denver, Colorado) {Brian Diamond is a comedian who gets some of his comedic material from being hearing with deaf parents} [*]

Dupree educational fund. (1990, December). Deaf Life: Deaf Life Plus, 3 (6), 19. [UNIV DEAF Periodicals]

Dying hero finds solace by signs. (1945, February). The Cavalier, 5 (6), 1 {Letter from Lt. Cmdr. - and surgeon - George M. McClure, Jr., U.S.N., to his father} [Gallaudet University Archives]

East, V. K. (1985, December 8). Children of the deaf live in two worlds. Tennessean, pp. 6E-7E. (Nashville, Tennessee) [Gallaudet University Archives, "Children of deaf adults" subject vertical file]

Edelstein, A. J. (1985, December 8). CBS launches 2nd season with sitcoms [The week's highlights]. Reporter Dispatch. (White Plains, New York) {Brief mention of Love is Never Silent and that Yonkers native Sid Caesar has a co-starring role as a Greek pawnbroker} [Gallaudet University Archives, "Parent-child relationship - deaf adults" subject vertical file]

Edward F., son of Benjamin Elkins [Photo and caption]. (1918, March). The Silent Worker, 30 (6), 107. {Edward is on the U.S.S. North Dakota after enlisting in the Navy, November, 1916} [UNIV DEAF Periodicals]

Edward Mayne and Calford Johnson [Photo and caption]. (1923, March). The Silent Worker, 35 (5), 230. {Edward is 4 1/2 years old and Calford is 8 months old. The parents, Mr. and Mrs. Morris, are of Devils Lake, North Dakota. Father is an instructor in printing at the North Dakota School for the Deaf} [UNIV DEAF Periodicals]

Edwards, E. (1990, July 9). Developing potential: Teacher works with gifted kids. Kenosha Life, p. 7. (Kenosha, Wisconsin) [*]

Eisenberger, L. (1979, June 19). Youngster aide to handicapped parents. The News Tribune. (Woodbridge, New Jersey) [Gallaudet University Archives, "Children of deaf adults" subject vertical file]

Eklof, D. (1993, November). CODA reflections. CODA Connection, 10 (4), 9. [UNIV DEAF Periodicals]

Eli Savanick. (1993, Aug/Sept). CODA Connection, 10 (3), 9. [UNIV DEAF Periodicals]

Elizabeth Benson dies; ex-Dean at Gallaudet. (1972, December 12). Evening Star. (Washington, D. C.) [Gallaudet University Archives, "Elizabeth English Benson: Obituary, memorial service" biographical subject vertical file]

Elizabeth Benson named editor. (1964, February 21). The Washington Post. (Washington, D. C.) {Dr. Elizabeth E. Benson, dean of women at Gallaudet College, has been named associate editor of The American Annals of the Deaf} [Gallaudet University Archives, "Elizabeth English Benson, Associate Editor of the American Annals of the Deaf" biographical subject vertical file]

Elizabeth Benson now 2nd lieutenant [photo]. (1945, April). The Cavalier (Akron Edition), 5 (8), 1. [Gallaudet University Archives]

(#) Elizabeth Benson visitor at school: W. A. C. teacher of speech reading at hospital calls here. (n.d.). (Newspaper unidentified) [Gallaudet University Archives, "World War II" subject vertical file]

Elizabeth English Benson. (1972, December 18). Newsday. (Long Island, New York) [Gallaudet University Archives, "Elizabeth English Benson: Obituary, memorial service" biographical subject vertical file]

Elizabeth Weeks Bennison [Photo and caption]. (1918, May). The Silent Worker, 30 (8), 148. {The photo is of 8-months-old Elizabeth, daughter of Mr. and Mrs. William Bennison, of Trenton, N. J. Caption says "Betty is now 10 months old and, like most other children of deaf parents, enjoys full possession of the sense of hearing."} [UNIV DEAF Periodicals]

Elkins, E. F. (1994, December). [Letter to the editor]. Views, 11 (11), 20. (Registry of Interpreters for the Deaf newsletter) {About his opposition to the formation of a special interest group for codas} [UNIV DEAF Periodicals]

Elstad, Benson honored by student groups. (1966, May-June). The Gallaudet Record, 11 (9), 2. {On May 25, at the 1966 annual awards day of Gallaudet College, it was announced that Dean Benson had been named 1966 Woman of the Year by the Women's Recreation Association} [Gallaudet University Archives and the "Elizabeth English Benson, citations and awards" biographical subject vertical file]

E. M. Gallaudet's birthday honored. (1944, February 18). The Buff and Blue, 52 (8), pp. 1, 4. (Student newspaper of the Gallaudet Student Body Government) [UNIV Archives]

Ensenat, D. (1994, November). The CODA Distinguished Service Award established. CODA Connection, 11 (4), 2. [UNIV DEAF Periodicals]

Ensenat, D. (1997, May). [Letter to the editor]. CODA Connection, 14 (2), 8. {Response to the proposal for an official "Christian Coda" group session} [UNIV DEAF Periodicals]

Eron, C. (1986, November 7). Book world: The trials of a silent love, review of *A loss for words* by Lou Ann Walker. The Washington Post, pp. C6-C7. (Washington, D. C.) [UNIV Newspapers Microfilm]

Expert on Sign Language to address Masquers. (1968, November 19). Courant. (Hartford, Connecticut) [Gallaudet University Archives, "Louie Fant" biographical vertical file]

Faculty members busy in varied activities. (1960, February). The Gallaudet Record, 5 (2), 3. [Gallaudet University Archives and "Louie Fant" biographical vertical file]

Fail, G. (Ed.). (1952, August). Swinging 'round the nation [Photo with caption]. The Silent Worker, 4 (12), 14-21. {The Carlos W. Seegmillers of Ogdon, Utah, are mentioned along with their children Stephen, Carlos, Jr., and Patricia} [UNIV DEAF Periodicals]

Fail, G. (Ed.). (1965, May). NEWS from 'round the Nation [Photo and caption]. The Deaf American, 17 (9), 15. {Jerry Connor is featured} [UNIV DEAF Periodicals]

A fair deal for deaf parents [Editorial]. (1990, February). The Silent News, 22 (2), 2. [UNIV DEAF Periodicals]

Fairweather, J. (1995, November). My place: A poem. <u>CODA Connection, 12</u> (4), 4. [UNIV DEAF Periodicals]

FAMILY: Jim and Diana Merchant play game with Derek and Jessica. (1980, March-April). <u>The Washingtonian, 84</u> (4), 7-9. (Newsletter of the Washington School for the Deaf, Vancouver) [UNIV DEAF Periodicals]

Family life in the deaf community. (1994, January). <u>British Deaf News, 25</u> (1), 9-11. [UNIV DEAF Periodicals]

Fant, L. (1962, December). Miss Kenney, go home? <u>The New Mexico Progress, 55</u> (3), 1. (Publication of the New Mexico School for the Deaf, Santa Fe, New Mexico - This article was rejected by <u>Harper's Magazine</u> but reprinted in <u>The Silent Worker</u>) [Gallaudet University Archives, "Louie Fant" biographical vertical file]

Fant, L. (1974-1975, Winter). Ameslan. <u>Gallaudet Today, 5</u> (2), 1-2. [Gallaudet University Archives and "Louie Fant" biographical vertical file]

Fant, L. J., Jr. (1971, June). Mr. Fant replies to Mr. Prickett [Letter to the editor]. <u>The Deaf American, 23</u> (10), 32-33. [UNIV DEAF Periodicals]

Farninham, M. (1974, May). To the Reverend Louis W. Foxwell [Poem]. <u>Deaf Fellowship News,</u> 2. (Chicago Temple, Chicago, Illinois) [Gallaudet University Archives, "Louis W. Foxwell" biographical vertical file]

Feature: The year of the family. (1995, January). <u>British Deaf News, 25</u> (1), 9-11. [UNIV DEAF Periodicals]

Feds forget "basic arithmetic." (1982, July/August). <u>Up Front, 2</u> (11). {Quotes from Louise Fletcher's Commencement address to graduates of Gallaudet College, May, 1982} [Gallaudet University Archives, "Louise Fletcher" biographical vertical file]

Feiner, P. (1986, Sept. 28). Living in a silent world [Letters to the editor] . <u>The New York Times Magazine,</u> 102. [UNIV Newspapers Microfilm]

Feinstein, J. (1978, August 5). Deaf patient beats the system. <u>The Washington Post.</u> (Washington, D. C.) [Gallaudet University Archives, "Court litigation - deaf" subject vertical file]

Felton, D. (1966, August 2). Baby again ordered taken from deaf couple: Infant becomes pawn in legal battle between Judge and Court. <u>The Los Angeles Times</u> (part 2), p. 1. (Los Angeles, California - Another reference to the same article is from the <u>San Fernando Valley News</u>) {About the Christensen custody case} [*]

Fetherston, D. (1985, December 9). An eloquent story of the non-hearing. <u>Newsday.</u> (Long Island, New York) {Positive review of *Love is Never Silent* that focuses on the three deaf actors, Ed Waterstreet, Phyllis Frelich and Julianna Fjeld. Ten-year-old Susan Ann Curtis wrote to the producer Dorothea Petrie for the part of Margaret as a young girl. Susan, like her character, "is the hearing child of deaf parents and knows sign language."} [Gallaudet University Archives, "Parent-child relationship - deaf adults" subject vertical file]

Fighting child abuse [Photo and caption]. (1990, April 9). <u>Times-News.</u> (Twin Falls, Idaho) [*]

Fink, L. (1986, February). Abstract: A child's subculture, the experience of growing up in the deaf culture. <u>CODA Newsletter, 3</u> (1), 5. [UNIV DEAF Periodicals]

Finnell, M. N. (1961, November). My parents are deaf. <u>Life Workshop Quarterly, 7</u> (2), 1. (National publication for the parents of hearing impaired children) [Gallaudet University Archives, "Mabel N. Finnell" biographical vertical file]

First WAC in Paris daughter of deaf. (1944, November). The Cavalier, 5 (3), 1. {Pfc. Pfunder is the daughter of Mr. and Mrs. William Pfunder of Akron, Ohio} [Gallaudet University Archives]

Fishman, D. J. (1992, January). 1991: Human biology, out of the mouths - and hands - of babes. Discover, 13 (1), 66. (Reprinted in the April, 1995, issue of Deaf Life, 7 (10), 3, 22-23. [UNIV DEAF Periodicals]) [UNIV Periodicals]

(*) Flanagan, R. (1990, May). My bicultural experience [The 1990 CODA Millie Brother Scholarship winning essay]. CODA Connection, 7 (2), 6. (Reprinted in D. Prickett & R. Prickett (Eds.), Richness in our diversity: Proceedings of the tenth International CODA Conference, Research Triangle Park, North Carolina, July 27-30, 1995 (p. 120). Santa Barbara, CA: Children of Deaf Adults. [On order]) [UNIV DEAF Periodicals]

Flander, J. (1984, October 2). TV Tonight: TV talk. Cape Cod Times. (Hyannis, Massachusetts) {"Louise Fletcher speaks and signs simultaneously as she pays tribute to Thomas Gallaudet on An American Portrait on channel 6 and 7."} [Gallaudet University Archives, "Louise Fletcher" biographical vertical file]

Flander, J. (1985, December 9). Made-for-TV Alice offers great change [TV highlights]. Rocky Mountain News. (Denver, Colorado) {Brief positive mention of Love is Never Silent. A "remarkable drama about the isolation of the deaf."} [Gallaudet University Archives, "Parent-child relationship - deaf adults" subject vertical file]

Flash!!! Dr. Elizabeth Benson to speak at convention banquet. (1952, August). Empire State News, 14 (3), 1, 4. (Official organ of the Empire State Association of the Deaf) {Dr. Benson will speak at the convention banquet, August 30, 1952, at the Hotel Utica} [Gallaudet University Archives, "Elizabeth English Benson, Addresses to various organizations" biographical subject vertical file]

Fleese, K. (1995, May). Mothers' group helps members handle concerns. Deaf Community News: Massachusetts State Association of the Deaf, 18 (5), 3. (Boston, Massachusetts) [UNIV DEAF Periodicals]

Fleishman, A. (1989, January 15). Lon Chaney not deaf. Sun-Sentinel. (Ft. Lauderdale, Florida) [Gallaudet University Archives, "Lon Chaney" biographical vertical file]

A flock has lost its shepherd. (1974, March 29). The Sign Post, 3 (7), 14. [Gallaudet University Archives, "Louis W. Foxwell" biographical vertical file]

Flood, J. T. (1962, February 10). Miss Benson signs for V. P. Johnson: Gallaudet's Dean Benson Columbus dinner speaker. The Ohio Chronicle, 99 (18), 1. (Publication of the Ohio School for the Deaf, Columbus) {Includes a photo of Dean Elizabeth Benson signing Vice President Lyndon Johnson. Includes a summary of her speech and events around her visit to Columbus} [Gallaudet University Archives, "Elizabeth English Benson, Addresses to various organizations" biographical subject vertical file]

Florida agency drops suit, parents keep son. (1986, June). Gallaudet Alumni Newsletter, 20 (12), 4. [Gallaudet University Archives]

Flynn, L. (1992, June). Consumers speak out on...the cost of interpreting services. Views, 9 (6), 1, 4-5. (Registry of Interpreters for the Deaf newsletter. Reprinted in the May, 1992, issue of the CODA Connection, 9 (2), 7. [UNIV DEAF Periodicals]) [UNIV DEAF Periodicals]

Foggy Bottom. (1956, January). <u>The George Washington University Federalist,</u> 29. {Miss Elizabeth Benson is mentioned as one of those honored as alumnae of distinction at the Fall tea of Columbian Women} [Gallaudet University Archives, "Elizabeth English Benson, citations and awards" biographical subject vertical file]

Fox, C. (1990, April 16-30). Sign in here: Sign Language and interpreting programs offer challenges and jobs. <u>Valley Outlook,</u> pp. 4, 22. (San Fernando Valley, California) [Gallaudet University Archives, "Children of deaf adults" subject vertical file]

Fradkin, P. (1967, May 23). Court overrules jurist, says deaf-mute pair may adopt boy. <u>The Los Angeles Times,</u> 86 (part 1), pp. 1, 23. (See the <u>San Fernando Valley News</u> for the same article) [*]

Frances, E. (1973, May). America's Teacher of the Year. <u>Ladies' Home Journal, 40</u> (5), 68, 70. [Gallaudet University Archives, "Parent-child relationship - deaf adults" and "Jack Ensworth" biographical vertical file]

Francis, T. M. (1996, March). Special Interest Groups: HIDP SIG [Letter to the editor]. <u>Views, 13</u> (3), 4. (Registry of Interpreters for the Deaf newsletter) [UNIV DEAF Periodicals]

Freedman, S. (1997, May). [Letter to the editor]. <u>CODA Connection, 14</u> (2), 8. {Response to the proposal for an official "Christian Coda" group session} [UNIV DEAF Periodicals]

Friedman, D. (1985, December 9). Let's hear it for *Love is Never Silent* [Television review]. <u>Daily News.</u> (Philadelphia, Pennsylvania) {A very positive review pointing out "the lion's share of the credit must go to Mare Winningham, Phyllis Frelich and Ed Waterstreet, who not only make their characters believable, but memorable."} [Gallaudet University Archives, "Love is Never Silent" subject vertical file]

Friend in need [Photo and caption]. (1985, December 8). <u>Star.</u> (Indianapolis, Indiana) {Photo of Margaret Ryder (Mare Winningham) looking longingly at the radio in a Greek pawnshop owned by Mr. Petrakis (Sid Caesar) in the new TV movie, *Love is Never Silent*} [Gallaudet University Archives, "Parent-child relationship - deaf adults" subject vertical file]

Friess, S. (1973, August 23). Young hands allow others to hear. <u>Macomb Daily,</u> pp. 1A, 4A. (Mt. Clemens, Michigan) [Gallaudet University Archives, "Parent-child relationship - deaf adults" subject vertical file]

Fultz quads [Letters to the editor]. (1969, February). <u>Ebony, 24</u> (4), 14, 16-17. {Written in response to a story about the Fultz quadruplets in the November, 1968, <u>Ebony.</u> Letters were by Gwendolyn Copper, Christine Griffin, Jeanne E. Little, Jerald Wilson, and Enid Richardson} [Gallaudet University Archives, "Parent-child relationship - deaf adults" subject vertical file]

Funeral of Mr. and Mrs. Cook's only child [Photo and story]. (1903, November). <u>The Silent Worker, 16</u> (2), 21. {Willie Cook was an only child "and he was remarkably bright with all his faculties perfect." Parents are members of the Mission to the Deaf at St. Paul's Protestant Cathedral, Los Angeles, California. Apparently Willie "stepped right in front of" a car on the Los Angeles Electric Railway line. "Poor Willie did not seem to know another car was coming."} [UNIV DEAF Periodicals]

Funeral services held for former Dean of Women, Elizabeth Benson. (1973, January 26). <u>The Buff and Blue,</u> 86 (7), pp. 8-9. (Student newspaper of the Gallaudet Student Body Government) {Obituary that summarizes Dr. Benson's life work, honors and service} [Gallaudet University Archives, "Elizabeth English Benson, honorary degree, Doctor of Letters" biographical subject vertical file]

Furey, J. (1983, December 8). Speaking off-hand...Sign language teacher "repaying deaf people" in entertaining style. Statesman-Journal. (Salem, Oregon) [Gallaudet University Archives, "Louie Fant" biographical vertical file]

Gallaudet Alumni News: Six receive awards at Charter Day banquet. (1996, Summer). Gallaudet Today, 26 (4), 26-27. {Reports that Dr. Cesare Magarotto of Italy (who is hearing and parents were deaf) received the Laurent Clerc Cultural Fund's Edward Miner Gallaudet Award} [Gallaudet University Archives or RESERVE]

Gallaudet College official is chosen for award. (1962, May 14). The Evening Star. (Washington, D. C.) {Miss Elizabeth Benson, dean of women at Gallaudet College, to receive award for outstanding achievement from the Alumni Association of the State teachers College at Towson, Maryland} [Gallaudet University Archives, "Elizabeth English Benson, citations and awards" biographical subject vertical file]

Gallaudet Dean of Women to be honored. (1962, May 17). The Uptown Citizen. (Washington, D. C.) {Miss Elizabeth Benson, dean of women at Gallaudet College, will receive an award for outstanding achievement from the Alumni Association of the State Teachers College at Towson, Baltimore, Maryland} [Gallaudet University Archives, "Elizabeth English Benson, citations and awards" biographical subject vertical file]

(#) Gallaudet Dean of Women to be honored at Towson. (1962, May). (City and newspaper unidentified) {On June 4, Gallaudet College will confer on Miss Elizabeth Benson, Dean of Women at Gallaudet College, an honorary Doctor of Letters Degree. This will be the 98th commencement exercises at the college} [Gallaudet University Archives, "Elizabeth English Benson, citations and awards" biographical subject vertical file]

Gallaudet grads featured on national TV special. (1967, April). The Gallaudet Record, 12 (6), 2. [Gallaudet University Archives and "Louie Fant" biographical vertical file]

(#) Gallaudet plans memorial service for Miss Benson. (1972, December or 1973, January). Frederick News. (Frederick, Maryland) [Gallaudet University Archives, "Elizabeth English Benson: Obituary, memorial service" biographical subject vertical file]

Gallaudet's Dean of Women gets rosy Mother's Day. (1963, May 13). The Washington Post. (Washington, D. C.) {Elizabeth Benson was named 1963 Mother of the Year by Alpha Sigma Pi Fraternity of Gallaudet} [Gallaudet University Archives, "Elizabeth English Benson, citations and awards" biographical subject vertical file]

Gallaudet teacher cited by newspaper. (1944, December 19). The Buff and Blue, 53 (3), pp. 1, 3. (Student newspaper of the Gallaudet Student Body Government) [UNIV Archives]

Gallimore, F. (1994, February). CODA Super Hero. Illustrated by Frank Gallimore. CODA Connection, 11 (1), 6. [UNIV DEAF Periodicals]

Gallimore, F. E. (1994, February). A Coda's point of view. CODA Connection, 11 (1), 1, 6. [UNIV DEAF Periodicals]

Gallimore, F. E. (1997, November). The luck of a Coda [The 1997 CODA Millie Brother Scholarship winning essay]. CODA Connection, 14 (4), 4-5. [UNIV DEAF Periodicals]

Gallo, A. (1992, May 28). Shirley Bassett wins Liberty Bell Award. The Johnstown Republic, 1 (5), p. 1. (Johnstown, Pennsylvania) [*]

(*) Galloway, G. (1990, Fall). Raising hearing kids: A deaf mother remembers the joys and trials of parenthood.

Gallaudet Today, 21 (1), 6-7. [Gallaudet University Archives or RESERVE]

Galloway, M. (1994, Summer). A wild ride: Acting novice Vic Galloway starts at the top in a new movie starring Meryl Streep. Gallaudet Today, 24 (4), 14-18. [Gallaudet University Archives or RESERVE]

Gardella, K. (1985, December 8). Actress speaks of her *Silent* role: Mare Winningham's dash for an Emmy. Daily News. (New York) {Focus is an interview with one of the stars of *Love is Never Silent* who says her experience on the set was "emotional" partly because of the challenge to sign and speak in her role of Margaret Ryder, the hearing daughter of deaf parents} [Gallaudet University Archives, "Parent-child relationship -deaf adults" subject vertical file]

Garretson, M. D. (1949, November). A Maryland personality...Harry G. Benson. The Silent Worker, 2 (3), 5-6. [UNIV DEAF Periodicals]

Garron, B. (1985, December 8). Even when words fail to communicate...*Love is Never Silent*. Star (TV and radio), pp. I-1, I-4. (Kansas City, Missouri) {A positive review. Although there is a focus on actress Mare Winningham, "it is difficult to single out any one actor for special praise [because] the supporting stars are equally excellent."} [Gallaudet University Archives, "Parent-child relationship - deaf adults" subject vertical file]

Gellman, B. (1997a, March 14). Jordanian soldier kills 7 Israeli girls: Colleagues at border overpower "madman;" Hussein condemns "vile crime." The Washington Post, 120th year, No. 99, pp. A1, A34. (Washington, D. C.) {It was reported that one of the teenagers was Adi Malka, the hearing daughter of deaf parents} [UNIV Newspapers]

Gellman, B. (1997b, March 17). Hussein, on his knees, begs forgiveness for massacre: Jordanian King visits families of slain Israeli girls. The Washington Post, 120th year, No. 102, pp. A1, A13. (Washington, D. C.) {It was reported that one of the teenagers was Adi Malka, the hearing daughter of deaf parents} [UNIV Newspapers]

George, D. W. (1893, July 20). Should the deaf marry the deaf? In T. F. Fox, O. Hanson & R. P. McGregor (Eds.), Proceedings of the World's Congress of the Deaf and the Report of the Fourth Convention of the National Association of the Deaf, held at the Memorial Art Palace, Chicago, Illinois, July 18th, 20th and 22nd, 1893 (pp. 112-115). Washington, DC: National Association of the Deaf. (The author is from Jacksonville, Illinois) [Gallaudet University Archives]

Gibson, L. S. (1995, January). Book review: *In silence - growing up hearing in a deaf world* by Ruth Sidransky. British Deaf News, 25 (1), 15. [UNIV DEAF Periodicals]

Gibson, L. S. (1996, March). Book review: *Mother father deaf - Living between sound and silence* by Paul Preston. British Deaf News, 26 (3), 11. [UNIV DEAF Periodicals]

Gilje, S. C. (1958, December). One of our interpreters...Woman with the flying fingers: Seattle woman devotes her talent to service of the deaf. The Silent Worker, 11 (4), 3-4. [UNIV DEAF Periodicals]

Gillett, Dr. (1891, February 26). Deaf-mute marriages, we can see no good reason why they should not marry: The present state of society due to education, and some of the best methods in use in the public school system came from teaching the deaf. The Silent Worker, 4 (29), 1. (Refers to his article from the October 31, 1890, issue of Science - first name is not mentioned) {Says it is not a "calamity" to have a "deaf and dumb child." "Dr. [Edward Miner] Gallaudet and Dr. [Alexander Graham] Bell object to my 'wholesale encouragement of the intermarriage of the deaf;' one advising the marriage of the deaf with hearing persons as the ideal marriage, and the other of the congenital with the non-congenital deaf." Urges the deaf to marry whomsoever they please but not in "undue haste."

Those deaf who have deaf offspring largely "belong to families in which the tendency to deafness inheres." "If it is improper for the deaf to marry, it is as much so for their relatives to enter wedlock" because of this tendency to deafness within the family} [UNIV DEAF Periodicals]

Girl Scouts' world of arts. (1968, August 15). Tablet. (Brooklyn, New York) [Gallaudet University Archives, "Louie Fant" biographical vertical file]

Glidden, E. (1976, September 12). Happy deaf couple adopts a very special baby. Pentecostal Evangel, 12-13. {Earl and Margie Claussen of Normal, Illinois, wanted to adopt a hearing child from Korea. They learned about an opportunity through an Assemblies of God missionary to Korea who spoke of the homeless children there. The Holt Agency rejected their request because they "doubted that a hearing child in a deaf home would be able to develop good speech patterns." After intervention from many parties, their daughter, Kathleen Lynn, arrived in February, 1976} [Gallaudet University Archives, "Parent-child relationship - deaf adults" subject vertical file]

Goldberg, A. (1997a, September). [Letter to the editor]. CODA Connection, 14 (3), 11, 13. (Letter is printed again on page 9) [UNIV DEAF Periodicals]

Goldberg, A. (1997b, November). Mother Father Deaf Day news from NJCODA! CODA Connection, 14 (4), 1. [UNIV DEAF Periodicals]

Goldstein, A. (1976, August 7). Bernard Hale dreams of "City" for the deaf. Herald. (Miami, Florida) [Gallaudet University Archives, "Bernard Hale" biographical vertical file]

Goldstein, A. (1990, April 17). From 1-room school to top U-Md. post: Chancellor brings reputation as low-key, broad-minded. The Washington Post, No. 113, pp. A1, A6. (Washington, D. C.) {Dr. Donald Langenberg is the hearing son of deaf parents, Ernest and Fern [Newton] Langenberg, both graduates of Gallaudet University. In 1990, he became Chancellor of the University of Maryland system of 11 campuses. His doctoral degree is in nuclear physics and he came to this position from the Presidency of the University of Chicago} [UNIV Newspapers Microfilm]

Goligoski, B. (1976, April 14). Deaf parents, hearing children: Despite boys young age, family can communicate. St. Paul Dispatch (Metro Life section), pp. C37, C39. (St. Paul, Minnesota) [Gallaudet University Archives, "Parent-child relationship - deaf adults" subject vertical file]

Goodson, J. (1997, May). From the mailbox [Letter to the editor]. CODA Connection, 14 (2), 4. [UNIV DEAF Periodicals]

Goodstein, A. (1981). Three generations of loving memories. The Deaf American, 34 (3), 10-16. [UNIV DEAF Periodicals]

Goodstein, L. (1990, September 2). Once the final hurdle for immigrants, Ellis will bear witness to their legacy: "Isle of hope, isle of tears" becomes museum of passage to America. The Washington Post. (Washington, D. C. - 2 pages) [UNIV Newspapers Microfilm]

Goudas, J. N. (1985, December 8). Lovely Mare Winningham speaks volumes in *Love is Never Silent*. News. (Buffalo, New York) {A positive review which focuses on Winningham} [Gallaudet University Archives, "Parent-child relationship - deaf adults" subject vertical file]

Gould, H. (1976, April 15). Hal's hunches: The feeling is mutual. The Gaithersburg Gazette. (Gaithersburg,

Maryland) [Gallaudet University Archives, "Louise Fletcher" biographical vertical file]

Grace, B. (1985, December 9). Girl is voice for deaf parents in moving *Love is Never Silent* [Television review]. <u>Chronicle,</u> pp. 1, 11. (Houston, Texas) {A positive review} [Gallaudet University Archives, "Parent-child relationship - deaf adults" subject vertical file]

Graduation speech interpreted [Photo and caption]. (1965, June 15). <u>The Evening Star.</u> (Washington, D. C.) {Bradshaw Mintener, an attorney, is the speaker for Gallaudet's 101st commencement and Miss Elizabeth Benson, dean of women, interprets} [Gallaudet University Archives, "Elizabeth English Benson, interpreter in the Language of Signs" biographical subject vertical file]

Graham, D. (1995, November). OHCODA corner. <u>CODA Connection, 12</u> (4), 4. (OHCODA is the acronym used within CODA for those who are "only hearing children of deaf adults" in their families...meaning they have one or more deaf siblings) [UNIV DEAF Periodicals]

Graham, D. (1997, February). More comments about CODA-LA 1996! [Letter]. <u>CODA Connection, 14</u> (1), 10. [UNIV DEAF Periodicals]

Grayson, R. (1949, November). Kentucky air hostess is daughter of deaf couple. <u>The Silent Worker, 2</u> (3), 21. {Brief story about Helen Jane Embry, oldest daughter of Mr. and Mrs. Zedock Embry of Louisville, who is a hostess for Delta Airlines. She is a trained nurse, her sister Monica is now in nurses training in a Louisville hospital and youngest sister, Emma, is in high school} [UNIV DEAF Periodicals]

The Great Grotesque [Editorial]. (1930, August 27). <u>The Cleveland Press,</u> No. 16318, p. 8. (Cleveland, Ohio) {About Lon Chaney who had just died} [*]

Green, F. (1984, January 27). Signs of dignity for the deaf. <u>Union,</u> pp. D1-D2. (San Diego, California) [Gallaudet University Archives, "Louie Fant" biographical vertical file]

(#) Griffin, Sgt. J. R. (1944). Wounded soldiers know WAC medical aide has good story. <u>The Daily Oklahoman.</u> (Oklahoma City, Oklahoma - date unspecified) {Story about Corporal Elizabeth Benson who teaches "stricken deaf" soldiers to lip read or "hear" again} [Gallaudet University Archives, "World War II" subject vertical file]

Griffing, W. T.. (Ed.). (1952, June). The educational front and parents department. <u>The Silent Worker, 4</u> (10), 10. [UNIV DEAF Periodicals]

Groff, B. (1987, July 7). Deaf mom had confidence her kids would speak well. <u>Reading Eagle,</u> pp. 19-20. (Reading, Pennsylvania) [Gallaudet University Archives, "Parent-child relationship - deaf adults" subject vertical file]

Grossinger, V. (1993, July-August). Vicki Grossinger: Deaf mother. <u>TBC News,</u> No. 60, 8. {Talks about the birth of their third son (the first two were deaf) and that the doctor suggested he have a hearing test. She told him: "That won't be necessary. It doesn't matter to me whether my son is Deaf or not. Being a strong, healthy son is more important." She goes on to express the desire for the best "Bi-Bi" education possible for them} [UNIV DEAF Periodicals]

Grossman, E. (1983a, February 25). Actress grew up with the sounds of silence. <u>The Shelby Daily Star,</u> p. 7. (Shelby, North Carolina) {About Louise Fletcher} [Gallaudet University Archives, "Louise Fletcher" biographical vertical file]

Grossman, E. (1983b, March 1). Growing up with the sounds of silence. <u>News-Free Press,</u> pp. 1-2. (Chattanooga, Tennessee) {About Louise Fletcher} [Gallaudet University Archives, "Louise Fletcher" biographical vertical file]

Grossman, E. (1983c, April 12). Louise Fletcher: Growing up with the sounds of silence. <u>Review.</u> (Reidsville, North Carolina) {About Louise Fletcher} [Gallaudet University Archives, "Louise Fletcher" biographical vertical file]

Guslin, C. (1986, October 6). People picks & pans: *A Loss for Words* by Lou Ann Walker [Book review]. <u>People Weekly, 26</u> (14), 23-24. [UNIV Periodicals]

Gwiasda, S. B. (1994, February 22). Bridging the gap: Hearing children are ears for deaf parents. <u>Telegraph Herald,</u> p. 94D. (Dubuque, Iowa) {Features a photo of Diane Tekippe, who is deaf, and her son Steven who is three. Ruth Ruen of East Dubuque, Illinois, is also interviewed. She is the oldest of three siblings who are hearing and had deaf parents} [Gallaudet University Archives, "Hearing children of deaf parents" subject vertical file]

Hailey, J. R. (1972, December 15). Elizabeth Benson, ex-Dean at Gallaudet [Obituary]. <u>The Washington Post.</u> (Washington, D. C.) [Gallaudet University Archives, "Elizabeth English Benson: Memorials" biographical subject vertical file]

Hall, B. (1996, September). Region III report: Region III conference promotes education, understanding and action on important issues - over 300 attend. <u>Views, 13</u> (8), 8-9. (Registry of Interpreters for the Deaf newsletter) {Reports among other things that Bonnie Kraft's keynote presentation was on "CODA and hearing interpreter issues."} [UNIV DEAF Periodicals]

Halligan, C. (1992, November). Masters of balance [Poem]. <u>CODA Connection, 9</u> (4), 4, 7. [UNIV DEAF Periodicals]

Hanford woman develops ASL course training program. (1988, February 16). <u>Sentinel.</u> (Hanford, California) {Reports that Cheri Smith is director of a project with Ken Mikos and Ella Mae Lentz at the Vista College, Berkeley, California. Cheri Smith is hearing and has deaf parents} [Gallaudet University Archives, "American Sign Language - teaching" vertical file]

Hansen, S. (1989, February 10). SCE's Cheryl Ruiz speaks a silent language. <u>Edison News,</u> 1-4. (Southern California Edison Company newsletter) [*]

Harrington, R. (1993, November 7). The power and the harmony. <u>The Washington Post Magazine,</u> 16-18. (Washington, D. C.) [*]

Harrington, R. (1994, October 7). *Deaf*: An eloquent silence. <u>The Washington Post,</u> pp. B1, B7. (Washington, D. C.) {Review of the French documentary on the French Deaf community, *In the Land of the Deaf*} [UNIV Newspapers Microfilm]

Harrison, S. E. (1979, April 4). Aiding parents a challenge. <u>Chronicle.</u> (Muskegon, Michigan) [Gallaudet University Archives, "Parent-child relationship - deaf adults" subject vertical file]

Harvey, M. A. (1985, July/August). Between two worlds: One psychologist's view of the hard of hearing person's experience. <u>Self Help for Hard of Hearing People, 6</u> (4), 4-5. [UNIV DEAF Periodicals]

Hassell, J. (1960, October). Fifty years an interpreter: Miriam Michaels Johnson honored by Austinites, daughter of the late Rev. John W. Michaels completes half century as interpreter, given silver service set in appreciation. The Silent Worker, 13 (2), 7. (Reprinted from the September, 1960, issue of The Baptist Messenger, publication of the Texas Baptist Conference [UNIV DEAF Periodicals]) [UNIV DEAF Periodicals]

(*) **Hatrak-Cundy, L. (1987, February).** A forum...for an exchange of...Public Opinion....: Hearing children of deaf parents, patronizing attitudes. The NAD Broadcaster, 9 (2), 15. {Linda, the deaf parent of hearing children, takes a firm stand against putting these children in a position to interpret for parents. "The television-made movie *Love is Never Silent* is a sad part of our history when deaf adults depended on their hearing children to communicate with the outside world...Those hearing children who are exposed to interpreting early in their childhood tend to grow up with patronizing attitudes toward the deaf community." A sweeping statement but is reflective of some people within the deaf community} [UNIV DEAF Periodicals]

(*) **Hatrak-Cundy, L. (1988, January).** Mother knows best column: What are objectives of CODA? The NAD Broadcaster, 10 (1), 21. (Reprinted in the November, 1988, issue of the CODA Newsletter, 5 (4), 7. [UNIV DEAF Periodicals]) [UNIV DEAF Periodicals]

(*) **Hatrak-Cundy, L. (1989, March).** Mother knows best column. The NAD Broadcaster, 11 (3), 13. {Discusses the question "How do hearing children of deaf parents learn signs?"} [UNIV DEAF Periodicals]

(*) **Hatrak-Cundy, L. (1991, February).** What are the trends for deaf parents in the '90s? CODA Connection, 8 (1), 6. [UNIV DEAF Periodicals]

Hay, J. (1994, January). Face to face with John Hay: Anne Bain [Interview]. British Deaf News, 25 (1), 14-15. [UNIV DEAF Periodicals]

Hayden, B. (1985a, December 9). Deaf parents, daughter learn the power of mutual respect [Television review]. Evening Journal. (Wilmington, Delaware) {A positive review of *Love is Never Silent*. The film "draws its strength, credibility, and to a degree, uniqueness from the performances of Frelich and Waterstreet. Both actors are deaf."} [Gallaudet University Archives, "Parent-child relationship - deaf adults" subject vertical file]

Hayden, B. (1985b, December 9). NBC airs a story of love, understanding and deafness [Television preview]. Democrat-Chronicle. (Rochester, New York) {*Love is Never Silent* airs tonight an "unusual television movie."} [Gallaudet University Archives, "Love is Never Silent" subject vertical file]

H. Daniel Drake Jr.: Hearing aid specialist [Obituary]. (1992, January 29). The Washington Post. (Washington, D. C.) [Gallaudet University Archives, "H. Daniel Drake, Jr." subject vertical file]

Head, K. M. (1979, November 27). Mountain moments: Handicapped? News. (Middlesboro, Kentucky) [Gallaudet University Archives, "Parent-child relationship - deaf adults" subject vertical file]

Hear, hear!!! (1988, March 5). The Boston Herald. (Boston, Massachusetts) {Reports that Louise Fletcher and Nanette Fabray went to Capitol Hill to speak on behalf of the deaf before the House Subcommittee on Health and the Environment} [Gallaudet University Archives, "Louise Fletcher" biographical vertical file]

Hearing children bear burden. (1974, July 21). News-Tribune. (Takoma, Washington) {Laura Clark of South Takoma and hearing daughter of Mr. and Mrs. Edward C. Hall, and Mrs. Bruce (Sandra) Brinkerhoff, hearing daughter of Mr. and Mrs. Bobby Kosanovich of Fife, Washington, share their experiences growing up in a deaf household} [Gallaudet University Archives, "Parent-child relationship - deaf adults" subject vertical file]

The hearing children of deaf parents in Finland. (1985, February). CODA Newsletter, 2 (1), 5. {Research results obtained in 1975 by Pertti Taimisto are reported} [UNIV DEAF Periodicals]

Hearing student enjoys deaf school. (1987, March). World Around You: A publication of Pre-College Programs, Gallaudet University, 5. Washington, DC: Gallaudet University, Pre-College Programs. {Brian Colins is a new student at the Indiana School for the Deaf} [Gallaudet University Archives]

(#) Helander, C. (n.d.). "The Devil made me do it." CCRID Sign Post, 1-2. (Newsletter of the Central California Registry of Interpreters for the Deaf) [*]

Helen Keller, Jane Addams: "Saints" to be honored [Religious News column]. (1970, February 7). The Evening Star. (Washington, D. C.) {Announces that these two eminent American women will be honored at Washington Cathedral and Dean Elizabeth Benson of Gallaudet College will interpret the service in sign language assisted by Pauline Shahan, Shirley Jordan and Thomas Bull of the Gallaudet staff} [Gallaudet University Archives, "Elizabeth English Benson, interpreter in the Language of Signs" biographical subject vertical file]

Henderson, K. (1995). A theatregoer's notebook: Beautiful signs. Billboard, 58. {About Alan Champion, Broadway interpreter, and a coda} [*]

Henderson, S. (1988, Sept./Oct.). A man of a thousand faces: Colorado's Lon Chaney. Colorado Homes and Lifestyles, 48-51. [Gallaudet University Archives, "Lon Chaney" biographical vertical file]

Hendrickson, P. (1991, August 8). Masters of the sounds of silence: Interpreters for the deaf, speaking out. The Washington Post, pp. D1, D2. (Washington, D. C.) [UNIV Newspapers Microfilm]

Herbst, C. (1998, February). Not all Codas. CODA Connection, 15 (1), 4. [UNIV DEAF Periodicals]

Heredity [Editorial]. (1921, April). The Silent Worker, 33 (7), 237. {"Heredity is a subject which requires years of hard study to comprehend...With "superficial knowledge of the laws of heredity [some] are ever ready to aid hasty and harsh legislation...The deaf may be the victims of such cruel laws...Why cannot some deaf student make [the study of genetics] his life's work?"} [UNIV DEAF Periodicals]

Herr, M. B. (Ed.). (1929, November). Trains with me: Some interesting highlights on the life of Dr. Bell as told by one of his pupils to Milton B. Herr, information supervisor, Philadelphia. The Telephone News, 25 (11), 3-7. (The Bell Telephone Company of Pennsylvania employee newsletter) [Gallaudet University Archives, "Alexander Graham Bell - biographical" subject vertical file]

Hiaasen, R. (1990, November 3). The inner voices: Author Ruth Sidransky's *In silence* is about growing up in a hearing society. The Palm Beach Post, pp. 1D, 7D. (Palm Beach, Florida) [*]

Hicks, J. (1997, September). Koda korner: My experience at camp. CODA Connection, 14 (3), 12, 18. {Jessica Hicks, a 15-year-old koda from Michigan, describes her experience at a deaf youth leadership camp where there were four other kodas (hearing kids of deaf adults)} [UNIV DEAF Periodicals]

Higbie, A. (1995, March 27). Curse of the Oscar. The New York Times, 144 (No. 50,013), p. C15. {About Louise Fletcher and others} [UNIV Newspapers - Microfilm]

Hill, M. (1985, December 9). An emotional film that is one of the best ever on TV. The Evening Sun. (Baltimore, Maryland) {Positive review of *Love is Never Silent*. "This is a tremendous television movie, a film that is able to evoke a particular era in the country's history and a particularly poignant time of life of everyone's personal history. Along the way, it teaches a few basic lessons of sacrifice, commitment, hard work and love, as well as teaching you a lot about being deaf."} [Gallaudet University Archives, "Love is Never Silent" subject vertical file]

Hines, L. (1993, February). My Coda friends...A poem. CODA Connection, 10 (1), 8. [UNIV DEAF Periodicals]

Hink, G. M. (1954, January). Children of the deaf..."Randy Merriman, MC." The Silent News, 6 (5), 12. [UNIV DEAF Periodicals]

Hirst, D. (1997, March 14). Aftermath of a massacre: Shooting shatters the king's peace. The (Manchester) Guardian Daily, p. 13. (England - Story reported from Beirut, Lebanon) {It was reported that one of the teenagers was Adi Malka, the hearing daughter of deaf parents} [C]

His phantom faces still live: Chaney's grotesque movie roles survive in fans' memories. (1930, August 26). The Cleveland Press, No. 16317, pp. 1, 13. (Cleveland, Ohio) [*]

(*) Hoffman, V. (1993, Aug/Sept). Full circle [The 1993 CODA Millie Brother Scholarship essay winner]. CODA Connection, 10 (3), 11. (Reprinted in D. Prickett & R. Prickett (Eds.), Richness in our diversity: Proceedings of the tenth International CODA Conference, Research Triangle Park, North Carolina, July 27-30, 1995 (pp. 122-123). Santa Barbara, CA: Children of Deaf Adults. [On order]) [UNIV DEAF Periodicals]

Hoffmeister, B. (1997a, February). One generation thick: Coda heritage. CODA Connection, 14 (1), 7, 13. [UNIV DEAF Periodicals]

Hoffmeister, B. (1997b, May). One generation thick: Common ground. CODA Connection, 14 (2), 5, 16. (Dated March 30, 1997) [UNIV DEAF Periodicals]

Hoffmeister, B. (1997c, September). One generation thick: We are codas forever. CODA Connection, 14 (3), 5. [UNIV DEAF Periodicals]

Hoffmeister, B. (1997d, November). One generation thick: Marie Philip, 1953-1997. CODA Connection, 14 (4), 11-12. [UNIV DEAF Periodicals]

Hoffmeister, B. (1998, May). One generation thick. CODA Connection, 15 (2), 4, 17. [UNIV DEAF Periodicals]

(*) Hoffmeister, M. P. (1987, November). CODA rap [Poem]. CODA Newsletter, 4 (4), 3. (Mary is called the CODA Rap Queen - Reprinted in the November, 1997, CODA Connection, 14 (4), 14. [UNIV DEAF Periodicals]) [UNIV DEAF Periodicals]

Hoffmeister, R. (1991, Fall). Book review: *In silence: Growing up hearing in a deaf world* by Ruth Sidransky. Gallaudet Today, 22 (1), 25. [Gallaudet University Archives or RESERVE]

Hokanson, K. A. (1953, December). Children of the deaf...An undersea sailor. The Silent News, 6 (4), 12. {Dustin Shattuck, Jr., is a radar operator on the submarine U.S.S. Blackfin, on duty in Pacific waters. He is 19 years old and the "son of Mr. and Mrs. Dustin Shattuck, Sr., of La Center, Washington, and a grandson of the late Mr. and Mrs. Frank B. Shattuck, well-known among the deaf circles of San Francisco."} [UNIV DEAF Periodicals]

Holcomb, R. K. (1951a, March). Children of the deaf...You hear them on the air. The Silent Worker, 3 (6), 5. {Story about Waldemar and Ramon Krohn, sons of Albert J. Krohn who taught printing and was coach at the South

Dakota School for the Deaf and Marion (Karney) Krohn, a graduate of the Wisconsin School for the Deaf. After Ramon left the Marines, he got involved in a radio station in his home town, Sioux Falls, South Dakota, and had his own show called the Bob King Show. Many of the boys' accomplishments are enumerated} [UNIV DEAF Periodicals]

Holcomb, R. K. (1951b, May). Children of the deaf..Three is not a crowd. The Silent Worker, 3 (9), 11. {Article about the accomplishments of Clinton Jr., Jack and Bob Ensworth, the hearing sons of Mr. and Mrs. Clinton Ensworth of Akron, Ohio} [UNIV DEAF Periodicals]

Holdren, N. L. (1996, April). Exceptional customer service. Views, 13 (4), 16-17. (Registry of Interpreters for the Deaf newsletter) [UNIV DEAF Periodicals]

Holland, G. (1969, March). Deaf and hearing students together...A school for children of deaf parents. The Deaf American, 21 (7), 9-12. [UNIV DEAF Periodicals]

Holsopple, B. (1985, December 9). NBC offers uplifting story on child of deaf parents [Television review]. News-Sentinel. (Knoxville, Tennessee) {Positive review of *Love is Never Silent*. A "poignant but uplifting story written and performed with sensitivity and skill." About "40 'walk-on' parts were also played by non-hearing men and women."} [Gallaudet University Archives, "Love is Never Silent" subject vertical file]

Honey, C. (1989, September 21). Signs of love: Children of deaf parents straddle two worlds. The Grand Rapids Press, pp. D1-D2. (Grand Rapids, Michigan) [*]

Honored. (1943, June). The FRAT: Official Publication of the National Fraternal Society of the Deaf, 40th year, No. 11, 4. {Quoting from the Keowee Courier (Walhalla, South Carolina) that a United States vessel will be named in honor of Allison P. Rhodes, who died in battle in the southwest Pacific. He was the son of Brother and Mrs. G. E. Rhodes of Walhalla} [UNIV DEAF Periodicals]

Honoring our parents; Mother, Father Deaf Day on April 27th. (1997, April). The NAD Broadcaster, 19 (4), 16. [UNIV DEAF Periodicals]

(#) Horine, D. (1976). The role won her an Oscar, but...Louise Fletcher reveals: Working in a real mental hospital while filming *Cuckoo's Nest* drove me nuts. The Enquirer. (Date unspecified) [Gallaudet University Archives, "Louise Fletcher" biographical vertical file]

Hospitals in Maryland, New York sued over deaf access: Request for interpreter refused, says 8-year-old girl and her mother. (1997, June). Newswaves for Deaf and Hard-of-Hearing People, 1 (6), 4. [UNIV DEAF Newspapers]

Housing community for deaf criticized. (1979, November 20). News-American. (Baltimore, Maryland) {The Rev. Louis Foxwell, director of the Deaf referral service [in Baltimore], has proposed a 300-unit apartment complex supported by a federal rent subsidy to help meet the housing needs of the deaf."} [Gallaudet University Archives, "Rev. Louis W. Foxwell, Jr." biographical vertical file]

Houston, Tex. - ship christened in sign language (Photo and caption). (1943, July). The Silent Cavalier, 3 (11), 3. {Caption reads: "Ship christened in sign language - with the sign of the cross, Mrs. G. E. Rhodes, of Walhalla, S.C., indicates the words 'I christen thee' at the launching of the USS Rhodes, a destroyer escort, at the Brown Ship-building Co. here. Lt. Comdr. G. C. Hotchkiss holds the champagne bottle while Mrs. Rhodes...gives the ship the name of her son, Lt. (j.g.) Allison P. Rhodes, who died in the attack on the Solomons. - The Washington Evening

Star, July 1, 1943 - A.P. Wirephoto."} [Gallaudet University Archives]

Howard, C. (1973, June). Son of deaf parents: 1973 National Teacher of the Year. The Deaf American, 25 (10), 24. (Reprinted from the May, 1973, issue of the Scholastic Teacher [*]) {About John Arthur "Jack" Ensworth in his 15th year teaching at Kenwood Elementary School, Bend, Oregon. The award was sponsored by The Council of Chief State School Officers, the Encyclopaedia Britannica and the Ladies' Home Journal} [UNIV DEAF Periodicals]

Howe, D. (1994, October 7). On screen: Touching visit with the Deaf. The Washington Post. (Washington, D. C.) {Review of the French documentary about life without sound: *In the Land of the Deaf*} [UNIV Newspapers Microfilm]

Howson, J. W. (1922, May). The Argonaut. The Silent Worker, 34 (18), 293-295, 297. {On page 295 is a photo of 2-year-old Virginia Ann White, a native Californian and child of deaf parents, with the title "Youthful Argonauts." Another photo of her appears on page 297} [Gallaudet University Archives]

(*) Hoza, J. (1987, November). For my parents (who are deaf) [Poem]. CODA Newsletter, 4 (4), 6. [UNIV DEAF Periodicals]

Huff, D. (1989, March 28). For family Bergan, all the signs are go: DeMatha star gets his point across. The Washington Post, p. B4. (Washington, D. C.) {Story about Tracy Bergan, senior point guard for DeMatha High School in Maryland. His parents, Gordon and Laura Bergan, and his younger brother, Stefan, are deaf} [UNIV Newspapers Microfilm]

Hunter, G. (1982, June). The day I grew up: First prize 1982 youth writing contest - $4000. scholarship. Guideposts, 2-4, cover. {Cover photo of Greg Hunter, senior at Lone Grove High School, Lone Grove, Oklahoma, with the question: "Have you ever felt embarrassed by your parents? Read this Youth Contest winner's story." Greg talks about his life with deaf parents} [Gallaudet University Archives, "Parent-child relationship - deaf adults" subject vertical file]

Hurst, J. (1977, March 20). The second season of Louise Fletcher. Chicago Tribune, pp. 20-21, 36, 38, 40. (Illinois) [Gallaudet University Archives, "Louise Fletcher" biographical vertical file]

Hurwitz, B. (1987, June 26). Readers' views: "Shining examples" [Letter to the editor]. Times-Union. (Rochester, New York) {Bernard Hurwitz of Penfield, New York, comments on Kathleen Wagner's article about Joely Parker and her deaf parents ["Signs of the times at Athena Commencement," Rochester Times-Union (June 18, 1987). He was also a graduating senior at Penfield High School in Rochester at the time and explains that interpreters were provided for the exercises. He also describes how much his upbringing was like that of other children} [*]

Hurwitz, B. (1988, February). [Guest editorial]. CODA Newsletter, 5 (1), 1-3. [UNIV DEAF Periodicals]

Huss, J. A. (1990, November). [Letter to the editor]. CODA Connection, 7 (4), 3. [UNIV DEAF Periodicals]

Huss, J. A. (1992, November). Children being used as interpreters in legal and medical settings [Letter to the editor]. CODA Connection, 9 (4), 3-4. [UNIV DEAF Periodicals]

Hutchinson, B. (1980, August 19). Deaf parents rear "Remarkable family." Spartanburg Herald, p. A6. (Spartanburg, South Carolina) [Gallaudet University Archives, "Parent-child relationship - deaf adults" subject vertical file]

Hyman, B. (1993a, June). My Jewish identity: Irving Linden. <u>Congregation News: Temple Beth Solomon of the Deaf, 32</u> (9), 4-5, 8. (Los Angeles, California) [UNIV DEAF Periodicals]

Hyman, B. (1993b, July/Aug). My Jewish identity: Hyman and Esther Aheroni. <u>Congregation News: Temple Beth Solomon of the Deaf, 32</u> (10), 6-7. (Los Angeles, California) [UNIV DEAF Periodicals]

Idema, J. (1989, April, 4). Parental deafness as a fact of life [Review of the book *Useful gifts* by Carole Glickfeld]. <u>Chicago Tribune.</u> (Illinois) [*]

Ingram, R. M. (1973, April). An interpreting story. <u>The Deaf American, 25</u> (8), 24. [UNIV DEAF Periodicals]

Inman, J. (1985, December 8). Fantasy sometimes flies in new *Alice* [Television review]. <u>Star.</u> (Indianapolis, Indiana) {A new musical version of *Alice in Wonderland* vies with *Love is Never Silent* for viewership on Monday night. There is a positive review of *Love*. "The script is both sensitive and compelling, and the production captures beautifully the dingy Depression-era tenement in which the Ryders first live, symbolizing the fear and mistrust which they feel."} [Gallaudet University Archives, "Love is Never Silent" subject vertical file]

In memoriam: Michele "Micki" Zinkovich. (1987, May). <u>CODA Newsletter, 4</u> (2), 5. [UNIV DEAF Periodicals]

Innerst, C. (1981, October 26). Agency lifts hope of deaf. <u>The Bulletin.</u> (Philadelphia, Pennsylvania) {This is an article in a series about United Way member agencies and affiliates in Philadelphia. This one focuses on the Association for Jewish Children and sign language instructor Lee Fink who is a coda and works with deaf families with hearing children} [Gallaudet University Archives, "Parent-child relationship - deaf adults" subject vertical file]

Innerst, C. (1986a, Nov. 24). A will to preserve Deaf culture. <u>Insight: The Washington Times (Health section),</u> pp. 50-51. (Washington, D. C.) {Proud to be deaf, David and Sharon Staehle are parents of 3 1/2 month old Beth. They also want their subculture to endure. David's image of family included "two children who were deaf...It took much convincing on the part of his wife that it would make no difference if their children were deaf or hearing." The article describes their adjustments to parenting, marriage patterns in the deaf community and issues around mainstreaming} [*]

Innerst, C. (1986b, December 1). Parents instill pride in deaf culture. <u>The Washington Times,</u> p. 4A. (Washington, D. C.) {A modified version of the 1986a article above. "To hearing people, Mr. Staehle's wish to beget handicapped children may seem an anomaly."} [Gallaudet University Archives, "Parent-child relationship - deaf adults" subject vertical file]

Inspired by Gospel and African rhythms, Sweet Honey in the Rock delivers political punch a capella. (1990, May 28). <u>People Weekly, 33</u> (21), 108. [UNIV Periodicals]

Intermarriage of the deaf [Editorial]. (1920, October). <u>The Silent Worker, 33</u> (1), 18. {The first of three articles on this topic will appear. They are by Mr. Fred De Land, editor of <u>The Volta Review.</u> "Scientific research has disclosed the fact that deafness is increased by consanguineous marriages and the National Association of the Deaf has gone on record as discouraging such marriages among the deaf." Mr. De Land urges others to "combat any such legislation" forbidding marriage among the deaf as undesirable and unwise} [UNIV DEAF Periodicals]

Interpreters meet in Washington. (1965, Feb-March). <u>The Gallaudet Record, 10</u> (5), 3. {Describes a meeting January 28-29, of the Registry of Interpreters for the Deaf. Mentions that Dr. Elizabeth Benson, Professor of Education and Dean of Women at Gallaudet College, is vice president of the RID} [Gallaudet University Archives, "Elizabeth English Benson, conferences and workshops attended, biographical subject vertical file]

The interpreting, deaf, and coda communities are shocked and saddened by the unexpected death of Judie Husted. (1998, May). CODA Connection, 15 (2), 19. {Includes a personal note from coda Judy Kraft and some remarks from Dan Burch, RID President, about Judie} [UNIV DEAF Periodicals]

Interview with Dr. Kathy Jankowski: The newest deaf superintendent of a deaf school. (1993, September). The NAD Broadcaster, 15 (9), 1, 4-5. {Lists the current 16 deaf superintendents. "Also listed are the hearing children of our community (CODA - Children of Deaf Adults) who have chosen to work within the deaf world and have become superintendents of deaf schools." Named are Oscar P. Cohen, Hugh T. Prickett, Luther B. Prickett, Marvin B. Sallop, W. Winfield McChord, Jr., and Hank Klopping} [UNIV DEAF Periodicals]

In the Ohio State University. (1925, January). The Silent Worker, 37 (4), 192. {Quoted is an article from The Ohio Chronicle (publication of the Ohio School for the Deaf [Institution for the Education of the Deaf and Dumb], Columbus) which lists the names of six "children of deaf parents" enrolled at Ohio State University. "There may be others. But this is sufficient to show the value the deaf place on the education of their children. It bears out what has been said so many times in the Chronicle that the deaf aim at the best for their children and will stop at nothing to attain it. It speaks for their patriotism and the high quality of their zeal and enterprise. The children will doubtless take care of themselves, because they are fine specimens of American manhood and womanhood."} [UNIV DEAF Periodicals]

Introducing: The funny forum, this is from the Deaf-L internet group, what a great example of Deaf/coda humor! (1997, May). CODA Connection, 14 (2), 19. [UNIV DEAF Periodicals]

Is marriage a failure? - Our views of this very much disputed question. (1889, February 28). The Silent Worker - Trenton, 2 (11), 4. {A commentary for the deaf to associate among themselves as well as to interact with the hearing community} [Gallaudet University Archives]

Is she world's youngest interpreter? [Photo and story]. (1984, September). The Silent News, 16 (9), 1. (Reprinted from the Staten Island Advance, New York, June 27, 1984) {Sabrina Marinaro is six and the daughter of Robert and Maida Marinaro of Staten Island, New York. Sabrina sang 21 songs "in sign for most of her deaf relatives at the [Academy of St. Dorothy] Kindergarten graduation ceremony so that they understood everything...."} [UNIV DEAF Periodicals]

Jacobs, S. (1985, May). Sneak preview! Abstract, native signers and second language signers: Their development as bilingual and bicultural interpreters. CODA Newsletter, 2 (2), 4. [UNIV DEAF Periodicals]

Jacobs, S. (1990, February). I-N-T-R-O-D-U-C-I-N-G Coda Talk column. CODA Connection, 9 (1), 1, 7-8. [UNIV DEAF Periodicals]

Jacobs, S. (1992, May). Coda Talk column. CODA Connection, 9 (2), 9. [UNIV DEAF Periodicals]

Jacobs, S. (1994a, January). Our unforgettable "Bi-Bi family" night. Bay Area CODA Chronicles, 3, 5, 8. (Newsletter of the Oakland/San Francisco, California, Bay Area CODA chapter) {Bi-Bi families are those "with deaf and hearing members." Sheila Jacobs talks about a pioneering new approach to mental health she calls "Double Pride" and illustrates some expressions of this work} [*]

Jacobs, S. (1994b, February). The birth of Double Pride. CODA Connection, 11 (1), 8. [UNIV DEAF Periodicals]

Jacobs, S., & Rexroat, N. (1987, June). Micki Zinkovich Bonfiglio: A rare, successful and mysterious woman.

NorCRID News, 1, 8-9. (Newsletter of the Northern California Registry of Interpreters for the Deaf) {A memorial tribute to Micki who died May 4th at the young age of 28 from a rare form of cancer. She was a coda, "EXCELLENT interpreter," film-maker, performer and staunch ally of the Deaf community} [*]

Jacobson, S. (1989, July 13). Woman's involvement calms deaf parents. Crofton News-Crier, 16 (27), p. 1. {Michael and Karyl Hummel are deaf and have two children, Michelle, 12, who is hearing, and Karlin Michael, who is "hearing impaired." They were attending the Deaf Way Conference at Gallaudet University. "Michelle walked between her parents' car and trailer police and witnesses said. Not realizing where she was, her father pulled away and caught his daughter under the trailer, dragging her 102 feet, according to police." Sheri Pick, former secretary at Gallaudet, happened upon the scene and interpreted} (Community newspaper: Crofton, Maryland) [*]

(*) Jaech, T. A. (1981). The Jaech family: From dad with love...dear kids. The Deaf American, 34 (3), 5-7. [UNIV DEAF Periodicals]

Jaluvka, L. (1984, June 20). Folks eager to learn, share starting club for deaf adults. The Sun, Family Scene section, p. B1. (Durham, North Carolina) [*]

James, C. (1994, September 14). Discovering eloquence amid silent gestures [Film review]. The New York Times. {Review of the film about the French deaf community, In the Land of the Deaf} [UNIV Newspapers Microfilm]

James Cagney star of the forthcoming movie on the life of Lon Chaney [Photo and caption]. (1957, January 10). The Johnson County Democrat. (Olathe, Kansas) {Photo is of James Cagney with Marjorie Ramsey who is formerly of Olathe, Kansas and serves as technical advisor on the film Cagney stars in: Man of a Thousand Faces. Her parents, Mr. and Mrs. C. N. Ramsey, are deaf and have retired from the faculty of the Kansas School for the Deaf. The text of a letter from Cagney to her parents accompanies the photo. This follows: "Marjorie, in a letter to her parents, says of the sign language used in the picture, 'The deaf may think all the actors sign too slowly but we did it deliberateely [sic]...for a feeling of pantomime to tie in with his [Chaney's] career later on as a silent, pantomime actor.'"} [Gallaudet University Archives, "Lon Chaney" biographical vertical file]

James, V. R. (1997, February). More comments about CODA-LA 1996! CODA Connection, 14 (1), 10, 17. [UNIV DEAF Periodicals]

Janson, R. (1988, May 22). Signs of the times: A language evolves from the hands of the deaf. Kalamazoo Gazette, pp. C1-C2. (Kalamazoo, Michigan) [Gallaudet University Archives, "Children of deaf adults" subject vertical file]

Jeffers, T. (1992, Aug/Sept). Trudy's story. CODA Connection, 9 (3), 6. {Reaching out to coda friends in a crisis helped "ME survive my dad's heart attack."} [UNIV DEAF Periodicals]

Jeffers, T. (1995, February). [Letter to the editor]. Views, 12 (2), 20. (Registry of Interpreters for the Deaf newsletter) {Rebuttal to a letter from Earl Elkins (December, 1994) and his opposition to the formation of a special interest group for codas} [UNIV DEAF Periodicals]

Jeffers, T. (1996, February). Mother Father Deaf Day: The first annual Mother, Father Deaf Day will be Sunday, April 28, 1996. CODA Connection, 13 (1), 6. [UNIV DEAF Periodicals]

Jeffers, T., & Pace, C. (1996, May). Mother Father Deaf Day. CODA Connection, 13 (2), 7-8. {A heart-warming story by Carol Pace. "My mother lived in a nursing home for three years before she died...The isolation she experienced her last few years of life bothered me, so I decided to do something." Besides getting her Masters of

Social Work degree, she struck up a friendship with two deaf ladies in nursing homes. She says, "I don't know where this will lead me. I'm sure there are hundreds of lonely Deaf adults in nursing homes. For now, I'm enjoying my two new Deaf friends and my mother's memories are stronger than ever."} [UNIV DEAF Periodicals]

Jensen, J. A. (1996, January 22). Daughter lends a hand in helping dad: She interprets for deaf workers at Haynes. Kokomo Tribune, p. 1. (Kokomo, Indiana) {About Elizabeth Rother whose parents are deaf} [Gallaudet University Archives, "Hearing children of deaf parents" subject vertical file]

John Fail, Jr., 21-year-old son of Mr. and Mrs. John Fail of Long Beach, California, serves as quartermaster.... (1960, September). The Silent Worker, 13 (1), 37. [UNIV DEAF Periodicals]

Johnson, E. (1959, January 6). Deaf parents "made" star. Los Angeles Daily Mirror. (Los Angeles, California - Reprinted in the March, 1959 edition of The Silent Worker, 11 (7), 3-5: "Daughter of deaf parents...Louise Fletcher shows promise as dramatic actress, attributes much of her talent to lifetime of familiarity with the Sign language...has appeared in recent television shows." {About Louise Fletcher, called "Hollywood's Cinderella girl of 1959."} [UNIV DEAF Periodicals]

Johnson, J. (1987, September 27). Personalities: The straight scoop. Inquirer. (Philadelphia, Pennsylvania) {The question is asked: Who was the actress before Marlee Matlin who used sign language for the deaf when accepting an Academy Award? Answer: Louise Fletcher} [Gallaudet University Archives, "Louise Fletcher" biographical vertical file]

Johnson, J. (1996, November). The impact of my coda experience [The 1996 CODA Millie Brother Scholarship essay winner]. CODA Connection, 13 (4), 4-5. [UNIV DEAF Periodicals]

Johnson, S. (1978, Dec. 26). Center uses clout for the deaf. Detroit Free Press. (Detroit, Michigan) [Gallaudet University Archives, "Court litigation - deaf" file]

Johnson, S. (1979, March 5). Law center battles for rights of deaf. Oregonian. (Portland, Oregon) [Gallaudet University Archives, "Parent-child relationship - deaf adults" subject vertical file]

Johnson sees higher goals for America. (1964, June 7). The Sunday Star, p. A14. (Washington, D. C.) {President Johnson spoke at the centennial banquet of Gallaudet College. Dr. Elizabeth Benson "interpreted his words to the audience as he spoke."} [Gallaudet University Archives, "Elizabeth English Benson, interpreter in the Language of Signs" biographical subject vertical file]

Johnstone, M. (1986a, January 13). Deaf parents, hearing children critique Love Never Silent. On the Green: A weekly publication for Gallaudet staff and faculty, 16 (12), 1-2. [Gallaudet University Archives]

Johnstone, M. (1986b, Spring). Love is Never Silent: Superb acting, but...Reactions vary widely among deaf parents, hearing children. Gallaudet Today, 16 (3), 9-14. {Some deaf parents who have hearing children were interviewed. They were: Kit Schreiber, Francis Higgins, Don Pettingill, Eugene Bergman, Dwight Rafferty, Eugene and Stella Stangarone, Iona and Winfield McChord, Sr., and Celia May Baldwin. The following hearing children (now adults) of deaf parents were interviewed for their opinions about the film: Earl Elkins, Diana Lusker, Eugene McVicker, Dr. John Schuchman, Dr. Paul Higgins, Dr. Winfield McChord Jr., Mary Anne Royster and James Stangarone} [Gallaudet University Archives or RESERVE]

Jones, E. G., & Topmiller, M. (1996, July). Deaf fathers' interactions with hearing infants and toddlers. NCAST National News (Nursing Child Assessment Satellite Training Programs), 12 (3), 4-5, 8. [*]

ARTICLES

Jones-Davis, G. (1998, March 29). Blindness and insight [Book reviews of *Planet of the Blind* by Stephen Kuusisto and *Close to the Bone: Memoirs of Hurt, Rage and Desire* edited by Laurie Stone]. The Washington Post (Book World section), p. 4. (Washington, D. C.) [UNIV Newspapers Microfilm]

Jordan, I. K. (1978, December 8). Do deaf mothers make bad mothers? The Buff and Blue, 88 (5), p. 6. (Student newspaper of the Gallaudet Student Body Government) {Dr. Jordan, the first deaf president of Gallaudet University was, in 1978, professor of psychology at Gallaudet. Here he comments on the Clinical Psychiatry Newsletter article by Drs. Galenson and Shopper, two psychiatrists. "This article is anything but professional - it is the pits of amateurism...The article is so full of overly generalized statements, gross exaggerations and what looks to me like patently false information about deaf mothers that it is an insult to the intelligence of the reader."} [Gallaudet University Archives and "Parent-child relationship - deaf adults" subject vertical file]

Jordan, L. (1973, April 17). Teacher of the year believes in paddling with love. The Oregonian, pp. 14-15. (Bend, Oregon) {Jack Ensworth, who has deaf parents, teaches sixth grade at Bend, Oregon's Kenwood Elementary School and became National Teacher of the Year. His mother wrote of her pride: "Son, you have done more than words can tell for the cause of deaf-mute parents. You have proven beyond a doubt that they are capable of rearing their children to become productive achievers."} [Gallaudet University Archives, "Parent-child relationship - deaf adults" subject and "Jack Ensworth" biographical vertical file]

Joyce, D. G. (1996, Aug/Sept). [Letter to the editor]. CODA Connection, 13 (3), 11. {About the organization's efforts on behalf of kodas (kids of deaf adults)} [UNIV DEAF Periodicals]

Joynes, J. W. (1976, February 8). Foxwell's hands spread the word to his flock. News-American. (Baltimore, Maryland) [Gallaudet University Archives, "Rev. Louis W. Foxwell, Jr." biographical vertical file]

J. R. Fortune ordained priest in Durham, N. C. (1945, May). The Cavalier, 5 (9), 1. {About James Robertson Fortune} [Gallaudet University Archives]

Julianna Fjeld: New director - in the age of light, struggle and success. (1991, November-December). The World Around You: A publication of Pre-College Programs, Gallaudet University, 6-7. Washington, DC: Gallaudet University, Pre-College Programs. [Gallaudet University Archives]

Jury clears five in sterilization case. (1979, February 17). The Washington Post. (Washington, D. C.) {Georgia Mae Downs, a 27 year old "deaf mute mother of two" claimed she was sterilized in 1973 against her will after having two children out of wedlock. This was in Bangor, Maine} [Gallaudet University Archives, "Court litigation - deaf" subject vertical file]

Justice returns a child [Editorial]. (1978, March 3). The Los Angeles Times (part 2), p. 4. (Los Angeles, California) {Ray and Patricia Riley are deaf and their 5-year-old hearing daughter was taken from them because, as the social work report noted, they "were both deaf and had difficulty communicating with the girl, who, as a result, lagged far behind the verbal skills that are normal for a child of her age" and because "the mother had a history of emotional problems" and because "they were unable to provide proper care for" her. The Southern California Center for the Law and Deaf in Los Angeles helped them regain custody. This was in San Bernardino County, California} [*]

Just snap-shots [Photo and caption]. (1921, November). The Silent Worker, 34 (2), 59. {Photo of Wallace Archie, son of Mr. and Mrs. Carl P. Magnuson, of Duluth, Minnesota} [UNIV DEAF Periodicals]

Kafer, K. (1981, October 11). Sign-language services open church to deaf flock. News-American, pp. 1B, 4B.

(Baltimore, Maryland) [Gallaudet University Archives, "Rev. Louis W. Foxwell, Jr." biographical vertical file]

Kaika, M. (1996-97, Winter). Finding each other: The Alumni Office helps a mother and son reunite after 29 years. <u>Gallaudet Today, 27</u> (2), 20-24. [Gallaudet University Archives or RESERVE]

Kampert, P. (1991, October 2). Easing the isolation: Music has a starring role at the Center on Deafness. <u>Chicago Tribune (Tempo - section 5),</u> 145th year, No. 275, p. 3. (Chicago, Illinois) [*]

Kantrowitz, B., & Witherspoon, D. (1986, September 22). Family: Bridge to a world of sound, hearing children reach out for their deaf parents. <u>Newsweek, 108,</u> 72. {Positive review of Lou Ann Walker's book, *A Loss for Words*. Marianne Turk and her deaf father Frank Turk, Mary Ann Klein, hearing daughter of Harry and Flo Grossinger, and Louise Fletcher, hearing daughter of the Rev. and Mrs. Robert C. Fletcher of Alexandria, Virginia, are interviewed} [UNIV Periodicals]

Kendall, J. (1978, March 2). Deaf couple win custody of daughter: 1-year ordeal. <u>The Los Angeles Times,</u> pp. 1, 6. (Los Angeles, California) [Gallaudet University Archives, "Court litigation - deaf" subject vertical file]

Kennedy, H. (1966, July 27). Deaf couple win 1st round in adoption fight. <u>The Los Angeles Times</u> (part 2, Editorials), p. 1. (See same article in the <u>San Fernando Valley News</u>) {Mr. and Mrs. Wayne Christiansen of Torrance, California, have cared for their 9-month-old foster baby since he was a few days old. He was taken away from them even after the County Bureau of Adoptions approved their adoption application. Superior Court Judge A. A. Scott denied their application saying "the couple's home is not 'normal' because the parents do not communicate in the customary way." The Second District Court of Appeals ordered the child returned to them} [*]

Kenworthy, J. (1961, July). The boon of silence. <u>National Business Woman, 40</u> (7), 4-7. (Magazine of the National Federation of Business and Professional Women's Clubs) {A general article about the achievements of deaf female graduates of Gallaudet, deafness, and the communication hurdles the deaf graduates of Gallaudet have overcome. There are pictures of Dean of Women Elizabeth Benson interpreting for Vice President Lyndon B. Johnson who spoke at commencement exercises this year} [Gallaudet University Archives, "Elizabeth English Benson, interpreter in the Language of Signs" biographical subject vertical file]

Kernan, M. (1976, May 16). Louise Fletcher: Heeding the call of a family tradition of service. <u>The Washington Post,</u> p. M3. (Washington, D. C.) [Gallaudet University Archives, "Louise Fletcher" biographical vertical file]

(*) Khalil, L. (1988, Winter). Phobia. <u>The Deaf American, 38</u> (1), 19-20. [UNIV DEAF Periodicals]

King, A. (1978, March 19). All the world's a stage, but for the Deaf the play is pantomime: Isolated and misunderstood, a San Bernardino couple was forced into a drama that nearly cost them their children. <u>The Los Angeles Times.</u> (Los Angeles, California) [Gallaudet University Archives, "Court litigation - deaf" subject vertical file]

Kinsey, J. A. (1992, February). CODA video review: *Hidden Signs*, a video by Micki Zinkovich. <u>CODA Connection, 9</u> (1), 6. [UNIV DEAF Periodicals]

Kinsey, J. A. (1994a, January 20). Hospitals need an interpreter policy: Forum section. <u>The Herald Sun,</u> p. A9. (Durham, North Carolina) [*]

Kinsey, J. A. (1994b, February). Thank you Codas! <u>CODA Connection, 11</u> (1), 7. {After her Deaf mother passed

Right margin tab: ARTICLES

away, Jo Ann and her family received a great deal of support from her CODA family and community} [UNIV DEAF Periodicals]

Kinsey, J. A. (1996, Aug/Sept). Post conference cruise great fun! CODA Connection, 13 (3), 7-8. [UNIV DEAF Periodicals]

Kirchner, C. (1995, September/October). The inclusive environment: The fourth of a six part series on education. Hearing Health, 11 (5), 37-38, 40. [UNIV DEAF Periodicals]

Kirkwood, D. H. (1992, November). Gorlin takes over helm at annual IHS convention: Emotional highlight. The Hearing Journal, 45 (11), 53-55. {Louise Fletcher addressed the International Hearing Society's Dallas, Texas, meeting. Speaking about her deaf parents, she recounts the moments leading up to and since receiving the Best Actress Award for her role in *One Flew Over the Cuckoo's Nest* in 1976} [Gallaudet University Archives, "Louise Fletcher" biographical vertical file]

Kischer-Browne, K. (1997, November). Deaf music [Story]. CODA Connection, 14 (4), 5. [UNIV DEAF Periodicals]

***Kiss and Tell* is Drama Club comedy. (1960, February).** The Gallaudet Record, 5 (2), 4. {Professors Elizabeth Benson and Edward Scouten were joint interpreters for this modern comedy by Frederick Hugh Herbert} [Gallaudet University Archives and "Elizabeth English Benson, interpreter in the Language of Signs" biographical subject vertical file]

Koda Korner: The circle of friendship [Poem]. (1998, May). CODA Connection, 15 (2), 6. (The editor thanks "my Koda buddy JJ!" for submitting this piece) [UNIV DEAF Periodicals]

Konner, B., & Konner, L. (1993, May 29). The night I "read" my first sitcom: How a woman's love affair with TV blossomed after she learned about closed captioning. TV Guide, 41 (22), Issue No. 2096, pp. 24-26. (By Bernice Konner as told to Linda Konner) [C]

Konner, L. (1977, April). Silent lives: My parents' deafness was not something that had to be spelled out to me. It was always there, something that I simply had to accept. Seventeen, 36 (4), 38, 42. [Gallaudet University Archives, "Hearing children of deaf parents" subject vertical file]

Konner, L. (1987, May). I was my parents' radio: As a child, I only knew that I could hear and they couldn't. Glamour Magazine, 85 (5), 228, 231-232, 234. [DEAF 306.874 K66i, 1987]

Kopas, J. (1992, March). Children of Deaf Adults: Ode on misconceptions of deafness. DCARA News, 6. (Newsletter of the Deafness Advocacy, Counseling and Referral Agency serving the San Francisco Bay Area. Main office is in San Leandro, California) [UNIV DEAF Periodicals]

Kowalewski, L., & Kowalewski, F. (Eds.). (1955, February). The answer box, this month's question is: As the deaf parent of a normal child what was your greatest problem in his upbringing? The Silent Worker, 7 (6), 31. {Responses are from Bert Neathery, Mrs. Barbara Babbini, Calton James, Walter M. Lester, Sr., Alfred and Josephine Skogen and Felix and Laura Kowalewski} [UNIV DEAF Periodicals]

Kraft, B. (1989a, May). The CODA forum: Focus, deaf codas [Letter from Bonnie Kraft]. CODA Newsletter, 6 (2), 5. [UNIV DEAF Periodicals]

Kraft, B. (1989b, July/August). From the mailbox [Letter to Betty Colonomos]. <u>TBC News,</u> No. 16, 4. {Letter in support of Betty Colonomos' letter in <u>TBC NEWS,</u> No. 14} [UNIV DEAF Periodicals]

Kraft, B. S. (1992, May). [Letter to the editor]. <u>CODA Connection, 9</u> (2), 3. {Response to the "Coda Talk" column by Sheila Jacobs} [UNIV DEAF Periodicals]

Kraft, B. (1995a, February). [Letter to the editor]. <u>Views, 12</u> (2), 20. (Registry of Interpreters for the Deaf newsletter) {Response to a letter from Earl Elkins (December, 1994) and his opposition to the formation of a special interest group for codas} [UNIV DEAF Periodicals]

Kraft, B. (1995b, Spring). Reaction to Region I. <u>The Communicator: Newsletter of the Massachusetts Registry of Interpreters for the Deaf,</u> 5. [*]

Kraft, B. (1995c, Spring). Being allies to each other. <u>The Communicator: Newsletter of the Massachusetts Registry of Interpreters for the Deaf,</u> 8. [*]

Kraft, B. (1996a, March). Special Interest Groups [Letter to the editor]. <u>Views, 13</u> (3), 4. (Registry of Interpreters for the Deaf newsletter) [UNIV DEAF Periodicals]

Kraft, B. (1996b, Aug/Sept). Deaf voices panel controversial. <u>CODA Connection, 13</u> (3), 8. [UNIV DEAF Periodicals]

Kraft, B. (1997a, February). Deaf parents? Get over it! <u>CODA Connection, 14</u> (1), 16. [UNIV DEAF Periodicals]

Kraft, B. (1997b, May). Dear readership [Note from the editor]. <u>CODA Connection, 14</u> (2), 7. {Response to the proposal for an official "Christian Coda" group session} [UNIV DEAF Periodicals]

Kraft, B. (1997c, May). [Editorial]. <u>CODA Connection, 14</u> (2), 2. {Misconceptions about CODA and her experiences over the years} [UNIV DEAF Periodicals]

Kraft, B. (1997d, September). Dear Codas [Editorial]. <u>CODA Connection, 14</u> (3), 2, 11, 17. [UNIV DEAF Periodicals]

Kraft, B. (Ed.). (1997e, September). Sharing a parent's pain. <u>CODA Connection, 14</u> (3), 10. {A letter from one child of a Holocaust survivor to another is reprinted with commentary from the editor and several questions. "Some of the sadness reported [in the letter] of not being able to communicate with a parent well or share in a parent's experience [of the Holocaust] reminds me of what some codas have reported feeling...Do we feel a similar kind of guilt for being hearing? Given that the existence of a Deaf Community today is also a remarkable testament to survival, would the process of documenting a parent's life story help create new ways of communicating together? Do we owe this to the next generations of our families? Maybe we should think of putting our family's stories on video, too."} [UNIV DEAF Periodicals]

Kraft, B. S. (1987, June). The only child of deaf parents. <u>Deaf Community News: Massachusetts State Association of the Deaf,</u> 3. (Boston, Massachusetts) [UNIV DEAF Periodicals]

Kraft, E. (1998, May). Guest editorial: Hello all the folks of Codas, Bonnie Kraft's friends. <u>CODA Connection, 15</u> (2), 2. {Elinor Kraft, the editor's mother, expresses her thanks to codas for their support and love during her illness} [UNIV DEAF Periodicals]

A
R
T
I
C
L
E
S

Larcen, D. (1989, April 7). A bridge to celebrity: Hartford kindergartner stars in made-for-TV film. The Hartford Courant (Connecticut Living section), pp. D1, D6. (Hartford, Connecticut) {Kim and John Silva are the deaf parents of Allison Silva, age 6 and hearing, who stars in *Bridge to Silence* with Marlee Matlin. John teaches at the American School for the Deaf and Kim teaches Sign Language for West Hartford's Continuing Education Program. The family is interviewed about their involvement in the filming} [*]

Latz, R. (1996, Aug/Sept). A personal response... CODA Connection, 13 (3), 9. [UNIV DEAF Periodicals]

Lawrence, S. (1994, September). No Dr. Spock for parents of deaf children? [Letter to the editor]. Deaf Life, 7 (3), 6-7. [UNIV DEAF Periodicals]

Layton, A. B., Jr. (1979, February 8). Deaf mother testifies about her sterilization. Daily News. (Bangor, Maine) [Gallaudet University Archives, "Court litigation - deaf" subject vertical file]

LBJ lauds graduates, but class doesn't hear. (1966, June 14). Record-American. (Boston, Massachusetts) {Accompanying photo shows Louis Fant "translating" for President Johnson} [Gallaudet University Archives, "Louie Fant" subject vertical file]

Leach, E. (1980, January 24). Signing off on overseas odyssey: She taught Malaysian deaf to communicate. Valley News. (Van Nuys, California) [Gallaudet University Archives, "Marie Greenstone" biography vertical file]

Learn to sign by video. (1985, May 1). Cache Citizen. (Cache County, Lewiston, Utah) [Gallaudet University Archives, "Children of deaf adults" and "American Sign Language - teaching" subject vertical files]

Legon, J. (1991, August 12). Child interpreters: Innocence, or more, may be lost in the translation. Boston Globe, pp. 1, 16. (Boston, Massachusetts - Article excerpted in the May, 1992, issue of the CODA Connection, 9 (2), 6. [UNIV DEAF Periodicals]) {Jeanine is 9 years old and the only English-speaking member of her immigrant family. She interpreted from Chinese to English for her pregnant mother in the hospital for the first two hours of the delivery. The article discusses issues around the fact that 42% of the 57,000 students in the Boston public schools come from homes where the principle language spoken is not English. Lowry Hemphill, Harvard University professor, is also interviewed. Parallels to hearing children interpreting for their deaf parents are pointed out} [*]

Lending an ear. (1988, March 7). The Detroit News. (Detroit, Michigan) {Reports that Louise Fletcher and Nanette Fabray went to Capitol Hill to speak for the deaf before the House Subcommittee on Health and the Environment} [Gallaudet University Archives, "Louise Fletcher" biographical vertical file]

Leon, K. (1964, June). A U.S. Navy news release...U.S. Navy's silent ambassador to Japan [Photo and story]. The Silent News, 16 (10), 3-4, cover. [UNIV DEAF Periodicals]

Lerch, K. (1992, February). Found new [A poem]. CODA Connection, 9 (1), 8. [UNIV DEAF Periodicals]

Lerch, K. (1995, Aug/Sept). [Letter to the editor]. CODA Connection, 12 (3), 8. [UNIV DEAF Periodicals]

Lessard, J. (1990, April 20). Deaf finally finding acceptance: Awareness week part of effort to aid understanding. East Oregonian, 115th year, No. 95, pp. 8B or 8E. (Pendleton, Oregon) [*]

Lessig, H. (1988, February 19). Interpreter helps testimony. Press-Enterprise, pp. 1, 14. (Bloomsburg, Pennsylvania) [Gallaudet University Archives, "Court litigation - deaf" subject vertical file]

Levin, A. (1977, January). The silent parent: The first in a series of disabled parent/disabled child interviews. Mainstream: Advocate of San Diego County's Able-Disabled, 2 (3), 3-4. (San Diego, California) {Interview with Jay D. Wilson, San Diego County interpreter for the deaf, who has deaf parents, grandparents, aunts and uncles on both sides of the family} [Gallaudet University Archives, "Parent-child relationship - deaf adults" subject vertical file]

Levitan, L. (1990, June). Entertainment book review: Irreconcilable differences? [Book review of *Never the Twain Shall Meet: The communications debate* by Richard Winefield, Gallaudet University Press, 1987]. Deaf Life, 2 (12), 6. [UNIV DEAF Periodicals]

Levitan, L. (1991, July). Entertainment book review: Remembrance of things past [Book review of *In silence: Growing up hearing in a deaf world* by Ruth Sidransky]. Deaf Life, 4 (1), 8. [UNIV DEAF Periodicals]

Levitan, L. (1992, April). Entertainment book review: Golden hands, review of *Our father Abe, the story of a deaf shoe repairman* by Harvey L. Barash, M.D., and Eve Barash Dicker. Deaf Life, 4 (10), 8. [UNIV DEAF Periodicals]

Lewellen, J. (1960, July). She preaches in the world of silence: The Rev. Constance Elmes of Chicago helps deaf people lead full, confident, happy lives. This is the inspiring story of her ministry. Every Woman's Family Circle, 72d-72g. {About The Rev. Constance Elmes, a coda, and pastor to her deaf congregation in Chicago Temple First Methodist Church, Chicago, Illinois} [Gallaudet University Archives, "Constance Elmes" biographical vertical file]

Lewis, J. (1985, November). My parents are deaf: There's really no other way to say it. Should you feel sorry for me? No, there's nothing to feel sorry for. Should I be treated any differently? I don't think so, because I'm not different. My family is just as normal as the next. My parents can do everything but hear [Your words column]. Seventeen, 44 (11), 114. {Janet Lewis is 17 years old and from Scranton, Pennsylvania, and talks about what it's like to have deaf parents and lessons she's learned} [UNIV Periodicals]

Lewis, P. (1976, April 29). Kids growing up unheard can tear a family. The Washington Star, pp. B1-B2. (Washington, D. C.) {Story about Louise Fletcher, Robert and Estelle Fletcher, her deaf parents, and hearing siblings Georgianna and John} [Gallaudet University Archives, "Parent-child relationship - deaf adults" subject vertical file]

Life with sounds of silence. (1983, May 26). News-Gazette. (Martinez, California) [Gallaudet University Archives, "Louise Fletcher" biographical vertical file]

Lilliston, L. (1968, June 5). Normal child fitting into deaf household [Photo and caption]. The Los Angeles Times, pp. 1, 8. (Los Angeles, California) [Gallaudet University Archives, "Wayne Christensen" biographical vertical file]

Lindholm, T. (1959, February). Richard West's tribute to Dr. Rice...The Deaf of the Philippines. The Silent Worker, 11 (6), 3-5. {Dr. Delight Rice was the hearing daughter of deaf parents and taught at the Wisconsin School for the Deaf. She established a school for the deaf and blind in Manila, Philippine Islands in 1907 and taught there for 18 years. She received an honorary Doctor of Pedagogy degree from Gallaudet College in 1955. Richard West pays tribute to Dr. Rice. He was educated at the school she founded in the Philippine Islands and served six terms as president of the Philippine Association of the Deaf. Delia Delight Rice was born in 1883 and died October 9, 1964} [UNIV DEAF Periodicals]

Lindholm, T. (Ed.). (1965, February). Humor among the deaf: G. Flora Hoag [and photo]. The Deaf American, 17 (6), 10. {Reported is the death of Mrs. G. Flora (nee Axtell) Hoag, in Berkeley, California, January 11, 1965. She was a graduate of the Minnesota School for the Deaf. Mentioned also is that her son, Dr. Ralph Hoag, is a specialist on education of the deaf in the U.S. Office of Education, Washington, D.C.} [UNIV DEAF Periodicals]

(*) **Lindner, D. (1993, Spring).** How you can help your kids adjust. Accent on Living, 38, 35-36. (Magazine that provides information about new products, travel ideas, medical news, housing, adjustment, inspiration and other areas of interest to mobility impaired individuals. Located in Bloomington, Illinois) {Mother has systemic lupus} [*]

Linnett, L. (1993a, September). CODA - American style. British Deaf News Supplement, 24 (9), 1. [UNIV DEAF Periodicals]

Linnett, L. (1993b, September). Hearing - Me, Mother Father Deaf. British Deaf News Supplement, 24 (9), 1. [UNIV DEAF Periodicals]

Linnett, L. (1993c, September). H-MFD. British Deaf News Supplement, 24 (9), 1. [UNIV DEAF Periodicals]

(#) **Lip-reading skill wins Wac commission (n.d.).** (Source and city unidentified) [Gallaudet University Archives, "World War II" subject vertical file]

Litchfield, A. (1986, February). Coda in the classroom [Letter from Ada Litchfield]. CODA Newsletter, 3 (1), 3. [UNIV Deaf Periodicals]

Lloyd, K. (1998, January). Brisbane bottom line: The WFD World Congress may just be the best deal in town. WFD News, 11 (1), 17-18. (Publication of the World Federation of the Deaf) {Announces the XIII World Congress of the World Federation of the Deaf that will occur July 25-August 1, 1999 in Brisbane, Australia. In addition, a CODA retreat will occur after the Congress} [UNIV DEAF Periodicals]

(##) **Lon Chaney, famous mimic who won world's applause by characterizations, dies. (1930, August 26).** Buffalo Times, p. 1. (Buffalo, New York) [*]

(#) **Lon Chaney famous son of deaf parents: Actor a genius at pantomime, learned from speech with deaf. (n.d.).** Ephpheta Newsletter. (A Catholic monthly for the deaf. A publication of the New York Xavier Ephpheta Society) {About the origins of Chaney's acting genius: his mother's bedside. Lon Chaney cared for his mother after she became an invalid and her hands were silenced from rheumatism. He was in the fourth grade. "His care of his mother, there in the bed...was his laboratory and classroom in a great workday school of acting."} [UNIV DEAF Periodicals and the Gallaudet University Archives, "Lon Chaney" biographical vertical file]

(##) **Lon Chaney, movie star: Movie world mourns noted mystery man, grotesque character of silver screen was believed on road to recovery. (1930, August 26).** Buffalo Times, p. 1. (Buffalo, New York) [*]

Lon Chaney's life: Learned mimicry by amusing mute mother; goes to movies from Vaudeville. (1930, August 29). The Cleveland Press, No. 16320, p. 17. (Cleveland, Ohio) [*]

Lon Chaney - Thousand faces. (1946, February). The Ohio Chronicle. (Publication of the Ohio School for the Deaf, Columbus. Reprinted from the Washington, D. C., Herald) [Gallaudet University Archives, "Lon Chaney" biographical vertical file]

The London H-MFD group. (1994, January). Hearing parents? How odd! British Deaf News, 25 (1), 13. (This H-MFD article commemorates the International Year of the Family) {Describes what happens when hearing adults who have deaf parents in England get together. Thoughts about the future of the London H-MFD (Hearing-me, mother father deaf) group are shared} [UNIV DEAF Periodicals]

Long, E. F. (1918a, April). Stray straws [Photos]. The Silent Worker, 30 (7), 120-121. {Mentions that many teachers, officers and sons of teachers and officers in American Schools for the Deaf are serving in the Army or Navy. Edmund H. Booth, the grandson of Iowa's "grand old deaf man," the late Edmund Booth, is pictured} [UNIV DEAF Periodicals]

Long, E. F. (1918b, May). Stray straws [Photo]. The Silent Worker, 30 (8), 139. {Mentions that Charles Owen Comp of Omaha, Nebraska, is the only son of Mr. and Mrs. Charles Comp (Eva Owen), both graduates of the Illinois School for the Deaf. A photo of him at the age of 19 is included. He is reported to be entering the United States Naval Academy at Annapolis, Maryland, soon} [UNIV DEAF Periodicals]

(#) Loos, R. (1988, October 23). Why David forgot how to talk. Sun Herald. (Melbourne, Australia?) {Ms. Trish Wright-Cullinane is interviewed about their special playgroup at Stanmore in Sydney's inner-west which is run by the Deaf Society of Australia. It is a playgroup for one to five-year-old hearing children who have deaf parents. They attempt to provide them with language and social skills to "catch up" before they enter pre-school or primary school}

Losacano, L. (1989, Fall). Growing up with deaf parents: My parents are deaf.... Voice, 5 (2), 10-12. [UNIV DEAF Periodicals]

(#) Louise Fletcher: Being a mom isn't so cuckoo. (n.d.). The Star. (City unidentified) {Includes two photos of Louise Fletcher with her sons Andrew, 12, and John, 13, at home in Bel Air, California} [Gallaudet University Archives, "Louise Fletcher" biographical vertical file]

Louise Fletcher crusading for the deaf. (1982, December 3). Post and Times Star. (Covington, Kentucky) {Reports that Louise Fletcher is meeting the press in various cities to talk about the program on PBS called *To Hear, a Celebration of Sound*} [Gallaudet University Archives, "Louise Fletcher" biographical vertical file]

Louise Fletcher's parents deaf: Dream realized in world of silence. (1976, April 8). Record. (Stockton, California) [Gallaudet University Archives, "Louise Fletcher" biographical vertical file]

(#) Louise Fletcher's understanding sister. (n.d.). (Publication and location unidentified) [Gallaudet University Archives, "Louise Fletcher" biographical vertical file]

Love is Never Silent (1985). (1986, November 28). Telegraph. (Alton, Illinois) {Reports a repeat showing of the film that won the 1986 Emmy for Outstanding Drama Special. Although it "lacks the edge and quirky vitality that some of us prize in drama...It is well-done.. a first-class tear-jerker" that "reaches a fine pitch of pathos."} [Gallaudet University Archives, "Love is Never Silent" subject vertical file]

Love is Never Silent [Photo and caption]. (1985, December 9). Evening Item. (Lynn, Massachusetts) {Reports *Love is Never Silent* will be on NBC, Monday evening} [Gallaudet University Archives, "Love is Never Silent" subject vertical file]

Love is Never Silent [Photo and caption]. (1986, December 7). Journal. (Providence, Rhode Island) {Reports a repeat showing of this Emmy-winning movie} [Gallaudet University Archives, "Love is Never Silent" subject vertical file]

Love is Never Silent production honored at Kennedy Center. **(1987, Jan.-Feb.).** Gallaudet Alumni Newsletter, 21 (4), 2. (See the February, 1986, issue of the CODA Newsletter, 3 (1), 3, for the article "CODA on the screen" with responses to the airing of this film on December 9, 1985 [UNIV DEAF Periodicals]) [Gallaudet University

A
R
T
I
C
L
E
S

Archives]

Love matters. (1967, September 21). The Wichita Eagle. (Wichita, Kansas - See the letter to the editor by D. C. Sherman, September 29th, entitled "Love conquers many things") {Short article noting it's "heartwarming to read that a deaf couple in California finally has won a battle to adopt a 2-year-old boy with normal hearing."} [Gallaudet University Archives, "Parent-child relationship: Deaf adults" subject vertical file]

Loving family [Photo and caption]. (1985, December 8). Tennessean. (Nashville, Tennessee) {Reports *Love is Never Silent* will be on Channel 4, Monday evening. Story is on page 14} [Gallaudet University Archives, "Love is Never Silent" subject vertical file]

Ludovico, R. G. (1950, April). Children of the deaf: The Fauths of Pennsylvania. The Silent Worker, 2 (8), 7-8. [UNIV DEAF Periodicals]

Luke, C. (1989, February). Murdered girl was voice and ears for deaf mother. The Silent News, 21 (2), 5. [UNIV DEAF Periodicals]

Lupo, F. (1943, November 24). Private Benson is honored visitor. The Buff and Blue, 52 (3), p. 1. (Student newspaper of the Gallaudet Student Body Government) [UNIV Archives]

LU spotlight: Singing to the deaf. (1987, May). Fundamentalist Journal, 6 (5), 42. (Liberty University publication, Lynchburg, Virginia) [*]

Luther, M. (1976, April 11). Deaf parents see dream come true: Used Sign Language on TV to talk to mother, father. Gazette. (Kalamazoo, Michigan) [Gallaudet University Archives, "Louise Fletcher" biographical vertical file]

Lynch, K. (1997, February). A Coda reaches out. CODA Connection, 14 (1), 19. [UNIV DEAF Periodicals]

Machniak, S. (1977, September). Growing up normal: Growing up with deafness. Hints Newsletter, 10 (9), 2-3. (Official monthly newsletter of Tarrant County Services for the Hearing Impaired, Fort Worth, TX 76110 Reprinted as a guest editorial in Gallaudet Today, 8 (2), 10-11. [Gallaudet University Archives or RESERVE]) [*]

Machniak, S. (1991, Aug/Sept). CODA song [Verse]. CODA Connection, 8 (3), 2. (Song to be sung to the tune of "Lola" by the Kinks. Sara is from Austin, Texas) [UNIV DEAF Periodicals]

Mackell, R., Jr. (1992, May 9). Johnstown woman wins state Bar award. The Tribune-Democrat, p. A3. (Philadelphia, Pennsylvania) [*]

Mairs, N. (1990, November 8). Vivid images get buried under verbiage [Book review of *In silence: Growing up hearing in a deaf world* by Ruth Sidransky]. The Los Angeles Times, p. E18. (Los Angeles, California) [*]

(#) Mandrell, J. (1994?). A quick tour of the Deaf Nation [Review of the film *In the Land of the Deaf*]. New York Newsday. [*]

Manners, D. (1976, February 29). Mean Nurse Ratched: Fletcher - extraordinary life. Herald-Examiner. (Los Angeles, California) [Gallaudet University Archives, "Louise Fletcher" biographical vertical file]

The man of a thousand faces: A sketch of Lon Chaney. (1940, February). Digest of the Deaf, 2 (5), 8-11.

(Condensed from an article in the September, 1930, <u>The Literary Digest, 106,</u> pages 37, 40, 42 and 44 - His first name was Alonzo) [Gallaudet University Archives, "Lon Chaney" biographical vertical file]

Man of many faces dons death mask [Photos and caption]. (1930, August 26). <u>Buffalo Times (Final Edition),</u> p. 1. (Buffalo, New York) {Five photos are of Chaney: two candid shots and three from various film roles} [*]

Man of thousand faces takes but one to grave: Versatile actor will play final role in drama of death tomorrow. (1930, August 27). <u>The Los Angeles Times, 49</u> (part 2), pp. 1, 5. (Los Angeles, California) {Funeral arrangements and obituary for Lon Chaney Sr., silent film star} [*]

Marcus, A. (1993, May). CODA/KODA down under. <u>CODA Connection, 10</u> (2), 4. [UNIV DEAF Periodicals]

Marcus, A. L. (1994, May/June). Present and future. <u>TBC News,</u> No. 68, 3. [UNIV DEAF Periodicals]

Marcus-Lieberman, A. J. (1993a, Aug/Sept). My two earths: A poem. <u>CODA Connection, 10</u> (3), 5. [UNIV DEAF Periodicals]

Marcus-Lieberman, A. J. (1993b, Aug/Sept). Silence inside: A poem. <u>CODA Connection, 10</u> (3), 5. [UNIV DEAF Periodicals]

Marcus-Lieberman, A. J. (1993c, Aug/Sept). Talk to me: A poem. <u>CODA Connection, 10</u> (3), 5. [UNIV DEAF Periodicals]

Mare Winningham [Photo and caption]. (1985, December 8). <u>Press.</u> (Pittsburgh, Pennsylvania) {Reports *Love is Never Silent* will be on NBC, Monday, at 9 p.m.} [Gallaudet University Archives, "Love is Never Silent" subject vertical file]

Mare Winningham sees what she "hears" on NBC-TV drama. (1985, December 8). <u>Maine Sunday Telegram</u> [TV Week, p. 4F. (Portland, Maine) {A positive review of the film *Love is Never Silent*. Mare Winningham is an Emmy-winning young actress who played "the hearing daughter of deaf-mute parents" in this drama. Describes her efforts under teacher Lou Fant, to learn Sign Language for the part of Margaret} [Gallaudet University Archives, "Love is Never Silent" subject vertical file]

Mare Winningham's toughest role tonight as child of deaf parents. (1985, December 9). <u>Jersey Journal.</u> (Jersey City, New Jersey) {An interview with Winningham and her struggle to learn Sign Language for *Love is Never Silent*} [Gallaudet University Archives, "Love is Never Silent" subject vertical file]

Marjorie Clere interprets medical program. (1973, July-August). <u>The Deaf American, 25</u> (11), 34. (Article appears in the "RID Interprenews" section) {Kay Russell's "Ladies Day" program on WSYR-TV in Syracuse, New York, is interpreted into American Sign Language by coda Marjorie Clere} [UNIV DEAF Periodicals]

Marklein, M. B. (1989, July 10). Parents meet challenges of child-rearing creatively. <u>USA Today,</u> p. D5. [UNIV Newspapers]

Marriage a failure. (1889, January 31). <u>The Silent Worker - Trenton, 2</u> (10), 1. {Reports the Literary Society in Columbus, Ohio, debated this question and answered affirmatively: "...a mute wife and a deaf husband ought to redeem matrimony and make it a 'howling' success."} [Gallaudet University Archives]

Marten, M. (1978, March 3). Custody battle over girl seen as victory for deaf. <u>Herald Examiner.</u> (Los Angeles,

California) [Gallaudet University Archives, "Court litigation - deaf" and "Parent-child relationship - deaf adults" subject vertical files]

Martin, M. (1993, August). Obituaries: Friends and family mourn 9-year old drowning victim. The Silent News, 25 (8), 21. (Reprinted from the Cleveland, Ohio, Plain Dealer, June 26, 1993) [UNIV DEAF Periodicals]

McAleavey, M. (1998, February). View from a Goda [Grandchild of Deaf Adult]. CODA Connection, 15 (1), 1, 7-8. {Marc is the son of long-time CODA member and Indiana representative, Judy McAleavey} [UNIV DEAF Periodicals]

McCann, J. A. (1992, Aug/Sept). Don't forget the children - the hearing children born to deaf parents. CODA Connection, 9 (3), 4. [UNIV DEAF Periodicals]

McConnell, L. (1995-96, Winter). Mothers and babies: Researchers study mother-child interaction and child development. Preview: Pre-College Programs, Gallaudet University, 5-7. [Gallaudet University Archives]

McDermott, J. (1982, June). What's the top winner like? Guideposts, 5-7, cover. {Cover photo of Greg Hunter with the question: "Have you ever felt embarrassed by your parents? Read this Youth Contest winner's story."} [Gallaudet University Archives, "Parent-child relationship - deaf adults" subject vertical file]

McDouglas, M. (1990, November). Children of deaf parents. Deaf USA, 4 (36), 3. [UNIV DEAF Periodicals]

McGee, J. (1994, May). Letters to the editor. CODA Connection, 11 (2), 5. {Discusses reasons she and others may not be involved in the organization CODA} [UNIV DEAF Periodicals]

McIntosh, R. A. (1995, April/May). Mixed couples: Mixed communication. Hearing Health, 11 (3), 23-24. [UNIV DEAF Periodicals]

McIntyre, B. (1978, September 19). Deaf couple raising children successfully. Record. (Stockton, California) [Gallaudet University Archives, "Parent-child relationship - deaf adults" subject vertical file]

(*) McKenna, K. E. (1995, Aug/Sept). My family room: The 1995 CODA [Millie Brother] Scholarship essay winner. CODA Connection, 12 (3), 6. (Reprinted in D. Prickett & R. Prickett (Eds.), Richness in our diversity: Proceedings of the tenth International CODA Conference, Research Triangle Park, North Carolina, July 27-30, 1995 (pp. 128-129). Santa Barbara, CA: Children of Deaf Adults. [On order]) [UNIV DEAF Periodicals]

McKinney, K. (1976, April 11). Their link with "other world" - Korean baby. Pantagraph, p. B10. (Bloomington-Normal, Illinois) [*]

McLendon, W. (1962, October 13). Singing star tells Gallaudet students: She's not beaten by missing a beat. The Washington Post. (Washington, D. C.) {Nanette Fabray stars in Mr. President, an Irving Berlin musical playing at the National Theater. She met with Gallaudet College students and discussed her own life "with a hearing defect."} [Gallaudet University Archives, "Elizabeth English Benson, interpreter in the Language of Signs" biographical subject vertical file]

McLeod, M. (1991, August). Death on the doorstep: As the police searched for clues, they began to ask, is some killer playing a game with us? Readers Digest, 139 (832), 135-140. (Reprinted from the Florida Magazine: The Sunday Supplement of Orlando Sentinel, May 12, 1991) {Subject is a coda} [UNIV Periodicals]

McSheffery, B. (1992, May). Dear Sheila [Letter to the editor]. <u>CODA Connection, 9</u> (2), 4. [UNIV DEAF Periodicals]

Mears, S. (1997, February). Her voice [Poem]. <u>CODA Connection, 14</u> (1), 18. [UNIV DEAF Periodicals]

Mellott, K. (1998, February 26). Sounding a horn for world's deaf: Mount Aloysius educators recruiting students in Central America. <u>The Tribune-Democrat,</u> p. A3. (Johnstown, Pennsylvania) {Article about coda Shirley Bassett and her forthcoming trip to interview and assess many poor deaf young people who are candidates for the Mount Aloysius College's Cooperative Association of States for Scholarships program funded through the United States Agency for International Development} [*]

Memorial service for Elizabeth Benson. (1973, January 10). <u>On the Green, 2</u> (9), 1. [Gallaudet University Archives]

Mental Health Services for Deaf Adults and Children Program (MENDAC). (1991, May). <u>CODA Connection, 8</u> (2), 3. (MENDAC is at the Seigel Institute, Humana-Michael Reese Medical Center, Chicago, Illinois) {Review of the *Pathways for Parenting* video-based parenting program which was developed by Lutheran Social Services of Michigan. Linda Tebelman, MSW, coordinated the project. It's designed to educate Deaf parents of hearing children} [UNIV DEAF Periodicals]

The message of Academy Awards [Letters to the editor]. (1976, April 4). <u>The Los Angeles Times, 95</u> (part 9), p. 2. (Los Angeles, California) {William Westmiller of Hollywood, Chris Stanford of San Clemente, Bruce Gross of Sherman Oaks, and Mark Stern of Sepulveda (all in California) write about Louise Fletcher receiving the 1975 Academy Award for Best Actress} [Gallaudet University Archives, "Louise Fletcher" biographical vertical file]

Middelton-Moz, J., & Fedrid, E. (1987, July-August). The many faces of grief: What many immigrants, Holocaust survivors, Native Americans/Alaskans have in common with adult children of alcoholics. <u>Changes, 2</u> (4), 8-9, 32-34. [*]

Middleton, T. H. (1972, September 26). Light Refractions: What is the opposite of "postpone"? <u>World, 1</u> (7), 80. [Gallaudet University Archives, "Louie Fant" biographical vertical file]

Military funeral for Lieutenant Underhill. (1939, January 16). <u>The Buff and Blue, 47</u> (7), p. 1. (Student newspaper of the Gallaudet Student Body Government) {Describes a West Point Military Academy funeral for Lieutenant James D. Underhill, only son of Mr. and Mrs. Odio W. Underhill, who left Gallaudet in 1908, and were employees at the North Carolina School for the Deaf} [Gallaudet University Archives]

(*) Millar, A. (1995, November). The commitment to succeed [The 1995 CODA Millie Brother Scholarship essay winner]. <u>CODA Connection, 12</u> (4), 6. (Reprinted in D. Prickett & R. Prickett (Eds.), <u>Richness in our diversity: Proceedings of the tenth International CODA Conference, Research Triangle Park, North Carolina, July 27-30, 1995</u> (pp. 130-131). Santa Barbara, CA: Children of Deaf Adults. [On order]) [UNIV DEAF Periodicals]

Miller, M. (1997, March 14). Rogue Jordan soldier kills 7 Israeli schoolgirls. <u>The Los Angeles Times,</u> pp. A1, A10. (Los Angeles, California - Referred to by Elliot Aheroni in "The President's Forum" in the May, 1997, <u>CODA Connection, 14</u> (2), 3-4. [UNIV DEAF Periodicals]) {It was reported that one of the teenagers was Adi Malka, the hearing daughter of deaf parents} [*]

Miller, R. (1985, December 9). Superb drama sounds off on problems of the deaf. Mercury News, pp. 1E, 5E. (San Jose, California) {A very positive review of *Love is Never Silent*. "An extraordinary film that I consider the very best of the 38 TV movies the networks have aired so far this season...Emmy nominations should flock to this movie."} [Gallaudet University Archives, "Love is Never Silent" subject vertical file]

Minister is shot and killed by youths outside home. (1974, April 3). The Evening Sun, 128 (142), pp. A1, A3. (Baltimore, Maryland) [Gallaudet University Archives, "Louis W. Foxwell" biographical vertical file]

Ministry to the deaf: They hear not - but they see. (1960, March). Together Magazine, 4 (3), 61-64. (Publication of the United Methodist Church) [Gallaudet University Archives, "Louis W. Foxwell" biographical vertical file]

Mink, E. (1985, December 9). Film transcends "Handicap" tag [Television/radio review]. Post-Dispatch. (St. Louis, Missouri) {A very positive review of the film *Love is Never Silent* which "becomes a story of the universal struggle between parent and child over freedom."} [Gallaudet University Archives, "Love is Never Silent" subject vertical file]

(#) Miss Benson first to win commission. (n.d.). The Washington Post. (Washington, D. C.) [Gallaudet University Archives, "World War II" subject vertical file]

Miss Benson honored by Gallaudet. (1963, September 30). The News, p. 6. (Frederick, Maryland) {Dean of Women, Elizabeth Benson, and President Leonard M. Elstad have been awarded lifetime "honorary membership in the Student Body Government of Gallaudet College. They have the distinction of being the first and only honorary members of the organization."} [Gallaudet University Archives, "Elizabeth English Benson, citations and awards" biographical subject vertical file]

Miss Benson is honored by fraternity at Gallaudet. (1963, May 13). The News. (Frederick, Maryland) {Alpha Sigma Pi Fraternity at Gallaudet College has named Miss Elizabeth Benson "1963 Mother of the Year."} [Gallaudet University Archives, "Elizabeth English Benson, citations and awards" biographical subject vertical file]

Miss Benson to receive degree. (1962, May 12). The News, p. 1. (Frederick, Maryland) {On June 4, Gallaudet College will confer on Miss Elizabeth Benson, Dean of Women at Gallaudet College, an honorary Doctor of Letters Degree. This will be the 98th commencement exercises at the college} [Gallaudet University Archives, "Elizabeth English Benson, citations and awards" biographical subject vertical file]

Miss Benson wins "Mother" title here. (1963, July 19). Star. (Washington, D. C.) {Alpha Sigma Pi Fraternity at Gallaudet College has named Miss Elizabeth Benson "1963 Mother of the Year."} [Gallaudet University Archives, "Elizabeth English Benson, citations and awards" biographical subject vertical file]

Miss Elizabeth Benson. (1973, February). Charles Thompson Memorial Hall Newsletter, 17 (2), 4. [Gallaudet University Archives, "Elizabeth English Benson: Obituary, memorial service" biographical subject vertical file]

Miss Elizabeth E. Benson....[Photo and caption]. (1963, April-May). The Buff and Blue, 71 (6), p. 1. (Student newspaper of the Gallaudet Student Body Government) {Photo of "President John F. Kennedy after a special program commemorating 'Hire the Handicapped Week.' Miss Benson served as interpreter for the senior class of Gallaudet who attended by official invitation from President Kennedy."} [Gallaudet University Archives and "Elizabeth English Benson, interpreter in the Language of Signs" biographical subject vertical file]

Missing: Children of Germany's deaf people. (1991, November-December). The World Around You: A publication of Pre-College Programs, Gallaudet University, 7 (14), 4. Washington, DC: Gallaudet University, Pre-

College Programs. [Gallaudet University Archives]

Miss Jo Ann Harrison, daughter of Mr. and Mrs. Edward R. Harrison.... (1961, April). The Silent Worker, 13 (8), 20. [UNIV DEAF Periodicals]

Miss Mary Benson, noted teacher of deaf, dies in Baltimore, Md. [Obituary]. (1984, September 28). The Frederick Post. (Frederick, Maryland) {Mary Benson, sister of Elizabeth English Benson, was born January 26, 1903 and died at the age of 81. She had taught 38 years at the Maryland School for the Deaf in Frederick and several years at four other school programs for the deaf} [Gallaudet University Archives, "Mary Alice Benson: 1903-1984" biographical subject vertical file]

Misurelli, D. (1985a, August 14). Bristol woman "talks" to deaf Russian couple: Part I of two parts. Westosha Report, No. 560, pp. 1, 22. (Twin Lakes, Wisconsin - See excerpts in the November, 1985, issue of the CODA Newsletter, 2 (4), 2-3. [UNIV DEAF Periodicals] Also reported in an article titled "CODA cross-culture" in the November, 1985, issue of the CODA Newsletter, 2 (4), 2-3. [UNIV DEAF Periodicals]) [*]

Misurelli, D. (1985b, August 21). Leningrad deaf couple, Bristol traveler break communication barrier by "signing": Part II of two parts. Westosha Report, No. 561, pp. 1-3. (Twin Lakes, Wisconsin - See excerpts in the November, 1985, issue of the CODA Newsletter, 2 (4), 2-3. [UNIV DEAF Periodicals] Also reported in an article titled "CODA cross-culture" in the November, 1985, issue of the CODA Newsletter, 2 (4), 2-3. [UNIV DEAF Periodicals]) [*]

Misurelli, D. (1985c, October 5). Trip to Leningrad. Chicago Tribune (Sunday Magazine), p. 16. (Illinois - See excerpts in the November, 1985, issue of the CODA Newsletter, 2 (4), 2-3. [UNIV DEAF Periodicals] Also reported in an article titled "CODA cross-culture" in the November, 1985, issue of the CODA Newsletter, 2 (4), 2-3. [UNIV DEAF Periodicals]) [*]

Mom and me [Photos with captions]. (1988, May 8). Fort Worth Star-Telegram. (Fort Worth, Texas) [Gallaudet University Archives, "Parent-child relationship - deaf adults" subject vertical file]

Moore, M. S., & Levitan, L. (1993, July). When deaf people meet deaf parents of a new baby, they always ask if the baby's deaf or hearing. Why? ["For hearing people only" column]. Deaf Life, 6 (1), 10-11. [UNIV DEAF Periodicals]

Moore, M. S., & Levitan, L. (1994, January). What problems, difficulties, or challenges would a "hearing and deaf" couple face as they relate to one another (i.e., dating, marriage)? ["For hearing people only" column]. Deaf Life, 6 (7), 10-11. [UNIV DEAF Periodicals]

Moore, M. S., & Levitan, L. (1995, January). My wife is deaf. I'm hearing. When we enter the deaf community, why do I feel like I'm from an alien nation? I want to fit in...but how? ["For hearing people only" column]. Deaf Life, 7 (7), 6-7. [UNIV DEAF Periodicals]

Moore, M. S., & Levitan, L. (1996, November). Why are deaf people against universal infant hearing screening? Isn't it a good idea to detect hearing loss as soon as possible? ["For hearing people only" column]. Deaf Life, 9 (5), 8-9. [UNIV DEAF Periodicals]

Moore, M. S., & Levitan, L. (1997, October). Are hard-of-hearing people part of the Deaf community? ["For hearing people only" column]. Deaf Life, 10 (4), 8-9. [UNIV DEAF Periodicals]

Morba, R. (1997, February). My inspiration. CODA Connection, 14 (1), 8. [UNIV DEAF Periodicals]

Moreland, C. (1997, September). Coda ambassadors go "Down Under." CODA Connection, 14 (3), 14. {Events surrounding her trip to Australia} [UNIV DEAF Periodicals]

Morrison, M. (1998, April). Marlee Matlin has a firm grip on reality. Mervyns California view, 40-42, 44-45, cover. (Advertising magazine of the California Mervyn apparel stores) {Marlee Matlin, her husband Kevin Grandalski, and their 2-year-old daughter, Sarah, are featured} [*]

Most beloved and endeared...Dr. Rice visits Philippine deaf, blind. (1961, October). The Silent Worker, 14 (2), 6. {An article from the Manila Free Press is quoted extensively. Dr. Delight Rice is the hearing daughter of deaf parents. She was a teacher at the Wisconsin School for the Deaf. She is now 73 years old but 50 years ago she founded the School for the Deaf and the Blind in Manila, the Philippines, in 1911. This article describes her arrival for the school's 50th anniversary celebration and the honors that await her. In 1955, Gallaudet College bestowed an honorary Doctor of Pedagogy degree on her. Delia Delight Rice was born in 1883 and died October 9, 1964} [UNIV DEAF Periodicals]

Most children of deaf can hear. (1975, March 17). Flatbush Life. (Brooklyn, New York - weekly) [Gallaudet University Archives, "Parent-child relationship - deaf adults" subject vertical file]

Mother, father deaf day April 28. (1996, April). The NAD Broadcaster, 18 (4), 34. [UNIV DEAF Periodicals]

Mother, Father Deaf Day. (1998, April). The Silent News, 30 (4), 37. [UNIV DEAF Periodicals]

Mother of the Year. (1963, May 14). The Washington Daily News. (Washington, D. C.) {The Alpha Sigma Pi Fraternity of Gallaudet College named Elizabeth Benson, dean of Women, "Mother of the Year."} [Gallaudet University Archives, "Elizabeth English Benson, citations and awards" biographical subject vertical file]

Movies serve as milestones. (1985, December 5). Enquire Journal. (Monroe, North Carolina) {Features Mare Winningham who stars in *Love is Never Silent*} [Gallaudet University Archives, "Love is Never Silent" subject vertical file]

Mr. and Mrs. Morris Laharty of New Orleans [Photos and caption]. (1922, March). The Silent Worker, 34 (6), 213. {Before her marriage, Mrs. Laharty was Miss Frieda Stern of Brooklyn, New York. Pictured is Bernard Laharty, born July 30, 1921. He is 5 1/2 months old. "The child is a fine wide awake boy."} [UNIV DEAF Periodicals]

Mr. and Mrs. Peter Schindorff. (1921, December). The Silent Worker, 34 (3), 99. {Article about the "mute and deaf residents of Fostoria, Ohio, [who] have a most interesting and accomplished family of two sons and a daughter, all three of them physically normal and 100 percent American citizens." The article and photo feature the military record of Clarence D. Schindorff and ends by saying, "Clarence has a brother, Claude Lester Schindorff, nine years old, a smart, healthy young fellow with promising qualities. They have a fine young sister, Catherine, four years old."} [UNIV DEAF Periodicals]

Mrs. Alfred J. Owens [Photo and caption]. (1918, March). The Silent Worker, 30 (6), 105. {The daughter of Mr. and Mrs. E. Harden of St. Louis, she is a bookkeeper and office assistant at the New York (Fanwood) School for the Deaf} [UNIV DEAF Periodicals]

Mrs. Gilbert Grosvenor, Bell's daughter, dies. (1965, January). The Deaf American, 17 (5), 14. [UNIV DEAF

Periodicals]

Mullins, J. (1984, January 11). Toddler masters sign language. <u>The Sumter Daily Item,</u> p. 4B. (Sumter, South Carolina) {Story about Kenny and Ida Potter and their 14-month-old daughter Julia. Written by a staff writer with <u>The Coalfield Progress</u> of Norton, Virginia} [Gallaudet University Archives, "Hearing children of deaf parents" subject vertical file]

A musical for the deaf. (1973, December). <u>Fundamentalist Journal,</u> 18. (Liberty University publication, Lynchburg, Virginia) [*]

Myers, R. (Ed.). (1989, May). CODA resource section. <u>CODA Connection, 6</u> (2), 4. {Review of the chapter discussing hearing children of deaf parents in Michael Harvey's book, *Psychotherapy with Deaf and Hard-of-Hearing Persons: A Systemic Model* and the film *Bridge to Silence* with six-year-old Allison Silva of Hartford, Connecticut} [UNIV DEAF Periodicals]

Myers, R. (1992, February). A personal exploration: On developing my Coda center [Editorial]. <u>CODA Connection, 9</u> (1), 3-4. [UNIV DEAF Periodicals]

N.A.D. gift. (1943, December). <u>The FRAT: Official Publication of the National Fraternal Society of the Deaf, 41st year, No. 5,</u> 6. {Press release from the American Red Cross} [UNIV DEAF Periodicals]

NAD meets CODA. (1986, August). <u>CODA Newsletter, 3</u> (3), 3. [UNIV DEAF Periodicals]

Nakamura, D. (1994, February 19). Bergan scores, but not alone: Loyola challenges Maryland tonight. <u>The Washington Post,</u> 117th year, No. 76, p. D4. (Washington, D. C.) {About Tracy Bergan of Maryland who is Loyola College's basketball career assists leader. His deaf parents are Gordon and Laura Bergan} [UNIV Newspapers Microfilm]

Names and faces: Rocky marriage smoothed a career. (1988, March 7). <u>The Detroit Free Press.</u> (Detroit, Michigan) {Reports that Louise Fletcher, Nanette Fabray and the Redskins' Larry Brown testified before the House Subcommittee on Health and the Environment sharing their personal experiences with hearing loss} [Gallaudet University Archives, "Louise Fletcher" biographical vertical file]

National acclaim for work of Rev. Elmes. (1945, April). <u>The Cavalier (Akron Edition), 5</u> (8), 3. [Gallaudet University Archives]

Navarro, M. (1981, December 7). Boy, 11, explains his kidney transplant: Five months of difficult medical procedures made this lad into a specialist. <u>San Francisco Examiner.</u> (California) {Bobby Toops and his parents Robert and Kathleen are featured} [*]

Necrology: Alexander Graham Bell. (1924). In <u>American Instructors of the Deaf: Report of the Proceedings of the twenty-third meeting of the Convention of American Instructors of the Deaf, June 25-30, 1923, at Belleville, Ontario, Canada</u> (p. 265). Washington, DC: Government Printing Office. (Bell's mother and wife were deaf) [DEAF 370.72 C6p, 23rd, 1923]

Necrology: Bess Michaels Riggs (August 27, 1887-October 14, 1935). (1936). In <u>Report of the Proceedings of the twenty-ninth meeting of the Convention of American Instructors of the Deaf, Jacksonville, Illinois, June 17-21, 1935</u> (p. 283). Washington, DC: Government Printing Office. {Riggs was the hearing daughter of The Rev. & Mrs. John Michaels of Richmond, Virginia. She graduated from Vassar College in 1910 and Gallaudet College in 1911.

After teaching in public schools for 15 years, and then at the Tennessee School for the Deaf for 2 years, Bess served as superintendent of the Arkansas School for the Deaf from 1926-1935. She died at the age of 48} [DEAF 370.72 C6p, 29th, 1935]

Necrology: William Kavanaugh Argo (October 8, 1857-April 14, 1921). (1924). In American Instructors of the Deaf: Report of the Proceedings of the twenty-third meeting of the Convention of American Instructors of the Deaf, June 25-30, 1923, at Belleville, Ontario, Canada (p. 264). Washington, DC: Government Printing Office. {Argo was the hearing son of deaf parents. He was born October 8, 1857, in Garrard County, Kentucky and died April 14, 1921. He received B.A., M.A., and honorary LL.D. degrees from Center College. He taught at the Kentucky School for the Deaf, then became superintendent. He was also superintendent of the Colorado School for the Deaf from 1888 to 1921} [DEAF 370.72 C6p, 23rd, 1923]

Nelson, H. (1966, July 7). Deaf couple's child-raising ability questioned. The Los Angeles Times, 85 (part 2), p. 1. (Also see San Fernando Valley News) {About the Christensen adoption case} [*]

Nelson, K. (1996, July/August). Region V conference: PAH!!!!! Views, 13 (7), 14-16. (Registry of Interpreters for the Deaf newsletter) [UNIV DEAF Periodicals]

News from Gallaudet College: Schuchman named dean. (1971, June). The Deaf American, 23 (10), 10. [UNIV DEAF Periodicals]

Newsfronts of the world: Lyndon's unheard talk [Photo and caption]. (1961, June 9). Life Magazine. {Vice President Lyndon B. Johnson spoke at the 97th Commencement exercises of Gallaudet College. Dean of Women Elizabeth Benson "interpreted vigorously at his side."} [Gallaudet University Archives, "Elizabeth English Benson, interpreter in the Language of Signs" biographical subject vertical file]

Newsmakers. (1976, April 12). Newsweek, 87 (15), 39. {About the Academy Awards and Louise Fletcher is mentioned} [UNIV Periodicals and Gallaudet University Archives, "Louise Fletcher" biographical vertical file]

Newsmen unable to contact Fulmer. (1955, January 18). Sentinel-Record. (Hot Springs, Arkansas) [Gallaudet University Archives, "Parent-child relationship - deaf adults" subject vertical file]

Noblin, S. (1997, February). Getting past difference. CODA Connection, 14 (1), 6. (Reprinted from an AT & T Relay Center newsletter) [UNIV DEAF Periodicals]

Non-hearing actress Phyllis Frelich... [Photo and caption]. (1985, December 8). Standard Times. (New Bedford, Massachusetts) {Photo of deaf actors Phyllis Frelich and Ed Waterstreet who star in *Love is Never Silent*} [Gallaudet University Archives, "Love is Never Silent" subject vertical file]

Normal child to stay with deaf-mute couple: "Merriest Christmas ever." (1967, December 25). Ft. Lauderdale News, p. 22A. (Ft. Lauderdale, Florida) [Gallaudet University Archives, "Parent-child relationship - deaf adults" subject vertical file]

Normal fellows possess proper background for teaching deaf. (1939, October 25). The Buff and Blue, 48 (2), p. 1. (Student newspaper of the Gallaudet Student Body Government) {"Kenneth F. Huff's inspiration to teach the deaf came from his parents, both of whom are deaf."} [Gallaudet University Archives]

Norris, D. (1988, November 8). Telling his life story: Local man recalls poignant memories from silent childhood. Herald-Republic, pp. 1-2. (Yakima, Washington) [Gallaudet University Archives, "Children of deaf adults" subject vertical file]

Norton, E. (1969, September 30). National Theater of the Deaf on tour again with new shows: Talented and gifted personnel. <u>Record-American.</u> (Boston, Massachusetts) [Gallaudet University Archives, "Louie Fant" subject vertical file]

Noteworthy: Interpreters for deaf parents, it's the law! (1989, January/February). <u>Perspectives in Education and Deafness, 7</u> (3), 23. [UNIV DEAF Periodicals]

Novels turned his head: An educated, wealthy man deserts his wife and children. (1888, April 30). <u>The Deaf-Mute Times, 1</u> (3), 3. {About Atwood J. Sellers, a 22 year old engaged in farming: "Mr Sellers received a college education. He was a great novel and story paper reader, and to too much of this kind of reading is attributed his disappearance. He is a descendant of one of the oldest families in Chester county and has many relatives living in Philadelphia and Darby. He has deen [sic] suffering from a pulmonary trouble, and Dr. Perdue, the attending physician, says he noticed strong evidences of weakness of mind, caused by over-study and reading." Not sure this is about a deaf family and am curious about it's inclusion in <u>The Deaf-Mute Times</u>} [Gallaudet University Archives]

NTD Founders: Where are they now? [Trial issue]. (1987). <u>Deaf Life,</u> 12-22. {Photo and story about Lou Fant (whose parents were deaf) are included. <u>Deaf Life</u> started regular publication in July, 1988} [UNIV DEAF Periodicals]

NTS news: Profile of a recently certified interpreter - Kristen L. Schwall, Arkansas. (1991, July-August). <u>VIEWS, 8</u> (3), 30-31. (Registry of Interpreters for the Deaf newsletter) [UNIV DEAF Periodicals]

Nuernberger, N. (1968, January). The Christensen adoption story. <u>The Deaf American, 20</u> (5), 7-8. [UNIV DEAF Periodicals]

Obituaries: Deaf church rites for Rev. Foxwell. (1974, April 4). <u>News-American.</u> (Baltimore, Maryland) [Gallaudet University Archives, "Louis W. Foxwell" biographical vertical file]

Obituaries: Ron Coffey, June 27, 1994. (1995, Spring). <u>CTN Magazine, 2</u> (1), 15. (Formerly published as <u>Coming Together Newsletter,</u> a national deaf lesbian, gay, and bisexual publication) [*]

Of love and language. (1991, April). <u>Deaf Life: Deaf Life Plus, 3</u> (10), 10. [UNIV DEAF Periodicals]

Olivier, J. (1893, July 20). Should the deaf marry the deaf? Translated by Thomas Francis Fox. In T. F. Fox, O. Hanson & R. P. McGregor (Eds.), <u>Proceedings of the World's Congress of the Deaf and the Report of the Fourth convention of the National Association of the Deaf, held at the Memorial Art Palace, Chicago, Illinois, July 18th, 20th and 22nd, 1893</u> (pp. 110-112). Washington, DC: National Association of the Deaf. (Mr. Jean Olivier is from Ajen, France) [Gallaudet University Archives]

Olsen, G. W. (1986, October). Deafinitely ours column: Frelich, Waterstreet star in Hallmark Hall of Fame's *Love is Never Silent.* <u>NAD Broadcaster, 8</u> (10), 1, 9. [UNIV DEAF Periodicals]

On deaf ears [Photo and caption]. (1985, December 8). <u>Commercial Appeal.</u> (Memphis, Tennessee) {Photo of deaf actors Phyllis Frelich and Ed Waterstreet and Mare Winningham who star in *Love is Never Silent*} [Gallaudet University Archives, "Love is Never Silent" subject vertical file]

118th Commencement held. (1982, May 24). <u>On the Green: A weekly publication for Gallaudet staff and faculty,</u>

A R T I C L E S

12 (32), 1, 3.   {Actress Louise Fletcher addresses graduates of Gallaudet College, May 17, 1982}   [Gallaudet University Archives]

One-man show for the Deaf. (1975, January 23). Post-Intelligencer. (Seattle, Washington) [Gallaudet University Archives, "Louie Fant" biographical vertical file]

On Phoenix (Ariz.) KPHO-TV...Talking hands and realistic views on communication. (1966, September). The Deaf American, 19 (1), 49-50. [UNIV DEAF Periodicals]

(#) (##) On signs, intimacy, and otherness. (1986?). Grey City Journal. (Student publication, University of Chicago) {Samuel Jay Petersen, in a letter to the editor entitled "Portrayal of deaf parents criticized," rebuts the portrayal of deaf people by Lou Ann Walker, author of *A Loss for Words*, and in this article. His parents are deaf and he is hearing}

Orangutan stars on CBS. (1985, March 24). The Florida Keys Keynoter. (Marathon, Florida - The Los Angeles Times Syndicate) {About Louise Fletcher} [Gallaudet University Archives, "Louise Fletcher" biographical vertical file]

Oscar asides. (1979, April 10). New York Post. (New York) {Best Actress Jane Fonda uses Sign Language at the 51st annual Academy Awards and is likened to Louise Fletcher who did the same in 1976 [Gallaudet University Archives, "Louise Fletcher" biographical vertical file]

And other school notes: Green Acres school gets new director. (1962, May 30). The Washington Daily News. (Washington, D. C.) {Briefly mentions that Miss Elizabeth E. Benson of Gallaudet College and several others will receive Honorary Doctors of Letters degrees from Gallaudet College at their 98th commencement, June 4th} [Gallaudet University Archives, "Elizabeth English Benson, honorary degree, Doctor of Letters" biographical subject vertical file]

Padden, D., & Padden, A. (Eds.). (1972, Dec-1973, Jan). Mileposts: In memoriam, 1932 - On Dec. 23, Elizabeth E. Benson, G-'32. Gallaudet Alumni Newsletter, 7 (3), 3. [Gallaudet University Archives]

Padden, D., & Padden, A. (Eds.). (1976, June 1). Mileposts column: General, 1926 and 1928. Gallaudet Alumni Newsletter, 10 (15), 1, 5. {Proud parents, the Rev. Dr. and Mrs. Robert C. Fletcher, and their daughter, Louse Fletcher} [Gallaudet University Archives]

Padden, D., & Padden, A. (Eds.). (1993, April). Mileposts column: In memoriam, 1976 - Eli Savanick, G-'76. Gallaudet Alumni Newsletter, 27 (7), 3. [Gallaudet University Archives]

Padden, T. (1996, February). A deaf mother's column. British Deaf News, 27 (2), 15. {An interesting column mainly addressing issues deaf children of deaf and hearing parents face in England. Tessa responds to letters she receives from concerned parents on a variety of topics. It's rare, but I have seen one brief mention of the hearing child in a family with deaf siblings} [UNIV DEAF Periodicals]

Pair held in slaying of cleric. (1974, April 11). The Washington Post. (Washington, D. C.) [Gallaudet University Archives, "Louis W. Foxwell" biographical vertical file]

Palmer, S., & Reeder, T. (1989, October 17). My story: "You're not like the rest of us." Woman's World: The Woman's Weekly, 10 (42), 16-17, cover. (Sheila Palmer told her story to Theresa Reeder. Listed in the index as a cover story with this title: "She cursed the miracle that made her different from the people she loved.") {Sheila

Palmer's hearing acuity was unknown until she was seven years old and enrolled at the Tennessee School for the Deaf. Her parents, siblings and twin, grandparents, aunt and nieces are all deaf} [*]

Panara, J. (1990, December). How times have changed for hearing children of deaf parents. The Silent News, 22 (12), 6. [UNIV DEAF Periodicals]

Parent-infant interaction in the first year of life. (1987, Winter/Spring). Research at Gallaudet, 4-5. (Report from the Center for Studies in Education and Human Development, Gallaudet Research Institute, Gallaudet University) [Gallaudet University Archives]

Parents' deafness was problem for Louise Fletcher's family. (1976, April 8). Journal. (Montgomery, Alabama) [Gallaudet University Archives, "Louise Fletcher" biographical vertical file]

Parlato, S., Jr. (1997, September). Deafness and eye [Poem]. CODA Connection, 14 (3), 15. (Reprinted from the April, 1997, Silent News [UNIV DEAF Periodicals]) [UNIV DEAF Periodicals]

Parsons, R. (1969, March 13). Deaf parents can bring up normal children. Missourian. (Columbia, Missouri) [Gallaudet University Archives, "Parent-child relationship - deaf adults" subject vertical file]

Pearlman, C. (1991, Spring). Debbie Alexander. Radio Chicago, 14-15. (Chicago, Illinois) [*]

Pearson, J. C. (1990, February). For your information: School ordered to help deaf parents, precedent setting ruling for the NAD Legal Defense Fund. CODA Connection, 7 (1), 6. [UNIV DEAF Periodicals]

(#) People and places: Austin Texas. (1979, November). SAA Newsletter, 12. (Austin, Texas - State Archives Association?) {Reports Louise Fletcher was doing research in the archives records of the Texas State School for the Deaf at the Texas State Archives} [Gallaudet University Archives, "Louise Fletcher" biographical vertical file]

People in the news: Joyous reunion. (1978, March 4). Daily News. (Bangor, Maine) [Gallaudet University Archives, "Court litigation - deaf" subject vertical file]

Perl, L. (1994, July/August). Deaf couple sues state for $18 million: Jackson couple claims Dept. of Social Services took their kids with no evidence. The Deaf Michigander, 2 (9-10), 1. (Reprinted from The Detroit News) [UNIV DEAF Periodicals]

(*) Perry-Sheridan, N. (1995, October). "I was told not to have children:" A serious spinal injury didn't stop one woman from becoming a mother. Parents Magazine 121-122, 124. [UNIV Periodicals]

Personal mention. (1988, March 5). Houston Chronicle. (Houston, Texas) {Reports that Nanette Fabray and Louise Fletcher went to Capitol Hill to speak on behalf of the deaf} [Gallaudet University Archives, "Louise Fletcher" biographical vertical file]

Peters, J., & McNamara, J. (1987, September 2). Honor student knifed. Daily News NYC, pp. 1-2. (New York) [*]

(#) Petersen, S. J. (1986). Portrayal of deaf parents criticized [Letter to the editor]. Grey City Journal. (Student publication, University of Chicago - Date unspecified) {Mr. Petersen is hearing and has deaf parents. He criticizes the depiction of deaf people by Lou Ann Walker in her book A Loss for Words and in an article, "On signs, intimacy, and otherness" in this same newspaper} [*]

141

Petitto, L. (1986, September 28). Living in a silent world [Letters to the editor]. The New York Times Magazine, p. 102. {Response to Lou Ann Walker's article of August 31 ["Outsider in a silent world"]} [UNIV Newspapers Microfilm]

Pictorial highlights of Charter Day. (1981, May). Gallaudet Alumni Newsletter, 15 (13), 1. {Pictures of events celebrating the life of "Bennie," Dr. Elizabeth Benson} [Gallaudet University Archives]

Pietila, A. (1979, November 20). Home like prison, deaf woman testifies. The Sun, pp. C1, C4. (Baltimore, Maryland) [Gallaudet University Archives, "Rev. Louis W. Foxwell, Jr." biographical vertical file]

Pioneer of deaf, blind education in Philippines...Honors pour on Dr. Delight Rice. (1962, February). The Silent Worker, 14 (6), 3, cover. {Dr. Rice is the hearing daughter of deaf parents. She taught at the Wisconsin School for the Deaf and then founded the School for the Deaf and Blind in Manila. She taught in the Philippines from 1907 to 1923. This article describes the honors bestowed on her at the school's 50th anniversary. Delia Delight Rice was born in 1883 and died October 9, 1964} [UNIV DEAF Periodicals]

Pope, R. (1998, May). Untitled [Poem]. CODA Connection, 15 (2), 17. [UNIV DEAF Periodicals]

Popkey, D. (1988a, June 5). Girl raised as deaf now interprets: I am part of both worlds; member of deaf family was "caught" hearing. The Idaho Statesman, 24th year, 316th issue, pp. A1, A10. (Boise, Idaho - There is another title: "Girl raised as deaf now interprets: Woman who once hid ability to hear, talk, uses experience to aid others") {About Sheila Palmer} [*]

Popkey, D. (1988b, June 27). Until age 7, woman didn't know she could hear, speak. The Knoxville Journal, pp. A1, A5. (Knoxville, Tennessee) {About Sheila Palmer} [*]

Porrelli, P. J. (1979, November 16). Pomona youngster handles big task as "ears" for deaf parents. Progress Bulletin. (Pomona, California) [Gallaudet University Archives, "Parent-child relationship - deaf adults" subject vertical file]

Portage couple, deaf-mutes, work out own system of rearing family. (1956, June 12). Sentinel-Tribune. (Bowling Green, Ohio) [Gallaudet University Archives, "Parent-child relationship - deaf adults" subject vertical file]

Porter, S. H. (1917, October). John K. Cloud: Ambulance driver for the deaf in France. The Silent Worker, 30 (1), 6. {Story behind how John K. Cloud got to France and a letter from him from the Front in France, August 23, 1917} [UNIV DEAF Periodicals]

Pregnant deaf woman needs an interpreter in delivery room: NAD-LDF files suit for hospital services. (1978, September). Silent News, 10 (9), 1. [Gallaudet University Archives, "Court litigation - deaf" subject vertical file]

President Johnson surprises graduating class. (1966, May-June). The Gallaudet Record, 11 (9), 1-2. {Photo shows Associate Professor of Education Louie Fant interpreting commencement remarks of President Lyndon Johnson} [Gallaudet University Archives]

President Kennedy addresses annual meeting participants. (1963, July-August). Performance the story of the handicapped, 4-5. (Publication of the President's Committee on Employment of the Handicapped) {President Kennedy greets the Senior Class of Gallaudet College for the Deaf. Miss Elizabeth Benson is one of the interpreters} [Gallaudet University Archives, "Elizabeth English Benson, interpreter in the Language of Signs" biographical subject vertical file]

Preston, C. (1996, Aug/Sept). A newcomer's perspective. <u>CODA Connection, 13</u> (3), 9. [UNIV DEAF Periodicals]

Preston, C. (1997, September). [Letter to the editor]. <u>CODA Connection, 14</u> (3), 7. [UNIV DEAF Periodicals]

Preston, P. (1996, Aug/Sept). [Letter to the editor]. <u>CODA Connection, 13</u> (3), 13. {About the flood disaster that devastated his parent's home} [UNIV DEAF Periodicals]

Prickett, H. (1971, March). [Letter to the editor]. <u>The Deaf American, 23</u> (7), 30-31. [UNIV DEAF Periodicals]

Prickett, H. (1992, May). CODA youth and deaf parents. <u>CODA Connection, 9</u> (2), 1, 4-5. [UNIV DEAF Periodicals]

Prickett, H. (1993a, Aug/Sept). Book review: *Dummy's Little Girl*. <u>CODA Connection, 10</u> (3), 6. [UNIV DEAF Periodicals]

Prickett, H. (1993b, November). Biloxi gets blown away by Sheila Jacobs at Southeastern Regional Conference! <u>CODA Connection, 10</u> (4), 1, 4. [UNIV DEAF Periodicals]

Prickett, H. (1993c, November). Like me [A poem]. <u>CODA Connection, 10</u> (4), 7. (Reprinted from the proceedings of the first CODA conference, Fremont, California, 1986. [DEAF 306.874 C44c, 1986]) [UNIV DEAF Periodicals]

Prickett, H. (1995, November). [Letter to the editor]. <u>CODA Connection, 12</u> (4), 9. [UNIV DEAF Periodicals]

Prickett, H. (1996, November). [Letter to the editor]. <u>CODA Connection, 13</u> (4), 8. [UNIV DEAF Periodicals]

Prickett, H. (1997, September). [Letter to the editor]. <u>CODA Connection, 14</u> (3), 11. [UNIV DEAF Periodicals]

Prickett, H. T. (1987, February). [Review of the book *A Loss for Words* by Lou Ann Walker]. <u>CODA Newsletter, 4</u> (1), 5. [UNIV DEAF Periodicals]

Prickett, R. (1997, August 4). "Building Bridges" breaks new ground. <u>On the Green: A Weekly Published for Gallaudet University Staff and Faculty, 27</u> (15), 4. [UNIV DEAF Newsletters]

Prime time players: Gallaudet graduates star in *Love is Never Silent*. (1986, Spring). <u>Gallaudet Today, 16</u> (3), 6-8. [Gallaudet University Archives or RESERVE]

Private Benson on duty at hospital. (1944, February). <u>The Silent Cavalier, 4</u> (6), 1. (Reprinted from <u>The Frederick News-Post,</u> Frederick, Maryland) [Gallaudet University Archives]

Profiles of notable CODAS. (1997, February). <u>CODA Connection, 14</u> (1), 4. (Reprinted in the May, 1998, issue of <u>The Silent News, 30</u> (5), B12) [UNIV DEAF Periodicals]

Pvt. Benson starts WAC basic training. (1943, September). <u>The Silent Cavalier, 4</u> (1), 1. [Gallaudet University Archives]

Pyers, J. (1998, May). Twentysomething tidbits. <u>CODA Connection, 15</u> (2), 7. {Jennie Pyers is a 24 year old coda and supports the idea of a "Generation Xer" forum in the CODA newsletter} [UNIV DEAF Periodicals]

Qualey, J. S. (1945, August). Deaf mute kills wife, child, thinks he was not loved. The Cavalier, 5 (12), 1. {It's mentioned that the child is a "normal infant." See the related editorial on page two: "Sensationalism and the Deaf."} [Gallaudet University Archives]

Radetsky, P. (1994, August). Silence, signs, and wonders. Discover, 15 (8), 60-68. (Reprinted in the April, 1995, issue of Deaf Life, 7 (10), 10-17, 19-21. [UNIV DEAF Periodicals]) [UNIV Periodical Abstracts Ondisc]

Ralston, A. (1985, September 28). Living in a silent world [Letters to the editor]. The New York Times Magazine, p. 102. [*]

Rancke, C. (1990, November). [Letter to the editor]. CODA Connection, 7 (4), 3-4. [UNIV DEAF Periodicals]

Read, M. A. (1979, March 13). The public forum: Second-class citizenship [Letter to the editor]. Progress Bulletin. (Pomona, California) [Gallaudet University Archives, "Court litigation - deaf" and "Parent-child relationship - deaf adults" subject vertical files]

(#) (##) Rebecca is just six, but she sounds out the world for her deaf family. (1995?). The Echo. (Talaght, Dublin, Ireland)

Receive appointments. (1945, April). WAC News Letter, 2 (9), 7. {Announces that Elizabeth M. Benson of Frederick, Maryland, is the first to receive a second lieutenant appointment in the Women's Army Corps under the new War Department directive} [Gallaudet University Archives, "World War II" subject vertical file]

Receives medal. (1944, September). The Cavalier, 5 (1), 1. {Mrs. Margaret T. Lindsay of Charlottesville, Virginia, received the Purple Heart certificate and Purple Heart Medal awarded her son, Donald Charles Taylor, carpenter's mate, first class, United States Navy} [Gallaudet University Archives]

Record player is sought to help mutes child learn speech. (1956, January 29). The Fresno Bee. (Fresno, California) {The Fresno County Society for Crippled Children is asking for the donation of a phonograph player to help 18 month old "Jack" learn to speak. His parents are deaf} [Gallaudet University Archives, "Parent-child relationship - deaf adults" subject vertical file]

Reid, J. (1988a, November 10). Signing a universal means of communication. American (The American Scene section). (Waterbury, Connecticut) {Feature story about Frank Coppola, hearing son of deaf parents} [Gallaudet University Archives, "Hearing children of deaf parents" subject vertical file]

Reid, J. (1988b, November 10). Signing a valuable communication skill. Waterbury Republican, p. 108. (Waterbury, Connecticut) {Feature story about Frank Coppola, hearing son of deaf parents} [Gallaudet University Archives, "Hearing children of deaf parents" subject vertical file]

Reiter Brandwein, D. (1991, July-Aug). Book review - another perspective on *Growing up hearing in a deaf world.* Views, 8 (3), 27. (Registry of Interpreters for the Deaf Newsletter) [UNIV DEAF Periodicals]

Remarks of President Lyndon B. Johnson at the Gallaudet Centennial Banquet. (1964, July-August). The Silent Worker, 16 (11), cover, 7. {Verbatim transcript of President Johnson's remarks. On the cover is a photo of Elizabeth Benson interpreting for President Johnson at the Gallaudet Centennial Banquet} [UNIV DEAF Periodicals]

Reppert, R. H. (1992a, February). Deaf culture: My heritage, a tribute to my deaf parents. Deaf Culture Today: Assemblies of God Newsletter, 4-5. [UNIV DEAF Periodicals]

Reppert, R. H. (1992b, February). My parents were different. The NAD Broadcaster, 14 (2), 24-25. [UNIV DEAF Periodicals]

Researcher seeks deaf adoptive parents. (1990, May-June). Gallaudet Alumni Newsletter, 24 (6), 4. {Barbara J. White, associate professor in the Department of Social Work at Gallaudet University, is a deaf adoptive mother. She wants to research the unique experiences of other deaf people who have successfully adopted children. She plans to publish her findings in professional journals in social work and adoption} [Gallaudet University Archives]

Reuben C. Stephenson dead. (1925, January). The Silent Worker, 37 (4), 195. {Mentions that "He was married to Josephine Hatterley, daughter of a prominent piano dealer, who bore him three fine hearing and speaking girls."} [UNIV DEAF Periodicals]

Reunion [Photo and caption]. (1978, March 3). San Francisco Chronicle. (California) {Story about 6-year-old Ruth Riley reunited with her deaf parents a year after a San Bernardino county judge placed her "in a foster home after deciding she was 'verbally retarded.'" The Riley's are African-American} [Gallaudet University Archives, "Court litigation - deaf" subject vertical file]

Rev. Louis Foxwell dies: Taught the deaf in Md. (1974, April 5). The Washington Star-News. (Washington, D. C.) [Gallaudet University Archives, "Louis W. Foxwell" biographical vertical file]

Rhein, D. (1985, December 8). A sensitive drama about a family living with deafness and hearing. Des Moines Register. (Des moines, Iowa) {A positive review of *Love is Never Silent*} [Gallaudet University Archives, "Love is Never Silent" subject vertical file]

Richards, B. (1974, April 6). Friend of deaf slain during holdup. The Washington Post, pp. B1, B6. (Washington, D. C.) [Gallaudet University Archives, "Louis W. Foxwell" biographical vertical file]

RID - A long look back - 30 years ago this month [Photo and article]. (1995, January). Views, 12 (1), 6, 21. (Registry of Interpreters for the Deaf newsletter) {The Registry of Interpreters for the Deaf was established in June, 1964, at Ball State University. A significant organizational meeting occurred in Washington, D. C., in January, 1965. Among the participants listed in attendance are the following codas: Mrs. Lillian Beard, Texas; Dr. Elizabeth Benson, Dean of Women, Gallaudet College; Mr. Louie Fant, Jr., Associate Professor, Gallaudet College; Mrs. Virginia Lewis, Executive Secretary, Associates in Anesthesiology; Mrs. Shirley Stein, Assistant Professor, Gallaudet College; Mr. David Watson, an author from Wisconsin; and Mr. Joseph Youngs, Superintendent, Governor Baxter School for the Deaf, Maine} [UNIV DEAF Periodicals]

(#) Riker, B. (1969, Spring). Daughter of deaf couple teaches the handicapped. The Los Angeles Times. (Los Angeles, California - date unidentified) {About Joyce (Linden) Groode} [*]

Rippe, V. (1990, November 3). The inner voices: Growing up with deaf parents means being depended upon to communicate with the world. The Palm Beach Post: Accent, Inside, South Palm Beach Country Living, pp. D1, D7. (Palm Beach, Florida) [*]

Riste, T. (1971, September 17). Emotion takes over in *Man and the City*. The Arizona Daily Star. (Tucson, Arizona) [Gallaudet University Archives, "Louie Fant" biographical vertical file]

Rittenberg, S. B. (1966, December). Lt. Col. Melvin S. Weil, Jr., son of deaf parents, makes good. The Deaf American, 19 (4), 11-12. [UNIV DEAF Periodicals]

A
R
T
I
C
L
E
S

(*) Ritter, D. (1993, Aug/Sept). Realizing new goals [The 1993 CODA Millie Brother Scholarship essay winner]. CODA Connection, 10 (3), 10. (Reprinted in D. Prickett & R. Prickett (Eds.), Richness in our diversity: Proceedings of the tenth International CODA Conference, Research Triangle Park, North Carolina, July 27-30, 1995 (p. 124). Santa Barbara, CA: Children of Deaf Adults. [On order]) [UNIV DEAF Periodicals]

Robertson, N. (1976a, April 5). The Fletchers, family that heard the silent thanks. The New York Times (Family/Style section), p. 36. {About Louise Fletcher} [Gallaudet University Archives, "Louise Fletcher" biographical vertical file]

Robertson, N. (1976b, April 7). Emotional isolation ends in hand-signaled tears. Citizen Patriot. (Jackson, Michigan - The New York Times News Service) {Robert and Estelle Fletcher, their children Georgianna and John, are interviewed about their response to Louise receiving the Oscar for her performance in *One Flew Over the Cuckoo's Nest*} [Gallaudet University Archives, "Louise Fletcher" biographical vertical file]

Robertson, N. (1976c, April 7). Actress' hands signal "my dream come true." Wilmington Morning Star, p. 6. (Wilmington, Delaware) [Gallaudet University Archives, "Louise Fletcher" biographical vertical file]

Robertson, N. (1976d, April 8). Louise Fletcher: Her dream a long time coming true. The Springfield Union. (Springfield, Massachusetts - The New York Times News Service) [Gallaudet University Archives, "Louise Fletcher" biographical vertical file]

Robertson, N. (1976e, April 8/March 28). Silent thanks heard loud and clear: In the Fletchers' world of silence, love isn't kept quiet. Chicago Tribune. (Chicago, Illinois) [Gallaudet University Archives, "Louise Fletcher" biographical vertical file]

Robertson, N. (1976f, April 9). Life in spaces, silences of Fletcher home. Hartford Times. (Hartford, Connecticut) {About Louise Fletcher} [Gallaudet University Archives, "Louise Fletcher" biographical vertical file]

Robertson, N. (1976g, April 10). Moving moment on Oscar show. State Journal. (Madison, Wisconsin - The New York Times News Service) [Gallaudet University Archives, "Louise Fletcher" biographical vertical file]

Robertson, N. (1976h, April 16). Actress presented silent Oscar to her parents. The Milwaukee Journal. (Milwaukee, Wisconsin - New York Times Service) [Gallaudet University Archives, "Louise Fletcher" biographical vertical file]

Robertson, N. (1976i, April 18). Oscar winner saluted world of silence. Sun. (Las Vegas, Nevada) [Gallaudet University Archives, "Louise Fletcher" biographical vertical file]

Rockstroh, D. (1984, June 13). Mom gets by with kids' help. Mercury News. (San Jose, California) [Gallaudet University Archives, "Parent-child relationship - deaf adults" subject vertical file]

Rocky's language [Photo and caption]. (1962, September 12). The Washington Post, p. D4. (Washington, D. C.) {Rocky Graziano, former world middleweight champion, spoke to students at Gallaudet College. He was deaf from an accident during a period in his youth. Elizabeth Benson, Dean of Women, interprets} [Gallaudet University Archives, "Elizabeth English Benson, interpreter in the Language of Signs" biographical subject vertical file]

Rogers, P. (1993, Spring). Feature interpreter: Judy Beldon. Gallaudet Interpreting Service Newsletter, 5. (Gallaudet University, Washington, D. C.) [*]

Romero, D. (1965, July-August). That's my pop: Emerson Romero, Mr. Versatility... The Deaf American, 17 (11), 9-11. [UNIV DEAF Periodicals]

Rosenbaum, D. (1992, November). Despite first negative impression hearing author is friend of deaf. Deaf USA, 6 (60), 17, 26. [UNIV DEAF Periodicals]

Rosenberg, H. (1985, December 9). *Love is Never Silent* is most eloquent drama. News. (Buffalo, New York) {A very positive review. "You just have to love this story, which is the sum of many contributions...Emmys? The line forms here...If you ever doubted how much of acting is nonverbal, though, watch Waterstreet and especially Frelich, who...just...*soars*. Watch her eyes. Watch her body. She's extraordinary, brilliant. Pick your superlative." Co-executive producer Julianna Fjeld is fortunate the film was produced at all. "The project was rejected by ABC and CBS, which wanted hearing actors to pay the deaf parents."} [Gallaudet University Archives, "Love is Never Silent" subject vertical file]

Rosenthal, R. (1973, April 15). For whom Bell toiled [Book review of *BELL: Alexander Graham Bell and the Conquest of Solitude* by Robert V. Bruce]. The Washington Post (Book World section). (Washington, D. C.) [Gallaudet University Archives, "Alexander Graham Bell - biographical" subject vertical file]

Roshak, S. (1997, September). Dear codas [Letter to the editor]. CODA Connection, 14 (3), 10. [UNIV DEAF Periodicals]

Ross, M. (1997, September/October). Seeking an identity: The personal and social identity of hard-of-hearing people is different from that of people who are physiologically deaf, or who consider themselves socially and culturally Deaf. Hearing Health, 13 (5), 15-18. [UNIV DEAF Periodicals]

Rosson, J. (1961, May 29). Speed up education, Vice President urges. The Evening Star. (Washington, D. C.) {Vice President Johnson addresses the 97th Commencement at Gallaudet College. "Representative [Homer] Thornberry, whose parents were deaf, introduced the Vice President in the sign language of the deaf." Elizabeth Benson, dean of women, "translated his words into sign language."} [Gallaudet University Archives, "Elizabeth English Benson, interpreter in the Language of Signs" biographical subject vertical file]

Rothenberg, F. (1985, December 9). *Never Silent* is golden: Hallmark presentation homage to families [TV review]. Tribune. (Tulsa, Oklahoma) {A very positive review of *Love is Never Silent*. "The real honestly depicted dilemma in [this film] is that, since birth, Margaret has suffered as both 'we' and 'them.'"} [Gallaudet University Archives, "Love is Never Silent" subject vertical file]

Rothenberg, F. (1986, December 1). *Love* a knockout production. Pioneer Press Dispatch. (St. Paul, Minnesota) {A very positive review of *Love is Never Silent* which repeats on Television this week. It's a "universal story about family tensions arising when a child seeks to disengage and leaves the parental nest. In another more powerful sense, though, it's an off-center track leading its hearing audience through uncharted, illuminating realms."} [Gallaudet University Archives, "Love is Never Silent" subject vertical file]

Rothwell, K., & Summers, J. (1994, December). Tucker gets tough: Forget your stereotypical image of a Deaf person - Maryland School for the Deaf's first Deaf superintendent is young, brash, and an outspoken champion of Deaf rights. Frederick Magazine, 10 (6), 22-25. (Frederick, Maryland) {Changes instituted at the Maryland School for the Deaf by the new deaf superintendent are described. "Teachers at MSD who were not proficient in ASL continue to take courses in the language, and Tucker is so adamant that ASL is the most obvious form of communication for the Deaf community [that] he strives only to hire interpreters who are Children of Deaf Adults [codas]."} [*]

Rovner, S. (1985, December 9). *Never Silent* runs deep. <u>The Washington Post.</u> (Washington, D. C.) {A very positive review of *Love is Never Silent*. "This is a play about human relationships, soaring far beyond the confines of problems between people who can hear and people who can't."} [Gallaudet University Archives, "Parent-child relationship - deaf adults" subject vertical file]

Royster, M. A. (1981). The Roysters: Deaf parents, a personal perspective. <u>The Deaf American, 34</u> (3), 18-22. [UNIV DEAF Periodicals]

Rubin, P. (1994, October 13-19). The silent survivor: A lonely, deaf teenager became a sexual plaything for men - and an enigma for law enforcement. Finally, someone cared enough to bring her tormentors to justice. <u>Phoenix New Times, 25</u> (41), pp. 22-26, 28, cover. (Phoenix, Arizona) {About Helen Young, foster parent and Sign Language interpreter who is a coda} [*]

Rubin, S. (1987, April 6). A family's quiet, loving communication: Deaf parents teach their children independence. <u>San Francisco Chronicle,</u> pp. 18, 21. (California) [Gallaudet University Archives, "Parent-child relationship - deaf adults" subject vertical file]

Rudin-Braschi, H. (1988, November 9). Food is language of love for cook born of deaf couple: Fremonter learned importance of balance at meals. <u>Mercury-News.</u> (San Jose, California) {Judith Anne Harris grew up in the Bronx with deaf parents. She learned early-on to cook in the Eastern European style from her maternal grandmother and mother. Her mother "worked in the New York sweatshops as a seamstress and [her] father worked as an engraver." Judy works at the California School for the Deaf in Fremont and shares some recipes here for traditional Jewish favorites} [Gallaudet University Archives, "Children of deaf adults" subject vertical file]

Ruge, R. (1990, February). Dad: Wilbur J. Ruge. <u>CODA Connection, 7</u> (1), 6-7. [UNIV DEAF Periodicals]

Ruth, D. (1985a, December 9). *Love is Never Silent* speaks out beautifully [Television review]. <u>Sun-Times.</u> (Chicago, Illinois) {A very positive review. "One of those dramas that restores your faith in television as a instrument for quality entertainment and more importantly - for communication...will be talked about for some time to come."} [Gallaudet University Archives, "Love is Never Silent" subject vertical file]

Ruth, D. (1985b, December 9). TV offers a sign of the times: Producer hires deaf actors to play hearing-impaired. <u>Sun-Times,</u> pp. 49, 58. (Chicago, Illinois) {A very positive review of *Love is Never Silent*. Interview with Phyllis Frelich and Ed Waterstreet through interpreter and coda Lou Fant. They "offer bravura performances."} [Gallaudet University Archives, "Love is Never Silent" subject vertical file]

Sacks, O. (1992, Fall). [Letters] *Our Father Abe.* <u>Gallaudet Today, 23</u> (1), 30. [Gallaudet University Archives or RESERVE]

Saks, A. (1974, October). Phonetype equals freedom. <u>Hearing, 29</u> (10), 299-302. (Journal name changed to <u>Soundbarrier</u>) [UNIV DEAF Periodicals]

Sanders, C. L. (1968, November). The Fultz quads: Grown-up, disappointed and bitter [Speaking of People column]. <u>Ebony, 24</u> (1), 212-214, 216-218, 220, 222. {Anne, Catherine, Alice and Louise Fultz created a sensation as "the world's only Negro identical quadruplets" when they were born on May 23, 1946, in Reidsville, North Carolina. Their mother, Annie Fultz, "had been left a deaf-mute by spinal meningitis at two years old." They are now 22 years old but were adopted by Charles and Elma Pearl Saylor when they were 10 years old. The story dwells on the Quads and the downward spiral of their lives after being highly publicized Pet Milk advertising babies. There's no mention of the circumstances of their adoption by the Saylors (Pet Milk had provided Mrs. Saylor as a nurse to look after them when they were babies). See "Fultz quads [Letters to the editor]" for further comments from Ebony readers} [UNIV Periodicals - Microfilm]

Sanders, D. (1985, December 9). *Love is Never Silent* inspires with joyful, uplifting scenes. Rocky Mountain News. (Denver, Colorado) {A very positive review: engrossing, realistic family drama with stunning performances} [Gallaudet University Archives, "Love is Never Silent" subject vertical file]

Sanders, J. (1997, September). Koda poetry: Talking with hands [Poem]. CODA Connection, 14 (3), 18. (Jessica is from Wisconsin and wrote this poem April 27, 1995) [UNIV DEAF Periodicals]

Sanderson, G. (1997, February). More comments about CODA-LA 1996! [Letter]. CODA Connection, 14 (1), 10. [UNIV DEAF Periodicals]

Sanderson, G. R. (1995, Aug/Sept). CODA and HEARING interpreters. CODA Connection, 12 (3), 5. [UNIV DEAF Periodicals]

Sanderson, G. R. (1996, Aug/Sept). Codas in the arts panel. CODA Connection, 13 (3), 10. [UNIV DEAF Periodicals]

Sanderson, G. R. (1997, May). [Letter to the editor]. CODA Connection, 14 (2), 8-9. {Response to the proposal for an official "Christian Coda" group session} [UNIV DEAF Periodicals]

Sante, L. (1996, May 12). Living in tongues: For a Belgian child growing up in suburban New Jersey, there were three words for home. The New York Times (Sunday Magazine), pp. 31-34. (Excerpts reprinted in the November, 1996, issue of the CODA Connection, 13 (4), 6-7. [UNIV DEAF Periodicals]) [*]

Sante, L. (1998, January-February). Heart without a country: Why *Mon Coeur* speaks one language and my brain another. Utne Reader, No. 85, 61-66. [UNIV Periodicals]

Saunders, W. (1971, September 17). Well-manicured TV look gives way to casual style. Rocky Mountain News. (Denver, Colorado) [Gallaudet University Archives, "Louie Fant" biographical vertical file]

Scarborough, E. (1976, June 14). Living with the deaf: For a child it means responsibility.... The Charlotte Observer, pp. 3C, 8C. (Charlotte, North Carolina) [Gallaudet University Archives, "Parent-child relationship - deaf adults" subject vertical file]

Schafer, T. (1997a, September). ...and President Schafer's first forum. CODA Connection, 14 (3), 3-4. [UNIV DEAF Periodicals]

Schafer, T. (1997b, November). The President's Forum: Kneading CODA. CODA Connection, 14 (4), 3. [UNIV DEAF Periodicals]

Schrader, S. L. (1997, March). Georgia makes deaf history - House speaker agreed to interpreter. The Silent News, 29 (3), 4 [UNIV DEAF Periodicals]

Schuchman, J. S. (1987, Spring). Book reviews: *A loss for words.* Gallaudet Today, 17 (3), 28-30. [Gallaudet University Archives or RESERVE]

Schuchman, J. S. (1992, Summer). Book review: *Our father Abe, the story of a deaf shoe repairman* by Harvey

L. Barash and Eva Barash Dicker. <u>Gallaudet Today, 22</u> (4), 32. [Gallaudet University Archives or RESERVE]

Schuchman, J. S. (1997, Spring). Book review: *The Silents* by Charlotte Abrams. <u>Gallaudet Today, 27</u> (3), 28. [Gallaudet University Archives or RESERVE]

Schuchman, S. (1989, November). Coda spouses: A report by Stan Schuchman. <u>CODA Newsletter, 6</u> (4), 3-4. [UNIV DEAF Periodicals]

Schuchman, S. (1995, Aug/Sept). CODA in London. <u>CODA Connection, 12</u> (3), 5. [UNIV DEAF Periodicals]

Scott, J. (1987, May 23). A 911 plea that failed as wife died brings suit. <u>The Los Angeles Times.</u> (Los Angeles, California) [Gallaudet University Archives, "Court litigation - deaf" subject vertical file]

Scott-Gibson, L. (1994, January). Book review: *In silence - growing up hearing in a deaf world* by Ruth Sidransky. <u>British Deaf News, 25</u> (1), 15. [UNIV DEAF Periodicals]

Scott-Gibson, L. (1995, March). Book review: *Mother father deaf - living between sound and silence* by Paul Preston. <u>British Deaf News, 26</u> (3), 11. [UNIV DEAF Periodicals]

Secretary of Defense highlights MTC dedication. (1973, April 5). <u>Fort Sam Houston Patriot, 4</u> (14), pp. 8, 13. (Published in the interest of personnel at Ft. Sam Houston, Texas) {A new building at the U.S. Army Medical Training Center will be named "The Elizabeth E. Benson Dormitory." Miss Mary Alice Benson of Frederick, Maryland, is pictured with Secretary Richardson} [Gallaudet University Archives, "Elizabeth English Benson: Memorials" biographical subject vertical file]

Sela, I. (1990, Fall). An international perspective: Israel's first interpreter recalls growing up in the deaf community. <u>Gallaudet Today, 21</u> (1), 8-9. {Condensed version of an address given as part of an international panel at the 1989 international conference of Children of Deaf Adults in Westminster, Maryland} [Gallaudet University Archives or RESERVE]

Selvage, S. (1991, October 15). America's forgotten children: They are children who should be at play, who ought to be having fun. Instead, they are caring for adults who should be caring for them, but can't. <u>Woman's World Magazine,</u> 7. {About the experiences of children in immigrant families} [*]

Sensationalism and the Deaf [Editorial]. (1945, August). <u>The Cavalier, 5</u> (12), 2. (See the related article by J. S. Qualey on page 1: "Deaf mute kills wife, child, thinks he was not loved.") [Gallaudet University Archives]

Separate apartments for deaf challenged. (1979, November 24). <u>The Washington Post.</u> (Washington, D. C.) [Gallaudet University Archives, "Rev. Louis W. Foxwell, Jr." biographical vertical file]

Seremeth-Graves, D. (1998, February). Hi Bonnie [Letter to the editor]. <u>CODA Connection, 15</u> (1), 8. [UNIV DEAF Periodicals]

Seven normals popular with undergraduate student body. (1940, October 31). <u>The Buff and Blue, 49</u> (2), p. 1. (Student newspaper of the Gallaudet Student Body Government) {Describes Miss Lorraine Frater's interest in the deaf through her deaf parents} [Gallaudet University Archives]

Seven recognized for their work with the deaf. (1967, May-June). <u>The Gallaudet Record, 12</u> (7), 3. {Dr. Elizabeth E. Benson, Dean of Women at Gallaudet College, was named Phi Kappa Zeta Sorority's Woman of the

Year} [Gallaudet University Archives and "Elizabeth English Benson, interpreter in the Language of Signs" biographical subject vertical file]

Shales, T. (1976a, March 30). *Cuckoo's Nest* takes the four top Oscars. Record-Searchlight. (Redding, California) [Gallaudet University Archives, "Louise Fletcher" biographical vertical file]

Shales, T. (1976b, March 30). It's "Cuckoo" time in Hollywood. The New York Post. (New York) [Gallaudet University Archives, "Louise Fletcher" biographical vertical file]

Shannon, C. (1996, Spring). "Mommy, you're deaf." ALDA News: The Official Newsletter of the Association of Late-Deafened Adults, 10 (1), 1-5, 17. [UNIV DEAF Periodicals]

Shannon, M. M. (1987, July 2). A good sign: Couple spend lives, raise children without hearing. Review. (Lake Oswego, Clackamas County, Oregon) [Gallaudet University Archives, "Parent-child relationship - deaf adults" subject vertical file]

Shaw, T. (1976, July). Louise Fletcher's own story: "I never cried when I was a child, because there was no one to hear me"... but now the world listens! Motion Picture Magazine, 65 (785), 26-27, 37. [Gallaudet University Archives, "Parent-child relationship - deaf adults" subject vertical file]

She acts as interpreter [Photo and caption]. (1922, July). The Silent Worker, 34 (10), 390. (Article reprinted from the Duluth Herald - Duluth, Minnesota - January 28, 1922) {Mrs. B. E. Ursin, daughter of Prof. Lars M. Larsen, has helped the Duluth Home Demonstration Bureau extend their work "to the deaf and dumb, and instructive classes have been given them in sewing and nutrition."} [UNIV DEAF Periodicals]

Sheffield, C. (1993, August 14). Writing autobiography therapeutic after growing up in deaf world. Northeast Mississippi Daily Journal, 120 (136), pp. B1, back page. (Tupelo, Mississippi) {About Doris Isbell Crowe, author of *Dummy's Little Girl*} [*]

Sheffield, J. (1995, Aug/Sept). New RID special interest group: HIDP. CODA Connection, 12 (3), 7. {HIDP is the acronym for the Hearing Interpreters with Deaf Parents special interest group (SIG) within the Registry of Interpreters for the Deaf organization} [UNIV DEAF Periodicals]

Sherman, D. C. (1967, September 29). Love conquers many things [Letter to the editor]. The Wichita Eagle. (Wichita, Kansas) {The author, from Wichita, Kansas, responds to a September 21, Wichita Eagle editorial titled "Love matters" that reports on the Court of Appeals and the California Supreme Court rulings "regarding a deaf couple's attempted adoption of a two-year old boy with normal hearing."} [Gallaudet University Archives, "Parent-child relationship - Deaf adults" subject vertical file]

Shettle, A. (1997, Summer). Building families: Deaf parents who adopt face challenges and rewards. Gallaudet Today, 27 (4), 8-14. {Includes some deaf parent families who have adopted hearing children} [UNIV DEAF Periodicals]

She works to bridge gap: In college atmosphere. (1974, November 21). The State. (Columbia, South Carolina) {Story about Matilda "Til" Collins, a freshman at Erskine College, daughter of Mr. and Mrs. Robert F. Collins of Carson, California} [Gallaudet University Archives, "Hearing children of deaf parents" and "American Sign Language - teaching" subject vertical files]

(#) Shipley, A. (1985, August). Only children talked. CODA Newsletter, 2 (3), 5. (Reprinted from the

Spring/1982, issue, page 5, of an unidentified publication) [UNIV DEAF Periodicals]

(#) Shorr, V. (1987, November 22). She's only mean onscreen: For actress Louise Fletcher, playing villains is just part of the job. The Daily News, p. 5. (City unidentified) [*]

Shultz-Myers, S. (1991, February). Books: Review of Ruth Sidransky's *In silence: Growing up hearing in a deaf world.* CODA Connection, 8 (1), 1, 4-5. (Reprinted in the July-August, 1991, issue of Views, 8 (3), 26-27, 29. [UNIV DEAF Periodicals]) [UNIV DEAF Periodicals]

Shultz-Myers, S. (1992a, May). [Letter to the editor]. CODA Connection, 9 (2), 3-4. {About Sheila Jacobs' model parts theory} [UNIV DEAF Periodicals]

Shultz-Myers, S. (1992b, Aug./Sept.). Report on "Parts workshop." CODA Connection, 9 (3), 9. [UNIV DEAF Periodicals]

Sid Caesar plays a Greek pawnshop owner...[Photo and caption]. (1985, December 8). Chronicle. (Houston, Texas) {*Love is Never Silent* to air on Television Channel 2, Monday at 8 p.m.} [Gallaudet University Archives, "Love is Never Silent" subject vertical file]

Sidransky, R. (1990, October). "You are my dictionary:" My father was deaf, yet he taught me how to listen. Reader's Digest, 101, 7-8, 10-12. {Condensed from *In Silence* by Ruth Sidransky} [UNIV Periodicals]

Sidransky, R. (1992, February 21). Autobiography, *In Silence*: She moved from the world of the deaf to the world of the hearing - and truly belonged in neither. Scholastic Scope, 4-9. {Excerpt from the book by Ruth Sidransky} [Gallaudet University Archives, "Parent-child relationship - deaf adults" subject vertical file]

Siegel, A. (1988, December 8). Signing their way through a trial. Santa Maria Times. (Santa Maria, California) {The case of the People vs. John Doe is described. The defendant was deaf but did not understand Sign Language or any other form of communication. They found he understood fingerspelled Spanish. Pamela Larsson-Toscher was one of the interpreters. Her parents were deaf missionaries in Jamaica where Pamela grew up} [Gallaudet University Archives, "Court litigation - interpreting for the deaf" subject vertical file]

Siegel, D. (1991, April). Book review: Silent love, a daughter opens hearing world for parents. The Jewish Monthly, 20. [*]

Signing class popular. (1988, January 20). Journal Record. (Oklahoma City, Oklahoma) {Patty Bagley works at South Community Hospital and teaches a popular 12-week American Sign Language class. Her mother is deaf. She has also been the interpreter for the past six years at St. Patrick's Church in Oklahoma City} [Gallaudet University Archives, "Children of deaf adults" subject vertical file]

Sign language. (1988, April 29). Vidette Messenger. (Valparaiso, Indiana) [Gallaudet University Archives, "Children of deaf adults" and "American Sign Language - teaching" vertical files]

Sign language film on "Noah" planned. (1977, February 3). Daily News. (Camarillo, California) [Gallaudet University Archives, "Louie Fant" biographical vertical file]

Sign language is words made visible. (1981, December 10). The Forum, p. 31. (Fargo-Moorhead, North Dakota) [Gallaudet University Archives, "Children of deaf adults" subject vertical file]

Silent comic entertains deaf. (1956, April 12). Herald-Star. (Steubenville, Ohio) [Gallaudet University Archives, "Parent-child relationship - deaf adults" subject vertical file]

SILENT NEWS advice column: *Dear Stella* gets letter about Codas! (1997, February). CODA Connection, 14 (1), 18. (In the December, 1996, issue of The Silent News there was a letter about codas) [UNIV DEAF Periodicals]

(#) Silent victory. (1967, September 18). (City and newspaper unidentified) {Reports that Wayne and Madeline Christensen of Torrance, California, were formally granted adoption of "Scott James Richardson by the California Superior Court after nearly two years of court litigation. They had become foster parents to Scott whose hearing is normal when he was one month old. "They were denied a petition for adoption on the grounds that "the Christensens could not provide a normal home for the boy."} [Gallaudet University Archives, "Parent-child relationship - deaf adults" subject vertical file]

Silva, T. (1993, August 8). Breaking the sound barrier: Book tells tale of growing up in deaf world. Rome News-Tribune, C1. (Rome, Georgia) {About Cave Spring resident Doris Crowe, author of *Dummy's Little Girl*} [*]

Simon, J. (1995, November 5). Season in the sun [Book review of *The First Man* by Albert Camus]. The Washington Post, Book World, 25 (45), p. 5. (Washington, D. C.) [UNIV Newspapers Microfilm]

Six mutes in one family. (1889, January 31). The Silent Worker, 2 (10), 2. {Reports that the Wisconsin Institution [School for the Deaf] has in attendance six pupils from one family} [UNIV DEAF Periodicals]

Six receive awards at Charter Day banquet. (1996, Summer). Gallaudet Today, 26 (4), 26-27. (Gallaudet Alumni News section) {Dr. Cesare Magarotto of Italy, whose parents are deaf, receives the Laurent Clerc Cultural Fund Edward Miner Gallaudet Award} [Gallaudet University Archives or RESERVE]

Skyer, M. (1994, Spring). My deaf dad, the singer. ALDA News: The Official Newsletter of the Association of Late-Deafened Adults, 8 (1), 2. {Melissa is 11 years old and has learned "that there are two sides to having a late-deafened parent."} [UNIV DEAF Periodicals]

SLA quarterly special reports: Interpreting for the performing arts. (1992, Spring). SLA Inc. Quarterly, 5 (1), 4-5. (Newsletter of Sign Language Associates, Silver Spring, Maryland) [UNIV DEAF Periodicals]

Smith, D. (1981, September 24). Interpreter gives deaf Arkansans a voice in court. Arkansas Gazette. (Little Rock, Arkansas) [Gallaudet University Archives, "Court litigation - deaf" subject vertical file]

Smith, F. (1986, November 27). Signing is popular elective: At Wake Forest Elementary. The Wake Weekly, pp. 3B. (Wake Forest, North Carolina) [Gallaudet University Archives, "Parent-child relationship - deaf adults" subject vertical file]

Smith, J. L. (Ed.). (1928, September 26). Sid Smith [Obituary]. The Companion by and for the Deaf, 54 (1), 12. (Newsletter of the Minnesota School for the Deaf, Faribault, Minnesota) {Sidney Chandler Smith was born in Faribault, February 28, 1893. He was the hearing son of Dr. and Mrs. J. L. Smith of Nevis, Minnesota. He became involved with the moving picture industry in Hollywood. He played leading roles in comedy films. He enlisted in the Army during World War I in 1917. He played with Thomas Meighan in *The Ne'er Do Well*, filmed in Panama. His death was from acute gastritis and he was laid to rest in Hollywood Memorial Cemetery} [Gallaudet University Archives]

Smith, R. (1990, May). Codas - Who are they?...What are they? <u>Deaf Culture Today, 1</u> (1), 7. (Springfield, Missouri: Publication of the Deaf Culture Ministries of the Assemblies of God) {Rod describes his and Katie Lerch's presentation about the church serving the hearing children in deaf families at the forthcoming 1990 National Deaf Convention. Rod is a nationally appointed home missionary in the Assemblies of God. Both are codas} [UNIV DEAF Periodicals]

Snedigar, P. (1992, March). Hearing children of deaf parents face ignorant comments. <u>DCARA News,</u> 6. (Newsletter of the Deafness Advocacy, Counseling and Referral Agency serving the San Francisco Bay Area. Main office in San Leandro, California) {Pam is a staff member of DCARA and a coda. In this column she asks for deaf community feedback and if there is interest in a workshop for deaf parents with hearing children, if the hearing children with deaf parents would like a workshop, or other opportunities for group support} [UNIV DEAF Periodicals]

Some sons of deaf parents in the war service [Photos and captions]. (1918, February). <u>The Silent Worker, 30</u> (5), 87. (Article reprinted from the <u>Duluth Herald,</u> - Duluth, Minnesota - January 28, 1922) {Pictured are Earle A. Bigelow, son of Mr. and Mrs. Frank W. Bigelow; Harry, son of Mr. and Mrs. H. Stengele, of Plainfield, New Jersey; Walter B. George, son of Mr. and Mrs. James B. George, Portland, Oregon; James F. Donnelly, Jr., son of Mr. and Mrs. James F. Donnelly, of Richmond Hill, New York; Cyrus Merrell, son of the late A. N. Merrell who graduated from the Illinois School; and Orvis D. Dantzer, son of Rev. C. Dantzer} [UNIV DEAF Periodicals]

Son lost at sea. (1944, June). <u>The Silent Cavalier, 4</u> (9), 3. {Mrs. Margaret Lindsay of Charlottesville, Virginia, was informed by the Bureau of Naval Personnel, Navy Department, that her 33 year old son, Donald C. Taylor, missing since March 27, 1942, is presumed to have died April 5, 1944} [Gallaudet University Archives]

Son of deaf couple with paratroopers. (1944, February). <u>The Silent Cavalier, 4</u> (6), 1. {About 2nd Lt. Frank Johnstone, Jr., son of Mr. and Mrs. Frank Johnstone, Sr., of Salt Lake City, Utah} [Gallaudet University Archives]

Son of E. C. Smoak leads Marines on Bougainville. (1944, January). <u>The Silent Cavalier, 4</u> (5), 1. (Source: <u>Tri-State News</u>) [Gallaudet University Archives]

Son of Lindholms gets West Point appointment. (1959, September). <u>The Silent Worker, 12</u> (1), 12. [UNIV DEAF Periodicals]

Son of W. L. Coffey killed in Anzio battle. (1944, December). <u>The Silent Cavalier, 5</u> (4), 1. [Gallaudet University Archives]

Sons of deaf in sports news. (1950, March). <u>The Silent Worker, 2</u> (7), 29. {Reports the appearance of articles in two different Los Angeles daily papers of photographs of hearing sons of deaf parents in basketball attire: <u>The Los Angeles Daily News</u> had a photo of Vic Larson, son of Mr. and Mrs. Levi Larson, regular guard for Pepperdine University; <u>The Los Angeles Times</u> pictured Aaron Seandel, son of Mr. and Mrs. Julius Seandel, playing for San Jose College} [UNIV DEAF Periodicals]

Sons of deaf parents in the war service [Photos and captions]. (1918a, April). <u>The Silent Worker, 30</u> (7), 126. {Pictured are the following: Harry H. McLachan, son of Mr. and Mrs. Robert H. McLachan, of Detroit, Michigan - "He was president of his class and was graduated with high honor from the Flint high school, Michigan, June 14th, 1911. He was a favorite among the students and a very fine boy. He studied medicine at Ann Arbor, Michigan, for three years;" Herbert Wickline Tucker, son of Mr. and Mrs. Arthur G. Tucker, of Richmond, Virginia; Joseph and Frank La Londe, sons of Mr. and Mrs. La Londe, well known deaf residents of Oswego, New York; and Laurent Gallaudet Tucker, son of Mr. and Mrs. Arthur G. Tucker, of Richmond, Virginia} [UNIV DEAF Periodicals]

Sons of deaf parents in the war service [Photo and caption]. (1918b, May). The Silent Worker, 30 (8), 141. {Photo of Lieutenant Weston Jenkins, Jr., oldest son of Mrs. Weston Jenkins} [UNIV DEAF Periodicals]

Sons of deaf parents in the war service [Photos and captions]. (1918c, June). The Silent Worker, 30 (9), 167. {Pictured are the following: Joseph H. Marksbury, Jr., son of Mrs. J. H. Marksbury of Kansas City, Missouri; George M. Van Allen, son of the Rev. and Mrs. H. Van Allen, Utica, New York; David Delroy, eldest son of Mrs. Eva Delroy, of Troy, New York; and Thomas K. Garth, son of Mr. and Mrs. John Garth of Webster Groves, Missouri} [UNIV DEAF Periodicals]

Sons of the deaf in the war [Photos and captions]. (1917, November). The Silent Worker, 30 (2), 23. {Pictured are Herbert, son of Mr. and Mrs. Beurmann, of Yonkers, New York and George H. Cloud who volunteered for service when two years under draft age. His brother John is in France driving the ambulance presented by the deaf of the United States} [UNIV DEAF Periodicals]

Sons return [from Army service]. (1945, December). The Cavalier, 6 (4), 5. {Mr. & Mrs. Lee R. Harris' son, T/Sgt. Oliver R. Harris, arrived home in Sebring, Ohio, and their son-in-law George A. Wright, was discharged from service as well} [Gallaudet University Archives]

Sontag, D. (1987, March 13). Children who speak for their parents. Chicago Tribune, pp. 1, 3. (Chicago, Illinois) [*]

South African woman, 58, now says baby isn't hers. (1969, July 20). The New York Times. {A 58-year-old grandmother, Mrs. Johanna Duplessis and her "deaf mute" husband, Dawie, are at the center of this controversy. They won't say where the baby came from} [Gallaudet University Archives, "Parent-child relationship - deaf adults" subject vertical file]

Spanjer, A. (1997, November). Food for thought. CODA Connection, 14 (4), 8. [UNIV DEAF Periodicals]

Spellman, J. F. (1988, Summer). A book review....By another hearing child of Deaf parents: *A loss for words, the story of deafness in a family* by Lou Ann Walker. The Deaf American, 38 (2), 19-21. [UNIV DEAF Periodicals]

Spencer, R. (1989, September 29). Art: Freedom to fight. Scene: Santa Barbara News-Press, pp. 1, 25-27. (Santa Barbara, California) [*]

Stangarone, J. (1977, September). Hearing children of deaf parents. Hints Newsletter, 10 (9). (Reprinted from Interprenews, Registry of Interpreters for the Deaf) [UNIV DEAF Periodicals]

Star tracks: Fletcher's young man. (1977, July 11). People Weekly, 8 (2), 58. [UNIV Periodicals - Microfilm]

Stecker, A. H. (1965, March). Michael Skropeta: Baker on the rise. The Deaf American, 17 (7), 9-10. {Pictured are the three Skropeta children, Susan, Kim and Carl} [UNIV DEAF Periodicals]

Sterling, A. (1997, November). Dear Rabbi and Peggy [Letter]. CODA Connection, 14 (4), 7, 14. (Reprinted from the Temple Beth El newsletter "some time ago.") {A touching memorial to a beloved parent} [UNIV DEAF Periodicals]

Sterling, P. (1958, October 26). Silent world of the deaf. Detroit Free Press, pp. 1D-2D. (Detroit, Michigan) [Gallaudet University Archives, "Parent-child relationship - deaf adults" subject vertical file]

Sternberg, M. L. A. (1971, April). Joanne Greenberg receives first Kenner Award. The Deaf American, 23 (8), 15. [UNIV DEAF Periodicals]

Stewart, D. A. (1996-97, Winter). A Journey into the DEAF-WORLD. Gallaudet Today, 27 (2), 34. {"I did wonder what emotions the two hearing authors struggled with before agreeing to pen their thoughts on the Deaf-World." One of the hearing authors is Harlan Lane. The other is coda Robert Hoffmeister} [Gallaudet University Archives or RESERVE]

Stodghill, M. (1988, February 22). ALL EYES: In sign language class, it's all in the movement. Duluth News-Tribune. (Duluth, Minnesota) [Gallaudet University Archives, "American Sign Language - teaching" subject vertical file]

Stolberg, M. (1980, November 2). Determined to work, he's caught in maze. Pittsburgh Press, pp. A1, A10. (Pittsburgh, Pennsylvania) {The legal maze in dealing with the Social Security Administration is described after Gerald Rossmont lost his job. He and his deaf wife, Christine, have three hearing children: Tina, 5, Paul, 4 and Michelle, 3 years old} [Gallaudet University Archives, "Court litigation - interpreting for the deaf" subject vertical file]

(#) (##) Stolicker, G. (1973, December). Lisa's home is one of quiet love. Oakland Press. (Pontiac, Michigan?)

Stormont, P. (1955, April 8). These parents never have heard their son's laughter, shouts: But Mr. and Mrs. Tappen, who are deaf mutes, manage their home, family without difficulty. Saginaw News. (Saginaw, Michigan) [Gallaudet University Archives, "Parent-child relationship - deaf adults" subject vertical file]

Straight, K. W. (1986, November/December). Editor's story: Sibling meets CODA and parent. The Endeavor, 2. (The newsletter of the American Society for Deaf Children, Silver Spring, Maryland. Reviewed in the May, 1987, issue of the CODA Newsletter, 4 (2), 2. [UNIV DEAF Periodicals]) [UNIV DEAF Periodicals]

Suit: Deafness cost couple children. (1994, September). The Silent News, 26 (9), 1. (Reprinted from the Associated Press, August 4, 1994) {Gerald and Keri Webb are suing the Jackson County and the Michigan state Department of Social Services for 18 million dollars. Their daughter, Angie, was put up for adoption} [UNIV DEAF Periodicals]

Sullivan, F. B. (Ed.). (1978, November-December). Irresponsible statements [Editorial]. The FRAT: Official Publication of the National Fraternal Society of the Deaf, 76th year, No. 2, 4. {Comments on the August issue of Clinical Psychiatry News where two physicians, both women, are quoted at a press conference. "Both agreed that deaf mothers generally do not make good mothers." The author goes on to describe the angry response of the deaf community. Some met with one of the physicians and her staff at the Lexington School for the Deaf. "It did not appear she was able to pacify her audience, and she admitted that only four deaf mothers were involved in an experiment - hardly enough to qualify for legitimate research." Comments about the other physician's defense, which was printed in a later issue of this same publication, are made} [UNIV DEAF Periodicals]

Sumac, J. (1997, November). Mother, Father Deaf talented much [Poem]. CODA Connection, 14 (4), 14. [UNIV DEAF Periodicals]

Suplee, C. (1998, January 19). Turning to the deaf for signs of innate language ability. The Washington Post (Science section), p. A3. (Washington, D. C.) [UNIV Newspapers Microfilm]

(#) (##) Swederlin, M. (1975, July). Family lives by signs. The Morning Herald. (City unidentified)

Swenson, S. E. (1993, April/May). She provides ears so deaf can serve: Sign Language pro serves deaf jurors [Photo and story]. The Professional INTERPRETER, 8-9. (Reprinted from The Bakersfield Californian, January 16, 1993) {Faye Wilkie, a Sign Language interpreter in Kern County, California, is featured. She was born in Oklahoma to deaf parents} [UNIV DEAF Periodicals]

Swiller, J. (1993, Fall). New developments: The story of a life, a scholarship fund honors the memory of Earl Higgins. Gallaudet Today, 24 (1), 30. {At the age of 29, in Los Angeles, California, Earl Higgins died trying to save an 11-year-old drowning child. His deaf father, Francis Higgins, graduated from Gallaudet College in 1936 and taught there for 42 years. He shared a letter from President Ronald Reagan: "Earl died a hero - he gave his life to save another. You must be proud."} [UNIV DEAF Periodicals]

Taste of Sunrise **opens on April 11. (1997, April 3).** On the Green: A Weekly Published for Gallaudet University Staff and Faculty, 27 (10), 2. Washington, DC: Gallaudet University Department of Publications and Production. [Gallaudet University Archives]

Teachers hurdle communication barrier to teach deaf children. (1959, April 15). The Pointer, 3 (8), 1, 3. (Newsletter of the Covina, California, School District) {Article features Ann Doty and Mabel Finnell who are teaching deaf students in their district. There is also a photo of Mabel Finnell, who is hearing and her parents are deaf, providing auditory/speech training to a student} [Gallaudet University Archives, "Marie Greenstone" biographical vertical file]

Tears at White House for Teacher of the Year: Son of deaf mutes honored for his ability to form a love of learning in his students. (1973, April 25). Philadelphia Inquirer. (Philadelphia, Pennsylvania) [Gallaudet University Archives, "Parent-child relationship - deaf adults" subject vertical file]

Terry, A. T. (1918, March). Eugenics. The Silent Worker, 30 (6), 95-96. [Gallaudet University Archives]

Terry, A. T. (1920, December). One night at our club. The Silent Worker, 33 (3), 83-85. {Photo of William Howe Phelps, founder of the Los Angeles Club for the Deaf and his older son} [Gallaudet University Archives]

Terry, C. (1985a, December 7). "Hall of Fame" story features deaf actors. The News and Courier/The Evening Post, p. 27F. (Charleston, South Carolina) {Positive review of the film *Love is Never Silent*. "A splendidly solid, straightforward production...This, assuredly, is no 'Handicap of the Month' vehicle."} [Gallaudet University Archives, "Love is Never Silent" subject vertical file]

Terry, C. (1985b, December 8-14). *Silent* is a sign of fine, powerful drama [Review of the film *Love is Never Silent* by their TV/Radio critic]. Chicago Tribune (TV Week), pp. 3, 9, cover. (Chicago, Illinois) {A very positive review of the film *Love is Never Silent*. Quotes Mare Winningham who plays the part of the hearing daughter: The actress "Louise [Fletcher - who is hearing and has deaf parents] called after finding out that I'd gotten the role...She told me that the hearing children of the deaf are either 'the most responsible people you'll ever meet or the most extraordinarily messed up.' Only she didn't say *messed*."} [Gallaudet University Archives, "Love is Never Silent" subject vertical file]

Terry, C. (1985c, December 9). Deaf actors play key roles in movie *Love is Never Silent*. Review Journal. (Las Vegas, Nevada) {Positive review of the film *Love is Never Silent* to be shown tonight on television} [Gallaudet University Archives, "Love is Never Silent" subject vertical file]

Terry, C. (1985d, December 9). Hallmark film deals with hearing daughter, deaf parents [Film review]. World, pp. A8, A9. (Tulsa, Oklahoma) {A very positive review of the film *Love is Never Silent*. The film succeeds "because of the natural talent (and quick-study adaptability) of Mare Winningham as the young woman who eventually comes to terms with the concept of both silence and of self."} [Gallaudet University Archives, "Love is Never Silent" subject vertical file]

Terry, C. (1985e, December 9). *Silent* simple, sensitive drama. Pioneer Press Dispatch. (St. Paul, Minnesota) {Positive review of the film *Love is Never Silent.* "A splendidly solid, straightforward production - no flashy surprises here - simple without being smarmy, sensitive without being sappy."} [Gallaudet University Archives, "Love is Never Silent" subject vertical file]

Terry, D. (1997, November). A silent house [The 1997 CODA Millie Brother Scholarship winning essay]. CODA Connection, 14 (4), 4-5. [UNIV DEAF Periodicals]

Testimonial honors Elizabeth Benson. (1969, October 7). The Frederick News-Post, p. A6. (Frederick, Maryland) [Gallaudet University Archives, "Elizabeth English Benson: Memorials" biographical subject vertical file]

Their ideas of the deaf. (1892, October 27). The Silent Worker, 5 (7), 7. (Reprinted from the Rome Register - Rome, New York) [Gallaudet University Archives]

This is one of the three clubmobiles...[Photo and caption]. (1943, September). The Silent Cavalier, 4 (1), 1. {The American National Association of the Deaf (NAD) collected enough money to purchase three ambulance station wagon clubmobiles and presented them to the American Red Cross} [Gallaudet University Archives]

Thomas, D. (1930, August 30). Lon Chaney's life: Master of make-up attained probably greatest role in "Quasimodo," Hugo's Hunchback. The Cleveland Press, No. 16321, p. 3. (Cleveland, Ohio) [*]

Thomas, R. M. (1955, February 13). Silence can be lively, too: Couple who cannot speak nor hear enjoy entertainment on television. The Columbus Dispatch, p. 3. (Columbus, Ohio) [Gallaudet University Archives, "Parent-child relationship - deaf adults" subject vertical file]

(##) Thomason, B., & Clifford, K. (1972). The disabled person and family dynamics. Accent on Living, 17, 20-35. (Magazine that provides information about new products, travel ideas, medical news, housing, adjustment, inspiration and other areas of interest to mobility impaired individuals. Located in Bloomington, Illinois)

Three Russian diplomats speak at Gallaudet. (1966, November 21). The Washington Post. (Washington, D. C.) {Elizabeth Benson translated remarks and responses to questions from students made by three first secretaries from the Soviet Embassy} [Gallaudet University Archives, "Elizabeth English Benson, interpreter in the Language of Signs" biographical subject vertical file]

Together again [Photo and caption]. (1978, March 3). The Los Angeles Times (part 2), p. 1. (Los Angeles, California) {"Six-year-old Ruth Riley as she was reunited with her parents, Ray and Patricia Riley, both of whom are deaf, in San Bernardino. A judge had ordered the child returned to the Rileys from a foster home where she was placed a year ago because the parents couldn't speak and offer verbal stimulation." To my knowledge, the only record of a Black Deaf family involved in a custody battle} [*]

Tomlinson, K. (1984, Fall). "Is your Mom an Indian?" Growing up with deaf parents. Scene, 7-10. (Magazine published twice a year by the Department of Journalism, California State University, Northridge) [*]

Top choice [Photo and caption]. (1986, November 30). Register-Star. (Rockford, Illinois) {Reports a rebroadcast of a Hallmark Hall of Fame presentation, *Love is Never Silent*} [Gallaudet University Archives, "Love is Never

Silent" subject vertical file]

Topliff, A. (1994, November). CODA as a community. <u>CODA Connection, 11</u> (4), 1. [UNIV DEAF Periodicals]

Topliff, A. (1997, September). Some thoughts from Ann Topliff... [Letter to the editor]. <u>CODA Connection, 14</u> (3), 7. {Mentions an article she read about a father who took his young son to Sicily to meet relatives. "In Sicily, the family stories become real. And it is from these stories that we understand ourselves: What we are and why we are. One of my Sicilian cousins says if one feels connected to his past, if he knows the family stories and understands them, he has a foundation on which to build his life." Ann goes on to say "To me, this is what CODA is all about. It is family. It is a place where we can share our stories and listen to stories and learn about ourselves."} [UNIV DEAF Periodicals]

Tousignant, M. (1996, June 3). Life sounds good to them: Va. couple abide by the maxim that deafness is "No Big Deal." <u>The Washington Post,</u> 119th year, No. 181, pp. A1, A4. (Washington, D. C.) [UNIV Newspapers Microfilm]

Trammer, M. L. (1977, October 30). Catonsville college sponsors meeting on needs of deaf. <u>The Sun.</u> (Baltimore, Maryland) [Gallaudet University Archives, "Rev. Louis W. Foxwell, Jr." biographical vertical file]

Translation for the deaf [Photo and caption]. (1964, June 8). <u>Indianapolis Star.</u> (Indianapolis, Indiana) {President Johnson's remarks at the centennial banquet at Gallaudet College are interpreted by Elizabeth Benson} [Gallaudet University Archives, "Elizabeth English Benson, interpreter in the Language of Signs" biographical subject vertical file]

Treesberg, J. (1992, May). "Louder than words," Coda letters: A memorial for Alan Dalton. <u>CODA Connection,</u> 9 (2), 5. {Reports the publication of Alan Dalton's writings} [UNIV DEAF Periodicals]

Trotto, T. J. (1990, May). Hearing power: A personal perspective. <u>Deaf Life, 2</u> (11), 12-15. {The misperception that hearing people are superior to deaf people is here called "hearing power." The author chronicles a variety of put-downs he experienced dating a hearing woman. The lesson is that the deaf and hearing worlds are rich but different. Hearing people need to respect this difference} [UNIV DEAF Periodicals]

Trounson, R. (1997a, March 14). At school, anguish and despair. <u>The Washington Post,</u> 120th year, No. 99, p. A34. (Washington, D. C.) {It was reported that one of the teenagers was Adi Malka, the hearing daughter of deaf parents} [UNIV Newspapers]

Trounson, R. (1997b, March 17). Jordan King grieves with families of slain Israelis. <u>The Los Angeles Times,</u> pp. A1, A14. (Los Angeles, California) {It was reported that one of the teenagers was Adi Malka, the hearing daughter of deaf parents} [*]

Tubergen, J. M., Jr. (1951, June). Children of the deaf...Caroline Leiter in Japan for Uncle Sam. <u>The Silent Worker, 3</u> (10), 7-8. {Caroline Marie Leiter is the hearing daughter of Harrison M. and Katherine Leiter. She served in the WAVES from 1944-1946. When she re-enlisted, Japan was her destination until 1950. At a meeting of the Chicago Club for the Deaf she reported among other things that the status of the deaf in Japan is that of "outcasts." The CCD collected over $200. to send Caroline after she went back to Japan. The money was given to the Osaka School for the Deaf and purchased much needed materials} [UNIV DEAF Periodicals]

Turner, D. (1989, June 26). Woman raised as deaf discovers the truth. <u>Times-News,</u> pp. D1-D2. (Twin Falls, Idaho) {Sheila Palmer was sent to the Tennessee School for the Deaf in Knoxville at the age of seven. Within two months they "discovered" her ability to hear. She was born into a very large all deaf family. She is now a Sign Language interpreter at the College of Southern Idaho} [*]

TV News. (1973, June 20). <u>On the Green: A Weekly Published for Gallaudet University Staff and Faculty, 2</u> (22), 1. {Reports that Louie Fant will be featured in a new situation comedy, *Thicker than Water*."} [Gallaudet University Archives, "Louie Fant" biographical vertical file]

Two boys held in murder of Rev. Foxwell: Pair of teen-agers arrested in slaying of Rev. Foxwell. (1974, April 10). <u>The Evening Sun, 128</u> (148), p. 1. (Baltimore, Maryland) [Gallaudet University Archives, "Louis W. Foxwell" biographical vertical file]

Two Deans to leave posts: Dean Benson will retire. (1970, April 9). <u>The Buff and Blue, 78</u> (14), pp. 1-2. (Student newspaper of the Gallaudet Student Body Government) {After 44-years as a member of the faculty, and as Dean of Women of Gallaudet College since 1950, Elizabeth Benson will retire July 1. Dean George Detmold is to resign in the Fall} [Gallaudet University Archives]

Two women...two cultures..one ideal..: M. J. Bienvenu, Betty Colonomos. (1989, April). <u>The World Around You: A publication of Pre-College Programs, Gallaudet University,</u> 8-9. Washington, DC: Gallaudet University, Pre-College Programs. [Gallaudet University Archives]

Types of children of deaf parents [Photos and caption]. (1917a, November). <u>The Silent Worker, 30</u> (2), 33. {Pictured are Edwin and Clara Weckel, children of Mr. and Mrs. John F. Weckel of Canton, Ohio} [UNIV DEAF Periodicals]

Types of children of deaf parents [Photos and caption]. (1917b, December). <u>The Silent Worker, 30</u> (3), 53. {Pictured are the following members of the Thomas family of Yonkers, New York: William F. Thomas, Mrs. W. W. W. Thomas and Margaret E., and Murray Campbell Thomas} [UNIV DEAF Periodicals]

Types of children of deaf parents [Photos and captions]. (1918a, March). <u>The Silent Worker, 30</u> (6), 108. {Pictured are: Visoen Elizabeth (age 7), Newton Reed, (age 5 1/2), and Asa Stewart (age 9) all children of Hugo A. Holcombe of Bremerton, Washington; and Mrs. Samuel Kohn and son of New York} [UNIV DEAF Periodicals]

Types of children of deaf parents [Photo and caption]. (1918b, May). <u>The Silent Worker, 30</u> (8), 141. {Pictured are Ruamah and Ervin, children of Mr. and Mrs. Gabriel Frank of Jersey City, New Jersey. "The little girl is six years old and the baby boy is nine months old. Both can hear and talk. The mother was Edna R. Lockwood before marriage."} [UNIV DEAF Periodicals]

Types of children of deaf parents [Photo and caption]. (1918c, June). <u>The Silent Worker, 30</u> (9), 165. {Pictured is Catherine Terry, daughter of Mr. and Mrs. Howard Terry of Hollywood, California} [UNIV DEAF Periodicals]

Types of children of deaf parents [Photo and caption]. (1920a, October). <u>The Silent Worker, 33</u> (1), 27. {Pictured is eight-year-old Helen Mary, "hearing daughter" of Mr. and Mrs. Albert Janak of Temple, Texas} [UNIV DEAF Periodicals]

Types of children of deaf parents [Photo and caption]. (1920b, December). <u>The Silent Worker, 33</u> (3), 85. {Pictured is the two-year-old son of Mr. and Mrs. Samuel Tong, Chickasha, Oklahoma} [UNIV DEAF Periodicals]

Types of children of deaf parents [Photo and caption]. (1921a, February). <u>The Silent Worker, 33</u> (5), 163.

{Pictured is Vernon Overbeck, "hearing son of Mr. and Mrs. J. W. Hale, of Ft. Worth, Texas."} [UNIV DEAF Periodicals]

Types of children of deaf parents [Photos and captions]. (1921b, April). The Silent Worker, 33 (7), 239. {Pictured are Frances and Betsy, children of Mr. and Mrs. C. L. Talbot, Dallas, Texas, ages twelve and thirteen; and six month old Teddy, Jr., son of Mr. and Mrs. Theodore V. Ercoliani of Pittsfield, Massachusetts} [UNIV DEAF Periodicals]

Types of children of deaf parents [Photos and captions]. (1921c, June). The Silent Worker, 33 (9), 343. {Pictured are Lillian May, 12-month-old daughter of Mr. and Mrs. George Wainwright of Trenton, New Jersey and Harry A. Watts, Jr., three and a half year-old grandson and "inseparable companion of Mrs. C. J. Jackson, of Atlanta, Ga. This little boy, although blessed with perfect hearing and speech, is quite an expert in the use of the sign language."} [UNIV DEAF Periodicals]

Types of children of deaf parents [Photo and caption]. (1921d, July). The Silent Worker, 33 (10), 357. {Pictured is Leonard B. Dickerson, Jr., son and only child of Mr. and Mrs. Dickerson of Atlanta, Georgia} [UNIV DEAF Periodicals]

Types of children of deaf parents [Photos and captions]. (1921e, October). The Silent Worker, 34 (1), 14. {Photos of the following are shown: Mrs. D. Wasserman and son of New York City; Georgia Maryland Thompson, granddaughter of Mrs. Emma Morris of Cave Spring, Georgia; Alfred C., son of Max M. Lubin of New York City; Margaret, daughter of Mr. and Mrs. J. F. Lonergan, New York City; Edmund McQ, 18 months old and Tom, Jr., 4 years old, sons of Mr. and Mrs. Tom Myers, Charlotte, North Carolina; and Muriel, daughter of Mr. and Mrs. F. A. Brown, New York City} [UNIV DEAF Periodicals]

Types of children of deaf parents [Photo and caption]. (1921f, October). The Silent Worker, 34 (1), 21. {Pictured is "Henry Raymond Glover, Jr., 8 months, 22 lbs., hearing son of Mr. and Mrs. H. Raymond Glover of Columbia," South Carolina} [UNIV DEAF Periodicals]

Types of children of deaf parents [Photos and captions]. (1921g, November). The Silent Worker, 34 (2), 56. {The following pictures are featured: Ingval J. Dahl, Jr., son of Mr. and Mrs. I. J. Dahl of Duluth, Minnesota; Sarah Elizabeth, eleven months, daughter of Mr. and Mrs. W. H. Chambers of Knoxville, Tennessee; Thomas and Dominic, nine and eight respectively, sons of Leon La Porte of Detroit, Michigan; Charlotte Eva, two-year-old "hearing daughter" of Mr. and Mrs. W. J. C. Hodges of Atlanta, Georgia; Claude and Catherine Schindorff, "hearing children" of Mr. and Mrs. Peter Schindorff of Fostoria, Ohio; and Carol Eickhoff, age four years, "daughter of the National Association of the Deaf."} [UNIV DEAF Periodicals]

Types of children of deaf parents [Photos and captions]. (1921h, December). The Silent Worker, 34 (3), 112. {Pictured are Clifford Ayers, age nine, son of Mr. and Mrs. K. B. Ayers of Akron, Ohio; Dorothy Phyllis Fraser, 12-month-old granddaughter of Mrs. Ella B. Lloyd of Trenton, New Jersey; and J. Fred Haberstroh, Jr., son of Mr. and Mrs. J. Fred Haberstroh of New York City} [UNIV DEAF Periodicals]

Types of children of deaf parents [Photo and caption]. (1921i, December). The Silent Worker, 34 (3), 99. {Pictured are Irene Engh, two and a half years old, and Helen, four months, daughters of Mr. and Mrs. Erick Engh of Minneapolis, Minnesota. Mother was Grace I. Wentz} [UNIV DEAF Periodicals]

Types of children of deaf parents [Photos and captions]. (1922a, January). The Silent Worker, 34 (4), 136. {Pictured are the following: Wallace Dickinson Edington, Jr., 8-month-old "hearing son" of Mr. and Mrs. Wallace D. Edington of Washington, D. C.; George Brown Bedford, 5-month-old "hearing son" of Mr. and Mrs. George

Bedford of Keyport, New Jersey; and Dorothy Mae Huffman, two-year-old "hearing daughter" of Mr. and Mrs. Chester B. Huffman of Columbus, Ohio} [UNIV DEAF Periodicals]

Types of children of deaf parents [Photos and captions]. (1922b, March). The Silent Worker, 34 (6), 215. {Pictured are the following: Hugh Graham, Jr., (age 14), Eugene Graham (12), Emily Graham (8), sons and daughter of Mr. and Mrs. Hugh Graham Miller of Shelby, North Carolina (mother was Miss Margaret LeGrand before marriage); and Alice Virginia, daughter of Mr. and Mrs. Wm. F. Jones of Chicago, Illinois} [UNIV DEAF Periodicals]

Types of children of deaf parents [Photos and captions]. (1922c, April). The Silent Worker, 34 (7), 271. {Featured are photographs of the following: Kathleen W. Hill, "hearing daughter" of Mr. and Mrs. Troy E. Hill, Austin, Texas; Maxine Dorothy Gould, "four year old hearing daughter" of Mr. and Mrs. Lyman N. Gould of Mobile, Alabama, who "can talk and is bright as a new dollar;" Dorothy Goetz, six years old, daughter of Mr. and Mrs. Harley E. Goetz (nee Florence Ethel) of Wapakoneta, Ohio; and William Frederick (fourteen), Murray Campbell (twelve), Margaret Elizabeth (seven) and Stuart Watson (three), children of Mr. W. W. W. Thomas of Yonkers, New York} [UNIV DEAF Periodicals]

Types of children of deaf parents [Photos and captions]. (1922d, July). The Silent Worker, 34 (10), 381. {Featured are Master Robert C. Goth, son of Mr. and Mrs. Simon A. Goth of Detroit, Michigan; and Albert McGhee, son of Mr. and Mrs. A. S. McGhee of Philadelphia, Pennsylvania} [UNIV DEAF Periodicals]

Types of children of deaf parents [Photos and captions]. (1922e, October). The Silent Worker, 35 (1), 19. {Featured are photographs of the following: John Harvey and Dorothy Gwendolyn Horner, son and daughter of Mr. and Mrs. John T. Horner of Akron, Ohio; and Allen Daggett, fourteen-year-old "boy scout hero, son of deaf parents. He gave his life that another might live. The deed brought forth a letter of sympathy from President Harding."} [UNIV DEAF Periodicals]

Types of children of deaf parents [Photos and captions]. (1922f, November). The Silent Worker, 35 (2), 69. {Photos are of the following are featured: Grace and Harry, children of Mr. and Mrs. Harry Calkin of Jersey City, New Jersey. "Both children can hear and speak." Mrs. Margaret Bothner Lounsbury and her sons, George and Theodore W. Both are in military uniform} [UNIV DEAF Periodicals]

Types of children of deaf parents [Photos and captions]. (1923a, January). The Silent Worker, 35 (4), 157. {Featured are photos of Mrs. Agnes O'Brien Ahl, daughter of John F. O'Brien of New York City; and S. Dorris Faulpel, daughter of Mr. and Mrs. George Faulpel of Frederick, Maryland} [UNIV DEAF Periodicals]

Types of children of deaf parents [Photos and captions]. (1923b, February). The Silent Worker, 35 (5), 193. {Featured are photos of the following: Ruamah and Ervin, children of Mr. and Mrs. Gabriel Franck of Jersey City, New Jersey; and James Dennis Underhill in his Boy Scout uniform} [UNIV DEAF Periodicals]

Types of children of deaf parents [Photos and captions]. (1923c, May). The Silent Worker, 35 (8), 324. {Featured are the following photographs: Dorothy Fraser, grandchild of Mrs. Ella B. Lloyd of Trenton; Ralph Lee Mealer, Jr., 20-months-old "hearing son" of Mr. and Mrs. R. L. Mealer of Cottondale, Alabama; Stuart Watson Thomas, son of Mr. and Mrs. William W. Thomas of Yonkers, New York; son of Mr. and Mrs. George Murphy, daughter of Lilly Gwin Andreweski and son of Mr. and Mrs. Clifford Thompson; Norman, son of Mr. and Mrs. Charles T. Hummer of Jersey City, New Jersey; Raymond and Mildred, children of Mr. and Mrs. Hubert B. West of Fairfield, Iowa; Winston and Joyce, children of Mr. and Mrs. Beach who are graduates of the Michigan School for the Deaf and live in Civic Park, Michigan} [UNIV DEAF Periodicals]

Types of children of deaf parents [Photos and captions]. (1923d, June). The Silent Worker, 35 (9), 383. {Six photos of the following are featured: Rita Kate Kaminsky, daughter of Mr. and Mrs. Manuel Kaminsky of New York City; Priscilla Alden Sweeney, "hearing daughter" of Mr. and Mrs. Miles Sweeney of Trenton, New Jersey; Frankie Marguerite Clark, "hearing daughter" of Mr. and Mrs. Adrian Clark of Austin, Texas; Raymond August Frick, grandchild of Mr. and Mrs. M. H. Small; Estela Rendon, daughter of Mr. and Mrs. J. D. Rendon of Loredo, Texas; and Melvin Wail, Jr., son of Mr. and Mrs. Melvin Wail of Bermingham [sic], Alabama. "Can hear, of course."} [UNIV DEAF Periodicals]

Types of children of deaf parents [Photos and captions]. (1923e, July). The Silent Worker, 35 (10), 433. {Three photos are featured: Grace Maxine Long, born October 23, 1911 in Council Bluffs, Iowa and the oldest daughter of Mr. Harry G. Long and Mrs. Mabel Fritz Long (She's "talented in more ways than one for she shines in school as the best speller and reader...."); Birtsel Lockwood Earnst, three-year-old hearing son of Mr. and Mrs. E. B. Earnst of Jersey City, New Jersey; and Marjorie Donovan, youngest child of Mr. and Mrs. Geo. N. Donovan of New York City} [UNIV DEAF Periodicals]

Types of children of deaf parents: Two chums [Photo and caption]. (1921, July). The Silent Worker, 33 (10), 357. {Pictured are J. Guerry Bishop, Jr., son of Mr and Mrs. J. Guerry Bishop, and Billy Gholdston, Jr., son of Mr. and Mrs. William E. Gholdston, all of Atlanta, Georgia. "The mothers of these little boys have been life-long chums."} [UNIV DEAF Periodicals]

Typical children of deaf parents: Amiee Lefferson Cook [Photo and caption]. (1903, November). The Silent Worker, 16 (2), 21. {Amiee was born October 4, 1901, and her parents, who were pupils at the New Jersey School for the Deaf, live in Asbury Park, New Jersey. "The little girl is certainly a most beautiful child."} [UNIV DEAF Periodicals]

Typical children of deaf parents: Claude E., Walter H., and Joseph H. Penrose [Photo and caption]. (1903, January). The Silent Worker, 15 (5), 74. {Pictured are the children of Mr. & Mrs. Joseph Penrose of New Market, New Jersey} [UNIV DEAF Periodicals]

Typical children of deaf parents: George and Catherine Lloyd [Photo and caption]. (1902, October). The Silent Worker, 15 (2), 21. {Pictured are Mrs. R. B. Lloyd and her two children, George and Catherine. At fifteen, George is one of the youngest members of Trenton High School. Catherine is nine and attends the Hamilton School where her aunt is the principal} [UNIV DEAF Periodicals]

Typical children of deaf parents: Gladys E. Penrose [Photo and caption]. (1904, February). The Silent Worker, 16 (5), 73. {Gladys is the eight-month-old child of Mr. & Mrs. Joseph Penrose of New Market, New Jersey} [UNIV DEAF Periodicals]

Typical children of deaf parents [Letter to the editor and photos]. (1905, February). The Silent Worker, 17 (5), 76. {The author sends along photographs of Edith Una Long, eldest daughter of Mr. J. Schuyler Long of Council Bluffs, Iowa, and Beth Thompson, the only child of Mr. and Mrs. Zach B. Thompson, also of Council Bluffs. This fascinating letter is dated December 27, 1904 and is signed "E. F. L."} [UNIV DEAF Periodicals]

Typical children of deaf parents: Lucille Berg [Photo and caption]. (1904, December). The Silent Worker, 17 (3), 42. {Lucille is the daughter of Mr. & Mrs. Albert Berg of Indianapolis, Indiana} [UNIV DEAF Periodicals]

Typical children of deaf parents: Ruth Jessie Anderson [Photo and caption]. (1903, November). The Silent Worker, 16 (2), 21. {Ruth is the six-year-old daughter of Mr. & Mrs. G. Walfrid Anderson of Olathe, Kansas} [UNIV DEAF Periodicals]

Uhland, E. (1988, August 3). Children of the deaf: Helping them speak is goal of new program at Cleary School. The Village Herald (weekly), 3A, 10A, cover. (East Setauket, New York) [Gallaudet University Archives, "Children of deaf adults" subject vertical file]

(#) Uhlig, M. A. (1985, January 21?). Boy, 16, is slain standing up for a girl. (Newspaper unidentified - Queens, New York) [*]

Using sign language... [Photo and caption]. (1961, May 29). The Evening Star, p. A1. (Washington, D. C.) {Vice President Johnson spoke at Gallaudet College's 97th graduation ceremony. Elizabeth Benson translates his speech} [Gallaudet University Archives, "Elizabeth English Benson, interpreter in the Language of Signs" biographical subject vertical file]

Valente, J. (1982, May 18). Actress Fletcher raps cuts in aid to deaf at Gallaudet Graduation. The Washington Post (Metro section), p. B9. (Washington, D. C.) [Gallaudet University Archives, "Parent-child relationship - deaf adults" subject vertical file]

Van Buren, A. (Ed.). (1997, April 17). Dear Abby [Column]. The News-Review, p. 12. (Roseburg, Oregon) {Letter to Dear Abby from Barbara Lincoln, Coordinator, House Ear Institute Lead Line, Los Angeles: "I am the mother of a 28-year-old son who is deaf. He is a contributing member of his community and a wonderful father to his beautiful 3-year-old hearing son." She shares two sources of information and support available to other hearing parents with deaf children} [*]

Veltri, D. (1996, Aug/Sept). A HOHA experiences CODA. CODA Connection, 13 (3), 7, 10. [UNIV DEAF Periodicals]

Vernon, M. (1974, April-May). Miracle man of deafness: Rev. Louis Foxwell. The Maryland Bulletin, 94 (4), 86-91. (Publication of the Maryland School for the Deaf, Frederick, Maryland) [UNIV DEAF Periodicals and Gallaudet University Archives, "Louis W. Foxwell" biographical vertical file]

Victor, R. (1964, March 12). Parents' deafness no bar to warm, happy family life for Barashes: Children set fine academic record; daughter, mate to teach handicapped. The Capital Times. (Madison, Wisconsin) [Gallaudet University Archives "Eva Barash Dicker" subject vertical file]

Victory Fund goes to Red Cross: One of three Clubmobiles in Army show. (1943, November 24). The Buff and Blue, 52 (3), p. 1. (Student newspaper of the Gallaudet Student Body Government) [UNIV Archives]

Video, J. (1989, March 23). Hanks gets *Big* on video, as Dreyfuss rules Parador. Star (Tinley Park Edition). (Oak Forest, Illinois) {Reports the release of *A Summer to Remember* by MCA Home Video} [Gallaudet University Archives, "Louise Fletcher" biographical vertical file]

Villasenor, R. (1967, June 2). Deaf-mute couple win long fight for custody of boy, two. The Los Angeles Times, p. 1. (See also San Fernando Valley News) [Gallaudet University Archives, "Court litigation - deaf" subject vertical file]

Virginia Ann White [Photo and caption]. (1922, May). The Silent Worker, 34 (18), 297. {One of several photos in an article titled "The Argonaut" by J. W. Howson, pages 293-295, 297. There is another photo of Virginia at age two on page 295 under the title "Youthful Argonauts."} [UNIV DEAF Periodicals]

Voice, K. (1986, May). From SODA to CODA. CODA Newsletter, 3 (2), 4. [UNIV DEAF Periodicals]

(##) Wagner, K. (1987, June 18). Sign of the times at Athena Commencement. Times-Union. (Rochester, New York) {An interpreter will be provided for Joely Parker's deaf parents at her graduation exercises. See the related letter to the editor by Bernard Hurwitz, June 26, 1987}

Walker, L. A. (1982, July 12). Vanilla fires: Rejected by a hearing world, a deaf gang finds brotherhood and protection on New York's streets. People Weekly, 18 (1), 24-29. [UNIV Periodicals]

Walker, L. A. (1985, June 20). Children of the disabled face special pressures. The New York Times (Home Section), pp. C1, C6. (Published as "When a parent is disabled" on this same date in another edition of this newspaper, pp. 21, 23. [*] A description of this article appears in the August, 1985, issue of the CODA Newsletter, 2 (3), 3. [UNIV DEAF Periodicals]) {Describes the additional responsibilities children of the disabled take on whether their parents are blind, deaf or physically or mobility impaired. Several authorities are quoted and anecdotal stories from several adults who had disabled parents are included} [UNIV Newspapers Microfilm]

Walker, L. A. (1986a, August 31). Outsider in a silent world: The author heard and spoke for her parents, yet deafness was something separate she could never really know. The New York Times Magazine, pp. 20-21, 28, 31, 33. [Gallaudet University Archives, "Parent-child relationship - deaf adults" subject vertical file]

Walker, L. A. (1986b, September 14). The sounds of silence: Growing up with deaf parents. San Francisco Chronicle (This World), pp. 9, 20. (California) [*]

Walker, L. A. (1986c, September 22). Striking a fragile and precious balance. Newsweek, 108, 72. {Excerpts from *A Loss for Words* by Lou Ann Walker} [UNIV Periodicals]

Walker, L. A. (1986d, December 15). A dutiful, hearing child of deaf parents grows up to find herself at a loss for words. People Weekly, 26 (24), 93-94, 96, 98. [UNIV Periodicals]

Walker, L. A. (1987, March). The empty crib: Little Joey meant everything in the world to his mom and dad. Why would anyone want to take him away from the parents who loved him so? Ladies' Home Journal, 104, (3), 76, 154-155, 157-158. {"The state of Florida takes an infant from his deaf parents."} [Gallaudet University Archives, "Parent-child relationship - deaf adults" subject vertical file]

Walker, L. A. (1989a, April 23). How deaf people are seizing power over their own lives: "I know how to ask for what I want." The Washington Post (Parade, the Sunday Newspaper Magazine), pp. 4-6. (Washington, D. C. - Cover title: "Finally they're being heard, a personal story by Lou Ann Walker") [*]

Walker, L. A. (1989b, December/1990, January). Last gasp: Louder than words. NewYork Woman, 4, 164. [*]

Walker, L. A. (1996, December). Signs of love: A mother builds a bridge between her daughter and her deaf parents. Parents Magazine, 71 (12), 169-171. (Under the heading "Family life: Generations") [*]

Walter, T. (1985, December 9). Moving film finds a voice in the silence. () {A positive review of the film *Love is Never Silent*} [Gallaudet University Archives, "Love is Never Silent" subject vertical file]

Walter, V. (1987-88, Winter). In der Nacht: An unusual exhibit depicts the Nazi persecution of deaf people. Gallaudet Today, 18 (2), 6-11. {The article includes a story about Rose Feld. There is a photograph of Rose with her daughter, Esther, after the war} [Gallaudet University Archives or RESERVE]

Walter, V. (1990, Fall). The ties that bind: Hearing children and deaf parents talk about being a family. Gallaudet

A
R
T
I
C
L
E
S

Today, 21 (1), 2-11. {Featured are the Kensicki family, the Dillehay family, the Bull family, the Agboola family, the Galloway family, the Corbett family, and the Sutcliffe family} [Gallaudet University Archives or RESERVE]

Walter, V., & Willigan, B. A. (1996, Summer). Creating a new community: A private developer and concerned deaf people are working together to make a community for deaf adults a reality. Gallaudet Today, 26 (4), 11-17. {The developer's grandparents are deaf. They have made efforts to get feedback from the deaf and coda communities in the planning stages of this retirement community} [Gallaudet University Archives or RESERVE]

Want careful statistics. (1890, May 29). The Silent Worker, 3 (23), 3. (Reprinted from the Missouri Record, a publication of the Missouri School for the Deaf, Fulton, Missouri) {One subscriber received a "D. and D. Marriage Record" and returned it to Dr. E. A. Fay. There is interest in this study because of a "theory of Prof. Alexander Graham Bell that marriages among the deaf have a tendency to produce a deaf variety of the human race."} [Gallaudet University Archives]

Washburn, D. (1985, December 8). Hallmark special opens eyes, ears to silent worlds. News, pp. 1F, 5F. (Birmingham, Alabama) {A positive review of the film *Love is Never Silent*. Mentions a conversation that actress Louise Fletcher, who is from Birmingham, and Mare Winningham had after Winningham got the part of Margaret} [Gallaudet University Archives, "Love is Never Silent" subject vertical file]

Waterhouse, H. (1955, June 22). "Cry relay": Baby just signals deaf mute parents. Beacon Journal. (Akron, Ohio) [Gallaudet University Archives, "Parent-child relationship - deaf adults" subject vertical file]

Wedding bells have rung...Petsy Lynch: Blue Ribbon horsewoman. (1962, June). The Silent Worker, 14 (10), 6-7. [UNIV DEAF Periodicals]

Weil, M. (1995, December 13). Obituaries: Homer Thornberry dies at 86, nominated to Supreme Court. The Washington Post, 119th year, No. 8, p. D4. (Washington, D. C.) {William Homer Thornberry was born in Austin, Texas, on January 9, 1909 to parents who were deaf. "He sold newspapers to help support himself and his widowed mother after his father died and worked his way through the University of Texas, where he received degrees in law and business." "In 1963, he spoke at commencement exercises at Gallaudet University, delivering the first part of his speech in sign language." President John F. Kennedy nominated him to the U.S. District Court in 1963. President Lyndon Johnson nominated Judge Thornberry to the Supreme Court in 1968} [UNIV Newspapers Microfilm]

Weinraub, B. (1995, March 27). Oscar's glory is fleeting: Ask one who knows. The New York Times, 144 (No. 50,013), pp. C11, C15. {"Louise Fletcher, the actress who won the Academy Award for her performance as Nurse Ratched in the film *One Flew Over the Cuckoo's Nest*, is profiled as a textbook example of an artist for whom an Oscar amounted to very little." - NewsAbs} [UNIV Newspapers Microfilm]

Weinrib, A. (1993, November). Books: The "thousand faces" of actor Lon Chaney. The Silent News, 25 (11) H1, H7. [UNIV DEAF Periodicals]

Weinstock, R. B. (1993, November). In the deep South: A tale of two brothers [Sports and Recreation column]. The Silent News, 25 (11), 41. (Reprinted from the TFA - Television for All - news of September 17, 1993) [UNIV DEAF Periodicals microfilm]

Weissmann, G. (1987, July 26). The tribe that wears white. The New York Times Book Review, 136 (Section 7) (No. 47,212), pp. 1-2. {Review of *Becoming a doctor: A journey of initiation in Medical School* by Melvin Konner} [UNIV Newspapers Microfilm]

Wentzel, M. (1979, November 20). Many deaf persons held cut off from social services. <u>Evening Sun.</u> (Baltimore, Maryland) [Gallaudet University Archives, "Rev. Louis W. Foxwell, Jr." biographical vertical file]

We taught a six year old to talk back to his mother [Advertisement]. (1992, April). <u>Deaf Life, 4</u> (10), 32. {This is an Easter Seals public service announcement. A deaf mother is looking closely at the fingerspelling on her son's hands. The caption reads: "His first word was 'Mom.' But he didn't speak it. He spelled it with his hands. Because his mom was deaf. Yet with the help of Easter Seals, he learned to tell her everything a mother wants to hear. Give to Easter Seals. Give the power to overcome."} [UNIV DEAF Periodicals]

Whisenant, M. (1998, February). What am I thankful for? <u>CODA Connection, 15</u> (1), 8. [UNIV DEAF Periodicals]

White, B. R. (1949, October). The editor's page: Children of deaf parents. <u>The Silent Worker, 2</u> (2), 31. {The editor gives some thought to the "idea prevalent among a great number of persons unacquainted with the deaf" that children born to deaf parents "are below par mentally, or that they possess some other woefully inadequate physical equipment." He goes on to counter this misconception and that "children of deaf parents are among the outstanding citizens of the land."} [UNIV DEAF Periodicals]

White, C. (1989, November). Catherine in the CODA community! <u>Soundbarrier,</u> No. 30, 9. {Report on the Children of Deaf Adults conference, Westminster, Maryland, USA, July 15-18, 1989} [UNIV DEAF Periodicals]

Whiteside, K. (1993, November 29). People: Tracy Bergan. <u>Sports Illustrated, 79</u> (22), 66. [UNIV Periodicals]

Who's who in the Deaf World. (1925, January). <u>The Silent Worker, 37</u> (4), 190. {In all of the biographies listed, mentioned also is whether they have deaf relatives and hearing children} [UNIV DEAF Periodicals]

Will, G. F. (1986, October 27). Immersed in a sea of silence: An old woman, born deaf, dreams in Sign Language. People will dream, no matter what. <u>Newsweek, 108,</u> 112. [UNIV Periodicals]

Willard, T. (1994, June). Media watch: <u>Sacramento Bee</u> stings its readers with insensitivity. <u>The Silent News, 26</u> (6), 4. (Sacramento, California) [UNIV DEAF Periodicals]

William N. Llewellyn [Photo and caption]. (1918, March). <u>The Silent Worker, 30</u> (6), 105. {Photo is of the nineteen year old son of Mr. and Mrs. Edward Llewellyn of Los Angeles, California} [UNIV DEAF Periodicals]

(*) Williams, B. T. (1993, Spring). Parenting with a disability - does it make a difference? <u>Accent on Living, 38,</u> 32-36. (Magazine that provides information about new products, travel ideas, medical news, housing, adjustment, inspiration and other areas of interest to mobility impaired individuals. Located in Bloomington, Illinois) {Two families are featured: one parent has Kugelberg-Welander muscular dystrophy and in the other family a parent has a limp as a birth defect. An interview with the children is reported. A rehabilitation counselor says, "However, these kids [whose parents are disabled] can be a little more compassionate - more appreciative of life."} [*]

Williams, M. (1994, February 21). Then and now: Remembering a great romance. <u>People Weekly, 41,</u> 13. {About Louise Fletcher} [UNIV Periodicals - microfilm]

Williams, S. (1993, August). A. B. [sic] Bell life story featured in miniseries. <u>The Silent News, 25</u> (8), 28-29. (From the Associated Press, July 18, 1993) [UNIV DEAF Periodicals]

Wilson, D. (1969, October). Real Estate syndicator Katz... Can the children of deaf parents succeed? You bet your

167

life! The Deaf American, 22 (2), 7. [UNIV DEAF Periodicals]

Wilson, M. R. (1998, May). Words [Poem]. CODA Connection, 15 (2), 17. [UNIV DEAF Periodicals]

With English children [Photo]. (1943, August). The Silent Cavalier, 3 (12), 3. {Photo of Staff Sergeant Murray Faupel, son of Prof. and Mrs. George H. Faupel, Sr., of the Maryland State School for the Deaf, Frederick, Maryland. Picture was taken May, 1943} [Gallaudet University Archives]

With the alumni, 1930-1939: Elizabeth E. Benson. (1962, July). The Newsletter, 6. (Publication of The George Washington University and it's alumni) {Mentions that Benson received an honorary Doctor of Letters degree at Gallaudet's Commencement in June. She received her B. A. degree from George Washington University in 1931} [Gallaudet University Archives, "Elizabeth English Benson, honorary degree, Doctor of Letters" biographical subject vertical file]

Wolfe, D. (1997, May). Kids who are different [Poem]. CODA Connection, 14 (2), 17. (Reprinted from Parade Magazine, 10/27/96 - written by Digby Wolfe for Goldie Hawn) [UNIV DEAF Periodicals]

Wolfe, L. (1990, September 2). Pompano woman tells of her life with deaf parents. The Miami Herald, p. C8. (Miami, Florida) [*]

Woodford, D. (1993, September). [Letter to the editor]. British Deaf News Supplement, 24 (9), 1. [UNIV DEAF Periodicals]

Woolfe, R. (Ed.). (1996, March). Face to face with Ramon Woolfe: Ben Steiner. British Deaf News, 27 (3), 14-15. {Ben Steiner is interviewed about his deaf mother and reasons for moving from interpreting for the BBC TV "See Hear" program to his new post as lecturer at Wolverhampton University, teaching on interpreting issues} [UNIV DEAF Periodicals]

World isn't silent' [sic] for deaf Willmar native. (1974, July 8). Willmar Tribune. (Willmar, Minnesota) [Gallaudet University Archives, "Parent-child relationship - deaf adults" subject vertical file]

Worth watching [Photo and caption]. (1985, December 8). Star. (Kansas City, Missouri) {See the related story on pages I-1 and I-4 by Barry Garron} [Gallaudet University Archives, "Love is Never Silent" subject vertical file]

Wriede, A. (1923, October). A sketch of Harry Gilmor Benson. The Maryland Bulletin, 44 (1), 8-9. (Publication of the Maryland School for the Deaf, Frederick, Maryland) {Mentions two girls in their family, Mary Alice and Elizabeth English} [Gallaudet University Archives and the "Elizabeth English Benson, biographical information and news clippings" biographical subject vertical file]

Young, I. (1987, May). Spotlight: Sweet Honey in the Rock. Essence: The Magazine for Today's Black Woman, 92-94, 158-161. {Shirley Childress, who is hearing and has deaf parents, is a member of this singing ensemble as a Sign Language interpreter} [UNIV Periodicals]

Youngs, J. P., Jr. (1973, July-August). Dr. Elizabeth E. Benson. The Deaf American, 25 (11), 32-33. (Article appears in the "RID Interprenews" section) {This tribute is written by Dr. Joseph P. Youngs, Jr., Superintendent of the Governor Baxter State School for the Deaf, Portland, Maine, and a coda himself} [Gallaudet University Archives, "Elizabeth English Benson: Obituary, memorial service" biographical subject vertical file]

Younkin, L. (1990, January/February). Between two worlds: Welcomed by neither Black nor deaf people, deaf

Blacks can find themselves in a virtual no-man's land. The Disability Rag, 11 (1), 30-33. [UNIV DEAF Periodicals]

"You're the gift" Denver Colorado Conference a smashing success! (1997, September). CODA Connection, 14 (3), 1, 6. [UNIV DEAF Periodicals]

Youthful Argonauts [Photos and captions]. (1922a, March). The Silent Worker, 34 (6), 211. {Pictures are of members of one family: Donia Jean Brodrick and Raymond Depew. Their mother is Emily Fariss Depew Brodrick of Berkeley, California} [UNIV DEAF Periodicals]

Youthful Argonauts [Photo and caption]. (1922b, May). The Silent Worker, 34 (8), 295. {Picture is of Virginia Ann White, two years old, of Berkeley, California} [UNIV DEAF Periodicals]

Zabytko, I. (1989, July 23). Life and deafness as seen by Ruthie [Review of the book *Useful gifts* by Carole L. Glickfeld]. Orlando Sentinel. (Orlando, Florida) [*]

Zito, T. (1973, April 19). Teacher of the Year. The Washington Post. (Washington, D. C.) {About John A. Ensworth, a 46-year-old 6th grade teacher in Bend, Oregon. First Lady Pat Nixon at a White House ceremony announced Ensworth was selected as the 1973 National Teacher of the Year. In its 22nd year, this program is sponsored by the Encyclopedia Britannica, the Council of Chief State School Officers, and the *Ladies Home Journal*} [Gallaudet University Archives, "Parent-child relationship - deaf adults" subject vertical file]

A
R
T
I
C
L
E
S

IV

CODA:

CONFERENCE PROCEEDINGS

ARTICLES AND CHAPTER

NEWSLETTERS

CODA

International CODA (Children of Deaf Adults, Inc.) conferences have produced a wealth of anecdotal and other resource material. These proceedings are available by writing to CODA Inc., at P.O. Box 30715, Santa Barbara, CA 93130-0715 Internet: <http://www.gallaudet.edu/~rgpricke/coda/index.html> Information about subscribing to the CODA Connection is available by looking at the section on INTERNATIONAL RESOURCES under CODA, Inc.

Abarbanell, A. (Ed.). (1997a). How to tell stories [Workshop]. In R. Shipman (Ed.), "Once upon a time...:" Proceedings of the twelfth annual International CODA Conference, Denver, Colorado, July 10-13, 1997 (pp. 111-112). Santa Barbara, CA: Children of Deaf Adults. (Nine unattributed poems were produced) [DEAF 306.874 I57o, 1997]

Abarbanell, A. (1997b). Once upon a time...: Wrap-up. In R. Shipman (Ed.), "Once upon a time...:" Proceedings of the twelfth annual International CODA Conference, Denver, Colorado, July 10-13, 1997 (pp. 114-115). Santa Barbara, CA: Children of Deaf Adults. [DEAF 306.874 I57o, 1997]

Aftercare [Breakout summary]. (1994). In R. Shipman (Ed.), Recollections: A decade of CODA, proceedings of the eighth International CODA Conference, Spokane, Washington, July 15-18, 1993 (p. 68). Santa Barbara, CA: Children of Deaf Adults. [DEAF 306.847 I57r, 1993]

Aheroni, E. (Ed.). (1989). Parents with a second disability [Summary of group discussion]. In T. H. Bull (Ed.), New beginnings, new directions: Proceedings of the third National CODA Conference, Denver, Colorado, August 13-15, 1988 (p. 55). Santa Barbara, CA: Children of Deaf Adults. [DEAF 306.874 N3, 1988]

Aheroni, E. (Ed.). (1990). Codas and personal relationships [Group #2 notes]. In T. H. Bull (Ed.), CODA: A diverse community, proceedings of the fourth National CODA Conference, Westminster, Maryland, July 15-18, 1989 (p. 83). Santa Barbara, CA: Children of Deaf Adults. [DEAF 306.874 N3, 1989]

Aheroni, E. (1992). The agony and the empathy [Keynote address]. In R. Childress & K. Austin-Hemelt (Eds.), CODA: Family of origin/family of choice, proceedings of the seventh International CODA Conference, New Orleans, July 16-19, 1992 (pp. 8-23). Santa Barbara, CA: Children of Deaf Adults. [DEAF 306.874 I57c, 1992]

Aheroni, E. (1994). Wrap up session [Closing speech and comments from others]. In R. Shipman (Ed.), Recollections: A decade of CODA, proceedings of the eighth International CODA Conference, Spokane, Washington, July 15-18, 1993 (pp. 78-95). Santa Barbara, CA: Children of Deaf Adults. [DEAF 306.847 I57r, 1993]

Aheroni, E. (Ed.). (1997). Voices: A Deaf voice roundtable [Panel]. In S. Schmidt-Boe, (Ed.), "Everyone is a star": The 11th annual international CODA conference proceedings, Buena Park, California, July 11-14, 1996 (pp. 57-60). Santa Barbara, CA: Children of Deaf Adults. (Moderator: Elliot Aheroni of California. Panel members: Alan Abarbanell, Illinois; Dave Eklof, Wisconsin; Bonnie Kraft, Massachusetts; Paula Olejarz, Virginia; and Marvin Sallop, Texas) [On order]

Ammons, D. K. (1989). Reflections on CODA III: A Deaf-coda's perspective of CODA III. In T. H. Bull (Ed.), New beginnings, new directions: Proceedings of the third National CODA conference, Denver, Colorado, August 13-15, 1988 (pp. 81-82). Santa Barbara, CA: Children of Deaf Adults. [DEAF 306.874 N3, 1988]

Anonymous. (1997). Once upon a time...: My memories of CODArado '97. In R. Shipman (Ed.), "Once upon a time...:" Proceedings of the twelfth annual International CODA Conference, Denver, Colorado, July 10-13, 1997 (pp. 121-122, 124-125, 127-128). Santa Barbara, CA: Children of Deaf Adults. (Five pieces were submitted to be credited as "anonymous") [DEAF 306.874 I57o, 1997]

Atencio, J. (1997). Once upon a time...: My memories of CODArado '97. In R. Shipman (Ed.), "Once upon a time...:" Proceedings of the twelfth annual International CODA Conference, Denver, Colorado, July 10-13, 1997 (p. 122). Santa Barbara, CA: Children of Deaf Adults. [DEAF 306.874 I57o, 1997]

(*) Baldwin, D. R. (1996). Winning essay: The 1992 CODA Millie Brother Scholarship. In D. Prickett & R.

Prickett (Eds.), <u>Richness in our diversity: Proceedings of the tenth International CODA Conference, Research Triangle Park, North Carolina, July 27-30, 1995</u> (p. 121). Santa Barbara, CA: Children of Deaf Adults. (Reprinted from the Aug/Sept, 1992, edition of the <u>CODA Connection, 9</u> (3), 5. [UNIV DEAF Periodicals]) [On order]

Bass, J. (Ed.). (1992). Male codas and significant others [Notes from session II]. In T. H. Bull (Ed.), <u>A CODA Retreat: Coming home, proceedings of the fifth National CODA Conference, Austin, Texas, July 14-17, 1990</u> (p. 61). Santa Barbara, CA: Children of Deaf Adults. [DEAF 306.874 N3, 1990]

Berman, H. (Ed.). (1987/1994). Codas and mental health [Breakout group summaries]. In T. H. Bull, S. D. Rutherford & S. Jacobs (Eds.), <u>Celebration and exploration of our heritage: Proceedings of the first National CODA Conference, Fremont, California, August 8-10, 1986</u> (Rev. ed., pp. 56-57). Santa Barbara, CA: Children of Deaf Adults. (The first edition was edited by S. Rutherford & S. Jacobs [DEAF 306.874 N4, 1986]) [DEAF 306.874 N37c, 1986b]

Berman, H. (1992a). Coming home [Keynote address]. In T. H. Bull (Ed.), <u>A CODA retreat: Coming home, proceedings of the fifth National CODA Conference, Austin, Texas, July 14-17, 1990</u> (pp. 10-17). Santa Barbara, CA: Children of Deaf Adults. [DEAF 306.874 N3, 1990]

Berman, H. (1992b). Rage and anger [Notes]. In T. H. Bull (Ed.), <u>A CODA retreat: Coming home, proceedings of the fifth National CODA Conference, Austin, Texas, July 14-17, 1990</u> (pp. 34-37). Santa Barbara, CA: Children of Deaf Adults. [DEAF 306.874 N3, 1990]

Berman, H., Morton, D., & Stansfield, M. (Eds.). (1987a/1994). Introduction [Wrap up of three topics]. In T. H. Bull, S. D. Rutherford & S. Jacobs (Eds.), <u>Celebration and exploration of our heritage: Proceedings of the first National CODA Conference, Fremont, California, August 8-10, 1986</u> (Rev. ed., p. 52). Santa Barbara, CA: Children of Deaf Adults. (The first edition was edited by S. Rutherford & S. Jacobs. [DEAF 306.874 N37c, 1986] - Author order is Stansfield, Morton and Berman in the revised edition) [DEAF 306.874 N37c, 1986b]

Berman, H., Morton, D., & Stansfield, M. (Eds.). (1987b/1994). Summary of the seven coda group discussions [Introduction and wrap up]. In T. H. Bull, S. D. Rutherford & S. Jacobs (Eds.), <u>Celebration and exploration of our heritage: Proceedings of the first National CODA Conference, Fremont, California, August 8-10, 1986</u> (Rev. ed., pp. 42-48). Santa Barbara, CA: Children of Deaf Adults. (The first edition was edited by S. Rutherford & S. Jacobs. [DEAF 306.874 N4, 1986] - The seven group facilitators were Diane Morton, Hank Berman, Millie Stansfield, Millie Brother, Forrest Orr, Robert Pollard and Susan Rutherford) [DEAF 306.874 N37c, 1986b]

Bettini, N. (1996). Memoirs and participant reflections [About the conference]. In D. Prickett & R. Prickett (Eds.), <u>Richness in our diversity: Proceedings of the tenth International CODA Conference, Research Triangle Park, North Carolina, July 27-30, 1995</u> (p. 114). Santa Barbara, CA: Children of Deaf Adults. [On order]

Blackman, C. (1997a). Memories, reflections and poetry: Memoirs. In S. Schmidt-Boe, (Ed.), <u>"Everyone is a star": The 11th annual international CODA conference proceedings, Buena Park, California, July 11-14, 1996</u> (p. 70). Santa Barbara, CA: Children of Deaf Adults. [On order]

Blackman, C. (1997b). Once upon a time...: My memories of CODArado '97. In R. Shipman (Ed.), <u>"Once upon a time...:" Proceedings of the twelfth annual International CODA Conference, Denver, Colorado, July 10-13, 1997</u> (p. 123). Santa Barbara, CA: Children of Deaf Adults. [DEAF 306.874 I57o, 1997]

Blackman, C. H. (1996). Memoirs and participant reflections [About the conference]. In D. Prickett & R. Prickett (Eds.), <u>Richness in our diversity: Proceedings of the tenth International CODA Conference, Research Triangle Park,</u>

North Carolina, July 27-30, 1995 (pp. 108-109). Santa Barbara, CA: Children of Deaf Adults. [On order]

Boe. S. (1997). Memories, reflections and poetry: Memoirs. In S. Schmidt-Boe, (Ed.), "Everyone is a star": The 11th annual international CODA conference proceedings, Buena Park, California, July 11-14, 1996 (pp. 69-70). Santa Barbara, CA: Children of Deaf Adults. [On order]

Boesen, S. (Ed.). (1992). Codas and their children [Summary]. In T. H. Bull (Ed.), A CODA retreat: Coming home, proceedings of the fifth National CODA Conference, Austin, Texas, July 14-17, 1990 (pp. 45-46). Santa Barbara, CA: Children of Deaf Adults. [DEAF 306.874 N3, 1990]

Bonser, P., & Bonser, J. (1997). Pioneering CODA - Australia [Keynote address]. In S. Schmidt-Boe, (Ed.), "Everyone is a star": The 11th annual international CODA conference proceedings, Buena Park, California, July 11-14, 1996 (pp. 41-49). Santa Barbara, CA: Children of Deaf Adults. [On order]

(*) Bourne, F. S. (1996). "Your parents are Deaf? I'm sorry. How did you get lucky?" [The 1994 CODA Millie Brother Scholarship winning essay]. In D. Prickett & R. Prickett (Eds.), Richness in our diversity: Proceedings of the tenth International CODA Conference, Research Triangle Park, North Carolina, July 27-30, 1995 (pp. 125-126). Santa Barbara, CA: Children of Deaf Adults. (Reprinted from the November, 1994, edition of the CODA Connection, 11 (4), 8. [UNIV DEAF Periodicals]) [On order]

(*) Bowe, D. W. (1996). What my father taught me [The 1994 CODA Millie Brother] Scholarship essay winner. In D. Prickett & R. Prickett (Eds.), Richness in our diversity: Proceedings of the tenth International CODA Conference, Research Triangle Park, North Carolina, July 27-30, 1995 (p. 127). Santa Barbara, CA: Children of Deaf Adults. (Reprinted from the November, 1994, edition of the CODA Connection, 11 (4), 9. [UNIV DEAF Periodicals]) [On order]

Brother, M. (Ed.). (1983, November). CODA Newsletter [Introductory issue]. Santa Barbara, CA: Children of Deaf Adults. (6 pages) [UNIV DEAF Periodicals]

Brother, M. (Ed.). (1984, February-1988, November). CODA Newsletter. Santa Barbara, CA: Children of Deaf Adults. (International newsletter of Children of Deaf Adults. Write CODA, P.O. Box 30715, Santa Barbara, CA 93130-0715) [UNIV DEAF Periodicals]

Brother, M. (1987a/1994). CODA: Past, present, and future [Summary]. In T. H. Bull, S. D. Rutherford & S. Jacobs (Eds.), Celebration and exploration of our heritage: Proceedings of the first National CODA Conference, Fremont, California, August 8-10, 1986 (Rev. ed., pp. 61-66). Santa Barbara, CA: Children of Deaf Adults. (The first edition was edited by S. Rutherford & S. Jacobs. [DEAF 306.874 N4, 1986]) [DEAF 306.874 N37c, 1986b]

Brother, M. (1987b/1994). Welcome and remarks. In T. H. Bull, S. D. Rutherford & S. Jacobs (Eds.), Celebration and exploration of our heritage: Proceedings of the first National CODA Conference, Fremont, California, August 8-10, 1986 (Rev. ed., pp. 13-14). Santa Barbara, CA: Children of Deaf Adults. (The first edition was edited by S. Rutherford & S. Jacobs. [DEAF 306.874 N4, 1986]) [DEAF 306.874 N37c, 1986b]

Brother, M. (1989a). CODA founder's welcome. In T. H. Bull (Ed.), New beginnings, new directions: Proceedings of the third National CODA Conference, Denver, Colorado, August 13-15, 1988 (pp. 14-16). Santa Barbara, CA: Children of Deaf Adults. [DEAF 306.874 N3, 1988]

Brother, M. (Ed.). (1989b). CODA newcomers group [Summary]. In T. H. Bull (Ed.), New beginnings, new

C
O
D
A

directions: Proceedings of the third National CODA Conference, Denver, Colorado, August 13-15, 1988 (p. 51). Santa Barbara, CA: Children of Deaf Adults. [DEAF 306.874 N3, 1988]

Brother, M. (1990a). CODA: Past, present, future. In T. H. Bull (Ed.), Reflections: Codas and cultures, proceedings of the second National CODA Conference, Rochester, New York, August 21-23, 1987 (3rd rev. ed., pp. 65-67). Santa Barbara, CA: Children of Deaf Adults. (Date is listed as August 23, 1987. The Gallaudet University Library also has the first edition [DEAF 306.874 N3, 1987] and the second edition [DEAF 306.874 N3, 1987b]) [DEAF 306.874 N3, 1987a]

Brother, M. (1990b). Conference welcoming remarks. In T. H. Bull (Ed.), CODA: A diverse community, proceedings of the fourth National CODA Conference, Westminster, Maryland, July 15-18, 1989 (p. 11). Santa Barbara, CA: Children of Deaf Adults. [DEAF 306.874 N3, 1989]

Brother, M. (1990c). Introduction to newcomers group session. In T. H. Bull (Ed.), CODA: A diverse community, proceedings of the fourth National CODA Conference, Westminster, Maryland, July 15-18, 1989 (p. 12). Santa Barbara, CA: Children of Deaf Adults. [DEAF 306.874 N3, 1989]

Brother, M. (1990d). Report on the First International CODA meeting, Helsinki, Finland, July 27, 1987. In T. H. Bull (Ed.), Reflections: Codas and cultures, proceedings of the second National CODA Conference, Rochester, New York, August 21-23, 1987 (3rd rev. ed., pp. 63-64). Santa Barbara, CA: Children of Deaf Adults. (The Gallaudet University Library also has the first edition [DEAF 306.874 N3, 1987] and the second edition [DEAF 306.874 N3, 1987b]) [DEAF 306.874 N3, 1987a]

Brother, M. (1990e). Report on the international CODA planning meeting. In T. H. Bull (Ed.), CODA: A diverse community, proceedings of the fourth National CODA Conference, Westminster, Maryland, July 15-18, 1989 (pp. 109-110). Santa Barbara, CA: Children of Deaf Adults. [DEAF 306.874 N3, 1989]

Brother, M. (1990f). Welcoming remarks. In T. H. Bull (Ed.), Reflections: Codas and cultures, proceedings of the second National CODA Conference, Rochester, New York, August 21-23, 1987 (3rd rev. ed., pp. 17-19). Santa Barbara, CA: Children of Deaf Adults. (The Gallaudet University Library also has the first edition [DEAF 306.874 N3, 1987] and the second edition [DEAF 306.874 N3, 1987b]) [DEAF 306.874 N3, 1987a]

Brother, M. (1992a). Welcome to the newcomers orientation. In T. H. Bull (Ed.), A CODA Retreat: Coming home, proceedings of the fifth National CODA Conference, Austin, Texas, July 14-17, 1990 (p. 9). Santa Barbara, CA: Children of Deaf Adults. [DEAF 306.874 N3, 1990]

Brother, M. (1992b). Newcomer's orientation session. In R. Childress & K. Austin-Hemelt (Eds.), CODA: Family of origin/family of choice, proceedings of the seventh International CODA Conference, New Orleans, July 16-19, 1992 (pp. 6-7). Santa Barbara, CA: Children of Deaf Adults. [DEAF 306.874 I57c, 1992]

Brother, M. (1994a). Keynote address. In R. Shipman (Ed.), Recollections: A decade of CODA, proceedings of the eighth International CODA Conference, Spokane, Washington, July 15-18, 1993 (pp. 31-39). Santa Barbara, CA: Children of Deaf Adults. [DEAF 306.847 I57r, 1993]

Brother, M. (Ed.). (1994b). Welcome to newcomers group [and panel presentation]. In R. Shipman (Ed.), Recollections: A decade of CODA, proceedings of the eighth International CODA Conference, Spokane, Washington, July 15-18, 1993 (pp. 8-19). Santa Barbara, CA: Children of Deaf Adults. (Moderator: Millie Brother. Panel members: Dave Eklof, Margaret Collier and Dale Dyal) [DEAF 306.847 I57r, 1993]

Brother, M. (Ed.). (1995). Welcome to newcomers group [and panel presentation]. In K. Bruno & D. Eklof (Eds.), You're among friends, welcome home: Proceedings of the 9th annual International CODA Conference, Oconomowoc, Wisconsin, July 14-17, 1994 (pp. 8-17). Santa Barbara, CA: Children of Deaf Adults. (Moderator: Millie Brother. Panel members: Mark Whisenant, Laureen Newmann Feldhorn, Andrea Goldberg and Dennis Joyce) [DEAF 306.874 I57a, 1995]

Brother, M. (1996a). Memoirs and participant reflections [About the conference]. In D. Prickett & R. Prickett (Eds.), Richness in our diversity: Proceedings of the tenth International CODA Conference, Research Triangle Park, North Carolina, July 27-30, 1995 (p. 108). Santa Barbara, CA: Children of Deaf Adults. [On order]

Brother, M. (Ed.). (1996b). Newcomer orientation and panel. In D. Prickett & R. Prickett (Eds.), Richness in our diversity: Proceedings of the tenth International CODA Conference, Research Triangle Park, North Carolina, July 27-30, 1995 (pp. 31-41). Santa Barbara, CA: Children of Deaf Adults. (Moderator: Millie Brother. Panel members: Sally Roshak, Jay Wolf, Cindy Blackman and Amy Mathews) [On order]

Brother, M. (1996c). What CODA is and is not... In D. Prickett & R. Prickett (Eds.), Richness in our diversity: Proceedings of the tenth International CODA Conference, Research Triangle Park, North Carolina, July 27-30, 1995 (p. 8). Santa Barbara, CA: Children of Deaf Adults. (Originally published in the Aug/Sept., 1987, issue of the CODA Newsletter, 4 (3), 1-2. [UNIV DEAF Periodicals] Also reprinted in T. H. Bull (Ed.), A CODA Retreat: Coming home, proceedings of the fifth National CODA Conference, Austin, Texas, July 14-17, 1990 (p. 8). Santa Barbara, CA: Children of Deaf Adults. [DEAF 306.874 N3, 1990]) [On order]

Brother, M. (1997a). Memories, reflections and poetry: Memoirs. In S. Schmidt-Boe, (Ed.), "Everyone is a star": The 11th annual international CODA conference proceedings, Buena Park, California, July 11-14, 1996 (p. 70). Santa Barbara, CA: Children of Deaf Adults. [On order]

Brother, M. (Ed.). (1997b). Newcomer orientation and panel. In S. Schmidt-Boe, (Ed.), "Everyone is a star": The 11th annual international CODA conference proceedings, Buena Park, California, July 11-14, 1996 (pp. 23-28). Santa Barbara, CA: Children of Deaf Adults. (Moderator, Millie Brother of California. Panelists: Jim Sewell, North Carolina; Nancy Holdren, Georgia; Bert Pickell, California; and Shelly Snow, Missouri) [On order]

Brother, M. (1997c). Once upon a time...: My memories of CODArado '97. In R. Shipman (Ed.), "Once upon a time...:" Proceedings of the twelfth annual International CODA Conference, Denver, Colorado, July 10-13, 1997 (pp. 124-125). Santa Barbara, CA: Children of Deaf Adults. [DEAF 306.874 I57o, 1997]

Brother, M. (Ed.). (1997d). Once upon a time...: Newcomers panel. In R. Shipman (Ed.), "Once upon a time...:" Proceedings of the twelfth annual International CODA Conference, Denver, Colorado, July 10-13, 1997 (pp. 38-52). Santa Barbara, CA: Children of Deaf Adults. (Moderator: Millie Brother, Santa Barbara, California. Panelists: Linda Morgan, Kansas City, Missouri; Renee Mabini, Denver, Colorado; Doug Schmidt, Portland, Oregon; and Cindy Etheredge, Orange, California) [DEAF 306.874 I57o, 1997]

Bruno, K. (Ed.). (1995-present). WisCODA News [Newsletter]. Waukesha, WI: WisCODA. (Newsletter of the Wisconsin chapter of Children of Deaf Adults. Write WisCODA News, 2603C N. University Dr., Waukesha, WI 53188) [*]

Bruno, K. (1996). Memoirs and participant reflections [About the conference]. In D. Prickett & R. Prickett (Eds.), Richness in our diversity: Proceedings of the tenth International CODA Conference, Research Triangle Park, North Carolina, July 27-30, 1995 (p. 106). Santa Barbara, CA: Children of Deaf Adults. [On order]

C
O
D
A

Bruno, K., & Eklof, D. (Eds.). (1995). You're among friends, welcome home: Proceedings of the 9th annual International CODA Conference, Oconomowoc, Wisconsin, July 14-17, 1994. Santa Barbara, CA: Children of Deaf Adults. (96 pages) [DEAF 306.874 I57a, 1995]

Bull, T. H. (Ed.). (1986, November-1990, Spring). DC/CODA Newsletter. Washington, DC: DC/CODA. (Newsletter of the Washington D. C. - Metropolitan area chapter of Children of Deaf Adults. Write DC/CODA, P.O. Box 2352, 800 Florida Ave., N.E., Washington, DC 20002-3695) [*]

Bull, T. H. (1989a). Editor's introduction. In T. H. Bull (Ed.), New beginnings, new directions: Proceedings of the third National CODA Conference, Denver, Colorado, August 13-15, 1988 (pp. 12-13). Santa Barbara, CA: Children of Deaf Adults. [DEAF 306.874 N3, 1988]

Bull, T. H. (Ed.). (1989b). New beginnings, new directions: Proceedings of the third National CODA Conference, Denver, Colorado, August 13-15, 1988. Santa Barbara, CA: Children of Deaf Adults. (127 pages) [DEAF 306.874 N3, 1988]

Bull, T. H. (Ed.). (1990a). Appendix II: CODA bibliography, abstracts and resources. In T. H. Bull (Ed.), Reflections: Codas and cultures, proceedings of the second National CODA Conference, Rochester, New York, August 21-23, 1987 (3rd rev. ed., pp. 81-117). Santa Barbara, CA: Children of Deaf Adults. (The Gallaudet University Library also has the first edition [DEAF 306.874 N3, 1987] and the second edition [DEAF 306.874 N3, 1987b]) [DEAF 306.874 N3, 1987a]

Bull, T. H. (Ed.). (1990b). CODA: A diverse community, proceedings of the fourth National CODA Conference, Westminster, Maryland, July 15-18, 1989. Santa Barbara, CA: Children of Deaf Adults. (149 pages) [DEAF 306.874 N3, 1989]

Bull, T. H. (1990c). Introduction by the editor. In T. H. Bull (Ed.), Reflections: Codas and cultures, proceedings of the second National CODA Conference, Rochester, New York, August 21-23, 1987 (3rd rev. ed., pp. 15-16). Santa Barbara, CA: Children of Deaf Adults. (The Gallaudet University Library also has the first edition [DEAF 306.874 N3, 1987] and the second edition [DEAF 306.874 N3, 1987b]) [DEAF 306.874 N3, 1987a]

Bull, T. H. (Ed.). (1990d). Reflections: Codas and cultures, proceedings of the second National CODA Conference, Rochester, New York, August 21-23, 1987 (3rd rev. ed.). Santa Barbara, CA: Children of Deaf Adults. (117 pages - Also see the first edition [DEAF 306.874 N3, 1987] and revised edition [DEAF 306.874 N3, 1987b]) [DEAF 306.874 N3, 1987a]

Bull, T. H. (Ed.). (1992a). A CODA retreat: Coming home, proceedings of the fifth National CODA Conference, Austin, Texas, July 14-17, 1990. Santa Barbara, CA: Children of Deaf Adults. (90 pages) [DEAF 306.874 N3, 1990]

Bull, T. H. (1992b). Introduction [By the editor]. In T. H. Bull (Ed.), A CODA Retreat: Coming home, proceedings of the fifth National CODA Conference, Austin, Texas, July 14-17, 1990 (p. 7). Santa Barbara, CA: Children of Deaf Adults. [DEAF 306.874 N3, 1990]

Bull, T. H. (1994). CODA means....[Poem]. In R. Shipman (Ed.), Recollections: A decade of CODA, proceedings of the eighth International CODA Conference, Spokane, Washington, July 15-18, 1993 (p. 72). Santa Barbara, CA: Children of Deaf Adults. [DEAF 306.847 I57r, 1993]

Bull, T. H. (1996). Memoirs and participant reflections: Ordinary Miracles. In D. Prickett & R. Prickett (Eds.),

Richness in our diversity: Proceedings of the tenth International CODA Conference, Research Triangle Park, North Carolina, July 27-30, 1995 (p. 105). Santa Barbara, CA: Children of Deaf Adults. [On order]

Bull, T. H., & Jacobson, M. (Eds.). (1995). Your mythic journey [Poems from breakout session]. In K. Bruno & D. Eklof (Eds.), You're among friends, welcome home: Proceedings of the 9th annual International CODA Conference, Oconomowoc, Wisconsin, July 14-17, 1994 (pp. 71-72). Santa Barbara, CA: Children of Deaf Adults. {Various writings by Jean Whitt, Beth McSheffey, Dan Roche, Tom Bull, MJ Tanzar, Margaret Collier, Lise R. St. Louis, Mariann Jacobson and Rosie Shipman} [DEAF 306.874 I57a, 1995]

Bull, T. H., Rutherford, S. D., & Jacobs, S. (Eds.). (1994). Celebration and exploration of our heritage: Proceedings of the first National CODA Conference, Fremont, California, August 8-10, 1986 (Rev. ed). Santa Barbara, CA: Children of Deaf Adults. (88 pages) [DEAF 306.874 N37c, 1986b]

Cacciatore, G. (1997). Once upon a time...: My memories of CODArado '97. In R. Shipman (Ed.), "Once upon a time...:" Proceedings of the twelfth annual International CODA Conference, Denver, Colorado, July 10-13, 1997 (p. 123). Santa Barbara, CA: Children of Deaf Adults. [DEAF 306.874 I57o, 1997]

Castle, D. (1997). Memories, reflections and poetry: Memoirs. In S. Schmidt-Boe, (Ed.), "Everyone is a star": The 11th annual international CODA conference proceedings, Buena Park, California, July 11-14, 1996 (p. 71). Santa Barbara, CA: Children of Deaf Adults. [On order]

Chapman-Smith, A. (1997). Memories, reflections and poetry: Memoirs. In S. Schmidt-Boe, (Ed.), "Everyone is a star": The 11th annual international CODA conference proceedings, Buena Park, California, July 11-14, 1996 (p. 71). Santa Barbara, CA: Children of Deaf Adults. [On order]

Childress, P. (Ed.). (1992). Codas with multi-handicapped parent(s) [Notes from group session]. In T. H. Bull (Ed.), A CODA retreat: Coming home, proceedings of the fifth National CODA Conference, Austin, Texas, July 14-17, 1990 (p. 52). Santa Barbara, CA: Children of Deaf Adults. [DEAF 306.874 N3, 1990]

Childress, R. (1992). Dawn disappearing: For my father who is deaf [Poem]. In R. Childress & K. Austin-Hemelt (Eds.), CODA: Family of origin/family of choice, proceedings of the seventh International CODA Conference, New Orleans, July 16-19, 1992 (pp. 49-50). Santa Barbara, CA: Children of Deaf Adults. [DEAF 306.874 I57c, 1992]

Childress, R., & Austin-Hemelt, K. (Eds.). (1993). CODA: Family of origin/family of choice, proceedings of the seventh International CODA Conference, New Orleans, July 16-19, 1992. Santa Barbara, CA: Children of Deaf Adults. (62 pages) [DEAF 306.874 I57c, 1992]

Coda interpreters [Summary]. (1992). In R. R. Myers (Ed.), CODA: At the Oasis, proceedings of the sixth International CODA Conference/Retreat, Chicago, Illinois, July 19-22, 1991 (p. 69). Santa Barbara, CA: Children of Deaf Adults. [DEAF 306.874 C44co, 1991]

Coda interview on National Public Radio, Chicago (91.5 FM). (1992). In R. R. Myers (Ed.), CODA: At the Oasis, proceedings of the sixth International CODA Conference/Retreat, Chicago, Illinois, July 19-22, 1991 (pp. 77-85). Santa Barbara, CA: Children of Deaf Adults. [DEAF 306.874 C44co, 1991]

Coda parts [Breakout summary]. (1994). In R. Shipman (Ed.), Recollections: A decade of CODA, proceedings of the eighth International CODA Conference, Spokane, Washington, July 15-18, 1993 (pp. 66-67). Santa Barbara, CA: Children of Deaf Adults. [DEAF 306.847 I57r, 1993]

C
O
D
A

Codas and abuse [Breakout]. (1992). In R. Childress & K. Austin-Hemelt (Eds.), <u>CODA: Family of origin/family of choice, proceedings of the seventh International CODA Conference, New Orleans, July 16-19, 1992</u> (p. 32). Santa Barbara, CA: Children of Deaf Adults. [DEAF 306.874 I57c, 1992]

Codas and elderly parents [Summary]. (1992). In R. R. Myers (Ed.), <u>CODA: At the Oasis, proceedings of the sixth International CODA Conference/Retreat, Chicago, Illinois, July 19-22, 1991</u> (p. 59). Santa Barbara, CA: Children of Deaf Adults. [DEAF 306.874 C44co, 1991]

Codas and the Deaf community [Summary]. (1992). In R. R. Myers (Ed.), <u>CODA: At the Oasis, proceedings of the sixth International CODA Conference/Retreat, Chicago, Illinois, July 19-22, 1991</u> (pp. 66-67). Santa Barbara, CA: Children of Deaf Adults. [DEAF 306.874 C44co, 1991]

Codas as interpreters [Breakout summary]. (1994). In R. Shipman (Ed.), <u>Recollections: A decade of CODA, proceedings of the eighth International CODA Conference, Spokane, Washington, July 15-18, 1993</u> (pp. 62-63). Santa Barbara, CA: Children of Deaf Adults. [DEAF 306.847 I57r, 1993]

Codas as interpreters [Breakout summary]. (1995). In K. Bruno & D. Eklof (Eds.), <u>You're among friends, welcome home: Proceedings of the 9th annual International CODA Conference, Oconomowoc, Wisconsin, July 14-17, 1994</u> (pp. 65-66). Santa Barbara, CA: Children of Deaf Adults. [DEAF 306.874 I57a, 1995]

Codas as parents [Breakout]. (1992). In R. Childress & K. Austin-Hemelt (Eds.), <u>CODA: Family of origin/family of choice, proceedings of the seventh International CODA Conference, New Orleans, July 16-19, 1992</u> (p. 33). Santa Barbara, CA: Children of Deaf Adults. [DEAF 306.874 I57c, 1992]

Codas as parents [Breakout summary of two sessions]. (1995). In K. Bruno & D. Eklof (Eds.), <u>You're among friends, welcome home: Proceedings of the 9th annual International CODA Conference, Oconomowoc, Wisconsin, July 14-17, 1994</u> (pp. 40, 63-64). Santa Barbara, CA: Children of Deaf Adults. [DEAF 306.874 I57a, 1995]

Codas in the Deaf community [Breakout]. (1992). In R. Childress & K. Austin-Hemelt (Eds.), <u>CODA: Family of origin/family of choice, proceedings of the seventh International CODA Conference, New Orleans, July 16-19, 1992</u> (p. 34). Santa Barbara, CA: Children of Deaf Adults. [DEAF 306.874 I57c, 1992]

Codas with addictive behaviors [Breakout summary]. (1995). In K. Bruno & D. Eklof (Eds.), <u>You're among friends, welcome home: Proceedings of the 9th annual International CODA Conference, Oconomowoc, Wisconsin, July 14-17, 1994</u> (p. 53). Santa Barbara, CA: Children of Deaf Adults. [DEAF 306.874 I57a, 1995]

Codas with [an] alcoholic parent [Breakout summary]. (1995). In K. Bruno & D. Eklof (Eds.), <u>You're among friends, welcome home: Proceedings of the 9th annual International CODA Conference, Oconomowoc, Wisconsin, July 14-17, 1994</u> (pp. 59-60). Santa Barbara, CA: Children of Deaf Adults. [DEAF 306.874 I57a, 1995]

Collier, M. (1997). Once upon a time...: My memories of CODArado '97. In R. Shipman (Ed.), <u>"Once upon a time..." Proceedings of the twelfth annual International CODA Conference, Denver, Colorado, July 10-13, 1997</u> (pp. 129-130). Santa Barbara, CA: Children of Deaf Adults. [DEAF 306.874 I57o, 1997]

Colonomos, B. (1995). These 1994 conference proceedings are dedicated to the memory of Ronald Lloyd Coffey, August 9, 1960 - June 27, 1994. In K. Bruno & D. Eklof (Eds.), <u>You're among friends, welcome home: Proceedings of the 9th annual International CODA Conference, Oconomowoc, Wisconsin, July 14-17, 1994</u> (pp. 5-7). Santa Barbara, CA: Children of Deaf Adults. {Remarks delivered in memory of Ronald Lloyd Coffey by Betty Colonomos} [DEAF 306.874 I57a, 1995]

Colonomos, B. (1997a). Foundations of interpreting processes for coda interpreters: Pre-conference workshop. In S. Schmidt-Boe, (Ed.), "Everyone is a star": The 11th annual international CODA conference proceedings, Buena Park, California, July 11-14, 1996 (pp. 21-22). Santa Barbara, CA: Children of Deaf Adults. [On order]

Colonomos, B. (1997b). Foundations of interpreting process for coda interpreters: Pre-conference workshop. In R. Shipman (Ed.), "Once upon a time...:" Proceedings of the twelfth annual International CODA Conference, Denver, Colorado, July 10-13, 1997 (p. 23). Santa Barbara, CA: Children of Deaf Adults. [DEAF 306.874 I57o, 1997]

(*) Colonomos, M. (1997a). Coda child [Poem]: Memories, reflections and poetry. In S. Schmidt-Boe, (Ed.), "Everyone is a star": The 11th annual international CODA conference proceedings, Buena Park, California, July 11-14, 1996 (p. 72). Santa Barbara, CA: Children of Deaf Adults. (Reprinted in R. Shipman (Ed.), "Once upon a time...:" Proceedings of the twelfth annual International CODA Conference, Denver, Colorado, July 10-13, 1997 (p. 106). Santa Barbara, CA: Children of Deaf Adults. [DEAF 306.874 I57o, 1997]) [On order]

(*) Colonomos, M. (1997b). Coda love [Poem]. In R. Shipman (Ed.), "Once upon a time...:" Proceedings of the twelfth annual International CODA Conference, Denver, Colorado, July 10-13, 1997 (p. 107). Santa Barbara, CA: Children of Deaf Adults. (Reprinted from the February, 1997, issue of the CODA Connection, 14 (1), 18. Also reprinted in the November, 1997, CODA Connection, 14 (4), 14. [UNIV DEAF Periodicals]) [DEAF 306.874 I57o, 1997]

(*) Colonomos, M. (1997c). Coda oscars [Poem]: Memories, reflections and poetry. In S. Schmidt-Boe, (Ed.), "Everyone is a star": The 11th annual international CODA conference proceedings, Buena Park, California, July 11-14, 1996 (p. 72). Santa Barbara, CA: Children of Deaf Adults. [On order]

Colonomos, M. (1997d). CODA process [Poem]. In R. Shipman (Ed.), "Once upon a time...:" Proceedings of the twelfth annual International CODA Conference, Denver, Colorado, July 10-13, 1997 (p. 108). Santa Barbara, CA: Children of Deaf Adults. [DEAF 306.874 I57o, 1997]

(*) Colonomos, M. (1997e). Coda voice [Poem]: Memories, reflections and poetry. In S. Schmidt-Boe, (Ed.), "Everyone is a star": The 11th annual international CODA conference proceedings, Buena Park, California, July 11-14, 1996 (pp. 71-72). Santa Barbara, CA: Children of Deaf Adults. (Reprinted in R. Shipman (Ed.), "Once upon a time...:" Proceedings of the twelfth annual International CODA Conference, Denver, Colorado, July 10-13, 1997 (p. 109). Santa Barbara, CA: Children of Deaf Adults. [DEAF 306.874 I57o, 1997]) [On order]

(*) Colonomos, M. (1997f). CODA wall [Poem]: Memories, reflections and poetry. In S. Schmidt-Boe, (Ed.), "Everyone is a star": The 11th annual international CODA conference proceedings, Buena Park, California, July 11-14, 1996 (p. 72). Santa Barbara, CA: Children of Deaf Adults. (Reprinted in R. Shipman (Ed.), "Once upon a time...:" Proceedings of the twelfth annual International CODA Conference, Denver, Colorado, July 10-13, 1997 (p. 110). Santa Barbara, CA: Children of Deaf Adults. [DEAF 306.874 I57o, 1997]) [On order]

Colonomos, M. (1997g). CODA world [Poem]. In R. Shipman (Ed.), "Once upon a time...:" Proceedings of the twelfth annual International CODA Conference, Denver, Colorado, July 10-13, 1997 (p. 105). Santa Barbara, CA: Children of Deaf Adults. (Reprinted int he May, 1998, issue of the CODA Connection, 15 (2), 17. [UNIV DEAF Periodicals]) [DEAF 306.874 I57o, 1997]

Conference overview. (1992). In R. Childress & K. Austin-Hemelt (Eds.), CODA: Family of origin/family of choice, proceedings of the seventh International CODA Conference, New Orleans, July 16-19, 1992 (p. 47). Santa Barbara, CA: Children of Deaf Adults. [DEAF 306.874 I57c, 1992]

C
O
D
A

181

Croll, L. (1997). Memories, reflections and poetry: Memoirs. In S. Schmidt-Boe, (Ed.), "Everyone is a star": The 11th annual international CODA conference proceedings, Buena Park, California, July 11-14, 1996 (pp. 73-74). Santa Barbara, CA: Children of Deaf Adults. [On order]

Czerny, T. (1997a). Back to our roots: Interpreting coda style, pre-conference workshop. In R. Shipman (Ed.), "Once upon a time...:" Proceedings of the twelfth annual International CODA Conference, Denver, Colorado, July 10-13, 1997 (p. 24). Santa Barbara, CA: Children of Deaf Adults. [DEAF 306.874 I57o, 1997]

Czerny, T. (1997b). Once upon a time...: My memories of CODArado '97. In R. Shipman (Ed.), "Once upon a time...:" Proceedings of the twelfth annual International CODA Conference, Denver, Colorado, July 10-13, 1997 (p. 122). Santa Barbara, CA: Children of Deaf Adults. [DEAF 306.874 I57o, 1997]

Czubek, T. (Ed.). (1992). Self exploration [Notes]. In T. H. Bull (Ed.), A CODA retreat: Coming home, proceedings of the fifth National CODA Conference, Austin, Texas, July 14-17, 1990 (p. 68). Santa Barbara, CA: Children of Deaf Adults. [DEAF 306.874 N3, 1990]

Davis, L. J. (Ed.). (1992a). Male codas and significant others [Notes from session I]. In T. H. Bull (Ed.), A CODA retreat: Coming home, proceedings of the fifth National CODA Conference, Austin, Texas, July 14-17, 1990 (p. 60). Santa Barbara, CA: Children of Deaf Adults. [DEAF 306.874 N3, 1990]

Davis, L. J. (1992b). Midnight at the Oasis [Poem]. In T. H. Bull (Ed.), A CODA retreat: Coming home, proceedings of the fifth National CODA Conference, Austin, Texas, July 14-17, 1990 (pp. 4-5). Santa Barbara, CA: Children of Deaf Adults. [DEAF 306.874 N3, 1990]

Davis, L. J. (1992c). Silence [Poem]. In T. H. Bull (Ed.), A CODA Retreat: Coming home, proceedings of the fifth National CODA Conference, Austin, Texas, July 14-17, 1990 (p. 5). Santa Barbara, CA: Children of Deaf Adults. [DEAF 306.874 N3, 1990]

(*) Dollard, V. (1988). Shared memories. In T. H. Bull (Ed.), Reflections: Codas and cultures, proceedings of the second National CODA Conference, Rochester, New York, August 21-23, 1987 (3rd rev. ed., pp. 74-75). Santa Barbara, CA: Children of Deaf Adults. (Reprinted from the Winter/Spring, 1988, NTID Focus, 24-25. A publication of the National Technical Institute for the Deaf, Rochester, New York. [UNIV DEAF Periodicals] The Gallaudet University Library also has the first edition [DEAF 306.874 N3, 1987] and the second edition [DEAF 306.874 N3, 1987b]) [DEAF 306.874 N3, 1987a]

Earley, M. (1997). Once upon a time...: My memories of CODArado '97. In R. Shipman (Ed.), "Once upon a time...:" Proceedings of the twelfth annual International CODA Conference, Denver, Colorado, July 10-13, 1997 (p. 124). Santa Barbara, CA: Children of Deaf Adults. [DEAF 306.874 I57o, 1997]

Eklof, D. (Ed.). (1991-1995). WisCODA News [Newsletter]. Cottage Grove, WI: WisCODA. (Newsletter of the Wisconsin chapter of Children of Deaf Adults. Write WisCODA News, 2603C N. University Dr., Waukesha, WI 53188) [*]

Eklof, D. (Ed.). (1993, November-1995, November). CODA Connection [Newsletter]. Santa Barbara, CA: CODA, Children of Deaf Adults. [UNIV DEAF Periodicals]

Elderly parents [Breakout]. (1992). In R. Childress & K. Austin-Hemelt (Eds.), CODA: Family of origin/family of choice, proceedings of the seventh International CODA Conference, New Orleans, July 16-19, 1992 (p. 35). Santa Barbara, CA: Children of Deaf Adults. [DEAF 306.874 I57c, 1992]

Elderly parents [Breakout summary]. (1995). In K. Bruno & D. Eklof (Eds.), You're among friends, welcome home: Proceedings of the 9th annual International CODA Conference, Oconomowoc, Wisconsin, July 14-17, 1994 (pp. 56-58). Santa Barbara, CA: Children of Deaf Adults. [DEAF 306.874 I57a, 1995]

Ensenat, D. (Ed.). (1992). Coda sibling relationships [Group session notes]. In T. H. Bull (Ed.), A CODA retreat: Coming home, proceedings of the fifth National CODA Conference, Austin, Texas, July 14-17, 1990 (p. 47). Santa Barbara, CA: Children of Deaf Adults. [DEAF 306.874 N3, 1990]

Family communication [Breakout]. (1992). In R. Childress & K. Austin-Hemelt (Eds.), CODA: Family of origin/family of choice, proceedings of the seventh International CODA Conference, New Orleans, July 16-19, 1992 (p. 36). Santa Barbara, CA: Children of Deaf Adults. [DEAF 306.874 I57c, 1992]

Family communication [Breakout summary]. (1994). In R. Shipman (Ed.), Recollections: A decade of CODA, proceedings of the eighth International CODA Conference, Spokane, Washington, July 15-18, 1993 (pp. 52-53). Santa Barbara, CA: Children of Deaf Adults. [DEAF 306.847 I57r, 1993]

Family communication [Breakout summary from two sessions]. (1995). In K. Bruno & D. Eklof (Eds.), You're among friends, welcome home: Proceedings of the ninth annual International CODA Conference, Oconomowoc, Wisconsin, July 14-17, 1994 (pp. 44, 48-49). Santa Barbara, CA: Children of Deaf Adults. [DEAF 306.874 I57a, 1995]

Family composition and interaction [Summary]. (1992). In R. R. Myers (Ed.), CODA: At the Oasis, proceedings of the sixth International CODA Conference/Retreat, Chicago, Illinois, July 19-22, 1991 (p. 60). Santa Barbara, CA: Children of Deaf Adults. [DEAF 306.874 C44co, 1991]

Family of origin to one of choice [Breakout]. (1992). In R. Childress & K. Austin-Hemelt (Eds.), CODA: Family of origin/family of choice, proceedings of the seventh International CODA Conference, New Orleans, July 16-19, 1992 (p. 37). Santa Barbara, CA: Children of Deaf Adults. [DEAF 306.874 I57c, 1992]

Family of origin to one of choice [Breakout summary]. (1994). In R. Shipman (Ed.), Recollections: A decade of CODA, proceedings of the eighth International CODA Conference, Spokane, Washington, July 15-18, 1993 (p. 49). Santa Barbara, CA: Children of Deaf Adults. [DEAF 306.847 I57r, 1993]

Fant, L., Jr. (1990). Blessings from my parents' deafness [Keynote address]. In T. H. Bull (Ed.), CODA: A diverse community, proceedings of the fourth National CODA Conference, Westminster, Maryland, July 15-18, 1989 (pp. 43-51). Santa Barbara, CA: Children of Deaf Adults. [DEAF 306.874 N3, 1989]

Fant, L., Jr. (1992). Wrap up. In T. H. Bull (Ed.), A CODA retreat: Coming home, proceedings of the fifth National CODA Conference, Austin, Texas, July 14-17, 1990 (pp. 69-70). Santa Barbara, CA: Children of Deaf Adults. [DEAF 306.874 N3, 1990]

Father and son relationships [Summary notes]. (1992). In T. H. Bull (Ed.), A CODA retreat: Coming home, proceedings of the fifth National CODA Conference, Austin, Texas, July 14-17, 1990 (p. 57). Santa Barbara, CA: Children of Deaf Adults. [DEAF 306.874 N3, 1990]

Fathers and sons [Breakout summary]. (1994). In R. Shipman (Ed.), Recollections: A decade of CODA, proceedings of the eighth International CODA Conference, Spokane, Washington, July 15-18, 1993 (p. 61). Santa Barbara, CA: Children of Deaf Adults. [DEAF 306.847 I57r, 1993]

C
O
D
A

Fire and ice [Breakout]. (1992a). In R. Childress & K. Austin-Hemelt (Eds.), <u>CODA: Family of origin/family of choice, proceedings of the seventh International CODA Conference, New Orleans, July 16-19, 1992</u> (p. 41). Santa Barbara, CA: Children of Deaf Adults. [DEAF 306.874 I57c, 1992]

Fire and ice [Summary]. (1992b). In R. R. Myers (Ed.), <u>CODA: At the Oasis, proceedings of the sixth International CODA Conference/Retreat, Chicago, Illinois, July 19-22, 1991</u> (pp. 61-62). Santa Barbara, CA: Children of Deaf Adults. [DEAF 306.874 C44co, 1991]

Fire and ice - Level 2 [Breakout summary]. (1994). In R. Shipman (Ed.), <u>Recollections: A decade of CODA, proceedings of the eighth International CODA Conference, Spokane, Washington, July 15-18, 1993</u> (p. 57). Santa Barbara, CA: Children of Deaf Adults. [DEAF 306.847 I57r, 1993]

Fire and ice II [Breakout summary from two sessions]. (1995). In K. Bruno & D. Eklof (Eds.), <u>You're among friends, welcome home: Proceedings of the ninth annual International CODA Conference, Oconomowoc, Wisconsin, July 14-17, 1994</u> (pp. 38-39, 67). Santa Barbara, CA: Children of Deaf Adults. [DEAF 306.874 I57a, 1995]

(*) Flanagan, R. (1996). My bicultural experience [The 1990 CODA Millie Brother Scholarship winning essay]. In D. Prickett & R. Prickett (Eds.), <u>Richness in our diversity: Proceedings of the tenth International CODA Conference, Research Triangle Park, North Carolina, July 27-30, 1995</u> (p. 120). Santa Barbara, CA: Children of Deaf Adults. (Reprinted from the May, 1990, edition of the <u>CODA Connection, 7</u> (2), 6. [UNIV DEAF Periodicals]) [On order]

Francis, T. (1997). Once upon a time...: My memories of CODArado '97. In R. Shipman (Ed.), <u>"Once upon a time...:" Proceedings of the twelfth annual International CODA Conference, Denver, Colorado, July 10-13, 1997</u> (p. 122). Santa Barbara, CA: Children of Deaf Adults. [DEAF 306.874 I57o, 1997]

Gay and Lesbian codas [Summary]. (1992). In R. R. Myers (Ed.), <u>CODA: At the Oasis, proceedings of the sixth International CODA Conference/Retreat, Chicago, Illinois, July 19-22, 1991</u> (p. 71). Santa Barbara, CA: Children of Deaf Adults. [DEAF 306.874 C44co, 1991]

Gay, Lesbian and bisexuals [Breakout summary]. (1994). In R. Shipman (Ed.), <u>Recollections: A decade of CODA, proceedings of the eighth International CODA Conference, Spokane, Washington, July 15-18, 1993</u> (p. 69). Santa Barbara, CA: Children of Deaf Adults. [DEAF 306.847 I57r, 1993]

Gay, Lesbian, bi-sexual, and transgender session [Breakout summary, second session]. (1995). In K. Bruno & D. Eklof (Eds.), <u>You're among friends, welcome home: Proceedings of the ninth annual International CODA Conference, Oconomowoc, Wisconsin, July 14-17, 1994</u> (p. 37). Santa Barbara, CA: Children of Deaf Adults. [DEAF 306.874 I57a, 1995]

Gay / Lesbian / Bisexual / Transgender [Summary from first breakout session]. (1995). In K. Bruno & D. Eklof (Eds.), <u>You're among friends, welcome home: Proceedings of the ninth annual International CODA Conference, Oconomowoc, Wisconsin, July 14-17, 1994</u> (p. 70). Santa Barbara, CA: Children of Deaf Adults. [DEAF 306.874 I57a, 1995]

Graham, D. (Ed.). (1996-present). <u>Michigan CODA</u> [Newsletter]. Pearl Beach, MI: Michigan CODA. (Newsletter of the Michigan chapter of Children of Deaf Adults. Write Michigan/CODA, P.O. Box 847, Pearl Beach, MI) [*]

Grief and loss [Breakout]. (1992). In R. Childress & K. Austin-Hemelt (Eds.), <u>CODA: Family of origin/family</u>

of choice, proceedings of the seventh International CODA Conference, New Orleans, July 16-19, 1992 (p. 42). Santa Barbara, CA: Children of Deaf Adults. [DEAF 306.874 I57c, 1992]

Grief and loss [Breakout summary]. (1994). In R. Shipman (Ed.), Recollections: A decade of CODA, proceedings of the eighth International CODA Conference, Spokane, Washington, July 15-18, 1993 (p. 54). Santa Barbara, CA: Children of Deaf Adults. [DEAF 306.847 I57r, 1993]

Grief and loss [Breakout summary]. (1995). In K. Bruno & D. Eklof (Eds.), You're among friends, welcome home: Proceedings of the ninth annual International CODA Conference, Oconomowoc, Wisconsin, July 14-17, 1994 (p. 50). Santa Barbara, CA: Children of Deaf Adults. [DEAF 306.874 I57a, 1995]

Hazel-Jones, D. (1996). Memoirs and participant reflections [About the conference]. In D. Prickett & R. Prickett (Eds.), Richness in our diversity: Proceedings of the tenth International CODA Conference, Research Triangle Park, North Carolina, July 27-30, 1995 (p. 107). Santa Barbara, CA: Children of Deaf Adults. [On order]

Hazel-Jones, D. (1997). Once upon a time...: My memories of CODArado '97. In R. Shipman (Ed.), "Once upon a time...:" Proceedings of the twelfth annual International CODA Conference, Denver, Colorado, July 10-13, 1997 (p. 123). Santa Barbara, CA: Children of Deaf Adults. [DEAF 306.874 I57o, 1997]

Hines, L. (Ed.). (1990). Coda interpreters and non-coda interpreters: Friends? [Notes from a group session]. In T. H. Bull (Ed.), CODA: A diverse community, proceedings of the fourth National CODA Conference, Westminster, Maryland, July 15-18, 1989 (pp. 88-89). Santa Barbara, CA: Children of Deaf Adults. [DEAF 306.874 N3, 1989]

(*) Hoffman, V. (1996). Full circle [The 1993 CODA Millie Brother Scholarship essay winner]. In D. Prickett & R. Prickett (Eds.), Richness in our diversity: Proceedings of the tenth International CODA Conference, Research Triangle Park, North Carolina, July 27-30, 1995 (pp. 122-123). Santa Barbara, CA: Children of Deaf Adults. (Reprinted from the Aug/Sept, 1993, edition of the CODA Connection, 10 (3), 11. [UNIV DEAF Periodicals]) [On order]

Hoffmeister, B. (1997). Deaf culture and storytelling - one generation thick: Pre-conference workshop. In R. Shipman (Ed.), "Once upon a time...:" Proceedings of the twelfth annual International CODA Conference, Denver, Colorado, July 10-13, 1997 (pp. 25-35). Santa Barbara, CA: Children of Deaf Adults. [DEAF 306.874 I57o, 1997]

(*) Hoffmeister, M. P. (1990). CODA rap song. In T. H. Bull (Ed.), Reflections: Codas and cultures, proceedings of the second National CODA Conference, Rochester, New York, August 21-23, 1987 (3rd rev. ed., p. 5). Santa Barbara, CA: Children of Deaf Adults. - The Gallaudet University Library also has the first edition [DEAF 306.874 N3, 1987] and the second edition [DEAF 306.874 N3, 1987b] - Also reprinted in the November, 1987, issue of the CODA Newsletter, 4 (4), 3 and also reprinted in the November, 1997, issue of the CODA Connection, 14 (4), 14. [UNIV DEAF Periodicals]) [DEAF 306.874 N3, 1987a]

(*) Hoza, J. (1990). For my parents (who are Deaf) [Poem]. In T. H. Bull (Ed.), Reflections: Codas and cultures, proceedings of the second National CODA Conference, Rochester, New York, August 21-23, 1987 (3rd rev. ed., p. 9). Santa Barbara, CA: Children of Deaf Adults. (The Gallaudet University Library also has the first edition [DEAF 306.874 N3, 1987] and the second edition [DEAF 306.874 N3, 1987b]) [DEAF 306.874 N3, 1987a]

Huss, J. S. (1997). Once upon a time...: My memories of CODArado '97. In R. Shipman (Ed.), "Once upon a time...:" Proceedings of the twelfth annual International CODA Conference, Denver, Colorado, July 10-13, 1997 (pp. 119-120). Santa Barbara, CA: Children of Deaf Adults. [DEAF 306.874 I57o, 1997]

InterCoda relations [Summary]. (1992). In R. R. Myers (Ed.), <u>CODA: At the Oasis, proceedings of the sixth</u> <u>International CODA Conference/Retreat, Chicago, Illinois, July 19-22, 1991</u> (p. 64). Santa Barbara, CA: Children of Deaf Adults. [DEAF 306.874 C44co, 1991]

Inter-Coda relations [Summary from two sessions]. (1994). In R. Shipman (Ed.), <u>Recollections: A decade of</u> <u>CODA, proceedings of the eighth International CODA Conference, Spokane, Washington, July 15-18, 1993</u> (pp. 55, 65). Santa Barbara, CA: Children of Deaf Adults. [DEAF 306.847 I57r, 1993]

Interpreting issues [Breakout]. (1992). In R. Childress & K. Austin-Hemelt (Eds.), <u>CODA: Family of origin/family</u> <u>of choice, proceedings of the seventh International CODA Conference, New Orleans, July 16-19, 1992</u> (p. 38). Santa Barbara, CA: Children of Deaf Adults. [DEAF 306.874 I57c, 1992]

Intimacy [Breakout]. (1992). In R. Childress & K. Austin-Hemelt (Eds.), <u>CODA: Family of origin/family of</u> <u>choice, proceedings of the seventh International CODA Conference, New Orleans, July 16-19, 1992</u> (p. 43). Santa Barbara, CA: Children of Deaf Adults. [DEAF 306.874 I57c, 1992]

Intimacy [Breakout summary from two sessions]. (1995). In K. Bruno & D. Eklof (Eds.), <u>You're among friends,</u> <u>welcome home: Proceedings of the ninth annual International CODA Conference, Oconomowoc, Wisconsin, July</u> <u>14-17, 1994</u> (pp. 52, 54-55). Santa Barbara, CA: Children of Deaf Adults. [DEAF 306.874 I57a, 1995]

Intimacy [Summary]. (1992). In R. R. Myers (Ed.), <u>CODA: At the Oasis, proceedings of the sixth International</u> <u>CODA Conference/Retreat, Chicago, Illinois, July 19-22, 1991</u> (p. 63). Santa Barbara, CA: Children of Deaf Adults. [DEAF 306.874 C44co, 1991]

Intimacy [Summary notes from three groups]. (1994). In R. Shipman (Ed.), <u>Recollections: A decade of CODA,</u> <u>proceedings of the eighth International CODA Conference, Spokane, Washington, July 15-18, 1993</u> (pp. 58-60). Santa Barbara, CA: Children of Deaf Adults. [DEAF 306.847 I57r, 1993]

Jacobs, S. (1987a/1994). Introduction. In T. H. Bull, S. D. Rutherford & S. Jacobs (Eds.), <u>Celebration and</u> <u>exploration of our heritage: Proceedings of the first National CODA Conference, Fremont, California, August 8-10,</u> <u>1986</u> (Rev. ed., pp. 9-12). Santa Barbara, CA: Children of Deaf Adults. (The first edition was edited by S. Rutherford & S. Jacobs [DEAF 306.874 N37c, 1986]) [DEAF 306.874 N4, 1986b]

Jacobs, S. (Ed.). (1987b/1994). Our coda identity [Panel presentation]. In T. H. Bull, S. D. Rutherford & S. Jacobs (Eds.), <u>Celebration and exploration of our heritage: Proceedings of the first National CODA Conference, Fremont,</u> <u>California, August 8-10, 1986</u> (Rev. ed., pp. 34-41). Santa Barbara, CA: Children of Deaf Adults. (Moderator: Sheila Jacobs. Panel members: Joyce Groode, Hugh Prickett and Lynnette Taylor - The first edition was edited by S. Rutherford & S. Jacobs [DEAF 306.874 N37c, 1986]) [DEAF 306.874 N4, 1986b]

Jacobs, S. (Ed.). (1989). What CODA means to me [Panel presentation]. In T. H. Bull (Ed.), <u>New beginnings, new</u> <u>directions: Proceedings of the third National CODA Conference, Denver, Colorado, August 13-15, 1988</u> (pp. 18-31). Santa Barbara, CA: Children of Deaf Adults. (Moderator: Sheila Jacobs. Panel members: Bonnie Kraft, Carol Mullis and Tom Bull) [DEAF 306.874 N3, 1988]

Jacobs, S. (Ed.). (1990a). Codas: Coping with loss [Group discussion summary]. In T. H. Bull (Ed.), <u>CODA: A</u> <u>diverse community, proceedings of the fourth National CODA Conference, Westminster, Maryland, July 15-18, 1989</u> (pp. 95-97). Santa Barbara, CA: Children of Deaf Adults. [DEAF 306.874 N3, 1989]

Jacobs, S. (Ed.). (1990b). Codas with deaf and hearing siblings [Summary of breakout session]. In T. H. Bull

(Ed.), <u>CODA: A diverse community, proceedings of the fourth National CODA Conference, Westminster, Maryland, July 15-18, 1989</u> (pp. 35-36). Santa Barbara, CA: Children of Deaf Adults. [DEAF 306.874 N3, 1989]

Jacobs, S. (Ed.). (1990c). Mental health for codas [Summary of roundtable group discussions]. In T. H. Bull (Ed.), <u>Reflections: Codas and cultures, proceedings of the second National CODA Conference, Rochester, New York, August 21-23, 1987</u> (3rd rev. ed., pp. 47-49). Santa Barbara, CA: Children of Deaf Adults. (The Gallaudet University Library also has the first edition [DEAF 306.874 N3, 1987] and the second edition [DEAF 306.874 N3, 1987b]) [DEAF 306.874 N3, 1987a]

Jacobs, S. (Ed.). (1990d). Taking care of ourselves [Group discussion session notes]. In T. H. Bull (Ed.), <u>CODA: A diverse community, proceedings of the fourth National CODA Conference, Westminster, Maryland, July 15-18, 1989</u> (pp. 79-80). Santa Barbara, CA: Children of Deaf Adults. [DEAF 306.874 N3, 1989]

Jacobs, S. (1997). Pioneering C. O. D. A.: Welcome back to California - right back where we started from! [Opening remarks]. In S. Schmidt-Boe, (Ed.), <u>"Everyone is a star": The 11th annual international CODA conference proceedings, Buena Park, California, July 11-14, 1996</u> (pp. 29-40). Santa Barbara, CA: Children of Deaf Adults. [On order]

Jacobs, S., & Hines, L. (Eds.). (1989). Loss in the coda family: Problems and solutions [Summary of group discussion]. In T. H. Bull (Ed.), <u>New beginnings, new directions: Proceedings of the third National CODA Conference, Denver, Colorado, August 13-15, 1988</u> (pp. 56-59). Santa Barbara, CA: Children of Deaf Adults. [DEAF 306.874 N3, 1988]

Jacobs, S., Singleton, J., & Washington, S. (Eds.). (1990). OHCODAS: Only Hearing (sibling) Codas, summary of breakout group session. In T. H. Bull (Ed.), <u>CODA: A diverse community, proceedings of the fourth National CODA Conference, Westminster, Maryland, July 15-18, 1989</u> (pp. 37-40). Santa Barbara, CA: Children of Deaf Adults. [DEAF 306.874 N3, 1989]

Jacobson, M. (Ed.). (1990a). Identifying our community [Panel discussion]. In T. H. Bull (Ed.), <u>Reflections: Codas and cultures, proceedings of the second National CODA Conference, Rochester, New York, August 21-23, 1987</u> (3rd rev. ed., pp. 35-46). Santa Barbara, CA: Children of Deaf Adults. (Moderator, Mariann Jacobson. Panel members: Florence Hughes, Brian Miceli, Sheila Jacobs and Ethel House - The Gallaudet University Library also has the first edition [DEAF 306.874 N3, 1987] and the second edition [DEAF 306.874 N3, 1987b]) [DEAF 306.874 N3, 1987a]

Jacobson, M. (1990b). Reflections: Codas-only group [Session I]. In T. H. Bull (Ed.), <u>Reflections: Codas and cultures, proceedings of the second National CODA Conference, Rochester, New York, August 21-23, 1987</u> (3rd rev. ed., p. 53). Santa Barbara, CA: Children of Deaf Adults. (The Gallaudet University Library also has the first edition [DEAF 306.874 N3, 1987] and the second edition [DEAF 306.874 N3, 1987b]) [DEAF 306.874 N3, 1987a]

Jacobson, M. (1990c). Reflections: Codas-only group [Session II]. In T. H. Bull (Ed.), <u>Reflections: Codas and cultures, proceedings of the second National CODA Conference, Rochester, New York, August 21-23, 1987</u> (3rd rev. ed., pp. 55-56). Santa Barbara, CA: Children of Deaf Adults. (The Gallaudet University Library also has the first edition [DEAF 306.874 N3, 1987] and the second edition [DEAF 306.874 N3, 1987b]) [DEAF 306.874 N3, 1987a]

Jacobson, M. (Ed.). (1991-present). <u>CODA/NJ Newsletter.</u> Edison, NJ: Children of Deaf Adults, New Jersey. (Newsletter of the New Jersey chapter of Children of Deaf Adults. Write CODA/NJ, 58 Harrison Ave., Edison, NJ 08837 - Other editors have been Dennis Joyce and Andrea Goldberg) [*]

Jacobson, M. (1997). Once upon a time...: My memories of CODArado '97. In R. Shipman (Ed.), <u>"Once upon a time...:" Proceedings of the twelfth annual International CODA Conference, Denver, Colorado, July 10-13, 1997</u> (pp. 128-129). Santa Barbara, CA: Children of Deaf Adults. [DEAF 306.874 I57o, 1997]

James, V. (1997). Memories, reflections and poetry: Memoirs. In S. Schmidt-Boe, (Ed.), <u>"Everyone is a star": The 11th annual international CODA conference proceedings, Buena Park, California, July 11-14, 1996</u> (pp. 74-75). Santa Barbara, CA: Children of Deaf Adults. [On order]

Jeffers, T. (Ed.). (1992). Codas in dysfunctional families [Notes from session I]. In T. H. Bull (Ed.), <u>A CODA retreat: Coming home, proceedings of the fifth National CODA Conference, Austin, Texas, July 14-17, 1990</u> (p. 48). Santa Barbara, CA: Children of Deaf Adults. [DEAF 306.874 N3, 1990]

Jeffers, T. (1995). Keynote address. In K. Bruno & D. Eklof (Eds.), <u>You're among friends, welcome home: Proceedings of the ninth annual International CODA Conference, Oconomowoc, Wisconsin, July 14-17, 1994</u> (pp. 20-32). Santa Barbara, CA: Children of Deaf Adults. [DEAF 306.874 I57a, 1995]

Jeffers, T. (1996). Memoirs and participant reflections [About the conference]. In D. Prickett & R. Prickett (Eds.), <u>Richness in our diversity: Proceedings of the tenth International CODA Conference, Research Triangle Park, North Carolina, July 27-30, 1995</u> (p. 106). Santa Barbara, CA: Children of Deaf Adults. [On order]

Jones, M. (Ed.). (1990). An opportunity for discussion with Lou Ann Walker [Notes from topic group discussion]. In T. H. Bull (Ed.), <u>CODA: A diverse community, proceedings of the fourth National CODA Conference, Westminster, Maryland, July 15-18, 1989</u> (pp. 100-101). Santa Barbara, CA: Children of Deaf Adults. [DEAF 306.874 N3, 1989]

Jucha, L. (Ed.). (1992). Relationships and intimacy [Notes from session II]. In T. H. Bull (Ed.), <u>A CODA retreat: Coming home, proceedings of the fifth National CODA Conference, Austin, Texas, July 14-17, 1990</u> (p. 67). Santa Barbara, CA: Children of Deaf Adults. [DEAF 306.874 N3, 1990]

Kalaher, L. (Ed.). (1990). Genetics and deafness [Notes from topic group discussion]. In T. H. Bull (Ed.), <u>CODA: A diverse community, proceedings of the fourth National CODA Conference, Westminster, Maryland, July 15-18, 1989</u> (pp. 103-104). Santa Barbara, CA: Children of Deaf Adults. [DEAF 306.874 N3, 1989]

Kamenski, N. (Ed.). (1990). Coda siblings (hearing coda issues): Summary of breakout group session. In T. H. Bull (Ed.), <u>CODA: A diverse community, proceedings of the fourth National CODA Conference, Westminster, Maryland, July 15-18, 1989</u> (p. 34). Santa Barbara, CA: Children of Deaf Adults. [DEAF 306.874 N3, 1989]

Kinderknecht, T. (1997). Once upon a time...: My memories of CODArado '97. In R. Shipman (Ed.), <u>"Once upon a time...:" Proceedings of the twelfth annual International CODA Conference, Denver, Colorado, July 10-13, 1997</u> (p. 121). Santa Barbara, CA: Children of Deaf Adults. [DEAF 306.874 I57o, 1997]

Kinsey, J. A. (Ed.). (1991-present). <u>CODA/NC Newsletter.</u> Durham, NC: Children of Deaf Adults, North Carolina. (Newsletter of the North Carolina chapter of Children of Deaf Adults. Write CODA/NC, 1510 Cotherstone Dr., Durham, NC 27712) [*]

Kinsey, J. A. (Ed.). (1992). Codas in dysfunctional families [Notes from session II]. In T. H. Bull (Ed.), <u>A CODA retreat: Coming home, proceedings of the fifth National CODA Conference, Austin, Texas, July 14-17, 1990</u> (p. 49). Santa Barbara, CA: Children of Deaf Adults. [DEAF 306.874 N3, 1990]

Kraft, B. (Ed.). (1995-present). CODA Connection [Newsletter]. Santa Barbara, CA: CODA - Children of Deaf Adults. [UNIV DEAF Periodicals]

Kraft, B. (1996). Coda interpreters and hearing interpreters: Building bridges [Pre-conference workshop address]. In D. Prickett & R. Prickett (Eds.), Richness in our diversity: Proceedings of the tenth International CODA Conference, Research Triangle Park, North Carolina, July 27-30, 1995 (pp. 21-30). Santa Barbara, CA: Children of Deaf Adults. [On order]

Kraft, B. (1997). Once upon a time...: You're the gift, telling our stories [Keynote speech]. In R. Shipman (Ed.), "Once upon a time...:" Proceedings of the twelfth annual International CODA Conference, Denver, Colorado, July 10-13, 1997 (pp. 75-84). Santa Barbara, CA: Children of Deaf Adults. [DEAF 306.874 I57o, 1997]

Langholtz, D. (Ed.) (1987/1994). Summary of the Deaf participants group discussion. In T. H. Bull, S. D. Rutherford & S. Jacobs (Eds.), Celebration and exploration of our heritage: Proceedings of the first National CODA Conference, Fremont, California, August 8-10, 1986 (Rev. ed., pp. 49-51). Santa Barbara, CA: Children of Deaf Adults. (The first edition was edited by S. Rutherford & S. Jacobs [DEAF 306.874 N4, 1986]) [DEAF 306.874 N37c, 1986b]

Latz, R. (1997a). Memories, reflections and poetry: Memoirs. In S. Schmidt-Boe, (Ed.), "Everyone is a star": The 11th annual international CODA conference proceedings, Buena Park, California, July 11-14, 1996 (pp. 75-76). Santa Barbara, CA: Children of Deaf Adults. [On order]

Latz, R. (1997b). Introduction to "Lost child, found man" [Poem]. In R. Shipman (Ed.), "Once upon a time...:" Proceedings of the twelfth annual International CODA Conference, Denver, Colorado, July 10-13, 1997 (pp. 101-102). Santa Barbara, CA: Children of Deaf Adults. [DEAF 306.874 I57o, 1997]

Latz, R. (1997c). Lost child, found man [Poem]. In R. Shipman (Ed.), "Once upon a time...:" Proceedings of the twelfth annual International CODA Conference, Denver, Colorado, July 10-13, 1997 (p. 103). Santa Barbara, CA: Children of Deaf Adults. [DEAF 306.874 I57o, 1997]

Lerch, K., & Schuchman, S. (Eds.). (1990). Codas and spouses [Topic group discussion session notes]. In T. H. Bull (Ed.), CODA: A diverse community, proceedings of the fourth National CODA Conference, Westminster, Maryland, July 15-18, 1989 (pp. 98-99). Santa Barbara, CA: Children of Deaf Adults. [DEAF 306.874 N3, 1989]

Levin, G. M. (1989). Silent peace [Poem]. In T. H. Bull (Ed.), New beginnings, new directions: Proceedings of the third National CODA Conference, Denver, Colorado, August 13-15, 1988 (pp. 3-4). Santa Barbara, CA: Children of Deaf Adults. [DEAF 306.874 N3, 1988]

Linden, J. (1997). Stargazing [Closing remarks]. In S. Schmidt-Boe, (Ed.), "Everyone is a star": The 11th annual international CODA conference proceedings, Buena Park, California, July 11-14, 1996 (pp. 61-63). Santa Barbara, CA: Children of Deaf Adults. [On order]

Linnett, L. (1996a). Memoirs and participant reflections: Yes! Something very familiar is going on here. In D. Prickett & R. Prickett (Eds.), Richness in our diversity: Proceedings of the tenth International CODA Conference, Research Triangle Park, North Carolina, July 27-30, 1995 (pp. 111-113). Santa Barbara, CA: Children of Deaf Adults. [On order]

Linnett, L. (Ed.) (1996b). Report from the meeting..."Hearing children of deaf parents." World Federation of the

CODA

189

Deaf (WFD) Conference, Vienna, Austria, July 13, 1995. In D. Prickett & R. Prickett (Eds.), <u>Richness in our diversity: Proceedings of the tenth International CODA Conference, Research Triangle Park, North Carolina, July 27-30, 1995</u> (pp. 95-96). Santa Barbara, CA: Children of Deaf Adults. [On order]

Love, C. (Ed.). (1992). Family composition [Notes from session I]. In T. H. Bull (Ed.), <u>A CODA retreat: Coming home, proceedings of the fifth National CODA Conference, Austin, Texas, July 14-17, 1990</u> (p. 55). Santa Barbara, CA: Children of Deaf Adults. [DEAF 306.874 N3, 1990]

Machniak, S. (1989). Reflections on CODA III: CODA newcomer's perspective. In T. H. Bull (Ed.), <u>New beginnings, new directions: Proceedings of the third National CODA Conference, Denver, Colorado, August 13-15, 1988</u> (p. 79). Santa Barbara, CA: Children of Deaf Adults. [DEAF 306.874 N3, 1988]

Marcus, A. (1990a). Conference wrap-up No. 1. In T. H. Bull (Ed.), <u>CODA: A diverse community, proceedings of the fourth National CODA Conference, Westminster, Maryland, July 15-18, 1989</u> (pp. 111-112). Santa Barbara, CA: Children of Deaf Adults. [DEAF 306.874 N3, 1989]

Marcus, A. (Ed.). (1990b). Taking care of ourselves [Group discussion session notes]. In T. H. Bull (Ed.), <u>CODA: A diverse community, proceedings of the fourth National CODA Conference, Westminster, Maryland, July 15-18, 1989</u> (p. 81). Santa Barbara, CA: Children of Deaf Adults. [DEAF 306.874 N3, 1989]

Marcus, A. (Ed.). (1992). Coping skills 101 [Notes from sessions I and II]. In T. H. Bull (Ed.), <u>A CODA retreat: Coming home, proceedings of the fifth National CODA Conference, Austin, Texas, July 14-17, 1990</u> (pp. 53-54). Santa Barbara, CA: Children of Deaf Adults. [DEAF 306.874 N3, 1990]

Marcus, A. (1994). A thorny crown. In R. Shipman (Ed.), <u>Recollections: A decade of CODA, proceedings of the eighth International CODA Conference, Spokane, Washington, July 15-18, 1993</u> (p. 77). Santa Barbara, CA: Children of Deaf Adults. [DEAF 306.847 I57r, 1993]

(*) McKenna, K. E. (1996). My family room: The 1995 CODA [Millie Brother] Scholarship essay winner. In D. Prickett & R. Prickett (Eds.), <u>Richness in our diversity: Proceedings of the tenth International CODA Conference, Research Triangle Park, North Carolina, July 27-30, 1995</u> (pp. 128-129). Santa Barbara, CA: Children of Deaf Adults. (Reprinted from the Aug/Sept, 1995, edition of the <u>CODA Connection, 12</u> (3), 6. [UNIV DEAF Periodicals]) [On order]

(*) Millar, A. (1996). The commitment to succeed [The 1995 CODA Millie Brother Scholarship essay winner]. n D. Prickett & R. Prickett (Eds.), <u>Richness in our diversity: Proceedings of the tenth International CODA Conference, Research Triangle Park, North Carolina, July 27-30, 1995</u> (pp. 130-131). Santa Barbara, CA: Children of Deaf Adults. (Reprinted from the November, 1995, edition of the <u>CODA Connection, 12</u> (4), 6. [UNIV DEAF Periodicals]) [On order]

Miller, M. (Ed.). (1989). Program for non-coda family members [Summary of group discussion]. In T. H. Bull (Ed.), <u>New beginnings, new directions: Proceedings of the third National CODA Conference, Denver, Colorado, August 13-15, 1988</u> (pp. 60-67). Santa Barbara, CA: Children of Deaf Adults. [DEAF 306.874 N3, 1988]

Moreland, C. (1996). A CODA memoir [About the conference]. In D. Prickett & R. Prickett (Eds.), <u>Richness in our diversity: Proceedings of the tenth International CODA Conference, Research Triangle Park, North Carolina, July 27-30, 1995</u> (pp. 109-110). Santa Barbara, CA: Children of Deaf Adults. [On order]

Morgan, L. L. (1997). Once upon a time...: My memories of CODArado '97. In R. Shipman (Ed.), <u>"Once upon</u>

a time...:" Proceedings of the twelfth annual International CODA Conference, Denver, Colorado, July 10-13, 1997 (p. 125). Santa Barbara, CA: Children of Deaf Adults. [DEAF 306.874 I57o, 1997]

Morton, D. (Ed.). (1987/1994). Codas and relationships [Notes from group discussion]. In T. H. Bull, S. D. Rutherford & S. Jacobs (Eds.), Celebration and exploration of our heritage: Proceedings of the first National CODA Conference, Fremont, California, August 8-10, 1986 (Rev. ed., pp. 54-56). Santa Barbara, CA: Children of Deaf Adults. (The first edition was edited by S. Rutherford & S. Jacobs [DEAF 306.874 N4, 1986]) [DEAF 306.874 N37c, 1986b]

Multi-cultural codas [Breakout]. (1992). In R. Childress & K. Austin-Hemelt (Eds.), CODA: Family of origin/family of choice, proceedings of the seventh International CODA Conference, New Orleans, July 16-19, 1992 (p. 39). Santa Barbara, CA: Children of Deaf Adults. [DEAF 306.874 I57c, 1992]

Myers, L. (Ed.). (1989). CODA business planning meeting [Report]. In T. H. Bull (Ed.), New beginnings, new directions: Proceedings of the third National CODA Conference, Denver, Colorado, August 13-15, 1988 (pp. 71-74). Santa Barbara, CA: Children of Deaf Adults. [DEAF 306.874 N3, 1988]

Myers, L. (Ed.). (1990). Codas and personal relationships [Group #3 notes]. In T. H. Bull (Ed.), CODA: A diverse community, proceedings of the fourth National CODA Conference, Westminster, Maryland, July 15-18, 1989 (pp. 84-85). Santa Barbara, CA: Children of Deaf Adults. [DEAF 306.874 N3, 1989]

Myers, L. (Ed.). (1992). Mother/daughter relationships [Notes]. In T. H. Bull (Ed.), A CODA retreat: Coming home, proceedings of the fifth National CODA Conference, Austin, Texas, July 14-17, 1990 (p. 62). Santa Barbara, CA: Children of Deaf Adults. [DEAF 306.874 N3, 1990]

Myers, R. (Ed.). (1989, February-1993, September). CODA Connection [Newsletter]. Santa Barbara, CA: CODA - Children of Deaf Adults. [UNIV DEAF Periodicals]

Myers, R. (Ed.). (1990). Codas and personal relationships [Group #1 notes]. In T. H. Bull (Ed.), CODA: A diverse community, proceedings of the fourth National CODA Conference, Westminster, Maryland, July 15-18, 1989 (p. 82). Santa Barbara, CA: Children of Deaf Adults. [DEAF 306.874 N3, 1989]

Myers, R. (Ed.). (1992). Pathological vs. cultural views on the coda experience [Notes]. In T. H. Bull (Ed.), A CODA retreat: Coming home, proceedings of the fifth National CODA Conference, Austin, Texas, July 14-17, 1990 (p. 65). Santa Barbara, CA: Children of Deaf Adults. [DEAF 306.874 N3, 1990]

Myers, R. R. (Ed.). (1992). CODA: At the Oasis, proceedings of the sixth International CODA Conference/Retreat, Chicago, Illinois, July 19-22, 1991. Santa Barbara, CA: Children of Deaf Adults. (85 pages) [DEAF 306.874 C44co, 1991]

Nelson, D. (Ed.). (1995-present). ICODA Newsletter. Round Lake Beach, IL: ICODA. (Newsletter of the Indiana chapter of Children of Deaf Adults. Write ICODA, 1403 Juneway Terrace, Round Lake Beach, IL 60073) [*]

Networking and aftercare [Breakout summary]. (1995). In K. Bruno & D. Eklof (Eds.), You're among friends, welcome home: Proceedings of the ninth annual International CODA Conference, Oconomowoc, Wisconsin, July 14-17, 1994 (pp. 68-69). Santa Barbara, CA: Children of Deaf Adults. [DEAF 306.874 I57a, 1995]

Networking, chapter development and aftercare [Summary]. (1992). In R. R. Myers (Ed.), CODA: At the Oasis, proceedings of the sixth International CODA Conference/Retreat, Chicago, Illinois, July 19-22, 1991 (p. 68). Santa

C
O
D
A

191

Barbara, CA: Children of Deaf Adults. [DEAF 306.874 C44co, 1991]

Newcomers [Breakout]. (1992). In R. Childress & K. Austin-Hemelt (Eds.), <u>CODA: Family of origin/family of choice, proceedings of the seventh International CODA Conference, New Orleans, July 16-19, 1992</u> (p. 40). Santa Barbara, CA: Children of Deaf Adults. [DEAF 306.874 I57c, 1992]

Noble, G. (Ed.). (1992). Rage and anger workshop [Notes]. In T. H. Bull (Ed.), <u>A CODA retreat: Coming home, proceedings of the fifth National CODA Conference, Austin, Texas, July 14-17, 1990</u> (p. 38). Santa Barbara, CA: Children of Deaf Adults. [DEAF 306.874 N3, 1990]

Older codas [Breakout summary]. (1995). In K. Bruno & D. Eklof (Eds.), <u>You're among friends, welcome home: Proceedings of the ninth annual International CODA Conference, Oconomowoc, Wisconsin, July 14-17, 1994</u> (pp. 61-62). Santa Barbara, CA: Children of Deaf Adults. [DEAF 306.874 I57a, 1995]

Older codas - Elderly parents [Breakout summary]. (1994). In R. Shipman (Ed.), <u>Recollections: A decade of CODA, proceedings of the eighth International CODA Conference, Spokane, Washington, July 15-18, 1993</u> (p. 64). Santa Barbara, CA: Children of Deaf Adults. [DEAF 306.847 I57r, 1993]

Only hearing codas [Summary]. (1992). In R. R. Myers (Ed.), <u>CODA: At the Oasis, proceedings of the sixth International CODA Conference/Retreat, Chicago, Illinois, July 19-22, 1991</u> (p. 70). Santa Barbara, CA: Children of Deaf Adults. [DEAF 306.874 C44co, 1991]

Orbke, L. (1997). Once upon a time...: My memories of CODArado '97. In R. Shipman (Ed.), <u>"Once upon a time...:" Proceedings of the twelfth annual International CODA Conference, Denver, Colorado, July 10-13, 1997</u> (pp. 126-127). Santa Barbara, CA: Children of Deaf Adults. [DEAF 306.874 I57o, 1997]

Orr, L. (Ed.). (1990). Who am I? (Codas-only group) [Summary notes from roundtable group discussion]. In T. H. Bull (Ed.), <u>Reflections: Codas and cultures, proceedings of the second National CODA Conference, Rochester, New York, August 21-23, 1987</u> (3rd. rev. ed., pp. 51-52). Santa Barbara, CA: Children of Deaf Adults. (The Gallaudet University Library also has the first edition [DEAF 306.874 N3, 1987] and the second edition [DEAF 306.874 N3, 1987b]) [DEAF 306.874 N3, 1987a]

Our heritage [Breakout summary]. (1994). In R. Shipman (Ed.), <u>Recollections: A decade of CODA, proceedings of the eighth International CODA Conference, Spokane, Washington, July 15-18, 1993</u> (pp. 50-51). Santa Barbara, CA: Children of Deaf Adults. [DEAF 306.847 I57r, 1993]

Our heritage [Breakout summary]. (1995). In K. Bruno & D. Eklof (Eds.), <u>You're among friends, welcome home: Proceedings of the ninth annual International CODA Conference, Oconomowoc, Wisconsin, July 14-17, 1994</u> (p. 43). Santa Barbara, CA: Children of Deaf Adults. [DEAF 306.874 I57a, 1995]

Pappas, D. (Ed.). (1990-1994). <u>Chicagoland/CODA Newsletter.</u> Chicago: Chicagoland/CODA. (Newsletter of the Chicago area chapter of Children of Deaf Adults. Now Illinois CODA: Write Diana Nelson, 1403 Juneway Terrace, Round Lake Beach, Illinois 60073) [*]

Pappas, D. (Ed.). (1992). Female codas and their significant others [Notes from session I]. In T. H. Bull (Ed.), <u>A CODA retreat: Coming home, proceedings of the fifth National CODA Conference, Austin, Texas, July 14-17, 1990</u> (p. 58). Santa Barbara, CA: Children of Deaf Adults. [DEAF 306.874 N3, 1990]

Powell, J. (Ed.). (1994). Panel discussion: Past, present and future. In R. Shipman (Ed.), <u>Recollections: A decade</u>

of CODA, proceedings of the eighth International CODA Conference, Spokane, Washington, July 15-18, 1993 (pp. 20-29). Santa Barbara, CA: Children of Deaf Adults. (Moderator, Janie Powell. Panel members: Amy Williamson, Kathleen Hemelt, Della Goswell and Judy Singleton) [DEAF 306.847 I57r, 1993]

Powell, J. (Ed.). (1997). Once upon a time...opening panel: What keeps you coming back to CODA? In R. Shipman (Ed.), "Once upon a time...:" Proceedings of the twelfth annual International CODA Conference, Denver, Colorado, July 10-13, 1997 (pp. 55-68). Santa Barbara, CA: Children of Deaf Adults. (Moderator, Janie Powell. Panelists: Linda Hines, Mark Whisenant, Darlene Graham, Sammy Milburn and Tom Bull) [DEAF 306.874 I57o, 1997]

Preston, C. (1997). Memories, reflections and poetry: Memoirs. In S. Schmidt-Boe, (Ed.), "Everyone is a star": The 11th annual international CODA conference proceedings, Buena Park, California, July 11-14, 1996 (p. 76). Santa Barbara, CA: Children of Deaf Adults. [On order]

Preston, P. (Ed.). (1990). An "only Coda" session [Notes]. In T. H. Bull (Ed.), CODA: A diverse community, proceedings of the fourth National CODA Conference, Westminster, Maryland, July 15-18, 1989 (pp. 31-33). Santa Barbara, CA: Children of Deaf Adults. [DEAF 306.874 N3, 1989]

Preston, P. M. (1996). Unfinished business: Stories of diversity [Keynote address]. In D. Prickett & R. Prickett (Eds.), Richness in our diversity: Proceedings of the tenth International CODA Conference, Research Triangle Park, North Carolina, July 27-30, 1995 (pp. 43-57). Santa Barbara, CA: Children of Deaf Adults. [On order]

Prickett, D. (1989a). Reflections on CODA III: Coda and coda-daughters' perspective. In T. H. Bull (Ed.), New beginnings, new directions: Proceedings of the third National CODA Conference, Denver, Colorado, August 13-15, 1988 (p. 77). Santa Barbara, CA: Children of Deaf Adults. [DEAF 306.874 N3, 1988]

Prickett, D. (Ed.). (1989b). Regional discussion group #1 [Summary]. In T. H. Bull (Ed.), New beginnings, new directions: Proceedings of the third National CODA Conference, Denver, Colorado, August 13-15, 1988 (pp. 46-47). Santa Barbara, CA: Children of Deaf Adults. [DEAF 306.874 N3, 1988]

Prickett, D. (1996). Memoirs and participant reflections [About the conference]. In D. Prickett & R. Prickett (Eds.), Richness in our diversity: Proceedings of the tenth International CODA Conference, Research Triangle Park, North Carolina, July 27-30, 1995 (p. 115). Santa Barbara, CA: Children of Deaf Adults. [On order]

Prickett, D., & Prickett, R. (Eds.). (1990, Fall-Present). DC/CODA Newsletter. Washington, DC: DC/CODA. (Newsletter of the Washington, D. C. - Metropolitan area chapter of Children of Deaf Adults. Write DC/CODA, P.O. Box 2352, 800 Florida Ave., N.E., Washington, DC 20002-3695) [*]

Prickett, D., & Prickett, R. (Eds.). (1996). Richness in our diversity: Proceedings of the tenth International CODA Conference, Research Triangle Park, North Carolina, July 27-30, 1995. Santa Barbara, CA: Children of Deaf Adults. (138 pages) [On order]

Prickett, H. (1987a/1994). Life sounds [Poem]. In T. H. Bull, S. D. Rutherford & S. Jacobs (Eds.), Celebration and exploration of our heritage: Proceedings of the first National CODA Conference, Fremont, California, August 8-10, 1986 (Rev. ed., p. 7). Santa Barbara, CA: Children of Deaf Adults. (The first edition was edited by S. Rutherford & S. Jacobs [DEAF 306.874 N4, 1986]) [DEAF 306.874 N37c, 1986b]

Prickett, H. (1987b/1994). Like me [Poem]. In T. H. Bull, S. D. Rutherford & S. Jacobs (Eds.), Celebration and exploration of our heritage: Proceedings of the first National CODA Conference, Fremont, California, August 8-10,

C
O
D
A

1986 (Rev. ed., p. 6). Santa Barbara, CA: Children of Deaf Adults. (The first edition was edited by S. Rutherford & S. Jacobs [DEAF 306.874 N4, 1986]) [DEAF 306.874 N37c, 1986b]

Prickett, H. (1989a). Closing remarks and wrap up. In T. H. Bull (Ed.), New beginnings, new directions: Proceedings of the third National CODA Conference, Denver, Colorado, August 13-15, 1988 (pp. 83-89). Santa Barbara, CA: Children of Deaf Adults. [DEAF 306.874 N3, 1988]

Prickett, H. (1989b). Reflections on CODA III: Coda and coda-parents' perspective. In T. H. Bull (Ed.), New beginnings, new directions: Proceedings of the third National CODA Conference, Denver, Colorado, August 13-15, 1988 (p. 78). Santa Barbara, CA: Children of Deaf Adults. [DEAF 306.874 N3, 1988]

Prickett, H. (1990). Conference wrap-up #2. In T. H. Bull (Ed.), CODA: A diverse community, proceedings of the fourth National CODA Conference, Westminster, Maryland, July 15-18, 1989 (pp. 113-114). Santa Barbara, CA: Children of Deaf Adults. [DEAF 306.874 N3, 1989]

Prickett, H. (Ed.). (1992). Older codas discussion [Notes]. In T. H. Bull (Ed.), A CODA retreat: Coming home, proceedings of the fifth National CODA Conference, Austin, Texas, July 14-17, 1990 (p. 64). Santa Barbara, CA: Children of Deaf Adults. [DEAF 306.874 N3, 1990]

Prickett, H. (1996a). A challenge to love [Closing remarks]. In D. Prickett & R. Prickett (Eds.), Richness in our diversity: Proceedings of the tenth International CODA Conference, Research Triangle Park, North Carolina, July 27-30, 1995 (pp. 79-88). Santa Barbara, CA: Children of Deaf Adults. [On order]

Prickett, H. (1996b). Memoirs and participant reflections: I remember the feeling of love. In D. Prickett & R. Prickett (Eds.), Richness in our diversity: Proceedings of the tenth International CODA Conference, Research Triangle Park, North Carolina, July 27-30, 1995 (p. 107). Santa Barbara, CA: Children of Deaf Adults. (Written under the name "Papa Bear") [On order]

Prickett, H. T. (1996). Papa Bear [Poem]. In D. Prickett & R. Prickett (Eds.), Richness in our diversity: Proceedings of the tenth International CODA Conference, Research Triangle Park, North Carolina, July 27-30, 1995 (p. 16). Santa Barbara, CA: Children of Deaf Adults. [On order]

Prickett, H. T. (1997). Memories, reflections and poetry: Memoirs. In S. Schmidt-Boe, (Ed.), "Everyone is a star": The 11th annual international CODA conference proceedings, Buena Park, California, July 11-14, 1996 (pp. 76-77). Santa Barbara, CA: Children of Deaf Adults. [On order]

Prickett, R. (1996). Memoirs and participant reflections [About the conference]. In D. Prickett & R. Prickett (Eds.), Richness in our diversity: Proceedings of the tenth International CODA Conference, Research Triangle Park, North Carolina, July 27-30, 1995 (p. 111). Santa Barbara, CA: Children of Deaf Adults. [On order]

Rancke, C. (1992). Position paper in opposition to the inclusion of non-codas at the annual CODA meeting. In T. H. Bull (Ed.), A CODA Retreat: Coming home, proceedings of the fifth National CODA Conference, Austin, Texas, July 14-17, 1990 (pp. 82-83). Santa Barbara, CA: Children of Deaf Adults. [DEAF 306.874 N3, 1990]

Random memories. (1992). In R. Childress & K. Austin-Hemelt (Eds.), CODA: Family of origin/family of choice, proceedings of the seventh International CODA Conference, New Orleans, July 16-19, 1992 (p. 46). Santa Barbara, CA: Children of Deaf Adults. [DEAF 306.874 I57c, 1992]

Rembiszewski, B. (1997). Once upon a time...: My memories of CODArado '97. In R. Shipman (Ed.), "Once upon a time...:" Proceedings of the twelfth annual International CODA Conference, Denver, Colorado, July 10-13, 1997 (p. 121). Santa Barbara, CA: Children of Deaf Adults. [DEAF 306.874 I57o, 1997]

Reports from the "National Action-Plan" Committee meetings. (1990). In T. H. Bull (Ed.), Reflections: Codas and cultures, proceedings of the second National CODA Conference, Rochester, New York, August 21-23, 1987 (3rd rev. ed., pp. 57-61). Santa Barbara, CA: Children of Deaf Adults. (The Gallaudet University Library also has the first edition [DEAF 306.874 N3, 1987] and the second edition [DEAF 306.874 N3, 1987b]) {Group discussion reports were summarized. Contact persons were identified as Diana Lusker (Funding sources); Ronald L. Coffey (Special Interest Forum); Cathy Illi (Publicity/Outreach); Betty Colonomos (Report by Liza Orr: CODA: Goals, purpose, membership, name, logo committee); Liz O'Brien (Parent education); and Brenda Stansbury (Organizational structure)} [DEAF 306.874 N3, 1987a]

(*) Ritter, D. (1996). Realizing new goals [The 1993 CODA Millie Brother Scholarship essay winner]. In D. Prickett & R. Prickett (Eds.), Richness in our diversity: Proceedings of the tenth International CODA Conference, Research Triangle Park, North Carolina, July 27-30, 1995 (p. 124). Santa Barbara, CA: Children of Deaf Adults. (Reprinted from the Aug/Sept, 1993, edition of the CODA Connection, 10 (3), 10. [UNIV DEAF Periodicals]) [On order]

Rocke, D. (Ed.). (1992). Adjusting to the hearing world: Communication problems and codas [Notes from session II]. In T. H. Bull (Ed.), A CODA retreat: Coming home, proceedings of the fifth National CODA Conference, Austin, Texas, July 14-17, 1990 (pp. 43-44). Santa Barbara, CA: Children of Deaf Adults. [DEAF 306.874 N3, 1990]

Ruge, R. (Ed.). (1989a). Alternate communication styles of parents [Summary]. In T. H. Bull (Ed.), New beginnings, new directions: Proceedings of the third National CODA Conference, Denver, Colorado, August 13-15, 1988 (p. 54). Santa Barbara, CA: Children of Deaf Adults. [DEAF 306.874 N3, 1988]

Ruge, R. (1989b). Reflections on CODA III: A coda sibling's perspective. In T. H. Bull (Ed.), New beginnings, new directions: Proceedings of the third National CODA Conference, Denver, Colorado, August 13-15, 1988 (p. 80). Santa Barbara, CA: Children of Deaf Adults. [DEAF 306.874 N3, 1988]

Ruge, R. (Ed.). (1989c). Regional discussion group #3 [Summary]. In T. H. Bull (Ed.), New beginnings, new directions: Proceedings of the third National CODA Conference, Denver, Colorado, August 13-15, 1988 (p. 49). Santa Barbara, CA: Children of Deaf Adults. [DEAF 306.874 N3, 1988]

Ruiz, S. (1997). Once upon a time...: My memories of CODArado '97. In R. Shipman (Ed.), "Once upon a time...:" Proceedings of the twelfth annual International CODA Conference, Denver, Colorado, July 10-13, 1997 (p. 126). Santa Barbara, CA: Children of Deaf Adults. [DEAF 306.874 I57o, 1997]

Rutherford, S. D. (1987/1994). Dynamics of a bicultural identity [Keynote presentation]. In T. H. Bull, S. D. Rutherford & S. Jacobs (Eds.), Celebration and exploration of our heritage: Proceedings of the first National CODA Conference, Fremont, California, August 8-10, 1986 (Rev. ed., pp. 22-33). Santa Barbara, CA: Children of Deaf Adults. (The first edition was edited by S. Rutherford & S. Jacobs [DEAF 306.874 N4, 1986]) [DEAF 306.874 N37c, 1986b]

Rutherford, S. D., & Jacobs, S. (Eds.). (1987). Celebration and exploration of our heritage: Proceedings of the first National CODA Conference, Fremont, California, August 8-10, 1986. Santa Barbara, CA: Children of Deaf Adults. (119 pages) [DEAF 306.874 C44c, 1986]

Sallop, M. (Ed.). (1990a). "The Big Meeting": A report. In T. H. Bull (Ed.), <u>CODA: A diverse community, proceedings of the fourth National CODA Conference, Westminster, Maryland, July 15-18, 1989</u> (pp. 107-108). Santa Barbara, CA: Children of Deaf Adults. [DEAF 306.874 N3, 1989]

Sallop, M. (Ed.). (1990b). The tri-cultural coda experience [Summary of breakout group session]. In T. H. Bull (Ed.), <u>CODA: A diverse community, proceedings of the fourth National CODA Conference, Westminster, Maryland, July 15-18, 1989</u> (pp. 41-42). Santa Barbara, CA: Children of Deaf Adults. [DEAF 306.874 N3, 1989]

Sallop, M. B. (Ed.). (1989). Regional discussion group #2 [Summary]. In T. H. Bull (Ed.), <u>New beginnings, new directions: Proceedings of the third National CODA Conference, Denver, Colorado, August 13-15, 1988</u> (p. 48). Santa Barbara, CA: Children of Deaf Adults. [DEAF 306.874 N3, 1988]

Sanderson, G. (Ed.). (1987/1994). Coda panel: A look across the ages. In T. H. Bull, S. D. Rutherford & S. Jacobs (Eds.), <u>Celebration and exploration of our heritage: Proceedings of the first National CODA Conference, Fremont, California, August 8-10, 1986</u> (Rev. ed., pp. 58-60). Santa Barbara, CA: Children of Deaf Adults. (Moderator, Gary Sanderson. Panel members: Elizabeth Crisswell, Johanna Larson, Ralph Neesam and Mark Seeger. The first edition was edited by S. Rutherford & S. Jacobs [DEAF 306.874 N4, 1986]) [DEAF 306.874 N37c, 1986b]

Sanderson, G. (Ed.). (1992). Coda panel [On the topic of how we communicate]. In R. Childress & K. Austin-Hemelt (Eds.), <u>CODA: Family of origin/family of choice, proceedings of the seventh International CODA Conference, New Orleans, July 16-19, 1992</u> (pp. 24-30). Santa Barbara, CA: Children of Deaf Adults. (Moderator: Gary Sanderson. Panel members: Sari Freedman, Bob Hoffmeister, Billy Collins and Ron Gallimore) [DEAF 306.874 I57c, 1992]

Sanderson, G. (1997a). Codas in the arts [Panel]. In S. Schmidt-Boe, (Ed.), <u>"Everyone is a star": The 11th annual international CODA conference proceedings, Buena Park, California, July 11-14, 1996</u> (p. 56). Santa Barbara, CA: Children of Deaf Adults. [On order]

Sanderson, G. (1997b). Memories, reflections and poetry: Memoirs. In S. Schmidt-Boe, (Ed.), <u>"Everyone is a star": The 11th annual international CODA conference proceedings, Buena Park, California, July 11-14, 1996</u> (p. 77). Santa Barbara, CA: Children of Deaf Adults. [On order]

Schmidt-Boe, S. (Ed.). (1997). <u>"Everyone is a star": The 11th annual international CODA conference proceedings, Buena Park, California, July 11-14, 1996.</u> Santa Barbara, CA: Children of Deaf Adults. (82 pages) [On order]

Schuchman, J. S. (Ed.). (1990). Images of codas in film and television [Topic group discussion notes]. In T. H. Bull (Ed.), <u>CODA: A diverse community, proceedings of the fourth National CODA Conference, Westminster, Maryland, July 15-18, 1989</u> (p. 102). Santa Barbara, CA: Children of Deaf Adults. [DEAF 306.874 N3, 1989]

Schuchman, S. (1989). My experience as a coda [Keynote address]. In T. H. Bull (Ed.), <u>New beginnings, new directions: Proceedings of the third National CODA Conference, Denver, Colorado, August 13-15, 1988</u> (pp. 32-44). Santa Barbara, CA: Children of Deaf Adults. [DEAF 306.874 N3, 1988]

Schuchman, S. (1992). A position paper in support to the inclusion of non-codas at the annual CODA meeting. In T. H. Bull (Ed.), <u>A CODA Retreat: Coming home, proceedings of the fifth National CODA Conference, Austin, Texas, July 14-17, 1990</u> (pp. 80-82). Santa Barbara, CA: Children of Deaf Adults. [DEAF 306.874 N3, 1990]

Shipman, R. (Ed.). (1994). <u>Recollections: A decade of CODA, proceedings of the eighth International CODA Conference, Spokane, Washington, July 15-18, 1993.</u> Santa Barbara, CA: Children of Deaf Adults. (119 pages)

[DEAF 306.847 I57r, 1993]

Shipman, R. (Ed.). (1997). "Once upon a time...:" Proceedings of the twelfth annual International CODA Conference, Denver, Colorado, July 10-13, 1997. Santa Barbara, CA: Children of Deaf Adults. (146 pages) [DEAF 306.874 I57o, 1997]

Shultz, S. (Ed.). (1990a). Bilingual/bicultural: Who am I? [Notes from a discussion session]. In T. H. Bull (Ed.), CODA: A diverse community, proceedings of the fourth National CODA Conference, Westminster, Maryland, July 15-18, 1989 (pp. 90-92). Santa Barbara, CA: Children of Deaf Adults. [DEAF 306.874 N3, 1989]

Shultz, S. (Ed.). (1990b). CODA, a diverse community [Panel]. In T. H. Bull (Ed.), CODA: A diverse community, proceedings of the fourth National CODA Conference, Westminster, Maryland, July 15-18, 1989 (pp. 13-27). Santa Barbara, CA: Children of Deaf Adults. (Moderator, Shirley Shultz. Panel members: Elliott Aheroni, Joyce Groode, Marvin Sallop, Paul Preston and Nancy Kamenski) [DEAF 306.874 N3, 1989]

Shultz-Myers, S. (Ed.). (1992). Coda panel: What "coming home" means to me. In T. H. Bull (Ed.), A CODA retreat: Coming home, proceedings of the fifth National CODA Conference, Austin, Texas, July 14-17, 1990 (pp. 18-33). Santa Barbara, CA: Children of Deaf Adults. (Moderator: Shirley-Shultz Myers. Panel members: Pam Timpson, Darlene Prickett, Jerry Bass, Jenny Singleton and Carol Mullis) [DEAF 306.874 N3, 1990]

Sibling issues [Breakout summary]. (1994). In R. Shipman (Ed.), Recollections: A decade of CODA, proceedings of the eighth International CODA Conference, Spokane, Washington, July 15-18, 1993 (pp. 47-48). Santa Barbara, CA: Children of Deaf Adults. [DEAF 306.847 I57r, 1993]

Sibling issues [Breakout summary]. (1995). In K. Bruno & D. Eklof (Eds.), You're among friends, welcome home: Proceedings of the ninth annual International CODA Conference, Oconomowoc, Wisconsin, July 14-17, 1994 (p. 41). Santa Barbara, CA: Children of Deaf Adults. [DEAF 306.874 I57a, 1995]

Siblings together [Breakout summary]. (1994). In R. Shipman (Ed.), Recollections: A decade of CODA, proceedings of the eighth International CODA Conference, Spokane, Washington, July 15-18, 1993 (p. 46). Santa Barbara, CA: Children of Deaf Adults. [DEAF 306.847 I57r, 1993]

Siblings together [Summary from two sessions]. (1995). In K. Bruno & D. Eklof (Eds.), You're among friends, welcome home: Proceedings of the ninth annual International CODA Conference, Oconomowoc, Wisconsin, July 14-17, 1994 (pp. 45-47). Santa Barbara, CA: Children of Deaf Adults. [DEAF 306.874 I57a, 1995]

Sidransky, R. (1992). Keynote address [And question and answer period]. In R. R. Myers (Ed.), CODA: At the Oasis, proceedings of the sixth International CODA Conference/Retreat, Chicago, Illinois, July 19-22, 1991 (pp. 38-52). Santa Barbara, CA: Children of Deaf Adults. [DEAF 306.874 C44co, 1991]

Singleton, J. (Ed.). (1992). Hidden parts: Tales never told [Opening panel presentation]. In R. R. Myers (Ed.), CODA: At the Oasis, proceedings of the sixth International CODA Conference/Retreat, Chicago, Illinois, July 19-22, 1991 (pp. 20-31). Santa Barbara, CA: Children of Deaf Adults. (Moderator, Jenny Singleton. Panel members: Sheila Jacobs, Bonnie Mendelson, Sue Washington, Charlie Rancke and Lenny Davis) [DEAF 306.874 C44co, 1991]

Smallwood, F. (Ed.). (1992). Female codas and their significant others [Notes from session II]. In T. H. Bull (Ed.), A CODA retreat: Coming home, proceedings of the fifth National CODA Conference, Austin, Texas, July 14-17, 1990 (p. 59). Santa Barbara, CA: Children of Deaf Adults. [DEAF 306.874 N3, 1990]

CODA

Smith, B. J. (1997). Once upon a time...: My memories of CODArado '97. In R. Shipman (Ed.), "Once upon a time...:" Proceedings of the twelfth annual International CODA Conference, Denver, Colorado, July 10-13, 1997 (pp. 125-126). Santa Barbara, CA: Children of Deaf Adults. [DEAF 306.874 I57o, 1997]

Smith, R. (Ed.). (1990). Working with codas under 18 years old. In T. H. Bull (Ed.), CODA: A diverse community, proceedings of the fourth National CODA Conference, Westminster, Maryland, July 15-18, 1989 (pp. 93-94). Santa Barbara, CA: Children of Deaf Adults. [DEAF 306.874 N3, 1989]

Sound expressions [Breakout summary]. (1994). In R. Shipman (Ed.), Recollections: A decade of CODA, proceedings of the eighth International CODA Conference, Spokane, Washington, July 15-18, 1993 (p. 70). Santa Barbara, CA: Children of Deaf Adults. [DEAF 306.847 I57r, 1993]

Stansfield, M. (Ed.). (1987/1994). Codas and the world of work [Group discussion notes]. In T. H. Bull, S. D. Rutherford & S. Jacobs (Eds.), Celebration and exploration of our heritage: Proceedings of the first National CODA Conference, Fremont, California, August 8-10, 1986 (Rev. ed., pp. 52-54). Santa Barbara, CA: Children of Deaf Adults. (The first edition was edited by S. Rutherford & S. Jacobs [DEAF 306.874 N4, 1986]) [DEAF 306.874 N37c, 1986b]

Staton, D. (1996). Memoirs and participant reflections: What did I learn or experience at CODA Conference 1995? In D. Prickett & R. Prickett (Eds.), Richness in our diversity: Proceedings of the tenth International CODA Conference, Research Triangle Park, North Carolina, July 27-30, 1995 (p. 115). Santa Barbara, CA: Children of Deaf Adults. [On order]

Stogis, K. (Ed.). (1997). Once upon a time...: Storytelling panel. In R. Shipman (Ed.), "Once upon a time...:" Proceedings of the twelfth annual International CODA Conference, Denver, Colorado, July 10-13, 1997 (pp. 86-98). Santa Barbara, CA: Children of Deaf Adults. (Moderator, Kas Stogis. Panelists: Dale Dyal, Dave Eklof, Alan Marcus and Paula Olejarz) [DEAF 306.874 I57o, 1997]

Tanzar, M. J. (1995). Wrap up [Closing remarks and comments from participants]. In K. Bruno & D. Eklof (Eds.), You're among friends, welcome home: Proceedings of the ninth annual International CODA Conference, Oconomowoc, Wisconsin, July 14-17, 1994 (pp. 73-88). Santa Barbara, CA: Children of Deaf Adults. [DEAF 306.874 I57a, 1995]

Taylor, L. (1987/1994). Bigger than the Empire State Building [Performance piece]. In T. H. Bull, S. D. Rutherford & S. Jacobs (Eds.), Celebration and exploration of our heritage: Proceedings of the first National CODA Conference, Fremont, California, August 8-10, 1986 (Rev. ed., pp. 76-84). Santa Barbara, CA: Children of Deaf Adults. (The first edition was edited by S. Rutherford & S. Jacobs [DEAF 306.874 N4, 1986]) [DEAF 306.874 N37c, 1986b]

Therapeutic expressions [Breakout summary]. (1994). In R. Shipman (Ed.), Recollections: A decade of CODA, proceedings of the eighth International CODA Conference, Spokane, Washington, July 15-18, 1993 (pp. 71, 73-76). Santa Barbara, CA: Children of Deaf Adults. {Poems are by Darlene P., L. H., J. K., and M. C. Two others on pages 72 and 77 are by Tom Bull and Alan Marcus and are listed elsewhere in this section} [DEAF 306.847 I57r, 1993]

Timpson, P. (Ed.). (1990). CODA chapter development [Notes from topic group discussion]. In T. H. Bull (Ed.), CODA: A diverse community, proceedings of the fourth National CODA Conference, Westminster, Maryland, July 15-18, 1989 (pp. 105-106). Santa Barbara, CA: Children of Deaf Adults. [DEAF 306.874 N3, 1989]

Timpson, P. (Ed.). (1992). Non-signing codas [Notes]. In T. H. Bull (Ed.), <u>A CODA retreat: Coming home, proceedings of the fifth National CODA Conference, Austin, Texas, July 14-17, 1990</u> (p. 63). Santa Barbara, CA: Children of Deaf Adults. [DEAF 306.874 N3, 1990]

Topliff, A. (Ed.). (1989a). Elderly deaf parents [Summary of group discussion]. In T. H. Bull (Ed.), <u>New beginnings, new directions: Proceedings of the third National CODA Conference, Denver, Colorado, August 13-15, 1988</u> (pp. 52-53). Santa Barbara, CA: Children of Deaf Adults. [DEAF 306.874 N3, 1988]

Topliff, A. (1989b). Welcome to Colorado. In T. H. Bull (Ed.), <u>New beginnings, new directions: Proceedings of the third National CODA Conference, Denver, Colorado, August 13-15, 1988</u> (p. 17). Santa Barbara, CA: Children of Deaf Adults. [DEAF 306.874 N3, 1988]

Topliff, A. (1997). Once upon a time...: My memories of CODArado '97. In R. Shipman (Ed.), <u>"Once upon a time...:" Proceedings of the twelfth annual International CODA Conference, Denver, Colorado, July 10-13, 1997</u> (pp. 117-119). Santa Barbara, CA: Children of Deaf Adults. [DEAF 306.874 I57o, 1997]

Topliff, A., & Dorman, E. (1997). Once upon a time...Conference introduction. In R. Shipman (Ed.), <u>"Once upon a time...:" Proceedings of the twelfth annual International CODA Conference, Denver, Colorado, July 10-13, 1997</u> (pp. 6-8). Santa Barbara, CA: Children of Deaf Adults. [DEAF 306.874 I57o, 1997]

Toth, S., Jr. (Ed.). (1992). Relationships and intimacy [Notes from session I]. In T. H. Bull (Ed.), <u>A CODA retreat: Coming home, proceedings of the fifth National CODA Conference, Austin, Texas, July 14-17, 1990</u> (p. 66). Santa Barbara, CA: Children of Deaf Adults. [DEAF 306.874 N3, 1990]

Toth, S., Jr., & Bass, J. (Eds.). (1990). Being a coda: The male perspective [Group discussion notes]. In T. H. Bull (Ed.), <u>CODA: A diverse community, proceedings of the fourth National CODA Conference, Westminster, Maryland, July 15-18, 1989</u> (pp. 86-87). Santa Barbara, CA: Children of Deaf Adults. [DEAF 306.874 N3, 1989]

Townsend-Handscomb, D. (Ed.). (1990). International coda panel. In T. H. Bull (Ed.), <u>CODA: A diverse community, proceedings of the fourth National CODA Conference, Westminster, Maryland, July 15-18, 1989</u> (pp. 53-76). Santa Barbara, CA: Children of Deaf Adults. (Moderator: Darren Townsend-Handscomb, Ilford, Essex, England. Panel members: Peter Bonser, Petersham, New South Wales, Australia; Catherine White, Tralee, County Kerry, Ireland; Brigitte Francois, Brussels, Belgium; Maureen Jones, Calgary, Alberta, Canada; Rosana Famularo, Buenos Aires, Argentina; Israel Sela, Tel-Aviv, Israel) [DEAF 306.874 N3, 1989]

Velez, M. (Ed.). (1994-present). <u>CODA Chronicles: Bay Area CODA Newsletter.</u> Oakland, CA: Bay Area CODA. (Newsletter of the Northern California chapter of Children of Deaf Adults. Write CODA/Bay Area, 4076 Whittle Ave. Oakland, CA 94602) [*]

Velez, M. (Ed.). (1997). Codas in the arts [Panel]. In S. Schmidt-Boe, (Ed.), <u>"Everyone is a star": The 11th annual international CODA conference proceedings, Buena Park, California, July 11-14, 1996</u> (p. 56). Santa Barbara, CA: Children of Deaf Adults. (Moderator: Michael Velez. Panel members: Lenny Davis, New York; Ron Hillas, Jack Jason, Sharon Neumann-Solow and Gary Sanderson, all from California) [On order]

Walker, L. A. (1990). Keynote address. In T. H. Bull (Ed.), <u>Reflections: Codas and cultures, proceedings of the second National CODA Conference, Rochester, New York, August 21-23, 1987</u> (3rd rev. ed., pp. 20-28). Santa Barbara, CA: Children of Deaf Adults. (The Gallaudet University Library also has the first edition [DEAF 306.874 N3, 1987] and the second edition [DEAF 306.874 N3, 1987b]) [DEAF 306.874 N3, 1987a]

C
O
D
A

Washington, S. (Ed.). (1992a). Adjusting to the hearing world: Communication problems and codas [Session I group discussion notes]. In T. H. Bull (Ed.), <u>A CODA retreat: Coming home, proceedings of the fifth National CODA Conference, Austin, Texas, July 14-17, 1990</u> (pp. 41-42). Santa Barbara, CA: Children of Deaf Adults. [DEAF 306.874 N3, 1990]

Washington, S. (Ed.). (1992b). Codas with elderly parents [Group discussion notes]. In T. H. Bull (Ed.), <u>A CODA retreat: Coming home, proceedings of the fifth National CODA Conference, Austin, Texas, July 14-17, 1990</u> (pp. 50-51). Santa Barbara, CA: Children of Deaf Adults. [DEAF 306.874 N3, 1990]

Washington, S. (Ed.). (1992c). Family composition [Notes from session II]. In T. H. Bull (Ed.), <u>A CODA retreat: Coming home, proceedings of the fifth National CODA Conference, Austin, Texas, July 14-17, 1990</u> (p. 56). Santa Barbara, CA: Children of Deaf Adults. [DEAF 306.874 N3, 1990]

Weed, S. A. (1997). Once upon a time...: My memories of CODArado '97. In R. Shipman (Ed.), <u>"Once upon a time...:" Proceedings of the twelfth annual International CODA Conference, Denver, Colorado, July 10-13, 1997</u> (p. 127). Santa Barbara, CA: Children of Deaf Adults. [DEAF 306.874 I57o, 1997]

What is Deaf culture [Summary]. (1992). In R. R. Myers (Ed.), <u>CODA: At the Oasis, proceedings of the sixth International CODA Conference/Retreat, Chicago, Illinois, July 19-22, 1991</u> (p. 65). Santa Barbara, CA: Children of Deaf Adults. [DEAF 306.874 C44co, 1991]

Whisenant, M. (1996). Memoirs and participant reflections [About the conference]. In D. Prickett & R. Prickett (Eds.), <u>Richness in our diversity: Proceedings of the tenth International CODA Conference, Research Triangle Park, North Carolina, July 27-30, 1995</u> (p. 114). Santa Barbara, CA: Children of Deaf Adults. [On order]

Whisenant, M. (1997). My walk - CODA [Poem]. In R. Shipman (Ed.), <u>"Once upon a time...:" Proceedings of the twelfth annual International CODA Conference, Denver, Colorado, July 10-13, 1997</u> (p. 104). Santa Barbara, CA: Children of Deaf Adults. [DEAF 306.874 I57o, 1997]

Williamson, A. (Ed.). (1996). Diversity panel discussion. In D. Prickett & R. Prickett (Eds.), <u>Richness in our diversity: Proceedings of the tenth International CODA Conference, Research Triangle Park, North Carolina, July 27-30, 1995</u> (pp. 69-77). Santa Barbara, CA: Children of Deaf Adults. (Moderator: Amy Williamson. Panel members: JoAnn Huss, Alan Izaguirre, Agnes Muse and Dave Eklof) [On order]

Women only [Breakout summary]. (1995). In K. Bruno & D. Eklof (Eds.), <u>You're among friends, welcome home: Proceedings of the ninth annual International CODA Conference, Oconomowoc, Wisconsin, July 14-17, 1994</u> (p. 51). Santa Barbara, CA: Children of Deaf Adults. [DEAF 306.874 I57a, 1995]

Woodward, J. (1987/1994). Deaf parents - hearing children: International perspectives [Keynote presentation]. In T. H. Bull, S. D. Rutherford & S. Jacobs (Eds.), <u>Celebration and exploration of our heritage: Proceedings of the first National CODA Conference, Fremont, California, August 8-10, 1986</u> (Rev. ed., pp. 15-21). Santa Barbara, CA: Children of Deaf Adults. (The first edition was edited by S. Rutherford & S. Jacobs [DEAF 306.874 N4, 1986]) [DEAF 306.874 N37c, 1986b]

Woodward, J. C. (Ed.). (1987/1994). Hearing children of hearing parents discussion [Group summary]. In T. H. Bull, S. D. Rutherford & S. Jacobs (Eds.), <u>Celebration and exploration of our heritage: Proceedings of the first National CODA Conference, Fremont, California, August 8-10, 1986</u> (Rev. ed., pp. 51-52). Santa Barbara, CA: Children of Deaf Adults. (The first edition was edited by S. Rutherford & S. Jacobs [DEAF 306.874 N4, 1986]) [DEAF 306.874 N37c, 1986b]

Yeager, R. (1990). CODA: Psychological implications [Keynote presentation]. In T. H. Bull (Ed.), <u>Reflections:</u> <u>Codas and cultures, proceedings of the second National CODA Conference, Rochester, New York, August 21-23,</u> <u>1987</u> (3rd rev. ed., pp. 29-33). Santa Barbara, CA: Children of Deaf Adults. (The Gallaudet University Library also has the first edition [DEAF 306.874 N3, 1987] and the second edition [DEAF 306.874 N3, 1987b]) [DEAF 306.874 N3, 1987a]

You don't have to do it all [Breakout]. (1992). In R. Childress & K. Austin-Hemelt (Eds.), <u>CODA: Family of</u> <u>origin/family of choice, proceedings of the seventh International CODA Conference, New Orleans, July 16-19, 1992</u> (p. 44). Santa Barbara, CA: Children of Deaf Adults. [DEAF 306.874 I57c, 1992]

You don't have to do it all [Breakout summary]. (1994). In R. Shipman (Ed.), <u>Recollections: A decade of CODA,</u> <u>proceedings of the eighth International CODA Conference, Spokane, Washington, July 15-18, 1993</u> (p. 56). Santa Barbara, CA: Children of Deaf Adults. [DEAF 306.847 I57r, 1993]

You don't have to do it all [Breakout summary]. (1995). In K. Bruno & D. Eklof (Eds.), <u>You're among friends,</u> <u>welcome home: Proceedings of the ninth annual International CODA Conference, Oconomowoc, Wisconsin, July</u> <u>14-17, 1994</u> (p. 42). Santa Barbara, CA: Children of Deaf Adults. [DEAF 306.874 I57a, 1995]

Zamora, J. A. M. (Ed.). (1989). Regional discussion group #4 [Summary]. In T. H. Bull (Ed.), <u>New beginnings,</u> <u>new directions: Proceedings of the third National CODA Conference, Denver, Colorado, August 13-15, 1988</u> (p. 50). Santa Barbara, CA: Children of Deaf Adults. [DEAF 306.874 N3, 1988]

C
O
D
A

V

Ph.D. DISSERTATIONS

AND M. A. THESES

T
H
E
S
E
S

For future research:

The <u>American Annals of the Deaf,</u> official publication of the Conference of Educational Administrators Serving the Deaf and the Convention of American Instructors of the Deaf, publishes an annual reference issue in April. A section on "research on deafness" lists deafness-related doctoral dissertations completed in the previous year. The <u>Annals</u> was founded in 1847 and is the oldest educational journal for the deaf in the world. Their internet address provides additional information:

<http://www.gallaudet.edu:80/~pcnmpaad/index.html>

University Microfilms International has an extensive data base on CD-Rom. Check the "International Resources" section for further details.

Akiyama, R. M. (1981, September). Social sensitivity in hearing children of deaf parents. Unpublished master's thesis in child development, University of California, Davis. (51 pages) [DEAF 306.874 A94s, 1981]

Althaus, C. L. (1986, April). Mother-infant interactive behaviors: The impact of maternal deafness. (Doctoral dissertation, University of Virginia, 1984). Dissertation Abstracts International, 46 (10-B), 3586. (University Microfilms International No. 85-15,501 - 122 pages) [DEAF Microfilm 1972 1984]

Babb, R. L. (1969). The legal rights of the Deaf. Unpublished Graduate Project and master's thesis, Department of Special and Rehabilitation Education, National Leadership Training Program, San Fernando Valley State College at Northridge, California. (31 pages) [On order]

Bakker, P. (1987, October). Hearing children of deaf parents. In Autonomous languages: Signed and spoken languages created by children in the light of Bickerton's Language Bioprogram Hypothesis, University of Amsterdam, Institute for General Linguistics, No. 53 (pp. 26-30). Amsterdam: University of Amsterdam. (97 pages - Slightly different version of this thesis was written in 1985-1986 at the University of Amsterdam) [DEAF 401.93 B34a, 1987]

Balkind, S. K. (1994). The process of writing and rationale for "I love you daddy, but I hate that you're sick." Unpublished master's thesis in education, Bank Street College of Education, New York. (52 pages - Not available from University Microfilms International) [*]

Barba, S. M., & Slocum, S. A. (1993). Experiences of deaf adoptive parents throughout the adoption process. Unpublished M. S. W. thesis, Department of Social Work, Gallaudet University, Washington, DC (113 pages) [DEAF 362.734 B37e, 1993]

Blane, K. K. (1995, September). Hearing children of deaf parents: A bicultural approach. (Doctoral dissertation - Psy.D., Graduate Institute of Professional Psychology, University of Hartford). Dissertation Abstracts International, 56 (03), 1692B. (University Microfilms International No. 95-23,264 - 108 pages) [DEAF Microfilm 3669 1995]

Blankenstijn, C. J. K., & Bogaerde, B. v. d. (1989, November). Hand in hand: Tweetalige aspecten in het taalaanbod van drie dove moeders aan hun horende kinderen [Hand in hand: Bilingual aspects in the language input of three deaf mothers to their hearing children]. Unpublished master's thesis, Institute for General Linguistics, Amsterdam, The Netherlands. (143 pages - In Dutch - Need translation - Not available from University Microfilms International) {Bilingual aspects in the language input from three deaf mothers to their hearing children - ages 0.4 months to 1.5 years} [DEAF 401.93 B52h, 1989]

Blaskey, P. F. (1984, October). Socialization and personality development in hearing children of deaf parents. (Doctoral dissertation, College of Education, Temple University, 1983). Dissertation Abstracts International, 45 (04), 1271B. (University Microfilms International No. 84-10,182 - 114 pages) [DEAF Microfilm 1015 1983]

Boese, R. J. (1971, May). Native Sign Language and the problem of meaning. Unpublished doctoral dissertation, Department of Sociology, University of California, Santa Barbara. (University Microfilms International No. 72-07,449 - 395 pages - The author was Canadian and his parents were deaf) [DEAF Copy 1: 420 B63n, 1971 and DEAF Microfilm 512 1971]

Boster, S. J. (1981, December). Attitudes toward marriage in the deaf. Unpublished M. A. thesis, Graduate School, University of Texas at Austin. (67 pages) [On order]

Brelje, H. W., Jr. (1971, May). A study of the relationship between the articulation and vocabulary of hearing impaired parents and their normally hearing children. Unpublished doctoral dissertation, University of Portland. (58 pages - Not available from University Microfilms International. Listed in American Doctoral Dissertations, 1971 edition - Summarized briefly in M. Vernon's article in P. J. Fine (Ed.), Deafness in infancy and early childhood. [DEAF 362.7 F5d, 1974]) [DEAF 155.646 B7s, 1971]

Buchino, M. A. (1989, August). Hearing children of deaf parents: Personal perspectives. (Doctoral dissertation, University of Cincinnati, Department of Special Education, 1988). Dissertation Abstracts International, 50 (02), 409A. (University Microfilms International No. 89-08,448 - 227 pages) [DEAF Microfilm 2448 1988]

Buck, F. M. (1980, November). The influence of parental disability on children: An exploratory investigation of the adult children of spinal cord injured fathers. (Doctoral dissertation, clinical psychology, University of Arizona, Tucson). Dissertation Abstracts International, 41 (05), 1905B. (University Microfilms International No. 80-25,220 - 142 pages) [*]

(*) Bunde, L. T. (1976). Theory of ministry: Deaf parents - hearing children, toward a greater understanding of the unique aspects, needs, and problems relative to the communication factors caused by deafness. Unpublished doctor of ministry thesis, project report, summary article, Luther Theological Seminary, St. Paul, Minnesota. (51 pages) Available from Luther Northwestern Theological Seminary Library, 2375 Como Ave., St. Paul, MN 55108. (Also see the booklet published in 1979 as Deaf parents-hearing children: Toward a greater understanding of the unique aspects, needs and problems relative to the communication factors caused by deafness. Washington, DC: Registry of Interpreters for the Deaf, Signograph Series No. 1. - 100 pages - [DEAF 306.87 B87d, 1979] Also available from Ephphatha Services, American Lutheran Church, 422 S. 5th Street, Minneapolis, MN 55415 - 83 pages [*]) [DEAF 306.874 B87d, 1979b]

Busch, P. (1996). School-age hearing siblings' perceptions of parental competency in deaf-parented families. Unpublished doctoral dissertation, College of Nursing, University of Arizona, Tucson. [*]

Carmel, S. J. (1987, September). A study of Deaf culture in an American urban Deaf community. (Doctoral dissertation, Department of Anthropology, American University, Washington, DC). Dissertation Abstracts International, 48 (03), 684A. (University Microfilms International No. 87-12,617 - 471 pages) [DEAF 306.1 C3s, 1987 and DEAF Microfilm 2178 1987]

Chappell, E. H. (1987). Word categories of a hearing child of deaf parents. Unpublished master's thesis in Speech Pathology, Department of Speech-Language-Hearing: Sciences and Disorders, University of Kansas. (128 pages) [DEAF 401.93 C45w, 1987]

Charlson, E. S. (1990, May). Social cognition and self-concept of hearing adolescents with deaf parents. (Doctoral dissertation, Graduate Group in Special Education, University of California, Berkeley, with San Francisco State University, 1989). Dissertation Abstracts International, 50 (11), 3520A. (University Microfilms International No. 90-06,588 - 134 pages) [DEAF Microfilm 2566 1989]

Cline, R. O. (1967, August). Selected communication skills of normal hearing children born to deaf parents. Unpublished master's thesis, Department of Speech and Drama, University of Kansas, Lawrence, Kansas. (49 pages) [DEAF Microfilm 1800 1967 - bad quality microfilm and oversized for microfilm printer]

Cole, E. B. (1981, January). Vocalization development of a normally hearing infant of deaf parents. (Doctoral dissertation, University of Cincinnati, 1980). Dissertation Abstracts International, 41 (07), 2976A. (University Microfilms International No. 80-29,656 - 157 pages) [DEAF Microfilm 692 1980]

Crimi, C. J. (1995, January). The use of interpersonal skills training to enhance social support among parents who are mentally retarded and at risk for child maltreatment: A feasibility study. (Doctoral dissertation, School of Social Work, University of Washington). Dissertation Abstracts International, 56 (07), 2870A. (94 pages - Not available from University Microfilms International) [*]

DeLuigi, D. M. (1991, September). The relationship between parental hearing status and self-concept of deaf and hearing children. (Doctoral dissertation, Pace University, New York). Dissertation Abstracts International, 52 (03), 1747B. (University Microfilms International No. 91-14,487 - 110 pages) [DEAF Microfilm 3067 1991]

Elder, M. S. (1997, May). The search for synchrony: A hearing infant with deaf parents. (Unpublished doctoral thesis, Teacher's College, Columbia University, New York, 1996). Dissertation Abstracts International, 57 (11), 4593A. (University Microfilms International No. 97-13,874 - 128 pages) [Deaf Microfilm 3837 1997]

Falconer, J. A. (1978, January). Identification of deaf and hearing speakers by children with deaf parents and children unfamiliar with deafness. Unpublished M. A. thesis, Department of Psychology, Case Western Reserve University, Cleveland, Ohio. (26 pages) [DEAF 152.15 F34i, 1978]

Falconer, J. A. (1979, January). Expressive non-verbal communication by hearing children of deaf parents. (Doctoral dissertation, Department of Psychology, Case Western Reserve University, Cleveland, Ohio, 1978). Dissertation Abstracts International, 39 (07), 3508B. (University Microfilms International No. 79-01,513 - 36 pages) [DEAF Microfilm 483 1978]

Feldman, D. D. (1974, Winter). A comparative examination of the language ability of pre-school hearing children of deaf and of hearing parents. (Unpublished master's thesis, School of Education, California State University, Long Beach, July, 1974). Master's Abstracts International, 12 (04), 389. (University Microfilms International No. M-6,357 - 81 pages) [DEAF Microfilm 618 1974]

Fink, L. A. W. (1985). A child's subculture: The experience of growing up in the Deaf culture, a project based upon an independent investigation. Unpublished M. S. W. thesis, Smith College School for Social Work, Northampton, Massachusetts. (81 pages - Abstract reprinted in the February, 1986, issue of the CODA Newsletter, 3 (1), 5. [UNIV DEAF Periodicals]) [DEAF 305.23 F5c, 1985]

Garner, D. H. (1984, April). An investigation of the comprehensibility of manually-coded English texts versus spoken English texts by normally-hearing adults. (Doctoral dissertation, Department of Human Development, University of Maryland, College Park, Maryland, 1983). Dissertation Abstracts International, 44 (10), 2931A. (University Microfilms International No. 84-02,565 - 176 pages) [DEAF Microfilm 3679 1983]

Gorman, P. P. (1960, February). Certain social and psychological difficulties facing the deaf person in the English community. Unpublished doctoral dissertation, University of Cambridge. (328 pages - Pierre Patrick Gorman was a librarian at the Royal National Institute for the Deaf, RNID, London) [DEAF 301.1 G6c, 1960]

Gosselin, D. (1994). School-aged hearing childrens perceptions of family life in deaf-parented families. Unpublished master's thesis, University of Arizona, Tucson. [*]

Halpern, K. P. (1989). Hearing and deaf parents' reactions to deafness in their child. Unpublished M. S. thesis, Emerson College. (71 pages) [*]

Hartley, G. M. (1989, June). Aspects of the home care of young deaf children of deaf parents. (Unpublished doctoral dissertation, University of Nottingham, United Kingdom, 1988). Dissertation Abstracts International, 49

THESES

207

(12), 3884A. (University Microfilms Inc., No. AAC D-84,729 - 359 pages) [DEAF Microfilm 3614 1988]

(*) Higgins, P. C. (1978, March). The Deaf community: Identity and interaction in a hearing world. (Doctoral dissertation, Department of Sociology, Northwestern University, 1977). Dissertation Abstracts International, 38 (09), 5723A. (University Microfilms International No. 78-711 - 189 pages) [DEAF Microfilm 345 1977] (Published in 1980 as Outsiders in a hearing world: Sociology of deafness. Beverly Hills, CA: Sage Publications) [DEAF 305 H5o, 1980]

Huddleston, D. J. (1986). Development of form, content, and use in the language of a normal hearing child of deaf parents. Unpublished master's thesis, South Carolina State College (now University), Orangeburg, South Carolina. (63 pages) [*]

Ingram, R. M. (1985). Recognition memory among Sign Language interpreters. Unpublished master's thesis, Brown University. (Subsequently published in two parts: [1] R. M. Ingram (1988, Spring). Interpreters' recognition of structure and meaning. Sign Language Studies, 58, 21-36. [UNIV RESERVE] Reprinted in D. Cokely (Ed.), Sign Language interpreters and interpreting (pp. 99-119). Burtonsville, MD: Linstok Press, 1992. [DEAF 418.02 S53, 1992] [2] R. M. Ingram (1985). Simultaneous interpretation of Sign Languages: Semiotic and psycholinguistic perspectives. Multilingua, 4 (2), 91-102. [*]) {Subjects were hearing interpreters with deaf parents} [*]

(*) Janson, J. L. (1996, September). Issues surrounding hearing children of deaf adults. Unpublished doctoral - Psy.D. thesis, School of Professional Psychology, Wright State University, Dayton, Ohio. (52 pages. In addition, the appendix contains a "Therapist's Guide for the CODA Workbook" - 8 pages - and a "CODA Workbook" - 41 pages) [*]

Johnson, H. A. (1981, January). A longitudinal ethnographic investigation of the development of interactional strategies by a normally hearing infant of deaf parents. (Doctoral dissertation, University of Cincinnati, 1980). Dissertation Abstracts International, 41 (07), 3281A-3282A. (University Microfilms International No. 80-29,671 - 112 pages) [DEAF Microfilm 690 1980]

Jones, E. G. (1987, June). Deaf adults as parents: A descriptive study. (Doctoral dissertation, College of Nursing, University of Arizona, Tucson, 1986). Dissertation Abstracts International, 47 (12), 4824B. (University Microfilms International No. 87-02,346 - 218 pages - Need author's permission to order) [DEAF Microfilm 3740 1987]

Jones, M. L. (1976, November). A longitudinal investigation into the acquisition of question formation in English and American Sign Language by three hearing children with deaf parents. (Doctoral dissertation, University of Illinois at Urbana-Champaign). Dissertation Abstracts International, 37 (05), 2831A. (University Microfilms International No. 76-24,111 - 77 pages) [DEAF Microfilm 260 1976]

Kanda, J. H. (1989, October). Characteristics of certified Sign Language interpreters including patterns of brain dominance. (Doctoral dissertation, Department of Educational Leadership, Brigham Young University, Provo, Utah, December, 1988). Dissertation Abstracts International, 50 (04), 863A. (University Microfilms International No. 89-07,503 - 199 pages) [DEAF Microfilm 2484 1988]

Kannapell, B. M. (1985, July). Language choice reflects identity choice: A sociolinguistic study of deaf college students. (Doctoral dissertation, Georgetown University, Washington, DC). Dissertation Abstracts International, 47 (01), 165A. (University Microfilms International No. 86-06,902 - 382 pages - Published in 1993 by Linstok Press, Inc., Burtonsville, Maryland, under the title Language choice and identity. [DEAF 3306.44 K3la, 1993]) [DEAF Microfilm 1937 1985]

Kettrick, C. (1986, June). Cerebral lateralization for ASL and English in Deaf and hearing native and non-native signers. (Doctoral dissertation, Department of Linguistics, University of Washington, 1985). Dissertation Abstracts International, 46 (12), 3706A. (University Microfilms International No. 86-03,108 - 134 pages) [DEAF Microfilm 1877 1985]

Kilroy, L. (1995, October). An exploratory study of the adaptive and emotional experiences of hearing children of deaf parents. (Doctoral dissertation, California School of Professional Psychology, Los Angeles). Dissertation Abstracts International, 56 (04), 2331B. (University Microfilms International No. 95-26,781 - 264 pages) [DEAF Microfilm 3697 1995]

Leven, R. (1981, May). Hearing children of deaf parents: A pilot study. Unpublished paper presented as partial fulfillment of the master's degree in education, Department of Education of Exceptional Children, San Francisco State University. (61 pages) [On order]

Liedel, J. A. (1997, April). Personality types and interpersonal styles of interpreters for deaf and hard of hearing individuals: Implications for administrators in K-12 educational settings. (Doctoral dissertation, Department of Educational Services and Research, The Ohio State University, Columbus, 1996). Dissertation Abstracts International, 57 (10), 4326A. (University Microfilms International No. 97-10,606 - 230 pages) [DEAF Microfilm 3825 1997]

Livingston, R. H. (1997, March). Growing up hearing with deaf parents: The influences on adult patterns of relating and on self/other awareness. (Doctoral dissertation, Graduate School of Arts and Sciences, Teacher's College, Columbia University, New York). Dissertation Abstracts International, 58 (09), 5127B. (University Microfilms International No. 98-09,738 - 205 pages) [DEAF 306.874 L58g, 1997]

Lynch, A. A. (1988, May). Adult hearing offspring of deaf parents: A study of personality variables. Unpublished master's thesis in counseling, California State University, Hayward. (65 pages - Not available from University Microfilms International) [*]

Maestas y Moores, M. J. (1981, January). A descriptive study of communication modes and pragmatic functions used by three prelinguistic, profoundly deaf mothers with their infants one to six months of age in their homes. (Doctoral dissertation, Department of Special Education, University of Minnesota, 1980). Dissertation Abstracts International, 41 (07), 3049A-3050A. (University Microfilms International No. 81-02,121 - 121 pages) [DEAF Microfilm 920 1980]

Mallory, B. L. (1992, Fall). Deaf parents of hearing children: Aspects of parenting performance. Unpublished doctoral dissertation, Department of Educational Psychology, University of Alberta, Edmonton, Alberta, Canada. (189 pages - Not available from University Microfilms International) [DEAF 306.874 M34d, 1992]

Marshall, K. G. (1979, May). A comparison of the self concepts of normally hearing offspring of deaf parents with those of normally hearing offspring of normally hearing parents. (Doctoral dissertation, School of Special Education and Rehabilitation, University of Northern Colorado, Greeley, 1978). Dissertation Abstracts International, 39 (11), 6699A. (University Microfilms International No. 79-10,307 - 73 pages) [DEAF Microfilm 515 1978]

McIntosh, R. A. (1995, December). Self-disclosure in deaf-hearing, deaf-deaf, and hearing-hearing married couples: A look at frequency, value, and contexts in relation to marital satisfaction. (Doctoral dissertation, Department of Speech Communication, University of Texas at Austin). Dissertation Abstracts International, 56 (06), 2045A. (University Microfilms International No. 95-34,883 - 179 pages) [DEAF Microfilm 3721 1995]

THESES

McKee, D. E. (1988, October). An analysis of specialized cognitive functions in deaf and hearing signers. (Doctoral dissertation, School of Education, University of Pittsburgh, 1987). Dissertation Abstracts International, 49 (04), 768A. (University Microfilms International No. 88-09,180 - 182 pages) [DEAF Microfilm 2297 1987]

Meilicke, M. J. (1994, June). Auditory processing in hearing children of deaf parents. (Doctoral dissertation, Department of Psychology, United States International University, San Diego, California, 1993). Dissertation Abstracts International, 54 (12), 6479B-6480B. (University Microfilms International No. 94-10,267 - 248 pages) [DEAF Microfilm 3594 1993]

Morrison, A. Y. (1986). A case study of a hearing child with deaf parents. Unpublished master's thesis in Speech and Language Pathology, Department of Speech-Language-Hearing: Sciences and Disorders, Division of Speech and Drama, University of Kansas. (66 pages) [DEAF 401.93 M67c, 1986]

Murphy, J. E. (1987). Language acquisition in hearing children of deaf parents. Unpublished M.Sp.Th. thesis, Department of Speech Pathology and Audiology, University of Queensland, Australia. (Not available from University Microfilms International) [On order]

Nichols, M. L. (1990, May). The self-esteem of normal children of mothers with mental retardation: An exploratory study. (Doctoral dissertation, Division of Counseling and Educational Psychology and the Graduate School, University of Oregon, August, 1989). Dissertation Abstracts International, 50 (11), 3529A. (University Microfilms International No. 90-10,143 - 211 pages) [*]

Oyer, E. J. (1969, December). Relationship of homemakers' hearing losses to family integration. (Doctoral dissertation, Home Economics, Michigan State University). Dissertation Abstracts International, 30 (06), 2781B. (101 pages) [DEAF Microfilm 3314 1969]

Paquin, M. M. (1993, June). The superior nonverbal intellectual performance of deaf children of deaf parents: An investigation of the genetic hypothesis. (Doctoral dissertation, California School of Professional Psychology, Berkeley/Alameda, California). Dissertation Abstracts International, 53 (12), 6568B. (University Microfilms International No. 93-12,790 - 74 pages) [DEAF Microfilm 3527 1992]

(*) Preston, P. M. (1993, March). Mother father deaf: Identity on the margins of culture. (Doctoral dissertation, Department of Medical Anthropology, University of California, San Francisco and Berkeley, 1992). Dissertation Abstracts International, 53 (09), 3270A. (University Microfilms International No. 93-03,549 - 397 pages) (Published in 1994 as *Mother father deaf: Living between sound and silence*, Harvard University Press, Cambridge, MA. [DEAF 306.874 P73m, 1994]) {The author is hearing and has deaf parents. "Based on 150 interviews with adult hearing children of deaf parents throughout the United States...[this book] is rich in anecdote and analysis, remarkable for its insights into a family life normally closed to outsiders." - *Booklist* "I have no doubt that Preston's work is now the major study on this topic and will be so regarded by researchers in deafness and anyone interested in the study of culture and its transmission through the family...Preston's interviews will lay to rest many of the stereotypes and myths that exist in both the media and the literature of deafness." John S. Schuchman, Gallaudet University - book jacket - highly recommended} [DEAF Microfilm 2915 1992]

Quick, S. (1996). Deaf mother's views of family life in families with deaf parents and hearing children. Unpublished M. S. thesis, College of Nursing, University of Arizona, Tucson. (108 pages) [DEAF 306.874 Q84d, 1996]

Richmond-Welty, E. D. (1996). Visual interaction styles of twins born to deaf parents. Unpublished master's thesis, cognitive psychology, Wayne State University, Detroit, Michigan. (63 pages) [*]

Rienzi, B. A. M. (1984, July). The deaf parent/hearing child family: Family adaptability and the influential power of the child. (Doctoral dissertation, Department of Clinical Psychology, California School of Professional Psychology, Fresno, 1983). Dissertation Abstracts International, 45 (01), 364B. (University Microfilms International No. 84-09,551 - 189 pages) [DEAF Microfilm 1047 1983]

Riley, K. E. (1997). Family functioning in a deaf-parented family with hearing adolescents: An illustrative case study. Unpublished doctoral dissertation, College of Nursing, University of Arizona, Tucson. [*]

Rutherford, S. D. (1988, March). A study of American deaf folklore. (Doctoral dissertation, Department of Deaf Studies, Language, Culture and Group Identity, University of California, Berkeley, May, 1987). Dissertation Abstracts International, 48 (09), 2420A. (University Microfilms International No. 87-26,354 - 232 pages - Published with the same title in 1993 by Linstok Press, Burtonsville, MD. [DEAF 398.2 R87s, 1993]) [DEAF Microfilm 2253 1987]

Sanders, M. W. (1984, December). An examination of the academic achievement and social/emotional adjustment of normally hearing children reared by deaf parents. (Doctoral dissertation, University of Tennessee, Knoxville). Dissertation Abstracts International, 45 (06), 1923B. (University Microfilms International No. 84-21,405 - 55 pages) [DEAF Microfilm 1215 1984]

Schetina, K. R. (1979, June). An exploratory study of deaf parents and their hearing children. Unpublished M. S. W. thesis, Graduate School of Social Welfare, University of California, Los Angeles. (151 pages - Not available through University Microfilms International) [DEAF 306.874 S33e, 1979]

Schiff, N. B. (1977, January). The development of form and meaning in the language of hearing children of deaf parents. (Doctoral dissertation, Columbia University, New York, 1976). Dissertation Abstracts International, 37 (07), 4289A-4290A. (University Microfilms International No. 76-29,860 - 190 pages) [DEAF Microfilm 620 1976]

Searls, J. M. (1990, August). A study of parental deafness as a factor in the development of self-concept in samples of deaf and hearing college students. (Doctoral dissertation, Department of Counseling and Development, American University, Washington, DC., 1989). Dissertation Abstracts International, 51 (02), 418A. (University Microfilms International No. 90-14,654 - 117 pages) [DEAF Microfilm 2469 1990]

Selph, B. S. (1992). Hearing children of deaf parents: A bicultural/bilingual perspective. Unpublished master's thesis, Department of Sociology, University of North Carolina, Charlotte. (143 pages) [*]

Shapiro, C. F. (1986). The parenting skills of deaf parents: A parent and child assessment, a project based upon an independent investigation. Unpublished M. S. W. thesis, School for Social Work, Smith College, Northampton, Massachusetts. (82 pages) [On order]

Siedlecki, T., Jr. (1992, August). The acquisition of American Sign Language phonology by young children of deaf parents. (Doctoral dissertation, University of Virginia, 1991). Dissertation Abstracts International, 53 (02), 1085B. (University Microfilms International No. 92-19,292 - 211 pages) [DEAF Microfilm 2952 1991]

Stewart, D. L. (1986). A comparison of a deaf mother's speech intonation to that of her normally hearing son. Unpublished master's thesis, Department of Speech-Language-Hearing: Sciences and Disorders and the Graduate Faculty, University of Kansas. (125 pages) [DEAF 401.93 S73c, 1986]

Szymoniak, E. (1977). Attitudes toward deafness: Children of deaf parents. Unpublished master's thesis, Iowa State University of Science and Technology, Ames, Iowa. (84 pages) [DEAF 303.38 S9a, 1977]

THESES

211

Tendler, R. (1976, February). Maternal correlates of differentiation in hearing children of the deaf. (Doctoral dissertation, Ferkauf Graduate School of Humanities and Social Sciences, Yeshiva University, New York, 1975). Dissertation Abstracts International, 36 (08), 4183B. (University Microfilms International No. 76-4,563 - 118 pages) [DEAF Microfilm 201 1975]

Todd, P. H., III. (1972). From Sign Language to speech: Delayed acquisition of English by a hearing child of deaf parents. Unpublished doctoral dissertation, Department of Psychology, University of California, Berkeley. (253 pages - Not available from University Microfilms International. Listed in the 1973 edition of American Doctoral Dissertations) {Dr. Ursula Bellugi at the Salk Institute for Biological Studies in La Jolla, California, served on Peyton Todd's dissertation committee. This piqued her interest in American Sign Language and the rest is history} [DEAF 472 T6f, 1972]

Topmiller, M. J. (1996). A comparison of deaf and hearing fathers' interactions with their hearing infants and toddlers. Unpublished M. S. thesis, College of Nursing, University of Arizona, Tucson. (116 pages) [On order]

(#) Walton, J. M. (1992, December). Development of vocalizations and communicative acts of a hearing infant in a deaf environment. Unpublished master's thesis in Speech-Language Pathology, Emerson College, Boston. (71 pages - pages 27, 43, 50, 56, 60, 68-69 are missing in the Emerson College Library copy - Not available from University Microfilms International) [DEAF 401.93 W34d, 1992]

Watkins, R. V. (1987, May). Language acquisition in a hearing child of deaf parents: A study of language errors. Unpublished master's thesis, Child Language Program and Graduate School, University of Kansas. (115 pages) [DEAF 401.93 W37l, 1987]

Waxman, R. P. (1996). A longitudinal study of deaf and hearing mothers' use of visual-tactile attention strategies with deaf and hearing children. (Doctoral dissertation, The American University, Washington, DC). Dissertation Abstracts International, 57 (09), 5952B. (University Microfilms International No. 97-06,132 - 84 pages) [DEAF Microfilm 3846 1996]

Waxman, R. P. (1997, February). Differing patterns of dyadic interaction during free-play between deaf and hearing mothers and their deaf and hearing children. (Master's thesis, Department of Psychology, The American University, Washington, DC., 1996). Master's Abstracts International, 35 (01), 355. (52 pages - Not available for interlibrary loan) [C]

Weiner, M. T. (1997, December). Raising bicultural and bilingual children: Deaf parents' perceptions. (Doctoral dissertation, Department of Human Development, University of Maryland, College Park). Dissertation Abstracts International. (155 pages - University Microfilms International) [On order]

Weisbach, E. I. (1976). A descriptive study of the language development of four normal children of deaf-mute parents. Unpublished project submitted for the Seminar in Learning Disabilities, Graduate Division, Glassboro State College (now Rowan University), Glassboro, New Jersey. (30 pages) [DEAF 401.93 W447d, 1976]

White, B. J. (In progress). The effects of perceptions of social support and entitlement on family functioning in Deaf-parented adoptive families. (D.S.W. dissertation, National Catholic School of Social Service, Catholic University of America, Washington, DC).

(*) Winefield, R. M. (1981, December). Bell, Gallaudet, and the Sign Language debate: An historical analysis of the communication controversy in education of the deaf. (Doctoral dissertation, Harvard University). Dissertation Abstracts International, 42 (06), 2536A. (University Microfilms International No. 81-25,504 - 278 pages - Published in 1987 by the Gallaudet University Press as *Never the Twain Shall Meet: Bell, Gallaudet, and the Communication Debate.* [DEAF 371.301 W5n, 1987]) [DEAF Microfilm 742 1981]

**T
H
E
S
E
S**

VI

VIDEO AND AUDIO TAPES,

FILMS AND COMPACT DISCS

VIDEO

About being deaf. (1978). 30 minutes. Color. Sound. Captioned. Director, Ray Williams. Producer, Nancy Rosenblatt. Student intern, Toby Silver. {Timothy Medina interviews a hearing mother of a deaf child and Carol Pace, a hearing child (now adult) of deaf parents} [Use limited to Gallaudet University campus only - GA: UNIV Cable TV U-Matic 1223]

Academy Awards ceremonies. (1976, March 29). 3 minutes. Color. Sound. VHS. Beverly Hills, CA: The Academy of Motion Picture Arts and Sciences, 8949 Wilshire Blvd., Beverly Hills, CA 90211-1972 (310) 247-3000 (Internet: <http://www.ampas.org>) {Louise Fletcher accepts the 1975 Academy Award for Best Actress for her role as Nurse Ratched in the 1975 movie, *One Flew Over the Cuckoo's Nest*, and signs her thanks to her deaf parents at the 48th Annual Academy Awards ceremonies. The film won four oscars: Best Actor (Jack Nicholson), Best Actress, Best Picture and Best Directing (Milos Forman)} [*]

American culture: the Deaf perspective. (1984). 116 minutes. Color. Sound. Signed. Produced by the San Francisco Public Library with the assistance of D.E.A.F. Media Inc., Berkeley, California. (Program 1: Deaf Heritage; program 2: Deaf Folklore; program 3: Deaf Literature; program 4: Deaf Minorities) {A four-part series exploring the culture and heritage of Deaf Americans} [Use limited to Gallaudet University campus only - GA: UNIV Cable TV, VHS 25, UNIV RESERVE]

ASL pah! Deaf student's perspectives on their language. (1992). 65 minutes. Color. VHS. Producers: Clayton Valli, Ceil Lucas, Esme Farb and Paul Kulick. Director Dennis Cokely. Write SMI, Sign Media Inc., Linstok Press, 4020 Blackburn Lane, Burtonsville, MD 20866 (No voice-over - There is also an accompanying 65-page booklet) [GA: UNIV Cable TV, VHS 90]

Beauty and the beast: Sticks and stones (CBS Series). (1989). 60 minutes. Color. Sound. Producer, George R. R. Martin. Co-producers: Alex Gansa and Howard Gordon. Creator, Ron Koslow. Writers: Howard Gordon and Alex Gansa. Director, Bruce Malmuth. {A coda undercover cop is emotionally involved with a deaf gang member} [GA: UNIV Cable TV U-Matic 3051]

The best of Zoom: Helping my parents, Alberta. (1976). 7 minutes. Color. Sound. 16 mm film. Produced by WGBH Educational Foundation, Boston, for the PBS children's program *Zoom*. Write Films, Inc., 1144 Wilmette Ave., Wilmette, IL 60091 {Alberta, the hearing daughter of deaf parents, describes how she helps her parents by interpreting. Alberta wants to work with deaf people when she grows up so she can share what she has learned. A very positive portrait of a Deaf, Black family} [*]

Beth Ann Dukes [CD]. (1996). 43 minutes. Compact disc and cassette tape. Produced by Beth Ann Dukes and Phil Medley. Order from Miller-Dukes Enterprises, P.O. Box 790, Woodbury, GA 30293 (# BAD 1711-2 - Beth Ann Dukes is hearing and her parents are deaf) {The album is dedicated to "my mom," Rosemary Smith Dukes and contains the song "Mom and Dad." "Mom and Dad: thank you for encouraging me to be creative in music. Even though you couldn't hear my music, you felt it in your hearts, and thank you for my first set of drums when I was a little girl" - Liner notes} [*]

Beyond silence (Jenseits der Stille). (1996). 107 minutes. Color. In German with English subtitles. Director, Caroline Link. Producers: Jakob Claussen, Thomas Wöbke and Luggi Waldleitner. Writers: Caroline Link and Beth Serlin. Cast: Tatjan Trieb, Sylvie Testud, and Sybille Canonica. Emmanuelle Laborit and Howie Seago are deaf actors. Production company: Claussen Wöbke Filmproduktion, GmbH/Roxy-Film GmbH Production, Herzog-Wilhelm Str. 27, Munich 80331, Germany. (Shown at the Fifth Annual RECENT FILMS FROM GERMANY series sponsored by The Goethe Institute of Washington, D. C., in January, 1996. Tied for the Grand Prix award for Best Picture at the 10th Tokyo International Film Festival, 1997. Winner, Best Picture, Vancouver Film Festival. Shown at the London Film Festival, 1997. Nominated for an Academy Award for Best Foreign Language Film, 1997.

VIDEO

Shown at the Twelfth Annual Washington, D. C. International Film Festival - Filmfest DC - April 22-May 3, 1998) {"Lara is a pretty, precocious nine-year old who has always skated between two worlds: the silent one of her loving parents, Martin and Kai, who are deaf, and the hearing world of Martin's family, school and music. As her parents' interpreter, Lara must sacrifice time from her own schooling and endure the taunts of classmates. The close-knit family is rent apart when Aunt Clarissa, Martin's wealthy, self-centered sister, takes an interest in Lara's future. The rift comes in the form of a clarinet passed from Clarissa to Lara -- following her passion for music leads to an inexorable separation between Lara and her father. Through striking out on her own, Lara must find a way to bridge silence and sound. Director Caroline Link gives us a warm but realistic portrayal of family relationships and the capacity within us to understand another world which we can never fully inhabit. T. Hanna" - From the 1996 Mill Valley (California) Film Festival book} [*]

Big story: Born - a son: NBC-TV. (1955, June 17). 30 minutes. Black and white. {The story is about a welfare agency's attempt to take a newborn infant away from a deaf/blind couple} [*]

Biography: Alexander Graham Bell, voice of invention. (1996). 50 minutes. Color. Sound. VHS. Produced by the Art and Entertainment Television Networks. Order AAE-14146 from Art and Entertainment Television Networks, (800) 344-6336. {"His drive to help his deaf mother communicate led to one of the most important inventions of the 20th century. But the telephone was only one of many notable contributions he made to fields ranging from medicine to aviation" - Biography shop} [*]

Biography: Lon Chaney Jr., son of a thousand faces. (1995). 50 minutes. Color. Sound. VHS. Produced by the Art and Entertainment Television Networks. Order AAE-14057 from Art and Entertainment Television Networks, (800) 344-6336. {"He was a stillborn baby whose father shocked him into life by plunging him in an icy lake. As a famous actor he shocked movie audiences worldwide with his classic portrayals of monsters like the Wolf Man. Lon Chaney, Jr., inherited more than his father's name. The son of the silent-era 'Man of a Thousand Faces' was a gifted performer in his own right...For the first time since his death, family member share their memories of the troubled actor - from his strained relationship with his father to the problems with alcoholism and self-doubt that marked the last years of his career...." - Biography shop} [*]

The Bridge. (1992). 60 minutes. Color. Written and directed by William Moses, faculty member at Gallaudet University. Play presented in American Sign Language. Washington, DC: Gallaudet University. Order No. VTB from Deaf Mosaic, Department of Television, Film and Photography, Gallaudet University, 800 Florida Ave., N.E., Washington, DC 20002 [GA: UNIV Cable TV, VHS 288]

CBS Morning News. (1986, October 26). (Reported in the November, 1986, issue of the CODA Newsletter, 3 (4), 2 [UNIV DEAF Periodicals]) {An interview with Lou Ann Walker about her book, *A Loss for Words*} [*]

CBS Movie of the Week: Bridge to silence. (1989). 95 minutes. Color. Sound. Closed-captioned. Fries Entertainment, Inc. Producer, Charles Fries. Director, Karen Arthur. Screenplay by Louisa Burns-Bisogno. Starring Lee Remick as the hearing mother and Marlee Matlin as her deaf daughter. Allison Silva is a 6-year-old coda who played the daughter and another coda, Candace Broecker, played the part of Marlee Matlin's best friend. Also starred Josef Sommer and Michael O'Keefe. (An auditions announcement for the role of the hearing granddaughter was published in the November, 1988, issue of the CODA Connection, 5 (4), 5. [UNIV DEAF Periodicals] She had to be between the ages of four and seven and be a fluent signer) {This is the story of a young deaf widow battling her hearing mother for custody of her (the deaf daughter's) hearing child} [GA: UNIV Cable TV U-Matic 3086]

Dateline: Baby Talk (NBC-TV). (1996, May 7). 9 minutes. Color. Sound. Closed-captioned. Producer, Ruth Chenetz Gaffin. Editor: Robert Q. Allen. Moderator: Jane Pauley. Write Dateline NBC, 30 Rockefeller Plaza, New

York, NY 10112 (800) 420-2626 <dateline@nbc.com> {An interview with Drs. Linda Acredolo and Susan Goodwyn, authors of <u>Baby Signs: How to talk with your baby before your baby can talk</u>} [*]

Dateline: Hear no evil (NBC-TV). (1997, July 14). 21 minutes. Color. Sound. Closed captioned. Reporter, Sara James. Producer, Lisa Freed. Write Dateline NBC, 30 Rockefeller Plaza, New York, NY 10112 (800) 420-2626 <dateline@nbc.com> {Keri Knickerbocker Webb and her Canadian husband, Gerald Webb, have sought and lost custody of their hearing daughter, Angie Genevieve. The court allowed Keri's step mother-in-law, Diane Knickerbocker, to adopt her. The Webbs have not seen their daughter for six years and have two other children, one of whom was taken away from them for a short period of time. This case involves the Department of Social Services in Jackson County, Michigan} [*]

Deaf Culture lecture: Cultural differences. (1994). 35 minutes. Color. Sound. VHS. Closed-captioned. In American Sign Language with English voice-over by Bonnie Sherwood. Order video No. 8I from Sign Enhancers, Inc., P.O. Box 12687, Salem, OR 97309-0687 {Nathie Marbury, a Black Deaf mother of two hearing children, shares humorous and poignant stories. Several are from experiences with her daughters: their need for eye-contact, Deaf Culture leave-taking rituals and the overnight (hearing) friend} [GA: UNIV Cable TV, VHS 388]

Deaf Culture lecture: Shared wisdom for families. (1996). 45 minutes. Color. Sound. VHS. Closed-captioned. In American Sign Language with English voice-over by Janet Maxwell. Order video No. 8L from Sign Enhancers, Inc., P.O. Box 12687, Salem, OR 97309-0687 {Nathie Marbury, a Black Deaf mother of two hearing children, shares parenting stories: how deaf parents test their infant's hearing status; advice to deaf parents who have hearing children and those who have both hearing and deaf children; and wisdom for deaf parents who have deaf children} [GA: UNIV Cable TV, VHS 514]

Deaf Culture lecture: Tools for a cross-cultural adventure. (1996). 45 minutes. Color. Sound. VHS. Closed-captioned. In American Sign Language with English voice-over by Janet Maxwell. Order video No. 8K from Sign Enhancers, Inc., P.O. Box 12687, Salem, OR 97309-0687 {Nathie Marbury, a Black Deaf mother of two hearing children, shares an eclectic, autobiographical and humorous series of stories that illustrate the numerous cross-cultural conflicts (hearing and Deaf) one experiences growing up hearing in a family with deaf parents. A touching and poignant reminder of the need for education within the community} [GA: UNIV Cable TV, VHS 515]

Deaf Mosaic: Adoption of deaf children by deaf families. Program No. 110. (1985, February). 28 minutes. Color. Signed, sound and open captioned. Washington, DC: Gallaudet University. Order No. DM 110 from Deaf Mosaic, Department of Television, Film and Photography, Gallaudet University, 800 Florida Ave., N.E., Washington, DC 20002. {Rachel Harris visits the homes of five adopted deaf children. Susan Wrightson with Associated Catholic Charities, Baltimore, Maryland, is interviewed. Diane Duval, who set up an adoption program in Korea, is interviewed} [GA: UNIV Cable TV U-Matic 2550]

Deaf Mosaic: Adoption services bring a deaf family together with a Russian child who needs a home. Program No. 902. (1993, June). 28 minutes. Color. Sound. VHS. Signed, sound and open captioned. Washington, DC: Gallaudet University. Order No. DM 902 from Deaf Mosaic, Department of Television, Film and Photography, Gallaudet University, 800 Florida Ave., N.E., Washington, DC 20002 {Tammy and Jerome Kerchner set about to adopt a deaf child from a Russian orphanage. They worked with Susan Wrightson, Coordinator at Adoption Advocates for Hearing Impaired Children of Baltimore, Maryland. They have to make an adjustment similar to hearing parents who unexpectedly find they have a deaf child. Nearly three-year-old Arthur is hearing} [GA: UNIV Cable TV U-Matic 2550]

Deaf Mosaic: The Alexander Graham Bell Association of the Deaf. Program No. 607. (1990, November). 28 minutes. Color. Sound. Signed and closed-captioned. Washington, DC: Gallaudet University. Order No. DM 607

V
I
D
E
O

from Deaf Mosaic, Department of Television, Film and Photography, Gallaudet University, 800 Florida Ave., N.E., Washington, DC 20002 {Background on the organization and the founder whose mother was deaf} [GA: UNIV Cable TV U-Matic 2550]

Deaf Mosaic: The Bi-Cultural Center [TBC] in Riverdale, Maryland. Program No. 508. (1989, November). 28 minutes. Color. Signed and open captioned. Produced by Mike Montagnino. Washington, DC: Gallaudet University. Order No. DM 508 from Deaf Mosaic, Department of Television, Film and Photography, Gallaudet University, 800 Florida Ave., N.E., Washington, DC 20002 {In this segment Betty Colonomos, who is hearing and parents are deaf, and M. J. Bienvenu, who is deaf, are interviewed about the philosophy and goals of The Bicultural Center} [GA: UNIV Cable TV U-Matic 2550]

Deaf Mosaic: A bridge between. Program No. 212. (1987, February). 28 minutes. Color. Sound. Signed and open captioned. Produced by Tony Hornick and Annjoy Marcus. Washington, DC: Gallaudet University. Order No. DM 212 from Deaf Mosaic, Department of Television, Film and Photography, Gallaudet University, 800 Florida Ave., N.E., Washington, DC 20002 {Hornick interviews Lou Ann Walker, author of *A Loss for Words*, about why she wrote the book and public and deaf community reaction} [GA: UNIV Cable TV U-Matic 2550]

Deaf Mosaic, clips from recent programs: *Cagney and Lacey*, *Sesame Street*, and *Love is Never Silent*. Program No. 411. (1989, January). 28 minutes. Color. Sound. VHS. Signed and open captioned. Washington, DC: Gallaudet University. Order No. DM 902 from Deaf Mosaic, Department of Television, Film and Photography, Gallaudet University, 800 Florida Ave., N.E., Washington, DC 20002 [GA: UNIV Cable TV U-Matic 2550]

Deaf Mosaic: Interview with TV producer Julianna Fjeld. Program No. 209. (1986, November). 28 minutes. Color. Sound. Signed and open captioned. Washington, DC: Gallaudet University. Order No. DM 209 from Deaf Mosaic, Department of Television, Film and Photography, Gallaudet University, 800 Florida Ave., N.E., Washington, DC 20002 {Jane Norman interviews Julianna Fjeld, co-executive producer of *Love is Never Silent*, the Hallmark Hall of Fame made-for-television adaptation of Joanne Greenberg's novel, *In This Sign*. Fjeld received the coveted Emmy for best dramatic program in 1986} [GA: UNIV Cable TV U-Matic 2550]

Deaf Mosaic: Julianna Fjeld interviewed by Jane Norman. Program No. 607. (1990, November). 28 minutes. Color. Sound. VHS. Signed and closed-captioned. Washington, DC: Gallaudet University. Order No. DM 607 from Deaf Mosaic, Department of Television, Film and Photography, Gallaudet University, 800 Florida Ave., N.E., Washington, DC 20002 {Jane Norman interviews Fjeld about receiving the Emmy for *Love is Never Silent* and what that means for career opportunities for other deaf persons} [GA: UNIV Cable TV U-Matic 2550]

Deaf Mosaic: KODA, a national organization for Kids of Deaf Adults. Program No. 908. (1993, December). 28 minutes. Color. Sound. VHS. Signed and open captioned. Washington, DC: Gallaudet University. Order No. DM 908 from Deaf Mosaic, Department of Television, Film and Photography, Gallaudet University, 800 Florida Ave., N.E., Washington, DC 20002 {Deaf members of the Washington, D. C. Metropolitan area KODA organization and two hearing children of deaf parents are interviewed} [GA: UNIV Cable TV U-Matic 2550]

Deaf Mosaic: Mosaic Memoirs, Program No. 507. (1989, October). 28 minutes. Color. Sound. Signed and open captioned. Washington, DC: Gallaudet University. Order No. DM 507 from Deaf Mosaic, Department of Television, Film and Photography, Gallaudet University, 800 Florida Ave., N.E., Washington, DC 20002 {This segment looks back on the controversy between manual and oral education and discusses the disagreement between Edward Miner Gallaudet and Alexander Graham Bell, both hearing but both also had deaf mothers} [GA: UNIV Cable TV U-Matic 2550]

Deaf Mosaic: Mosaic Memoirs, Program No. 604. (1990, August). 28 minutes. Color. Sound. Signed and closed-captioned. Washington, DC: Gallaudet University. Order No. DM 604 from Deaf Mosaic, Department of Television, Film and Photography, Gallaudet University, 800 Florida Ave., N.E., Washington, DC 20002 {This edition highlights the 1880 International Conference on Education of the Deaf, Milan, Italy. Edward Miner Gallaudet (who was hearing and his mother was deaf) headed the five member United States delegation. Members of that Conference voted 160 to four in favor of the oral method to educate the deaf} [GA: UNIV Cable TV U-Matic 2550]

Deaf Mosaic: Performing Arts Special, the role of deaf people in theater, film, television and dance, program No. 411. (1989, January). 27 minutes. Color. Sound. VHS. Signed and open captioned. Producers: John Mullen and Faith Powell. Washington, DC: Gallaudet University. Order No. DM 411 from Deaf Mosaic, Department of Television, Film and Photography, Gallaudet University, 800 Florida Ave., N.E., Washington, DC 20002 {In the "film" segment there is an interview with Dr. John S. Schuchman, history professor, Gallaudet University, and author of <u>Hollywood speaks: Deafness and the film entertainment industry,</u> and the hearing son of deaf parents. In the "television" segment there is an interview with Emmy award winner Julianna Fjeld, co-executive producer of *Love is Never Silent*, with several clips from this Hallmark Hall of Fame made-for-television movie} [GA: UNIV Cable TV U-Matic 2550]

Deaf Mosaic: Prime time, Rochester's new deaf television program, *HEY, Listen!* Program No. 504. (1989, June). 28 minutes. Color. Sound. Signed and open captioned. Washington, DC: Gallaudet University. Order No. DM 504 from Deaf Mosaic, Department of Television, Film and Photography, Gallaudet University, 800 Florida Ave., N.E., Washington, DC 20002 {An interview with Arden Coulston who is hearing and whose parents are deaf. He's the creator of *HEY, Listen!*} [GA: UNIV Cable TV U-Matic 2550]

Deaf Mosaic: Publisher's review, author and historian Dr. John Schuchman on *Hollywood speaks*, his history of deaf people in film and television. Program No. 408. (1988, October). 28 minutes. Color. Sound. Signed and open captioned. Washington, DC: Gallaudet University. Order No. DM 408 from Deaf Mosaic, Department of Television, Film and Photography, Gallaudet University, 800 Florida Ave., N.E., Washington, DC 20002 (Dr. Schuchman, professor of history and former Dean of Gallaudet University, is hearing and had deaf parents) [GA: UNIV Cable TV U-Matic 2550]

Deaf Mosaic: Registry of Interpreters for the Deaf. Program No. 706. (1991, October). 28 minutes. Color. Sound. Signed and open captioned. Washington, DC: Gallaudet University. Order No. DM 706 from Deaf Mosaic, Department of Television, Film and Photography, Gallaudet University, 800 Florida Ave., N.E., Washington, DC 20002 {Discusses the history of interpreting in the Deaf community with a clip from *Love is Never Silent* where Margaret, as a young girl, interprets an important event for her parents} [GA: UNIV Cable TV U-Matic 2550]

Deaf Mosaic: Signs Across America. Program No. 201 (1986, March). 28 minutes. Color. Sound. Signed and open captioned. Producer: Faith Powell. Washington, DC: Gallaudet University. Order No. DM 201 from Deaf Mosaic, Department of Television, Film and Photography, Gallaudet University, 800 Florida Ave., N.E., Washington, DC 20002 {Rachel Stone-Harris interviews Edgar Shroyer, a hearing educator whose parents are deaf and the author of <u>Signs Across America</u>} [GA: UNIV Cable TV U-Matic 2550]

Deaf Mosaic: Tony award-winning deaf actress Phyllis Frelich. Program No. 504. (1989, June). 28 minutes. Color. Sound. Signed and open captioned. Washington, DC: Gallaudet University. Order No. DM 504 from Deaf Mosaic, Department of Television, Film and Photography, Gallaudet University, 800 Florida Ave., N.E., Washington, DC 20002 {Ms. Frelich is interviewed as she receives the Annie Glenn Award at the 8th Annual Awards of the National Council on Communicative Disorders, a branch of the American Speech Language and Hearing Association, at the Kennedy Center, Washington, D. C. She is recognized not only for her 1980 Tony Award winning performance in *Children of a Lesser God* but for her Emmy-nominated role as the mother in *Love is Never Silent* and her role in the CBS-TV film *Bridge to Silence* among others} [GA: UNIV Cable TV U-Matic 2550]

Deaf Mosaic: The biggest difference, TRIPOD, An innovative Los Angeles program for deaf children. Program No. 409. (1988, November). 28 minutes. Color. Sound. Signed and open captioned. Producer, Mary Lou Novitsky. Washington, DC: Gallaudet University. Order No. DM 409 from Deaf Mosaic, Department of Television, Film and Photography, Gallaudet University, 800 Florida Ave., N.E., Washington, DC 20002 {TRIPOD stands for "Toward Rehabilitation by Parents of the Deaf." Carl Kirchner, who is hearing and has deaf parents, is interviewed about this innovative educational program for deaf and hearing children} [GA: UNIV Cable TV U-Matic 2550]

Dick Wolfsie Show, A. M. Indiana: WTHR, Channel 13, Indianapolis. (1988, March 30). 60 minutes. Color. Sound. VHS. Interpreted into American Sign Language. {In the program on "Deaf Community issues," Wolfsie interviews Jerry Bass, Evelyn Thompson and George Perry about what it was like to grow up hearing with deaf parents} [*]

Families with deaf children: Discovering your needs and exploring your choices, parents talk with parents about having a deaf child. (1996). 27 minutes. Color. Sound. VHS. Co-produced by Malinda Eccarius and Kevin Williams at the Center for Hearing Loss in Children. Boys Town Press, 13603 Flanagan Blvd., Boys Town, NE 68010 (800) 282-6675 {One Deaf parent expresses difficulty accepting his deaf child; a coda parent with a deaf child talks about making educational choices} [GA: UNIV Cable TV, VHS 529]

Hearing children of deaf parents. (1982). 58 minutes. Color. Sound. Signed. Washington, DC: Gallaudet College Television. (Part of the Roger Beach lecture series) {Agnes Muse, Mary Ann Royster and Mary Turk, discuss their experiences growing up as hearing children of deaf parents} [For individual use only by permission of the Counseling Department, Gallaudet University Graduate School, GA: UNIV Cable TV U-Matic 1928]

HEY, Listen! Show No. 3: Deaf/hearing, mixed marriages. (1988, Fall). 30 minutes. Color. Sound. VHS. Closed-captioned with voice over. Producer/creator: Arden Coulston. Jacqueline Schertz is the host. Visual Communication Services, Inc., 36 St. Paul St., Suite 104-108, Rochester, New York 14604-1308 {"Deaf/hearing couples talk about their experiences coexisting with two cultures. While sometimes sad, often funny, the discussion is always warm and honest."} [*]

HEY, Listen! Show No. 6: Deaf parents/hearing children. (1988, Spring). 30 minutes. Color. Sound. VHS. Closed-captioned with voice over. Producer/creator: Arden Coulston. Jacqueline Schertz is the host. Visual Communication Services, Inc., 36 St. Paul St., Suite 104-108, Rochester, New York 14604-1308 {Interviewed are deaf parents who have hearing children: Sharon Cagle, Sam and Marjorie Bell Holcomb. Bonnie Kraft, the hearing daughter of deaf parents also appears. "Deaf parents are entertained, enlightened, and inspired by Bonnie Kraft, a hearing child of deaf adults. Bonnie's stories are sad, funny, heartwarming, and educational." - Flyer} [*]

HEY, Listen! Show No. 12: CODA, Children of Deaf Adults. (1988, Fall). 30 minutes. Color. Sound. VHS. Closed-captioned with voice over. Producer/creator: Arden Coulston. Associate producer, Elizabeth Bell-Coulston. Jacqueline Schertz is the host. Produced in cooperation with WUHF-31 television. Visual Communication Services, Inc., 36 St. Paul St., Suite 104-108, Rochester, New York 14604-1308 {"Three hearing adults of deaf parents share their stories about growing up. Amusing at times and touching as well. Three very different experiences." Florence Hughes, Arden Coulston and Dorothy Cimo Baldassare are interviewed} [*]

Hidden signs: A daughter's journey toward acceptance of her mother's deafness. (1990). 21 minutes. Color. Sound. VHS or 16mm film. Open captioned. Produced and directed by Micki Zinkovich. Write Pyramid Film and Video, P.O. Box 1048, Santa Monica, CA 90406-9957. Contact: Micki's Memorial Fund, P.O. Box 1907,

Benicia, CA 94510 {Micki Zinkovich was hearing and had deaf parents. She died of cancer before this film was completed. Her family and friends finished the project as a memorial tribute to her} [*]

The hunchback of Notre Dame. (1923). 92 minutes. Black and white. Sound. Carl Laemmle presents Victor Hugo's classic starring Lon Chaney. Adapted by Perley Poor Sheehan; scenario, Edward T. Lowe, Jr.; director, Wallace Worsely. Universal Pictures. {Quasimodo is born terribly deformed and abandoned by his family. The priest Frollo raises him in isolation. One of his duties is to ring the huge bells at the cathedral which causes his deafness. "The star, Lon Chaney, was the son of deaf parents. Adapted from the novel: Notre Dame de Paris. The first film version of Victor Hugo's novel. Quasimodo, the misshapen deaf and half-blind bellringer of Notre Dame de Paris, sacrifices his life to save Esmerelda, a gypsy girl who once befriended him, from Jehan, the hunchback's evil master and brother to the Chief Priest of the cathedral." - Gallaudet catalogue} [GA: UNIV Cable TV U-Matic 1290]

Hunter: Cries of silence. (1991, March 15). 60 minutes. Color. Sound. One episode of the NBC-TV series. Producer, Victor. A. Schiro. Writer, David H. Balkan. Director, Peter Crane. Performers: Phyllis Frelich, Fred Dryer, Lauren Lane, Courtney Barilla, Pierrette Grace and Melissa Hayden. Stephen J. Cannell Productions. {A deaf parent seeks Hunter's help to locate her runaway hearing child} [GA: UNIV Cable TV U-Matic 3209]

I never promised you a rose garden. (1977). 90 minutes. Black and white. Sound. VHS. Distributed by Warner Home Video, 4000 Warner Blvd, Burbank, CA 91522 {A disturbed 16-year-old travels downward to madness in this gripping version of the best-seller by Joanne Greenberg. An emotional experience well done. Received an Academy Award nomination for Best Adapted Screenplay - originally written under the pseudonym Hannah Green} [*]

Interview with Bernice Turk, Frank Turk, and Marianne Turk. (1985). 30 minutes. Color. Sound. Signed. Channel 4 NBC News, Washington, D. C. {The Turk family discusses the experiences of deaf parents and hearing children} [Use limited to Gallaudet University campus only - GA: UNIV Cable TV U-Matic 2634]

In the land of the deaf. (1992/1994). 99 minutes. Color. Sound. VHS. Spoken French and French Sign Language. English subtitles. Produced by Les Films d'ici. Directed by Nicholas Philibert. Distributed by International Film Circuit Inc., P.O. Box 1151, Old Chelsea Station, New York, New York 10011. Also distributed by Sign Enhancers, Inc., P.O. Box 12687, Salem, OR 97309-0687 {Full-length documentary on the French Deaf Culture: 1989-1992} [GA: UNIV Cable TV, VHS 406 - UNIV RESERVE, VHS 406]

Intimate strangers. (In progress, 1985). Color. Sound. Produced by Lynnette Taylor. {A portrait of three generations in a family: a hearing grandmother, Deaf mother, and bi-lingual daughter} [*]

An introduction to American Deaf Culture: Identity. (1988). 50 minutes. Color. Sound. VHS. In American Sign Language with English voice-over. Introduction by Betty Colonomos. Moderator, MJ Bienvenu. Write SMI, Sign Media, Inc., Film and Video Tape Production Services, 4020 Blackburn Lane, Burtonsville, MD 20866. (Fifth videotape in a series on American Deaf Culture) {Conversation among deaf panel and audience members. The cultural membership within the Deaf Community of hearing children of deaf parents is discussed among other topics} [GA: UNIV Cable TV, VHS 33]

Johnny Belinda (1948). 103 minutes. Black and white. Sound. Starring Jane Wyman, Lew Ayres, Charles Bickford, Agnes Morehead and Stephen McNally. Based on the play of the same name by Elmer Harris. Available from MGM/United Artists, MGM/Pathe Home Video, 10000 W. Washington Blvd., Culver City, CA 90232-2728 310-280-8000 #M600761-V. (See the numerous references to this film in Hollywood speaks: Deafness and the film entertainment industry, by J. S. Schuchman) {Schuchman explains that Belinda McDonald is raped by the rural

**V
I
D
E
O**

Nova Scotia town bully who then tries to take the baby from her "convincing the village that a dummy is an unfit mother" (p. 53)} [Captioned by R. W. Bennett in 1987, use limited to educational institutions serving the deaf. GA: UNIV Cable TV, U-Matic 2859]

Johnny Belinda: CBS (1984, August 31). 95 minutes. Color. Sound. Starring Richard Thomas, Dennis Quaid, Candy Clark, Roberts Blossom, Fran Ryan, Rosanna Arquette, and the deaf actress Julianna Fjeld. Producer: Stanley Bass. Director, Anthony Page. Based on the play of the same title by Elmer Harris. Available from USA Home Video, c/o Lieberman International Video Entertainment, 15400 Sherman Way, Van Nuys, CA 91410 818-908-0303 USA#63528-V. (See J. S. Schuchman's book, Hollywood speaks: Deafness and the film entertainment industry, p. 147, for more description) {A Vista volunteer tries to set up a nutrition program and befriends a deaf woman whom he tries to help} [Captioned verbatim by Gallaudet Television, 1984. Use limited to Gallaudet University campus only. GA: UNIV Cable TV, U-Matic 2368]

(#) Koshish. (1970). Color. Sound. (Reviewed in J. S. Schuchman's book, Hollywood speaks: Deafness and the film entertainment industry, p. 125. Urbana, IL: University of Illinois Press, 1988. [DEAF 791.43 S3h, 1988]) [*]

Legacy of learning series: [Interview with] Lou Fant with program host Sharon Neumann Solow. (1995). 55 minutes. Color. In American Sign Language with English voice-over. Closed-captioned. Order tape No. LEG-1. Available from Sign Enhancers, Inc., P.O. Box 12687, Salem, OR 97309-0687 (Both Fant and Neumann Solow are hearing and were raised in deaf families) [GA: UNIV Cable TV, VHS 493]

Legacy of learning series: [Interview with] Sharon Neumann Solow with program host Lou Fant. (1995). 55 minutes. Color. In American Sign Language with English voice-over. Closed-captioned. Order tape No. LEG-2. Available from Sign Enhancers, Inc., P.O. Box 12687, Salem, OR 97309-0687 (Both Neumann Solow and Fant are hearing and were raised in deaf families) [GA: UNIV Cable TV, VHS 493]

The listening hand: ABC-TV. (1956, March 6). 30 minutes. Black and white. [*]

Live at SMI (video No. 256): Elinor Kraft. (1994). 90 minutes. Color. Sound. VHS. Produced by Sign Media, Inc. Directed by Dennis Cokely. English translation and voice-over by Bonnie Kraft. Write SMI: Sign Media, Inc., 4020 Blackburn Lane, Burtonsville, MD 20866 {Elinor Kraft is the mother of Bonnie Kraft, well-known coda (child of deaf adults) and story teller. Elinor shares two stories from Canadian deaf parents who have deaf and hearing children. She also "demonstrates that she can take even the simplest experience and transform it into a funny and entertaining one. Her humorous stories about herself and her family will definitely tickle your funny bone!" - video jacket} [*]

Live at SMI (video No. 251): Gilbert Eastman. (1994). 90 minutes. Color. Sound. VHS. Directed by Dennis Cokely. Voice-over interpretation by Don Renzulli. Write SMI: Sign Media, Inc., 4020 Blackburn Lane, Burtonsville, MD 20866 {"In this one-man show Gil not only pokes fun at his fictitious 'Aunt Erma,' but also presents a twenty minute classic entitled *Epic*."} [GA: UNIV Cable TV, VHS 168]

A loss for words on audio cassette. (1987). 5 cassettes. 6 1/4 hours. Write Recorded Books, Inc., P.O. Box 79, Charlotte Hall, MD 20622 {Unabridged narration of Lou Ann Walker's book, *A Loss for Words: A Story of Deafness in the Family*, by Barbara McCulloh} [*]

Lou Fant on "What do you think I know that you want to know?" (1998, January 8). 180 minutes. Color. In ASL with spoken English voice-over. Available at the National Center on Deafness (NCOD) at the California State University - Northridge (CSUN), California, Library. Internet: <http://www.ncod.csun.edu> {Videotaped presentation at the NCOD 16th annual Interpreter Symposium, CSUN, January 7-9, 1998: Lou Fant imparts some of the knowledge and experience he has gained as a preacher, teacher, government bureaucrat, actor and Sign Language interpreter. Skill development is included}

Love is Never Silent, Hallmark Hall of Fame: NBC-TV. (1985, December 1). 90 Minutes. Color. Sound. Executive producer, Julianna Fjeld. {A Hallmark Hall of Fame production based on the 1970 novel, <u>In this sign,</u> by Joanne Greenberg, this Emmy Award winning film aired on NBC, December 9, 1985} [GA: UNIV Cable TV U-Matic 2632]

The man and the city, Hands of love: ABC-TV. (1971, September 11). 60 minutes. Color. (Reviewed in J. S. Schuchman's book, <u>Hollywood speaks: Deafness and the film entertainment industry,</u> p. 138. Urbana, IL: University of Illinois Press, 1988. [DEAF 791.43 S3h, 1988]) {Deaf parents try to adopt a hearing foster child; features Lou Fant in the role of a deaf parent} [*]

Man of a thousand faces: The story of Lon Chaney, Hollywood's master of disguise. (1957/1992). 122 minutes. Black and white. Hi-fi sound. VHS. Starring James Cagney, Dorothy Malone, Jane Greer, Marjorie Rambeau, Jim Backus, Roger Smith and Robert Evans. Distributed by MCA/Universal Home Video, Inc. (MCA #80706), 70 Universal City Plaza, Suite 435, Los Angeles, CA 91608. {Autobiography of Lon Chaney, Sr.} [GA: UNIV Cable TV, VHS 108]

Mom and Dad can't hear me: ABC After School Special, the teenage years. (1978). 47 minutes. Color. Sound. Executive producer, Daniel Wilson. Producer, Fram Sears. Teleplay: Irma Reichert and Daryl Warner. Director, Larry Elikann. Performers: Rosanna Arquette, Priscilla Pointer and Stephen Elliot. Write Time Life Videos, 1271 Avenue of the Americas, New York, New York 10020 {A teenage girl, new in town, feels ashamed to have new friends meet her deaf parents} [GA: UNIV Cable TV U-Matic 1244]

Mr. Holland's Opus (1996). 143 minutes. Color. Closed-captioned. Hi-Fi Stereo. Director: Stephen Herek. Richard Dreyfuss stars in his Oscar-nominated role as a teacher trying to get by in this uplifting drama. Also starring Glenne Headley, Olympia Dukakis, and Jay Thomas. Distributed by Buena Vista Home Movies, Burbank, CA 91521 {Carl Kirchner was the American Sign Language and Deaf Culture consultant and one of the on-screen interpreters} [GA: UNIV Cable TV, VHS 522]

My daddy's ears are broken: Man alive series. (1990). 27 minutes. Color. Sound. VHS. Toronto, Canada: Canadian Broadcasting Corporation. Distributed by Filmakers Library, New York. Write Linda Gottesman, Filmakers Library, 124 E 40th St., Suite 901, New York, New York 10016 (212) 355-6545 (See the review by A. Wilson in "Journal articles and book chapters" section) {Documents experiences of three adults with hearing loss in adapting and sensitizing family members and business associates. A small child describes hearing loss this way: "My daddy's ears are broken."} [*]

(#) Ne'er do well. (1915). (Available at the Library of Congress, Washington, D. C.) {Sydney Smith's parents were deaf, he was hearing} [*]

One flew over the cuckoo's nest. (1975/1993). 129 minutes. Color. Sound. VHS. Closed captioned. Directed by Milos Forman. Producers: Saul Zaentz and Michael Douglas. Starring Jack Nicholson and Louise Fletcher both in Academy Award winning performances. Available from Republic Pictures, 12636 Beatrice Street, Los Angeles, CA 90066-0930 (VHS #5922) {Based on the novel by Ken Kesey: Set in a mental ward, the story revolves around McMurphy, whose rebelliousness pits him against Nurse Ratched and the full spectrum of institutional repression} [C]

(#) Our silent love (Chichi To Ko). (1969). Sound. (Reviewed in J. S. Schuchman's book, <u>Hollywood speaks:</u>

225

Deafness and the film entertainment industry, p. 125. Urbana, IL: University of Illinois Press, 1988 [DEAF 791.43 S3h, 1988]) [*]

The "PAH" side story. (Forthcoming). 90 minutes. Color. VHS. Filmed by Sign Media Inc., Burtonsville Commerce Center, 4020 Blackburn Lane, Burtonsville, MD 20866. {"This original play (loosely based on West Side Story) was developed and presented by the 1993 class of the Indiana School for the Deaf...centers around the challenges faced by a Deaf girl and a hearing boy who are attracted to each other despite the naive, negative perceptions of their peer groups." SMI brochure - The hearing boy acting the part was in actuality also a coda}

(*) Parenting: Bringing two worlds together [Videotapes]. (1992). 180 minutes. Color. VHS. In American Sign Language without voice-over. Developed by the Northern Virginia Resource Center for Deaf and Hard of Hearing Persons (NVRC), the Mount Vernon Center for Community Mental Health, the Virginia Department for the Deaf and Hard of Hearing and the Rev. Katherine Chipps, Holy Trinity Ministry of the Deaf. Consultant: Jennifer C. Witteborg. Distributed by NVRC. Write NVRC, 10363 Democracy Lane, Fairfax, VA 22030 (Part of a kit that contains these two 90-minute videotapes and an eight lesson loose-leaf manual - 206 pages - Title on the manual: Parenting skills: Bringing together two worlds, one home, two cultures, [DEAF 649.1 P373, 1992]) {On the videotape are interviews with 21 deaf parents about their experiences raising hearing children and interviews with two hearing children of deaf parents - Highly recommended} [GA: UNIV Cable TV, VHS 485]

Passport without a country. (1992/1993). 47 minutes. Color. Sound. VHS. Open captions. Written, produced and directed by Cameron Davie at Griffith University and Queensland University of Technology, Queensland, Australia. Narrator, Graham Webster. Contact Centre for Deafness Study and Research, Griffith University. Available from Films for the Humanities and Sciences, P.O. Box 2053, Princeton, NJ 08543. {About "the hearing children of deaf parents who are born into a unique culture, and often learn sign language before they learn to speak. They are becoming known as Codas - Children of Deaf Adults...This documentary provides an intimate glimpse into the lives of seven Codas, from their earliest memories of childhood to where they find themselves now. There are many happy recollections, but there are also painful ones, and we gradually learn of the dilemmas facing Codas who are searching for their identity. As one Coda points out, it's like having a passport that is not accepted by the country in which you were born." - video jacket. Highly recommended} [GA: UNIV Cable TV, VHS 279]

(*) Pathways for parenting video: A video program for deaf parents with hearing children. (1987). 66 minutes. Three videocassettes. Color. Signed. Open captioned. Produced by Linda Tebelman. Part 1: Our baby is hearing, 18 minutes; Part 2: Our child goes to school, 20 minutes; Part 3: From teenager to adult, 30 minutes. Contact: Lutheran Social Services of Michigan, Family Counseling and Education, 8131 E. Jefferson Ave., Detroit, MI 48214. (See the related Pathways for parenting video: parent's guide [DEAF 649.1 T42p, 1989, facilitator's guide] and the Pathways for parenting video: Facilitator's guide [DEAF 649.1 T42p, 1989, parent's guide] both by L. Tebelman. Also see the related Pathways for parenting booklets by Marjorie Neubacher [DEAF 649.1 N48p, 1987]) [GA: UNIV Cable TV, VHS 155]

People are talking. (1985, December 6). 60 minutes. Color. Sound. Interpreted into American Sign Language. (This interview is described in the February, 1986, issue of the CODA Newsletter, 3 (1), 2. [UNIV DEAF Periodicals]) {Interview with Janet Enos Perez, author of A sign of love, her sister Donna Lohse, and other family members on KPIX Television Channel 5, San Francisco, California. There is audience participation as well} [*]

The phantom of the opera. (1925/1985). 79/93 minutes. Silent. Black/white. Director, Rupert Julian. Producer, Carl Laemmle. Starring Lon Chaney, Mary Philbin and Norman Kerry. Based on the novel by Gaston Leroux. Write Universal Pictures or Goodtimes Movie Classics, 401 5th Ave., New York, New York 10016 {The classic silent film about a madman in the Paris Opera House and his evil control over a young starlet} [C]

Profiles in pride: KCBS-TV channel 2, Los Angeles. (1995, January 8). 1 minute. Color. Sound. Closed-captioned and open-captioned. {Joyce Linden, Associate Professor, California State University, Northridge, is profiled. She has received a President's Associate's Award and taught at CSUN for many years} [*]

The rivalry of Edward Miner Gallaudet and Alexander Graham Bell. (1982). 108 minutes. Color. Sound. Washington, DC: Gallaudet College Television. Janet Bailey and Kathy Markland are the interpreters. {Richard Winefield discusses the topic of his dissertation and the rivalry between these two well-known spokespersons on deafness during the 19th century. See Winefield's book published in 1987, Alexander Graham Bell - Edward Miner Gallaudet: Never the Twain Shall Meet, the Communications Debate} [GA: UNIV Cable TV U-Matic 1862]

The river wild. (1994). 112 minutes. Color. HI FI stereo surround sound. VHS. Closed-captioned. Starring Meryl Streep, Kevin Bacon, David Strathairn and also Victor Galloway as the deaf father. Available from MCA/Universal Home Video, Inc., (#82008) 70 Universal City Plaza, Universal City, CA 91608 [*]

Ron Coffey memorial service. (1994, July 30). 55 minutes. Color. Sound. VHS. In American Sign Language with spoken English accompaniment. Produced by SMI, Sign Media, Inc. Write SMI, Sign Media Inc., Linstok Press, 4020 Blackburn Lane, Burtonsville, MD 20866 {Memorial service for Ronald L. Coffey (August 9, 1960-June 27, 1994), American Sign Language interpreter-extraordinaire, coda, and beloved by all who knew him. Tributes by family members, professional colleagues and friends. Includes a touching video life retrospective} [*]

Say it with Sign No. 9: Wonderful Baby (Vol. 3, 3rd episode). (1980/1987). 30 minutes. Color. Sound. VHS. Producers: Sheldon I. Altfeld and Kathleen Gold. Director: John W. Mitchell. Produced by the Silent Network in association with KNBC. Order from Valiant Educational Videos, 21110 Nordhoff Street, Unit L, Chatsworth, CA 91311 or call (800) 266-2159 {Sharon Neumann Solow explains how her deaf parents devised ways to know when she was crying in her crib} [GA: UNIV Cable TV U-Matic 2321]

Say it with Sign No. 10: Baby and children (Vol. 3, 4th episode). (1980/1987). 30 minutes. Color. Sound. VHS. Producers: Sheldon I. Altfeld and Kathleen Gold. Director: John W. Mitchell. Produced by the Silent Network in association with KNBC. Order from Valiant Educational Videos, 21110 Nordhoff Street, Unit L, Chatsworth, CA 91311 or call (800) 266-2159 {Sharon Neumann Solow explains her ways of keeping secrets from her deaf parents when on the telephone} [GA: UNIV Cable TV U-Matic 2321]

Say it with Sign No. 18: Family II (Vol. 5, 4th episode). (1980/1987). 30 minutes. Color. Sound. VHS. Producers: Sheldon I. Altfeld and Kathleen Gold. Director: John W. Mitchell. Produced by the Silent Network in association with KNBC. Order from Valiant Educational Videos, 21110 Nordhoff Street, Unit L, Chatsworth, CA 91311 or call (800) 266-2159 {Sharon Neumann Solow introduces her deaf parents, hearing sister and hearing nephews. They have a conversation in Sign Language about hearing children growing up in a deaf household} [GA: UNIV Cable TV U-Matic 2321]

Sherry: The music Sign Language video. (1994). 29 minutes. Color. Sound. VHS. Closed-captioned. Producers: Sherry Hicks and Dan Veltri. Write Treehouse Video, San Francisco, California or UNI-QUE Productions, P.O. Box 14421, Berkeley, California 94712 {Sherry Hicks discusses her journey as hearing in a deaf family and how that affects her understanding of "musically inspired interpretation" into American Sign Language. Three songs illustrate this understanding} [UNIV Cable TV, VHS 247]

The signs of language. (1992/1993). 25 minutes. Color. Sound. Open captioned. VHS. Produced for the Centre for Deafness Studies and Research by the Educational Television Facility at Griffith University and Queensland University of Technology. Executive producer, Rob Care-Wickham. Producer, Cameron Davie. Directed by Cameron Davie. Written by Breda Carty. Award winner: United States Industrial Film and Video Festival, 1992.

V
I
D
E
O

Write Films for the Humanities and Sciences, Princeton, New Jersey. {This video "takes us into the Australian Deaf community and shows us the depth and range of deaf people's use of Australian Sign Language (Auslan). It gives us some fascinating insights into the nature of the language, and its place in the lives of the people who use it." - video box cover} [GA: UNIV Cable TV, VHS 281]

Signs of life: Australia's deaf community. (1989). 40 minutes. Color. Sound. Open captioned. VHS. Produced for the Deafness Resources Project by the A/V Production Unit, Brisbane College of Advanced Education, Australia. Project coordinator, Des Power. Produced and directed by Cameron Davie. {Interviewed are a deaf couple overjoyed to have two deaf children and Trevor Johnson, author of the first Australian Sign Language dictionary. He is hearing and has deaf parents} [GA: UNIV Cable TV, VHS 281]

Silent perspectives: Interview with Leo Jacobs. (1974). 30 minutes. Black and white. Sound. VHS. Signed. Producer, Edward Ingham. Director, Mort Bernstein. Host, George Attletweed. Produced by KCSM-TV, San Mateo, California. {An interview with Leo Jacobs, author of A deaf adult speaks out. Discusses hearing-deaf relationships} [GA: UNIV Cable TV U-Matic 760]

Silent perspectives: The many faces of Lou Fant. (1976). 31 minutes. Black and white. Sound. VHS. Signed. Producer, Dan Renzulli. Director, Rick Zanardi. Interviewer, George Attletweed. Produced by KCSM-TV, San Mateo, California. {Interview with Lou Fant who discusses American Sign Language and signs several songs} [GA: UNIV Cable TV U-Matic 1331]

60 Minutes, twenty-year retrospective: ABC Television. (1997, September 7). 8 minutes. Color. Sound. VHS. Closed captioned. Produced by Deluca Sheh and Norman Gorin. (Interpreters for both segments were codas: 1976, Carol Pace; 1997, Deborah Tomardy) {Host Mike Wallace interviewed Deeadra Blaylock in 1976 when she was an undergraduate student at Gallaudet College and again in 1997 when she and her husband (Scott Morrison) have four hearing children} [*]

(#) So you have hearing kids. (197-?). 50 minutes. Black and white. Sound. Moderator: Virginia Lewis. Produced by the Center for Continuing Education, Gallaudet College. {Panel of adults talk about familial relationships between deaf and hearing children and between children and deaf parents} [Use limited to Gallaudet University campus only - GA: UNIV Cable TV U-Matic 718]

The story of Alexander Graham Bell. (1939/1996). 110 minutes. Black and white. Sound. Producer, Darryl F. Zanuck. Director, Irving Cummings. Screenplay, Lamar Trotti. Starring Don Ameche, Loretta Young and Henry Fonda. Order video #1251 from Movies Unlimited (800) 523-0823 or Club Fox, P.O. Box 27, Minneapolis MN 55440-9176 {Story of the loves, sacrifices and final success of the man who invented the telephone and lived from 1847-1922} [GA: UNIV Cable TV U-Matic 803]

A summer to remember. (1984). 120 minutes. Color. Sound. VHS. Closed-captioned. Producers: Micheline H. Keller and Edward Gold. Editor, Les Green. Director, Robert Lewis. Teleplay by Scott Swanton. Performers: James Farentino, Tess Harper, Bridgette Andersen, Sean Justin Gerlis, Burton Young and Louise Fletcher. {The story of an unusual relationship that develops between a withdrawn deaf boy and an escaped orangutan. Louise Fletcher plays the role of a linguist who studies "signing" gorillas} [GA: UNIV Cable TV U-Matic 2481]

Sunday and Monday in silence. (1974). 55 minutes. Color. Sound. 16mm film. Write Heritage Visual Sales, Ltd., 508 Church Street, Toronto, Canada. {This British made film depicts two families learning to cope with deafness. Hearing parents in one family have two deaf sons. In the other family, Deaf parents have a hearing daughter} [*]

Tales from a clubroom. (1991). 118 minutes. Color. VHS. American Sign Language with voice-over. Written by Bernard Bragg and Eugene Bergman. Washington, DC: Gallaudet University. Order No. VTTFC from Gallaudet University, Department of TV, Film and Photography, 800 Florida Ave., N.E., Washington, DC 20002 {This two-act play takes place in a typical deaf club that can be found in any American city. Dr. Lawrence Newman, educator and former president of the National Association of the Deaf says: "The play makes clear that the need for a clubroom is a powerful need for deaf people, for here is not just a refuge from the world of sound but a place that is the shaker and the maker of lives, of customs and attitudes, a clearinghouse for moods and emotion. Here can be seen how the deaf communicate with each other in the highly effective, colorful, pithy, three-dimensional richness of ASL." The same can be said of the need hearing offspring of the deaf have to gather together} [GA: UNIV Cable TV, VHS 556]

The telephone: A quest for instant communication. (1996). 50 minutes. Color. Sound. VHS. Produced by the History Channel and Art and Entertainment Home Video. Order AAE-12230 from Art and Entertainment Television Networks, (800) 344-6336. {"It is absolutely essential to modern life - the most important, influential and effective communications tool ever developed. But the story of its invention is one of false starts, close calls and a bitter rivalry with an astonishing ending. All his life, Alexander Graham Bell was driven to create a machine to help the deaf speak and hear. Ultimately, it led to the invention of the telephone...See how Bell used an actual human ear from a cadaver to help understand the nature of sound, and how he enlisted the help of a young Thomas Edison in his quest...As we approach the dawn of the twenty-first century, it is astonishing to see how one man's speaking device has grown into the essential web that links humankind." - Biography shop} [*]

Telling stories. (1989). 88 minutes. Color. Sound. VHS. In American Sign Language with voice-over. Written and directed by William Moses. Music composed by Chris Patton. Produced and directed by Marin P. Allen. Washington, DC: Gallaudet University. Order No. VTTS from Gallaudet University, Department of TV, Film and Photography, 800 Florida Ave., N.E., Washington, DC 20002 {An international award-winning play. "Using symbols and myths drawn from the struggle between the world of the deaf and the world of the hearing, this nonverbal, gestural play fascinates audiences regardless of their knowledge of deafness or sign language." - catalogue} [GA: UNIV Cable TV, VHS 459]

Tomorrow Dad will still be deaf and other stories. (1997). 90 minutes. Color. Sound. VHS. In American Sign Language with captions and voice-over by Bonnie Kraft. Producer, Joe Dannis. Director: Yoon Lee. Interviewer, Ben Bahan. Storyteller, Bonnie Kraft. Available from DawnSignPress, 6130 Nancy Ridge Drive, San Diego, CA 92121. {"Whether you are Deaf or hearing, get ready for a completely absorbing experience. The wise and witty Bonnie Kraft will captivate you with true stories of her life as a **coda**, the hearing **child** of deaf adults. 'I Can hear, but my heart is Deaf,' she tells you. In this spirit, she has navigated both worlds to become a rising star on the stage of Deaf comedy. Now she voices and signs her way into your heart with serious humor about serious issues worthy of serious thought. *Cross-cultural aspects of the world of ASL [American Sign Language] and spoken English; a coda's perspectives on the Deaf community; behaviors, beliefs, and attitudes of the hearing; the place of codas in the Deaf culture....* BONNIE KRAFT, is a fourth-generation storyteller who discovered she was funny while attending weekly meetings of the Deaf club throughout her childhood. She parlayed her hysterical and heart-wrenching stories into a career as a teacher, interpreter, and speaker." - video jacket. Highly recommended} [*]

Wanna see ASL stories? Level I. (1979). 35 minutes. Color. Silent. Signed. Washington, DC: Gallaudet College Television. Produced by William M. Kemp. Directed by Vicki Leon. Art director, Paul Hunter Butler. {One of seven videocassettes of stories presented at the beginning, intermediate and advanced levels. One anecdote by a deaf mother explains how she discovered her baby could hear} [UNIV RESERVE VHS 1347]

What's eating Gilbert Grape. (1993). 118 minutes. Color. Stereo sound. Closed-captioned. VHS. Director: Lasse Hallstrom. Starring: Johnny Depp, Juliette Lewis, Leonardo DiCaprio, Darlene Cates and Mary Steenburgen.

Distributed by Paramount Communications Company, video #32955. (Rated PG-13) {Interesting to see family dynamics at play when the older, more responsible sibling takes care of a retarded brother and overweight mother. "Good fortune can happen in unexpected ways. Gilbert Grape's break came when she sputtered into town in a big silver camper that had engine trouble...a special movie that comes along rarely, one with exciting young stars, a heartwarming yet unpredictable story and performances that win raves...[a] flawless blend of comedy and drama that includes Leonardo DiCaprio's astonishing, universally acclaimed performance as Gilbert's mentally impaired younger brother." - video box} [*]

What's Up Gallaudet #24A. (1997, April 30). 25 minutes. Color. Sound. Signed. VHS. {Sherry Duhon of the Public Relations Office at Gallaudet University interviews Sherry Hicks about the forthcoming production of her one-woman show *PHOENIX the* at the Elstad Auditorium, May 2, 1997} [*]

W. H. (Bill) McGovern: Remembering a life lived in silence. (1985). 28 minutes. Color. Sound. VHS. Produced by TV Ontario and the Gerontological Society. Available from Filmakers Library, 124 40th Street, New York, New York 10016 (212) 808-4980 <Filminfo@aol.com> (Captioned version and study guide available) {"Bill McGovern was born deaf at the beginning of the century. His life, beautifully recounted, provides historical perspective on the progress society has made towards integrating the deaf into the community...His children - all hearing people - talk with honesty and perception about the experience of growing up with deaf parents." - Filmakers' catalogue} [*]

(#) Women today. (1991, September 1). Channel 4. {Dr. Elaine Jones is interviewed by Lupita Murillo: they discuss research about deaf parents} [*]

A world of quiet. (1984). 23 minutes. Color. Sound. Written and produced by Sheldon I. Altfeld and Kathleen Gold. Host, Robert Walden. Interpreter, Gary R. Sanderson. A KABC-TV-7 Public Affairs Presentation in association with The Silent Network. Order from Valiant Educational Videos, 21110 Nordhoff Street, Unit L, Chatsworth, CA 91311 or call (800) 266-2159 {"...A fascinating and informative exploration into the unique life-style of a deaf couple, James and Fran Ripplinger, and their **hearing** daughter, Laura...provides you with a close-up look at how they bridge the communication gap. Issues of dependency and independence are poignantly brought to the forefront as the Ripplingers prepare to deal with the inevitable departure of their daughter, whose adult life is just beginning and who has been their ears and connection to the hearing world for the last eighteen years." - brochure} [GA: UNIV Cable TV U-Matic 3189]

VII

INFORMATION ABOUT,

BY AND FOR

DEAF AND DISABLED

PARENTS

There are a number of possible sources of more information under this topic.

You might want to explore the following:

The Family Psychologist; Marriage and Family Review; Accent on Living; Law and Inequality; Children's Legal Rights Journal; Family Law Quarterly; Disability and Society, Sexuality and Disability, etc.

There are also a number of internet resources under "rehabilitation," "medical" and "parent chat" subjects. For example:

<http://www.bradingrao.com> (Parent's Place chat room for EDEN - Electronic Deaf Education Network)

<http://www.koda.org> (Seattle, Washington deaf parents organization)

(*) **Bail, S., & Littlefield, D. (1993).** Setting up a parent education program. In S. Polowe-Aldersley (Ed.), <u>Pride is with us: Proceedings of the 56th biennial meeting, Convention of American Instructors of the Deaf and the 64th annual meeting of the Conference of Educational Administrators Serving the Deaf, Baltimore, Maryland, June, 1993</u> (pp. 116-118). Bedford, TX: Convention of American Instructors of the Deaf. [Gallaudet University Archives]

(*) **Baranowski, E. (1983, March-April).** Childbirth education classes for expectant deaf parents: Because of communication barriers and cultural differences, expectant deaf parents need childbirth education classes adapted to their situation. <u>American Journal of Maternal Child Nursing, 8</u> (2), 143-146. [DEAF 618.24 B3c, 1983]

(*) **Bergmann, R. (1994, April).** Parent guidance of Deaf parents with deaf children: We need deaf parent counselors. <u>WFD News,</u> No. 1, 28-29. (A publication of the World Federation of the Deaf, founded by Cesare Magarotto who is hearing and whose parents are deaf. This article was also obtained off the internet on January 23, 1997 at <http://dww.deafworldweb.org:80/dww/pub/english/f/counselors.html> from the Deaf World Web) [UNIV DEAF Periodicals]

(*) **Blackman, J. A. (1986).** <u>Warning signals: Basic criteria for tracking at-risk infants and toddlers.</u> Washington, DC: National Center for Clinical Infant Programs. (13 pages) [DEAF 618.9209 B52w, 1986]

(*) **Brabham, B. T. (1994).** <u>My mom is handicapped: A "grownup" children's book.</u> Illustrated by Caleb Tims Brabham. Virginia Beach, VA: Cornerstone Publishing. (16 pages - P.O. Box 7972, Louisville, KY 40257 Proceeds go to support the Muscular Dystrophy Association: <http://www.educ.kent.edu/deafed/viiib8.html>) {A beautiful book for children written by a mother with MD and illustrated by her 9-year-old daughter} [*]

(*) **Brown, D. (1981).** All in the family: Disabled persons are parents, too. <u>Disabled U.S.A., 4</u> (3), 32-35. (Quarterly publication of the President's Committee on Employment of the Handicapped, Washington, DC 20120 The author is on the Communications staff of the President's Committee) {"The five mobility impaired parents interviewed for this article demonstrate skill in adapting to the demands of parenting. Further, in varying degrees, the lives of their children seem to have been enriched."} [*]

(*) **Burns, K. (1989).** <u>Our Mom.</u> New York: Franklin Watts. (A book for children with black and white photographs - 48 pages) {The author, paraplegic since an automobile accident in 1968, is pictured throughout with her four children doing a variety of daily activities to care for her family. A wheelchair helps her get about} [*]

(*) **Clark, J. G. (1982, August).** Counseling in a pediatric audiologic practice. <u>ASHA, 24</u> (8), 521-526. [UNIV DEAF Periodicals]

(*) **Cornwell, M. (1975a).** Blind and partially sighted parents. In <u>Early years</u> (pp. 138-143). London: Disabled Living Foundation. [UNIV Deaf 649.1 C6e, 1975]

(*) **Cornwell, M. (1975b).** Deaf and partially hearing parents. In <u>Early years</u> (pp. 144-149). London: Disabled Living Foundation. {Most of the material in this chapter was contributed by Diane Kenyon, a partially hearing mother of hearing children} [UNIV Deaf 649.1 C6e, 1975]

(*) **Cornwell, M. (1975c).** General considerations [for disabled parents]. In <u>Early years</u> (pp. 6-18). London: Disabled Living Foundation. [UNIV Deaf 649.1 C6e, 1975]

(*) **Deshen, S., & Deshen, H. (1989, Fall).** Brief communications: Managing at home, relationships between blind parents and sighted children. <u>Human Organization, 48</u> (3), 262-267. [C]

PARENTS

(*) Families first: A study of disabled parents of school-aged children and their families. (1997?) England: Association of Disabled Parents in the Norfolk Area. (45 pages - A "concise report" is also available. Write to PANDA, 145 Main Road, Clenchwarton, King's Lynn, Norfolk PE34 4DT United Kingdom or call 01553 768193) [*]

(*) Ford, N. M. (1984, April). Parent-education services for deaf adults. Journal of Rehabilitation of the Deaf, 17 (4), 1-3. [UNIV DEAF Periodicals]

(*) Galloway, G. (1990, Fall). Raising hearing kids: A deaf mother remembers the joys and trials of parenthood. Gallaudet Today, 21 (1), 6-7. [Gallaudet University Archives or RESERVE]

(*) Gatewood, J., Thomas, W., Musteen, Z., & Castleberry, E. (1992, Summer). Parenting skills for lower functioning deaf adults. Journal of the American Deafness and Rehabilitation Association, 26 (1), 26-29. [UNIV RESERVE]

(*) Gilhool, T. K., & Gran, J. A. (1985). Legal rights of disabled parents. In S. K. Thurman (Ed.), Children of handicapped parents: Research and clinical perspectives (pp. 11-34). Orlando, FL: Academic Press. [UNIV Deaf 306.874 C4, 1985]

(*) Gill-Williamson, L. M. (1991, June). The impact of a visually impaired parent on a family's decision making. Journal of Visual Impairment and Blindness, 85 (6), 246-248. [UNIV Periodicals]

(*) Griffith, A., & Scott, D. (Eds.). (1985). Marriage and children. In Looking back - looking forward: Living with deafness (pp. 200-201). Toronto, Canada: Canadian Hearing Society. [DEAF Copy 1: 362 L66, 1985]

(*) Haseltine, F. P., Cole, S. S., & Gray, D. B. (Eds.). (1995). Reproductive issues for persons with physical disabilities. Baltimore: Paul H. Brookes. (368 pages) [C]

(*) Hatrak-Cundy, L. (1987, February). A forum...for an exchange of...Public Opinion....: Hearing children of deaf parents, patronizing attitudes. The NAD Broadcaster, 9 (2), 15. {Linda, the deaf parent of hearing children, takes a firm stand against putting these children in a position to interpret for parents. "The television-made movie *Love is Never Silent* is a sad part of our history when deaf adults depended on their hearing children to communicate with the outside world...Those hearing children who are exposed to interpreting early in their childhood tend to grow up with patronizing attitudes toward the deaf community." A sweeping statement but is reflective of some people within the deaf community} [UNIV DEAF Periodicals]

(*) Hatrak-Cundy, L. (1988, January). Mother knows best column: What are objectives of CODA? The NAD Broadcaster, 10 (1), 21. (Reprinted in the November, 1988, issue of the CODA Newsletter, 5 (4), 7. [UNIV DEAF Periodicals]) [UNIV DEAF Periodicals]

(*) Hatrak-Cundy, L. (1989, March). Mother knows best column. The NAD Broadcaster, 11 (3), 13. {Discusses the question "How do hearing children of deaf parents learn signs?"} [UNIV DEAF Periodicals]

(*) Hatrak-Cundy, L. (1991, February). What are the trends for deaf parents in the '90s? CODA Connection, 8 (1), 6. [UNIV DEAF Periodicals]

(*) Held, M. (1975, May). Oral deaf parents communicate with their deaf infants. The Volta Review, 77 (5), 309-310. [UNIV DEAF Periodicals and DEAF Copy 1: 306.874 H44o, 1975]

(*) **Hoshimi, S. (1975).** Programs for parents in early education and cases. In International Congress on Education of the Deaf (Ed.), <u>Proceedings of the International Congress on Education of the Deaf, Tokyo, 1975</u> (pp. 247-249). Tokyo: The Organizing Committee, International Congress on Education of the Deaf. (The author is at the Sapporo School for the Deaf, Sapporo, Japan) [DEAF 370 I57p, 1975]

(*) **How can deaf parents raise their children in the Christian faith? (1978).** Grand Rapids, MI: Christian Literature for the Deaf. (4 pages) [DEAF 248.4 H6]

(*) **Inoue, K. (1975).** What should the school do for the children who have left school to start in life? In International Congress on Education of the Deaf (Ed.), <u>Proceedings of the International Congress on Education of the Deaf, Tokyo, 1975</u> (pp. 660-661). Tokyo: The Organizing Committee, International Congress on Education of the Deaf. [DEAF 370 I57p, 1975]

(*) **Jackson, A. B. (1996).** Pregnancy and delivery. <u>Sexuality and Disability, 14</u> (3), 211-219. [UNIV Periodicals]

(*) **Jacobson, D. S. (1995).** Rethinking expectations. In F. P. Haseltine, S. S. Cole & D. B. Gray (Eds.), <u>Reproductive issues for persons with physical disabilities</u> (pp. 49-52). Baltimore: Paul H. Brookes. [C]

(*) **Jacobson, N. (1995).** Learning about disability from children. In F. P. Haseltine, S. S. Cole & D. B. Gray (Eds.), <u>Reproductive issues for persons with physical disabilities</u> (pp. 63-65). Baltimore: Paul H. Brookes. [C]

(*) **Jaech, T. A. (1981).** The Jaech family: From dad with love...dear kids. <u>The Deaf American, 34</u> (3), 5-7. [UNIV DEAF Periodicals]

(*) **Janson, J. L. (1996, September).** <u>Issues surrounding hearing children of deaf adults.</u> Unpublished doctoral - Psy. D. thesis, School of Professional Psychology, Wright State University, Dayton, Ohio. (52 pages. In addition, the appendix contains a "Therapist's Guide for the CODA Workbook" - 8 pages - and a "CODA Workbook" - 41 pages) [*]

(*) (#) **Johnson, R. L. (1968).** Unique problems encountered in raising deaf and hearing children: Views of deaf parents of hearing children. (2 pages - source unidentified) {Mr. Johnson has five hearing children} [*]

(*) **Jones, E., Strom, R., & Daniels, S. (1989, December).** Evaluating the success of deaf parents. <u>American Annals of the Deaf, 134</u> (5), 312-316. [UNIV DEAF Periodicals]

(*) **Kane, J., & Shafer, C. M. (1970).** <u>Personal and family counseling services for the adult deaf: Final report.</u> Los Angeles: Family Service of Los Angeles. (74 pages) [DEAF Copy 1: 361.06 K33p, 1970 - microfiche]

(*) **Kelsall, J. (1992, December 1).** She can lip-read, she'll be all right: Improving maternity care for the deaf and hearing-impaired. <u>Midwifery, 8,</u> 178-183. [*]

(*) **Khalil, L. (1988, Winter).** Phobia. <u>The Deaf American, 38</u> (1), 19-20. [UNIV DEAF Periodicals]

(*) **Kirshbaum, M. (1988, June).** Parents with physical disabilities and their babies. <u>Zero to Three: A Bulletin of the National Center for Clinical Infant Programs, 7</u> (5), 8-15. Washington, DC: National Center for Clinical Infant Programs. [C]

(*) **Kirshbaum, M. (1994, Fall).** Family context and disability culture reframing: Through the Looking Glass. The Family Psychologist, 10 (4), 8-12. [*]

(*) **Kirshbaum, M. (1995).** Serving families with disability issues: Through the Looking Glass. Marriage and Family Review, 21 (1/2), 9-28. (Co-published simultaneously in 1995 in D. Guttmann & M. B. Sussman (Eds.), Exemplary social intervention programs for members and their families (pp. 9-28). New York: The Haworth Press.) [C]

(*) **Koester, L. S. (1992, October).** Intuitive parenting as a model for understanding parent-infant interactions when one partner is deaf. American Annals of the Deaf, 137 (4), 362-369. [UNIV DEAF Periodicals]

(*) **Lawrence, I. E. (1972).** Is justice deaf: What are the legal and constitutional rights of the deaf. Tallahassee, FL: Florida Registry of Interpreters for the Deaf. (33 pages - Ivan Lawrence is an attorney and associate professor of law) [DEAF 342.085 L3i, 1972]

(*) **Leigh, I. W. (1979, Spring).** The support a parent needs from the audiologist and speech pathologist. Hearing Rehabilitation Quarterly, 4 (1), 9. [UNIV DEAF Periodicals]

(*) **Levesque, R. J. R. (1996, Spring).** Maintaining children's relations with mentally disabled parents: Recognizing difference and the difference that it makes [Update]. Children's Legal Rights Journal, 16, 14-22. (Publication of the Children's Legal Rights Information and Training Program, Washington, D. C.) [C]

(*) **Lindner, D. (1993, Spring).** How you can help your kids adjust. Accent on Living, 38, 35-36. (Magazine that provides information about new products, travel ideas, medical news, housing, adjustment, inspiration and other areas of interest to mobility impaired individuals. Located in Bloomington, Illinois) {Mother has systemic lupus} [*]

(*) **Lundh, P. (1986, May).** A new baby-alarm based on tenseness of the cry signal. Scandinavian Audiology, 15 (4), 191-196. [UNIV DEAF Periodicals]

(*) **Mallory, B. L., Schein, J. D., & Zingle, H. W. (1991-1992, Winter).** Parenting resources of deaf parents with hearing children. Journal of the American Deafness and Rehabilitation Association, 25 (3), 16-30. [UNIV RESERVE]

(*) **Mallory, B. L., Schein, J. D., & Zingle, H. W. (1992, January).** Improving the validity of the PSNI [Parental Strengths and Needs Inventory] in assessing the performance of deaf parents of hearing children. American Annals of the Deaf, 137 (1), 14-21. [UNIV DEAF Periodicals]

(*) **Mann, H.G., & Sevigny-Skyer, S. (1989, July).** Deaf patients [sic: parents] and children: An innovative organization by and for deaf parents. Journal of the American Deafness and Rehabilitation Association, 23 (1), 14-16. [UNIV RESERVE]

(*) **Marafino, K. (1990).** Parental rights of persons with mental retardation. In B. Y. Whitman & P. J. Accardo (Eds.), When a parent is mentally retarded (pp. 163-189). Baltimore: Paul. H. Brookes Publishing Co. [C]

(*) **Mathews, J. (1992).** A mother's touch: The Tiffany Callo story. New York: Henry Holt & Company. (265 pages) {Tiffany Callo, a cerebral-palsied mother, fought the State of California for custody of her two sons} [C]

(*) **Mulhern, E. (1988, January).** How will you hear the baby cry? The Hearing Journal, 41 (1), 19-20. {A hearing ear dog is the perfect solution for this family} [UNIV DEAF Periodicals]

(*) **Murkin, R. W., & Womersley, R. (1978).** Health and safety. In <u>For young deaf people: A guide to everyday living</u> (pp. 130-183). Melbourne, Australia: Victorian School for Deaf Children. (281 pages) {In a segment titled "Pregnancy and child care" there are four pages in a "special note for deaf parents with a hearing child."} [UNIV DEAF Copy 1: 301.157 M8f, 1978]

(*) **Neubacher, M. (1987).** <u>Pathways for parenting, parents guide:</u> (1) <u>Our baby is hearing</u> (24 pages); (2) <u>Our child - two worlds</u> (40 pages); (3) <u>Adolescence to grown-up</u> (28 pages). Illustrated by Steve Schudlich. Detroit, MI: Lutheran Social Services of Michigan. Write Lutheran Social Services, 8131 E. Jefferson Avenue, Detroit, MI 48214. (See additional materials under Tebelman in this section) [DEAF 649.1 N48p, 1987]

(*) **Newbrough, J. R. (1985).** The handicapped parent in the community: A synthesis and commentary. In S. K. Thurman (Ed.), <u>Children of handicapped parents: Research and clinical perspectives</u> (pp. 181-193). Orlando, FL: Academic Press. [DEAF 306.874 C4, 1985]

(*) **Odegard, J. (1993).** The Americans with Disabilities Act: Creating "Family values" for physically disabled parents. <u>Law and Inequality, 11,</u> 533-563. (Publication of law students of the University of Minnesota Law School) [C]

(*) **Parenting: Bringing two worlds together [Videotapes]. (1992).** 180 minutes. Color. VHS. In American Sign Language without voice-over. Developed by the Northern Virginia Resource Center for Deaf and Hard of Hearing Persons (NVRC), the Mount Vernon Center for Community Mental Health, the Virginia Department for the Deaf and Hard of Hearing and the Rev. Katherine Chipps, Holy Trinity Ministry of the Deaf. Consultant: Jennifer C. Witteborg. Distributed by NVRC. Write NVRC, 10363 Democracy Lane, Fairfax, VA 22030 (Part of a kit that contains these two 90-minute videotapes and an eight lesson loose-leaf manual - 206 pages - Title on the manual: <u>Parenting skills: Bringing together two worlds, one home, two cultures,</u> [DEAF 649.1 P373, 1992]) {On the videotape are interviews with 21 deaf parents about their experiences raising hearing children and interviews with two hearing children of deaf parents - Highly recommended} [GA: UNIV Cable TV, VHS 485]

(*) **Parenting skills: Bringing together two worlds, one home, two cultures [Manual]. (1992).** (206 pages) Developed by the Northern Virginia Resource Center for Deaf and Hard of Hearing Persons (NVRC), the Mount Vernon Center for Community Mental Health, the Virginia Department for the Deaf and Hard of Hearing and the Rev. Katherine Chipps, Holy Trinity Ministry of the Deaf. Consultant: Jennifer C. Witteborg. Distributed by NVRC. Write NVRC, 10363 Democracy Lane, Fairfax, VA 22030 (Part of a kit that contains two 90-minute videotapes and this eight lesson loose-leaf manual. Title on the videotape: <u>Parenting: Bringing two worlds together.</u> [GA: UNIV Cable TV, VHS 485]) {There are eight lessons and accompanying materials designed to be utilized by a deaf facilitator over an eight-week period in conjunction with the videotapes. Topics covered: 1) introduction; 2) communication; 3) interpreting; 4) discipline; 5) values; 6) self esteem; 7) teens and future expectations; 8) other issues. - Highly recommended} [DEAF 649.1 P373, 1992]

(*) **Parks, S. (Ed.). (1984).** <u>HELP: When the parent is handicapped.</u> Palo Alto, CA: VORT Corp. (278 pages) {Adapted version of the Hawaii Early Learning Profile - HELP - activity guide, introduction and bibliography} [DEAF 649.1 P371h, 1984]

(*) **Pathways for parenting video: A video program for deaf parents with hearing children. (1987).** 66 minutes. Three videocassettes. Color. Signed. Open captioned. Produced by Linda Tebelman. Part 1: <u>Our baby is hearing,</u> 18 minutes; Part 2: <u>Our child goes to school,</u> 20 minutes; Part 3: <u>From teenager to adult,</u> 30 minutes. Contact: Lutheran Social Services of Michigan, Family Counseling and Education, 8131 E. Jefferson Ave., Detroit, MI 48214. (See the related <u>Pathways for parenting video: parent's guide</u> [DEAF 649.1 T42p, 1989, facilitator's guide] and the <u>Pathways for parenting video: Facilitator's guide</u> [DEAF 649.1 T42p, 1989, parent's guide] both by L. Tebelman.

Also see the related <u>Pathways for parenting booklets</u> by Marjorie Neubacher [DEAF 649.1 N48p, 1987]) [GA: UNIV Cable TV, VHS 155]

(*) **Pelarski, J., Poorbaugh, J., & Hines, J. (1973).** Tell it like it is. In National Conference on Program Development for and with Deaf People (Ed.), <u>Proceedings of National Conference on Program Development for and with Deaf People, Washington, D. C., October 9-12, 1973</u> (pp. 19-21). Washington, DC: Gallaudet College, Public Service Programs. (ERIC Document Reproduction Service No. ED 108 427 - 131 pages) [DEAF 361.8 N3p, 1973 or REFERENCE DESK]

(*) **Perry-Sheridan, N. (1995, October).** "I was told not to have children:" A serious spinal injury didn't stop one woman from becoming a mother. <u>Parents Magazine,</u> 121-122, 124. [UNIV Periodicals]

(*) **Pischke, M. E. (1995).** Parenting with a disability. In F. P. Haseltine, S. S. Cole & D. B. Gray (Eds.), <u>Reproductive issues for persons with physical disabilities</u> (pp. 57-60). Baltimore: Paul H. Brookes. [C]

(*) **Roberson, C. A. (1995).** I can do anything. In F. P. Haseltine, S. S. Cole & D. B. Gray (Eds.), <u>Reproductive issues for persons with physical disabilities</u> (pp. 43-46). Baltimore: Paul H. Brookes. [C]

(*) **Rogers, J., & Matsumura, M. (1995?).** <u>Mother-to-be: A guide to pregnancy and birth for women with disabilities.</u> Demos Vermande. [*]

(*) **Sackett, R. S. (1991, Fall).** Terminating parental rights of the handicapped. <u>Family Law Quarterly, 25</u> (3), 253-298. (Publication of the American Bar Association, section of Family Law, proceedings, Chicago, Illinois) [*]

(*) **Saito, I. (1975).** Marriage of the graduates of our school and problems involved. In International Congress on Education of the Deaf (Ed.), <u>Proceedings of the International Congress on Education of the Deaf, Tokyo, 1975</u> (pp. 675-678). Tokyo: The Organizing Committee, International Congress on Education of the Deaf. [DEAF 370 I57p, 1975]

(*) **Starkey Laboratories (Ed.). (1983).** <u>Suggestions for the family.</u> Eden Prarie, MN: Starkey Laboratories. (16 pages) [DEAF 306.87 S8, 1983]

(*) **Stone-Harris, R. (1983).** Deaf parents' perceptions of family life with deaf and/or hearing children. In G. D. Tyler (Ed.), <u>Rehabilitation and human services: Critical issues for the eighties, proceedings of the 1980 conference of the American Deafness and Rehabilitation Association, Cincinnati, 1980, Readings in deafness: Monograph No. 6</u> (pp. 5-9). Silver Spring, MD: American Deafness and Rehabilitation Association. [DEAF 361.06 A43m, 1980]

(*) **Stranik, M. K. (1986).** <u>The child care picture book: Especially for hearing impaired parents: (1) Baby is here! Basic newborn care. (2) Feeding your child: Nutrition for 6-24 months. (3) Healthy child, sick child: Child health issues. (4) Safe child and emergencies: Childproofing and first aid techniques. (5) Baby grows: Child development. (6) Baby plays: Play and stimulation.</u> St. Paul, MN: Hearing Impaired Health and Wellness Services, Hearing Impaired Parents Program, St. Paul-Ramsey Medical Center, 640 Jackson, St. Paul, MN 55101. [DEAF 649.1 C455, 1986]

(*) (##) **Stranik, M. K., Nelson, M., & Hornfeldt, D. (1986a).** <u>Emergencies.</u> St. Paul, MN: Hearing Impaired Parents Program, St. Paul-Ramsey Medical Center, MELD. [*]

(*) (##) Stranik, M. K., Nelson, M., & Hornfeldt, D. (1986b). Feeding your child after five months old. St. Paul, MN: Hearing Impaired Parents Program, St. Paul-Ramsey Medical Center, MELD. [*]

(*) (##) Stranik, M. K., Nelson, M., & Hornfeldt, D. (1986c). Safe child. St. Paul, MN: Hearing Impaired Parents Program, St. Paul-Ramsey Medical Center, MELD. [*]

(*) Stranik, M. K., Nelson, M., & Hornfeldt, D. (1986d). The middle of the night book for hearing impaired parents. St. Paul, MN: Hearing Impaired Parents Program, St. Paul-Ramsey Medical Center, MELD. (67 pages) [DEAF Copy 1: 649.1 M522, 1986]

(*) Stranik, M. K., Nelson, M., Meyer, V., & Hinkley, K. R.. (Eds.). (1986). The child care book especially for parents who are deaf and hard of hearing, book 4: Safe child and emergencies. Illustrations and design by Mary F. Nelson, Fred Gravatt and Linda L. Hinkley. St. Paul, MN: HIPP (Hearing Impaired Parents Program) and MELD, St. Paul-Ramsey Medical Center. (62 pages) [*]

(*) Stranik, M. K., Nelson, M., Meyer, V., & Leif, K. R. (Eds.). (1986a). The child care book especially for parents who are deaf and hard of hearing, book 1: Baby is here! Illustrations and design by Mary F. Nelson, Fred Gravatt and Linda L. Hinkley. St. Paul, MN: HIPP (Hearing Impaired Parents Program) and MELD, St. Paul-Ramsey Medical Center. (86 pages) [*]

(*) Stranik, M. K., Nelson, M., Meyer, V., & Leif, K. R. (Eds.). (1986b). The child care book especially for parents who are deaf and hard of hearing, book 2: Feeding your child. Illustrations and design by Mary F. Nelson, Fred Gravatt and Linda L. Hinkley. St. Paul, MN: HIPP (Hearing Impaired Parents Program) and MELD, St. Paul-Ramsey Medical Center. (61 pages) [*]

(*) Stranik, M. K., Nelson, M., Meyer, V., & Leif, K. R. (Eds.). (1986c). The child care book especially for parents who are deaf and hard of hearing, book 3: Healthy child/sick child. Illustrations and design by Mary F. Nelson, Fred Gravatt and Linda L. Hinkley. St. Paul, MN: HIPP (Hearing Impaired Parents Program) and MELD, St. Paul-Ramsey Medical Center. (61 pages) [*]

(*) Stranik, M. K., Nelson, M., Meyer, V., & Leif, K. R. (Eds.). (1986d). The child care book especially for parents who are deaf and hard of hearing, book 5: Baby grows. Illustrations and design by Mary F. Nelson, Fred Gravatt and Linda L. Hinkley. St. Paul, MN: HIPP (Hearing Impaired Parents Program) and MELD, St. Paul-Ramsey Medical Center. (52 pages) [*]

(*) Stranik, M. K., Nelson, M., Meyer, V., & Leif, K. R. (Eds.). (1986e). The child care book especially for parents who are deaf and hard of hearing, book 6: Baby plays. Illustrations and design by Mary F. Nelson, Fred Gravatt and Linda L. Hinkley. St. Paul, MN: HIPP (Hearing Impaired Parents Program) and MELD, St. Paul-Ramsey Medical Center. (52 pages) [*]

(*) Strom, R., Daniels, S., & Jones, E. (1988, Spring). Parent education for the deaf. Educational and Psychological Research, 8 (2), 117-128. [DEAF 649.1 S77p, 1988]

(*) Strom, R., Daniels, S., Wurster, S., & Jones, E. (1985, September). Deaf parents of normal hearing children. Journal of Instructional Psychology, 12 (3), 121-126. [*]

(*) Strom, R. D. (1985, April). Developing a curriculum for parent education. Family Relations, 34 (2), 161-167. [UNIV Periodicals]

(*) **Tebelman, L. (1989a).** Pathways for parenting video: facilitator's guide. Detroit, MI: Lutheran Social Services of Michigan. (146 pages) Write Lutheran Social Services of Michigan, Family Counseling and Education, 8131 E. Jefferson Avenue, Detroit, MI 48214. (See the related Pathways for parenting booklets by Marjorie Neubacher. [DEAF 649.1 N48p, 1987]) [DEAF 649.1 T42p, 1989, facilitator's guide]

(*) **Tebelman, L. (1989b).** Pathways for parenting video: parent's guide. Lutheran Social Services of Michigan, Detroit. (102 pages) Write Lutheran Social Services of Michigan, Family Counseling and Education, 8131 E. Jefferson Avenue, Detroit, MI 48214. (See the related Pathways for parenting booklets by Marjorie Neubacher. [DEAF 649.1 N48p, 1987]) [DEAF 649.1 T42p, 1989, parent's guide]

(*) **Thurman, S. K. (1985).** Ecological congruence in the study of families with handicapped parents. In S. K. Thurman (Ed.), Children of handicapped parents: Research and clinical perspectives (pp. 35-46). Orlando, FL: Academic Press. [DEAF 306.874 C4, 1985]

(*) **Urban, C. (1984).** Child custody issues for parents with disabilities. East Orange, NJ: Community Health Law Project. (32 pages) {Legal issues and opinions specific to New Jersey are surveyed} [*]

(*) **Watson, T. (1991, April).** A deaf parent's view. In National Council for Social Workers with Deaf People Training Committee (Ed.), Special needs or special breed? Hearing children of deaf adults (pp. 10-11). (24 pages) Write NCSWDP - 1st floor, Bedford House, 125-133 Camden High Street, London, England NW1 7JR. {Transcript of a paper presented at a one day seminar organized by the Training Committee of the National Council for Social Workers with Deaf People, NCSWDP, April 9, 1991} [DEAF 306.874 S632, 1992]

(*) **Watts, A. J. (1995, March/April).** Sticking it out! Managing a parent support group. Perspectives in Education and Deafness, 13 (5), 5-7, 11. [UNIV DEAF Periodicals]

(*) **White, G. W., & White, N. L. (1995).** The adoptive process: Challenges and opportunities for people with disabilities. In F. P. Haseltine, S. S. Cole & D. B. Gray (Eds.), Reproductive issues for persons with physical disabilities (pp. 107-115). Baltimore: Paul H. Brookes. [C]

(*) **Whitman, B. Y., Graves, B., & Accardo, P. J. (1990).** Parents learning together I: Parenting skills training for adults with mental retardation. In B. Y. Whitman & P. J. Accardo (Eds.), When a parent is mentally retarded (pp. 51-65). Baltimore: Paul. H. Brookes Publishing Co. [*]

(*) **Williams, B. T. (1993, Spring).** Parenting with a disability - does it make a difference? Accent on Living, 38, 32-36. (Magazine that provides information about new products, travel ideas, medical news, housing, adjustment, inspiration and other areas of interest to mobility impaired individuals. Located in Bloomington, Illinois) {Two families are featured: one parent has Kugelberg-Welander muscular dystrophy and in the other family a parent has a limp as a birth defect. An interview with the children is reported. A rehabilitation counselor says, "However, these kids [whose parents are disabled] can be a little more compassionate - more appreciative of life."} [*]

(*) **Williams, J. S. (1976, Spring).** Bilingual experiences of a deaf child. Sign Language Studies, 10, 37-41. [UNIV RESERVE]

(*) **Zola, I. K. (1995a).** A father's gift. In F. P. Haseltine, S. S. Cole & D. B. Gray (Eds.), Reproductive issues for persons with physical disabilities (pp. 117-118). Baltimore: Paul H. Brookes. [C]

(*) **Zola, I. K. (1995b).** And the children shall lead us. In F. P. Haseltine, S. S. Cole & D. B. Gray (Eds.), Reproductive issues for persons with physical disabilities (pp. 67-69). Baltimore: Paul H. Brookes. [C]

240

(*) Zola, I. K. (1995c). Is it all right to be sad? In F. P. Haseltine, S. S. Cole & D. B. Gray (Eds.), <u>Reproductive issues for persons with physical disabilities</u> (pp. 61-62). Baltimore: Paul H. Brookes. [C]

(*) Zola, I. K. (1995d). Tell me...tell me. In F. P. Haseltine, S. S. Cole & D. B. Gray (Eds.), <u>Reproductive issues for persons with physical disabilities</u> (pp. 97-102). Baltimore: Paul H. Brookes. [C]

(*) Zola, I. K. (1995e). Why Marcia is my favorite name. In F. P. Haseltine, S. S. Cole & D. B. Gray (Eds.), <u>Reproductive issues for persons with physical disabilities</u> (pp. 53-56). Baltimore: Paul H. Brookes. [C]

P
A
R
E
N
T
S

VIII

MISCELLANEOUS

PUBLICATIONS

This category includes the following types of materials:

monographs, reports, brochures, booklets, manuscripts, handbooks, internet articles, unpublished, difficult to obtain or unavailable papers. Materials from the Gallaudet University Archives such as vertical, manuscript, subject, biographical and other files are listed here. The Gallaudet University Archives is in the process of entering all file titles into their data base. They were only up to "F" at the time of publication.

Action program on the family. (1991). Translated by Anna Lena Nilsson. Leksand, Sweden: The Swedish National Association of the Deaf. (15 pages) {Discusses issues relative to hearing children of deaf parents in Sweden and family life of the deaf in Sweden} [DEAF 306.874 A27, 1991]

Alice Hanson Jones, 1959-1983. (n.d.). {Alice Hanson Jones was the daughter of Olof and Agatha Hanson. Alice taught economics at Washington University in St. Louis} [Gallaudet University Archives, SMSS (small manuscripts), papers and letters, open to the public without restrictions]

Alla's films. (1997, January). (Obtained off the internet at <http:nutcom.com/~ken/kibo.html>) {Alla Kliouka-Schaffer is a superstar Russian movie actress whose parents are deaf. She won the "Green Apple" (the equivalent of America's Oscar) Award for "Best Actress" in Russia on November 8, 1995. Here are a series of stills from her films: Cloudy Paradise, Nocturne Chopin, Body, Made in the USSR, Hammer & Sickle} [*]

Anderson, K. (1991). Remember child me [Short story]. (Personal communication)

(##) Anthony, M. R. (1993, July). Improving parenting skills: Deaf parents with hearing children. Paper presented at the 56th biennial meeting, Convention of American Instructors of the Deaf and the 64th annual meeting of the Conference of Educational Administrators Serving the Deaf, Baltimore, Maryland, June, 1993. (The author is at the Center on Deafness, Western Pennsylvania School for the Deaf, Pittsburgh, PA)

Bell, A. G. (1887a/1891/1969). Marriage: An address to the deaf. (14 pages - "An address delivered to the Members of the Literary Society of Kendall Green, Washington, D. C., March 6, 1891." See the second edition [Gallaudet University Archives] which has three additional pages: "Appendix. Consanguineous Marriages" dated May 22, 1891 - Also see A. G. Bell. (1891, March 12). "Upon marriage." Dr. Bell defines his position. Silent World, 5 (6), 1-4. [Gallaudet University Archives - DEAF Rare] (Dated May 22, 1891) [DEAF 306.81 B44m, 1891]) [Gallaudet University Archives - DEAF Rare]

Bell, A. G. (1887b/1969). Marriages of deaf mutes. Baddeck, Cape Breton, Nova Scotia: The Island Reporter. (Reprinted from the National Deaf Mute Gazette - photocopy - University Microfilms International, 1969 - 16 pages) {The names of deaf couples who were married between 1862 and 1868 are listed. No other explanations are given to describe the contents. Also mentioned are the location and date of the wedding and other incidental information as may be available. All entries are taken from the National Deaf Mute Gazette with month and year listed} [DEAF 306.8 B4m, 1887]

Bell, A. G. (1917). Graphical studies of marriages of the deaf. Washington, DC: Volta Bureau. (259 pages - Bell's mother and wife were deaf) [DEAF 312.5 B4g, 1917]

Bell, Dr. Alexander Graham. (n.d.). (Newspaper and other clippings open to the public without restriction) [Gallaudet University Archives, "Biographical" subject vertical files. Under his name you'll be able to find the following additional vertical files: Articles about; Articles written by; Books about; Family; Hall of Fame and A. G. Bell Museum; Miscellaneous; News clippings; Telephone invention by A. G. B.; Mabel Gardiner Hubbard Bell]

Bernard Hale. (n.d.). (Newspaper and other clippings open to the public without restriction) [Gallaudet University Archives, "Biographical" subject vertical file]

Blackmore, H. (1995). An Australian CODA's perspective. (2 pages - Obtained off the internet at <Deaf World Web> [*]

Block, S. (Ed.). (1972). Keeping up with your hearing children [Panel]. Unpublished transcript. (14 pages - Sam

Block was the moderator of this panel of deaf parents who volunteered to be on the panel) [National Information Center on Deafness, Gallaudet University, "Hearing children of deaf parents" subject vertical file]

Brother, M. (1980, November 24). An interview survey of hearing children of deaf parents: Common experiences in an uncommon environment. Unpublished paper, Department of Education, Gallaudet College, Washington, D. C. (19 pages) [DEAF 306.874 B7i, 1980]

Brother, M. (1985). Hearing child/deaf parent: Workshop ideas. (Personal communication) [*]

Brother, M., & Myhre, M. (Eds.). (1984/1985/1988). Hearing children of deaf parents: Bibliography. San Francisco: San Francisco Public Library, Deaf Services. (12-14 pages - Also published and distributed by the National Information Center on Deafness in 1986 and 1988 - 6 pages [*]) [DEAF 306.874 B7h]

Buckle, K. G. (1998). Professional Training and qualifications of CODA and non-CODA BSL/ASL Interpreters: Are they BOTH a Good Model of Practice? B. A. Honors thesis in Community and Youth Studies, Reading University, Earley, Reading, England. {Compares coda and non-coda interpreters in British Sign Language (BSL) users in England and American Sign Language (ASL) users in the United States} Manuscript in preparation.

Bull, T. H. (Ed.). (1993, March). Hearing children of deaf parents: Bibliography. Washington, DC: Gallaudet University, National Information Center on Deafness. (20 pages - publication #532: Internet: <http:www.gallaudet .edu/~nicd/pub10.html>) [DEAF 306.874016 B84h, 1993]

Bull, T. H. (Ed.). (1994, September). The CODA quilt: Background information [Booklet]. (24 pages) {The "CODA Quilt" was sewn together by Peggy Keough, deaf mother of Margaret Collier who is hearing. The quilt was sold during a live auction at the 1994 CODA Conference in Oconomowoc, Wisconsin, to raise funds for the CODA Millie Brother Scholarship Fund. The quilt is roughly 5' x 7' and beautifully displays international CODA conference T-shirts from 1986 to 1994. Two pillows with T-shirts from two other conferences were also auctioned. Booklet includes the following: background information on the quilt; photographs of the quilt, a pillow and Peggy Keough; photo and description of the "signature" on the back of the quilt; Margaret Collier's poem, "Chaotic Beginnings," about the quilt and her mother; an article about Peggy and her quilting that appeared in a Southern Baptist Women's publication; background and list of past recipients of the Millie Brother Scholarship; photo and names of the 19 members of the Washington, D. C. CODA chapter who contributed toward the winning bid; CODA Fact Sheet and Proceedings Order Form}

Bull, T. H. (1996, March). Coda-talk: Code switching literature of hearing offspring with Deaf parents. Unpublished paper presented to a course in the Department of Linguistics and Interpreting, Gallaudet University. [*]

Bull, T. H., & Witteborg, J. (forthcoming). If deaf parents want a deaf child, what happens when the child is born hearing? Paper presented at the Building Bridges conference, Strengthening home and school relationships for Deaf parents and their hearing children, Gallaudet University, Washington, D. C., May 1-3, 1997. Washington, DC: Gallaudet University, College for Continuing Education. Manuscript in preparation.

Carroll, C. (1993a). A father, a son, and a university: Edward Miner Gallaudet, 1837-1917. Washington, DC: National Information Center on Deafness, Gallaudet University. (8 pages) [DEAF 920 G33ca, 1993]

Carroll, C. (1993b). A father, a son, and a university: Thomas Hopkins Gallaudet, 1787-1851. Washington, DC: National Information Center on Deafness, Gallaudet University. (8 pages) [DEAF 920 G3ca, 1993]

Charlson, E. (1989). At-risk deaf parents and their children. In University of California, San Francisco, Center on Deafness, Research and Training: 1985-1989. San Francisco: University of California Center on Deafness. (Elizabeth Charlson was the principal investigator) [*]

Children of deaf adults (codas). (n.d.). (Newspaper and other clippings open to the public without restriction) [Gallaudet University Archives, "Deaf subject" subject vertical file]

Chism, S. C. (1996a). Father, Francis (Pa) [Poem]. (Personal communication)

Chism, S. C. (1996b). Mother [Poem]. (Personal communication)

Classic movie monsters. (1997). U.S. Postal Service. Write Stamps Worth Saving, U.S. Postal Service Philatelic Fulfillment Center, P.O. Box 449997, Kansas City, MO 64144-9997. (Commemorative stamps and first day issue packet) {A commemorative stamp and poster tribute to Lon Chaney, Bela Lugosi, Boris Karloff, and Lon Chaney, Jr., and their respective films: "Phantom of the Opera," "Dracula," "Frankenstein" and "The Mummy," and "The Wolf Man."} [*]

Collier, M. (1994, July). Chaotic beginnings [Poem]. (Personal communication) {Margaret Collier's poem about her mother's artistry in sewing the "CODA Quilt" in 1994}

Constance Elmes. (n.d.). (Newspaper and other clippings open to the public without restriction) [Gallaudet University Archives, "Biographical" subject vertical file]

Cooper, E. E. (1981). Deaf parents of hearing children handbook. Veneta, OR: Author. (34 pages) [DEAF 306.874 C66d, 1979]

(#) Deafinitely worth thinking about.....: Hearing children with Deaf parents [Pamphlet]. (n.d.). London: British Deaf Association. {A packet of 12 leaflets designed for Deaf persons to give hearing professionals. The one entitled "Hearing children with Deaf parents" has paragraphs on the following subjects: hearing children with Deaf parents; how do hearing children with Deaf parents learn to speak?; Deaf people as parents; hearing children as interpreters; contact with other families; and hearing adults with Deaf parents. It was "written by a Child of Deaf Parents." An accompanying video in British Sign Language outlines the information in each leaflet to help monolingual BSL users} [*]

Deaf parents/hearing children: A collection of articles. (1994). Distributed by the Danish Deaf Association, Foreningen Bórn af Dóve (Children of Deaf) and available from the Danish Deaf Association, Fensmarkgade 1, Postbox 704, DK-2200, Copenhagen N, Denmark. (27 pages) [DEAF 306.874 D423, 1994]

Dedication Ceremony [Program]. (1973, March 30). (3 pages) {From the U.S. Army Medical Training Center, Fort Sam Houston, Houston, Texas: includes biography, cover and program} [Gallaudet University Archives, "Elizabeth English Benson: Memorials" biographical subject vertical file]

Digest of past mailshots and newsletters: H-MFD. (1994, September). London: Hearing-Me Mother Father Deaf. (19 pages) {Digest of articles from newsletters number 1-4 of H-MFD, Hearing me-Mother/Father Deaf, the London based organization of hearing children of deaf parents} [*]

Discussion group A: Hearing children of deaf adults, a special needs group? (1992, January). In National Council for Social Workers with Deaf People Training Committee (Ed.), Special needs or special breed? Hearing children of deaf adults (p. 21). London: Training Committee of the National Council for Social Workers with Deaf

MISC

People, NCSWDP. (24 pages) Write NCSWDP, 1st floor, Bedford House, 125-133 Camden High Street, London, England NW1 7JR. {Summary from a one day seminar, April 19, 1991} [DEAF 306.874 S632, 1992]

Discussion group B: Strategies for intervention. (1992, January). In National Council for Social Workers with Deaf People Training Committee (Ed.), Special needs or special breed? Hearing children of deaf adults (p. 22). London: Training Committee of the National Council for Social Workers with Deaf People, NCSWDP. (24 pages) Write NCSWDP, 1st floor, Bedford House, 125-133 Camden High Street, London, England NW1 7JR. {Summary from a one day seminar, April 9, 1991} [DEAF 306.874 S632, 1992]

Discussion group C: Children of deaf adults, is there a role for SWDP? [Social Workers with Deaf Parents]. (1992, January). In National Council for Social Workers with Deaf People Training Committee (Ed.), Special needs or special breed? Hearing children of deaf adults (p. 23). London: Training Committee of the National Council for Social Workers with Deaf People, NCSWDP. (24 pages) Write NCSWDP, 1st floor, Bedford House, 125-133 Camden High Street, London, England NW1 7JR. {Summary from a one day seminar, April 9, 1991} [DEAF 306.874 S632, 1992]

Dispelling myths about deaf parenting. (1996). (2 pages - Excerpts reprinted in the February, 1997, issue of the CODA Connection, 14 (1), 5. [UNIV DEAF Periodicals]) {Part of a packet of materials assembled to accompany the "Mother Father Deaf Day" announcement, proclamation and press release. For further information check the "International resources" section under "Mother Father Deaf Day."} [*]

Dr. Elizabeth E. Benson, '32, Testimonial Dinner [Program]. (1969, September 27). {Elizabeth Benson, Dean of Women, Gallaudet College, was affectionately known as "Benny" by her many friends. There was a testimonial dinner held in her honor at the Presidential Arms on September 27, 1969} [Gallaudet University Archives, "Elizabeth English Benson, Testimonial Dinner" biographical subject vertical file]

Elizabeth English Benson: 1904-1972. (n.d.). (Archival/manuscript material and visual material open to the public without restriction - There are 17 separate vertical files: Addresses to various organizations; articles written by; Associate Editor of the American Annals of the Deaf; Biographical Information, news clippings; Board of Directors, resolutions; Citations and awards; Conferences and workshops attended; Faculty member of summer sessions and workshops; Gifts to the library; Honorary degree, Doctor of Letters; Interpreting in the Language of Signs; Memorials; National Association of Deans of Women; Obituary, memorial service, etc.; Radio appearances; Retirement as Dean of Women at Gallaudet; and Testimonial dinner [7/27/69]) [Gallaudet University Archives, "Biographical" subject vertical file]

Emmorey, K. (1994, March). Enhanced visual imagery in Deaf signers: Studies conducted at Gallaudet University. LaJolla, CA: The Salk Institute. (Personal communication) [*]

Emmorey, K. (1994, March). Recent results with CODAs: Enhanced visual imagery in Deaf and Hearing signers. LaJolla, CA: The Salk Institute. (Personal communication) [*]

Eva Barash Dicker. (n.d.). (Newspaper and other clippings open to the public without restriction) [Gallaudet University Archives, "Biographical" subject vertical file]

(*) Families first: A study of disabled parents of school-aged children and their families. (1997?) England: Association of Disabled Parents in the Norfolk Area. (45 pages - A "concise report" is also available. Write to PANDA, 145 Main Road, Clenchwarton, King's Lynn, Norfolk PE34 4DT United Kingdom or call 01553 768193) [*]

Family Life Day. (1972). Hearing children of deaf parents [Panel]. Unpublished transcript. Washington, DC: Gallaudet College, Public Service Programs. (8 pages) {Mervin Garretson was the moderator of this panel of seven participants listed by first name only} [National Information Center on Deafness, "Hearing children of deaf parents" subject vertical file]

(##) Franck-Smith, C. (1984). Hearing children of deaf parents: Deaf-hearing family dynamics. Unpublished senior thesis, University of California, Santa Cruz. (62 pages) [DEAF 306.874 F72H - pages 17-57 are missing]

Gallaudet, Edward Miner. (n.d.). (Newspaper and other clippings open to the public without restriction) [Gallaudet University Archives, "Biographical" subject vertical files]

(#) Garcia, M. (1990). Are we handicapping the children of the handicapped? Unpublished paper. (3 pages - Publication source unidentified) [*]

Garretson, M. D. (1969, September 27). To Elizabeth Benson [Poem]. {There was a testimonial dinner held in honor of Elizabeth Benson, Dean of Women, Gallaudet College, September 27, 1969. This poem was written for that occasion. Mervin D. Garretson is from the class of 1947} [Gallaudet University Archives, "Elizabeth English Benson, Testimonial Dinner" biographical subject vertical file]

Gilbert, L. A. (1996, Fall). Deaf characters in children's literature. Unpublished paper for the course "Classroom Applications of Sign Communication," Gallaudet University. (55 pages) {Lists several books that have coda characters in them - hearing children who have deaf parents}

Gilbert, L. J., DiPietro, L., & Gannon, J. R. (1993). Edward Miner Gallaudet: Man with a vision. Washington, DC: Gallaudet University Press. (8 pages) [DEAF 920 G33, 1933]

(#) Gober, P. (n.d.). Evaluating language scores: Preschool hearing children of deaf parents. Research project, McGehee Public Schools, McGehee, Arkansas. Write McGehee Public Schools, P.O. Box 767, McGehee, AR 71854 or Shirley J. Pine, Department of Communicative Disorders, University of Arkansas at Little Rock-University of Arkansas Medical Sciences, Little Rock, AR 72204. (2 page summary) [*]

Gold, J. (1998, February 13). Deaf parents suing to get interpreters. (The Associated Press) From the internet: pmoss@pluto.njcc.com February 17, 1998. {Victoria and Michael E. Murphy's attorney is Clara R. Smit, who is hearing and her parents are deaf}

Goldenthal, M. (1973, February 7). [Letter to Miss Mary Alice Benson of Frederick, Maryland]. {From the Commanding Colonel, Signal Corps, U.S. Department of the Army, Fort Sam Houston, Texas, notifying her that a new building for the United States Army Medical Training Center will be named the "Elizabeth E. Benson Dormitory" in honor of her late sister} [Gallaudet University Archives, "Elizabeth English Benson: Memorials" biographical subject vertical file]

(##) Goldin-Meadow, S., & Mylander, C. (1986, October). The development of morphology without a conventional language model: The resilience of levels of structure. Paper presented at the 11th Annual Boston University Conference on Language Development, Boston, MA. [*]

Goldstein, S. D., & Stone. E. A. (1982). Hearing children of deaf parents: A preliminary developmental study. Unpublished paper, New York University, New York. (25 pages) [On order]

(#) Greidovich, S. (n.d.). Language guide for parents. Unpublished paper. Washington, DC: Gallaudet College.

M
I
S
C

(5 pages) {Notes explain that this paper was prepared for "Operation Moving Ahead." Gratitude is given to Mrs. Ruth Peterson "for her [27] suggestions to deaf parents of young hearing children on possible wasy [sic] to use this guide." Includes a one page "Language guide for parents" with 23 points} [Gallaudet University Archives, "Parent-child relationship - deaf adults" subject vertical file]

(##) **Griffith, P. (1980).** The acquisition of the first few signs and words by a hearing child of deaf parents. Paper presented at the annual convention of the American Speech-Language and Hearing Association, Detroit.

H. Daniel Drake, Jr. (n.d.). (Newspaper and other clippings open to the public without restriction) [Gallaudet University Archives, "Biographical" subject vertical file]

Hearing children of deaf parents: Bibliography. (1995, December). London: Royal National Institute for the Deaf (RNID) Library. (6 pages) [*]

Hearing from the heart. (1996, April). Film proposal developed by David Cerf, San Francisco, California. (Personal communication)

Hicks, S. L. (1993). "PHOENIX the": A one act play, an autobiographic life-work in progress. Unpublished B. A. thesis, Performance Art and Humanities, New College, San Francisco, California. (32 pages) Contact UNI-QUE Productions, P.O. Box 14421, Berkeley, California 94712. E-Mail: <Sherrythe1@aol.com> {A one-woman-show presented in English, American Sign Language (ASL) and Coda-talk. Sherry Hicks breaks out with her own voice exploring issues of identity and liberation. This play has been performed in 1991 and 1993 at international conferences of CODA., (Children of Deaf Adults), at the Building Bridges Conference, May, 1997, Gallaudet University and a number of other locations}

Hicks, S. L. (1996, February). Triple tongues. 30 minutes. Unpublished play by Sherry Hicks. Directed by Sherry Glaser. First performed by the author at "BRAVA! For Women in the Arts, the eighth Annual Taking Shape! Series, New Works-in-Progress by Women Theater Makers," Brava Studio Theatre, 2180 Bryant Street, San Francisco, California, February 1-4, 1996. Contact UNI-QUE Productions, P.O. Box 14421, Berkeley, California 94712. E-Mail: <Sherrythe1@aol.com> (Sherry Glaser was the star of "Family Secrets" off-Broadway production, 1995) {About three generations of matriarch in a family: the hearing OHCODA daughter (Only Hearing Child of Deaf Adults), her deaf mother and her (the deaf mother's) hearing grandmother. Vignettes that cast a light on and engender understanding of the complexity of family dynamics}

Hils, M. (1998, February 18). Miramax placing bet on *Beyond [Silence]*. From the internet: From the newsroom of Reuters/Variety, Tuesday, February 17, 1998. Retrieved from <pmoos@pluto.njcc.com> {Reports that Miramax Films has acquired Jenseits Der Stille [Beyond Silence], the German-language film nominated for an Oscar in 1997 for Best Foreign Language film, from Bavaria Film International} [*]

(##) **Hohmann, G., & Buck, F. (1979, September).** Influence of parental disability characteristics on children's personality and behavior. Paper presented at the meeting of the American Psychological Association, New York.

(*) **How can deaf parents raise their children in the Christian faith? (1978).** Grand Rapids, MI: Christian Literature for the Deaf. (4 pages) [DEAF 248.4 H6]

Ingram, R. M. (1976, January). Preliminaries to the study of bilingualism in hearing children of deaf parents. Linguistics course paper, Brown University. (25 pages) [*]

In memoriam: Elizabeth E. Benson [Program]. (1973, January 18). [Gallaudet University Archives, "Elizabeth

English Benson: Obituary, memorial service" biographical subject vertical file]

Israelite, N., Ewoldt, C., & Hoffmeister, R., et. al. (Eds.). (1989, October). A review of the literature on the effective use of native Sign Language on the acquisition of a majority language by hearing impaired students: Final report to Her Majesty the Queen in the Right of Ontario as represented by Minister of Education, Ontario. (Research project No. 1170). Ontario, Canada: York University. (121 pages) [DEAF 305.773 I87b, 1992]

Jack Ensworth. (n.d.). (Newspaper and other clippings open to the public without restriction) [Gallaudet University Archives, "Biographical" subject vertical file]

Jacobs, S. (1984, Summer). Hearing children of deaf parents: Living with stigma. Unpublished paper submitted for a course in psychopathology at JFK University, Concord, CA. (23 pages) [*]

Johnson, J. M., & Watkins, R. V. (1989, April). The influence of ASL on the spoken English language development in a hearing child of deaf parents. Paper presented at the biennial meeting of the Society for Research in Child Development, Kansas City, Missouri. (7 pages) [*]

(*) (#) Johnson, R. L. (1968). Unique problems encountered in raising deaf and hearing children: Views of deaf parents of hearing children. (2 pages - source unidentified) {Mr. Johnson has five hearing children} [*]

Jones, R. J. (1983a, January 30). Letter to Homer and Alice [Hanson Jones]. {Richard's letter is written to his deaf grandmother, Agatha Hanson, and speaks of his grandfather, Olof, who was an ordained minister} [Gallaudet University Archives, "Alice Hanson Jones - papers" biographical subject vertical file]

Jones, R. J. (1983b, January 30). Letter to Mr. Douglas D. Bahl of Faribault, Minnesota. {Richard's grandparents, Olof and Agatha Hanson, were deaf. In this letter he mentions seeing a PBS biographical program about his grandfather who was an Episcopal priest. He goes on to say: "I remember from time to time to be grateful to my grandparents for being unafraid - they can't have been oblivious, can they? - of getting married and having children." He goes on to share how his own life seemed "particularly charmed."} [Gallaudet University Archives, "Alice Hanson Jones - papers" biographical subject vertical file]

(*) Kane, J., & Shafer, C. M. (1970). Personal and family counseling services for the adult deaf: Final report. Los Angeles: Family Service of Los Angeles. (74 pages) [DEAF Copy 1: 361.06 K33p, 1970 - microfiche]

Kibo's Mama (1997, January). {Short listing of films by Russian movie superstar Alla Kliouka whose parents are deaf. Obtained from <http://nutcom.com/~ken/kliouka.html> in January, 1997. See the reference under "Alla Kliouka" for stills from her movies} [*]

KODA: Kids of Deaf Adults (1992). (Personal communication) {A listing of information to be given to a hearing child's school teacher that explains their bi-cultural needs. Developed by Susan Robbins and Ann Meehan-Kalis and other deaf parents in the Maryland KODA group formed in 1992} [*]

Koziar, S. W. (1969, September 27). A salute to Benny [Poem]. {Elizabeth Benson was affectionately known as "Benny" by her many friends. There was a testimonial dinner held in her honor September 27, 1969. This poem was written for that occasion. Stephen Koziar is from the class of 1934 and it was read by Bette Hicks of the class of 1969} [Gallaudet University Archives, "Elizabeth English Benson, Testimonial Dinner" biographical subject vertical file]

Kraft, B. (1988). Faith and adversity. Unpublished B. A. thesis, Lesley College, Cambridge, MA. (55 pages) [*]

(#) Laboratory for Language and Cognitive Sciences: Bibliography. (n.d.). La Jolla, CA: Salk Institute Laboratory for Language and Cognitive Studies. (10 pages) [*]

Lane, H. (1997). Modality-appropriate stimulation and deaf-blind children and adults. Paper presented at the Hilton/Perkins National Conference on Deafblindness, the Individual in a Changing Society, Washington, D. C., June 6-9, 1997. [*]

(*) Lawrence, I. E. (1972). Is justice deaf: What are the legal and constitutional rights of the deaf. Tallahassee, FL: Florida Registry of Interpreters for the Deaf. (33 pages - Ivan Lawrence is an attorney and associate professor of law) [DEAF 342.085 L3i, 1972]

Leonard, D., & Leonard, T. (1986). DEAF ED: A trivia game in deafness. Clive, IA: Deaf Expressions Unlimited. Write Deaf Expressions Unlimited, P.O. Box 142, Clive, IA 50053-0142 (515) 253-0925 (Recommended for 17 years and older - Reported in the May, 1987, issue of the CODA Newsletter, 4 (2), 3. [UNIV DEAF Periodicals]) {Questions are in the following five categories: biology; culture; history and education; potpourri; and sports and leisure. A few questions are about hearing children of the deaf: Charlie Babb, Alexander Graham Bell, Elizabeth Benson, Lon Chaney, Lou Fant, Edward Miner Gallaudet, Sidney Homer, and others. Questions on other related subjects are asked} [*]

Lon Chaney. (n.d.). (Newspaper and other clippings open to the public without restriction) [Gallaudet University Archives, "Biographical" subject vertical file]

Lon Chaney: The man behind the thousand faces, [Poster]. (1993). Vestal, NY: Vestal Press, Ltd. Write Vestal Press, P.O. Box 97, Vestal, New York 13851-0097 {To accompany the book by Michael F. Blake, Lon Chaney: The man behind the thousand faces. See listing under "books."} [*]

Louie J. Fant. (n.d.). (Newspaper and other clippings open to the public without restriction) [Gallaudet University Archives, "Biographical" subject vertical file]

Louise Fletcher. (n.d.). (Newspaper and other clippings open to the public without restriction) [Gallaudet University Archives, "Biographical" subject vertical file]

Louis W. Foxwell, Jr. (n.d.). (Newspaper and other clippings open to the public without restriction) [Gallaudet University Archives, "Biographical" subject vertical file]

Louis W. Foxwell, Sr. (n.d.). (Newspaper and other clippings open to the public without restriction) [Gallaudet University Archives, "Biographical" subject vertical file]

Love is Never Silent. (n.d.). (Newspaper and other clippings open to the public without restriction) [Gallaudet University Archives, "Deaf subject" subject vertical file]

Lovley, S. (1996). Marriage, parenting, and romance after a hearing loss. In Now What?: Life after deaf (pp. 38-47). Published by the author. Write Sean Lovley, 2812 Nomad Court West, Bowie, MD 200716 [DEAF 612.85 L68n, 1996]

Luczak, R. (forthcoming). Whispers of a savage sort. Unpublished play performed in September, 1996, at the National Technical Institute for the Deaf, Department of Performing Arts, Rochester Institute of Technology, Rochester, New York. {One main character, a hearing son, hates what backstabbing has done to his deaf parents and wants to avenge it somehow} Manuscript in preparation.

Mabel Anne Northern Finnell. (n.d.). (Newspaper and other clippings open to the public without restriction) [Gallaudet University Archives, "Biographical" subject vertical file]

Malinowski, A. C. (1997). What does the sun sound like. Unpublished autobiographical one-woman play. (Actually a "work in progress." Vignettes have been performed in a variety of venues including the 12th International CODA Conference, Denver, Colorado, July, 1997 - Personal communication) {"About a hearing daughter's continuing journey to bridge the divergent worlds of her Deaf parents and the hearing world. These personal tales open a window on Deaf culture and the complexities of being a cultural tourist in a land of 'hearies.' Through storytelling, Sign Language, laughter and tears, these stories illuminate the universal struggle for identity, communication and community" - Personal communication}

Marie Greenstone. (n.d.). (Newspaper and other clippings open to the public without restriction) [Gallaudet University Archives, "Biographical" subject vertical file]

Mary Alice Benson: 1903-1984. (n.d.). (SMSS - small manuscripts, archival, manuscript material, clippings and visual material open to the public without restriction) [Gallaudet University Archives, "Biographical" subject vertical file]

(##) Mathis, S. L., III. (1973-1974). Hearing children of deaf parents. {Unpublished study made while the author held the Powrie Vaux Doctor Chair of Deaf Studies at Gallaudet College, Washington, D. C. - RNID bibliography}

Memorial service [Notes]. (1973, January 18). (11 pages) {Includes an introduction by Rev. Rudolph Gawlik; a quote from Ulysses by Tennyson; a message from Dr. Leonard M. Elstad: "Service to Gallaudet College;" "services to the world;" "Miss Benson and her girls;" and "'Benny' my friend." All unattributed} [Gallaudet University Archives, "Elizabeth English Benson: Memorials" biographical subject vertical file]

(#) (##) Moody, G. H. (1991). In limbo: The barriers to spiritual awareness, a request for spiritual and pastoral care for deaf people and their families - especially hearing children of deaf parentage. (Available from the author in England)

Myers, L. (1985, May). Developmental issues related to being a hearing child of deaf parents. (Personal communication)

Myers, R. R. (1985a, Spring). The organization of Children of Deaf Adults - how goals affect its functioning. Unpublished paper, School of Social Welfare, University of California, Berkeley. (10 pages) [*]

Myers, R. R. (1985b). The process of goal establishment: CODA (Children of Deaf Adults). Unpublished paper, University of California, Berkeley. (16 pages) [*]

National Council for Social Workers with Deaf People Training Committee (Ed.). (1992, January). Special needs or special breed? Hearing children of deaf adults. Occasional Paper No. 4. Disability Resource Team. London: Training Committee of the National Council for Social Workers with Deaf People, NCSWDP. (24 pages) Write NCSWDP, 1st floor, Bedford House, 125-133 Camden High Street, London, England NW1 7JR. (The papers by Karen Coutts and Catherine White were reprinted in Deafness: The Journal of the Sociology of Deafness, a publication of the British Deaf Association [UNIV DEAF Periodicals]) {Transcript summary from a one day seminar organised [sic] by the London Boroughs Disability Resource Team of the NCSWDP, April 9, 1991} [DEAF 306.874 S632, 1992]

(*) Neubacher, M. (1987). Pathways for parenting, parents guide: (1) Our baby is hearing (24 pages); (2) Our child

M
I
S
C

253

- two worlds (40 pages); (3) <u>Adolescence to grown-up</u> (28 pages). Illustrated by Steve Schudlich. Detroit, MI: Lutheran Social Services of Michigan. Write Lutheran Social Services, 8131 E. Jefferson Avenue, Detroit, MI 48214. (See additional materials under Tebelman in this section) [DEAF 649.1 N48p, 1987]

Parent-child relationship: deaf. (n.d.). (File is a mixture of deaf-child/hearing-parent and hearing-child/deaf-parent newspaper and other clippings. Open to the public without restriction) [Gallaudet University Archives, "Deaf subject" subject vertical file]

Parent-child relationship: deaf adults. (n.d.). (Newspaper and other clippings open to the public without restriction) [Gallaudet University Archives, "Deaf subject" subject vertical file]

Parent-child relationship: deaf children. (n.d.). (A few coda-related newspaper and other clippings but the bulk concern deaf-children/hearing parents. Open to the public without restriction) [Gallaudet University Archives, "Deaf subject" subject vertical file]

(*) Parenting skills: Bringing together two worlds, one home, two cultures [Manual]. (1992). (206 pages) Developed by the Northern Virginia Resource Center for Deaf and Hard of Hearing Persons (NVRC), the Mount Vernon Center for Community Mental Health, the Virginia Department for the Deaf and Hard of Hearing and the Rev. Katherine Chipps, Holy Trinity Ministry of the Deaf. Consultant: Jennifer C. Witteborg. Distributed by NVRC. Write NVRC, 10363 Democracy Lane, Fairfax, VA 22030 (Part of a kit that contains two 90-minute videotapes and this eight lesson loose-leaf manual. Title on the videotape: <u>Parenting: Bringing two worlds together,</u> [GA: UNIV Cable TV, VHS 485]) {There are eight lessons and accompanying materials designed to be utilized by a deaf facilitator over an eight-week period in conjunction with the videotapes. Topics covered: 1) introduction; 2) communication; 3) interpreting; 4) discipline; 5) values; 6) self esteem; 7) teens and future expectations; 8) other issues. - Highly recommended} [DEAF 649.1 P373, 1992]

Payne, J. E. (1989, Fall). <u>Hearing children of deaf parents: Are they really different? A report of an independent study for the Division of Behavioral Sciences and Human Services.</u> Undergraduate thesis, Sign Language interpretation, Maryville College, Maryville, Tennessee. (45 pages) [*]

Profiles of notable children of deaf adults. (1996). (1 page) {Part of a packet of materials assembled to accompany the "Mother Father Deaf Day" proclamation, announcement and press release. For further information check the "International resources" section under "Mother Father Deaf Day."} [*]

Quigley, S. P., Babbini-Brasel, B. E., & Montanelli, D. S. (1973). <u>Interpreters for deaf people: Selection, evaluation and classification.</u> Urbana-Champaign, IL: University of Illinois, Institute for Research on Exceptional Children. (31 pages) [DEAF 418.02 Q5i, 1973]

Robbins, C. (1993, June 7). My children's dilemma [Poem]. (Personal communication)

Saunders, S. (1994). Families sharing experiences. In Year of the Family Conference (Ed.), <u>Year of the family conference: Families sharing experiences</u> (pp. 14-15). Dublin: Cheeverstown House. (Organised by the Irish Deaf Women's Group and the Irish Deaf Society - The author is a hearing daughter of Deaf parents) [DEAF 306.87 Y42y, 1994]

Schein, J. D. (1968). <u>Deaf persons in the United States: A demographic sketch.</u> Paper delivered to the International Research Seminar on Deafness, Washington, D. C., May, 1968. (7 pages) [DEAF 301.32 S3dea, 1968]

Sciarabba, A. M. (1994, May). <u>Turning a deaf ear: Video and thesis presented to the University Honors Committee</u>

in fulfillment of the requirements for Department Honors in Corporate Communication, Southern Connecticut State University, 1994. (32 pages) Video: 4 minutes. Color. Sound. VHS. [*]

Searls, J. M. (1989). Parental deafness as a factor in self-concept of deaf and hearing college students: A poster presentation. Washington, DC: Gallaudet University. (14 pages) [DEAF 155.5 S42p, 1989]

Sewell, H. R. (1969, September 27). Benny [Poem]. {Elizabeth Benson, Dean of Women, Gallaudet College, was affectionately known as "Benny" by her many friends. There was a testimonial dinner held in her honor on September 27, 1969. This poem was written for that occasion. Helen Ross Sewell is from the class of 1948} [Gallaudet University Archives, "Elizabeth English Benson, Testimonial Dinner" biographical subject vertical file]

(#) Shipley, A. E. (1982). Only children talked. (Reprinted in the August, 1985, issue of the CODA Newsletter, 2 (3), 5. [UNIV DEAF Periodicals] The original source is unidentified) [*]

(#) (##) Siedlecki, T. (1993a). Development of American Sign Language phonology in young children of deaf parents: Acquisition of location. Unpublished manuscript. (See dissertation)

(#) (##) Siedlecki, T. (1993b). Development of American Sign Language phonology in young children of deaf parents: Acquisition of movement. Unpublished manuscript. (See dissertation)

Siple, P., Akamatsu, C. T., & Loew, R. C. (1990). Acquisition of American Sign Language by fraternal twins: A case study. Unpublished paper. (20 pages. Published in 1991 as "Emergence of American Sign Language in a set of fraternal twins" in P. Siple & S. D. Fischer (Eds.), Theoretical issues in Sign Language research: Vol. 2. Psychology (pp. 25-40). Chicago: University of Chicago Press. [DEAF 420 T43, v.2]) [*]

Spellman, E. D. (1973). Words from a deaf parent. Morganton, NC: North Carolina School for the Deaf. {All the advice given here is directed toward hearing parents who have deaf children} [DEAF 306.874 S63w, 1973]

Spitz, S. (1989). Hearing children. (Draft of a paper submitted for publication) {Susan Spitz is a free lance writer in New York City. This is a paper written when she was a student at the Columbia University Graduate School of Journalism} [*]

(*) Starkey Laboratories (Ed.). (1983). Suggestions for the family. Eden Prarie, MN: Starkey Laboratories. (16 pages) [DEAF 306.87 S8, 1983]

(*) Stranik, M. K. (1986). The child care picture book: Especially for hearing impaired parents: (1) Baby is here! Basic newborn care. (2) Feeding your child: Nutrition for 6-24 months. (3) Healthy child, sick child: Child health issues. (4) Safe child and emergencies: Childproofing and first aid techniques. (5) Baby grows: Child development. (6) Baby plays: Play and stimulation. St. Paul, MN: Hearing Impaired Health and Wellness Services, Hearing Impaired Parents Program, St. Paul-Ramsey Medical Center, 640 Jackson, St. Paul, MN 55101. [DEAF 649.1 C455, 1986]

(*) (##) Stranik, M. K., Nelson, M., & Hornfeldt, D. (1986a). Emergencies. St. Paul, MN: Hearing Impaired Parents Program, St. Paul-Ramsey Medical Center, MELD. [*]

(*) (##) Stranik, M. K., Nelson, M., & Hornfeldt, D. (1986b). Feeding your child after five months old. St. Paul, MN: Hearing Impaired Parents Program, St. Paul-Ramsey Medical Center, MELD. [*]

(*) (##) Stranik, M. K., Nelson, M., & Hornfeldt, D. (1986c). Safe child. St. Paul, MN: Hearing Impaired Parents

M
I
S
C

Program, St. Paul-Ramsey Medical Center, MELD. [*]

(*) **Stranik, M. K., Nelson, M., & Hornfeldt, D. (1986d).** The middle of the night book for hearing impaired parents. St. Paul, MN: Hearing Impaired Parents Program, St. Paul-Ramsey Medical Center, MELD. (67 pages) [DEAF Copy 1: 649.1 M522, 1986]

(*) **Stranik, M. K., Nelson, M., Meyer, V., & Hinkley, K. R.. (Eds.). (1986).** The child care book especially for parents who are deaf and hard of hearing, book 4: Safe child and emergencies. Illustrations and design by Mary F. Nelson, Fred Gravatt and Linda L. Hinkley. St. Paul, MN: HIPP (Hearing Impaired Parents Program) and MELD, St. Paul-Ramsey Medical Center. (62 pages) [*]

(*) **Stranik, M. K., Nelson, M., Meyer, V., & Leif, K. R. (Eds.). (1986a).** The child care book especially for parents who are deaf and hard of hearing, book 1: Baby is here! Illustrations and design by Mary F. Nelson, Fred Gravatt and Linda L. Hinkley. St. Paul, MN: HIPP (Hearing Impaired Parents Program) and MELD, St. Paul-Ramsey Medical Center. (86 pages) [*]

(*) **Stranik, M. K., Nelson, M., Meyer, V., & Leif, K. R. (Eds.). (1986b).** The child care book especially for parents who are deaf and hard of hearing, book 2: Feeding your child. Illustrations and design by Mary F. Nelson, Fred Gravatt and Linda L. Hinkley. St. Paul, MN: HIPP (Hearing Impaired Parents Program) and MELD, St. Paul-Ramsey Medical Center. (61 pages) [*]

(*) **Stranik, M. K., Nelson, M., Meyer, V., & Leif, K. R. (Eds.). (1986c).** The child care book especially for parents who are deaf and hard of hearing, book 3: Healthy child/sick child. Illustrations and design by Mary F. Nelson, Fred Gravatt and Linda L. Hinkley. St. Paul, MN: HIPP (Hearing Impaired Parents Program) and MELD, St. Paul-Ramsey Medical Center. (61 pages) [*]

(*) **Stranik, M. K., Nelson, M., Meyer, V., & Leif, K. R. (Eds.). (1986d).** The child care book especially for parents who are deaf and hard of hearing, book 5: Baby grows. Illustrations and design by Mary F. Nelson, Fred Gravatt and Linda L. Hinkley. St. Paul, MN: HIPP (Hearing Impaired Parents Program) and MELD, St. Paul-Ramsey Medical Center. (52 pages) [*]

(*) **Stranik, M. K., Nelson, M., Meyer, V., & Leif, K. R. (Eds.). (1986e).** The child care book especially for parents who are deaf and hard of hearing, book 6: Baby plays. Illustrations and design by Mary F. Nelson, Fred Gravatt and Linda L. Hinkley. St. Paul, MN: HIPP (Hearing Impaired Parents Program) and MELD, St. Paul-Ramsey Medical Center. (52 pages) [*]

(##) **Taimisto, P. (1975).** The emotional and cognitive development of the hearing children of deaf parents. (See the summary of results of this study in the February, 1985, issue of the CODA Newsletter, 2 (1), 5. [UNIV DEAF Periodicals]) {Reports on developments in Finland for hearing children with deaf parents}

(*) **Tebelman, L. (1989a).** Pathways for parenting video: facilitator's guide. Detroit, MI: Lutheran Social Services of Michigan. (146 pages) Write Lutheran Social Services of Michigan, Family Counseling and Education, 8131 E. Jefferson Avenue, Detroit, MI 48214. (See the related Pathways for parenting booklets by Marjorie Neubacher. [DEAF 649.1 N48p, 1987]) [DEAF 649.1 T42p, 1989, facilitator's guide]

(*) **Tebelman, L. (1989b).** Pathways for parenting video: parent's guide. Lutheran Social Services of Michigan, Detroit. (102 pages) Write Lutheran Social Services of Michigan, Family Counseling and Education, 8131 E. Jefferson Avenue, Detroit, MI 48214. (See the related Pathways for parenting booklets by Marjorie Neubacher. [DEAF 649.1 N48p, 1987]) [DEAF 649.1 T42p, 1989, parent's guide]

Treesberg, J. (Ed). (1992). Louder than words, coda letters: A memorial for Alan Dalton. Washington, DC: Louder Than Words. Write Judith Treesberg, P.O. Box 90934, Washington, DC 20090 [*]

Tubergen, J. (1991, April). Codas: Are they like White America? A study of hearing children of deaf parents. Unpublished term paper. (29 pages) [*]

(*) Urban, C. (1984). Child custody issues for parents with disabilities. East Orange, NJ: Community Health Law Project. (32 pages) {Legal issues and opinions specific to New Jersey are surveyed} [*]

(##) Voss, S. A. (1992, Spring). Children of deaf adults. Unpublished report of a senior thesis for the Division of Behavioral Sciences and Human Services, Sign Language interpreting, Maryville College, Maryville, Tennessee. (55 pages)

Wakabayashi, R., Ayers, G. E., Rivera, O. A., Saylor, L. Q., & Stewart, J. L. (Eds.). (1977). Unique problems of handicapped minorities: Awareness papers. Washington, DC: White House Conference on Handicapped Individuals. (Publication No. 18 - 20 pages) {Papers were prepared on the following populations: Asian Americans, Black Americans, Native Americans and those with Spanish Surnames. Interesting, almost no mention of hearing children of the deaf and parenting needs} [DEAF 362.84 U54, 1977]

Warren Wesley Fauth. (n.d.). (Newspaper and other clippings open to the public without restriction) [Gallaudet University Archives, "Biographical" subject vertical file]

(*) Watson, T. (1991, April). A deaf parent's view. In National Council for Social Workers with Deaf People Training Committee (Ed.), Special needs or special breed? Hearing children of deaf adults (pp. 10-11). (24 pages) Write NCSWDP - 1st floor, Bedford House, 125-133 Camden High Street, London, England NW1 7JR. {Transcript of a paper presented at a one day seminar organized by the Training Committee of the National Council for Social Workers with Deaf People, NCSWDP, April 9, 1991} [DEAF 306.874 S632, 1992]

Why was a long long train stretching after actress Alla Kliouka? (1995, November 9). {This is an interview from Komsomolskaya Pravda with the Russian Best Actress award winner whose parents are deaf. See the listing of Alla's movies under "Kibo's Mama." Obtained off the internet at <http://www.nutcom.com/~ken/interview.html>} [*]

World War II subject vertical files. (n.d.). (Several files of newspaper and other clippings open to the public without restriction) {Numerous references to children of the deaf: obituaries, those serving in the miliary, rank promotions, etc.} [Gallaudet University Archives subject vertical files]

Zeder, S. L. (1997, April). A taste of sunrise: Tuc's story. Unpublished play directed by Victoria Brown and performed at the Gallaudet University Theatre Arts Department in April, 1997. {Maizie is Tuc's hearing daughter and has a prominent role}

**M
I
S
C**

IX

INTERNATIONAL

RESOURCES

FOR FURTHER

INFORMATION

Caution: not all organizations listed here have services for deaf families with hearing children. For example, the American Speech-Language Hearing Association (ASHA) could be helpful in educating the public about the fact that NOT ALL hearing children in deaf families need speech therapy or have difficulty learning spoken language. Maybe someday they will be involved in educating their members (speech therapists, audiologists, speech pathologists, etc.) away from the medical/pathological model of Deaf parenting.

Check the following for additional organization information:

International Directory of Services for the Deaf published by the National Information Center on Deafness, Washington, D. C.

Also check the 1998 TDI National Directory and Guide compiled and published by Telecommunications for the Deaf, Inc., 8630 Fenton Street, Suite 604, Silver Spring, Maryland 20910-3803 USA 301-589-3786 (V) or 301-589-3797 (TTY) or internet: <http://www.tdi-online.org>

Internet resources:

The Spring, 1997, issue of Gallaudet Today, contains an article "On the Web" listing numerous organizations and their internet addresses (pp. 12-13). Search YAHOO! under the topic "Society and culture: Disabilities: Specific Disabilities: Deafness: Organizations" for their list. And, of course, many of the internet addresses listed in the following directories will themselves have hyper-links to other web sites.

<http://www.deafworldweb.org/dww/> (Deaf World Web National Directory of organizations)

<http://www.weizmann.ac.il/deaf-info/> (The "All you wanted to know about deafness" site)

<http://www.dpi.org> (Disabled People's International)

<http://www.DEAF-L> (Frequently Asked Questions - FAQ - web site)

<http://www.deafness.miningco.com/mlibrary.html> (Jamie Berke, host)

<http://www.deaflibrary.org> (Created by Karen Nakamura)

NAME: Accent on Living Magazine (USA)
Contact: Julie Cheever Starshak, Marketing Manager
Address: Gillum Road and High Drive, P.O. Box 700, Bloomington, Illinois 61702
Phone: 800-787-8444
E-Mail: <acntlvng@aol.com>
Internet: <http://www.blvd.com/accent/index.html>
Julie Cheever Starshak's parents started this magazine in 1953, four years after her dad had polio. On the cutting edge of getting ideas and information to the physically disabled: product information; medical updates; news of upcoming events; travel tips; how-to ideas and more. They also have an assortment of books on a variety of related topics. The oldest magazine of this type.

NAME: Alexander Graham Bell Association for the Deaf (AGB, USA)
Address: 3417 Volta Place, N.W., Washington, DC 20007
Phone: 202-337-5220 (V/TTY) 202-337-8314 (FAX)
E-Mail: <agbell2@aol.com>
Internet: <http://www.agbell.org>
Publications: The Volta Review, and Volta Voices
A nonprofit membership organization that was established in 1890 to empower persons who are hearing impaired to function independently by promoting universal rights and optimal opportunities to learn to use, maintain, and improve all aspects of their verbal communications, including their abilities to speak, speechread, use residual hearing, and process both spoken and written language.

NAME: American Association of People with Disabilities (AAPD, USA)
Address: 1819 H Street N.W., Suite 330, Washington, DC 20006
Phone: 800-840-8844 or 202-457-8168 and 202-457-0473 (FAX)
Internet: <http://www.aapd-dc.org/>
AAPD was launched on July 25, 1995, as a non-profit, non-partisan, cross-disability organization whose goals are unity, leadership and impact. Membership is $10.00 annually per individual. Dr. I. King Jordan, President of Gallaudet University, and Nancy Bloch, Executive Director of the National Association for the Deaf, are two of the 21 elected members of their board. With 49 million people with disabilities in the United States alone, AAPD was established to represent these 49 million Americans and to be a positive private-sector force to achieve the goal of full inclusion in American society and to form a unified front for the civil rights of people with disabilities.

NAME: American Speech-Language-Hearing Association (ASHA, USA)
Address: 10801 Rockville Pike, Rockville, Maryland 20852
Phone: 301-897-5700 (V/TTY) 1-800-498-2071 (V/TTY) 301-571-0457 (FAX)
Internet: <http://www.asha.org>
ASHA is the professional, scientific, and credentialing association for more than 91,000 audiologists, speech-language pathologists, and speech, language, and hearing scientists. Mission: to promote the interests of and provide the highest quality services for professionals in audiology, speech-language pathology, and speech and hearing science, and to advocate for people with communication disabilities.

DEAF: Association of Disabled Parents in the Norfolk Area (PANDA, England)
Address: PANDA, 145 Main Road, Clenchwarton, King's Lynn, Norfolk PE34 4DT United Kingdom
Phone: 01553 768193
PANDA has just published Families First which is a study of disabled parents of school-aged children and their families living mainly in West Norfolk and Cambridgeshire (United Kingdom). This report will interest disabled parents, and those working in the voluntary and statutory bodies which offer services and facilities to families,

RESOURCES

parents, children and disabled people. It was compiled from a survey which aimed to create accurate information about how disabled parents with school-aged children view and manage their lives. Subjects include: talking about disability with children; children and schools - parents' views on schools and schools' attitudes to disability; family activities and holidays; family prospects - effects of disability on family employment; children at work - helping, nursing and guiding at home; parents and the Law - experiences in courts concerning welfare of their children; medical matters - views on professionals, information and counseling; help and advice - who and what helps, and what doesn't. Available from PANDA. Large print and audio formats are available.

NAME: Association of Late-Deafened Adults (ALDA, USA)
Address: 10310 Main St., #274, Fairfax, Virginia, 22030
P.O. Box 641763, Chicago, IL 60664
Phone: 404-289-1596 (TTY hotline)
Internet: <http://www.alda.org>
Publication: ALDA NEWS
Formed in Chicago, Illinois, in 1987, ALDA's membership is international in scope. ALDA works collaboratively with other organizations around the world serving the needs of late-deafened people and extends a welcome to everyone, late deafened or not, who supports our goals.

NAME: Børn af Døve - Children of Deaf (Denmark, THE NETHERLANDS)
Contact: Danish Deaf Association
Address: Fensmarkgade 1, Postbox 704, DK-2200, Copenhagen N, Denmark.
See their publication, Deaf parents/hearing children: A collection of articles, in the "Miscellaneous" section.

NAME: British Deaf Association (BDA, London, ENGLAND)
Contact: Liz Bassett, Education/Youth Assistant
Address: 1-3 Worship Street, London EC2A 2AB ENGLAND
Phone: 0171-588 3520 (V) 0171-588 3529 (TEXT) 0171-588 3527 (FAX)
E-Mail: <ldap@ndirect.co.uk>
Internet: <http://www.bda.org.uk/bda1a.html>
The United States counterpart of the National Association of the Deaf. "To advance and protect the interests of Deaf people." They publish in cooperation with the Department of Health a pack of 12 pamphlets with the title: "**Deaf**initely worth thinking about....." Its purpose is to promote Deaf Awareness in schools and health services. One is entitled "Hearing children with Deaf parents" with several paragraphs on the following subjects: hearing children with Deaf parents; how do hearing children with Deaf parents learn to speak?; Deaf people as parents; hearing children as interpreters; contact with other families; and hearing adults with Deaf parents. It was "written by a Child of Deaf Parents." They also have a video in British Sign Language that outlines the information in each leaflet to help monolingual BSL users.

NAME: Camp Mark 7 (USA)
Contact: Lisa Flynn, Executive Director
Address: 93 Wilson Street A4, Marlboro, Massachusetts 01752
Phone: 508-624-7688 (TTY) 508-624-0956 (FAX)
E-Mail: <LisaFlynn@aol.com>
Internet: <http://www.members.aol.com/campmark7>
After May 15 contact: Camp Mark 7, 144 Mohawk Hotel Road, Old Forge, New York 13420
Phone: 315-357-6089 (V/TTY) 315-357-6403 (FAX)
Camp Mark 7 is located on the Fourth Lake of the Adirondack Mountains in Old Forge, New York. There is a large multi-level lodge with 31 bedrooms. Activities: waterskiing, tubing, kneeboarding, canoeing and sailing, outdoor games, tennis and basketball court. During the summer of 1998, there will be a camp program offered for hearing

kids of deaf adults from ages 11-15 the week of August 2-8, 1998 (KODA Week). There is a Deaf staff to operate the facilities but they hope to have a coda (hearing adult with deaf parents) coordinator and coda camp staff. CM7 is a subsidiary of Mark Seven Deaf Foundation.

NAME: Camp Tom Tom (USA)
Contact: Wendy An-Koch, Education Coordinator, Deaf Hearing Community Center
Address: Holy Spirit Lutheran Church, 2545 Franklin Avenue, Secane, Pennsylvania 19018
Phone: 610-534-4940 (TTY) 610-534-4942 (FAX)
E-Mail: <DHCCedu@aol.com>
This camp has outdoor activities, swimming, arts and crafts and more. They invite deaf campers, hearing siblings of deaf campers and children of deaf adults. Ages for each session, 4-7 and 8-11 year olds.

NAME: Catholic Charities of the Archdiocese of San Francisco - Hearing Impaired Program (USA)
Contact: Millie Stansfield, M.S., M.F.C.C., Deaf Family Coordinator
Address: 1801 Octavia Street, San Francisco, California 94109-4328
Phone: 415-749-3812 (V) 415-567-0540 (TTY) 415-567-0916 (FAX)
The Hearing Impaired Program was first established in 1976. Housed at St. Benedict's Church for the Deaf, it offers counseling, social services and advocacy to deaf individuals and families from all over the Bay Area. Catholic Charities, the not-for-profit service arm of the Archdiocese of San Francisco, is one of the Bay Area's largest human service organizations. The Deaf Parents Project (DPP) uses a bilingual/bicultural approach to enhance family relationships between deaf parents and their hearing children by developing skills in parenting, communicating and self-empowerment. The Deaf Parent Class is an integral part of the support system for deaf families and allows for them to create a "Community within a Community." These families learn how to better manage the two different cultures in their families (deaf and hearing). The children's groups are also an integral part of the overall program. Group activities provide an arena for the children to develop Sign Language communication skills, as well as a better understanding of, and comfort with, their Deaf culture.

NAME: Center for German Sign Language and Communication of the Deaf (Hamburg, GERMANY)
Contact: Guido Joachim, M.A., Librarian
Address: University of Hamburg Rothenbaumchaussee 45, 20148 Hamburg - Germany.
Phone: 49-40-4123-3239 or 49-40-4123-6578 (FAX)
E-Mail: <Gjoachim@rrz.uni-hamburg.de>
Internet: <http://www.Guido.Joachim@signlang.uni-hamburg.de>
See the following 1993 publication which lists 6,400 articles in 14 categories with an extensive index. G. H. G. Joachim & S. Prillwitz (Eds.), International Studies on Sign Language and Communication of the Deaf, Vol. 21. International bibliography of Sign Language. Hamburg, Germany: Signum Press.

NAME: Center on Deafness, Western Pennsylvania School for the Deaf (USA)
Contact: Helen B. Craig, Ph.D., Research Director
Address: Center on Deafness at WPSD, 300 East Swissvale Avenue, Pittsburgh, PA 15218
Phone: 412-244-4228 (V/TTY)
In 1991, the Center had a grant from the Pennsylvania State Department of Education to develop a program in family literacy for deaf families with hearing children. See their ERIC documents reported elsewhere. They have a series of brochures with the following over-all title: TIPS: Toward improved parenting skills for deaf parents with hearing children. Topics covered are: 1) Behavior management; 2) self-esteem; 3) your child's language development; 4) your child's speech development; 5) the Deaf parent in a hearing child's school; 6) safety; and 7) nutrition. They also have literacy material titled Literacy initiatives for families of deaf parents with hearing children: Project description and report.

R
E
S
O
U
R
C
E
S

NAME: Centre for Deaf Studies, School for Education, Research Unit, University of Bristol (ENGLAND)
Contact: Dr. Jim Kyle
Address: University of Bristol, 22 Berkeley Square, Bristol, BS8 IHP, UNITED KINGDOM
Phone: 0117 928 7080 (V) 0117 925 1370 (Minicom) 0117 925 7875 (FAX)
E-Mail: <Jim.Kyle@bristol.ac.uk>
Internet: <http://www.bris.ac.uk/> or <http://www.bris.ac.uk/Depts/DeafStudies/welcome.html>
Much of the Centre's focus seems to revolve around issues of deaf children within hearing families. Jim Kyle, Jennifer Ackerman and Bencie Woll have also been involved in a Research Project at the University of Bristol on "Hearing and deaf children of deaf families." Check their web site for their vast array of programs and research.

NAME: Child Development Center (CDC, USA)
Contact: Gail Solit, Director
Address: Gallaudet University, KDES, CDC, 800 Florida Avenue, N.E., Washington, DC 20002-3695
Phone: 202-651-5130 (V/TTY)
E-Mail: <gasolit@gallua.gallaudet.edu>
Internet: <http://www.gallaudet.edu/~precpweb/childev.html>
The CDC is an accredited campus child care center that began in 1984. CDC serves preschool and kindergarten children and their families who work and study at Gallaudet, University alumni parents, the deaf community and the general metropolitan area community. This is a 12-month program which has a special 8-week summer program that serves children up to age 10. The Center is accredited by the National Academy of Accredited Programs, a division of the National Association for the Education of Young Children. Since 1988, they have served deaf, hard-of-hearing and hearing toddlers, preschoolers, and kindergartners in an integrated child care program.

NAME: College for Continuing Education, Gallaudet University (CCE, USA)
Contact: Dr. Reggie Redding, Director
Address: Gallaudet University, 800 Florida Avenue, N.E., Washington, DC 20002
Phone: 202-651-6060 (V/TTY) 202-651-6074 (FAX)
E-Mail: <klwalker@gallua.gallaudet.edu>
Internet: <http://www.gallaudet.edu/~cceweb/>
For years CCE sponsored a variety of "family learning vacations" for families with deaf children, deaf-blind children, and others. They have provided a training seminar, "Developing Family Learning Programs for Deaf-Hearing Families." Their family life programs continue on a limited basis. In May of 1997, UCM co-sponsored the first-ever conference for deaf families with hearing children entitled, "Building Bridges: Strengthening Home and School Relationships for Deaf Parents and their Hearing Children." CCE is committed to maintaining excellence in learning and celebrating diversity by offering lifelong learning opportunities to deaf and hard-of-hearing individuals, as well as their families, friends and professionals serving them. In collaboration with the Gallaudet University academic divisions, CCE designs, develops, and delivers quality continuing education programs and outreach services through multiple formats to enhance the quality of life for deaf and hard-of-hearing people world-wide.

NAME: The Community Network (TCN, USA)
Contact: Darlene Goncz Zangara, Wee Too! Project Director
Address: 452 W. Market St., Xenia, Ohio 45385
Phone: 937-376-8700 (V/TTY) 937-376-8792 (V) 937-376-8788 (TTY)
The Wee Too! Team provides educational workshops for parents and professionals. These are specially designed to provide the information and strategies necessary to foster resiliency in young children with special needs. Other services: consultation; Wee Too Program/curriculum manuals; individual training; awareness activities for schools, agencies or community events. Many of these activities are for hearing families with deaf children but programs for deaf parents with hearing children are available.

NAME: CODA/AUSTRALIA (Children of Deaf Adults, NEW SOUTH WALES, AUSTRALIA)
Contact: Peter and Judie Bonser
Address: 3 Spey St., Winston Hills, NSW 2153, Australia
Phone: 011-612-9893-8555 (V/TTY) 011-612-9639-0373 (FAX)
E-Mail: <deafsoc@tig.com.au>
Peter and Judie Bonser are not only the founders, but the movers and shakers in the Australian CODA organization and have been recognized as such. In 1993 their group received funding for a 4-day camp for kodas, kids of deaf adults, that was very successful. Peter Bonser is an International Representative to the American CODA Board.

NAME: CODA - Children of Deaf Adults (CODA, USA, International)
Contact: Millie Brother, Founder
Address: P.O. Box 30715, Santa Barbara, California 93130-0715
Phone: 805-682-0977 (V/TTY)
Contact: Trudy Schafer, President
E-Mail: <Trudy_Schafer@harvard.edu>
Internet: <http://www.gallaudet.edu/~rgpricke/coda/index.html>
Publication: CODA Connection
Founded in 1983 and incorporated as a not-for-profit corporation in 1990, CODA is an international membership organization for hearing adults who have at least one deaf parent. Membership, activities and scope are international. CODA is an organization established for the purpose of promoting family awareness and individual growth in hearing children of deaf parents. This purpose is accomplished through providing educational opportunities, promoting self-help, organizing advocacy efforts, and acting as a resource for the membership and various communities. CODA is an organization that focuses on hearing children of deaf adults. Membership is primarily but not exclusively composed of hearing children of deaf parents. CODA addresses our bicultural experiences through conferences, support groups, and resource development. Voting membership is available to hearing offspring of deaf adult(s) and is $20. annually (US Funds only). Supporting membership (non-voting) is available for everyone else ($15. US annually). Both memberships come with a one-year subscription to the quarterly newsletter. On the CODA internet HOMEPAGE you'll find the following information: purpose and mission statements; history of CODA; international conferences; publications; calendar of events; how to join; local chapters; the Millie Brother Scholarship; the board of directors; internet directory of codas; and a guest book for visitor comments.

NAME: CODA/Bay Area (USA)
Contact: Michael Velez
Address: 1015 Esther Drive, Pleasant Hill, California 94523-4301
Phone: 510-235-7800 (V) 510-945-1949 (FAX)
Publication: CODA Chronicles
CODA chapter in the San Francisco-Oakland and Bay Area of Northern California.

NAME: CODA/Canada (Ontario, CANADA)
Contact: Anna P. Perry
Address: 9-11 Sedgeley Dr., Weston, Ontario M9R, Canada
E-Mail: <brianp@indirect.com>
There is no formally organized CODA chapter in Canada yet.

NAME: CODA-Chat on America On Line (Internet, International)
Contact: Dave Eklof
E-Mail: <WisCoda01@aol.com>
A monthly America On Line (AOL) chat room for hearing adults who have Deaf parents. You do not have to be a member of Children of Deaf Adults (CODA) to join in.

NAME: CODA/DC: Washington-Metropolitan Area (USA)
Contact: Roz Prickett
Address: P.O. Box 2352, 800 Florida Ave., N.E., Washington, DC 20002-3695
Phone: 202-651-5877 or 301-352-6883
E-Mail: <Tom.Bull@Gallaudet.edu> or <Roz.Prickett@Gallaudet.edu>
Internet: <http://www.gallaudet.edu/~rgpricke/coda/index.html>
This chapter of CODA was founded in 1986 by Hugh Prickett, Diana Lusker, Maryanne Royster and Tom Bull. The area served includes the Washington, D. C., Virginia and Maryland suburbs and region. They have a newsletter, bi-monthly dinners, partners group, retreats, picnics and other events.

NAME: CODA/Finland (Helsinki, FINLAND)
Contact: Raili Ojala, Secretary
Address: Box 65, 00401 Helsinki, Finland
Phone: +358-9-5803 570 (TTY) +358-9-5803 576 (FAX)
E-Mail: <raili.ojala@kl-deaf.fi>
A couple of years ago, Finland's Constitution was amended and mentions the "rights of those who use Sign Language" (covers codas too). They are now organized. The name is Kuurojen Vanhempien Kuulevien Lasten Yhdistysry [Association of Hearing Children of Deaf Parents]. President is Arto Kaartti. They are in the process of producing information and material packages for codas, deaf parents, schools, day care centres, social workers, etc. In 1975, a study was conducted (See the P. Taimisto reference in "Miscellaneous") indicating there were meetings of hearing children of deaf parents between 1976 and 1983. Since 1977, the Finnish Association of the Deaf has arranged courses for deaf families with hearing children "about bringing up a hearing child, [and] for the children about deafness and sign language."

NAME: CODA/Hawaii (USA)
Contact: Hugh Prickett
Address: 3440 Leahi Ave., Honolulu, Hawaii 96815
Phone: 808-739-0404
E-Mail: <jprickett@compuserve.com>
A new chapter of CODA which meets sporadically in Oahu but they hope to reach out to other islands.

NAME: CODA Inc. International Outreach (USA, International)
Contact: Tom Bull
Address: P.O. Box 2352, 800 Florida Ave., N.E., Washington, DC 20002-3695
Phone: 703-799-2239 (V/TTY) 202-651-5752 (FAX)
E-Mail: <Tom.Bull@Gallaudet.edu> or <Tomthe@aol.com>
Internet: <http://www.gallaudet.edu/~rgpricke/coda/index.html>
For information about CODA or to contribute resources to update the bibliography. Web site information is updated periodically. Hot links to related sites.

NAME: CODA/Illinois (ILCODA, USA)
Contact: Diana Nelson, President
Address: 1403 Juneway Terrace, Round Lake Beach, Illinois 60073
Phone: 847-546-0799
E-Mail: <mullis_the@media.com> or <jolycoda@aol.com>
Formerly the ChicagoLand CODA group, now serves the state of Illinois and surrounding areas. Chapter newsletter, Mother Father Deaf Day celebrations, dinners and retreats.

NAME: CODA Indiana (USA)

Contact: Judy McAleavey
Address: 7324 Brackenwood Circle South Drive, Indianapolis, Indiana 46260
Phone: 317-255-4299
E-Mail: <JudyMCODA@aol.com>
Chapter of CODA serving the Indiana state area.

NAME: CODA INTERNET CONNECTION (Internet Listserv, International)
Contact: Roz Prickett
Address: 4029J Emerald Lane, Bowie, Maryland 20716
Phone: 202-651-5704 or 301-352-6883
E-Mail: <Roz.Prickett@Gallaudet.edu>
Internet: <http://www.gallaudet.edu/~rgpricke/coda/index.html>
An international internet news service for hearing offspring of deaf adults. On the CODA HOMEPAGE there is a section for listing your internet address and a "comments" section to say who you are.

NAME: CODA/Michigan (USA)
Contact: Darlene Graham
Address: 9391 Pearl Beach Blvd., Pearl Beach, Michigan 48001
Phone: 810-794-3391
E-Mail: <dgraham@mchg.org>
State chapter of Children of Deaf Adults. Activities have been newsletter, Mother Father Deaf Day celebration, teen kodas gathering.

NAME: CODA/Minnesota (MinneCODA, USA)
Contact: Rubin Latz or Amy Mathews
Address: 205 Lilac Lane, Shoreview, Minnesota 55126-6209
Phone: 612-482-1822 or 612-405-0332
E-Mail: <RSLatz@aol.com> or <ALMathews@aol.com>
State chapter of Children of Deaf Adults. Activities: bi-monthly meetings; annual family holiday potluck. Dues, $10.00/year.

NAME: CODA/Netherlands (NETHERLANDS)
Contact: Mrs. Heinke Nederlof (Julia Stoel)
Address: Weerdstraat 57, 7941 XK Meppel
E-Mail: <v.neure-stoel@wxs.nl>

NAME: CODA/Nevada (USA)
Contact: Sammie Milburn
Address: P.O. Box 12175, Las Vegas, Nevada 89112
Phone: 702-454-1104
E-Mail: <Milsam@aol.com>
Chapter of CODA serving the state of Nevada.

NAME: CODA/New Jersey (NJCODA, USA)
Contact: Mariann Jacobson
Address: 58 Harrison Avenue, Edison, New Jersey 08837
Phone: 732-548-2571
E-Mail: <aggr01a@prodigy.com>
This chapter began in 1991. Dues are $7.50/year. There are monthly meetings and big family holiday party. They

RESOURCES

have annual one-day retreats and have been involved in New Jersey's Deaf Fest. Plan for a Mother Father Deaf Day celebration. Have been involved with a koda and koda parents group.

NAME: CODA/North Carolina (NC/CODA, USA)
Contact: JoAnn Kinsey
Address: 1510 Cotherstone Dr., Durham, North Carolina 27712
Phone: 919-477-0110
E-Mail: <nccoda@aol.com>
CODA chapter functioning in North Carolina since 1992. Activities: newsletter, dinners, retreats.

NAME: CODA/Southeastern Region (SECODA, USA)
Contact: Margaret Collier
Address: 1525 Lyncrest Avenue, Jackson, Mississippi 39202
Phone: 601-355-3222
E-Mail: <MKColl@aol.com>
For the last four years, the Southeastern (region of the United States) codas have had a retreat in early Spring. They have been held in Tennessee, Mississippi, Alabama, Georgia, and South Carolina.

NAME: CODA/Wisconsin (WisCODA, USA)
Contact: Kim Bruno
Address: 2446 Pebble Valley Road, Waukesha, Wisconsin 53188
E-Mail: <Mimi11995@aol.com>
Have had dinners, a newsletter, and an International Conference in their area. Kids of Deaf Adults contact is (WisKODA) at <frankbroder@globaldial.com>

NAME: Deaf Access Services Children's Center (DAS, USA)
Contact: Janell Bunn-Verdin, Director
        Peter C. Myers, Executive Director
Address: 540 South Market Street, Frederick, Maryland 21705-3104
Phone: 301-696-1550 (V/TTY) 301-695-6859 (FAX)
E-Mail: <deafaccess@juno.com>
Established in 1997, the DAS Children's Center is a state-licensed preschool and child care program designed to meet the unique needs of deaf children, their siblings, and hearing children with deaf parents. Children from the community at-large are also welcome.

NAME: Deaf Adoption News Service (DANS, Internet, USA)
Contact: Jamie Berke
E-Mail: <sberke@netcom.com>
Internet: <http://www.deafness.miningco.com/> or <http://www.erols.com/berke/deafchildren.html>
Free news service sending out information about waiting deaf and hard-of-hearing foreign children.

NAME: DEAF C.A.N.! Community Advocacy Network (USA)
Contact: Michelle R. Graham, MSW, Pathways for Parenting Coordinator
Address: 2111 Orchard Lake Road, #101, Sylvan Lake, Michigan 48320
Phone: 248-332-3331 (V) 248-332-3323 (TTY) 248-332-7334 (FAX)
E-Mail: <mgraham4@juno.com> or <deafcan@prodigy.net>
The Pathways to Parenting program is now operated through Deaf C.A.N. (Community Advocacy Network). A United Way Agency, DEAF C.A.N.! offers several programs: Pathways for Parenting video classes; five-week classes, Practical Parenting Series; and a monthly support group and Peaceful Parenting (one-to-one intervention).

They plan to add MELD: The Child Care Program especially for parents who are Deaf and Hard-of-Hearing providing practical information for child care in the first two years of life. Contact MELD's Minneapolis office, 612-332-7563.

NAME: Deaf Family Research Press (DFR Press, USA)
Contact: Thomas H. Bull
Address: P.O. Box 8417, Alexandria, Virginia 22306-8417
E-Mail: <TomThe@aol.com>
Internet: <http://www.gallaudet.edu/~gisweb/Tom.html>
Committed to publishing definitive quality reference materials in the area of Deaf parents and families with hearing children. Several publications forthcoming.

NAME: Deaf-Hearing Couples Communication Enrichment Network (DHC, Internet, International, USA)
Contact: Anne McIntosh, Ph.D., founder
Address: P.O. Box 1961, Davidson, North Carolina 28036
E-Mail: <mcintosh@vnet.net>
An international organization that reaches out to married or dating couples where one partner is hearing and the other is deaf. To join this listserv: e-mail <listproc@vnet.net> In the body: "subscribe DHC John Doe"

NAME: Deaf Mosaic (USA)
Address: Department of Television, Film and Photography, Gallaudet University
800 Florida Ave., N.E., Washington, DC 20002-3695
Phone: 202-651-5115 (TTY/V) 202-651-5124 (FAX)
While the television program is no longer being produced, you can get a catalogue listing their valuable collection of videotapes that are for sale.

NAME: Deaf World Web (DWW, Internet, International)
E-Mail: <dww@deafworldweb.org>
Internet address: <http://www.deafworldweb.org/dww/>
An international Web publication of the deaf. Check their online deaf encyclopedia under "C" for CODA there are international articles of interest. Check under "K" for KODA-related materials, information and other links.

NAME: Dissertation Abstracts International (DAI, USA)
Address: 300 N. Zeeb Rd., Ann Arbor, Michigan 48106
Phone: 313-761-4700 or 800-521-0600 x 3781
DAI distributes copies of M.A. theses and Ph.D. dissertations at nominal cost.

NAME: Double Pride (USA)
Contact: Sheila Jacobs, M.F.C.C.
Address: 1035 San Pablo Ave., Suite No. 5, Albany, California 94706
Phone: 510-528-9869
Presents workshops, consultations and retreats throughout the country for bilingual individuals and families in the Deaf Community. Sheila addresses the bicultural issues we face and ways to benefit from "Double Pride," pride in both our languages - American Sign Language (ASL) and English. She facilitates the exploration of the deaf and hearing parts within each of us, and conflicts they sometimes present, and the resolutions that are possible. Not available at the present time.

NAME: The Eli Savanick Memorial Fund (USA)
Contact: Millie Brother

R
E
S
O
U
R
C
E
S

269

Address: CODA, P.O. Box 30715. Santa Barbara, California 93130-0715

Internet: <http://www.gallaudet.edu/~rgpricke/coda/index.html>

This fund, established in 1993, honors the life and work of a coda, the late Eli Savanick, who was director of the International Center on Deafness at Gallaudet University for many years. As an early and ardent supporter of CODA, Eli is beloved for his dedication, humanity and many years of service. As CODA founder Millie Brother says, Eli "was a man who tread lightly upon all parts of the earth, yet left indelible marks." This fund enables codas from around the world to attend annual international conferences of CODA. Contributions can be sent to CODA, Inc. at the above address. CODA Inc. is a 501 (c) (3) non-profit, tax-exempt organization founded in 1983. Contributions are deductible as allowed by U.S. law.

NAME: ERIC (Educational Resources Information Center) Clearinghouse (ERIC, USA)
             ERIC Document Reproduction Service (EDRS)

Address: 7420 Fullerton Road, Suite 110, Springfield, Virginia 22153-2852

Phone: 800-443-ERIC (3742) or 703-440-1400 or 703-440-1408 (FAX)

E-Mail: <edrs@inet.ed.gov>

Internet: <http://www.edrs.com>

ERIC is a national information system on education with a large database of education materials. There are 16 ERIC clearinghouses that select and abstract the best of the professional literature on disabilities for inclusion. They publish and disseminate information and serve as a resource center for the general public and promote the dissemination of research which is available at nominal cost.

NAME: Five Acres: The Boys' and Girls' Aid Society of Los Angeles (USA)

Contact: Marla Petal

Address: 760 West Mountain View Street, Altadena, California. 91001-4996

Phone: 626-798-6793 (V) 626-698-9006 (TTY) 626-797-7722 (FAX)

E-Mail: <hn2716@handsnet.org>

Internet: <http://www.5acres.org>

Founded in 1888. They provide a 10-week parenting class for deaf and hard-of-hearing parents conducted in American Sign Language. This helps deaf and hard-of-hearing parents learn nurturing ways to encourage appropriate behavior, increase their empathy, build self-esteem and how to have fun as a family. Topics: child growth and development, discipline, communication and handling difficult feelings. Accredited member of the Child Welfare League of America. Participating member of United Way.

NAME: Friends of Libraries for Deaf Action (FOLDA, USA)

Contact: Alice Hagemeyer

Address: 2930 Craiglawn Road, Silver Spring, Maryland 20904-1816

Phone: 301-572-4134 (TTY)

E-Mail: <alhagemeyer@juno.com>

FOLDA has an extensive collection of deaf-related materials, both print and nonprint, they would like to use as the nucleus for a new deaf materials public lending library collection. Alice is an active member of the White House Conference on Libraries and Information Services Task Force, working with other delegates and library friends on a follow-up to the resolutions developed at the 1991 Conference. Their concern is to make deaf-related library materials available to the public, particularly the deaf community.

NAME: Gallaudet Research Institute (GRI, USA)

Contact: Dr. Tom Allen, Director

Address: Gallaudet University, 800 Florida Ave., N.E., Washington, DC 20002

E-Mail: <Thomas.Allen@Gallaudet.edu>

Internet: <http://www.gri.gallaudet. edu>

The GRI publishes a series of monographs and other research reports and have expressed an interest in encouraging and disseminating research on deaf families with hearing children.

NAME: Gallaudet University Archives (USA)
Contact: Archives Director
Address: Gallaudet University Learning Center, 800 Florida Ave., N.E., Washington, DC 20002
Phone: 202-651-5209 (TTY) 202-651-5213 (FAX)
E-Mail: <uhedberg@gallua.gallaudet.edu>
Internet: <http://www.gallaudet.edu/~archives/archives.html>
The Archives, established in 1967, is dedicated to the preservation of Deaf related collections, such as diaries, letters, scrapbooks, photographs, films, including University records, Pennsylvania School for the Deaf records, manuscripts or personal papers created by individuals or organizations. In addition, they have rare books and periodicals from the early progress and development of the Deaf community. The rare books focus on subjects such as education, sign language, history, pedagogy, physiology. Also they collect art works and artifacts produced by Deaf artists. The Archives houses 4,000,000 pages of archival papers, 2,000 rare books, 2,000 reports from various Deaf schools, 1,250,000 newspaper news clippings related to the Deaf community, 7,500 architectural drawings of Deaf schools, 1,600 films and videotapes, 86,000 photographs, 31,000 slides and 15,000 negatives. The oldest item is a book which was published in 1546.

NAME: Gallaudet University Library (USA)
Contact: Gallaudet University Learning Center
Address: Gallaudet University, 800 Florida Ave., N.E., Washington, DC 20002
Internet: <http://www.gallaudet.edu/~library/home.html>
Pathfinders: <http://www.gallaudet.edu/~library/new/deafguid.html>
Gallaudet University is a member of the Washington (D.C.) Research Library Consortium (WRLC) with combined holdings of more than 4.6 million volumes, over 5 million microform items, 24,000 serial subscriptions and extensive holdings in nonprint media, manuscripts, rare books and special collections. Member universities of the WRLC are: Southeastern University; American University; The Catholic University of America; Gallaudet University; George Mason University; The George Washington University; Marymount University; and the University of the District of Columbia. <http://www.consortium.org> These member libraries share an online electronic library system known as ALADIN (Access to Library and Database Information Network). ALADIN can be accessed through the Gallaudet University Library home page located at <http://www.gallaudet.edu/~library>. You can access their Deafness Collection through ALADIN. The library also has a series of "pathfinder" guides on a number of topics. Check the "Deaf Parents of Hearing Children" pathfinder which lists descriptors to search the ALADIN online catalog, ERIC, and PSYJ (PsychInfo). They also have links to the Library of Congress, and the University of Maryland library catalogs.

NAME: H-M. F. D. [Hearing me - Mother Father Deaf] (London, UNITED KINGDOM)
Contact: Linda Linnett
Address: 28 All Saints Close, Edmonton, London, England N9 9AT
Phone: 011-44181-803-6254 (V/FAX) 011-44181-981-1231 (V/TTY)
Publication: H-MFD newsletter
The British counterpart to Children of Deaf Adults in the United States. The first meeting was held at the 1990 British Deaf Association Centenary Congress in Brighton. Provides a forum for exploring our common experiences and to pass them on to younger H-MFD's (hearing-me, mother father deaf), as well as organizing social events on a regional basis. Linda Linnett is an International Representative to the American CODA Board.

NAME: HALF-n-HALF All-Coda Ensemble (USA)
Contact: Sherry Hicks or Michael Velez

Address: P.O. Box 14421, Berkeley, California 94702

Phone: 510-653-4232

E-Mail: <Sherrythe1@aol.com>

Since 1993, an ensemble of hearing adults who have deaf parents (codas) has created shows exploring the craft of "musically-inspired American Sign Language storytelling." Using music, dance, ASL storytelling and video, the audience gets an inside view into their Half Deaf, Half Hearing WORLD. Principal members are Sherry Hicks and Michael Velez. Others have been Sheila Jacobs, Pam Johnson, Karen Luttge and Nancy Holdren. They have performed at international CODA conferences since 1993 and at regional and national conventions of the Registry of Interpreters for the Deaf and on many other occasions.

NAME: Health and Wellness Program Serving Deaf and Hard of Hearing People at Regions Hospital (USA)

Address: Regions Hospital, 640 Jackson St., St. Paul, Minnesota 55101-2595

Phone: 612-221-2719 (V) 612-221-3258 (TTY)

E-Mail: <Kristen.L.Swan@HealthPartners.com>

Formerly the Hearing Impaired Health and Wellness Services (Program) and Hearing Impaired Parents Program. Former location of this program was at the St. Paul-Ramsey Medical Center which has been renamed Regions Hospital and Foundation.

NAME: Hearing Interpreters with Deaf Parents (HIDP) Special Interest Group (SIG) of the RID (Registry of Interpreters for the Deaf) (HIDP, USA)

Address: 8630 Fenton Street, Suite 324, Silver Spring, Maryland 20910-3803

Phone: 301-608-0050

Internet: <http://www.rid.org>

It is the mission of the RID to provide international, national, regional, state, and local forums and an organizational structure for the continued growth and development of the professions of interpretation and transliteration of American Sign Language and English. There are a number of Special Interest Groups (SIGs) within the RID. One of those is the HIDP SIG. Its mission is to advocate for the needs and interests of RID members who are hearing interpreters and transliterators of deaf parent(s) and to strengthen the ties between all members and officers of the RID by open recognition of the bilingual and bicultural diversity of the RID membership. More specifically: a) to promote awareness of the needs of hearing interpreters with deaf parents; b) to provide a forum for Interpreters and Transliterators with deaf parents; c) to foster an understanding within the general membership of the unique experiences and contributions which HIDPs bring to the field of Interpreting and Transliterating; d) to serve as a resource to the RID board, National Office of the RID, committees, and the membership on issues affecting interpreters, HIDPs, and the Deaf community; e) to recommend programs, activities and policies to the membership, Board of Directors, and the National Office that serve the interests and meet the needs of HIDPs; f) to provide a support group for hearing interpreters with deaf parents; g) to promote and review the development of position and free papers; h) to ensure the provision of the highest quality interpreting and transliterating services to Deaf and hard-of-hearing individuals based upon our cultural heritage; i) to encourage and promote career opportunity awareness for hearing individuals with deaf parents.

NAME: The International Deaf Queer Electronic 'Zine (Internet, International)

Contact: Dragonsani Renteria (Drago)

Address: P.O. Box 14431, San Francisco, California 94114

Phone: 415-626-9033 (FAX)

E-Mail: <ctnmag@aol.com>

Internet: <http://www.deafqueer.org>

Send press releases/announcements to: <FLASH@deafqueer.org>

An award-winning website published electronically since 1994, FLASH is a free supplement to CTN Magazine and brought to you by Drago and CTN Magazine (Coming Together News: The National Deaf Lesbian, Gay, Bi

Publication). News of interest to Deaf and Deaf community gays, lesbians, bisexuals and transgendered persons. They consider gay children of deaf adults, especially gay and lesbian coda interpreters, as members of their community. For example, in their "Deaf lost to AIDS" name list, they include coda interpreters and other hearing-signers who were "an active part of our community." Visit this list at <http://www.deafaids.net> or <http://www.deafqueer.org/AIDS/> Notify them to add any names. Send press releases and announcements to <DQRC@hooked.net>.

NAME: The Interpreter's Network (London, Ontario, CANADA, International)
Contact: Paul Cowley
Address: Suite 230, 1326 Huron Street, London, Ontario, Canada, N5V 2E2
Phone: 519-451-2327 (FAX)
E-Mail: <Pcowley@terpsnet.com>
Internet: <http://www.terpsnet.com>
An internet listserve and distribution network for interpreters whose working languages include a signed language. Membership information can be found at <http://www.terpsnet.com/Terpsnet-membership.html> Occasionally topics of interest to codas come up for discussion and debate.

NAME: Jewish Social Service Agency of Metropolitan Washington, DC (JSSA, USA)
Contact: Randy Myers, LCSW-C
Address: 6123 Montrose Road, Rockville, Maryland 20852
Phone: 301-881-3700 (V) 301-984-5662 (TTY)
E-Mail: <rmyers@gallua.gallaudet.edu>
From time to time JSSA provides a non-sectarian support group for hearing children of deaf parents ages 12-16. Participants explore: a) identity issues for a hearing child of deaf parents; b) managing the deaf and hearing worlds; c) communicating with deaf people; and d) feelings about having deaf parents. These sessions last one hour for eight weeks.

NAME: Kaleidoscope TV Website (Internet, International)
Internet address: <http://www.ktv-i.com>
With a National Advisory Board of over 250 nonprofit and professional health and disability organizations, these groups have helped Kaleidoscope create a health/disability website with information on medical breakthroughs, cutting edge technology, government health care, nutrition and lifestyles for persons with disabilities, their families, and professionals. There are also chat forums, news, features, and hot links. Based in San Antonio, Texas.

NAME: Kids of Deaf Adults (KODA-WA, USA)
Contact: Ms. Holly Jensen, M. A., C.M.H.C., President
Address: 15208 55th Ave. S.E., Everett, WA 98208
Phone: 206-316-6880 (TTY) 206-324-9433 (FAX)
E-Mail: <hollyj@smh.org>
Internet: <http://www.koda.org>
E-Mail Webmaster: <Gholte@aol.com>
A non-profit organization, founded in April, 1995. To promote family awareness and individual growth in hearing children of Deaf parents. In order to support the children's unique bilingual and bicultural upbringing, KODA provides education and supports to foster a positive integration of both hearing and deaf cultures into healthy personal identities in koda children. Deaf parents who have hearing children have formed support groups for themselves with activities for their young hearing children. Send relevant information and news to the KODA Webmaster. At their website there is a guest book to leave messages. Contact numbers of other KODA chapters are listed on their WEB page. {At the Building Bridges Conference in May, 1997, it was agreed by all Deaf and hard-of-hearing parents, codas and interested professionals present that KODA information should be directed through this Seattle,

273

R
E
S
O
U
R
C
E
S

Washington, group because they are incorporated and have a Homepage on the World Wide Web}

NAME: Kraft and Stewart (USA)
Contact: Bonnie Kraft (CI, CT, CSC) and Kelli Mills Stewart (CI, CT, CSC, Prov. SC:L
Address: P.O. Box 681, Medford, Massachusetts 02155
Phone: Ms. Stewart 508-667-9423 (V/TTY) or Ms. Kraft at 617-393-0339 (V/TTY)
E-Mail: <Kraft617@aol.com>
Purpose: A program for American Sign Language interpreters "Building Bridges" between coda interpreters and hearing interpreters. "Join colleagues in search of a better understanding of the dynamic between hearing interpreters raised in hearing homes and those raised in d/Deaf homes. Come to this open, interactive class and take one more step toward creating a climate of understanding and support."

NAME: The Laurent Clerc Elementary School (USA)
Address: 740 E. Seedway Blvd., Tucson, AZ 85719
Phone: 520-798-0847 V/TTY
E-Mail: <cng@theriver.com>
This new charter school is an ASL-based program accepting deaf and hearing children. This is a public school that for the first time allows hearing signing children in deaf families to be educated along with deaf signing peers. Hearing siblings of deaf children are able to attend the same school as their deaf siblings.

NAME: Library of Congress (USA)
Address: First St. and Independence Ave., S. E., Washington, DC 20003
Phone: General information: 202-707-5000 Reference Assistance: 202-707-6500
Internet: <http://www.loc.gov>
An outstanding resource for research.

NAME: Lutheran Social Services of Michigan, Pathways to Parenting Program (USA)
    See DEAF C.A.N.! Community Advocacy Network (above)

NAME: Mental Health Center at Gallaudet University (MHC, USA)
Contact: Barbara A. Brauer, Ph.D., Executive Director
Address: GUKCC, Gallaudet University, 800 Florida Avenue, N.E., Washington, DC 20002
Phone: 202-651-6080 (V/TTY)
Internet: <http://www.gallaudet.edu.
The Mental Health Center (MHC) at Gallaudet University is a cross-disciplinary training site for both graduate students in the Gallaudet departments of counseling, psychology, and social work and for graduate students from elsewhere. It is a combined program providing community and student mental health services. They provide confidential counseling, therapy, and assessment services to Gallaudet students, staff and faculty as well as to members of the Washington, D.C. Metropolitan community. Individual, group, couples, and family therapy is provided to meet the diverse needs of the university population and the surrounding community.

NAME: Metropolitan Washington Area Deaf Adoptive Parents Support Group (USA)
Contact: Barbara J. White
Address: Department of Social Work, Gallaudet University, 800 Florida Ave., N.E., Washington, DC 20002
Phone: 202-651-5160 (TTY)
E-Mail: <bjwhite@gallua.gallaudet.edu>
Publication: The Networker
The newsletter was begun in 1993. This is a support group for deaf adoptive parents and those interested in becoming one.

NAME: MELD for Parents who are Deaf and Hard of Hearing (MELD, USA)

(formerly Minnesota Early Learning Design)

Address: 123 North Third Street, Suite 507, Minneapolis, Minnesota 55401

Phone: 612-332-7563 (V/TTY) 612-344-1959 (FAX)

E-Mail: <meldctrl@aol.com>

Internet: <http://www.users.aol.com/meldctrl/index.html>

Since 1973, MELD has developed rich, culturally-sensitive publications that provide parents, and those who work with them, practical and essential information that enhances confidence and competence. MELD is a nationally recognized parent program designed to meet the comprehensive needs of the family in the first and most important years of a child's life. MELD has adapted its program for parents who are Deaf and hard-of-hearing. MELD's mission is to strengthen families at critical periods of transition in parenthood. MELD brings together groups of parents who have similar parenting needs, provides them with pertinent information and helps them develop into supportive peer groups. More recently their materials are directed to families in general, Spanish language parenting materials, and most recently materials for African American young mothers.

NAME: The Millie Brother Scholarship Fund (USA)

Contact: Dr. Robert J. Hoffmeister, Attention: CODA Scholarships

Address: Programs in Deaf Studies, Boston University, 605 Commonwealth Ave., Boston, Massachusetts 02215

Phone: 617-353-3205 (V/TTY)

Internet: <http://www.gallaudet.edu/~rgpricke/coda/index.html>

E-Mail: <Rhoff@bu.edu>

Since 1990, CODA International has awarded over $20,000.00 in scholarships to assist codas to pursue their post-high school educational goals. Applicants submit an essay describing their coda experience and how it has shaped them as an individual. The essay should include a description of future career aspirations. Each essay will be judged for organization, content, creativity, and a sense of purpose. Winning essays will be published in the CODA Connection newsletter. Write for an application. Contributions to this fund can be sent to CODA., P.O. Box 30715, Santa Barbara, California. 93130-1715. CODA Inc. is a 501 (c) (3) non-profit, tax-exempt organization founded in 1983. Contributions are deductible as allowed by U.S. law.

NAME: Mother Father Deaf Day (USA)

Contact: Trudy Schafer

Address: 28 Tremont St., Brighton, Massachusetts 02135

Internet: <http://www.gallaudet.edu/~rgpricke/coda/index.html>

E-Mail: <Trudy_Schafer@harvard.edu>

Begun in 1996, this annual event one Sunday in May offers members of CODA (Children of Deaf Adults) the opportunity to honor their Deaf parents and to recognize the gifts of culture and language they received. Proclamation: "Whereas, Children of Deaf Adults International (CODA), is an organization established for the purpose of promoting family awareness and individual growth in hearing children of Deaf adults, and Whereas, in it's 12th year, CODA International, has evolved into a viable, ongoing organization, intent on celebrating the heritage and culture passed on to us by our parents, and Whereas, this heritage is a source of pride for us, and Whereas, we are grateful to our parents and their friends for giving us this rich gift of culture and language, THEREFORE, be it resolved that We the members of CODA International, hereby declare the establishment of 'Mother, Father Deaf Day' to be celebrated annually."

NAME: National Association of the Deaf (NAD, USA)

Contact: Nancy J. Bloch, Executive Director

Address: 814 Thayer Avenue, Silver Spring, Maryland 20910-4500

Phone: 301-587-1788 (V) 301-587-1789 (TTY) 301-587-1791 (FAX)

E-Mail: <NADHQ@juno.com>

RESOURCES

Internet: <http://www.nad.org>
Publications: The NAD Broadcaster, The Deaf American Monograph (series)
Founded in 1880, the NAD is the nation's oldest and largest organization representing people with disabilities in the United States. The NAD safeguards the accessibility and civil rights of 28 million deaf and hard-of-hearing Americans in a variety of areas including education, employment, health care, social services and telecommunications.

NAME: National Black Deaf Advocates (NBDA, USA)
Contact: Albert Couthen, President
Address: P.O. Box 5465, Laurel, Maryland 29726 or P.O. Box 92168, Washington, DC 20090-2168
Phone: 301-206-2802 (TTY) 301-206-51-57 (FAX)
E-Mail: <couthen61@aol.com>
Internet: <http://www.bin.org/assocorg/nbda/nbdainf.html>
NBDA is a non-profit, tax exempt organization established in 1982. Membership is $15.00/year. It is the first and largest consumer organization of deaf and/or hard-of-hearing people of color in the United States. Promotes the well-being, culture, and empowerment of African-American persons who are deaf or hard-of-hearing. Through its mission, NBDA aims to strengthen the educational, cultural, social and economic advancement of deaf and hard-of-hearing African-Americans. There are 27 active chapters of NBDA. Black codas may contact Agnes Muse, Gallaudet University, P.O. Box 2352, Washington, DC 20002 Phone: 202-651-5111 or 301-567-5672 <ammuse@gallua.gallaudet.edu>

NAME: National Council on Disability (NCD, USA)
Address: 1331 F Street, N.W., Suite 1050, Washington, DC 20004-1007
Phone: 202-272-2004 (V) 202-272-2074 (TTY) 202-272-2022 (FAX) 1-888-206-6463
Internet: <http://www.ncd.gov>
The NCD reports U.S. Census Bureau statistics that between October, 1994, and January, 1995, approximately 54 million Americans reported some level of disability, and that 26 million described their disability as severe. In the period from 1991-1992 the numbers were nearly 49 million with a disability and 24 million who said their disability was severe.

NAME: National Information Center on Deafness (NICD, USA)
Contact: Loraine DiPietro, Director
Address: Gallaudet University, 800 Florida Ave., N.E., Washington, DC 20002-3695
Phone: 202-651-5051 (V) 202-651-5052 (TTY) 202-651-5054 (FAX)
E-Mail: <nicd@gallux.gallaudet.edu>
Internet: <http://www.gallaudet.edu/~nicd/>
The NICD is a centralized source of information about hearing loss and deafness. They collect, develop, and disseminate up-to-date information on deafness, hearing loss, and organizations and services for deaf and hard-of-hearing people. They also have a vertical file on "hearing children with deaf parents." Since 1984, they have disseminated a bibliography on "Hearing Children of Deaf Parents."

NAME: National Institute on Deafness and Other Communication Disorders (NIDCD)
Address: National Institutes of Health, Building 31, Room 1B-62, Bethesda, Maryland 20892-3456
Phone: 301-496-7243 (V) 301-402-0252 (TTY) 301-907-8830 (FAX) 800-241-1044 (V) 800-241-1055 (TTY)
E-Mail: <nidcd@aerie.com>
Internet: <http://www.nih.gov/nidcd/>
Established in 1988, NIDCD is one of the National Institutes of Health. Mission: to support biomedical and behavioral research and research training in the 7 areas of human communication: hearing, balance, smell, taste, voice, speech, and language.

NAME: National Parent Information Network (NPIN)
Contact: Anne S. Robertson
Address: University of Illinois at Urbana-Champaign, 51 Gerty Drive, Champaign, IL 61820
Phone: 800-583-4135 (V/TTY) 217-333-3767 (FAX)
E-Mail: <arobrtsn@uiuc.edu>
Internet: <http://www.ericps.crc.uiuc.edu/npin.npinhome.html>
    or <http://www.ericps.crc.uiuc.edu/fte/ftehome.html>
NPIN is funded by the U.S. Department of Education and is a project of the ERIC (Educational Resources Information Center) system which serves educators worldwide through 16 different locations around the country. NPIN is an Internet-based information network for parents, and for organizations and individuals who support parents. Those services include: 1) PARENT NEWS, an award wining Internet resource, updated monthly, with such items as current articles, books, organizations. community programming ideas, and interesting websites; 2) PARENTS AskERIC, a question and answer service for parents, teachers, administrators, and parent education specialists; 3) PARENTING Discussion List, an informal list of parents and professionals who work with parents, discussing current parenting issues; 4) Resources for Parents, and for those who work with parents: building a variety and perhaps the largest collection of current journals, articles and books on family life, child development, and parenting from birth through early adolescence.

NAME: National Softball Association of the Deaf (NSAD, USA)
Contact: Vance Rewolinski, Commissioner
Address: 6605 Kroltton Drive, Austin, Texas 78745
E-Mail: <officers@NSAD>
Internet: <http://nsad.org/>
NSAD is a non-profit recreational and competitive organization serving Deaf and Hard-of-Hearing regional softball organizations and players. It has been organizing national softball activities since 1976 and is incorporated in the state of Kansas in 1992. The NSAD is considering revising their policy to now allow codas to become associate NSAD members and be able to play on teams that have traditionally been only for deaf players.

NAME: National Technical Institute for the Deaf (NTID, USA)
Address: Rochester Institute of Technology, One Lomb Memorial Drive, Rochester, New York 14623-0877
Phone: 716-475-6400 (V/TTY)
Internet: <http://www.rit.edu/NTID>
Homepage: <http://www.rit.edu/%7e418www/>
NTID is a College of the Rochester Institute of Technology for deaf and hard-of-hearing students to obtain degrees in technical fields.

NAME: Northern Virginia Resource Center for Deaf and Hard of Hearing Persons (NVRC, USA)
Contact: Cheryl Heppner, Executive Director
Address: Courthouse Plaza Offices, 10363 Democracy Lane, Fairfax, Virginia 22030
Phone: 703-352-9056 (TTY) 703-352-9055 (V) 703-352-9058 (FAX)
E-Mail: <NVRCheryl@aol.com> or <NVRCinfo@aol.com>
Internet: <http://www.nvrc.org>
A service, referral and advocacy organization whose board is composed of deaf, hard-of-hearing and hearing members of the community. They have produced a parent education video and educational package for deaf parents with hearing children in 1992 which is highly recommended (see reference in the "Video and audio tapes..." section).

NAME: Parenting Advisory Council (PAC, USA)
Contact: Sylvia Stagnoli
Address: P.O. Box 135, Fairfax, Virginia 22030-0135

Phone: 703-385-2083 (V/TTY)

E-Mail: <ParentAdvC@aol.com>

The PAC was established in 1989 to meet the needs of Deaf parents in the community; specifically, classes which focus on the unique communication and cultural differences of Deaf parents raising hearing children. We are offering more classes for Deaf parents and are expanding the Parenting Program to include other groups within the Deaf and hard-of-hearing communities.

NAME: President's Committee on Employment of People with Disabilities (PCEPD, USA)

Address: 1331 F Street, N.W., Suite 300, Washington, DC 20004

Phone: 202-376-6200 (V) 202-376-6205 (TTY) 202-376-6219 (FAX)

E-Mail: <info@pcepd.gov>

Internet: <http://www.pcepd.gov>

Mission of PCEPD is to facilitate the communication, coordination and promotion of public and private efforts to enhance the employment of people with disabilities.

NAME: Registry of Interpreters for the Deaf (RID, USA)

Address: 8630 Fenton Street, Suite 324, Silver Spring, Maryland 20910-3803

Phone: 301-608-0050 (V) 301-608-0562 (TTY) 301-608-0508 (FAX)

Internet: <http://www.rid.org>

To provide international, national, regional, state and local forums and an organizational structure for the continued growth and development of the profession of interpretation and transliteration of American Sign Language and English. (See HIDP above)

NAME: The Ron Coffey Memorial Fund (USA)

Contact: Millie Brother

Address: CODA, P.O. Box 30715. Santa Barbara, California 93130-0715

Internet: <http://www.gallaudet.edu/~rgpricke/coda/index.html>

Ronald Lloyd Coffey died on June 27, 1994 at 7:13 a.m. He lived with AIDS for more than nine years. He was 33 years old. He was a coda. In 1981, Ron entered the Interpreter Training Program at Gallaudet. Over the years he evolved into a highly-respected and competent interpreter. He was unique in that he was able to work with a wide range of consumers who appreciated his skills and requested his services again and again. So many people loved Ron. He wanted to make a contribution, to change society. He was the only member of his family to earn a bachelor's degree. This fund was established in 1996 with money originally donated to the Center for Bicultural Studies, Inc. by Ron, and later by others in his memory. Awards will be given to help minority codas improve their skills in interpreting. Contributions to this fund can be sent to CODA, P.O. Box 30715, Santa Barbara, California. 93130-0715. CODA Inc. is a 501 (c) (3) non-profit, tax-exempt organization founded in 1983. Contributions are deductible as allowed by U.S. law.

NAME: Royal National Institute for Deaf People, Library (RNID, London, ENGLAND)

Contact: Mary Plackett, Librarian

Address: 330-332 Gray's Inn Road, London, England WC1X 8EE

Phone: 0171-915-1553 (V/Minicom) 0171-915-1443 (FAX)

E-Mail: <rnidlib@ucl.ac.uk>

Internet: <http://www.ucl.ac.uk/UCL-Info/Divisions/Library/RNID/mid.html>

The RNID library is a cooperative venture between the Royal National Institute for Deaf People and the University College London Library and is located on the grounds of the Royal National Throat Nose and Ear Hospital, London. The library covers all aspects of hearing, speech and language and specializes in literature on deafness - from academic journals, research reports and student textbooks to children's books and novels with deaf characters. Its collection of historical material has eared it a reputation as the archives of the deaf community. You do not have to be a member of the library in order to use its services. Check their internet resources for deaf studies at the following web site: <http://www.ucl.ac.uk/UCL-Info/Divisions/Library/RNID/deafin.html>

NAME: The Salk Institute for Biological Studies, Laboratory for Language and Cognitive Studies (USA)
Contact: Dr. Ursula Bellugi, Director
Address: 10010 North Torrey Pines Road, La Jolla, California 92037
Phone: 619-453-4100 ext. 222 or 619-453-5470 (TTY)
Internet: <http://www.salk.edu/index.html>

NAME: San Francisco Public Library, Deaf Services, Communications Center (USA)
Contact: Marti Goddard, Deaf Services Librarian
Address: Civic Center, San Francisco, California 94102
Phone: 415-557-4433 (TTY) or 415-557-4434 (V)
E-Mail: <Martig@SFPL.Lib.CA.US>
An excellent resource for the deaf and hard-of-hearing community in the Bay Area. Margaret Myhre, librarian in the 1980's edited with Millie Brother, CODA founder, a bibliography that was a "first." They continue to collect materials on deaf families with hearing children. In particular, see the vertical files on the following topics: Hearing Children of Deaf Parents; Parents and Parenting.

NAME: Self Help for the Hard of Hearing People (SHHH, USA)
Address: 7800 Wisconsin Ave., Bethesda, Maryland 20814
Phone: 301-657-2248 (V) 301-657-2249 (TTY)
Publication: SHHH journal
Internet: <http://www.shhh.org>
SHHH and our members are catalysts that make mainstream society more accessible to people who are hard-of-hearing. We strive to improve the quality of hard-of-hearing people's lives through education, advocacy and self help. Promotes awareness about and provides information on hearing loss, communication, assistive devices and alternative communication skills through publications, exhibits, and presentations.

NAME: Sign Talk Children's Centre Cooperative (CANADA)
Contact: Teresa Hope, Director
Address: 285 Pembina Highway, Winnipeg, Manitoba R3L 2E1
Phone: 204-475-8914 (TTY)
The Sign Talk Children's Centre is a specialized, quality daycare for children two to five years of age. It offers bilingual and bicultural programming in American Sign Language - ASL and English. Until "Sign Talk" was established in 1987 by a concerned group of Deaf parents, no daycare in North America could meet the special needs of Deaf parents and their children. See the two references by Evans and Zimmer on the Sign Talk Development Project.

NAME: TERPS-L Internet Listserv (Internet, International)
Contact: Paul Cowley
Address: The Interpreters Network, 1326 Huron Street, Suite 230, London, Ontario, Canada N5V 2E2
E-Mail: <paul.cowley@SHERIDANC.ON.CA>
Internet: <http://www.terpsnet.com>
Internet archive of TERPS-L: <http://www.findmail.com>
Internet LISTSERV for interpreters whose working languages include a Signed language. From time to time has information and discussions relevant to hearing children with deaf parents.

NAME: Through the Looking Glass (TLG, USA)

National Research and Training Center for Families of Adults with Disabilities
Contact: Paul Preston, Ph.D. and Megan Kirshbaum, Ph.D., Co-Directors
Address: 2198 Sixth Street, Suite 100, Berkeley, California 94710-2204
Phone: 800-644-2666 (V) 510-804-1616 (TTY) 510-848-4445 (FAX)
E-Mail: <TLG@lookingglass.org>
Internet: <http://www.lookingglass.org/>
Publication: Parenting with a Disability
TLG is funded by the U.S. Department of Education to be the National Resource Center for Parents with Disabilities. In the U.S. alone, there are more than 8 million families in which one or both parents have a disability. This National Center provides information, technical assistance and training for parents with disabilities, deaf parents, family members and professionals. Resources include: consultations on parent rights, custody, adoption, pregnancy and birthing, adaptive equipment for parents; a free international newsletter; a national parent-to-parent network for parents with disabilities and deaf parents; a national clearinghouse of resources and information, publications, and trainings, workshops and conferences, all for parents and professionals. TLG is a community non-profit organization which emerged from the independent living movement in 1982. Over the past 15 years, TLG has pioneered clinical and supportive services, training and research on families in which a parent or child has a disability. TLG's mission has been to create, demonstrate and encourage resources and model early intervention services which are non-pathological and empowering, and which integrate the perspectives of adults and parents with disabilities as well as parents of children with disabilities. Over 80% of TLG's staff have a disability, or are parents or children of persons with disabilities. In October 1997, TLG sponsored a historic meeting of the First International Conference on Parents with Disabilities and their Families. Check their LINKS at <http://www.lookingglass.org/ links.html>

NAME: UNI-QUE Productions (USA)
Contact: Sherry Hicks
Address: P.O. Box 14421, Berkeley, California 94712
E-Mail: <Sherrythe1@aol.com>
Producer and distributor of *Sherry: The Music Sign Language Video*.

NAME: University Microfilms International (UMI, USA)
Contact: Peggy Braun, serial sales office
Address: P.O. Box 1764, Ann Arbor, Michigan 48106-1764
        300 N. Zeeb Rd., Ann Arbor, Michigan 48106
Phone: 800-521-0600/3042 and 313-761-4700 or 313-665-5022 (FAX)
Doctoral dissertations and M.A. theses copies are available at nominal cost.

NAME: University of Amsterdam, Institute for General Linguistics (THE NETHERLANDS)
Contact: Profs. Dr. Anne E. Baker or Dr. Jane Coerts
Address: Spuistraat 210, 1012 VT Amsterdam, The Netherlands
Phone: 020-525-3864 (V) 020-525-3052/3021 (FAX)
Internet: <aebaker@let.uva.nl> or <j.a.coerts@let.uva.nl>
A number of research projects are under way in the areas of Sign Language of the Netherlands and deafness. Several of them are reported in their November, 1996, "Summary of Research and Teaching in the area of Sign Language of the Netherlands and Deafness." In particular, Dr. Beppie van den Bogaerde, is conducting research on "The role of language input in the acquisition of SLN (Sign Language of the Netherlands) by children learning it as their first language." Both deaf and hearing children are being studied. For further information contact her on E-Mail at <beppie@crystal.feo.hvu.nl>

NAME: University of Arizona, College of Nursing (USA)
Contact: Elaine Jones, Ph.D., R.N., Associate Professor, University of Arizona

Address: 1305 N. Martin, P.O. Box 210203, Tucson, Arizona 85721-0203
Phone: 520-626-6154
E-Mail: <ejones@rn1.nursing.arizona.edu>
Dr. Jones is also Director of Clinical Scholarship, College of Nursing, University of Arizona, and Adjunct Family Health Educator at the Community Outreach Program for the Deaf (COPD) and an Adjunct Perinatal Clinical Nurse Specialist at the University Medical Center. She has a final report available [E. Jones. (1990-1995). Family Functioning: Deaf Parents with Nondeaf Children. Tucson, Arizona: University of Arizona, College of Nursing. Funded by the National Institute of Nursing, NIH. (R01NR02665-05)] Here is an excerpt from that final report: "This study was one of the largest studies to date about Deaf-parented families. A comparative, descriptive study design was used to investigate Deaf parents' family functioning, with emphasis on Deaf parents' effectiveness in socialization of nondeaf children. Data was collected in sign language, using qualitative, quantitative, and observational methods. The final sample was 80 families (40 Deaf-parented and 40 comparison, nondeaf families) with a total of 324 individual family members. Children ranged in age from infancy to adolescence. Findings were noteworthy for 1) absence of significant differences in Deaf and hearing parents' scores on measures of family functioning and parent-child interactions and 2) concurrent identification of cultural differences in parent-child interactions, and some family values among Deaf-parented versus hearing families. A cultural perspective of Deafness, and Deaf-parented families suggests a markedly different approach to family health care for Deaf-parented families than a pathological perspective." (Personal communication)

NAME: The Western Region Outreach Center and Consortia, National Center on Deafness, California State University, Northridge - Library (NCOD at CSUN, USA)
Contact: Anthony Ivankovic, Resource Specialist
Address: CSUN, 18111 Nordhoff Street, Northridge, California 91330-8267
Phone: 818-677-2145 (V) 818-677-2665 (TTY) 818-677-4899 (FAX)
E-Mail: <anthony.ivankovic@csun.edu>
Internet: <http://www.csun.ncod.edu> or <http://www.csun.edu> or <http://www.library.csun.edu>

NAME: World Federation of the Deaf (WFD, International)
Address: c/o International Disability Centre, 13D, Chemin du Levant, F-01210 Ferney-Voltaire, FRANCE
Phone: General Secretary: +33-4-50-40-01-07 (FAX) President: +358-9-580-3770 (FAX)
E-Mail: <wfd@kl-deaf.fi>
Internet: <http://www.wfd@kl-deaf.fi>
Publication: WFD News
Founded September, 1951. Objectives/aims/principles: To promote the human and social rights of deaf persons, their full participation in society and equalization of opportunities; strengthen the status of sign language and advance educational opportunities for deaf persons; and promote their access to information. Stimulate the efforts of national associations of the deaf towards a better overall situation for the deaf community in each country. Render expertise in deafness and advocate the rights of deaf persons worldwide to the UN system. In the present programme, deaf persons and their organizations in developing countries are given priority. The WFD is made up of 116 national organizations of deaf people. The WFD holds consultative status in the United Nations structure.

NAME: Wyndholme Village - A Deaf Senior Community (USA)
Contact: Barbara Willigan, Executive Vice President
     c/o Lancelotta & Associates.
Address: 5052 Dorsey Hall Drive, Suite 203, Ellicott City, Maryland 21042
Phone: 800-242-9963 (TTY) 410-461-4444 (V) 410-730-6610 (FAX)
E-Mail: <wyndholme@aol.com>
Internet: <http://www.wyndholmevillage.com>
The only private, planned development designed for deaf senior citizens in the Washington, D. C. - Baltimore region.

R
E
S
O
U
R
C
E
S

The developer's grandparents are deaf. They have contacted the CODA community for input and invited codas as residents and advertised through the <u>CODA Connection.</u> They expect over 100 residences to be occupied by deaf seniors by December, 1998.

X

SUBJECT INDEX

AND

INTERNATIONAL RESOURCES

ALPHABETICAL LISTING

A

B

INDEX

C

D

E

F

G

H

310

I

L

M

Magarotto, Cesare

O

P

Q

R

S

INDEX

337

INDEX

INDEX

Y

Z

INTERNATIONAL RESOURCES
ALPHABETICAL LISTING

Accent on Living Magazine (USA)
Alexander Graham Bell Association for the Deaf (AGB, USA)
American Association of People with Disabilities (AAPD, USA)
American Speech-Language-Hearing Association (ASHA, USA)
Association of Disabled Parents in the Norfolk Area (PANDA, England)
Association of Late-Deafened Adults (ALDA, USA)

Børn af Døve - Children of Deaf (Denmark, THE NETHERLANDS)
British Deaf Association (BDA, London, ENGLAND)

Camp Mark 7 (USA)
Camp Tom Tom (USA)
Catholic Charities of the Archdiocese of San Francisco - Hearing Impaired Program (USA)
Center for German Sign Language and Communication of the Deaf (Hamburg, GERMANY)
Center on Deafness, Western Pennsylvania School for the Deaf (USA)
Centre for Deaf Studies, School for Education, Research Unit, University of Bristol (ENGLAND)
Child Development Center (USA)
College for Continuing Education, Gallaudet University (CCE, USA)
The Community Network (TCN, USA)
CODA/Australia (Children of Deaf Adults, New South Wales, AUSTRALIA)
CODA - Children of Deaf Adults (CODA, USA, International, and Internet)
CODA/Bay Area (USA)
CODA/Canada (Ontario, CANADA)
CODA-Chat on America On Line (Internet)
CODA/DC: Washington-Metropolitan Area (USA)
CODA/Finland (Helsinki, FINLAND)
CODA/Hawaii (USA)
CODA Inc. International Outreach (USA, International)
CODA/Illinois (ILCODA, USA)
CODA/Indiana (USA)
CODA INTERNET CONNECTION (Internet Listserv, International)
CODA/Michigan (USA)
CODA/Minnesota (MinneCODA, USA)
CODA/Netherlands (NETHERLANDS)
CODA/Nevada (USA)
CODA/New Jersey (NJCODA, USA)

CODA/North Carolina (NC/CODA, USA)
CODA/Southeastern Region (SECODA - USA)
CODA/Wisconsin (WisCODA, USA)

Deaf Access Services Children's Center (DAS, USA)
Deaf Adoption News Service (DANS, Internet, USA)
Deaf CAN! Community Advocacy Network (USA)
Deaf Family Research Press (DFR Press, USA)
Deaf-Hearing Couples Communication Enrichment Network (DHC, Internet, International, USA)
Deaf Mosaic (USA)
Deaf World Web (DWW, Internet, International)
Dissertation Abstracts International (DAI, Michigan, USA)
Double Pride (USA)

The Eli Savanick Memorial Fund (USA)
ERIC (Educational Resources Information Center) Clearinghouse (ERIC, USA)
    ERIC Document Reproduction Service (EDRS, USA)

Five Acres: The Boys' and Girls' Aid Society of Los Angeles (USA)
Friends of Libraries for Deaf Action (FOLDA, USA)

Gallaudet Research Institute (GRI, USA)
Gallaudet University Archives (USA)
Gallaudet University Learning Center - Library (USA)

H-M. F. D. (Hearing me - Mother Father Deaf) (London, UNITED KINGDOM)
Half-n-Half All-Coda Ensemble (USA)
Health and Wellness Program Serving Deaf and Hard-of-Hearing People at Regions Hospital (USA)
Hearing Interpreters with Deaf Parents (HIDP, USA)

The International Deaf Queer Electronic 'Zine (Internet, International)
The Interpreter's Network (London, Ontario, CANADA, International)

Jewish Social Service Agency of Metropolitan Washington, DC (JSSA, USA)

Kaleidoscope TV Website (Internet, International)
Kids of Deaf Adults (KODA-WA, USA and Internet)
Kraft and Stewart (USA)

The Laurent Clerc Elementary School (USA)
Library of Congress (USA)
Lutheran Social Services of Michigan (USA)
    See: Deaf CAN! Community Advocacy Network (USA)

Mental Health Center at Gallaudet University (MHC, USA)

Metropolitan Washington Area Deaf Adoptive Parents Support Group (USA)
MELD for Parents who are Deaf and Hard-of-Hearing (MELD, USA)
The Millie Brother Scholarship Fund (USA)
Mother Father Deaf Day (USA)

National Association of the Deaf (NAD, USA)
National Black Deaf Advocates (NBDA, USA)
National Council on Disability (NCD, USA)
National Information Center on Deafness (NICD, USA)
National Institute on Deafness and Other Communication Disorders (NIDCD, USA)
National Parent Information Network (NPIN, USA)
National Softball Association of the Deaf (NSAD, USA)
National Technical Institute for the Deaf (NTID, USA)
Northern Virginia Resource Center for Deaf and Hard of Hearing Persons (NVRC, USA)

Parenting Advisory Council (PAC, USA)
President's Committee on Employment of People with Disabilities (PCEPD, USA)

Registry of Interpreters for the Deaf (RID, USA)
The Ron Coffey Memorial Fund (USA)
Royal National Institute for Deaf People (RNID, London, ENGLAND)

The Salk Institute for Biological Studies, Laboratory for Language and Cognitive Studies (USA)
San Francisco Public Library: Deaf Services, Communications Center (USA)
Self Help for Hard of Hearing People (SHHH, USA)
Sign Talk Children's Centre Cooperative (Winnipeg, Manitoba, CANADA)

TERPS-L: Internet Listserv (Internet, International)
Through the Looking Glass (TLG, USA)
    National Research and Training Center for Families of Adults with Disabilities

UNI-QUE Productions (California, USA)
University Microfilms International (UMI, USA)
University of Amsterdam, Institute for General Linguistics (The Netherlands)
University of Arizona, College of Nursing (USA)

The Western Region Outreach Center and Consortia, National Center on Deafness,
    California State University, Northridge (USA)
World Federation of the Deaf (WFD, International)
Wyndholme Village - A Deaf Senior Community (USA)

INDEX

Hearing Children of Deaf Parents
A Pathfinder

SCOPE

The Gallaudet University Library contains much material relating to hearing children of deaf parents. This pathfinder is designed to help you find information and materials about hearing children of deaf parents. If you want the most recent information on this subject, you should plan to use periodicals (magazines and journals) found in the ERIC or ECER databases. Books will also be helpful and often more thorough, but they are usually not as current as periodicals.

Remember, this pathfinder will not tell you about all the materials the Library has about this topic. You must do the basic research yourself. This pathfinder will guide you to the appropriate places to begin your search for information. If you need further assistance, please ask at the Reference Desk.

BOOKS

Books are good places to get in-depth information and the historical background of an issue. Books are *not* good places to find *recent* information. *Hint:* Don't forget to check the bibliography (list of resources) at the end of most books to find other suggestions of where to find information!

You can find books about hearing children of deaf parents in the <u>Local Catalog</u> part of ALADIN by using the following keywords in the <u>Word Search</u>:

+"hearing children" +"family relationship"
+"parent child relationship" +"hearing children"
+"hearing children" +"deaf parents"

PERIODICALS

To find information about hearing children of deaf parents using the ERIC article database, access ERIC through the <u>Articles Databases</u> on ALADIN. You can use the following terms in a **keyword** search:

hearing children and deaf parents
coda and deafness

Some material may also be found through the **ECER** (Exceptional Child Education Resources) database. This is available through the Gallaudet University Library's World Wide Web home page:

http://www.gallaudet.edu/~library/lr/elecrsrc.html

In ECER, use the <u>Words Anywhere</u> search with the terms:

hearing children deaf parents

To find information in the psychology literature about hearing children of deaf parents, use the PsychInfo article databases **PSYJ** and **PSYB** on ALADIN. Use the **keyword** search with the following terms:

hearing children deaf parents

OTHER RESOURCES
Videotapes

Videotapes are available through the Circulation Desk. Most videotapes on this topic are not kept at the desk, and must be viewed through the Gallaudet cable TV system. You will need to request the videotapes at least two weekdays in advance. Use the <u>Local Catalog</u> part of ALADIN and the <u>Word Search</u> with the following terms:

+"hearing children" +"family relationship" +videorecording
+"parent child relationship" +"hearing children" +videorecording
+"hearing children" +"deaf parents" +videorecording

World Wide Web (WWW)

The organization Children of Deaf Adults (CODA) has a site on the WWW, which you can visit for more information about CODA itself:
http://www.gallaudet.edu/~rgpricke/coda/

For more information on hearing children of deaf parents, use the Infoseek search engine at:
http://www.infoseek.com
and run the following search:

+"hearing children" +"deaf parents"

Remember: If you have any questions, please ask a librarian at the Reference Desk.

Patrick Oberholtzer, 10/95
Revised by Tom Harrington, 3/3/97 and 3/31/98

ACKNOWLEDGMENTS

The following libraries and librarians have been wonderful and need to be acknowledged: the Center for German Sign Language and Communication of the Deaf, University of Hamburg, Guido Joachim, librarian; the Gallaudet University Archives, Ulf Hedberg, librarian, and Michael J. Olson, archives technician; the Gallaudet University Merrill Learning Center, Thomas Harrington, reference and instruction librarian, Carolyn Jones, Susan M. Davis, Sara Hamrick, Laura Jacobi, Lee B. Murphy, Jane Rutherford, and all their other fine staff; the Royal National Institute for the Deaf (RNID), London, England, Mary Plackett, librarian; the San Francisco Public Library, Deaf Services Library, Marti Goddard, librarian, and their staff; and lastly, the Western Region Outreach Center and Consortia, National Center on Deafness, California State University, Northridge, Anthony Ivankovic, resource specialist. Detailed information about these institutions can be found in the last section of this bibliography: "International Resources for Further Information."

I want to thank the individuals who have reviewed the resources section: Dr. Yerker Andersson, past President of the World Federation of the Deaf and Professor Emeritus of Sociology at Gallaudet University; Millie Brother, founder of CODA; Loraine DiPietro, Director of the National Information Center on Deafness, Gallaudet University; Anita B. Farb, Associate Executive Director, National Association of the Deaf; Dr. Jack R. Gannon, author of Deaf Heritage among other books; Cheryl Heppner, Executive Director of the Northern Virginia Resource Center for Deaf and Hard of Hearing Persons; Dr. Robert Hoffmeister, chair, Programs in Deaf Studies, Boston University; Dr. Janet Pray, Chair of the Department of Social Work, Gallaudet University; Dr. Paul Preston, Co-Director, National Resource Center for Parents with Disabilities, Berkeley, California; Krista Leitch Walker, program specialist, College for Continuing Education, Gallaudet University; Barbara J. White, Assistant Professor of Social Work, Gallaudet University; and Dr. Mary T. Weiner, Assistant Professor, Psychology, Gallaudet University. In addition, a debt of gratitude is owed to those who reviewed the manuscript and gave me very positive and constructive feedback as well as an encouraging endorsement. Many of them are themselves deaf or hard-of-hearing parents with hearing children, or are deaf or hearing professionals who have done research with deaf families with hearing children, or are codas. In one case, the reviewer has a deaf brother. Thank you all.

These families were willing to submit pictures for consideration and I thank them as well: Patrick and Sandi Atuonah (Maryland); Ernest and Kitty Davin (California); Jacob and Tilly Goedhard (Holland); Anthony and Mary Beth Heller (Virginia); Daniel and Charity (Reedy) Hines (Maryland); Brad and Cathy Holt (Washington); Anthony and Patty (Rule) Ivankovic; Barry and Holly Parker Jensen (Washington); Louis Lapides and Ann Meehan (Maryland); David and Daphne McGregor (Virginia); Edgar (Bernie) and Carie Palmer (Maryland); Kent and Judy Pfau (Colorado); Remingo and Daria Segura (Colorado); Dr. Ron Sutcliffe and Agnes Sutcliffe (Maryland); Peter and Mary Un (Maryland); Charles and Patricia Williams (Ohio); Raj and Jennifer (Grinder) Witteborg (Virginia); Darnell and Helen Woods (Washington, D.C.); and finally, Sam and Pat Yates (Maryland). A number of other families offered to help. I thank them for their interest and appreciate their efforts.

So many people have passed along references, articles, or otherwise been encouraging and supportive in small and large ways: Liz Bassett; Shirley Bassett; Dr. Ursula Bellugi; Liz Bezera; Mala Boyce; Millie Brother; Dr. Breda Carty; Dr. Elizabeth Charlson; Sylvia Chism, R.N.; Dr. Aaron Cicourel; Dr. David P. Corina; Albert Couthen; Wendelin A. Daniels; Cameron Davie; Dr. Leonard Davis; JohnMark Ennis; Daryl Frelich; Rosalyn Gannon; Laura-Jean Gilbert; Eline Goedhart; Paulette Goodman; Robert Hahn; Peter Hauser; Cheryl Heppner; Ron Hillas; Dr. Robert Hoffmeister; Gary Holte; Kathrine Hom; Sheila Hope-Palmer; Sue A. Hotto; Dr. Robert C. Johnson; Dr. Elaine Jones; Dr. Barbara Kannapell; Dr. Lynn Kilroy; Bonnie Kraft; Dr. Richard Kretschmer; Dr. Irene Leigh; Malina Lindell; Joyce Linden; Dr. Ruth H. Livingston; Chun Louie; Ruth Lowe; Dr. Arlene Malinowski; Dr. Barbara L. Mallory; Dr. Susan Mather; Dr. Ann McIntosh; Dr. David E. McKee; Dr. Jan Meilicke; Bonnie Mendelson; Julie Mertz; Randy Myers, MFCC; Kathleen Nash; Dee Pappas; Dr. Laura A. Petitto; Carol Plodin; Dr. Hugh Prickett; Rosanne Prickett; Jennie Pyers; Nancy B. Rarus; Ron Seagrave; Elaine L. Shaffer; Dr. Shirley Shultz-Myers; Dr. Pat Spencer; Millie Stansfield, MFCC; Barry Strassler; Dr. Beppie van den Bogaerde; Lou Ann Walker; Ivey P. Wallace; Barry White; J. Alan Wolf; William F. Wrede; Tom Wright; Mike Yared; and Enid L. Zafran. It's certain that many have been overlooked. Please accept my apologies.

Thanks go to some special persons who have been supportive and encouraging of this work. First of all, I should thank my children, Andrew, Daniell (especially for his DFR Press logo design), and Megan for their loving support over the years and good humor at my attention to detail. Also many friends within the International CODA community, but especially those within the Washington, D. C. CODA chapter, have given their encouragement and support. I want to specifically thank Susan Russell, Sherry Hicks, Sheila Jacobs, MFCC, Mariann Jacobson, Dennis Joyce, Bonnie Kraft, Dr. Alan Marcus, Agnes Muse, Cynthia Pearson, Darlene Prickett, Rosalyn Prickett, Trudy Schafer, Dr. Stan Schuchman, Dr. Pia Seagrave, and Jim Van Manen. My apologies to anyone overlooked, it was not intentional.